Praise for the First Edition

For anyone considering Groovy, or just interested in seeing what all of the fuss is around the features of dynamic languages, this book will deliver.

—Gregory Pierce, JavaLobby.org

Not just a language guide, this book presents the clear, readable, and enjoyable specification of Groovy … you should definitely read it.

—Alexander Popescu, Mindstorm

A real page-turner. Brilliant examples … all other programming books I know really fall behind.

—Dr. Gernot Starke

Excellent code samples … very readable.

—Scott Shaw, ThoughtWorks

Great, logical focus on language features.

—Norman Richards, author of *XDoclet in Action*

Destined to be the definitive guide. First rate!

—Glen Smith, Bytecode Pty Ltd.

Examples are clear, complete, and they work!

—David Sills, JavaLobby.org

Among the top five Manning books. For me personally, it's also a perception-changing and influential book.

—Weiqi Gao

The examples are the strongest part of the book—all assumptions are checked using assertions, and they have been run before printing so one can trust that they're faultless. Explanations are fine-grained so even inexperienced developers can read it with understanding.

—Marek Zganiacz, Comarch SA

Very readable, engaging, and does a great job of slotting Groovy into the broader world of software development. Highly recommended.

—Pan Pantziarka

Real computer LITERATURE.
—Johannes Link

To our families

Groovy in Action
Second Edition

DIERK KÖNIG
PAUL KING

WITH
GUILLAUME LAFORGE
HAMLET D'ARCY
CÉDRIC CHAMPEAU
ERIK PRAGT
AND JON SKEET

MANNING
SHELTER ISLAND

For online information and ordering of this and other Manning books, please visit
www.manning.com. The publisher offers discounts on this book when ordered in quantity.
For more information, please contact

> Special Sales Department
> Manning Publications Co.
> 20 Baldwin Road
> PO Box 761
> Shelter Island, NY 11964
> Email: orders@manning.com

Manning Publications Co.
20 Baldwin Road
PO Box 761
Shelter Island, NY 11964

Development editor:	Nermina Miller
Copyeditor:	Jodie Allen
Technical editor	Michael Smolyak
Proofreader:	Elizabeth Martin
Technical proofreader:	Gordon Dickens
Typesetter:	Dennis Dalinnik
Cover designer:	Marija Tudor

ISBN: 9781935182443
Printed in the United States of America

contents

            Introducing JSR-223   588 ▪ *The script engine manager
            and its script engines   589* ▪ *Compilable and invocable
            script engines   590* ▪ *Polyglot programming   592*

    16.7   Mastering CompilerConfiguration   592
            The import customizer   594 ▪ *The source-aware customizer   595
            Writing your own customizer   597* ▪ *The configscript
            compilation option   598*

    16.8   Choosing an integration mechanism   600
    16.9   Summary   601

PART 3   APPLIED GROOVY 603

17   *Unit testing with Groovy   605*

    17.1   Getting started   606
            Writing tests is easy   607 ▪ *GroovyTestCase: an
            introduction   608* ▪ *Working with GroovyTestCase   610*

    17.2   Unit testing Groovy code   611
    17.3   Unit testing Java code   614
    17.4   Organizing your tests   617
            Test suites   617 ▪ *Parameterized or data-driven testing   618
            Property-based testing   619*

    17.5   Advanced testing techniques   621
            Testing made groovy   622 ▪ *Stubbing and mocking   623
            Using GroovyLogTestCase   628* ▪ *Unit testing performance   629
            Code coverage with Groovy   631*

    17.6   IDE integration   634
            Using GroovyTestSuite   635 ▪ *Using AllTestSuite   637*

    17.7   Testing with the Spock framework   638
            Testing with mocks   639 ▪ *Data-driven Spock tests   642*

    17.8   Build automation   644
            Build integration with Gradle   644 ▪ *Build integration
            with Maven   647*

    17.9   Summary   649

foreword to the first edition

I first integrated Groovy into a project I was working on almost two years ago. There is a long and rich history of using "scripting languages" as a flexible glue to stitch together, in different ways, large modular components from a variety of frameworks. Groovy is a particularly interesting language from this tradition, because it doesn't shy away from linguistic sophistication in the pursuit of concise programming, especially in the areas around XML, where it is particularly strong. Groovy goes beyond the "glue" tradition of the scripting world to being an effective implementation language in its own right. In fact, while Groovy is often thought of and referred to as a scripting language, it really is much more than that.

It is traditional for scripting languages to have an uneasy relationship with the underlying linguistic system in which the frameworks are implemented. In Groovy's case, they have been able to leverage the underlying Java model to get integration that is smooth and efficient. And because of the linguistic similarities between Java and Groovy, it is fairly painless for developers to shift between programming in one environment and the other.

Groovy in Action by Dierk König and his coauthors is a clear and detailed exposition of what is groovy about Groovy. I'm glad to have it on my bookshelf.

JAMES GOSLING
CREATOR OF JAVA
DECEMBER 2006

preface

Nothing is more terrible than ignorance in action.

—Johann Wolfgang von Goethe

Thinking back to January 2007 when the first edition of this book hit the shelves, feels like time travel to the Middle Ages. The idea of using a programming language other than Java on the Java platform was widely considered frivolous. Today, a new language seems to pop up every other week, and we even go as far as designing languages for specific domains (DSLs) on a per-project basis.

This evolution of languages reflects a change in concerns. If performance were still our utmost concern, we would all be coding in a low-level language. But if performance is considered "good enough" for our purposes, we now turn our focus on human approachability.

Groovy has been a trendsetter for this development. Many Groovy features that ease the burden of developers are now commonplace in novel languages and may even find their way into newer versions of Java: literal declarations for common datatypes, simplified property access, null-safe dereferencing, closures, and more. Surprisingly many languages have adopted Groovy's optional typing strategy—few languages can claim to have static and dynamic *behavior* at the same time, though, the way Groovy has since version 2.

Just like Groovy, the first edition of this book set some trends as well. The idea of having every single listing as a self-testing piece of code resonated in the market and may be one reason why the book is among Manning's top-ten bestsellers of the decade.

The feedback for the first edition was overwhelming. We never expected to have so many great developers speaking so nicely about our work. We have no words to express this feeling of being proud and humbled at the same time. Most touching, though, was the stranger who once gave Dierk a pat on the back and mumbled, "Thank you for the book!" and then disappeared into the crowd. This book is for him.

We are fully aware that the first edition would have never been so successful if Groovy itself had been less appealing. The reason for Groovy's success is easy to see: it delivers its power in the most Java-friendly manner. It is Java's dynamic friend.

The development of Groovy, from version 1.0 covered in the first edition of this book until the current version 2.4, has closed what used to be a syntax gap by providing enums, annotations, generics, the classic for loop, nested classes, varargs, static imports, and the ability to use Groovy closures where Java 8 expects lambda expressions.

The Groovy project has progressed at a very high speed, not only in its core but also at its periphery. We see, for example, new usages of compile-time metaprogramming. This core feature gets instantly applied in the Spock testing framework, which in turn contributes back its "power assert" feature to the core. The community is buzzing and it has become a challenge to keep up to date with all the developments and activities.

It's only natural that many readers of the first edition of *Groovy in Action* (or "Gina" as we say for short) demanded an update that we are now happy to deliver as the second edition (codename "ReGina"). Our goal in this book is not only to rework the code examples, update the API description, and explain new features, but also to reflect the marketplace and the growth of the ecosystem. Groovy has evolved from a niche language to the default choice for dynamic programming on the Java platform for millions of developers.

Major financial organizations use Groovy to transfer billions of dollars every day, space agencies watch the stars with the help of Groovy, and satellite live-data streams are handled by Groovy code. Groovy is traveling the oceans, shipping containers around the globe, helping software developers automate recurring tasks, and running Mom's website. We felt an obligation to provide an up-to-date, solid, and comprehensive book to all these users.

Not only did Groovy and its environment change, we authors changed as well. We enjoyed the luxury of working on Groovy projects, introducing new team members to the language, running workshops and tutorials, recognizing struggles (and occasionally struggling ourselves), finding lots of unanticipated use cases while consulting, exploring new practices, using the toolset in anger, and generally facing the Groovy development reality. The book reflects these experiences.

In this second edition, we put more emphasis on the optional typing system, explain both dynamic and static metaprogramming in full depth, dive into type checking and static compilation, cover domain-specific languages, and introduce new modules that have evolved for user interfaces, testing, XML, JSON, database programing,

Web Services, dependency management, build automation, and concurrent programming as well as give you an updated overview of the Groovy ecosystem. We hope you
will find this updated book an enjoyable and rewarding read.

DIERK KÖNIG
PAUL KING

acknowledgments

Our publisher warned us that a second edition would be much more difficult. We did not understand that back then, but he was right. We needed to get more coauthors on board to account for the growth of Groovy and we are very grateful that Hamlet D'Arcy, Cédric Champeau, and Erik Pragt joined the group. Paul King invested an enormous amount of extra time and I (Dierk) am also very grateful to him for that.

We're deeply indebted to our technical reviewing team: Atul Khot, David McFarland, Jakob Mayr, Ken Shih, Paul Grebenc, Phillip Warner, Rick Wagner, Robert O'Connor, Ronald Tischliar, Scott Ruch, Vinod Panicker, and Vladimír Oraný, with special thanks to our technical editor Michael Smolyak and technical proofreader Gordon Dickens.

While the book was in development, readers could subscribe to Manning's Early Access Program (MEAP) to get the content early and to provide feedback. We received so many valuable suggestions that we cannot possibly list everyone's name, but we would like to say a big thank you to all of you! The MEAP ran longer than any other and while we are not proud of that record, we thank everyone for their patience and hope that you will find the book up-to-date and worth the wait.

Other friends helped with the book in one way or another: Andres Almiray, Bob Brown, Nick Chase, Andy Clement, Scott Davis, Marc Guillemot, Dr. Urs Hengartner, Arturo Herrero, Martin Huber, Roshan Dawrani, Wim Deblauwe, Dean DeChambeau, Gordon Dickens, Andrew Eisenberg, Jeremy Flowers, Dave Klein, Rupin Kotecha, Kenneth Kousen, Peter Ledbrook, Mac Liaw, Johannes Link, Joshua Logan, Chris Mair, Tsuyoshi Miyake, Vaclav Pech, Graeme Rocher, Baruch Sadogursky, Uwe Sauerbrei,

Erik Schwalbe, Larry Seltzer, Jim Shingler, Dan Sline, Glen Smith, David Stuve, Andre Steingress, Jochen Theodorou, Marija Tudor, Craig Walls, Dr. Hans-Dirk Walter, and Geertjan Wielenga.

The book would never had made it to the shelves without the support and guidance of everyone at Manning, especially our publisher Marjan Bace, our editors Nermina Miller and Maureen Spencer, and all the other great people who worked with us: Jodie Allen, Luke Bace, Jeff Bleiel, Olivia Booth, Candace Gillhoolley, Todd Green, Steven Hong, Cynthia Kane, Emily Macel, Elizabeth Martin, Tara McGoldrick Walsh, Mary Piergies, Christina Rudloff, Mike Stephens, and Kevin Sullivan.

Finally, very special thanks to James Gosling for writing the foreword to the first edition of *Groovy in Action*.

But most of all, we thank our families for their ongoing encouragement to pursue our ideas, their patience when we were once again physically or mentally absent, and their love that gives us a purpose in life. We love you.

about this book

Groovy in Action, Second Edition describes the Groovy language, presents the library classes and methods that Groovy adds to the standard Java Development Kit, and leads you through a number of topics that you are likely to encounter in your daily development work. The book has three parts:

- Part 1   The Groovy language
- Part 2   Around the Groovy library
- Part 3   Applied Groovy

An introductory chapter explains what Groovy is and then part 1 starts with a broad overview of Groovy's language features, before going into more depth about scalar and collective datatypes. The language description includes an explanation of the closure concept that is ubiquitous in Groovy, describing how it relates to and distinguishes itself from control structures. We present Groovy's model of object-orientation and its dynamic capabilities at both runtime and compile-time. Part 1 closes with a surprise: You can use Groovy as a static language as well!

Part 2 begins the library description with a presentation of Groovy's builder concept and its various implementations. An explanation of the GDK follows, with Groovy's enhancements to the Java standard library. This is the "beef" of the library description in part 2. The Groovy library shines with simple but powerful support for database programming and XML and JSON handling, and we include a detailed exposition of both topics. Another big advantage of Groovy is its all-out seamless integration with Java, and we explain the options provided by the Groovy library for setting this into action.

If part 1 was a tutorial and part 2 a reference, part 3 is about typical use cases for Groovy. It starts with a thorough exposition of how to use Groovy for test automation. Testing is an important topic in itself, but with Groovy even more so since Groovy developers seem to be very quality-oriented and even in otherwise plain-Java projects, Groovy is often used for testing because it is so convenient. Next, we want to use Groovy on multi-core machines and thus go into concurrent programming with Groovy. Another much-requested topic is using Groovy for domain specific languages, which we cover in a full, dedicated chapter. Part 3 ends with an overview of the Groovy ecosystem.

The book closes with an extensive series of helpful appendixes, which are intended to serve as quick references, cheat sheets, and detailed technical descriptions.

Who should read this book?

This book is for everyone who wants to learn Groovy as a new dynamic programming language. Existing Groovy users can use it to deepen their knowledge; and both new and experienced programmers can use it as a black-and-white reference. We found ourselves going to our own book to look up details that we had forgotten. Newcomers to Groovy will need a basic understanding of Java since Groovy is completely dependent on it; Java basics are not covered in our book.

Topics have been included that will make reading and understanding easier, but are not mandatory prerequisites: patterns of object-oriented design, Ant, Maven, JUnit, HTML, XML, JSON, Swing, and JavaFX. It is beneficial—but not required—to have been exposed to some other scripting language. This enables you to connect what you read to what you already know. Where appropriate, we point out similarities and differences between Groovy and other languages.

What's new in the second edition?

When starting the second edition, we considered adding visual clues or icons to the book so readers could quickly see what had changed from the first edition. We had to give up on that idea or the whole book would have been full of markers since there is hardly any paragraph that hasn't changed!

The second edition is a full rewrite. We dropped some chapters, reorganized others, and added new ones, so the book now has 20 chapters, up from 16, and a few hundred additional pages of genuinely new content. These changes reflect the evolution of the language and its use in the market.

Tackling the task of covering such a big topic needs many hands and we were very lucky that Hamlet Darcy, Cédric Champeau, and Erik Pragt joined the team. Hamlet authored the new chapters 9 "AST Transformations" and 20 "The Groovy Ecosystem." Cédric contributed his deep knowledge of Groovy internals to the new chapter 10 "Groovy as a static language" and helped to fine-tune chapters 7, 9, and 16. Erik got the laborious task of going through all changes to the Groovy standard library for chapter 12 "Working with the GDK" and fundamentally revised chapter 17 "Unit testing with Groovy" to cover the popular Spock testing framework.

Guillaume Laforge revised chapter 16 "Integrating Groovy" and shaped new chapter 19 "Domain Specific Languages (DSLs)" to address this important usage of Groovy.

Dierk König added chapter 19 "Concurrent Groovy with GPars" to show how well Groovy fits into the multi-core era. He also thoroughly revised and updated the core "language" chapters 1 through 6. Former chapter 7 was split into "Object orientation, Groovy style," and a new chapter 8 "Dynamic Programming with Groovy."

Paul King revised the "library" chapters 11 "Working with builders," 13 "Database programming with Groovy," and split the former XML chapter 14 into "Working with XML and JSON" and 15 "Interacting with Web Services" and extended the content to account for the rising importance of these Groovy usages. He also did the enormous work of going through every single page of the book to ensure consistency in style, wording, feel, and appearance. With so many authors and such diverse topics it is very difficult to keep the book coherent. If we finally managed to achieve this, it is thanks to Paul.

Code conventions and downloads

This book provides copious examples that show how you can make use of each of the topics covered. Source code in listings or in text appears in a `fixed-width font` like this to separate it from ordinary text. In addition, class and method names, object properties, and other code-related terms and content in text are presented using `fixed-width font`.

Occasionally, code is italicized, as in *reference*.`dump()`. In this case *reference* should not be entered literally but replaced with the content that is required, such as the appropriate reference.

Where the text contains the pronouns "I" and "we", the "we" refers to all the authors. "I" refers to the lead author of the respective chapter.

Most of the code examples contain Groovy code. This code is very compact so we present it "as is" without any omissions. Unless stated otherwise, you can copy and paste it into a new file and run it right away. In rare cases, when this wasn't possible, we have used ... (ellipses).

Java, HTML, XML, and command-line input can be verbose. In many cases, the original source code (available online) has been reformatted; we've added line breaks and reworked indentation to accommodate the page space available in the book. In rare cases, when even this was not enough, line-continuation markers were added.

Code annotations accompany many of the listings, highlighting important concepts. In some cases, numbered cueballs link to additional explanations that follow the listing.

You can download the source code for all of the examples in the book from the publisher's website at www.manning.com/GroovyinActionSecondEdition.

Keeping up to date

The world doesn't stop turning when you finish writing a book, and getting the book through production also takes time. Therefore, some of the information in any technical book becomes quickly outdated, especially in the dynamic world of agile languages.

This book covers Groovy 2.4. Groovy will see numerous improvements, and by the time you read this, it's possible that an updated version will have become available. New Groovy versions always come with a detailed list of changes. It is unlikely that any of the core Groovy concepts as laid out in this book will change significantly in the near future; and even then the emphasis is likely to be on *additional* concepts and features. Groovy has earned a reputation of caring deeply about backward compatibility. This outlook makes the book a wise investment, even in a rapidly changing world.

We will do our best to keep the online resources for this book reasonably up to date and provide information about language and library changes as the project moves on. Please check for updates on the book's web page at www.manning.com/GroovyinActionSecondEdition.

Author Online

Purchase of *Groovy in Action* includes free access to a private web forum run by Manning Publications where you can make comments about the book, ask technical questions, and receive help from the authors and from other users. To access the forum and subscribe to it, point your web browser to www.manning.com/GroovyinActionSecondEdition. This page provides information on how to get on the forum once you are registered, what kind of help is available, and the rules of conduct on the forum. It also provides links to the source code for the examples in the book, errata, and other downloads.

Manning's commitment to our readers is to provide a venue where a meaningful dialog between individual readers and between readers and the authors can take place. It is not a commitment to any specific amount of participation on the part of the authors, whose contribution to the AO remains voluntary (and unpaid). We suggest you try asking the authors some challenging questions lest their interest stray!

The Author Online forum and the archives of previous discussions will be accessible from the publisher's website as long as the book is in print.

About the cover illustration

The figure on the cover of *Groovy in Action, Second Edition* is a "Danzerina del Japon," a Japanese dancer, taken from a Spanish compendium of regional dress customs first published in Madrid in 1799. While the artist may have captured the "spirit" of a Japanese dancer in his drawing, the illustration does not accurately portray the looks, dress, or comportment of a Japanese woman or geisha of the time, compared to Japanese drawings from the same period. The artwork in this collection was clearly not researched first hand!

The book's title page states:

> *Coleccion general de los Trages que usan actualmente todas las Nacionas del Mundo desubierto, dibujados y grabados con la mayor exactitud por R.M.V.A.R. Obra muy util y en special para los que tienen la del viajero universal*

which we translate, as literally as possible, thus:

> *General collection of costumes currently used in the nations of the known world, designed and printed with great exactitude by R.M.V.A.R. This work is very useful especially for those who hold themselves to be universal travelers*

Although nothing is known of the designers, engravers, and workers who colored this illustration by hand, the "exactitude" of their execution is evident in this drawing. The "Danzerina del Japon" is just one of many figures in this colorful collection. Travel for pleasure was a relatively new phenomenon at the time and books such as this one were popular, introducing both the tourist as well as the armchair traveler to the exotic inhabitants, real and imagined, of other regions of the world.

Dress codes have changed since then and the diversity by nation and by region, so rich at the time, has faded away. It is now often hard to tell the inhabitant of one continent from another. Perhaps, trying to view it optimistically, we have traded a cultural and visual diversity for a more varied personal life. Or a more varied and interesting intellectual and technical life.

We at Manning celebrate the inventiveness, the initiative, and the fun of the computer business with book covers based on the rich diversity of regional life two centuries ago, brought back to life by the pictures from this collection.

about the authors

DIERK KÖNIG has worked for over 20 years as a professional software developer, architect, trainer, and consultant. Through his publications, conference appearances, trainings, workshops, and consulting activities, Dierk has reached more developers than he ever thought possible. He has worked with Canoo Engineering AG, Basle, Switzerland, since 2000, where he is a cofounder and enjoys being part of a thriving organization.

Dierk contributes to many open source projects, including Groovy, Grails, Open-Dolphin, Frege, and CanooWebTest. He joined the Groovy project in 2004 and has worked as a committer ever since. He presented Groovy to win the JAX Innovation Award 2007 and won the JAX Developer Challenge 2009 with his team.

He is an acknowledged reviewer and contributor to numerous books, including the classic *Extreme Programming Explained* (Kent Beck), *Test-Driven Development* (Kent Beck), *Agile Development in the Large* (Jutta Eckstein), *Unit Testing in Java* (Johannes Link), *JUnit and Fit* (Frank Westphal), *Refactoring in Large Software Projects* (Martin Lippert and Stephen Roock), *The Definitive Guide to Grails* (Graeme Rocher), and *Grails in Action* (Glen Smith, Peter Ledbrook).

In the course of authoring this second edition, Dierk became a happy husband and a proud father of a girl and a boy. You can follow him on twitter as @mittie.

DR. PAUL KING'S career spans technical and managerial roles in a number of organizations, underpinned by deep knowledge of the information technology and telecommunications markets and a passion for the creation of innovative organizations.

Throughout his career, Paul has provided technical and strategic consulting to hundreds of organizations in the U.S. and Asia Pacific. The early stages of Paul's career were highlighted by his contributions to various research fields, including object-oriented software development, formal methods, telecommunications, and distributed systems. He has had numerous publications at international conferences and in journals and trade magazines. He is an award-winning author and sought-after speaker at conferences.

Currently, Paul leads ASERT (Advanced Software Engineering, Research & Training), which is recognized as a world-class center of expertise in the areas of middleware technology, agile development, and internet application development and deployment. ASERT has experience teaching thousands of students in more than 15 countries, and has provided consulting services and development assistance throughout Asia Pacific to high-profile startups and government e-commerce sites. In his spare time, Paul is a taxi driver and homework assistant for his seven children and two grandchildren. You can follow him on twitter as @paulk_asert.

GUILLAUME LAFORGE has been the official Groovy project manager since the end of 2004, after having been a contributor and later a core committer on the project. He is also the specification lead for JSR-241, the ongoing effort to standardize the Groovy language through Sun's Java Community Process. Guillaume is Groovy's "public face" and often responds to interviews regarding Groovy and presents his project at conferences around the world, such as at JavaOne or Devoxx, where he recently spoke about how scripting can simplify enterprise development. Guillaume cofounded the G2One company, which focused on and further developed the Groovy and Grails technologies, later acquired by SpringSource; also VMware and its Pivotal spin-off. Guillaume recently joined Restlet as Product Ninja and Advocate.

CÉDRIC CHAMPEAU is a member of the Groovy core team. He is a passionate developer who started writing programs at the age of eight and learned it the hard way by manually typing magazine listings into an Amstrad PC1512. He worked several years in natural language processing where he used Groovy in multiple contexts, from a workflow engine to a DSL for linguists, and Lucene custom scoring. This is how he dived into the internals of the language and started contributing before becoming one of the core team members. He implemented many advanced Groovy features like compilation customizers, static compilation, traits, the markup template engine, and the recent support for Android.

HAMLET D'ARCY is a software engineer at Microsoft, founder of the Basel-based Hackergarten open source coding group, and can be found speaking at local and international user groups and conferences. He's a committer on the Groovy and CodeNarc projects and a contributor on a number of other projects (including the IDEA Groovy Plugin). He's passionate about learning new languages and different ways of thinking about problems. He blogs regularly at http://hamletdarcy.blogspot.com.

ERIK PRAGT is a passionate software developer with a broad range of experience in static languages like Java and Scala, and dynamic languages like Groovy, JavaScript, and Python. Having worked as a consultant for a broad range of customers, mostly in the Telecom, ISP, and banking sectors, Erik is now an independent freelance consultant. He founded the Dutch Groovy and Grails user group, and is a regular conference speaker and trainer. Erik spends most of his free time working on open source software. In the limited time he's not sitting behind the computer he can be found in the gym, riding his motorcycle, or diving, always looking for new inspiration, which he shares on twitter at @epragt.

JON SKEET Jon Skeet is a software engineer working for Google in London. He is probably best known for his contributions on Stack Overflow. He blogs, tweets (@jonskeet), speaks at conferences, and generally says too much and listens too little. For some years now, his primary open source contribution to the world has been Noda Time, a better .NET date and time API. He is the author of Manning's *C# in Depth, Third Edition*.

Part 1

The Groovy language

A good notation has subtlety and suggestiveness which at times makes it almost seem like a live teacher.

— Bertrand Russell
The World of Mathematics (1956)

Learning a new programming language is comparable to learning to speak a foreign language. You have to deal with new vocabulary, grammar, and language idioms. But this initial effort pays off multiple times. With the new language, you find unique ways to express yourself, you're exposed to new concepts and styles that add to your personal abilities, and you may even explore new perspectives on your world. This is what Groovy did for us, and we hope Groovy will do it for you, too.

The first part of this book introduces you to the language basics: the Groovy syntax, grammar, and typical idioms. We present the language by example as opposed to using an academic style.

You may skim this part on first read and revisit it before going into serious development with Groovy. If you decide to skim, please make sure you visit chapter 2 and its examples. They are cross-linked to the in-depth chapters so you can easily look up details about any topic that interests you.

One of the difficulties of explaining a programming language by example is that you have to start somewhere. No matter where you start, you end up needing to use some concept or feature that you haven't explained yet for your examples.

Section 2.3 serves to resolve this perceived deadlock by providing a collection of self-explanatory warm-up examples.

We explain the main portion of the language using its built-in datatypes and introduce expressions, operators, and keywords as we go along. By starting with some of the most familiar aspects of the language and building up your knowledge in stages, we hope you'll always feel confident when exploring new territory.

Chapter 3 introduces Groovy's practical approach to typing, examines the numeric and other primitive types that Groovy supports, and discusses strings and regular expressions.

Chapter 4 continues looking at Groovy's rich set of built-in types, examining those with a collection-like nature: ranges, lists, and maps.

Chapter 5 builds on the preceding sections and provides an in-depth description of the closure concept.

Chapter 6 touches on logical branching, looping, and shortcutting program execution flow.

Chapter 7 sheds light on the way Groovy builds on Java's object-oriented features adding support for multimethods and traits.

Chapter 8 looks at Groovy's dynamic programming capabilities.

Chapter 9 dives into compile-time metaprogramming and AST transformations.

Chapter 10, the final chapter in part 1, discusses Groovy as a static language.

At the end of part 1, you'll have the whole picture of the Groovy language. This is the basis for getting the most out of part 2, which explores the Groovy library: the classes and methods that Groovy adds to the Java platform. Part 3, "Applied Groovy," leads you through places where the power of Groovy is put into action.

Your way to Groovy 1

It isn't the mountains ahead to climb that wear you out; it's the pebble in your shoe.

—Muhammad Ali

You've heard of Groovy, maybe even installed the distribution and tried snippets from the online tutorials. Perhaps your project has adopted Groovy as a dynamic extension to Java and you now seek information about what you can do with it. You may have been acquainted with Groovy from using the Grails web application platform, the Griffon desktop application framework, the Gradle build system, or the Spock testing facility, and now look for background information about the language that these tools are built upon. This book delivers to that purpose, but you can expect even more from learning Groovy.

Groovy will give you quick wins, whether by making your Java code simpler to write, by automating recurring tasks, by modeling business logic in domain-specific languages (DSLs), or by supporting ad-hoc scripting for your daily work as a programmer. It'll give you longer-term wins by making your code simpler to *read*. Perhaps most important, it's a pleasure to use.

Learning Groovy is a wise investment. Groovy brings the power of advanced language features such as closures, dynamic methods, and the Meta Object Protocol (MOP) to the Java platform. Your Java knowledge will not become obsolete by walking the Groovy path. Groovy will build on your experience and familiarity with the Java platform, allowing you to pick and choose when you use which tool—and when to combine the two seamlessly.

Groovy follows a pragmatic "no drama"[1] approach: it obeys the Java object model and always keeps the perspective of a Java programmer. It doesn't force you into any new programming paradigm, but offers those advanced capabilities that you legitimately expect from a "top-of-stack" language.

This first chapter provides background information about Groovy and everything you need to know to get started. It starts with the Groovy story: why Groovy was created, what considerations drive its design, and how it positions itself in the landscape of languages and technologies. The next section expands on Groovy's merits and how they can make life easier for you, whether you're a Java programmer, a script aficionado, or an agile developer.

We strongly believe that there's only one way to learn a programming language: by trying it. We present a variety of scripts to demonstrate the compiler, interpreter, and shells, before listing plug-ins available for widely used IDEs and where to find the latest information about Groovy.

By the end of this chapter, you'll have a basic understanding of what Groovy is and how you can experiment with it.

We—the authors, the reviewers, and the editing team—wish you a great time programming Groovy and using this book for guidance and reference.

1.1 *The Groovy story*

At Groovy One 2004—a gathering of Groovy developers in London—James Strachan gave a keynote address telling the story of how he arrived at the idea of inventing Groovy.

He and his wife were waiting for a late plane. While she went shopping, he visited an internet cafe and spontaneously decided to go to the Python website and study the language. In the course of this activity, he became more and more intrigued. Being a seasoned Java programmer, he recognized that his home language lacked many of the interesting and useful features Python had invented, such as native language support for common datatypes in an expressive syntax and, more important, dynamic behavior. The idea was born to bring such features to Java.

---

[1] Thanks to Mac Liaw for this wording.

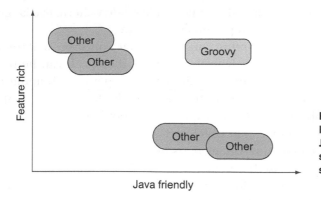

Figure 1.1 **The landscape of JVM-based languages. Groovy is a feature-rich and Java-friendly language—it excels at both sides instead of sacrificing one for the sake of the other.**

This led to the main principles that guide Groovy's development: to be a feature-rich and Java-friendly language, bringing the attractive benefits of dynamic languages to a robust and well-supported platform.

Figure 1.1 shows how this unique combination defines Groovy's position in the varied world of languages for the Java platform.[2] We don't want to offend anyone by specifying exactly where we believe any particular other language might fit in the figure, but we're confident of Groovy's position.

In the early days of Groovy, we were mainly asked how it'd compare to Java, Bean-Shell, Pnuts, and embedded expression languages. The focus was clearly on Java friendliness. Then the focus shifted to dynamic capabilities and the debate went on putting Groovy, JavaScript (Rhino), Jython, and JRuby side by side. Recently, we see more comparison with Clojure, Scala, Kotlin, Ceylon, Fan, Nice, Newspeak, and Frege. Most of them introduce the functional programming paradigm to the Java platform, which makes a comparison on the feature dimension rather difficult. They're simply different. Some other JVM languages like Alice and Fortress are even totally unrelated. By the time you read this, some new kids are likely to have appeared on the block and the pendulum may have swung in a totally different direction. But with the landscape picture shown in figure 1.1 you're able to also position upcoming languages.

Some languages may offer more advanced features than Groovy. Not so many languages may claim to fit equally well to the Java language. None can currently touch Groovy when you consider both aspects together: nothing provides a better combination of Java friendliness and a complete feature set.

With Groovy being in this position, what are its main characteristics?

1.1.1 *What is Groovy?*

Groovy is an optionally typed, dynamic language for the Java platform with many features that are inspired by languages like Python, Ruby, and Smalltalk, making them

---

[2] See www.is-research.de/info/vmlanguages/category/jvm-language/, which lists about 240 languages targeting the Java virtual machine (JVM).

available to Java developers using a Java-like syntax. Unlike other alternative languages, it's designed as a companion to, not a replacement for, Java.

Groovy is often referred to as a scripting language, and it works very well for scripting. It's a mistake to label Groovy purely in those terms, though. It can be precompiled into Java bytecode, integrated into Java applications, power web applications, add an extra degree of control within build files, and be the basis of whole applications on its own. Groovy, obviously, is too flexible to be pigeonholed.

What we *can* say about Groovy is that it's closely tied to the Java platform. This is true in terms of both implementation (many parts of Groovy are written in Java, with the rest being written in Groovy itself) and interaction. When you program in Groovy, in many ways you're writing a special kind of Java. All the power of the Java platform—including the massive set of available libraries—is there to be harnessed.

Does this make Groovy just a layer of syntactic sugar? Not at all. Although everything you do in Groovy *could* be done in Java, it'd be madness to write the Java code required to work Groovy's magic. Groovy performs a lot of work behind the scenes to achieve its agility and dynamic nature. As you read this book, try to think every so often about what would be required to mimic the effects of Groovy using Java. Many of the Groovy features that seem extraordinary at first—encapsulating logic in objects in a natural way, building hierarchies with barely any code other than what's *absolutely* required to compute the data, expressing database queries in the normal application language before they're translated into SQL, manipulating the runtime behavior of individual objects after they've been created—are tasks that Java wasn't designed for.

To quote a JavaOne slogan: Groovy is there for "extending the reach of Java."

Let's take a closer look at what makes Groovy so appealing, starting with how Groovy and Java work hand-in-hand.

1.1.2 *Playing nicely with Java: seamless integration*

Being Java friendly means two things: seamless integration with the Java Runtime Environment and having a syntax that's aligned with Java.

SEAMLESS INTEGRATION

Figure 1.2 shows the integration aspect of Groovy: it runs inside the JVM and makes use of Java's libraries (together called the Java Runtime Environment, or JRE). Groovy is only a new way of creating *ordinary* Java classes—from a runtime perspective, Groovy *is* Java with an additional JAR file as a dependency.

Consequently, calling Java from Groovy is a nonissue. When developing in Groovy, you end up doing this all the time without noticing. Every Groovy type is a subtype of

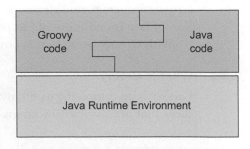

Figure 1.2 **Groovy and Java join together in a tongue-and-groove fashion.**

java.lang.Object. Every Groovy object is an instance of a type in the normal way. A Groovy date *is* a java.util.Date. You can call all methods on it that you know are available for a Date, and you can pass it as an argument to any method that expects a Date.

Calling into Java is an easy exercise. It's something that all JVM languages offer, at least the ones worth speaking of. They all make it possible, some by staying inside their own non-Java abstractions, and some by providing a gateway. Groovy is one of the few that does it its own way *and* the Java way at the same time, because there's no difference.

Integration in the opposite direction is just as easy. Suppose a Groovy class MyGroovyClass is compiled into MyGroovyClass.class and put on the classpath. You can use this Groovy class from within a Java class by typing

```
new MyGroovyClass(); // create from Java
```

You can then call methods on the instance, pass the reference as an argument to methods, and so forth. The JVM is blissfully unaware that the code was written in Groovy. This becomes particularly important when integrating with Java frameworks that call your class where you have no control over how that call is affected.

The "interoperability" in this direction is a bit more involved for alternative JVM languages. Yes, they may compile to bytecode but that doesn't mean much by itself, because one can produce valid bytecode that's totally incomprehensible for a Java caller. A language may not even be object-oriented and provide classes and methods. And even if it does, it may assign totally different semantics to those abstractions. Groovy, in contrast, fully stays inside the Java object model. Actually, compiling to class files is only one of many ways to integrate Groovy into your Java project. Chapter 16 on integration describes the full range of options. The integration ladder in figure 1.3 arranges the criteria by their significance.

One step up on the integration ladder and you meet the issue of references. A Groovy class may reference a Java class (that goes without saying) and a Java class may reference a Groovy class, as you've just seen. You can even have circular references and groovyc compiles them all transparently. Even better, the leading IDEs provide cross-language compile, navigation, and refactoring such that you rarely need to care about the project build setup. You're free to choose Java or Groovy when implementing any class for that matter. Such tight build-time integration is a challenge for every other language.

The next rung where candidates slip off is overloaded methods. Imagine you set out to implement the Java interface java.io.Writer in any non-Java language. It comes with three versions of write that take one parameter: write(int c), write(String str), and write(char[] buf). Implementing this in Groovy is trivial—it's *exactly* like in Java. The formal parameter types distinguish which methods you override. That's one of many merits of optional typing. Languages that are solely dynamically typed have no way of doing this.

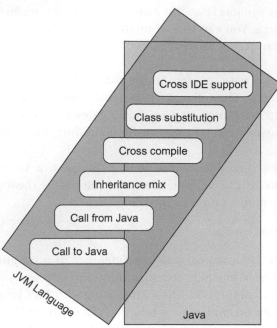

Figure 1.3   The integration ladder shows increasing cross-language support from simple calls for interoperability up to seamless tool integration.

But the buck doesn't stop here. The Java–Groovy mix allows annotations and interfaces being defined in either language and implemented and used in the other. You can subclass in any combination even with abstract classes and "sandwich" inheritance like Java–Groovy–Java or Groovy–Java–Groovy in arbitrary depth. It may look exotic at first sight but we actually needed this feature in customer projects. We'll come back to that. Of course, this integration presupposes that your language knows about annotations and interfaces like Groovy does.

True seamless integration means that you can take *any* Java class from a given Java codebase and replace it with a Groovy class. Likewise, you can take any Groovy class and rewrite it in Java, both without touching any other class in the code base. That's what we call a *drop-in replacement*, which imposes further considerations about annotations, static members, and accessibility of the used libraries from Java.

Generated bytecode can be more or less Java-tool friendly. There are more and more tools on the market that directly augment your bytecode, be it for gathering test coverage information or "weaving aspects" in. These tools don't only expect bytecode to be valid, but also to find well-known patterns in it such as the Java and Groovy compiler provide. Bytecode generated by other languages is often not digestible for such tools.

Alternative Java virtual machine (JVM) languages are often attributed as working "seamlessly" with Java. With the integration ladder in figure 1.3, you can check to what degree this applies: calls into Java, calls from Java, bidirectional compilation, inheritance intermix, mutual class substitutability, and tool support. We didn't even consider security, profiling, debugging, and other Java architectures. So much for the *platform* integration, now on to the syntax.

SYNTAX ALIGNMENT

The second dimension of Groovy's friendliness is its syntax alignment. Let's compare the different mechanisms to obtain today's date in various languages to demonstrate what alignment *should* mean:

```
import java.util.*;        // Java
Date today = new Date();   // Java

today = new Date()         // Groovy

require 'date'             # Ruby
today = Date.new           # Ruby

import java.util._         // Scala
var today = new Date       // Scala

(import '(java.util Date)) ; Clojure
(def today (new Date))     ; Clojure
(def today (Date.))        ; Clojure alternative
```

The Groovy solution is short, precise, and more compact than regular Java. Groovy doesn't need to import the java.util package or specify the Date type. This is very handy when using Groovy to evaluate user input. In those cases, one cannot assume that the user is proficient in Java package structures or willing to write more code than necessary. Additionally, Groovy doesn't require semicolons when it can understand the code without them. Despite being more compact, Groovy is fully comprehensible to a Java programmer.

The Ruby solution is listed to illustrate what Groovy avoids: a different packaging concept (require), a different comment syntax, and a different object-creation syntax. Scala introduces a new wildcard syntax with underscores and has its own way of declaring whether a reference is supposed to be (in Java terms) "final" or not (var vs. val). The user has to provide one or the other. Clojure doesn't support wildcard imports as of now, and shows two alternative ways of instantiating a Java class, both of which differ syntactically from Java.

Although all the alternative notations make sense in themselves and may even be more consistent than Java, they don't align as nicely with the Java syntax and architecture as Groovy does. Throw into the mix that Groovy is the only language besides Java that fully supports the Java notation of generics and annotations and you easily retrace why the Groovy syntax is placed perfectly aligned with Java.

Now you have an idea what Java friendliness means in terms of integration and syntax alignment. But how about feature richness?

1.1.3 *Power in your code: a feature-rich language*

Giving a list of Groovy features is a bit like listing moves a dancer can perform. Although each feature is important in itself, it's how well they work together that makes Groovy shine. Groovy has three main enhancements over and above those of Java: language features, libraries specific to Groovy, and additions to the existing Java standard classes (known as the Groovy Development Kit, or GDK). Figure 1.4 shows some of these enhancements and how they fit together. The shaded circles indicate the way that the features use each other. For instance, many of the library features rely heavily on language features. Idiomatic Groovy code rarely uses one feature in isolation; instead, it usually uses several of them together, like notes in a chord.

Unfortunately, many of the features can't be understood in just a few words. *Closures*, for example, are an invaluable language concept in Groovy, but the word on its own doesn't tell you anything. We won't go into all the details now, but here are a few examples to whet your appetite.

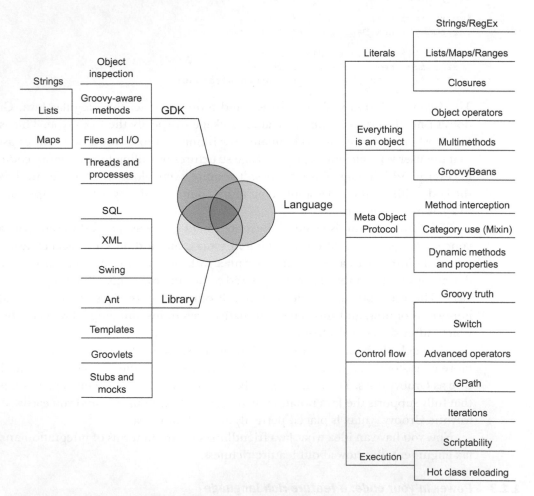

Figure 1.4   Many of the additional libraries and GDK enhancements in Groovy build on the new language features. The combination of the three forms a "sweet spot" for clear and powerful code.

LISTING A FILE: CLOSURES AND I/O ADDITIONS

Closures are blocks of code that can be treated as first-class objects: passed around as references, stored, executed at arbitrary times, and so on. Java's anonymous inner classes are often used this way, particularly with adapter classes, but the syntax of inner classes is ugly, and they're limited in terms of the data they can access and change.

File handling in Groovy is made significantly easier with the addition of various methods to classes in the `java.io` package. A great example is the `File.eachLine` method. How often have you needed to read a file, a line at a time, and perform the same action on each line, closing the file at the end? This is such a common task; it shouldn't be difficult. In Groovy, it isn't.

Let's put the two features together and create a complete program that lists a file with line numbers:

```
def number = 0
new File('data.txt').eachLine { line ->
    number++
    println "$number: $line"
}
```

which prints

```
1: first line
2: second line
```

The braces enclose the closure. It's passed as an argument to `File`'s new `eachLine` method, which in turn calls back the closure for each line that it reads, passing the current line as an argument.

PRINTING A LIST: COLLECTION LITERALS AND SIMPLIFIED PROPERTY ACCESS

The interfaces `java.util.List` and `java.util.Map` are probably the most widely used ones in Java, but there's little language support for them. Groovy adds the ability to declare list and map literals just as easily as you would a string or numeric literal, and it adds many methods to the collection classes.

Similarly, the JavaBean conventions for properties are almost ubiquitous in Java, but the language makes no use of them. Groovy simplifies property access, allowing for far more readable code.

Here's an example using these two features to print the package for each of a list of classes. Note that the word "clazz" isn't "class" because that would be a Groovy keyword—exactly like in Java. Although Java would allow a similar first line to declare an array, we're using a real list here—elements could be added or removed with no extra work:

```
def classes = [String, List, File]
for (clazz in classes) {
    println clazz.package.name
}
```

which prints

```
java.lang
java.util
java.io
```

In Groovy, you can even avoid such commonplace for loops by applying property access to a list—the result is a list of the properties. Using this feature, an equivalent solution to the previous code is

```
println( [String, List, File]*.package*.name )
```

which prints

```
[java.lang, java.util, java.io]
```

Pretty cool, eh? The star character is optional in the preceding code. It's added to emphasize that the access to package and name is *spread* over the list and thus applied to every item in it.

XML HANDLING THE GROOVY WAY: GPATH WITH DYNAMIC PROPERTIES

Whether you're reading it or writing it, working with XML in Java requires a considerable amount of work. Alternatives to the W3C DOM make life easier, but Java itself doesn't help you in language terms—it's unable to adapt to your needs. Groovy allows classes to act as if they had properties at runtime even if the names of those properties aren't known when the class is compiled. GPath was built on this feature, and it allows seamless XPath-like navigation of XML documents.

Suppose you have a file called customers.xml such as this:

```
<?xml version="1.0" ?>
<customers>
  <corporate>
    <customer name="Bill Gates"     company="Microsoft" />
    <customer name="Tim Cook"       company="Apple"     />
    <customer name="Larry Ellison"  company="Oracle"    />
  </corporate>
  <consumer>
    <customer name="John Doe" />
    <customer name="Jane Doe" />
  </consumer>
</customers>
```

You can print all the corporate customers with their names and companies using just the following code:

```
def customers = new XmlSlurper().parse(new File('customers.xml'))
for (customer in customers.corporate.customer) {
    println "${customer.@name} works for ${customer.@company}"
}
```

which prints

```
Bill Gates works for Microsoft
Tim Cook works for Apple
Larry Ellison works for Oracle
```

Note that Groovy cannot possibly know anything in advance about the elements and attributes that are available in the XML file. It happily compiles anyway. That's one capability that distinguishes a *dynamic* language.

A FRIENDLY LANGUAGE

Even trying to demonstrate just a few features of Groovy, you've seen other features in the preceding examples—string interpolation with GString, simpler for loops, optional typing, and optional statement terminators and parentheses, just for starters. The features work so well with each other and become second nature so quickly, you hardly notice you're using them.

Although being Java friendly and feature rich are the main driving forces for Groovy, there are more aspects worth considering. So far, we've focused on the hard technical facts about Groovy, but a language needs more than that to be successful. It needs to *attract* people. In the world of computer languages, building a better mousetrap doesn't guarantee that the world will beat a path to your door. It has to appeal to both developers and their managers, in different ways.

1.1.4 *Community driven but corporate backed*

For some people it's comforting to know that their investment in a language is protected by its adoption as a standard. This is one of the distinctive promises of Groovy. Groovy is a de-facto standard like Spring and, not coincidentally, it's endorsed by the same company. Groovy is also a "first-class citizen" in the Spring framework.

The size of the user base is a second criterion. The larger the user base, the greater the chance of obtaining good support and sustainable development. Groovy's user base has grown beyond all expectations and has recently reached the top 20 of the TIOBE (www.tiobe.com) index.[3] Recent polls suggest that Groovy is used in the majority of organizations that develop professionally with Java, much higher than any alternative language. Groovy is regularly covered in Java conferences and publications, and virtually any Java open source project that allows scripting extensions supports Groovy and has become an important item in many developers' CVs and job descriptions.

Many corporations support Groovy. Oracle integrates Groovy support in its Net-Beans IDE tool suite, presents Groovy at JavaOne, and pushes forward the idea of multiple languages on the JVM, as in the JSRs 223 (Scripting Integration) and 292 (InvokeDynamic). Oracle has a long-standing tradition of using Groovy in a number of products, just like other big players including IBM and SAP. While the development of Groovy has always been driven by its community, it also profited from financial backing. Sustainability of the Groovy development was first sponsored by Big Sky Technology, then by G2One and SpringSource (later acquired by VMware and then spun off as part of Pivotal). Since 2015, Groovy is run under the stewardship of the Apache Software Foundation (ASF). Big thanks to all that made this development possible!

---

[3] Groovy's ranking tends to jump around quite a lot for that index as TIOBE Software alters its algorithm.

Commercial support is also available if needed. Many companies offer training, consulting, and engineering for Groovy, including the ones that we authors work for: ASERT, Canoo, and Jworks.

Attraction is more than strategic considerations, however. Beyond what you can measure is a gut feeling that causes you to enjoy programming *or not.*

The developers of Groovy are aware of this feeling, and it's carefully considered when deciding on language features. After all, there's a reason for the name of the language.

> **GROOVY** "A situation or an activity that one enjoys or to which one is espe-
> cially well suited (found his groove playing bass in a trio). A very pleasurable
> experience; enjoy oneself (just sitting around, grooving on the music). To be
> affected with pleasurable excitement. To react or interact harmoniously."
> (http://dict.leo.org).

Working with Groovy feels like a partnership between you and the language, rather than a battle to express what's clear in your mind in a way the computer can understand.

Of course, while it's nice to "feel the groove," you still need to pay your bills. In the next section, we'll look at practical advantages Groovy will bring to your professional life.

1.2   What Groovy can do for you

Depending on your background and experience, you're probably interested in different features of Groovy. It's unlikely that anyone will require every aspect of Groovy in their day-to-day work, just as no one uses the whole of the mammoth framework provided by the Java standard libraries.

This section presents interesting Groovy features and areas of applicability for Java professionals; script programmers; and pragmatic, extreme, and agile programmers. We recognize that developers rarely have just one role within their jobs and may well have to take on each of these identities in turn. But it's helpful to focus on how Groovy helps in the kinds of situations typically associated with each role.

1.2.1   Groovy for the busy Java professional

If you consider yourself a Java professional, you probably have years of experience in Java programming. You know all the important parts of the Java Runtime API and most likely the APIs of a lot of additional Java packages.

But, be honest. There are times when you cannot easily leverage this knowledge. Consider an everyday task like searching through a number of websites for a particular word. If you're in a hurry you might even want to do the searching concurrently. You probably know several libraries and classes that could be effectively utilized to accomplish this ad-hoc task but, if you're like us, you probably consider coding the Java solution as just too much effort.

As you'll learn in this book, with Groovy you can quickly open the console and accomplish this task by typing just a few lines of code as shown here:

```
import static groovyx.gpars.GParsPool.withPool

def urls = [
    'http://www.groovy-lang.org',
    'http://gpars.codehaus.org',
    'http://gr8conf.org/'
]*.toURL()

println withPool {
    urls.collectParallel {
        it.text.findAll(~/[Gg]roovy/).size()
    }
}
```

At the time of writing, this produced the following list of three numbers:

```
[38, 13, 2]
```

With current versions of Java, the equivalent solution with its exception handling, thread management, and other scaffolding code is significantly harder to write and understand. Java 8 improves on this somewhat, thanks to the introduction of lambdas, but Groovy remains far ahead with regard to readability and ease of use.

Besides command-line availability and code beauty, Groovy allows you to bring dynamic behavior to Java applications, such as through expressing business rules that can be maintained while the application is running, allowing smart configurations, or even implementing DSLs.

You have the options of using static or dynamic types and working with precompiled code or plain Groovy source code with on-demand compiling. As a developer, you can decide where and when you want to put your solution "in stone" and where it needs to be flexible. With Groovy, you have the choice.

This should give you enough safeguards to feel comfortable incorporating Groovy into your projects so you can benefit from its features.

1.2.2 Groovy for the polyglot programmer

As a polyglot programmer, you may be versed in various kinds of languages and programming paradigms like Perl, Ruby, Python, Smalltalk, Lisp, Haskell, or Dylan. But the Java platform has an undeniable market share, and it's fairly common that folks like you work with the Java language to make a living. Corporate clients often run a Java standard platform (for example, JEE), allowing nothing but Java to be developed and deployed in production. You have no chance of getting your ultraslick foreign-language solution in there, so you bite the bullet, thinking all day, "If I only had [*your language here*], I could replace this whole method with a single line!" We confess to having experienced this kind of frustration.

Groovy can give you relief and bring back the fun of programming by providing advanced language features where you need them: in your daily work. By allowing you to call methods on *anything*, pass blocks of code around for immediate or later execution following a functional approach, augment existing library code with your own specialized semantics, and use a host of other powerful features, Groovy lets you express yourself clearly and achieve miracles with little code. Just sneak the groovy-all-*.jar file into your project's classpath, and you're there.

Today, software development is seldom a solitary activity, and your teammates (and your boss) need to know what you're doing with Groovy and what Groovy is about. This book aims to be a device you can pass along to others so they can learn, too. (Of course, if you can't bear the thought of parting with it, you can tell them to buy their own copies. We won't mind.)

1.2.3   *Groovy for pragmatic programmers, extremos, and agilists*

If you fall into this category, you probably already have an overloaded bookshelf, a board full of index cards with tasks, and an automated test suite that threatens to turn red at a moment's notice. The next iteration release is close, and there's anything but time to think about Groovy. Even uttering the word makes your pair-programming mate start questioning your state of mind.

One thing that we've learned about being pragmatic, extreme, or agile is that every now and then you have to step back, relax, and assess whether your tools are still sharp enough to cut smoothly. Despite the ever-pressing project schedules, you need to *sharpen the saw* regularly. In software terms, that means having the knowledge and resources needed and using the right methodology, tools, technologies, and languages for the task at hand.

Groovy will be your *house elf* for all automation tasks that you're likely to have in your projects. These range from simple build automation, continuous integration (CI), and reporting, up to automated documentation, shipment, and installation. The Groovy automation support leverages the power of existing solutions such as Ant, Maven, and Gradle while providing a simple and concise language means to control them. Groovy even helps with testing, both at the unit and functional levels, helping us test-driven folks feel right at home.

Hardly any school of programmers applies as much rigor and pays as much attention as we do when it comes to self-describing, intention-revealing code. We feel an almost physical need to remove duplication while striving for simpler solutions. This is where Groovy can help tremendously.

Before Groovy, I (Dierk) used other scripting languages (preferably Ruby) to sketch some design ideas, do a *spike* (a programming experiment to assess the feasibility of a task), and run a functional *prototype*. The downside was that I was never sure if what I was writing would *also* work in Java. Worse, in the end, I had the work of porting it over or redoing it from scratch. With Groovy, I can do all the exploration work *directly* on my target platform.

Real-life example

Recently, Guillaume and I did a spike on *prime number factorization.*[4] We started with a small Groovy solution that did the job cleanly but not efficiently. Using Groovy's interception capabilities, we unit-tested the solution and counted the number of operations. Because the code was clean, it was a breeze to optimize the solution and decrease the operation count. It would have been much more difficult to recognize the optimization potential in Java code. The final result can be used from Java as it stands, and although we certainly still have the option of porting the optimized solution to plain Java, which would give us another performance gain, we can defer the decision until the need arises.

The seamless interplay of Groovy and Java opens two dimensions of optimizing code: using Java for code that needs to be optimized for runtime performance, and using Groovy for code that needs to be optimized for flexibility and readability.

Along with all these tangible benefits, there's value in learning Groovy for its own sake. It'll open your mind to new solutions, helping you to perceive new concepts when developing software, whichever language you use.

No matter what kind of programmer you are, we hope you're now eager to get some Groovy code under your fingers. If you cannot hold back from looking at real Groovy code, look ahead at chapter 2.

1.3 Running Groovy

First, we need to introduce you to the tools you'll be using to run and optionally compile Groovy code. If you want to try these out as you read, you'll need to have Groovy installed, of course. Appendix A provides a guide for the installation process.

> **TIP** You can execute Groovy code—and most examples in this book—even without installing anything! Point your browser to http://groovyconsole .appspot.com/. This console is hosted on the Google app engine and is provided by Guillaume Laforge. Share and enjoy!

There are three commands to execute Groovy code and scripts, as shown in table 1.1. Each of the three different mechanisms of running Groovy is demonstrated in the following sections with examples and screenshots. Groovy can also be run like any ordinary Java program, as you'll see in section 1.4.2, and there's also a special integration with Ant that's explained in section 1.4.3.

We'll explore several options for integrating Groovy in Java programs in chapter 11.

---

[4] Every ordinal number N can be uniquely disassembled into factors that are prime numbers: $N = p_1 \times p_2 \times p_3$. The factorization problem is known to be hard. Its complexity guards cryptographic algorithms like the popular Rivest–Shamir–Adleman (RSA) algorithm.

Table 1.1 Commands to execute Groovy

Command	What it does
groovy	Starts the processor that executes Groovy scripts. Single-line Groovy scripts can be specified as command-line arguments.
groovysh	Starts the groovysh command-line shell, used to execute Groovy code interactively. By entering statements or whole scripts line by line into the shell, code is executed on the fly.
groovyConsole	Starts a graphical interface that's used to execute Groovy code interactively; moreover, groovyConsole loads and runs Groovy script files.

1.3.1 Using groovysh for a welcome message

Let's look at groovysh first because it's a handy tool for running experiments with Groovy. It's easy to edit and run Groovy interactively in this shell, and doing so facilitates seeing how Groovy works without creating and editing script files.

To start the shell, run groovysh (UNIX) or groovysh.bat (Windows) from the command line. You should get a command prompt like the following where you can enter Groovy code to receive a warm welcome:

```
Groovy Shell (2.4.0, JVM: 1.7.0_75)
Type ':help' or ':h' for help.
-----------------------------------------------------------------
groovy:000> "Welcome, " + System.properties."user.name"
===> Welcome, Dierk
groovy:000>
```

The shell is a good companion when you work on a remote server with only a text terminal available. For the more common case where you are working on a desktop or laptop machine, there are options that are even more comfortable as you'll see in a minute.

The shell can be started with a number of different command-line options that are well explained in the online documentation (www.groovy-lang.org/groovysh.html). The shell also understands useful commands, most notably help, which spares us listing all commands here. One explanation, though: the shell comes with the notion of an editing buffer that comes in to play when a statement or expression spans multiple lines. Class and method definitions are typical cases. The shell then keeps track of the line numbers and allows various commands on the buffer, like editing it in your system's text editor.

1.3.2 Using groovyConsole

groovyConsole is a Swing interface that acts as a minimal Groovy development editor. It lacks support for the command-line options supported by groovysh; however, it has a File menu to allow Groovy scripts to be loaded, created, and saved. Interestingly, groovyConsole is written in Groovy. Its implementation is a good demonstration of builders, which are discussed in chapter 11.

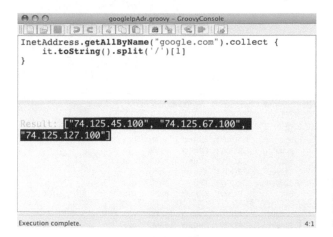

```
InetAddress.getAllByName("google.com").collect {
    it.toString().split('/')[1]
}
```

Result: ["74.125.45.100", "74.125.67.100", "74.125.127.100"]

Execution complete.   4:1

Figure 1.5 `groovyConsole` with a script in the edit pane that finds the IP addresses of google.com. The output pane captures the result.

groovyConsole takes no arguments and starts a two-paned window like the one shown in figure 1.5. The console accepts keyboard input in the upper pane. To run a script, either key in Ctrl-R or Ctrl-Enter, or use the Run command from the Action menu. When any part of the script code is selected, only the selected text is executed. This feature is useful for simple debugging or *single stepping* by successively selecting one or multiple lines.

groovyConsole comes with all the UI goodness that you expect from a Swing application.[5] Walk through the menus or read the documentation under www.groovy-lang.org/groovyconsole.html (you got the pattern by now, right?). The console comes with some pleasant surprises. For good reasons, we made it very "demo-friendly." Ctrl-Shift-L and Ctrl-Shift-S will make the code appear larger or smaller so that the audience can better see the code.

You can also drag and drop Groovy files from your filesystem right into the editor. But that's not all!

Figure 1.6 shows the Object Browser inspecting the returned list of IP addresses. It contains information about the ArrayList class in the header, with tabbed tables showing available variables, methods, and fields.

For easy browsing, you can sort columns by clicking the headers or reverse the sort with a second click. You can sort by multiple criteria by clicking column headers in sequence, and rearrange the columns by dragging the column headers.

By this means, you can easily find out which methods you can call on the object you're currently working on (same intent as code completion in IDEs), which type declared that method, and whether it comes from Groovy or Java. Let's try this out: click the Name header to sort by method names, then click Declarer, then click Origin. Now scroll down the list until you see Object as the declarer. Now you should see

---

[5] Thanks to Romain Guy, the UI expert and coauthor of *Filthy Rich Clients: Developing Animated and Graphical Effects for Desktop Java Applications* (Addison-Wesley Professional, 2007), who supported the Groovy team here.

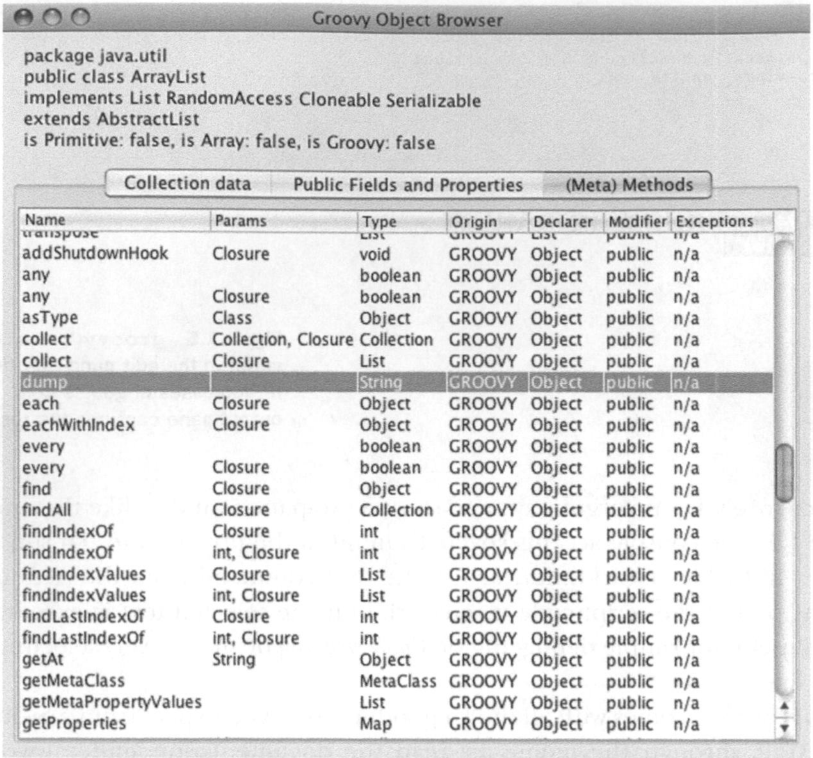

**Figure 1.6   The Groovy Object Browser when opened on an object of type
`ArrayList`, displaying the table of available methods in its bytecode and
registered meta-methods.**

the same as in figure 1.6: the list of all methods, including parameter types and return type, that Groovy adds to `java.lang.Object`. You'll learn more about these methods in chapter 12.

Highlighted is the method `dump()` that Groovy adds to all objects. Try it! Put it in the input field of the console. You'll see that it's like `toString()` but includes the internal state of the object.

Unless explicitly stated otherwise, you can put any code example in this book directly into `groovysh` or `groovyConsole` and run it there. The more often you do that, the quicker you'll get a feeling for the language.

1.3.3   *Using the groovy command*

The `groovy` command is used to execute Groovy programs and scripts. Listing 1.1 calculates the *golden ratio* that intersects a line into a smaller and bigger part such that the total line length relates to the bigger part like the bigger part relates to the smaller part. Composing paintings, photos, or UIs with the help of the golden ratio is considered pleasing to the human eye and has a long tradition in classic art. The pentagram that underlies the Groovy logo is composed of golden ratios.[6]

We calculate the golden ratio by narrowing down on the ratio of adjacent Fibonacci[7] numbers. The Fibonacci number sequence is a pattern where the first two numbers are 1 and 1, and every subsequent number is the sum of the preceding two. The ratio between fibo(n) and fibo($n - 1$) comes closer and closer to the golden ratio for increasing values of n.

We don't go into the details of the implementation right now. Think about it as arbitrary Groovy code, which for the beginning isn't quite as "Groovy idiomatic" as it could be. One little explanation anyway: `[-1]` refers to the last element in a list, `[-2]` to the last-but-one.

If you'd like to try this, copy the code into a file, and save it as Gold.groovy. The file extension doesn't matter much as far as the `groovy` executable is concerned, but naming Groovy scripts with a .groovy extension is conventional. One benefit of using this extension is that you can omit it on the command line when specifying the name of the script—instead of `groovy Gold.groovy`, you can just run `groovy Gold`.

Listing 1.1 Calculating the golden ratio with `Gold.groovy`

```
List fibo = [1, 1]                          ◁── Initial Fibonacci
List gold = [1, 2]                                numbers
                                                              Last gold
while ( ! isGolden( gold[-1] ) ) {          ◁──               candidate
    fibo.add( fibo[-1] + fibo[-2] )                     ◁──  Next Fibonacci
    gold.add( fibo[-1] / fibo[-2] )    ◁── Next golden        number
}                                          candidate

println "found golden ratio with fibo(${ fibo.size-1 }) as"
println fibo[-1] + " / " + fibo[-2] + " = " + gold[-1]
println "_" * 10 + "|"  + "_" * (10 * gold[-1])         Candidate
                                                        satisfies
                                                  ◁──   golden rule
def isGolden(candidate) {
    def small = 1
    def big = small * candidate            ◁──
    return isCloseEnough( (small+big)/big, big/small)      Bigger
}                                                          section

def isCloseEnough(a,b) { return (a-b).abs() < 1.0e-9 }
```

- **Golden ratio candidates** (labels left side)
- **Smaller section** (labels left side)

[6] For additional information about pentagrams and golden ratios, see http://en.wikipedia.org/wiki/Golden_ratio#Pentagram.

[7] Leonardo Pisano (1170–1250), a.k.a. Fibonacci, was a mathematician from Pisa (now a town in Italy). He introduced this number sequence to describe the growth of an isolated rabbit population. Although this may be questionable from a biological point of view, his number sequence plays a role in many different areas of science and art. For more information, you can subscribe to the *Fibonacci Quarterly*.

Run this file as a Groovy program by passing the filename to the `groovy` command. You should see the following output that prints the value, the last step of the calculation, and a visual indication of where the golden ratio intersects a given line:

```
found golden ratio with fibo(23) as
46368 / 28657 = 1.6180339882
_____|_____
```

The `groovy` command has many additional options that are useful for command-line scripting. For example, expressions can be executed by typing `groovy -e "println Math.PI"`, which prints `3.141592653589793` to the console. Section 12.3 will lead you through the full range of options, with numerous examples.

In this section, we've dealt with Groovy's support for simple ad-hoc scripting, but this isn't the whole story. The next section expands on how Groovy fits into a code-compile-run cycle.

1.4   Compiling and running Groovy

So far, we've used Groovy in direct[8] mode, where the code is directly executed without producing any executable files. In this section, you'll see a second way of using Groovy: compiling it to Java bytecode and running it as regular Java application code within a JVM, called precompiled mode. Both ways execute Groovy inside a JVM eventually, and both ways compile the Groovy code to Java bytecode. The major difference is when that compilation occurs and whether the resulting classes are used in memory or stored on disk.

1.4.1   Compiling Groovy with groovyc

Compiling Groovy is straightforward because it comes with a compiler called `groovyc`. The `groovyc` compiler generates at least one class file for each Groovy source file compiled. As an example, you can compile `Gold.groovy` from the previous section into normal Java bytecode by running `groovyc` on the script file like so:

```
groovyc -d classes Gold.groovy
```

In this case, the `groovyc` compiler outputs Java class files to a directory named `classes`, which you told it to do with the `-d` flag. If the directory specified with `-d` doesn't exist, it's created. When you're running the compiler, the name of each generated class file is printed to the console.

For each script, Groovy generates a class that extends `groovy.lang.Script`, which contains a `main` method so that Java can execute it. The name of the compiled class

---

[8] We avoid the term *interpreted* to make clear that Groovy code is never interpreted in the sense of traditional Perl/Python/Ruby/Bash scripts. It's always fully compiled into proper classes, even if that happens transparently.

matches the name of the script being compiled. More classes may be generated, depending on the script code.

Now that you've got a compiled program, let's see how to run it.

1.4.2 *Running a compiled Groovy script with Java*

Running a compiled Groovy program is identical to running a compiled Java program, with the added requirement of having the embeddable groovy-all-*.jar file in your JVM's classpath, which will ensure that all of Groovy's third-party dependencies will be resolved automatically at runtime. Make sure you add the directory in which your compiled program resides to the classpath, too. You then run the program in the same way you'd run any other Java program, with the `java` command:[9]

```
java -cp %GROOVY_HOME%/embeddable/groovy-all-2.4.0.jar;classes Gold
found golden ratio with fibo(23) as
46368 / 28657 = 1.6180339882
_____|_____
```

Note that the .class file extension for the main class shouldn't be specified when running with the `java` command.

All this may seem like a lot of work if you're used to building and running your Java code with Ant at the touch of a button. We agree, which is why the developers of Groovy have made sure you can do all of this easily in an Ant script.

Groovy comes with a `groovyc` Ant task that works pretty much like the `javac` task. See the details under www.groovy-lang.org/groovyc.html#_ant_task. But there's more! The `groovy` Ant task allows you to hook into the Ant build with whatever Groovy code you like. See http://docs.groovy-lang.org/next/html/documentation/#_the_groovy_ant_task.

When it comes to integrating Groovy into a larger project setup, there are even more options. One is using the Groovy Maven integration. A second option is to rely on the Groovy-based Gradle build system that we introduce in the "Gradle for Project Automation" section in chapter 20. A very lightweight option for dependency resolution is using Groovy's `@Grab` annotation as covered in "Using Grapes" in section 2.3.5. Groovy projects of any size are developed with IDE help anyway, and they all support the transparent cross-compile of Groovy and Java sources as we'll discuss next.

1.5 *Groovy IDE and editor support*

Depending on how you use Groovy—from command-line scripts through medium-sized all-Groovy applications up to multilanguage enterprise projects—you face very different needs for development support. On the small scale, a decent text editor is

---

[9] You should replace the .jar version (shown here as 2.4.0) with the version of Groovy you've installed. Also, the command line as shown applies to Windows shells. The equivalent on UNIX would be:
```
> java -cp $GROOVY_HOME/embeddable/groovy-all-2.4.0.jar:classes Gold
```

fine; however, on the large scale, you need the full story, including integrated cross-language unit testing, refactoring, debugging, and profiling support like all leading IDEs provide. This applies to literally all languages, but for Groovy, there's an additional consideration.

The Groovy compiler is by default very lenient when it comes to compile-time checking of code. It must be, because in a dynamic language, new methods[10] may become available at runtime that the compiler cannot foresee. Therefore, it cannot shield you from mistyped method names. But the IDE can warn you. It can highlight unknown method names and even apply so-called type inference to give better warnings and type-inferred code completion.

That's why IDE support is even more valuable for Groovy than it is for other programming languages. Some commonly used IDEs and text editors for Groovy are listed in the following sections. But this information is likely to be out of date as soon as it's printed. Stay tuned for updates for your favorite IDE.

Since Groovy 2.0, you can make the Groovy compiler behave more like you'd expect when using a traditional static language by enforcing type checking at compile time. This isn't done by default, but it is easily activated by annotating your code with `@TypeChecked` or `@CompileStatic`. In chapter 3, we'll dive into the details of typing in Groovy and explain the possible options, and we devote all of chapter 10 to static typing aspects of Groovy.

1.5.1 *IntelliJ IDEA plug-in*

JetBrains, the company behind IntelliJ IDEA, was the first to provide a compelling Groovy plug-in for its commercial IDE under the name JetGroovy, which today is bundled by default with their distribution (since version 8.0). The JetGroovy plug-in is now bundled with IDEA and split into two parts. The Groovy language support comes with the free open source IntelliJ IDEA Community Edition, and the Grails/Griffon support comes with the Ultimate Edition. No separate JetGroovy releases will be made. The development of this plug-in led to the first cross-language compiler for Groovy, which made bidirectional Java–Groovy compilation possible. JetBrains thankfully donated this compiler to the Groovy project and it has heavily influenced today's Groovy compiler.

Listing all the features of the IntelliJ Groovy plug-in would be a futile attempt. We wouldn't even know where to start. It may be enough to say that any Groovy code is so tightly integrated that the lines with Java begin to blur. The screenshot in figure 1.7 shows a Groovy script that produces this book from docbook format to PDF. Note that the method `getRepls()` has no return type and is thus dynamically typed. It returns a map where both keys and values are strings. Now see how in the structure pane (left bottom) the return type is listed as `Map<String,String>`.

This is type inference in action and it controls how code completion works in the trailing code and even how method calls on keys and values of that map are known to

---

[10] This applies to more than just method names, but we'll keep it short at the start.

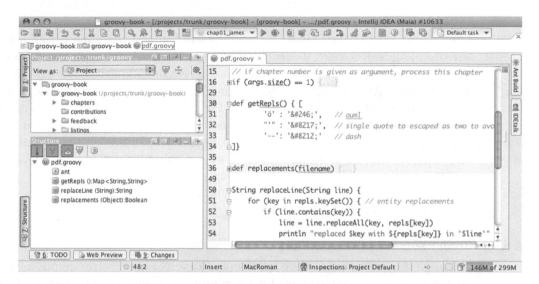

Figure 1.7 The special Groovy support in IntelliJ IDEA uses type inference to provide type safety where the compiler can't.

be of type `String`. As an example, in `line.contains(key)` the key must be a `String`, and because IntelliJ infers that it is, there's no warning marker.

Note that IntelliJ even understands the inferred type of `args` (it's `String[]`), and therefore it knows the available methods. This allows the IDE to provide code completion for all the methods on `args`. Beyond the native language support, IntelliJ offers goodies for various Groovy-based frameworks like Grails, Griffon, Gradle, Gant, and, by the time you're reading this, probably even more.

1.5.2 *NetBeans IDE plug-in*

NetBeans IDE[11] is an open source IDE sponsored by Oracle. Groovy support is a main focus for NetBeans since version 6.5. Since then, Groovy is part of the standard Java distribution of NetBeans IDE.

NetBeans 8.0, the current version, has good support for Groovy, Grails, Gradle, and Griffon. One of the compelling features of NetBeans IDE, besides it being open source, is the cross-language support for multiple languages, enabling one to easily combine Java, Groovy, JavaFx, and others in the same project. Furthermore, NetBeans IDE is always at the forefront of providing value-added services for the Groovy frameworks Grails and Griffon. The online documentation gives a good overview of the features. Also check out Geertjan Wielenga's[12] blog and the quick-start guide.[13]

---

[11] See "NetBeans IDE—The Smarter and Faster Way to Code," https://netbeans.org/features/.
[12] Geertjan's blog, "Random NetBeans Stuff," can be found at https://blogs.oracle.com/geertjan/.
[13] At www.netbeans.org/kb/docs/java/groovy-quickstart.html you'll find a document that gets you started with Groovy in NetBeans IDE.

1.5.3   *Eclipse plug-in*

The Groovy plug-in for Eclipse has a long tradition and has gone through a number of changes. Recently, its development has followed the approach of coercing the Groovy compiler into contributing to the Java model used by the Java Development Toolkit (JDT) to populate the workbench. This piggyback approach provides a deeply integrated developer experience for the Eclipse user and eliminates some pitfalls of traditional compilation approaches that have relied on stub generation. In fact, the compilation mechanism used by this plug-in has now been put into its own separate module so that it can be used outside of Eclipse with the Maven build tool.[14]

In addition, you can download a special bundled version of Eclipse with Groovy and Grails support called the Groovy and Grails Tool Suite, found at http://spring.io/tools.

1.5.4   *Groovy support in other editors*

Although they don't claim to be full-featured development environments, a lot of all-purpose editors provide support for programming languages in general and Groovy in particular.

The cross-platform JEdit editor comes with a plug-in for Groovy that supports executing Groovy scripts and code snippets. A syntax-highlighting configuration is available separately. More details are available at http://plugins.jedit.org/plugins/?Groovy.

For Mac users, there's the popular TextMate editor with its Windows equivalent simply called E. It comes with a Groovy and Grails bundle that you can install from MacroMate's bundle repository.

UltraEdit can easily be customized to provide syntax highlighting for Groovy and to start or compile scripts from within the editor. Any output goes to an integrated output window. A small sidebar lets you jump to class and method declarations in the file. It supports smart indentation and brace matching for Groovy. Besides the Groovy support, it's a feature-rich, quick-starting, all-purpose editor.

1.6   *Summary*

We hope that by now we've convinced you that you really want Groovy in your life. As a modern language built on the solid foundation of Java, with a great community of millions of users, and with corporate backing, Groovy has something to offer everyone, in whatever way they interact with the Java platform.

With a clear idea of why Groovy was developed and what drives its design, you should be able to see where features fit into the bigger picture as each is introduced in the coming chapters. Keep in mind the principles of Java integration and feature richness, making common tasks simpler and your code more expressive.

---

[14] For details and to download the latest Groovy Eclipse plug-in, see http://docs.groovy-lang.org/latest/html/documentation/tools-groovyeclipse.html.

Once you have Groovy installed, you can run it both directly as a script and after compilation into classes. If you've been feeling energetic, you may even have installed a Groovy plug-in for your favorite IDE. With this preparatory work complete, you're ready to see (and try!) more of the language itself. In the next chapter, we'll take you on a whistle-stop tour of Groovy's features to give you a better feeling for the shape of the language, before we examine each element in detail for the remainder of part 1.

Overture: Groovy basics

This chapter covers

- What Groovy code looks like
- Quickstart examples
- Groovy's dynamic nature

> *Do what you think is interesting, do something that you think is fun and worthwhile, because otherwise you won't do it well anyway.*
>
> —Brian Kernighan

This chapter follows the model of an overture in classical music, in which the initial movement introduces the audience to a musical topic. Classical composers weave euphonious patterns that are revisited, extended, varied, and combined later in the performance. In a way, overtures are the whole symphony *en miniature*.

In this chapter, we introduce many basic constructs of the Groovy language. First though, we cover two things you need to know about Groovy to get started: code appearance and assertions. Throughout the chapter, we provide examples to jumpstart you with the language, but only a few aspects of each example will be explained in detail—just enough to get you started. If you struggle with any of the examples, revisit them after having read the whole chapter.

An overture allows you to make yourself comfortable with the instruments, the sound, the volume, and the seating. So lean back, relax, and enjoy the Groovy symphony.

2.1 General code appearance

Computer languages tend to have an obvious lineage in terms of their look and feel. For example, a C programmer looking at Java code might not understand a lot of the keywords but would recognize the general layout in terms of braces, operators, parentheses, comments, statement terminators, and the like. Groovy allows you to start out in a way that's almost indistinguishable from Java and transition smoothly into a more lightweight, suggestive, idiomatic style as your knowledge of the language grows. We'll look at a few of the basics—how to comment-out code, places where Java and Groovy differ, places where they're similar, and how Groovy code can be briefer because it lets you leave out certain elements of syntax.

Groovy is *indentation-unaware,* but it's good engineering practice to follow the usual indentation schemes for blocks of code. Groovy is mostly unaware of excessive whitespace, with the exception of line breaks that end the current statement and single-line comments. Let's look at a few aspects of the appearance of Groovy code.

2.1.1 Commenting Groovy code

Single-line comments and multiline comments are exactly like those in Java, with an additional option for the first line of a script:

```
#!/usr/bin/env groovy
// some line comment
/* some multi
   line comment */
```

Here are some guidelines for writing comments in Groovy:

- The `#!` *shebang* comment is allowed only in the first line. The shebang allows UNIX shells to locate the Groovy bootstrap script and run code with it.
- `//` denotes single-line comments that end with the current line.
- Multiline comments are enclosed in `/* ... */` markers.
- Javadoc-like comments in `/** ... */` markers are treated the same as other multiline comments, but are processed by the `groovydoc` Ant task.

Other parts of Groovy syntax are similarly Java friendly.

2.1.2 Comparing Groovy and Java syntax

Most Groovy code—but not all—appears exactly as it would in Java. This often leads to the false conclusion that Groovy's syntax is a superset of Java's syntax. Despite the similarities, neither language is a superset of the other. Groovy currently doesn't support multiple initialization and iteration statements in the classic `for(init1,init2;test;inc1,inc2)` loop. As you'll see in listing 2.1, the language semantics can be slightly different even when the syntax is valid in both languages. For example, the `==` operator can give different results depending on which language is being used.

Beside those subtle differences, the overwhelming majority of Java's syntax is *part* of the Groovy syntax. This applies to:

- The general packaging mechanism.
- Statements (including `package` and `import` statements).
- Class, interface, enum, field, and method definitions including nested classes, except for special cases with nested class definitions inside methods or other deeply nested blocks.
- Control structures.
- Operators, expressions, and assignments.
- Exception handling.
- Declaration of literals, with the exception of literal array initialization where the Java syntax would clash with Groovy's use of braces. Groovy uses a shorter bracket notation for declaring lists instead.
- Object instantiation, referencing and dereferencing objects, and calling methods.
- Declaration and use of generics and annotations.

The added value of Groovy's syntax includes the following:

- Ease access to Java objects through new expressions and operators.
- Allow more ways of creating objects using literals.
- Provide new control structures to allow advanced flow control.
- Use annotations to generate invisible code, the so-called AST transformations that are described in chapter 9.
- Introduce new datatypes together with their operators and expressions.
- A backslash at the end of a line escapes the line feed so that the statement can proceed on the following line.
- Additional parentheses force Groovy to treat the enclosed content as an expression. We'll use this feature in section 4.3 when we cover more of the details about maps.

Overall, Groovy looks like Java, except more compact and easier to read thanks to these additional syntax elements. One interesting aspect that Groovy *adds* is the ability to leave things *out*.

2.1.3   *Beauty through brevity*

Groovy allows you to leave out some elements of syntax that are always required in Java. Omitting these elements often results in code that's shorter and more *expressive*. Compare the Java and Groovy code for encoding a string for use in a URL. For Java:

```
java.net.URLEncoder.encode("a b", "UTF-8");
```

For Groovy:

```
URLEncoder.encode 'a b', 'UTF-8'
```

By leaving out the package prefix, parentheses, and semicolon, the code boils down to the bare minimum.

The support for optional parentheses is based on the disambiguation and precedence rules as summarized in the Groovy Language Specification (GLS). Although these rules are unambiguous, they're not always intuitive. Omitting parentheses can lead to misunderstandings, even though the compiler is happy with the code. We prefer to include the parentheses for all but the most trivial situations. The compiler doesn't try to judge your code for readability—you must do this yourself.

Groovy automatically imports the packages `groovy.lang.*`, `groovy.util.*`, `java.lang.*`, `java.util.*`, `java.net.*`, and `java.io.*`, as well as the classes `java.math.BigInteger` and `BigDecimal`. As a result, you can refer to the classes in these packages without specifying the package names. We'll use this feature throughout the book, and we'll use fully qualified class names only for disambiguation or for pointing out their origin. Note that Java automatically imports `java.lang.*`, but nothing else.

There are other elements of syntax that are optional in Groovy too:

- In chapter 7, we'll talk about optional *return* statements.
- Even the ubiquitous dot becomes optional when the chaining method is called. For example, in combination with optional parentheses, the following code is legal in Groovy: `buy best of stocks`, which is short for `buy(best).of(stocks)`. Chapter 7 has the full description of these so-called command chains.
- Where Java demands *type declarations*, they either become optional in Groovy or can be replaced by `def` to indicate that you don't care about the type.
- Groovy makes *type casts* optional.
- You don't need to add the *throws* clause to your method signature when your method potentially throws a checked exception.

This section has given you enough background to make it easier to concentrate on each individual feature in turn. We're still going through them quickly rather than in great detail, but you should be able to recognize the general look and feel of the code. With that under your belt, we can look at the principal tool you're going to use to test each new piece of the language: assertions.

2.2 *Probing the language with assertions*

If you've worked with Java 1.4 or later, you're probably familiar with *assertions*. They test whether everything is right with the world as far as your program is concerned. Usually they live in your code to make sure you don't have any inconsistencies in your logic, for performing tasks such as checking preconditions at the beginning and postconditions and invariants at the end of a method, or for ensuring that method arguments are valid. In this book we'll use them to demonstrate the features of Groovy. Just as in test-driven development, where the tests are regarded as the ultimate demonstration of what a unit of code should do, the assertions in this book demonstrate the results of executing particular pieces of Groovy code. We use assertions to show not only what code can be run, but the result of running the code. This section will prepare you for reading the code examples in the rest of the book, explaining how assertions work in Groovy and how you'll use them.

Although assertions may seem like an odd place to start learning a language, they're our first port of call because you won't understand any of the examples until you understand assertions. Groovy provides assertions with the `assert` keyword. The following listing makes some simple assertions.

Listing 2.1   Using assertions

```
assert(true)
assert 1 == 1
def x = 1
assert x == 1
def y = 1; assert y == 1
```

Let's go through the lines one by one.

```
assert(true)
```

This introduces the `assert` keyword and shows that you need to provide an expression that you're asserting will be true.[1]

```
assert 1 == 1
```

This demonstrates that `assert` can take full expressions, not just literals or simple variables. Unsurprisingly, 1 equals 1. Exactly like Ruby or Scala but unlike Java, the `==` operator denotes *equality,* not *identity.* The parentheses were left out as well, because they're optional for top-level statements.

```
def x = 1
assert x == 1
```

This defines the variable x, assigns it the numeric value 1, and uses it inside the asserted expression. Note that nothing was revealed about the *type* of x. The `def` keyword means "dynamically typed."

```
def y = 1; assert y == 1
```

This is the typical style when asserting the program status for the current line. It uses two statements on the same line, separated by a semicolon. The semicolon is Groovy's statement terminator. As you've seen before, it's optional when the statement ends with the current line.

---

[1]   Groovy's meaning of truth encompasses more than a simple Boolean value, as you'll see in "The Groovy truth" in chapter 6.

What happens if an assertion fails? Let's see![2] For example:

```
def a = 5
def b = 9
assert b == a + a        ⟵┘  Expected
                              to fail
```

prints to the console (yes, really!):

```
Assertion failed:
                         ⟵┘  Expression
assert b == a + a             retained
       | |   | | |
       9 |   5 | 5       ⟵┤  Referenced
         |    10              values
       false   Subexpression
               values

        at snippet22_failing_assert.run(snippet22_failing_assert.groovy:3)
```

Pause and think about the language features required to provide such a sophisticated error message. You'll see more examples of Groovy's "power assert" feature when we discuss unit testing in chapter 17.

Assertions serve multiple purposes:

- They can be used to reveal the current program state, as they're used in the examples in this book. The one-line assertion in the previous example reveals that the variable y now has the value 1.
- They often make good replacements for line comments, because they reveal assumptions and verify them *at the same time.* The assertion reveals that, at this point, it's assumed that y has the value 1. Comments may go out of date without anyone noticing—assertions are always checked for correctness. They're like tiny unit tests sitting inside the real code.

Real-life example

One real-life example of the value of assertions is in your hands right now (or on your screen). This book is constructed such that all listings and the assertions they contain are maintained outside the actual text and linked into the text via file references. With the help of a little Groovy script, all the listings are evaluated before the normal production process even begins. For instance, the assertions in listing 2.1 were evaluated and found to be correct. If an assertion fails, the whole process stops with an error message.

The fact that you're reading a production copy of this book means the production process wasn't stopped and all assertions succeeded. This should give you confidence in the correctness of the Groovy examples provided. For the first edition, we did the same with MS Word using Scriptom (chapter 20) to control MS Word, and AntBuilder (chapter 11) to help with the building side. As we said before, the features of Groovy work best when they're used together.

---

[2] This code is one of the few listings that isn't executed as part of the book production.

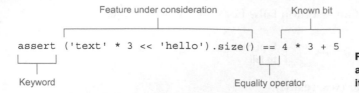

Figure 2.1   **A complex assertion, broken up into its constituent parts**

Most of the examples use assertions—one part of the expression will use the feature being described, and another part will be simple enough to understand on its own. If you have difficulty understanding an example, try breaking it up, thinking about the language feature being discussed and what you'd expect the result to be given your description, and then looking at what you've said the result will be, as checked at run-time by the assertion. Figure 2.1 breaks up a more complicated assertion into its constituent parts.

This is an extreme example—you'll often perform the steps in separate statements and then make the assertion itself short. The principle is the same, however: there's code that has functionality you're trying to demonstrate, and there's code that's trivial and can be easily understood without knowing the details of the topic at hand.

In case assertions don't convince you or you mistrust an asserted expression in this book, you can usually replace it with output to the console. A hypothetical assertion such as

```
assert x == 'hey, this is really the content of x'
```

can be replaced by

```
println x
```

which prints the value of x to the console. Throughout the book, we often replace console output with assertions for the sake of having self-checking code. This isn't a common way of presenting code in books,[3] but we feel it keeps the code and the results closer—and it appeals to our test-driven nature.

Assertions have a few more interesting features that can influence your programming style, and we'll return to them in section 6.2.4 where we'll cover them in more depth. Now that we've explained the tool you'll be using to put Groovy under the microscope, you can start seeing some of the features in use.

2.3   *Groovy at a glance*

Like many languages, Groovy has a language specification that breaks down code into statements, expressions, and so on. Learning a language from such a specification tends to be a dry experience and doesn't take you far toward the goal of writing useful Groovy code in the shortest possible amount of time. Instead, we'll present

---

[3] This was a genuine innovation in the first edition of this book, which was found so useful by other authors that they copied the concept. We don't mind. Everything that advances our profession is welcome.

simple examples of typical Groovy constructs that make up most Groovy code: classes, scripts, beans, strings, regular expressions, numbers, lists, maps, ranges, closures, loops, and conditionals.

Take this section as a broad but shallow overview. It won't answer all your questions, but it'll allow you to start experimenting with Groovy *on your own*. We encourage you to play with the language. If you wonder what would happen if you were to tweak the code in a certain way, try it! You learn best by experience. We promise to give detailed explanations in later, in-depth chapters.

2.3.1 Declaring classes

Classes are the cornerstone of object-oriented programming (OOP), because they define the blueprints from which objects are created.

Listing 2.2 contains a simple Groovy class named Book, which has an instance variable title, a constructor that sets the title, and a getter method for the title. Note that everything looks much like Java, except there's no accessibility modifier: methods are *public* by default.

> **Listing 2.2   A simple Book class**

```
class Book {
    private String title
    Book (String theTitle) {
        title = theTitle
    }
    String getTitle(){
        return title
    }
}
```

Please save this code in a file named Book.groovy, because we'll refer to it in the next section.

The code isn't surprising. Class declarations look much the same in most object-oriented languages. The details and nuts and bolts of class declarations will be explained in chapter 7.

2.3.2 Using scripts

Scripts are text files, typically with an extension of *.groovy, that can be executed from the command shell like this:

```
> groovy myfile.groovy
```

Note that this is very different from Java. In Groovy, you're executing the source code! An ordinary Java class is generated for you and executed behind the scenes. But from a user's perspective, it looks like you're executing plain Groovy source code.[4]

---

[4] Any Groovy code can be executed this way as long as it can be run; that is, it's either a script, a class with a main method, a Runnable, or a Groovy or JUnit test case.

Scripts contain Groovy statements without an enclosing `class` declaration. Scripts can even contain method definitions outside of class definitions to better structure the code. You'll learn more about scripts in chapter 7. Until then, take them for granted.

Listing 2.3 shows how easy it is to use the `Book` class in a script. You create a new instance and call the getter method on the object by using Java's *dot* syntax. Then you define a method to read the title backward.

Listing 2.3   Using the `Book` class from a script

```
Book gina = new Book('Groovy in Action')

assert gina.getTitle() == 'Groovy in Action'
assert getTitleBackwards(gina) == 'noitcA ni yvoorG'

String getTitleBackwards(book) {
    String title = book.getTitle()
    return title.reverse()
}
```

Note how you're able to invoke the method `getTitleBackwards` before it's declared. Behind this observation is a fundamental difference between Groovy and scripting languages such as Ruby. A Groovy script is fully constructed—that is, parsed, compiled, and generated—*before execution*. Section 7.2 has more details about this.

Another important observation is that you can use `Book` objects without explicitly compiling the `Book` class! The only prerequisite for using the `Book` class is that `Book.groovy` must reside on the classpath. The Groovy runtime system will find the file, compile it transparently into a class, and yield a new `Book` object. Groovy combines the ease of scripting with the merits of object orientation.

This inevitably leads to the question of how to organize larger script-based applications. In Groovy, the preferred way isn't to mesh numerous script files together, but instead to group reusable components into classes such as `Book`. Remember that such a class remains fully scriptable; you can modify Groovy code, and the changes are instantly available without further action.

It was pretty simple to write the `Book` class and the script that used it. Indeed, it's hard to believe that it can be any simpler—but it *can*, as you'll see next.

2.3.3   GroovyBeans

JavaBeans are ordinary Java[5] classes that expose *properties*. What is a property? That's not easy to explain, because it's not a single standalone concept. It's made up from a naming convention. If a class exposes methods with the naming scheme `getName()` and `setName(name)`, then the concept describes `name` as a property of that class. The `get` and `set` methods are called *accessor* methods. (Some people make a distinction between accessor and mutator methods, but we don't.) Boolean properties can use an `is` prefix instead of `get`, leading to method names such as `isAdult`.

---

[5]   This is prior to Java 8 where a new concept of properties as first-class citizens comes bundled with JavaFX 8.

A GroovyBean is a JavaBean defined in Groovy. In Groovy, working with beans is much easier than in Java. Groovy facilitates working with beans in three ways:

- Generating the accessor methods
- Allowing simplified access to all JavaBeans (including GroovyBeans)
- Simplifying registration of event handlers together with annotations that declare a property as *bindable*

The following listing shows how the `Book` class boils down to a one-liner defining the `title` property. This results in the accessor methods `getTitle()` and `setTitle(title)` being generated.

Listing 2.4   Defining the `BookBean` class as a GroovyBean

```
class BookBean {
  String title              <—| Property
}                              | declaration

def groovyBook = new BookBean()

groovyBook.setTitle('Groovy in Action')                        | Property use with
assert groovyBook.getTitle() == 'Groovy in Action'             | explicit getter calls

groovyBook.title = 'Groovy conquers the world'                 | Property use with
assert groovyBook.title == 'Groovy conquers the world'         | Groovy shortcuts
```

We also demonstrate how to access the bean in the standard way with accessor methods, as well as in the simplified way, where property access reads like direct field access.

Note that listing 2.4 is a fully valid script and can be executed *as is,* even though it contains a class declaration and additional code. You'll learn more about this construction in chapter 7.

Also note that `groovyBook.title` *is not* a field access. Instead, it's a shortcut for the corresponding accessor method. It'd work even if you'd explicitly declared the property longhand with a `getTitle()` method.

More information about methods and beans will be given in chapter 7.

2.3.4   *Annotations*

In Groovy, you can define and use annotations just like in Java, which is a distinctive feature among JVM languages. Beyond that, Groovy also uses annotations to mark code structures for special compiler handling. Let's have a look at one of those annotations that comes with the Groovy distribution: `@Immutable`.

A Groovy bean can be marked as immutable, which means that the class becomes `final`, all its fields become `final`, and you cannot change its state after construction. Listing 2.5 declares an immutable `FixedBean` class, calls the constructor in two different ways, and asserts that you have a standard implementation of `equals()` that supports comparison by content. With the help of a little `try-catch`, you assert that changing the state isn't allowed.

Listing 2.5   Defining the immutable `FixedBean` and exercising it

```
import groovy.transform.Immutable

@Immutable class FixedBook {          ←— AST
    String title                          annotation.
}
                                                          Positional
                                                          constructor.
def gina   = new FixedBook('Groovy in Action')        ←—
def regina = new FixedBook(title:'Groovy in Action')   ←——
                                                          Named-arg
                                                          constructor.
assert gina.title == 'Groovy in Action'
assert gina == regina                                  ←—
                                                          Standard
                                                          equals().
try {
    gina.title = "Oops!"                               ←——
    assert false, "should not reach here"
} catch (ReadOnlyPropertyException expected) {         Not
    println "Expected Error: '$expected.message'"      allowed!
}
```

It must be said that proper immutability isn't easily achieved without such help and
the annotation does actually much more than what you see in listing 2.5: it adds a correct `hashCode()` implementation and enforces *defensive copying* for access to all properties that aren't immutable by themselves.

Immutable types are always helpful for a clean design but they're indispensable for
concurrent programming: an increasingly important topic that we'll cover in chapter 18.

The `@Immutable` annotation is only one of many that can enhance your code with
additional characteristics. In the next section we'll briefly cover the `@Grab` annotation,
in chapter 8 we'll look at `@Category` and `@Mixin`, and in chapter 9 we'll cover the full
range of other annotations that come with the GDK.

Most Groovy annotations, like `@Immutable`, instruct the compiler to execute an
AST transformation. The acronym AST stands for abstract syntax tree, which is a representation of the code that the Groovy parser creates and the Groovy compiler works
on to generate the bytecode. In between, AST transformations can modify that AST
to sneak in new method implementations or add, delete, or modify any other code
structure. This approach is also called compile-time metaprogramming and isn't
limited to the transformations that come with the GDK. You can also provide your
own transformations!

2.3.5   *Using grapes*

Before continuing we should cover one of the other annotations that you'll see in
numerous places in the rest of the book. The `@Grab` annotation is used to explicitly
define your external library dependencies within a script. We sometimes use the term
grapes as friendly shorthand for our external Groovy library dependencies. In the
Java world, you might store your dependent libraries in a `lib` directory and add that
to your classpath and IDE settings, or you might capture that information in an Ivy,
Maven, or Gradle build file. Groovy provides an additional alternative that's very

handy for making scripts self-contained. The following listing shows how you might use it.

```
@Grab('commons-lang:commons-lang:2.4')
import org.apache.commons.lang.ClassUtils

class Outer {
  class Inner {}
}

assert !ClassUtils.isInnerClass(Outer)
assert ClassUtils.isInnerClass(Outer.Inner)
```

Here the use of the commons lang library is declared. It's used to make some assertions about two classes, ensuring that one of them is an inner class. At compile time and runtime that library will be downloaded if needed and added to the classpath. More details about @Grab and numerous related annotations can be found in appendix E.

2.3.6   *Handling text*

Just as in Java, character data is mostly handled using the java.lang.String class. But Groovy provides some tweaks to make that easier, with more options for string literals and some helpful operators.

GSTRINGS
In Groovy, string literals can appear in single or double quotes. The double-quoted version allows the use of placeholders, which are automatically resolved as required. This is a *GString*, and that's also the name of the class involved. The following code demonstrates a simple variable expansion, although that's not all GStrings can do:

```
def nick = 'ReGina'
def book = 'Groovy in Action, 2nd ed.'
assert "$nick is $book" == 'ReGina is Groovy in Action, 2nd ed.'
```

Chapter 3 provides more information about strings, including more options for GStrings, how to escape special characters, how to span string declarations over multiple lines, and the methods and operators available on strings. As you'd expect, GStrings are pretty neat.

REGULAR EXPRESSIONS
If you're familiar with the concept of regular expressions, you'll be glad to hear that Groovy supports them *at the language level*. If this concept is new to you, you can safely skip this section for the moment. You'll find a full introduction to the topic in chapter 3.

   Groovy makes it easy to declare regular expression patterns, and provides operators for applying them. Figure 2.2 declares a pattern with the slashy // syntax and uses the =~ find operator to match the pattern against a given string. The first example ensures that the string contains a series of digits; the second example replaces every digit with an x.

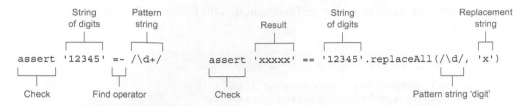

Figure 2.2   Regular expression support in Groovy through operators and slashy strings

Note that replaceAll is defined on java.lang.String and takes two string arguments. It becomes apparent that '12345' is a java.lang.String, as is the expression /\d/.

Chapter 3 explains how to declare and use regular expressions and goes through the ways to apply them.

2.3.7   Numbers are objects

Hardly any program can do without numbers, whether for calculations or (more frequently) for counting and indexing. Groovy *numbers* have a familiar appearance, but unlike in Java, they're first-class objects rather than primitive types.

In Java, you cannot invoke methods on primitive types. If x is of primitive type int, you cannot write x.toString(). On the other hand, if y is an object, you cannot use 2*y.

In Groovy, both are possible. You can use numbers with numeric operators, and you can also call methods on number instances. For example:

```
def x = 1
def y = 2
assert x + y == 3
assert x.plus(y) == 3
assert x instanceof Integer
```

The variables x and y are objects of type java.lang.Integer. Thus, you can use the plus method, but you can just as easily use the + operator.

This is surprising and a major lift to object orientation on the Java platform. Whereas Java has a small but ubiquitous part of the language that isn't object oriented at all, Groovy makes a point of using objects for everything. You'll learn more about how Groovy handles numbers in chapter 3.

2.3.8   Using lists, maps, and ranges

Many languages, including Java, only have direct support for a single collection type—an array—at the syntax level and have language features that only apply to that type. In practice, other collections are widely used, and there's no reason why the language should make it harder to use those collections than arrays. Groovy makes collection handling simple, with added support for operators, literals, and extra methods beyond those provided by the Java standard libraries.

LISTS

Java supports indexing arrays with a square bracket syntax, which we'll call the *subscript operator*. In Groovy the same syntax can be used with *lists*—instances of `java.util.List`—which allows adding and removing elements, changing the size of the list at runtime, and storing items that aren't necessarily of a uniform type. In addition, Groovy allows lists to be indexed outside their current bounds, which again can change the size of the list. Furthermore, lists can be specified as literals directly in your code.

The example in figure 2.3 declares a list of Roman numerals and initializes it with the first seven numbers.

The list is constructed such that each index matches its representation as a Roman numeral. Working with the list

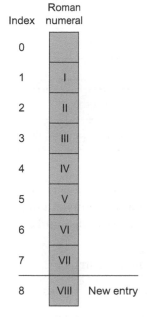

Figure 2.3 An example list where the content for each index is the Roman numeral for that index

looks like you're working with an array, but in Groovy, the manipulation is more expressive, and the restrictions that apply to arrays are gone:

```
def roman = ['', 'I', 'II', 'III', 'IV', 'V', 'VI', 'VII']    ←— List of Roman
assert roman[4] == 'IV'                            ←—           numerals

roman[8] = 'VIII'                ←—  List    List
assert roman.size() == 9             expansion    access
```

Note that there was no list item with index 8 when you assigned a value to it. You indexed the list outside the current bounds. We'll look at the list datatype in more detail in section 4.2.

SIMPLE MAPS

A *map* is a storage type that associates a key with a value. Maps store and retrieve values by key; lists retrieve them by numeric index.

Unlike Java, Groovy supports maps at the language level, allowing them to be specified with literals and providing suitable operators to work with them. It does so with a clear and easy syntax. The syntax for maps looks like an array of key–value pairs, where a colon separates keys and values. That's all it takes.

The example in figure 2.4 stores descriptions of HTTP[6] return codes in a map.

---

[6] The server returns these codes with every response. Your browser typically shows the mapped descriptions for codes above 400.

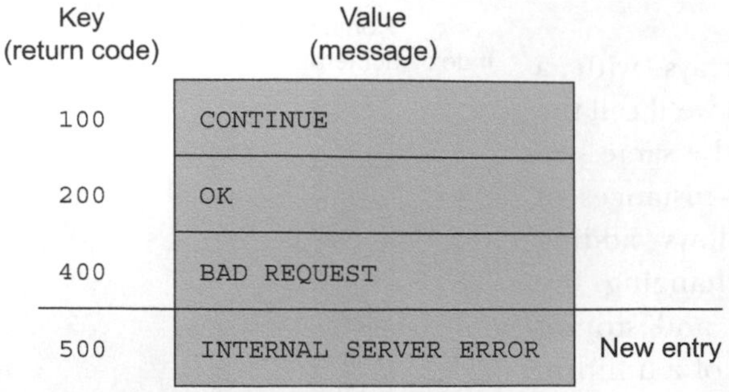

Key (return code)	Value (message)	
100	CONTINUE	
200	OK	
400	BAD REQUEST	
500	INTERNAL SERVER ERROR	New entry

Figure 2.4   An example map where HTTP return codes map to their respective messages

You can see the map declaration and initialization, the retrieval of values, and the addition of a new entry. All of this is done with a single method call explicitly appearing in the source code—and even that's only checking the new size of the map:

```
def http = [
      100 : 'CONTINUE',
      200 : 'OK',
      400 : 'BAD REQUEST'
]
assert http[200] == 'OK'
http[500] = 'INTERNAL SERVER ERROR'
assert http.size() == 4
```

Note how the syntax is consistent with that used to declare, access, and modify lists. The differences between using maps and lists are minimal, so it's easy to remember both. This is a good example of the Groovy language designers taking commonly required operations and making programmers' lives easier by providing a simple and consistent syntax. Section 4.3 gives more information about maps and their rich feature set.

RANGES

Although ranges don't appear in the standard Java libraries, most programmers have an intuitive idea of what a range is—effectively a start point and an end point, with an operation to move between the two in discrete steps. Again, Groovy provides literals to support this useful concept, along with other language features such as the `for` statement, which understands ranges.

The following code demonstrates the range literal format, along with how to find the size of a range, determine whether it contains a particular value, find its start and end points, and reverse it:

```
def x = 1..10
assert x.contains(5)
assert !x.contains(15)
assert x.size() == 10
assert x.from == 1
assert x.to == 10
assert x.reverse() == 10..1
```

These examples are limited because we're only trying to show what ranges do *on their own*. Ranges are usually used in conjunction with other Groovy features. Over the course of this book, you'll see a lot of range uses.

So much for the usual datatypes. We'll now come to closures, a concept that doesn't exist in Java, but which Groovy uses extensively.

2.3.9 *Code as objects: closures*

The concept of *closures* isn't a new one, but it has usually been associated with functional languages, allowing one piece of code to execute an arbitrary piece of code that has been specified elsewhere.

In object-oriented languages, the Method Object pattern has often been used to simulate the same kind of behavior by defining types, the sole purpose of which is to implement an appropriate single-method interface. The instances of those types can subsequently be passed as arguments to methods, which then invoke the method on the interface.

A good example is the `java.io.File.list(FilenameFilter)` method. The `FilenameFilter` interface specifies a single method, and its only purpose is to allow the list of files returned from the `list` method to be filtered while it's being generated.

Unfortunately, this approach leads to an unnecessary proliferation of types, and the code involved is often widely separated from the logical point of use. Java uses anonymous inner classes and, since Java 8, lambdas and method references to address these issues. Although similar in function, Groovy closures are much more versatile and powerful when it comes to reaching out to the caller's scope and putting closures in a dynamic execution context. Groovy allows closures to be specified in a concise, clean, and powerful way, effectively promoting the Method Object pattern to a first-class position in the language.

Because closures are a new concept to most Java programmers, it may take a little time to adjust. The good news is that the initial steps of using closures are so easy that you hardly notice what's so new about them. The "aha-wow-cool" effect comes later, when you discover their real power.

Informally, a closure can be recognized as a list of statements within braces, like any other code block. It optionally has a list of identifiers to name the parameters passed to it, with an `->` marking the end of the list.

It's easiest to understand closures through examples. Figure 2.5 shows a simple closure that's passed to the `List.each` method, called on a list [1, 2, 3].

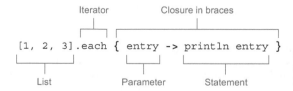

Figure 2.5 A simple example of a closure that prints the numbers 1, 2, and 3

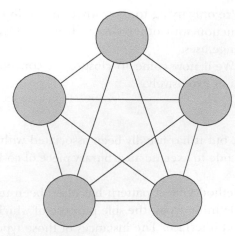

Figure 2.6   Five elements and their distinct connections, modeling five people (the circles) at a party clinking glasses with each other (the lines). Here there are 10 clinks.

The `List.each` method takes a single parameter—a closure. It then executes that closure for each of the elements in the list, passing in that element as the argument to the closure. In this example, the main body of the closure is a statement to print whatever is passed to the closure, namely the parameter called `entry`.

Let's consider a slightly more complicated question: If *n* people are at a party and everyone clinks glasses with everybody else, how many clinks do you hear?[7] Figure 2.6 sketches this question for five people, where each line represents one clink.

To answer this question, you can use `Integer`'s upto method, which does *something* for every `Integer` starting at the current value and going *up to* a given end value. You apply this method to the problem by imagining people arriving at the party one by one. As people arrive, they clink glasses with everyone who is already present. This way, everyone clinks glasses with everyone else exactly once.

Listing 2.7 calculates the number of clinks. You keep a running total of the number of clinks, and when each guest arrives, you add the number of people already present (the guest number − 1). Finally, you test the result using Gauss' formula[8] for this problem—with 100 people, there should be 4,950 clinks.

Listing 2.7   Counting all the clinks at a party using a closure

```
def totalClinks = 0
def partyPeople = 100
1.upto(partyPeople) { guestNumber ->
    clinksWithGuest = guestNumber-1            Modifies
    totalClinks += clinksWithGuest       <──┘  outer
}                                              scope
assert totalClinks == (partyPeople * (partyPeople-1)) / 2
```

---

[7] In computer terms: What is the maximum number of distinct connections in a dense network of *n* components?

[8] Johann Carl Friedrich Gauss (1777–1855) was a German mathematician. At the age of seven, his teacher wanted to keep the kids busy by making them sum up the numbers from 1 to 100. Gauss discovered this formula and finished the task correctly and surprisingly quickly. There are differing reports on how the teacher reacted.

How does this code relate to Java? In Java, you'd have used a loop like the following code snippet. The class declaration and main method are omitted for the sake of brevity:

```
// Java snippet
int totalClinks = 0;
int partyPeople = 100;
for(int guestNumber = 1;
        guestNumber <= partyPeople;
        guestNumber++) {
    int clinksWithGuest = guestNumber-1;
    totalClinks += clinksWithGuest;
}
```

Note that `guestNumber` appears four times in the Java code but only twice in the Groovy version. Don't dismiss this as a minor thing. The code should explain the programmer's intention with the simplest possible means, and expressing behavior with *two words rather than four* is an important simplification.

Also note that the `upto` method encapsulates and hides the logic of how to walk over a sequence of integers. That is, this logic appears only *one time* in the code (in the implementation of `upto`). Count the equivalent `for` loops in any Java project, and you'll see the amount of structural duplication inherent in Java. But while code duplication itself is bad, it's even more so an indicator for a lack of modularity! Groovy gives you more means to separate your code into its independent concerns such as how to walk a data structure and what to do at each step.

The example has another subtle twist. The *closure* updates the `totalClinks` variable, which is defined in the outer scope. It can do so because it has access to the *enclosing* scope. That's pretty tricky to do in Java, even with lambdas in Java 8.[9]

There's much more to say about the great concept of closures, and we'll do so in chapter 5.

2.3.10 Groovy control structures

Control structures allow a programming language to control the flow of execution through code. There are simple versions of everyday control structures like `if-else`, `while`, `switch`, and `try-catch-finally` in Groovy, just like in Java.

In conditionals, `null` is treated like `false`, and so are empty strings, collections, and maps. The `for` loop has a

```
for(i in x) { body }
```

notation, where x can be anything that Groovy knows how to iterate through, such as an iterator, an enumeration, a collection, a range, a map—or literally any object, as explained in chapter 6. In Groovy, the `for` loop is often replaced by iteration methods that take a closure argument. The following listing gives an overview.

---

[9] Java pours "syntax vinegar" over such a construct to discourage programmers from using it.

Listing 2.8   Control structures

```
if (false) assert false                              The if as
                                                     one-liner
if (null)
{
    assert false                     null is false
}
else
{                                    Blocks may start
    assert true                      on new line
}

def i = 0
while (i < 10) {                     Classic
    i++                              while
}
assert i == 10

def clinks = 0
for (remainingGuests in 0..9) {      The for in
    clinks += remainingGuests        range
}
assert clinks == (10*9)/2

def list = [0, 1, 2, 3]
for (j in list) {                    The for
    assert j == list[j]              in list
}

list.each() { item ->                The each method
    assert item == list[item]        with a closure
}

switch(3)  {
    case 1 : assert false; break     Classifer
    case 3 : assert true;  break     switch
    default: assert false
}
```

The code in listing 2.8 should be self-explanatory. Groovy control structures are reasonably close to Java's syntax, but we'll go into more detail in chapter 6.

That's it for the initial syntax presentation. You've got your feet wet with Groovy and you should have the impression that it's a nice mix of Java-friendly syntax elements with some new interesting twists.

Now that you know how to write your first Groovy code, it's time to explore how it gets executed on the Java platform.

2.4   *Groovy's place in the Java environment*

Behind the fun of Groovy looms the world of Java. We'll examine how Groovy classes enter the Java environment to start with, how Groovy augments the existing Java class library, and how Groovy gets its groove: a brief explanation of the dynamic nature of Groovy classes.

2.4.1   *My class is your class*

Mi casa es su casa—my home is your home. That's the Spanish way of expressing hospitality. Groovy and Java are just as generous with each other's classes. So far, when talking about Groovy and Java, we've compared the appearance of the source code. But the connection to Java is much stronger. Behind the scenes, all Groovy code runs inside the JVM, and follows Java's object model. Regardless of whether you write Groovy classes or scripts, they run as Java classes inside the JVM.

You can run Groovy classes inside the JVM in two ways:

- You can use `groovyc` to compile *.groovy files to Java *.class files, put them on Java's classpath, and retrieve objects from those classes via the Java classloader.
- You can work with *.groovy files directly and retrieve objects from those classes via the Groovy classloader. In this case, no *.class files are generated, but rather *class objects*—that is, instances of `java.lang.Class`. In other words, when your Groovy code contains the expression `new MyClass()`, and there's a `MyClass.groovy` file, it'll be parsed, a class of type `MyClass` will be generated and added to the classloader, and your code will get a new `MyClass` object as if it had been loaded from a *.class file. (We hope the Groovy programmers will forgive this oversimplification.)

These two methods of converting *.groovy files into Java classes are illustrated in figure 2.7. Either way, the resulting classes have the same format as classic Java classes. Groovy enhances Java at the *source-code level* but stays compatible at the *bytecode level.*

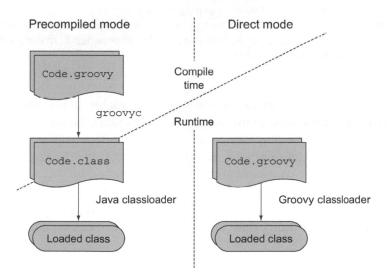

Figure 2.7   Groovy code can be compiled using `groovyc` and then loaded with the normal Java classloader, or loaded directly with the Groovy classloader.

2.4.2 GDK: the Groovy library

Groovy's strong connection to Java makes using Java classes from Groovy and vice versa exceptionally easy. Because they're the same thing, there's no gap to bridge. In the code examples, every Groovy object is instantly a Java object. Even the term *Groovy object* is questionable. Both are identical objects, living in the Java runtime.

This has an enormous benefit for Java programmers, who can fully leverage their knowledge of the Java libraries. Consider a sample string in Groovy:

```
'Hello World!'
```

Because this *is* a java.lang.String, Java programmers know that they can use JDK's String.startsWith method on it:

```
if ('Hello World!'.startsWith('Hello')) {
    // Code to execute if the string starts with 'Hello'
}
```

The library that comes with Groovy is an extension of the JDK library. It provides some new classes (for example, for easy database access and XML processing), but it also adds functionality to existing JDK classes. This additional functionality is referred to as the GDK,[10] and it provides significant benefits in consistency, power, and expressiveness.

Still have to write Java code? Don't get too comfortable...

Going back to plain Java and the JDK after writing Groovy with the GDK can often be an unpleasant experience! It's all too easy to become accustomed not only to the features of Groovy as a language, but also to the benefits it provides in making common tasks simpler within the standard library.

One example is the size method as used in the GDK. It's available on everything that's of some size: strings, arrays, lists, maps, and other collections. Behind the scenes, they're all JDK classes. This is an improvement over the JDK, where you determine an object's size in a number of different ways, as listed in table 2.1. We think you'd agree that the GDK solution is more consistent and easier to remember.

Groovy can play this trick by funneling all method calls through a device called MetaClass. This allows a dynamic approach to object orientation, only part of which involves adding methods to existing classes. You'll learn more about MetaClass in the next section.

---

[10] This is a bit of a misnomer because DK stands for development kit, which is more than just the library; it should also include supportive tools. We'll use this acronym anyway, because it's conventional in the Groovy community.

Table 2.1   Ways of determining sizes in the JDK

Type	Determine the size in JDK via ...	Groovy
`Array`	`length` field	`size()` method
`Array`	`java.lang.reflect.Array.getLength(array)`	`size()` method
`String`	`length()` method	`size()` method
`StringBuffer`	`length()` method	`size()` method
`Collection`	`size()` method	`size()` method
`Map`	`size()` method	`size()` method
`File`	`length()` method	`size()` method
`Matcher`	`groupCount()` method	`size()` method

When describing the built-in datatypes later in the book, we also mention their most prominent GDK properties. Appendix C contains the complete list.

To help you understand how Groovy objects can leverage the power of the GDK, we'll next sketch how Groovy objects come into being.

2.4.3   *Groovy compiler lifecycle*

Although the Java runtime understands compiled Groovy classes without any problem, it doesn't understand *.groovy source files. More work has to happen behind the scenes if you want to load *.groovy files dynamically at runtime.

Some relatively advanced Java knowledge is required to fully appreciate this section. If you don't already know a bit about classloaders, you may want to skip to the chapter summary and assume that magic pixies transform Groovy source code into Java bytecode at the right time. You won't have as full an understanding of what's going on, but you can keep learning Groovy without losing sleep. Alternatively, you can keep reading and not worry when things get tricky.

Groovy *syntax* is line-oriented, but the *execution* of Groovy code is not. Unlike other scripting languages, Groovy code isn't processed line-by-line in the sense that each line is interpreted separately.

Instead, Groovy code is fully parsed, and a class is generated from the information that the *parser* has built. The generated class is the binding device between Groovy and Java, and Groovy classes are generated such that their format is *identical* to Java bytecode.

Inside the Java runtime, classes are managed by a classloader. When a Java classloader is asked for a certain class, it usually loads the class from a *.class file, stores it in a cache, and returns it. Because a Groovy-generated class is identical to a Java class, it can also be managed by a classloader with the same behavior. The difference is that the Groovy classloader can also load classes from *.groovy files (and do parsing and class generation before putting it in the cache).

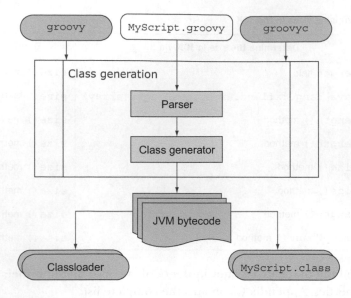

Figure 2.8 Flowchart of the Groovy bytecode generation process when executed in the runtime environment or compiled into *.class files. Different options for executing Groovy code involve different targets for the bytecode produced, but the parser and class generator are the same in each case.

Groovy can *at runtime* read *.groovy files as if they were *.class files. The class generation can also be done *before* runtime with the groovyc compiler. The compiler simply takes *.groovy files and transforms them into *.class files using the same parsing and class-generation mechanics.

GROOVY CLASS GENERATION AT WORK

Suppose you have a Groovy script stored in a file named MyScript.groovy, and you run it via groovy MyScript.groovy. The following are the class-generation steps, as shown in figure 2.8:

1 The file MyScript.groovy is fed into the Groovy parser.
2 The parser generates an AST that fully represents all the code in the file.
3 The Groovy class generator takes the AST and generates Java bytecode from it. Depending on the file content, this can result in multiple classes. Classes are now available through the Groovy classloader.
4 The Java runtime is invoked in a manner equivalent to running java MyScript.

Figure 2.8 also shows a second variant, when groovyc is used instead of groovy. This time, the classes are written into *.class files. Both variants use the same class-generation mechanism.

All this is handled behind the scenes and makes working with Groovy feel like it's an interpreted language, which it isn't. Classes are always fully constructed before runtime and don't change while running.[11]

---

[11] This doesn't preclude replacing a class at runtime, when the *.groovy file changes.

Given this description, you might legitimately ask how Groovy can be called a *dynamic* language if all Groovy code lives in the *static* Java class format. Groovy performs class construction and method invocation in a particularly clever way, as you'll see.

GROOVY IS DYNAMIC

What makes dynamic languages so powerful is their *dynamic method dispatch.* Allow yourself some time to let this sink in. It's not the dynamic typing that makes a dynamic language dynamic. It's the dynamic method dispatch.

In Grails, for example, you see statements like `Album.findByArtist('Oscar Peterson')` but the `Album` class has no such method! Neither has any superclass. No class has such a method! The trick is that method calls are funneled through an object called a `MetaClass`, which in this case recognizes that there's no corresponding method in the bytecode of `Album` and therefore relays the call to its `missingMethod` handler. This knows about the naming convention of Grails' dynamic finder methods and fetches your favorite albums from the database.

But because Groovy is compiled to regular Java bytecode, how is the `MetaClass` called? Well, the bytecode that the Groovy class generator produces is necessarily different from what the Java compiler would generate—not in format but in content. Suppose a Groovy file contains a statement like `foo()`. Groovy doesn't generate bytecode that reflects this method call directly, but does something like this:[12]

```
getMetaClass().invokeMethod(this, "foo", EMPTY_PARAMS_ARRAY)
```

That way, method calls are redirected through the object's `MetaClass`. This `MetaClass` can now do tricks with method invocations such as intercepting, redirecting, adding/removing methods at runtime, and so on. This principle applies to all calls from Groovy code, regardless of whether the methods are in other Groovy objects or are in Java objects. Remember: there's no difference.

> **TIP** The technically inclined may have fun running `groovyc` on some Groovy code and feeding the resulting class files into a decompiler such as Jad. Doing so gives you the Java code equivalent of the bytecode that Groovy generated.

Calling the `MetaClass` for every method call seems to imply a considerable performance hit, and, yes, this flexibility comes at the expense of runtime performance. But this hit isn't quite as bad as you might expect, because the `MetaClass` implementation comes with some clever caching and shortcut strategies that allow the Java just-in-time compiler and the hot-spot technology to step in. When you need near-Java performance, you can even use `@CompileStatic` (see chapter 10) and the generated code is no longer calling into the `MetaClass`.

A less obvious but perhaps more important consideration is the effect that Groovy's dynamic nature has on the compiler. Notice that, for example, `Album.find-ByArtist('Oscar Peterson')` isn't known at compile time but the compiler has to

---

[12] The actual implementation involves a few more redirections.

compile it anyway. Now if you've mistyped the method name by accident, a compiler cannot warn you. In fact, compilers have to accept almost any method call that you throw at them and the code will fail at runtime.[13] But don't despair! What the compiler cannot do, other tools can. Your IDE can do more than the compiler because it has contextual knowledge of what you're doing. It'll warn you on method calls that it cannot resolve and, in the preceding case, it even gives you code completion and refactoring support for Grails's dynamic finder methods.

A way of using dynamic code is to put the source in a string and ask Groovy to evaluate it. You'll see how this works in chapter 16. Such a string can be constructed literally or through any kind of logic. Be warned though: you can easily get overwhelmed by the complexity of dynamic code generation.

Here is an example of concatenating two strings and evaluating the result:

```
def code = '1 + '
code += System.getProperty('java.class.version')
assert code == '1 + 51.0'
assert 52.0 == evaluate(code)
```

Note that code is an ordinary string! It happens to contain '1 + 51.0' when running the code with Java 7,[14] which is a valid Groovy expression (a *script,* actually). Instead of having a programmer write this expression (say, println 1 + 51.0), the program puts it together at runtime. The evaluate method finally executes it.

Wait—didn't we claim that line-by-line execution isn't possible, and code has to be fully constructed as a class? How can code be *executed* like this? The answer is simple. Remember the left path in figure 2.7? Class generation can transparently happen at runtime. The only new feature here is that the class-generation input can also be a *string* like code rather than the content of a *.groovy file.

The ability to evaluate an arbitrary string of code is the distinctive feature of scripting languages. That means Groovy can operate as a scripting language although it's a general-purpose programming language in itself.

GROOVY CAN BE STATIC

Does the dynamic support within Groovy worry you? Do you think it might add performance penalties to your execution? Or do you worry that you might have reduced IDE support when writing your programs? We already told you not to despair because of the excellent tool support available even for Groovy in its most dynamic form. But if you still aren't reassured, you can force the Groovy compiler to do strict type checking (with elaborate type inference) by using the @TypeChecked annotation for pieces of code that you know to be free of dynamic features. The type checking mechanism is extensible so you can even provide stricter type checking than available in Java if you want.

---

[13] That is, the code fails at unit-test time, right?

[14] You should expect 49.0 if running using JDK5, 50.0 using JDK6, and 52.0 if using JDK8.

To see a glimpse of this feature, examine the following class definition:

```
class Universe {
  @groovy.transform.TypeChecked
  int answer() { "forty two" }
}
```

If you try to compile this you'll get a compilation error:

```
[Static type checking] - Cannot return value of type java.lang.String
on method returning type int
```

Without the @TypeChecked annotation, the code would fail at runtime with a Groovy-CastException. Chapter 10 has all the details.

2.5 Summary

That's it for our initial overview. Don't worry if you don't feel you've mastered everything we've covered—we'll go over it all in detail in the upcoming chapters.

We started by looking at how this book demonstrates Groovy code using assertions. This allows you to keep the features you're trying to demonstrate and the results of using those features close together within the code. It also lets you automatically verify that the listings are correct.

You got a first impression of Groovy's code notation and found it both similar to and distinct from Java at the same time. Groovy is similar with respect to defining classes, objects, and methods. It uses keywords, braces, brackets, and parentheses in a very similar fashion; however, Groovy's notation is more lightweight. It needs less scaffolding code, fewer declarations, and fewer lines of code to make the compiler happy. This may mean that you need to change the pace at which you read code: Groovy code says more in fewer lines, so you typically have to read more slowly, at least to start with.

Groovy is bytecode compatible with Java and obeys Java's protocol of full class construction before execution. But Groovy is still fully dynamic, generating classes transparently at runtime when needed. Despite the fixed set of methods in the bytecode of a class, Groovy can modify the set of available methods as visible from a Groovy caller's perspective by routing method calls through the MetaClass, which we'll cover in depth in chapter 8. Groovy uses this mechanism to enhance existing JDK classes with new capabilities, together named GDK.

You now have the means to write your first Groovy scripts. Do it! Grab the Groovy shell (groovysh) or the console (groovyConsole) and write your own code. As a side effect, you've also acquired the knowledge to get the most out of the examples that follow in the upcoming in-depth chapters.

For the remainder of part 1, we'll leave the surface and dive into the deep sea of Groovy. This may be unfamiliar, but don't worry. We'll return to sea level often enough to take some deep breaths of Groovy code *in action*.

Simple Groovy datatypes

This chapter covers

- Groovy's approach to typing
- Operators as method implementations
- Strings, regular expressions, and numbers

Do not worry about your difficulties in mathematics. I can assure you mine are still greater.

—Albert Einstein

Groovy supports a limited set of datatypes at the *language* level; that is, it offers constructs for literal declarations and specialized operators. This set contains the simple datatypes for strings, regular expressions, and numbers, as well as the collective datatypes for ranges, lists, and maps. This chapter covers simple datatypes; the next chapter introduces collective datatypes.

Before we go into details, we'll talk about Groovy's general approach to typing. With this in mind, you can appreciate Groovy's approach of treating everything as an object and all operators as method calls. You'll see how this improves the level of object orientation in the language compared to Java's division between primitive types and reference types.

We then describe the natively supported datatypes individually. By the end of this chapter, you'll be able to confidently work with Groovy's simple datatypes and have a whole new understanding of what happens when you write 1+1.

3.1 Objects, objects everywhere

In Groovy, everything is an object. It is, after all, an object-oriented language. Groovy doesn't have the slight "fudge factor" of Java, which is object-oriented apart from some built-in types. To explain the choices made by Groovy's designers, we'll first go over basics of Java's type system. We'll then explain how Groovy addresses the difficulties presented, and finally examine how Groovy and Java can still interoperate with ease due to automatic boxing and unboxing where necessary.

3.1.1 Java's type system: primitives and references

Java distinguishes between *primitive* types (such as boolean, short, int, double, float, char, and byte) and *reference* types (such as Object and String). There's a fixed set of primitive types, and these are the only types that have *value semantics*—where the value of a variable of that type is the actual number (or character, or true/false value). You cannot create your own value types in Java.

Reference types (everything apart from primitives) have *reference semantics*—the value of a variable of that type is only a reference to an object. Readers with a C/C++ background may wish to think of a reference as a pointer—it's a similar concept. If you change the value of a reference type variable, it has no effect on the object it was previously referring to—you're just making the variable refer to a different object or to no object at all. The reverse is true too: changing the *contents* of an object doesn't affect the value of a variable referring to that object.

You cannot call methods on values of primitive types, and you cannot use them where Java expects objects of type java.lang.Object. For each primitive type, Java has a *wrapper type*—a reference type that stores a value of the primitive type in an object. The wrapper for int, for example, is java.lang.Integer.

Conversely, operators such as * in 3 * 2 or a * b *aren't* supported for arbitrary[1] reference types in Java, but only for primitive types (with the notable exception of +, which is also supported for strings).

The Groovy code in listing 3.1 calls methods on seemingly primitive types (first with a literal declaration and then on a variable), which isn't allowed in Java where you need to explicitly create the integer wrapper to convince the compiler. While calling + on strings is allowed in Java, calling the - (*minus*) operator is not. Groovy allows both.

---

[1] From Java 5 onward, the autoboxing feature may kick in to unbox the wrapper object to its primitive payload and apply the operator.

Listing 3.1   Groovy supports primitive methods and object operators

```
(60 * 60 * 24 * 365).toString(); // invalid Java

int secondsPerYear = 60 * 60 * 24 * 365;
secondsPerYear.toString(); // invalid Java

new Integer(secondsPerYear).toString();

assert "abc" - "a" == "bc" // invalid Java
```

The Groovy way looks more consistent and involves some language sophistication that we're going to explore next.

3.1.2   *Groovy's answer: everything's an object*

To make Groovy fully object-oriented, and because at the JVM level Java doesn't support object-oriented operations such as method calls on primitive types, the Groovy designers decided to do away with primitive types. When Groovy needs to store values that would have used Java's primitive types, Groovy uses the wrapper classes already provided by the Java platform. Table 3.1 provides a complete list of these wrappers.

Table 3.1   Java's primitive datatypes and their wrappers

Primitive type	Wrapper type	Description
byte	java.lang.Byte	8-bit signed integer
short	java.lang.Short	16-bit signed integer
int	java.lang.Integer	32-bit signed integer
long	java.lang.Long	64-bit signed integer
float	java.lang.Float	Single-precision (32-bit) floating-point value
double	java.lang.Double	Double-precision (64-bit) floating-point value
char	java.lang.Character	16-bit Unicode character
boolean	java.lang.Boolean	Boolean value (true or false)

Any time you see what looks like a primitive literal value (the number 5, for example, or the Boolean value true) in Groovy source code, that's a reference to an instance of the appropriate wrapper class. For the sake of brevity and familiarity, Groovy allows you to declare variables as if they were primitive-type variables. Don't be fooled—the type used is really the wrapper type. Strings and arrays aren't listed in table 3.1 because they're already reference types, not primitive types—no wrapper is needed.

While we have the Java primitives under the microscope, so to speak, it's worth examining the numeric literal formats that Java and Groovy each use. They're slightly different because Groovy allows instances of java.math.BigDecimal and java.math.BigInteger to be specified using literals in addition to the usual binary floating-point types. Table 3.2 gives examples of each of the literal formats available for numeric types in Groovy.

Table 3.2 Numeric literals in Groovy

Type	Example literals
java.lang.Integer[a]	15, 0x1234ffff, 0b00110011, 100_000_000
java.lang.Long	100L, 2001[b]
java.lang.Float	1.23f, 4.56F
java.lang.Double	1.23d, 4.56D
java.math.BigInteger	123g, 456G
java.math.BigDecimal	1.23, 4.56, 1.4E4, 2.8e4, 1.23g, 1.23G

a. Project Coin introduced binary literals and underscores within integer constants as part of Java 7. You can use these features within Groovy even using older versions of the JDK.
b. The use of lowercase *l* as a suffix indicating Long is discouraged, as it can look like a 1 (number one). There's no difference between the uppercase and lowercase versions of any of the suffixes.

Notice how Groovy decides whether to use a BigInteger or a BigDecimal to hold a literal with a G suffix depending on the presence or absence of a decimal point. Notice also how BigDecimal is the default type of noninteger literals. BigDecimal will be used unless you specify a suffix to force the literal to be a Float or a Double.

3.1.3 *Interoperating with Java: automatic boxing and unboxing*

Converting a primitive value into an instance of a wrapper type is called *boxing* in Java and other languages that support the same notion. The reverse action—taking an instance of a wrapper and retrieving the primitive value—is called *unboxing*. Groovy performs these operations automatically for you where necessary. This is primarily the case when you call a Java method from Groovy. This automatic boxing and unboxing is known as *autoboxing*.

You've seen that Groovy is designed to work well with Java, so what happens when a Java method takes primitive parameters or returns a primitive return type? How can you call that method from Groovy? Consider the existing method in the java.lang.String class: int indexOf (int ch). You can call this method from Groovy like this:

```
assert 'ABCDE'.indexOf(67) == 2
```

From Groovy's point of view, you're passing an Integer containing the value 67 (the Unicode value for the letter *C*), even though the method expects a parameter of primitive type int. Groovy takes care of the unboxing. The method returns a primitive type

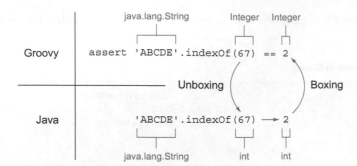

Figure 3.1   Autoboxing in action: an `Integer` parameter is unboxed to an `int` for the Java method call, and an `int` return value is boxed into an `Integer` for use in Groovy.

`int` that's boxed into an `Integer` as soon as it enters the world of Groovy. That way, you can compare it to the `Integer` with value 2 back in the Groovy script.

Figure 3.1 shows the process of going from the Groovy world to the Java world and back.

All of this is transparent—you don't need to do anything in the Groovy code to enable it. Now that you understand autoboxing, the question of how to apply operators to objects becomes interesting. We'll explore this question next.

3.1.4 *No intermediate unboxing*

If in `1+1` both numbers are objects of type `Integer`, you may be wondering whether those `Integer` objects are unboxed to execute the plus operation on primitive types.

The answer is no: Groovy is more object-oriented than Java. It executes this expression as `1.plus(1)`, calling the `plus()` method of the first `Integer` object, and passing[2] the second `Integer` object as an argument. The method call returns an `Integer` object of value 2.

This is a powerful model. Calling methods on objects is what object-oriented languages should do. It opens the door for applying the full range of object-oriented capabilities to those operators.

Let's summarize. No matter how literals (numbers, strings, and so forth) appear in Groovy code, they're always objects. Only at the border to Java are they boxed and unboxed. Operators are shorthand for method calls. Now that you've seen how Groovy handles types when you tell it what to expect, let's examine what it does when you don't give it any type information.

3.2   *The concept of optional typing*

So far, we haven't used any type declarations in the sample Groovy scripts—or have we? Well, we haven't used them in the way that you're familiar with in Java. We assigned strings and numbers to variables and didn't care about the type. Behind the scenes,

---

2 The phrase "passing an object" is short for "passing a reference to an object." In Groovy and Java alike, only references are passed as arguments: objects themselves are never passed.

Groovy implicitly assumes these variables to be of static type `java.lang.Object`. This section discusses what happens when a type *is* specified, and the pros and cons of doing it either way.

3.2.1 Assigning types

Groovy offers the choice of explicitly specifying variable types just as you do in Java. Table 3.3 gives examples of optional type declarations. It's tricky—anything talking about a "type declaration" makes us think it's a type being declared, not a variable. What we're really talking about is "variable declarations using optional typing," but that's a mouthful. We're normally an absolute stickler for getting terminology right, but if you'd like to fudge this slightly for the sake of more readable text, that's fine.

The `def` keyword is used to indicate that no particular type is specified.

Table 3.3   Example Groovy statements and the resulting runtime type

Statement	Type of value	Comment
`def a = 1`	`java.lang.Integer`	Implicit typing
`def b = 1.0f`	`java.lang.Float`	
`int c = 1`	`java.lang.Integer`	Explicit typing using the Java primitive type names
`float d = 1`	`java.lang.Float`	
`Integer e = 1`	`java.lang.Integer`	Explicit typing using reference type names
`String f = '1'`	`java.lang.String`	

As we stated earlier, it doesn't matter whether you declare a variable to be of type `int` or `Integer`. Groovy uses the reference type (`Integer`) either way.

It's important to understand that regardless of whether a variable's type is explicitly declared, the system is *type safe.* Unlike untyped languages, Groovy doesn't allow you to treat an object of one type as an instance of a different type without a well-defined conversion being available. You could never assign a `java.util.Date` to a reference of type `java.lang.Number`, in the hope that you'd end up with an object that you could use for calculation. That sort of behavior would be dangerous, which is why Groovy doesn't allow it any more than Java does.

3.2.2 Dynamic Groovy is type safe

We'll first look at Groovy's default dynamic behavior. It's important to understand that even when using all of its dynamic capabilities, Groovy is providing full type safety at runtime. In chapter 10, we'll explore how to make Groovy provide more type checking at compile time to match and even exceed the kind of checking you might expect from Java.

The web is full of heated discussions of whether static or dynamic typing is "better" while it often remains unclear what either should actually mean. *Static* is often associated with the appearance of type markers in the code. For instance, code such as

```
String greeting = readFromConsole()
```

is often considered static because of the `String` type marker, while unmarked code like

```
def greeting = readFromConsole()
```

is usually deemed *dynamic*. But it isn't as simple as that. In languages that support type inference[3] and have no dynamic behavior capabilities, it might be possible to fully statically type check the latter code, while in a fully dynamic language, it's not possible at compile time to type check the former code even with type markers. This is because in general solely dynamic languages cannot tell what type the `readFromConsole()` method will eventually return,[4] so there's little point in doing many of the traditional compile-time checks.[5]

By default, Groovy is very much a dynamic language. You can safely leave out type markers (and also type casts) in most scenarios and know that Groovy will do the appropriate runtime checks to ensure type safety when required. Because type markers are optional in Groovy, that concept is often called *optional typing*. The types are still there, of course, but you can choose not to make them explicit in your code.

All of that may sound as if type markers are superfluous, but they play an important role not only at runtime—for the method dispatch as you'll see in chapters 7 and 8—but also for our current concern: type-safe assignments.

Groovy uses type markers to enforce the Java type system at runtime. Yes, you've read this correctly: *Groovy enforces the Java type system!* But it only does so at runtime, where Java does so with a mixture of compile-time and runtime checks. Java enforces the type system to a large extent at compile time based on static information, which gives static typing its second meaning. The fact that Java does part of the work at runtime can easily be inferred from the fact that Java programs can still raise `Class-CastExceptions` and other runtime typing errors.

All this explains why the Groovy compiler[6] takes no issue with

```
Integer myInt = new Object()
println myInt
```

---

[3] And indeed Groovy, when using @TypeChecked or @CompileStatic, is one of them!

[4] It may, for example, be intercepted, relayed, or replaced by a different method.

[5] Groovy will still do some compile-time checks even when compiling dynamically. For instance, if you declare that a class implements an interface, Groovy requires that at compile time it contains the methods from the interface.

[6] Your IDE will present you a big warning, though. It can apply additional logic like data flow analysis and type inference to even discover more hidden assignment errors. It's your responsibility as a developer on how to deal with these warnings.

but when running the code, the cast from `Object` to `Integer` is enforced and you'll see

```
org.codehaus.groovy.runtime.typehandling.GroovyCastException:
    Cannot cast object 'java.lang.Object@5b0bc6'
    with class 'java.lang.Object' to class 'java.lang.Integer'
```

In fact, this is the same effect you see if you write a typecast on the right-hand side of the assignment in Java.

Consider this Java code:

```
Integer myInt = (Integer) returnsObject(); // Java!
```

The Java compiler will check whether `returnsObject()` returns an object of a type that can sensibly be cast to `Integer`. Let's assume that the declared return type is `Object`. That makes `Object` the *compile-time type*[7] of the `returnsObject()` reference. The hope is that at runtime it'll yield an `Integer`, which becomes its *runtime type*.[8]

The Groovy code

```
Integer myInt = returnsObject()
```

is the exact equivalent of the preceding Java code as far as the type handling is concerned. The Groovy compiler inserts type-casting logic for you that makes sure that the right-hand side of an assignment is cast to the type of the left-hand side. Consequently, when using the dynamic programming style as in

```
def myInt = returnsObject()
```

you'd cast to `Object` because that's assumed when `def` is used. But this can never have any effect because *every* object is at least of type `Object` and Groovy optimizes the cast away.

Declared types give you a number of benefits. They're means of documentation and communication, but most of all, they enable you to *reason about your code*. Consider this code snippet:

```
Integer myInt = returnsObject()
println(++myInt)
```

The second line is guarded by the first line; there's *no way* that it'd *ever* be called if `myInt` wasn't of type `Integer`. You can reason that the ++ operator will be found and work as expected.

As a second example, consider a method definition with a parameter that bears a type marker:

```
def printNext(Integer myInt) {
    println(++myInt)
}
```

---

[7] This is usually also called the *static* type but we avoid this term here to avoid further confusion.

[8] Often called the *dynamic* type—a term we avoid for the same reason.

There's *no possible way* that this method could *ever* be called with an argument that isn't of type Integer! Even though the compiler accepts code like printNext(new Object()), this will *never* result in calling the previous method. And now to a common misconception.

> **Groovy types aren't dynamic, they never change**
> If we could make the ink blink, we would! The word "dynamic" doesn't mean that the type of a reference, once declared, can ever change. Once you've declared Integer myInt, you cannot execute myInt = new Object(). This will throw a GroovyCast-Exception. You can only assign a value, which Groovy can cast to an Integer. As you see, the phrase "dynamic typing" can be misleading and is best avoided.

Type declarations and type casts also play an important role in the Groovy method dispatch that we'll examine in more detail in chapters 7 and 8. Casts come with some additional logic to make development easier.

3.2.3 *Let the casting work for you*

To complete the picture, Groovy actually applies convenience logic when casting, which is mainly concerned with casting primitive types to their wrapper classes and vice versa, arrays to lists, characters to integers, Java's type widening for numeric types, applying the "Groovy truth" (see chapter 6) for casts to boolean, calling toString() for casts to string, and so on. The exhaustive list can be looked up in DefaultType-Transformation.castToType.

Two notable features are baked into the Groovy type casting logic that may be surprising at first, but make for really elegant code: casting lists and maps to arbitrary classes. The following listing introduces these features by creating Point, Rectangle, and Dimension objects.

Listing 3.2 Casting lists and maps to arbitrary classes

```
import java.awt.*

Point topLeft = new Point(0, 0) // classic
Point botRight = [100, 100] // List cast
Point center = [x:50, y:50] // Map cast

assert botRight instanceof Point
assert center instanceof Point

def rect = new Rectangle()
rect.location = [0, 0] // Point
rect.size = [width:100, height:100] // Dimension
```

As you see from the listing, implicit runtime casting can lead to very readable code, especially in cases like property assignments where Groovy knows that rect.size is of type `java.awt.Dimension` and can cast your list or map of constructor arguments onto that. You don't have to worry about it: Groovy infers the type for you.

We've seen the value of type markers and pervasive casting. But because Groovy offers optional typing, what is the use case for omitting type markers?

3.2.4 The case for optional typing

Omitting type markers isn't only convenient for the lazy programmer who does ad-hoc scripting, but is also useful for relaying and duck typing. Suppose you get an object as the result of a method call, and you have to relay it as an argument to some other method call without doing anything with that object yourself:

```
def node = document.findMyNode()
log.info node
db.store node
```

In this case, you're not interested in finding out what the heck the actual type and package name of that node are. You're spared the work of looking them up, declaring the type, and importing the package. You also communicate: "That's just something."

The second use of unmarked typing is calling methods on objects that have no guaranteed type. This is often called *duck typing*, and it allows the implementation of generic functionality with high reusability.

> **Duck typing**
>
> As coined by the dynamic language community, "If it walks like a duck and quacks like a duck, it must be a duck." Weakly typed languages usually let you call any method or access any property on an object, even if you don't know at compile time or even at runtime that the object is of a known type that contains that method or property. This means you know the kind of objects you expect will have the relevant signature or property. It's an assumption. If you can call the method or access the property, it must be the type you were expecting—hence, it's a duck because it walks and quacks like a duck!
>
> Duck typing implies that as long as an object has a certain set of method signatures, it's interchangeable with any other object that has the same set of methods, regardless of whether the two have a related inheritance hierarchy.

For programmers with a strong Java background, it's not uncommon to start programming Groovy almost entirely using type declarations, and gradually shift into a more dynamic mode over time. This is legitimate because it allows everybody to use what they're confident with.

RULE OF THUMB Experienced Groovy programmers tend to follow this rule of thumb: as soon as you *think* about the type of a reference, declare it; if you're thinking of it as "just an object," leave the type out.

Whether or not you declare your types, you'll find that Groovy lets you do a lot more than you may expect. Let's start by looking at the ability to override operators.

3.3 Overriding operators

Overriding refers to the object-oriented concept of having types that specify behavior and subtypes that override this behavior to make it more specific. When a language bases its operators on method calls and allows these methods to be overridden, the approach is called *operator overriding*.

It's more conventional to use the term *operator overloading*, which means almost the same thing. The difference is that *overloading* suggests, at least to many Java programmers, that you have multiple implementations of a method (and thus the associated operator) that differ only in their parameter types.

We'll show you which operators can be overridden, show a full example of how overriding works in practice, and offer guidance on the decisions you need to make when operators work with multiple types.

3.3.1 Overview of overridable operators

As you saw in section 3.1.2, `1+1` is a convenient way of writing `1.plus(1)`. This is achieved by class `Integer` having an implementation of the `plus` method.

This convenient feature is also available for other operators. Table 3.4 shows an overview.

Table 3.4   Method-based operators

Operator	Name	Method	Works with
a + b	Plus	a.plus(b)	Number, String, StringBuffer, Collection, Map, Date, Duration
a – b	Minus	a.minus(b)	Number, String, List, Set, Date, Duration
a * b	Star	a.multiply(b)	Number, String, Collection
a / b	Divide	a.div(b)	Number
a % b	Modulo	a.mod(b)	Integral number
a++ ++a	Postincrement Preincrement	def v = a; a = a.next(); v a = a.next(); a	Iterator, Number, String, Date, Range
a-- --a	Postdecrement Predecrement	def v = a; a = a.previous(); v a = a.previous(); a	Iterator, Number, String, Date, Range
-a	Unary minus	a.unaryMinus()	Number, ArrayList

Table 3.4 Method-based operators

Operator	Name	Method	Works with
+a	Unary plus	`a.unaryPlus()`	`Number, ArrayList`
a ** b	Power	`a.power(b)`	`Number`
a | b	Numerical or	`a.or(b)`	`Number, Boolean, BitSet, Process`
a & b	Numerical and	`a.and(b)`	`Number, Boolean, BitSet`
a ^ b	Numerical xor	`a.xor(b)`	`Number, Boolean, BitSet`
~a	Bitwise complement	`a.bitwiseNegate()`	`Number, String` (the latter returning a regular expression pattern)
a[b]	Subscript	`a.getAt(b)`	`Object, List, Map, CharSequence, Matcher,` many more
a[b] = c	Subscript assignment	`a.putAt(b, c)`	`Object, List, Map, StringBuffer,` many more
a << b	Left shift	`a.leftShift(b)`	Integral number, also used like "append" to `String-Buffer, Writer, File, Socket, List`
a >> b	Right shift	`a.rightShift(b)`	`Number`
a >>> b	Right shift unsigned	`a.rightShift-Unsigned(b)`	`Number`
switch(a){ case b: }	Classification	`b.isCase(a)`	`Object, Class, Range, Collection, Pattern, Closure;` also used with `Collection c` in `c.grep(b)`, which returns all items of `c` where `b.isCase(item)`
a in b	Classification	`b.isCase(a)`	See previous row
a == b	Equals	`if (a implements Comparable) { a.compareTo(b) == 0 } else { a.equals(b) }`	`Object;` consider `hashCode()` [a]
a != b	Not equal	`!(a == b)`	`Object`

a. When overriding the `equals` method, Java strongly encourages the developer to also override the `hashCode()` method such that equal objects have the same hash code (whereas objects with the same hash code are not necessarily equal). See the Java API documentation of `java.lang.Object#equals`.

Table 3.4 **Method-based operators** *(continued)*

Operator	Name	Method	Works with
a <=> b	Spaceship	a.compareTo(b)	java.lang.Comparable
a > b	Greater than	a.compareTo(b) > 0	
a >= b	Greater than or equal to	a.compareTo(b) >= 0	
a < b	Less than	a.compareTo(b) < 0	
a <= b	Less than or equal to	a.compareTo(b) <= 0	
a as type	Enforced coercion	a.asType(typeClass)	Any type

The case of equals

Nothing is easier than determining whether a == b is true, right? Well, only at first sight if you want this to be a useful equality check. If both are null, they should count as equal. If they reference the same object, they're equal without the need for checking. In other words, a == a for all values of a.

But there's more! If a >= b and a <= b, then you can deduce that a == b, right? But this may impose a conflict if you have a Comparable object that doesn't implement the equals method consistently. This is why Groovy only looks at the compareTo method for Comparable objects when doing the equality check and ignores the equals method in this case. You can find the full logic implemented in the Groovy runtime under DefaultTypeTransformation.compareEqual(a,b).

You can easily use any of these operators with your own classes. Just implement the respective method. Unlike in Java, there's no need to implement a specific interface.

Strictly speaking, Groovy has even more operators in addition to those in table 3.4, such as the dot operator for referencing fields and methods. Their behavior can also be overridden. They come into play in chapter 7.

This is all good in theory, but let's see how it all works in practice.

3.3.2 *Overridden operators in action*

Listing 3.3 demonstrates an implementation of the == (*equals*) and + (*plus*) operators for a Money class. It's an implementation of the Value Object[9] pattern. You allow values of the same currency to be summed, but don't support multicurrency addition.

---

9 See a discussion of value objects at http://c2.com/cgi/wiki?ValueObject.

You implement `equals` indirectly by using the `@Immutable` annotation as introduced in section 2.3.4. Remember that `==` (or equals method) denotes object *equality* (equal values), not *identity* (same object instances).

```
import groovy.transform.Immutable              ❶ Overrides ==
                                                 operator
@Immutable
class Money {
    int     amount
    String  currency
                                               ❷ Implements +
    Money plus (Money other) {                   operator
        if (null == other) return this
        if (other.currency != currency) {
            throw new IllegalArgumentException(
                "cannot add $other.currency to $currency")
        }
        return new Money(amount + other.amount, currency)
    }
}
                                               ❸ Uses
Money   buck = new Money(1, 'USD')               overridden ==
assert buck
assert buck          == new Money(1, 'USD')    ❹ Uses
assert buck + buck == new Money(2, 'USD')        implemented +
```

Because every immutable object automatically gets a value-based implementation of `equals`, you get away with only a minimal declaration at ❶. The use of this operator is shown at ❸, where one dollar becomes equal to any other dollar. At ❷, the + operator isn't *overridden* in the strict sense of the word, because there's no such operator in `Money`'s superclass (`Object`). In this case, *operator implementing* is the best wording. This is used at ❹, where two `Money` objects are added.

We mentioned earlier in this section that Java programmers may already be familiar with method *overloading*. You can apply that concept even with operators by defining additional `plus` implementations. Let's look at a possible overload for the + operator. In listing 3.3, `Money` can only be added via the `plus` method to other `Money` objects. However, you might also want to be able to add `Money` with code like this:

```
assert buck + 1 == new Money(2, 'USD')
```

We can provide the additional method as follows:

```
Money plus (Integer more) {
    return new Money(amount + more, currency)
}
```

which overloads the `plus` method with a second implementation that takes an `Integer` parameter. The Groovy method dispatch finds the right implementation at runtime.

NOTE   Our plus operation on the Money class returns Money objects in both cases. We describe this by saying that Money's plus operation is *closed* under its type. Whatever operation you perform on an instance of Money, you end up with another instance of Money.

This example leads to the general issue of how to deal with different parameter types when implementing an operator method. We'll go through aspects of this issue in the next section.

3.3.3   *Making coercion work for you*

Implementing operators is straightforward when both operands are of the same type. Things get more complex with a mixture of types, say

```
1 + 1.0
```

This adds an Integer and a BigDecimal. What is the return type? Section 3.6 answers this question for the special case of numbers, but the issue is more general. One of the two arguments needs to be promoted to the more general type. This is called *coercion*.

   When implementing operators, there are three main issues to consider as part of coercion.

SUPPORTED ARGUMENT TYPES

You need to decide which argument types and values will be allowed. If an operator must take a potentially inappropriate type, throw an IllegalArgumentException where necessary. In the Money example, even though it makes sense to use Money as the parameter for the plus operator, you don't allow different currencies to be added together.

PROMOTING MORE SPECIFIC ARGUMENTS

If the argument type is a more specific one than your own type, promote it to *your* type and return an object of *your* type. To see what this means, consider how you might implement the + operator if you were designing the BigDecimal class, and what you'd do for an Integer argument.

   Integer is more specific than BigDecimal: every Integer value can be expressed as a BigDecimal, but the reverse isn't true. So for the BigDecimal.plus(Integer) operator, you'd consider promoting the Integer to BigDecimal, performing the addition, and then returning another BigDecimal—even if the result could accurately be expressed as an Integer.

HANDLING MORE GENERAL ARGUMENTS WITH DOUBLE DISPATCH

If the argument type is more general, call *its* operator method with *yourself* ("this," the current object) as an argument. Let *it* promote *you*. This is also called *double dispatch*,[10] and it helps to avoid duplicated, asymmetric, possibly inconsistent code. Let's reverse the previous example and consider Integer.plus(BigDecimal operand).

---

[10] Double dispatch is usually used with overloaded methods: a.method(b) calls b.method(a) where method is overloaded with method(TypeA) and method(TypeB).

We'd consider returning the result of the expression `operand.plus(this)`, delegating the work to `BigDecimal`'s `plus(Integer)` method. The result would be a `BigDecimal`, which is reasonable—it'd be odd for `1+1.5` to return an `Integer` but `1.5+1` to return a `BigDecimal`.

Of course, this is only applicable for *commutative*[11] operators. Test rigorously, and don't make the mistake of creating an endless cycle. If `Integer`'s `plus` is calling `BigInteger`'s `plus`, you better make sure that `BigInteger`'s `plus` doesn't call back to `Integer`!

GROOVY'S CONVENTIONAL BEHAVIOR

Groovy's general strategy of coercion is to return the most general type. Other languages such as Ruby try to be smarter and return the *least* general type that can be used without losing information from range or precision. The Ruby way saves memory at the expense of processing time. It also requires that the language promotes a type to a more general one when the operation would generate an overflow of that type's range. Otherwise, intermediary results in a complex calculation could truncate the result.

Now that you know how Groovy handles types in general, we can delve deeper into what it provides for each of the datatypes it supports at the language level. We begin with the type that's probably used more than any other non-numeric type: the humble string.

3.4 *Working with strings*

Considering how widely strings are used, many languages—including Java—provide few language features to make them easier to handle. Scripting languages tend to fare better in this regard than mainstream application languages, so Groovy takes on board some of those extra features. This section examines what's available in Groovy and how to make the most of the extra abilities.

Groovy strings come in two flavors: plain strings and GStrings. Plain strings are instances of `java.lang.String`, and GStrings are instances of `groovy.lang.GString`. GStrings allow placeholder expressions to be resolved and evaluated at runtime. Many scripting languages have a similar feature, usually called *string interpolation*, but it's more primitive than the GString feature of Groovy. Let's start by looking at each flavor of string and how it appears in code.

3.4.1 *Varieties of string literals*

Java allows only one way of specifying string literals: placing text in quotes "like this." If you want to embed dynamic values within the string, you have to either call a formatting method (made easier, but still far from simple, in Java 1.5) or concatenate each constituent part. If you specify a string with a lot of backslashes in it (such as a Windows filename or a regular expression), your code becomes hard to read, because you have to double the backslashes. If you want a lot of text spanning several lines in

---

[11] An operator is commutative if the operands can be exchanged without changing the result of the operation. For example, plus is usually required to be commutative (`a + b == b + a`) but minus is not (`a - b != b - a`).

the source code, you have to make each line contain a complete string (or several complete strings).

Groovy recognizes that not every use of string literals is the same, so it offers a variety of options. These are summarized in table 3.5.

Table 3.5   Summary of the string literal styles available in Groovy

Start/end characters	Example	Placeholder resolved?	Backslash escapes?
Single quote	`'hello Dierk'`	No	Yes
Double quote	`"hello $name"`	Yes	Yes

Triple single quote (`'''`)	`'''`
	
	`==========`
	
	`Total: $0.02`
	
	`==========`
	
	`'''`
		No	Yes

Triple double quote (`"""`)	`"""`
	
	`first $line`
	
	`second $line`
	
	`third $line`
	
	`"""`
		Yes	Yes

Forward slash	`/x(\d*)y/`	Yes	Occasionally
Dollar slash	`$/x(\d*)y/$`	Yes	Occasionally

The aim of each form is to specify the text data you want with a minimum of fuss. Each of the forms has a single feature that distinguishes it from the others:

- The single-quoted form never pays any attention to placeholders. This is closely equivalent to Java string literals.
- The double-quoted form is the equivalent of the single-quoted form, except that if the text contains unescaped dollar signs, the dollar sign introduces a placeholder, and the string will be treated as a GString instead of a plain string. GStrings are covered in more detail in the next section.
- The triple-quoted form (or *multiline* string literal) allows the literal to span several lines. New lines are always treated as \n regardless of the platform, but all other whitespace is preserved as it appears in the text file. Multiline string literals may also be GStrings, depending on whether single quotes or double quotes are used. Multiline string literals act similar to Ruby or Perl.
- The *slashy* form of string literal is also multiline but allows strings with backslashes to be specified simply without having to escape all the backslashes. This

is particularly useful with regular expressions, as you'll see later. There are only a few exceptions and limitations. Slashes are escaped with a backslash. A backslash can't appear as the last character of a slashy string. Dollar symbols that could introduce a placeholder but aren't meant to also need to be escaped. If you want to create a string with a backslash followed by a *u*, the backslash needs to be escaped so as not to be interpreted as a Unicode character, which happens in the earliest stages of parsing.[12]

- The *dollar slashy* form of string literal also allows strings with backslashes to be specified without having to escape all the backslashes. Only Unicode characters are escaped with a backslash. Dollar signs and slashes are escaped with a dollar sign. The other restrictions on backslashes you saw for normal slashy strings don't apply.

As we hinted earlier, Groovy uses a similar mechanism to Java for specifying special characters, such as linefeeds and tabs. In addition to the Java escapes, dollar signs can be escaped in double-quoted GStrings to allow them to be placed directly in such strings without the compiler assuming you're defining a GString placeholder. The full set of escaped characters is specified in table 3.6.

Table 3.6 Escaped characters as known to Groovy

Escaped special character	Meaning
\b	Backspace
\t	Tab
\r	Carriage return
\n	Linefeed
\f	Form feed
\\	Backslash
\$	Dollar sign
\uabcd	Unicode character *u* + *abcd* (where *a*, *b*, *c*, and *d* are hex digits)
\abc	Unicode character *u* + *abc* (where *a*, *b*, and *c* are octal digits, and *b* and *c* are optional)
\'	Single quote
\"	Double quote

Note that in a double-quoted string, single quotes don't need to be escaped, and vice versa. In other words, `'I said, "Hi."'` and `"don't"` both do what you hope they will.

---

[12] Escaping backslashes and dollars is slightly tricky in a slashy string and involves either using GString tricks or embedding Unicode escape sequences (for example, \u005C is the Unicode for a backslash). Here are three expressions involving slashy strings resulting in a string starting with a backslash followed by u2: /\u005Cu${1+1}/ or GString.EMPTY + '\\' + /u${1+1}/ or /${'\\'}u${1+1}/. A similar issue occurs if you want to use a dollar sign. This is a small (and rare) price to pay for the benefits available, however.

For the sake of consistency, both still *can* be escaped in each case. Likewise, dollar signs can be escaped in single-quoted strings, even though they don't need to be. This makes it easier to switch between the forms.

Note that Java uses single quotes for *character* literals, but as you've seen, Groovy cannot do so because single quotes are already used to specify *strings*.

But you can achieve the same as in Java when providing the type explicitly:

```
char a = 'x'
```

or

```
Character b = 'x'
```

The `java.lang.String` 'x' is cast into a `java.lang.Character`. If you want to coerce a string into a character at other times, you can do so in either of the following ways:

```
'x' as char
```

or

```
'x'.toCharacter()
```

As a GDK goody, there are more to* methods to convert a string, such as `toInteger`, `toLong`, `toFloat`, and `toDouble`.

Whichever literal form is used, unless the compiler decides it's a GString, it ends up as an instance of `java.lang.String`, just like Java string literals. So far, we've only teased you with allusions to what GStrings are capable of. Now it's time to spill the beans.

3.4.2 *Working with GStrings*

GStrings are like strings with additional capabilities.[13] They're literally declared in double quotes. What makes a double-quoted string literally a GString is the appearance of placeholders. Placeholders may appear in a full `${expression}` syntax or an abbreviated `$reference` syntax. See the examples in the following listing.

Listing 3.4   Working with GStrings

```
import static java.util.Calendar.*

def me      = 'Tarzan'
def you     = 'Jane'
def line    = "me $me - you $you"
assert  line == 'me Tarzan - you Jane'

TimeZone.default =  TimeZone.getTimeZone('GMT')
def date = new Date(0)
def dateMap = [y:date[YEAR]-1900, m:date[MONTH], d:date[DAY_OF_MONTH]]
def out = "Year $dateMap.y Month $dateMap.m Day $dateMap.d"
assert out == 'Year 70 Month 0 Day 1'

def tz = TimeZone.getTimeZone('GMT')
def format = 'd MMM YYYY HH:mm:SS z'
```

❶ Abbreviated dollar syntax

❷ Extended dot syntax

---

[13] `groovy.lang.GString` isn't actually a subclass of `java.lang.String`, and couldn't be, because String is final. But GStrings can usually be used as if they were strings—Groovy coerces them into strings when it needs to.

```
out = "Date is ${date.format(format, tz)} !"
assert out == 'Date is 1 Jan 1970 00:00:00 GMT !'
```
← **3** **Full syntax with braces**

```
def sql = """
SELECT FROM MyTable
  WHERE Year = $dateMap.y
"""
assert sql == """
SELECT FROM MyTable
  WHERE Year = 70
"""
```
4 **Multiline GStrings**

```
out = "my 0.02\$"
assert out == 'my 0.02$'
```
← **Escaped dollar sign**
← **Literal dollar sign**

Within a GString, simple references to variables can be dereferenced with the dollar sign. This simplest form is shown at **1**, whereas **2** shows this being extended to use property accessors with the dot syntax. You'll learn more about accessing properties in chapter 7.

The full syntax uses dollar signs and braces, as shown at **3**. It allows arbitrary Groovy expressions within the braces. The braces denote a *closure*.

In real life, GStrings are handy in templating scenarios. A GString is used to create the string for an SQL query. Groovy provides even more sophisticated templating support, as shown in chapter 8. If you need a dollar character within a template (or any other GString use), you must escape it with a backslash as shown in **4**.

Although GStrings behave like `java.lang.String` objects for all operations that a programmer is usually concerned with, they're implemented differently to capture the fixed and dynamic parts (the so-called *values*) separately. This is revealed by the following code:

```
def me        = 'Tarzan'
def you       = 'Jane'
def line      = "me $me - you $you"
assert line == 'me Tarzan - you Jane'
assert line instanceof GString
assert line.strings[0] == 'me '
assert line.strings[1] == ' - you '
assert line.values[0]  == 'Tarzan'
assert line.values[1]  == 'Jane'
```

> **Placeholder evaluation time**
>
> Each placeholder inside a GString is evaluated at declaration time and the result is stored in the GString object. By the time the GString *value* is converted into a `java.lang.String` (by calling its `toString` method or casting it to a string), each value gets written[14] to the string. Because the logic of how to write a value can be elaborate for certain types (most notably *closures*), this behavior can be used in advanced ways that make the evaluation of such placeholders appear to be lazy. See section D.2 of the cheat sheet appendix for an example of this.

---

[14] See `Writer.write(Object)` in section 12.2.3.

You've seen the Groovy language support for declaring strings. What follows is an introduction to the use of strings in the Groovy *library*. This will also give you a first impression of the seamless interplay of Java and Groovy. We start in typical Java style and gradually slip into Groovy mode, carefully watching each step.

3.4.3 *From Java to Groovy*

Now that you have your strings easily declared, you can have some fun with them. Because they're objects of type `java.lang.String`, you can call `String`'s methods on them or pass them as parameters wherever a string is expected, such as for easy console output:

```
System.out.print("Hello Groovy!");
```

This line is equally valid Java and Groovy. You can also pass a literal Groovy string in single quotes:

```
System.out.print('Hello Groovy!');
```

Because this is such a common task, the GDK provides a shortened syntax:

```
print('Hello Groovy!');
```

You can drop parentheses and semicolons, because they're optional and don't help readability in this case. The resulting Groovy style boils down to

```
print 'Hello Groovy!'
```

Looking at this last line only, you cannot tell whether this is Groovy, Ruby, Perl, or one of several other line-oriented scripting languages. It may not look sophisticated, but it boils down the code to its essence.

The next listing presents more of the mix-and-match between core Java and additional GDK capabilities. How would you judge the signal-to-noise ratio of each line?

Listing 3.5 A miscellany of string operations

```
String greeting = 'Hello Groovy!'

assert greeting.startsWith('Hello')

assert greeting.getAt(0) == 'H'
assert greeting[0] == 'H'

assert greeting.indexOf('Groovy') >= 0
assert greeting.contains('Groovy')

assert greeting[6..11] == 'Groovy'
assert 'Hi' + greeting - 'Hello' == 'Hi Groovy!'

assert greeting.count('o') == 3

assert 'x'.padLeft(3)       == '  x'
assert 'x'.padRight(3,'_') == 'x__'
```

```
assert 'x'.center(3)        == ' x '
assert 'x' * 3              == 'xxx'
```

These self-explanatory examples give an impression of what's possible with strings in Groovy. If you've ever worked with other scripting languages, you may notice that a useful piece of functionality is missing from listing 3.5: changing a string in place. Groovy cannot do so because it works on instances of java.lang.String and obeys Java's *invariant* of strings being *immutable*.

Before you say "What a lame excuse!" here's Groovy's answer to changing strings: although you cannot work on String, you can still work on StringBuffer![15] On a StringBuffer, you can work with the << (left shift) operator for appending and the subscript operator for in-place assignments. Using the << operator on String returns a StringBuffer. Here's the StringBuffer equivalent to listing 3.5:

```
def greeting = 'Hello'

greeting <<= ' Groovy'                                    ❶ Left shift
                                                            and assign
assert greeting instanceof java.lang.StringBuffer

greeting << '!'                                           ❷ Left shift on
                                                            StringBuffer
assert greeting.toString() == 'Hello Groovy!'

greeting[1..4] = 'i'                                      Substring 'ello'
                                                          becomes 'i'
assert greeting.toString() == 'Hi Groovy!'
```

NOTE Although the expression stringRef << string returns a StringBuffer, note that StringBuffer isn't automatically assigned to the stringRef ❶. When used on a String, it needs explicit assignment; on StringBuffer it doesn't. With a StringBuffer, the data in the existing object is changed ❷— with a String you can't change the existing data, so you have to return a new object instead. You might also note that a greeting was explicitly typed. It's effectively of type Object and can reference both String and String-Buffer values.

Throughout the next sections, you'll gradually add to what you've learned about strings as you discover more language features. String has gained several new methods in the GDK. You've already seen a few of these, but you'll see more as we talk about working with regular expressions and lists. The complete list of GDK methods on strings is listed in appendix C.

Working with strings is one of the most common tasks in programming, and for script programming in particular: reading text, writing text, cutting words, replacing phrases, analyzing content, search and replace—the list is amazingly long. Think about your own programming work. How much of it deals with strings?

---

[15] Future versions may use a StringBuilder instead. StringBuilder was introduced in Java 1.5 to reduce the synchronization overhead of StringBuffers. Typically, StringBuffers are used only in a single thread and then discarded—but StringBuffer itself is thread-safe, at the expense of synchronizing each method call.

Groovy supports you in these tasks with comprehensive string support, but that's not the whole story. The next section introduces *regular expressions*, which cut through text like a chainsaw: difficult to operate but extremely powerful.

3.5   *Working with regular expressions*

> *Once a programmer had a problem. He thought he could solve it with a regular expression. Now he had two problems.*
>
> —Jamie Zawinski

Suppose you had to prepare a table of contents for this book. You'd need to collect all the headings like "3.5 Working with regular expressions"—paragraphs that start with a number or with a number, a dot, and another number. The rest of the paragraph would be the heading. This would be cumbersome to code naïvely: iterate over each character; check whether it's a line start; if so, check whether it's a digit; if so, check whether a dot and a digit follow. Puh—lots of rope, and we haven't even covered numbers that have more than one digit.

Regular expressions come to the rescue. They allow you to declare such a pattern rather than programming it. Once you have the pattern, Groovy lets you work with it in numerous ways.

Regular expressions are prominent in scripting languages and have also been available in the Java library since JDK 1.4. Groovy relies on Java's *regex* (*reg*ular *ex*pression) support and adds three operators for convenience:

- The regex *find* operator, `=~`
- The regex *match* operator, `==~`
- The regex *pattern* operator, `~string`

An in-depth discussion about regular expressions is beyond the scope of this book. Our focus is on Groovy, not on regexes. We give the shortest possible introduction to make the examples comprehensible and provide you with a jumpstart. For additional information, see http://docs.oracle.com/javase/7/docs/api/java/util/regex/Pattern.html.

Regular expressions are defined by *patterns*. A pattern can be anything from a simple character, fixed string, or something like a date format made up of digits and delimiters, up to descriptions of balanced parentheses in programming languages. Patterns are declared by a sequence of symbols. In fact, the pattern description is a language of its own. Some examples are shown in table 3.7. Note that these are the raw patterns, not how they'd appear in string literals. In other words, if you stored the pattern in a variable and printed it out, this is what you'd want to see. It's important to make the distinction between the pattern itself and how it's represented in code as a literal.

A pattern like one of the examples in table 3.7 allows you to declare *what* you're looking for, rather than having to program *how* to find something.

Table 3.7 Simple regular expression pattern examples

Pattern	Meaning
`some text`	Exactly "some text."
`some\s+text`	The word "some" followed by one or more whitespace characters followed by the word "text."
`^\d+(\.\d+)?(.*)`	Our introductory example: headings of level one or two denoted by a line ^ start, one or more digits, and an optional dot followed by more digits. Parentheses are used for grouping. The question mark makes the first group optional. The second group contains the title, made of a dot for any character and a star for any number of such characters.
`\d\d/\d\d/\d\d\d\d`	A date formatted as exactly two digits followed by a slash, two more digits followed by a slash, followed by exactly four digits.

Next you'll see how patterns appear as literals in code and what can be done with them. We'll then revisit the initial example with a full solution, before examining some performance aspects of regular expressions and finally showing how they can be used for classification in `switch` statements and for collection filtering with the `grep` method.

3.5.1 Specifying patterns in string literals

How do you put the sequence of symbols that declares a pattern inside a string? In Java, this causes confusion. Patterns use lots of backslashes, and to get a backslash in a Java string literal, you need to double it. This leads to Java strings, which are very hard to read in terms of the raw pattern involved. It gets even worse if you need to match an actual backslash in your pattern—the pattern language escapes that with a backslash too, so the Java regex string literal needed to match a\b is `"a\\\\b"`.

Groovy does much better. As you saw earlier, there's the slashy form of string literal, which doesn't require you to escape the backslash character and still works like a normal GString. The following listing shows how to declare patterns conveniently.

Listing 3.6 Regular expression GStrings

```
assert "abc" == /abc/
assert "\\d" == /\d/

def    reference = "hello"
assert reference == /$reference/
```

Note that you have the choice to declare patterns in either kind of string: literal string with single quotes, GString with double quotes, or slashy strings.

> **TIP** Sometimes the slashy syntax interferes with other valid Groovy expressions such as line comments or numerical expressions with multiple slashes for division. When in doubt, put parentheses around your pattern like (/pattern/). Parentheses force the parser to interpret the content as an expression.

SYMBOLS

The key to using regular expressions is knowing the pattern symbols. For convenience, table 3.8 provides a short list of the most common ones. Put an earmark on this page so you can easily look up the table—you'll use it a lot.

Table 3.8   Regular expression symbols (excerpt)

Symbol	Meaning
.	Any character
^	Start of line (or start of document, when in single-line mode)
$	End of line (or end of document, when in single-line mode)
\d	Digit character
\D	Any character except digits
\s	Whitespace character
\S	Any character except whitespace
\w	Word character
\W	Any character except word characters
\b	Word boundary
()	Grouping
(x | y)	x or y, as in (Groovy|Java|Ruby)
\1	Backmatch to group one; for example, find doubled characters with (.) \1
x *	Zero or more occurrences of x
x +	One or more occurrences of x
x ?	Zero or one occurrence of x
x { m , n }	At least *m* and at most *n* occurrences of x
x { m }	Exactly *m* occurrences of x
[a-f]	Character class containing the characters a, b, c, d, e, f
[^a]	Character class containing any character except a
(?is:x)	Switches mode when evaluating x; i turns on ignoreCase, s means single-line mode

TIP   Symbols tend to have the same first letter as what they represent; for example, *d*igit, *s*pace, *w*ord, and *b*oundary. Uppercase symbols define the complement; think of them as a warning sign for *no.*

More to consider:

- Use grouping properly. The *expanding* operators such as * and + bind closely; ab+ matches abbbb. Use (ab)+ to match ababab.
- In normal mode, the expanding operators are *greedy*, meaning they try to match the longest substring that matches the pattern. Add an additional question mark after the operator to put them into *restrictive* mode. You may be tempted to extract the href from an HTML anchor element with this regex: href="(.*)". But href= "(.*?)" is probably better. The first version matches until the last double quote in your text; the latter matches until the next double quote.[16]

This is only a brief description of the regex pattern format, but a complete specification comes with your JDK, as part of the Javadoc for java.util.regex.Pattern. It may change marginally between JDK versions; for JDK 7, it can be found online at http://docs.oracle.com/javase/7/docs/api/java/util/regex/Pattern.html.

See the Javadoc to learn more about different evaluation modes, positive and negative look-ahead, back references, and posix characters.

It always helps to test your expressions before putting them into code. There are many online applications that allow interactive testing of regular expressions. You should be aware that not all regular expression pattern languages are exactly the same. You may get unexpected results if you take a regular expression designed for use in .NET and apply it in a Java or Groovy program. Although there aren't many differences, the differences that do exist can be hard to spot. Even if you take a regular expression from a book or a website, you should still test that it works in your code.

Once you've declared the pattern you want, you need to tell Groovy how to apply it. We'll explore a whole variety of uses.

3.5.2 Applying patterns

For a given string and pattern, Groovy supports the following tasks for regular expressions:

- Tell whether the pattern fully matches the whole string.
- Tell whether there's an occurrence of the pattern in the string.
- Count the occurrences.
- Do something with each occurrence.
- Replace all occurrences with some text.
- Split the string into multiple strings by cutting at each occurrence.

Listing 3.7 puts patterns into action. Unlike most other examples, this listing contains some comments. This reflects real life and isn't for illustrative purposes. The use of regexes is best accompanied by this kind of comment for all but the simplest patterns.

---

[16] This is only to explain the greedy behavior of regular expression, not to explain how HTML is parsed correctly, which would involve a lot of other topics such as ordering of attributes, spelling variants, and so forth.

Listing 3.7   Regular expressions

```
def twister = 'she sells sea shells at the sea shore of seychelles'

// twister must contain a substring of size 3
// that starts with s and ends with a
assert twister =~ /s.a/

def finder = (twister =~ /s.a/)
assert finder instanceof java.util.regex.Matcher

// twister must contain only words delimited by single spaces
assert twister ==~ /(\w+ \w+)*/

def WORD = /\w+/
matches = (twister ==~ /($WORD $WORD)*/)
assert matches instanceof java.lang.Boolean

assert !(twister ==~ /s.e/)

def wordsByX = twister.replaceAll(WORD, 'x')
assert wordsByX == 'x x x x x x x x x x'

def words = twister.split(/ /)
assert words.size() == 10
assert words[0] == 'she'
```

❶ Regex find operator usable in an if statement

❷ Find expression evaluates to a Matcher object

Regex match operator

Match expression evaluates to a Boolean

Match is full unlike find

Split returns a list of words

❶ and ❷ have an interesting twist. Although the regex *find* operator evaluates to a `Matcher` object, it can also be used as a Boolean conditional. We'll explore how this is possible when examining the "Groovy Truth" in chapter 6.

> **TIP**   To remember the difference between the `=~` *find* operator and the `==~` *match* operator (it looks like a burning match), recall that match is more restrictive, because the pattern needs to cover the whole string. The demanded coverage is "longer" just like the operator itself.

See your Javadoc for more information about the `java.util.regex.Matcher` object, such as how to walk through all the matches and how to work with *groupings* within each match.

COMMON REGEX PITFALLS

You don't need to fall into the regex traps yourself. We've already done this for you and we (the authors) have learned the following:

- When things get complex (note, this is *when*, not *if*), comment verbosely.
- Use the slashy syntax instead of the regular string syntax, or you'll get lost in a forest of backslashes.
- Don't let your pattern look like a toothpick puzzle. Build your pattern from subexpressions like WORD in listing 3.7.
- Put your assumptions to the test. Write some assertions or unit tests to test your regex against static strings. Please don't send us any more flowers for this advice; a tweet like "Assertions saved my life today! Thanks #ReGina." will suffice.

3.5.3 Patterns in action

You're now ready to do everything you wanted to do with regular expressions, except we haven't covered "do something with each occurrence." *Something* and *each* sounds like a cue for a closure to appear, and that's the case here. String has a method called eachMatch that takes a regex as a parameter along with a closure that defines what to do on each match.

> **What is a match?**
> A match is the occurrence of a regular expression pattern in a string. It's therefore a string: a substring of the original string. When the pattern contains groupings like in /begin(.*?)end/, you need to know more information: not just the string matching the whole pattern, but also what part of that string matched each group. Therefore, the match becomes a list of strings, containing the whole match at position 0 with group matches being available as match[n] where *n* is group number *n*. Groups are numbered by the sequence of their opening parentheses.

The match gets passed into the closure for further analysis. In the musical example in the next listing, each match is appended to a result string.

Listing 3.8 Working on each match of a pattern

```
def myFairStringy = 'The rain in Spain stays mainly in the plain!'

// words that end with 'ain': \b\w*ain\b
def wordEnding = /\w*ain/
def rhyme = /\b$wordEnding\b/
def found = ''
myFairStringy.eachMatch(rhyme) { match ->        ←─❶ String.eachMatch(regex){}
    found += match + ' '
}
assert found == 'rain Spain plain '

found = ''
(myFairStringy =~ rhyme).each { match ->         ←─❷ Matcher.each{}
    found += match + ' '
}
assert found == 'rain Spain plain '                        String.replaceAll(regex){}  ❸

def cloze = myFairStringy.replaceAll(rhyme){ it-'ain'+'___' }   ←─┐
assert cloze == 'The r___ in Sp___ stays mainly in the pl___!'
```

There are two different ways to iterate through matches with identical behavior: use String.eachMatch(Pattern) ❶, or use Matcher.each() ❷, where the Matcher is the result of applying the regex find operator to a string and a pattern. ❸ shows a special case for replacing each match with some dynamically derived content from the given closure. The variable it refers to the matching substring. The result is to replace "ain" with underscores, but only where it forms part of a rhyme.

To fully understand how the Groovy regular expression support works, we need to look at the `java.util.regex.Matcher` class. It's a JDK class that encapsulates knowledge about:

- How often and at what position a pattern matches.
- The groupings for each match.

The GDK enhances the `Matcher` class with simplified array-like access to this information. In Groovy, you can think about a *matcher* as if it was a list of all its *matches*. This is what happens in the following example that matches all nonwhitespace characters:

```
def matcher = 'a b c' =~ /\S/

assert matcher[0] == 'a'
assert matcher[1..2] == ['b','c']
assert matcher.size() == 3
```

This use case comes with an interesting variant that uses Groovy's *parallel assignment* feature that allows you to directly assign each match to its own reference.

```
def (a,b,c) = 'a b c' =~ /\S/

assert a == 'a'
assert b == 'b'
assert c == 'c'
```

It gets even more interesting with *groupings* in the match. If the pattern contains parentheses to define groups, then the result of asking for a particular match is an array of strings rather than a single one: the same behavior as we mentioned for `eachMatch`. Again, the first result (at index 0) is the match for the whole pattern. Consider this example, where each match finds pairs of strings that are separated by a colon. For later processing, the match is split into two groups, for the left and the right string:

```
def matcher = 'a:1 b:2 c:3' =~ /(\S+):(\S+)/

assert matcher.hasGroup()
assert matcher[0] == ['a:1', 'a', '1'] // 1st match
assert matcher[1][2] == '2' // 2nd match, 2nd group
```

In other words, what `matcher[0]` returns depends on whether the pattern contains groupings.

This also applies to the matcher's each method, which comes with a convenient notation for groupings. When the processing closure defines multiple parameters, the list of groups is distributed over them:

```
def matcher = 'a:1 b:2 c:3' =~ /(\S+):(\S+)/
matcher.each { full, key, value ->
    assert full.size()  == 3
    assert key.size()   == 1 // a,b,c
    assert value.size() == 1 // 1,2,3
}
```

This matcher matches three times, passing the full match and the two groups into the closure on each match. The preceding code snippet enables you to assign meaningful names to the group matches. We decided to call them key and value, which much better reveals their intent than match[1] and match[2] would.

Our advice is to use group names whenever the group count is fixed. Groovy supports the spreading of match groups over closure parameters for all methods that pass a match into a closure. For example, you can use it with the String.each-Match(regex){match->} method.

> **IMPLEMENTATION DETAIL** Groovy internally stores the most recently used matcher (per thread). It can be retrieved with the static property Matcher .lastMatcher. You can also set the index property of a matcher to make it look at the respective match with matcher.index = x. Both can be useful in some exotic corner cases. See Matcher's API documentation for details.

We'll revisit the Matcher class later in numerous places. It's particularly interesting because it plays so well with Groovy's approach of letting classes decide how to iterate over themselves and reusing that behavior pervasively.

Matcher and Pattern work in combination and are the key abstractions for regexes in Java and Groovy. You've seen Matcher, and we'll have a closer look at the Pattern abstraction next.

3.5.4 *Patterns and performance*

Finally, let's look at performance and the pattern operator ~string (note this is a tilde, not a minus sign). The pattern operator transforms a string into an object of type java.util.regex.Pattern. For a given string, this pattern object can be asked for a *matcher* object.

The rationale behind this construction is that patterns are internally backed by a *finite-state machine* that does all the high-performance magic. This machine is compiled when the pattern object is created. The more complicated the pattern, the longer the creation takes. In contrast, the *matching* process as performed by the machine is extremely fast.

The pattern operator allows you to split pattern-creation time from pattern-matching time, increasing performance by reusing the finite-state machine. The following listing shows a poor-man's performance comparison of the two approaches. The precompiled pattern version is at least twice as fast (although these kinds of measurements can differ wildly).

> **Listing 3.9   Increasing performance with pattern reuse**

```
def twister = 'she sells sea shells at the sea shore of seychelles'
// some more complicated regex:
// word that starts and ends with same letter
def regex = /\b(\w)\w*\1\b/
def many  = 100 * 1000
```

```
start = System.nanoTime()
many.times{                                    ❶ Find operator with implicit
    twister =~ regex                              pattern construction
}
timeImplicit = System.nanoTime() - start
                                               │ Explicit pattern
start = System.nanoTime()                        construction
pattern = ~regex
many.times{                                    │ Apply pattern
    pattern.matcher(twister)                     on a string
}
timePredef = System.nanoTime() - start

                                               │ At least twice as fast
assert timeImplicit > timePredef * 2             (possibly 3–5 times)
```

To find words that start and end with the same character, the \1 backmatch is used to refer to that character. Its use is prepared by putting the word's first character into a group, which happens to be group 1.

Note the difference in spelling in ❶. This isn't a =~ b but a= ~b. Tricky.

Use whitespace wisely

The observant reader may spot a language issue: What happens if you write a=~b without any whitespace? Is that the =~ *find* operator, or is it an assignment of the ~b pattern to a? For the human reader, it's ambiguous. Not so for the Groovy parser. It's greedy and will parse this as the *find* operator.

It goes without saying that being explicit with whitespace is good programming style, even when the meaning is unambiguous for the parser. Do it for the next human reader, which will probably be you.

Don't forget that performance should usually come second to readability—at least to start with. If reusing a pattern means bending your code out of shape, you should ask yourself how critical the performance of that particular area is before making the change. Measure the performance in different situations with each version of the code, and balance ease of maintenance with speed and memory requirements.

3.5.5   *Patterns for classification*

Listing 3.10 completes your journey through the domain of patterns. The Pattern object, as returned from the pattern operator, implements an isCase(String) method that's equivalent to a full match of that pattern with the string. This classification method is a prerequisite for using patterns conveniently with the in operator, the grep method, and in switch cases.

The example classifies words that consist of exactly four characters. The pattern, therefore, consists of the word character class \w followed by the {4} quantification.

Listing 3.10 Patterns for classification

```
def fourLetters = ~/\w{4}/

assert fourLetters.isCase('work')

assert 'love' in fourLetters

switch('beer'){
    case fourLetters: assert true; break
    default         : assert false
}

beasts = ['bear','wolf','tiger','regex']

assert beasts.grep(fourLetters) == ['bear','wolf']
```

> **TIP** Classifications read nicely with in, switch, and grep. It's rare to call classifier.isCase(candidate) directly, but when you see such a call, it's easiest to read it from right to left: "*candidate* is a case of *classifier*."

Patterns are also prevalent in the Groovy library (see the GDK reference in appendix C). These methods give you the convenient choice between using either a string that describes the regular expression (conventionally this parameter is called regex), or supplying a pattern object instead (conventionally called pattern).

At times, regular expressions can be difficult beasts to tame, but mastering them adds a new quality to all text-manipulation tasks. Once you have a grip on them, you'll hardly be able to imagine having programmed (some would say *lived*) without them. Writing this book without their help would have been very hard indeed. Groovy makes regular expressions easily accessible and straightforward to use.

This concludes our coverage of text-based types, but of course computers have always dealt with numbers as well as text. Working with numbers is easy in most programming languages, but that doesn't mean there's no room for improvement. Let's see how Groovy goes the extra mile when it comes to numeric types.

3.6   Working with numbers

We introduced the available numeric types and their declarations in section 3.1 and you've already seen that for decimal numbers, the default type is java.math.Big-Decimal. This is a feature to get around the most common misconceptions about floating-point arithmetic. We're going to look at which type is used where and what extra abilities have been provided for numbers in the GDK.

3.6.1   Coercion with numeric operators

It's always important to understand what happens when you use one of the numeric operators.

Most of the rules for the addition, multiplication, and subtraction operators are the same as in Java, but there are some changes regarding floating-point behavior, and

BigInteger and BigDecimal also need to be included. The rules are straightforward. The first rule to match the situation is used.

For the operations +, -, and *:

- If either operand is a Float or a Double, the result is a Double. (In Java, when only Float operands are involved, the result is a Float too.)
- Otherwise, if either operand is a BigDecimal, the result is a BigDecimal.
- Otherwise, if either operand is a BigInteger, the result is a BigInteger.
- Otherwise, if either operand is a Long, the result is a Long.
- Otherwise, the result is an Integer.

Table 3.9 depicts the scheme for quick lookup. Types are abbreviated by uppercase letters.

Table 3.9 Numerical coercion

+ - *	B	S	I	C	L	BI	BD	F	D
Byte	I	I	I	I	L	BI	BD	D	D
Short	I	I	I	I	L	BI	BD	D	D
Integer	I	I	I	I	L	BI	BD	D	D
Character	I	I	I	I	L	BI	BD	D	D
Long	L	L	L	L	L	BI	BD	D	D
BigInteger	BI	BI	BI	BI	BI	BI	BD	D	D
BigDecimal	BD	BD	BD	BD	BD	BD	BD	D	D
Float	D	D	D	D	D	D	D	D	D
Double	D	D	D	D	D	D	D	D	D

Other aspects of coercion behavior include:

- Like Java but unlike Ruby, no coercion takes place when the result of an operation exceeds the current range, except for the power operator.
- For division, if any of the arguments is of type Float or Double, the result is of type Double; otherwise the result is of type BigDecimal with the maximum precision of both arguments, rounded half up. The result is normalized—that is, without trailing zeros.
- Integer division (keeping the result as an integer) is achievable through explicit casting or by using the intdiv() method.
- The *shifting* operators are implemented with bit-shifting semantics only for types Integer and Long but you can implement them for other types, too, through operator overriding. They don't coerce to other types.

- The *power* operator coerces to the next best type that can take the result in terms of range and precision, in the sequence `Integer`, `Long`, `Double`.
- The *equals* operator coerces to the more general type before comparing.

Rules can be daunting without examples, so this behavior is demonstrated in table 3.10.

Table 3.10 Numerical expression examples

Expression	Result Type	Comments
`1f*2f`	`Double`	In Java, this would be `Float`.
`(Byte)1+(Byte)2`	`Integer`	As in Java, integer arithmetic is always performed in at least 32 bits.
`1*2L`	`Long`	
`1/2`	`BigDecimal (0.5)`	In Java, the result would be the integer 0.
`(int)(1/2)`	`Integer (0)`	This is normal coercion of `.BigDecimal` to `Integer`.
`1.intdiv(2)`	`Integer (0)`	This is the equivalent of the Java `1/2`.
`Integer.MAX_VALUE+1`	`Integer`	Non-*power* operators wrap without promoting the result type.
`2**30`	`Integer`	
`2**31`	`BigInteger`	The *power* operator promotes where necessary.
`2**3.5`	`Double`	
`2G+1G`	`BigInteger`	
`2.5G+1G`	`BigDecimal`	
`1.5G==1.5F`	`Boolean (true)`	`Float` is promoted to `BigDecimal` before comparison.
`1.1G==1.1F`	`Boolean (false)`	1.1 can't be exactly represented as a `Float` (or indeed a `Double`), so when it's promoted to `BigDecimal`, it isn't equal to the exact `BigDecimal` 1.1G but rather 1.100000023841858G.

The only surprise is that there's no surprise. In Java, results like in the fourth row are often surprising—for example, `(1/2)` is always 0 because when both operands of division are integers, only integer division is performed. To get `0.5` in Java, you need to write `(1f/2)`.

This behavior is especially important when using Groovy to enhance your application with user-defined input. Suppose you allow superusers of your application to specify a formula that calculates an employee's bonus, and a business analyst specifies it as businessDone * (1/3). With Java semantics, this will be a bad year for the poor employees.

3.6.2 GDK methods for numbers

The GDK defines all applicable methods from table 3.4 to implement overridable operators for numbers such as plus, minus, power, and so forth. They all work without surprises. In addition, the following methods fulfill their self-describing duty:

```
assert 1 == (-1).abs()
assert 2 == 2.5.toInteger()      // conversion
assert 2 == 2.5 as Integer       // enforced coercion
assert 2 == (int) 2.5            // cast
assert 3 == 2.5f.round()
assert 3.142 == Math.PI.round(3)
assert 4 == 4.5f.trunc()
assert 2.718 == Math.E.trunc(3)

assert '2.718'.isNumber()        // String methods
assert 5 == '5'.toInteger()
assert 5 == '5' as Integer
assert 53 == (int) '5'           // gotcha!
assert '6 times' == 6 + ' times' // Number + String
```

As you can see, there are various conversion possibilities: the toInteger() method (also available for Double, Float, and so on), enforced coercion with the as operator that calls the asType(class) method, and the humble cast.

> **WARNING!** Don't cast strings to numbers! In Groovy, you can cast a string of length 1 directly to a char. But char and int are essentially the same thing on the Java platform. This leads to the gotcha where '5' is cast to its Unicode value 53. Instead, use the type conversion methods.

More interestingly, the GDK also defines the methods times, upto, downto, and step. They all take a closure argument. Listing 3.11 shows these methods in action: times is just for repetition, upto is for walking a sequence of increasing numbers, downto is for decreasing numbers, and step is the general version that walks until the end value by successively adding a step width.

Listing 3.11 GDK methods on numbers

```
def store = ''
10.times{                        ⟵— Repetition
    store += 'x'
}
assert store == 'xxxxxxxxxx'

store = ''
1.upto(5) { number ->            ⟵┐ Walking up with
    store += number               │ loop variable
}
assert store == '12345'
```

```
store = ''
2.downto(-2) { number ->
    store += number + ' '
}
assert store == '2 1 0 -1 -2 '

store = ''
0.step(0.5, 0.1){ number ->
    store += number + ' '
}
assert store == '0 0.1 0.2 0.3 0.4 '
```

← Walking
   down

← Walking with
   step width

Calling methods on numbers can feel unfamiliar at first when you come from Java. Just remember that numbers are objects and you can treat them as such. As you've seen, numbers in Groovy work in a natural way and protect you against the most common errors with floating-point arithmetic. In most cases, there's no need to remember all details of coercion. When the need arises, this section may serve as a reference.

The strategy of making objects available in unexpected places starts to become an ongoing theme. You've seen it with numbers, and section 4.1 will show the same principle applied to ranges.

3.7   *Summary*

Contrary to popular belief, Groovy gives you the same type safety as Java, albeit at runtime instead of Java's mix of compile time and runtime. This approach is a prerequisite to enable the awesome power of dynamic language features such as synthesized methods, flexible bindings for scripts, templates and closures, and all the other metaprogramming goodness that we'll explore in the course of this book.

Making common activities more convenient is one of Groovy's main promises. Consequently, Groovy promotes even the primitive data types to first-class objects and implements operators as method calls to make the benefits of object orientation ubiquitously available.

Developer convenience is further enhanced by allowing a variety of means for string literal declarations, whether through flexible GString declarations or with the slashy syntax for situations where extra escaping is undesirable, such as regular expression patterns. GStrings contribute to another of Groovy's central pillars: concise and expressive code. This allows the reader a clearer insight into the runtime string value, without having to wade through reams of string concatenation or switch between format strings and the values replaced in them.

Regular expressions are well represented in Groovy, again confirming its comfortable place among other top-of-stack languages. Utilizing regular expressions is an everyday exercise, and a language that treated them as second-class citizens would be severely hampered. Groovy effortlessly combines Java's libraries with language support, retaining the regular expression dialect familiar to Java programmers with the ease of use found in scripting.

The Groovy way of treating numbers with respect to type conversion and precision handling leads to intuitive use, even for nonprogrammers. This becomes particularly important when Groovy scripts are used for smart configurations of larger systems where business users may provide formulas—for example, to define share-valuation details.

Strings, regular expressions, and numbers alike profit from numerous methods that the GDK introduces on top of the JDK. A clear pattern has emerged already—Groovy is a language designed for the ease of those developing in it, concentrating on making repetitive tasks as simple as they can be without sacrificing the power of the Java platform.

You'll soon see that this focus on ease of use extends far beyond the simple types that Java developers are used to having built-in language support for. The Groovy designers are well aware of other concepts that are rarely far from a programmer's mind. The next chapter shows how intuitive operators, enhanced literals, and extra GDK methods are also available with Groovy's collective datatypes: ranges, lists, and maps.

Collective
Groovy datatypes

4

This chapter covers
- Understanding Groovy's collective datatypes: ranges, lists, and maps
- How to declare them
- Operators and library methods for these types
- How to use them in action

The intuitive mind is a sacred gift and the rational mind is a faithful servant.
We have created a society that honors the servant and has forgotten the gift.

—Albert Einstein

The nice thing about computers is that they never get tired of repeatedly doing the same task. This is probably the singlemost important quality that justifies letting them take part in our lives. Searching through countless files or web pages, down-loading emails every 10 minutes, looking up all values of a stock symbol for the last quarter to paint a nice graph—these are only a few examples in which a computer needs to repeatedly process an item of a data collection. It's no wonder that a great deal of programming work is about collections.

Because collections are so prominent in programming, Groovy alleviates the tedium of using them by directly supporting datatypes of a collective nature: ranges, lists, and maps. Just as with simple datatypes, Groovy's support for collective datatypes encompasses new lightweight means for literal declaration, specialized operators, and numerous GDK enhancements.

The notation that Groovy uses to set its collective datatypes into action will be new to Java programmers, but as you'll see, it's easy to understand and remember. You'll pick it up so quickly that you'll hardly be able to imagine a time when you were new to the concept.

Despite the new notation possibilities, lists and maps have the very same semantics as in Java. This situation is slightly different for ranges, because they don't have a direct equivalent in Java. So let's start our tour with that topic.

4.1   *Working with ranges*

Think about how often you've written a loop like this:

```
for (int i=0; i<upperBound; i++){
   // do something with i
}
```

Most of us have done this thousands of times. It's so common that it is second nature. Does the code tell you what it does or how it does it?

After inspecting the variable, the conditional, and the incrementation, you see that it's an iteration starting at zero and not reaching the upper bound, assuming there are no side effects on i in the loop body. You have to go through the description of *how* the code works to find out *what* it does.

Next, consider how often you've written a conditional like this:

```
if (x >= 0 && x <= upperBound) {
   // do something with x
}
```

The same thing applies here: you have to inspect *how* the code works to understand *what* it does. Variable x must be between zero and an upper bound for further processing. It's easy to overlook that the upper bound is now inclusive.

We're not saying that we make mistakes using this syntax on a regular basis. We're not saying that you can't get used to (or indeed haven't gotten used to) the C-style for loop, as countless programmers have over the years. What we're saying is that it's harder than it needs to be; and, more important, it's *less expressive* than it could be. Can you understand it? Absolutely. Then again, you could understand this chapter if it were written entirely in capital letters—that doesn't make it a good idea, though.

Groovy allows you to reveal the meaning of such code pieces by providing the concept of a *range*. A range has a left bound and a right bound. You can do something for each element of a range, effectively iterating through it. You can determine whether a candidate element falls inside a range. In other words, a range is an interval plus a strategy for how to move through it.

By introducing the new concept of ranges, Groovy extends your means of expressing your intentions in the code.

We'll show you how to specify ranges, how the fact that they're objects makes them ubiquitously applicable, how to use custom objects as bounds, and how they're typically used in the GDK.

4.1.1 Specifying ranges

Ranges are specified using the double-dot range operator (..) between the left and right bounds. This operator has a low precedence, so you often need to enclose the declaration in parentheses. Ranges can also be declared using their respective constructors.

The ..< range operator specifies a half-exclusive range—that is, the value on the right isn't part of the range:

```
left..right
(left..right)
(left..<right)
```

Ranges usually have a lower left bound and a higher right bound. When this is switched it's called a *reverse* range. Ranges can also be any combination of the types we've described. The following listing shows these combinations and how ranges can have bounds other than integers, such as dates and strings. Groovy supports ranges at the language level with the special for-in-range loop.

Listing 4.1   Range declarations

```
assert (0..10).contains(0)
assert (0..10).contains(5)
assert (0..10).contains(10)                      Inclusive
                                                 ranges
assert (0..10).contains(-1) == false
assert (0..10).contains(11) == false

assert (0..<10).contains(9)                      Half-exclusive
assert (0..<10).contains(10) == false            ranges

def a = 0..10
assert a instanceof Range                     ❶ References
assert a.contains(5)                            to ranges

a = new IntRange(0,10)                           Explicit
assert a.contains(5)                             construction

assert (0.0..1.0).contains(1.0)                  Bounds
assert (0.0..1.0).containsWithinBounds(0.5)      checking

def today     = new Date()
def yesterday = today - 1                      ❷ Date ranges
assert (yesterday..today).size() == 2

assert ('a'..'c').contains('b')          ←──❸ String ranges

def log = ''
for (element in 5..9){
    log += element                               for-in-range
}                                                loop
assert log == '56789'
```

```
log = ''
for (element in 9..5){          Loop with
    log += element              reverse
}                               range
assert log == '98765'
```

```
log = ''
(9..<5).each { element ->       ❹  Half-exclusive,
    log += element                  reverse, each
}                                   with closure
assert log == '9876'
```

Note that we assign a range to a variable ❶. In other words, the variable holds a reference to an object of type groovy.lang.Range. We'll examine this feature further and see what consequences it implies.

Date objects can be used in ranges ❷ because the GDK adds the previous and next methods to date, which increases or decreases the date by one day.

> **NOTE**   The GDK also adds *minus* and *plus* operators to java.util.Date, which increases or decreases the date by so many days.

The String methods previous and next are added by the GDK to make strings usable for ranges ❸. The last character in the string is incremented or decremented, and overflow or underflow is handled by appending a new character or deleting the last character.

You can walk through a range with the each method, which presents the current value to the given closure with each step ❹. If the range is reversed, you walk through the range backward. If the range is half-exclusive, the walking stops before reaching the right bound.

4.1.2   *Ranges are objects*

Because every range is an object, you can pass a range around and call its methods. The most prominent methods are each, which executes a specified closure for each element in the range, and contains, which specifies whether or not a value is within a range.

Being first-class objects, ranges can also participate in the game of operator overriding (see section 3.3) by providing an implementation of the isCase method, with the same meaning as contains. That way, you can use ranges as grep filters and as switch cases. This is shown in the following listing.

Listing 4.2   Ranges are objects

```
def result = ''
(5..9).each { element ->        Iterating
    result += element           over a
}                               range
assert result == '56789'
```

```
assert 5 in 0..10
assert (0..10).isCase(5)

def age = 36
switch(age){
    case 16..20 : insuranceRate = 0.05 ; break          ❶ Ranges for
    case 21..50 : insuranceRate = 0.06 ; break             classification
    case 51..65 : insuranceRate = 0.07 ; break
    default: throw new IllegalArgumentException()
}
assert insuranceRate == 0.06

def ages = [20, 36, 42, 56]
def midage = 21..50                                     ❷ Filtering
assert ages.grep(midage) == [36, 42]                       with ranges
```

The use with the grep method ❷ is a good example for passing around range objects: the midage range gets passed as a parameter to the grep method.

Classification through ranges ❶ is what you'll often find in the business world: interest rates for different ranges of allocated assets, transaction fees based on volume ranges, and salary bonuses based on ranges of business done. Although technical people prefer using functions, business people tend to use ranges. When you're modeling the business world in software, classification by ranges can be very handy.

4.1.3   Ranges in action

Listing 4.1 made use of date and string ranges. In fact, any datatype can be used with ranges, provided that both of the following are true:

- The type implements next and previous; that is, it overrides the ++ and -- operators.
- The type implements java.lang.Comparable; that is, it implements compareTo, effectively overriding the <=> (*spaceship*) operator.

As an example, listing 4.3 implements a class Weekday that represents a day of the week. From the perspective of the code that uses the class, a Weekday has a value 'Sun' through 'Sat'. Internally, it's just an index between 0 and 6. A little list maps indexes to weekday name abbreviations.

We implement next and previous to return the respective new Weekday object. compareTo simply compares the indexes.

With this preparation, we can construct a range of working days and work our way through it, reporting the work done until we reach the well-deserved weekend. Oh, and our boss wants to assess the weekly work report. A final assertion does this on his behalf.

> **Listing 4.3   Custom ranges: weekdays**

```
class Weekday implements Comparable {
  static final DAYS = [
      'Sun', 'Mon', 'Tue', 'Wed', 'Thu', 'Fri', 'Sat'
  ]
  private int index = 0
```

```
Weekday(String day) {
  index = DAYS.indexOf(day)              Allows all
}                                        values

Weekday next() {
  return new Weekday(DAYS[(index + 1) % DAYS.size()])
}

Weekday previous() {
  return new Weekday(DAYS[index - 1])          Range bound
}                                           ❶ methods

int compareTo(Object other) {
  return this.index <=> other.index
}

String toString() {
  return DAYS[index]
}
}
def mon = new Weekday('Mon')
def fri = new Weekday('Fri')
                                      Working
def worklog = ''                      through
for (day in mon..fri) {               the week
  worklog += day.toString() + ' '
}
assert worklog == 'Mon Tue Wed Thu Fri '
```

This code can be placed inside one script file,[1] even though it contains both a class declaration and script code. The Weekday class is like an inner class to the script.

The implementation of previous ❶ is a bit unconventional. Although next uses the modulo operator in a conventional way to jump from Saturday (index 6) to Sunday (index 0), the opposite direction simply decreases the index. The index –1 is used for looking up the previous weekday name, and DAYS[-1] references the last entry of the days list, as you'll see in the next section. We construct a new Weekday('Sat'), and the constructor normalizes the index to 6.

Compared to the Java alternatives, ranges have proven to be a flexible solution. for loops and conditionals aren't objects, they cannot be reused, and they cannot be passed around, but ranges can. Ranges let you focus on *what* the code does, rather than *how* it does it. This is a pure declaration of your intent, as opposed to fiddling with indexes and boundary conditions.

Using custom ranges is the next step forward. Look actively through your code for possible applications. Ranges slumber everywhere, and bringing them to life can significantly improve the expressiveness of your code. With a bit of practice, you may

---

[1]   But don't call it Weekday.groovy, otherwise two clashing Weekday.class files will be produced, one for the script and one for the inner class.

find ranges where you never thought possible. This is a sure sign that new language concepts can change your perception of the world.

You'll shortly refer to your newly acquired knowledge about ranges when we explore the subscript operator on lists, the built-in datatype that we're going to cover next.

4.2 Working with lists

In a recent Java project, we had to write a method that takes a Java array and adds an element to it. This seemed like a trivial task, but we forgot how awkward Java programming could be. (We're spoiled from too much Groovy programming.) Java arrays cannot be changed in length, so you cannot add elements easily. One way is to convert the array to a `java.util.List`, add the element, and convert back. A second way is to construct a new array of `size+1`, copy the old values over, and set the new element to the last index position. Either way takes some lines of code.

But Java arrays also have their benefits in terms of language support. They work with the subscript operator to easily retrieve elements of an array by index like `myarray[index]`, or store elements at an index position with `myarray[index] = newElement`.

We'll demonstrate how Groovy lists give you the best of both approaches, extending the features for smart operator implementations, method overloading, and using lists as Booleans. With Groovy lists, you'll also discover new ways of leveraging the power of the Java Collections API.

4.2.1 Specifying lists

Listing 4.4 shows various ways of specifying lists. The primary way is with square brackets around a sequence of items, delimited with commas:

```
[item1, item2, item3]
```

The sequence can be empty to declare an empty list. Lists are by default of type `java.util.ArrayList` and can also be declared explicitly by calling the respective constructor. The resulting list can still be used with the subscript operator. In fact, this works with any type of list, as shown next with type `java.util.LinkedList`.

Lists can be created and initialized at the same time by calling `toList` on ranges.

Listing 4.4 Specifying lists

```
List myList = [1, 2, 3]

assert myList.size()     == 3
assert myList[0]         == 1
assert myList instanceof ArrayList

List emptyList = []
assert emptyList.size() == 0

List longList = (0..1000).toList()
assert longList[555] == 555
```

```
List explicitList = new ArrayList()
explicitList.addAll(myList)
assert explicitList.size() == 3
explicitList[0] = 10
assert explicitList[0] == 10

explicitList = new LinkedList(myList)
assert explicitList.size() == 3
explicitList[0] = 10
assert explicitList[0] == 10
```

❶ Fills from myList

We use the `addAll(Collection)` method from `java.util.List` ❶ to easily fill the lists. As an alternative, the collection to fill from can be passed right into the constructor, as done here with `LinkedList`.

For the sake of completeness, we need to add that lists can also be constructed by passing a Java array to Groovy. Such an array is subject to autoboxing—a list will be automatically generated from the array with its elements being autoboxed.

The GDK extends all arrays, collection objects, and strings with a `toList` method that returns a newly generated list of the contained elements. Strings are handled like lists of characters.

4.2.2   *Using list operators*

Lists implement some of the operators that you saw in section 3.3. Listing 4.4 contains two of them: the `getAt` and `putAt` methods to implement the subscript operator. But this is a simple use that works with a mere index argument. There's much more to the list operators than that.

SUBSCRIPT OPERATOR

The GDK overloads the `getAt` method with range and collection arguments to access a range or a collection of indexes. This is demonstrated in the next listing.

The same strategy is applied to `putAt`, which is overloaded with a `Range` argument, assigning a list of values to a whole sublist.

Listing 4.5   Accessing parts of a list with an overloaded subscript operator

```
myList = ['a','b','c','d','e','f']

assert myList[0..2]  == ['a','b','c']          getAt(Range)
assert myList[0,2,4] == ['a','c','e']          getAt(collection
                                                of indexes)

myList[0..2] = ['x','y','z']
assert myList == ['x','y','z','d','e','f']     putAt(Range)

myList[3..5] = []
assert myList == ['x','y','z']                 ❶ Removing
                                                 elements

myList[1..1] = [0, 1, 2]
assert myList == ['x', 0, 1, 2, 'z']           ❷ Adding
                                                 elements
```

Subscript assignments with ranges don't need to be of identical size. When the assigned list of values is smaller than the range or even empty, the list shrinks ❶. When the assigned list of values is bigger, the list grows ❷.

Ranges used within subscript assignments are a convenience feature to access Java's excellent sublist support for lists. See also the Javadoc for `java.util.List#sublist`.

In addition to positive index values, lists can be subscripted with negative indexes that count from the end of the list backward. Figure 4.1 shows how positive and negative indexes map to an example list `[0,1,2,3,4]`.

Consequently, you get the last entry of a nonempty list with `list[-1]` and the next-to-last with `list[-2]`. Negative indexes can also be used in ranges, so `list[-3..-1]` gives you the last three entries. When using a *reversed* range, the resulting list is reversed as well, so `list[4..0]` is `[4,3,2,1,0]`. In this case, the result is a new list object rather than a *sublist* in the sense of the JDK. Even mixtures of positive and negative indexes are possible, such as `list[1..-2]`, to cut away the first entry and the last entry.

Avoid negative indexes with half-exclusive ranges

Ranges in `List`'s subscript operator are `IntRanges`. Exclusive `IntRanges` are mapped to inclusive ones at construction time, before the subscript operator comes into play and can map negative indexes to positive ones. This can lead to surprises when mixing positive left and negative right bounds with exclusiveness; for example, `IntRange(0..<-2)` gets mapped to `(0..-1)`, such that `list[0..<-2]` is effectively `list[0..-1]`.

Although this is stable and works predictably, it may be confusing for the readers of your code, who may expect it to work like `list[0..-3]`. For this reason, this situation should be avoided for the sake of clarity.

Example list values		0	1	2	3	4		
Positive index		0	1	2	3	4	5	6
Negative index	−7	−6	−5	−4	−3	−2	−1		
	Out of bounds		In bounds				Out of bounds	

Figure 4.1 Positive and negative indexes of a list of length 5, with "in bounds" and "out of bounds" classification for indexes

ADDING AND REMOVING ITEMS

Although the subscript operator can be used to change any individual element of a list, there are also operators available to change the contents of the list in a more drastic way: plus(Object), plus(Collection), leftShift(Object), minus(Collection), and multiply. The following listing shows them in action. The plus method is overloaded to distinguish between adding an element and adding all elements of a collection. The minus method only works with collection parameters.

Listing 4.6   List operators involved in adding and removing items

```
myList = []

myList += 'a'                              <---  plus(Object)
assert myList == ['a']

myList += ['b','c']                        <---  plus(Collection)
assert myList == ['a','b','c']

myList = []                                    ┐ leftShift is
myList <<  'a' << 'b'                       <---┘ like append
assert myList == ['a','b']

assert myList - ['b'] == ['a']             <---┐ minus(Collection)

assert myList * 2 == ['a','b','a','b']     <---  Multiply
```

While we're talking about operators, it's worth noting that we've used the == operator on lists, happily assuming that it does what we expect. Now you see how it works: the equals method on lists tests that two collections have equal elements. See the Javadoc of java.util.List#equals for details.

CONTROL STRUCTURES

Groovy lists are more than flexible storage places. They also play a major role in organizing the execution flow of Groovy programs. The following listing shows the use of lists in Groovy's if, switch, and for control structures.

Listing 4.7   Lists taking part in control structures

```
myList = ['a', 'b', 'c']

assert myList.isCase('a')
assert 'b' in myList

def candidate = 'c'                                    ❶ Classifies by
switch(candidate){                                        containment
    case myList : assert true; break   <---┘
    default     : assert false
}                                                      ❷ Intersection
assert ['x','a','z'].grep(myList) == ['a']   <---┘        filter

myList = []
if (myList) assert false            <---┐ Empty lists
                                    ❸    are false
// Lists can be iterated with a 'for' loop
def expr = ''
```

```
for (i in [1,'*',5]){
    expr += i
}
assert expr == '1*5'
```
← **❹ Iterates over a list**

In **❶** and **❷**, you see the trick that you already know from patterns and ranges: implementing isCase and getting a grep filter and a switch classification for free. **❸** is a little surprising. Inside a Boolean test, empty lists evaluate to false. **❹** shows looping over lists or other collections and also demonstrates that lists can contain mixtures of types.

4.2.3 Using list methods

There are so many useful methods on the List type that we cannot provide an example for all of them in the language description. The large number of methods comes from the fact that the Java interface java.util.List is already fairly wide (25 methods in JDK 1.7 and 28 in JDK 1.8).

Furthermore, the GDK adds methods to the List interface, to the Collection interface, and to Object. Therefore, many methods are available on the List type, including all methods of Collection and Object.

Appendix C has the complete overview of all methods added to List by the GDK. The Javadoc of java.util.List has the complete list of its JDK methods.

While working with lists in Groovy, there's no need to be aware of whether a method stems from the JDK or the GDK, or whether it's defined in the List or Collection interface. But for the purpose of describing the Groovy List datatype, we fully cover the GDK methods on lists and collections, but not all combinations from overloaded methods and not what's covered in the previous examples. We provide only partial examples of the JDK methods that we consider important.

MANIPULATING LIST CONTENT

A first set of methods is presented in the following listing. It deals with changing the content of the list by adding and removing elements; combining lists in various ways; sorting, reversing, and flattening nested lists; and creating new lists from existing ones.

Listing 4.8 Methods to manipulate list content

```
assert [1,[2,3]].flatten() == [1,2,3]
assert [1,2,3].intersect([4,3,1])== [3,1]
assert [1,2,3].disjoint([4,5,6])

list = [1,2,3]
popped = list.pop()                                    ❶ Treating a list
assert popped == 3                                       like a stack
assert list == [1,2]

assert [1,2].reverse() == [2,1]
assert [3,1,2].sort() == [1,2,3]
                                                       ❷ Comparing
def list = [ [1,0], [0,1,2] ]                            lists by first
list = list.sort { a,b -> a[0] <=> b[0] }                element
assert list == [ [0,1,2], [1,0] ]
```

```
list = list.sort { item -> item.size() }
assert list == [ [1,0], [0,1,2] ]

list = ['a','b','c']
list.remove(2)
assert list == ['a','b']
list.remove('b')
assert list == ['a']

list = ['a','b','b','c']
list.removeAll(['b','c'])
assert list == ['a']

def doubled = [1,2,3].collect{ item ->
   item*2
}
assert doubled == [2,4,6]

def odd = [1,2,3].findAll{ item ->
   item % 2 == 1
}
assert odd == [1,3]
```

❸ Comparing lists by size

❹ Removing by index

❺ Removing by value

❻ Transforming one list into another

❼ Finding every element matching the closure

List elements can be of arbitrary type, including other nested lists. This can be used to implement lists of lists, the Groovy equivalent of multidimensional arrays in Java. For nested lists, the flatten method provides a flat view of all elements.

An intersection of lists contains all elements that appear in both lists. Collections can also be checked for being disjointed—that is, whether their intersection is empty.

Lists can be used like *stacks*, with usual stack behavior on push and pop ❶. The push operation is relayed to the list's << (left-shift) operator.

When list elements are comparable, there's a natural sort. Alternatively, the comparison logic of the sort can be specified as a closure ❷, ❸. The first example sorts lists of lists by comparing their entry at index 0. The second example shows that a single argument can be used inside the closure for comparison. In this case, the comparison is made between the results that the closure returns when fed each of the candidate elements.

Elements can be removed by index ❹ or by value ❺. We can also remove all the elements that appear as values in the second list. These removal methods are the only ones in the listing that are available in the JDK.

The collect method ❻ returns a new list that's constructed from what a closure returns when successively applied to all elements of the original list. In the example, we use it to retrieve a new list where each entry of the original list is multiplied by two. Other languages call such a method map, but we don't because it's so easily confused with the datatype of the same name.[2]

---

[2] The collect method's name was originally inspired from Smalltalk and is also used in C#, but several popular functional languages use map. Given the increased popularity of functional concepts, future versions of Groovy may supply a map alias for collect.

With `findAll` ❼, we retrieve a list of all items for which the closure evaluates to true. The example here uses the modulo operator to find all odd numbers.

Two issues related to changing an existing list are removing duplicates and `null` values. One way to remove duplicate entries is to convert the list to a datatype that's free of duplicates: a `Set`. This can be achieved by calling a `Set`'s constructor with that list as an argument, such as:

```
def x = [1,1,1]
assert [1] == new HashSet(x).toList()
assert [1] == x.unique()
```

If you don't want to create a new collection but want to keep working on your cleaned list, you can use the `unique` method, which ensures that the sequence of entries isn't changed by this operation.

Removing `null` from a list can be done by keeping all non-nulls—for example, with the `findAll` methods that you've seen previously:

```
def x = [1,null,1]
assert [1,1] == x.findAll{it != null}
assert [1,1] == x.grep{it}
```

You can see there's an even shorter version with `grep`, but to understand its mechanics, you need more knowledge about closures (see chapter 5) and the "Groovy truth" (see chapter 6). Just take it for granted until then.

ACCESSING LIST CONTENT
Lists have methods to query their elements for certain properties, iterate through them, and retrieve accumulated results.

Query methods include a `count` of given elements in the list, `min` and `max`, a `find` method that finds the first element that satisfies a closure, and methods to determine whether `every` or `any` element in the list satisfies a closure.

Iteration can be achieved as usual—forward with `each` or backward with `each-Reverse`.

Cumulative methods come in simple and sophisticated versions. The `join` method is simple: it returns all elements as a string, concatenated with a given string. The `inject` method is inspired by Smalltalk: it uses a closure to inject new functionality. That functionality operates on an intermediary result and the current element of the iteration. The first parameter of the `inject` method is the initial value of the intermediary result. In the following listing, we use this method to sum up all elements and then use it a second time to multiply them.

Listing 4.9 List query, iteration, and accumulation

```
def list = [1, 2, 3]

assert list.first()  == 1
assert list.head()   == 1
assert list.tail()   == [2, 3]
```

```
assert list.last()    == 3
assert list.count(2) == 1
assert list.max()     == 3
assert list.min()     == 1

def even = list.find { item ->
    item % 2 == 0                               Querying
}
assert even == 2

assert list.every { item -> item < 5 }
assert list.any   { item -> item < 2 }

def store = ''
list.each { item ->
    store += item
}
assert store == '123'

store = ''
list.reverseEach { item ->
    store += item                               Iterating
}
assert store == '321'

store = ''
list.eachWithIndex { item, index ->
    store += "$index:$item "
}
assert store == '0:1 1:2 2:3 '

assert list.join('-') == '1-2-3'

result = list.inject(0) { clinks, guests ->
    clinks + guests
}
assert result == 0 + 1 + 2 + 3
assert list.sum() == 6                          Accumulating

factorial = list.inject(1) { fac, item ->
    fac * item
}
assert factorial == 1 * 1 * 2 * 3
```

Understanding and using the `inject` method can be a bit challenging if you're new to the concept. Note that it's parallel to the iteration examples, with `store` playing the role of the intermediary result. The benefit is that you don't need to introduce that extra variable to the outer scope of your accumulation, and your closure has no side effects on that scope. Other languages often call this kind of method `fold` or `reduce`.

There are a host of additional GDK methods we don't have space to cover in detail, including `collate`, `collectMany`, `combinations`, `dropWhile`, `flatten`, `groupBy`, `permutations`, `take`, `transpose`, and `withIndex`. Consult the cheat sheet for lists in appendix D for a few more examples and the complete list of GDK methods for lists in the groovy-jdk documentation.[3]

The GDK also introduces two convenience methods for producing views backed by an existing list: `asImmutable` and `asSynchronized`. These methods use Java's `Collections.unmodifiableList` and `Collections.synchronizedList` to protect the list from unintended content changes and concurrent access. See these methods' Javadocs for more details on the topic.

4.2.4 Lists in action

After all the artificial examples, you deserve to see a real one. Here it is: we'll implement Tony Hoare's Quicksort[4] algorithm in listing 4.10. To make things more interesting, we'll do so in a generic way; we'll not demand any particular datatype for sorting. We'll rely on duck typing.[5] For our use, this means that as long as we can use the <, =, and > operators with the list items, we treat them as if they were comparable.

The goal of Quicksort is to be sparse with comparisons. The strategy relies on finding a good *pivot* element in the list that serves to split the list into two sublists: one with all elements smaller than the pivot, and the second with all elements bigger than the pivot. Quicksort is then called recursively on the sublists. The rationale behind this is that you never need to compare elements from one list with elements from the other list. If you always find the perfect pivot, which exactly splits your list in half, the algorithm runs with a complexity of $n \times \log(n)$. In the worst case, you choose a border element every time, and you end up with a complexity of n^2. In the next listing, we choose the middle element of the list, which is a good choice for the frequent case of preordered sublists.

Listing 4.10 Quicksort with lists

```
def quickSort(list) {
  if (list.size() < 2) return list
  def pivot  = list[list.size().intdiv(2)]
  def left   = list.findAll { item -> item <  pivot }
  def middle = list.findAll { item -> item == pivot }
  def right  = list.findAll { item -> item >  pivot }
  return quickSort(left) + middle + quickSort(right)
}

assert quickSort([])      == []
assert quickSort([1])     == [1]
assert quickSort([1,2])   == [1,2]
```

❶ Classify by pivot

Recursive calls

---

[3] Groovy JDK API Documentation describes the methods added to the JDK to make it more groovy: http://docs.groovy-lang.org/docs/latest/html/groovy-jdk/.

[4] For an explanation of Quicksort, sometimes called partition-exchange sort, see http://en.wikipedia.org/wiki/Quicksort.

[5] See section 3.2.4 "The case for optional typing" for more details.

```
assert quickSort([2,1])             == [1,2]                        ❷  Duck-typed
assert quickSort([3,1,2])           == [1,2,3]                          items
assert quickSort([3,1,2,2])         == [1,2,2,3]
assert quickSort([1.0f,'a',10,null]) == [null,1.0f,10,'a']  ◄─┐
assert quickSort('bca')             == 'abc'.toList()  ◄────┘  ❸  Duck-typed
                                                               structure
```

In contrast to what we said earlier, we use not two but three lists ❶. Use this implementation when you don't want to lose items that appear multiple times.

The duck-typing approach is powerful when it comes to sorting different types. We can sort a list of mixed content types ❷, or even sort a string ❸. This is possible because we didn't demand any specific type to hold the items. As long as that type implements size, getAt(index), and findAll, we're happy to treat it as a *sortable*. Actually, we use duck typing twice: for the items and for the structure.

> **NOTE** The sort method that comes with Groovy uses Java's sorting implementation that beats our example in terms of worst-case performance. It guarantees a complexity of $n \times \log(n)$. But we win on a different front.

Of course, this implementation could be optimized in multiple dimensions. Our goal is to be tidy and flexible, not the fastest on the block.

If we had to explain the Quicksort algorithm without the help of Groovy, we'd sketch it in pseudocode that looks exactly like listing 4.10. In other words, the Groovy code itself is the best description of what it does. Imagine what this can mean to your codebase, when all your code reads like it were a formal documentation of its purpose!

Another extremely common use case where Groovy's GDK methods for lists add real value is filter/map/reduce style processing of lists of your domain classes. We'll use a list of URLs but you could imagine a list of customers, invoices, shopping carts, or some other domain objects. Suppose we want to take a list of URLs, select only those having a port with certain characteristics, then transform some information from the URL, then sort the results, and finally combine the results into a single string. This can be done easily with a series of list GDK methods as shown in the following listing.

Listing 4.11   Processing lists of URLs

```
def urls = [
  new URL('http', 'myshop.com', 80, 'index.html'),
  new URL('https', 'myshop.com', 443, 'buynow.html'),
  new URL('ftp', 'myshop.com', 21, 'downloads')
]

assert urls
    .findAll{ it.port < 99 }
    .collect{ it.file.toUpperCase() }
    .sort()
    .join(', ') == 'DOWNLOADS, INDEX.HTML'
```

Prior to Java 8, the equivalent Java code to achieve this would be quite cluttered and cumbersome. The Groovy version is simple and very easy to understand in comparison.

The Java 8 version is substantially better and the good news is that you can leverage the Java 8 methods with a bit of Groovy syntactic sugar added to boot, as can be seen here:

```
// Groovy with Java 8
import java.util.stream.Collectors
def commaSep = Collectors.joining(", ")
assert urls.stream()
    .filter{ it.port < 99 }
    .map{ it.file.toUpperCase() }
    .sorted()
    .collect(commaSep) == 'DOWNLOADS, INDEX.HTML'
```

If you like what you see with these examples, there's even better news when you see how to perform such operations concurrently using GPars in chapter 18.

You've seen that lists are one of Groovy's strongest workhorses. They're always at hand; they're easy to specify inline, and using them is easy due to the operators supported. The plethora of available methods may be intimidating at first, but that's also the source of lists' power.

You're now able to add them to your carriage and let them pull the weight of your code.

The next section about maps will follow the same principles that you've seen for lists: extending the Java collection's capabilities while providing efficient shortcuts.

4.3 *Working with maps*

Suppose you were about to learn the vocabulary of a new language, and you set out to find the most efficient way of doing so. It'd surely be beneficial to focus on the words that appear most often in your texts. So, you'd take a collection of your texts and analyze the word frequencies in that text corpus.[6]

What Groovy mechanisms are available to do this? For the time being, assume that you can work on a large string. You have numerous ways of splitting this string into words. But how do you count and store the word frequencies? You can't have a distinct variable for each possible word you encounter. Finding a way of storing frequencies in a list is possible but inconvenient—more suitable for a brainteaser than for good code. Maps come to the rescue.

Some pseudocode to solve the problem could look like this:

```
for each word {
    if (frequency of word is not known)
        frequency[word] = 0
    frequency[word] += 1
}
```

This looks like the list syntax, but with strings as indexes rather than integers. In fact, Groovy maps appear like lists, allowing any arbitrary object to be used for indexing.

---

[6] Analyzing word frequencies in a text corpus is a common task in computer linguistics and is used for optimizing computer-based learning, search engines, voice recognition, and machine translation programs.

To describe the map datatype, we show how maps can be specified, which operations and methods are available for maps, some surprisingly convenient features of
maps, and, of course, a map-based solution for the word-frequency exercise.

4.3.1 *Specifying maps*

The specification of maps is analogous to the list specification that you saw in the
previous section. Just like lists, maps make use of the subscript operator to retrieve
and assign values. The difference is that maps can use any arbitrary type as an argument to the subscript operator, where lists are bound to integer indexes. Lists are
aware of the sequence of their entries, maps are generally not. Specialized maps like
`java.util.TreeMap` may have a sequence to their keys, though.

Simple maps are specified with square brackets around a sequence of items, delimited with commas. The key feature of maps is that the items are key–value pairs that
are delimited by colons:

```
[key1:value1, key2:value2, key3:value3]
```

In principle, any arbitrary type can be used for keys or values. When using exotic[7] types
for keys, you need to obey the rules as outlined in the Javadoc for `java.util.Map`.

The character sequence `[:]` declares an empty map. Maps are, by default, of type
`java.util.LinkedHashMap`, and can also be declared explicitly by calling the respective
constructor. The resulting map can still be used with the subscript operator. In fact, this
works with any type of map, as you see in the next listing with `java.util.TreeMap`.

Listing 4.12 Specifying maps

```
def myMap = [a:1, b:2, c:3]

assert myMap instanceof LinkedHashMap
assert myMap.size() == 3
assert myMap['a']    == 1

def emptyMap = [:]
assert emptyMap.size() == 0

def explicitMap = new TreeMap()
explicitMap.putAll(myMap)
assert explicitMap['a'] == 1

def composed    = [x:'y', *:myMap]          ← Spread operator
assert composed == [x:'y', a:1, b:2, c:3]
```

In the previous listing, we use the `putAll(Map)` method from `java.util.Map` to easily
fill the example map. One alternative would be to pass `myMap` as an argument to
`TreeMap`'s constructor.

---

[7] *Exotic* in this sense refers to types of which the instances change their `hashCode` during their lifetime. There
is also a corner case with GStrings if their values write themselves lazily.

For the common case of having keys of type String, you can leave out the string markers (single or double quotes) in a map declaration:

```
assert ['a':1] == [a:1]
```

Such a convenience declaration is allowed only if the key contains no special characters (it needs to follow the rules for valid identifiers) and isn't a Groovy keyword.

This notation can also get in the way when, for example, the content of a local variable is used as a key. Suppose you have local variable x with content 'a'. Because [x:1] is equal to ['x':1], how can you make it equal to ['a':1]? The trick is that you can force Groovy to recognize a symbol as an expression by putting it inside parentheses:

```
def x = 'a'
assert ['x':1] == [x:1]
assert ['a':1] == [(x):1]
```

It's rare to require this functionality, but when you need keys that are derived from local symbols (local variables, fields, properties), forgetting the parentheses is a likely source of errors.

4.3.2 Using map operators

The simplest operations with maps are storing objects in a map with a *key* and retrieving them back using that key. Listing 4.13 demonstrates how to do that. One option for retrieving is using the subscript operator. As you've probably guessed, this is implemented with Map's getAt method. A second option is to use the key like a *property* with a simple dot-key syntax. You'll learn more about properties in chapter 7. A third option is the get method, which additionally allows you to pass a default value to be returned if the key isn't yet in the map. If no default is given, null will be used as the default. If on a get(key,default) call the key isn't found and the default is returned, the (key,default) pair is added to the map.

Listing 4.13   Accessing maps (GDK map methods)

```
def myMap = [a:1, b:2, c:3]

assert myMap['a']        == 1        Retrieves
assert myMap.a           == 1        existing
assert myMap.get('a')    == 1        elements
assert myMap.get('a',0)  == 1

assert myMap['d']        == null     Attempts to
assert myMap.d           == null     retrieve missing
assert myMap.get('d')    == null     elements

assert myMap.get('d',0)  == 0        Default value
assert myMap.d           == 0

myMap['d'] = 1
assert myMap.d == 1                   Single putAt
myMap.d = 2
assert myMap.d == 2
```

Assignments to maps can be done using the subscript operator or via the dot-key syntax. If the key in the dot-key syntax contains special characters, it can be put into string markers, like so:

```
myMap = ['a.b':1]
assert myMap.'a.b' == 1
```

Just writing `myMap.a.b` wouldn't work here—that would be the equivalent of calling `myMap.getA().getB()`.

Listing 4.14 shows how information can easily be gleaned from maps, largely using core JDK methods from `java.util.Map`. Using `equals`, `size`, `containsKey`, and `containsValue` as in listing 4.14 is straightforward. The `keySet` method returns a *set* of keys, a collection that's flat like a list but has no duplicate entries and no inherent ordering. See the Javadoc of `java.util.Set` for details. To compare the `keySet` method against the list of known keys, we need to convert this list to a set. This is done with a small service method `toSet`.

The `value` method returns the list of values. Because maps have no idea how their keys are ordered, there's no foreseeable ordering in the list of values. To make it comparable with the known list of values, we convert both to a set.

Maps can be converted into a collection by calling the `entrySet` method, which returns a set of entries where each entry can be asked for its key and value property.

Listing 4.14 Query methods on maps

```
def myMap = [a:1, b:2, c:3]
def other = [b:2, c:3, a:1]

assert myMap == other                                    Call to equals

assert !myMap.isEmpty()
assert myMap.size()      == 3
assert myMap.containsKey('a')                            JDK methods
assert myMap.containsValue(1)
assert myMap.entrySet() instanceof Collection

assert myMap.any   {entry -> entry.value > 2 }           ❶ GDK methods
assert myMap.every {entry -> entry.key   < 'd'}      Set equals
assert myMap.keySet() == ['a','b','c'] as Set
assert myMap.values().toList() == [1, 2, 3]              List equals
```

The GDK adds two more informational methods to the JDK map type: any and every ❶. They work analogously to the identically named methods for lists: they return a Boolean value to tell whether *any* or *every* entry in the map satisfies a given closure.

Listing 4.14 makes use of the fact that a literally declared map is of type `LinkedHashMap` and we can therefore rely on the ordering of entries, keys, and values. This feature is so helpful and shields programmers from bugs that arise when relying on such a sequence for arbitrary maps. With the information about the map, we can iterate it over the entries or over keys and values separately. Because the sets that are returned from `keySet` and `entrySet` are collections, we can use them with the for-in-collection type loops. The following listing goes through some of the possible combinations.[8]

Listing 4.15 Iterating over maps (GDK)

```
def myMap = [a:1, b:2, c:3]

def store = ''
myMap.each { entry ->
    store += entry.key            Iterates over
    store += entry.value          entries
}
assert store == 'a1b2c3'

store = ''
myMap.each { key, value ->
    store += key                  Iterates
    store += value                over keys
}                                 and values
assert store == 'a1b2c3'

store = ''
for (key in myMap.keySet()) {
    store += key                  Iterates over
}                                 just keys
assert store == 'abc'

store = ''
for (value in myMap.values()) {
    store += value                Iterates over
}                                 just values
assert store == '123'
```

`Map`'s each method uses closures in two ways: passing one parameter into the closure means that it's an *entry*, and passing two parameters means it's a key and a value. The latter is more convenient to work with for common cases.

Map content can be changed in various ways, as shown in listing 4.16. Removing elements works with the original JDK methods. New capabilities that the GDK introduces are:

- Creating a `subMap` of all entries with keys from a given collection.
- `findAll` entries in a map that satisfy a given closure.
- `find` one entry that satisfies a given closure, where, unlike lists, there's no notion of a *first* entry because there's no ordering in maps.
- `collect` in a list whatever a closure returns for each entry, optionally adding to a given collection.

---

[8] The example uses a default Groovy map that retains order. When using other types of maps, the order in which these iteration methods return values may be undefined.

Listing 4.16   Changing map content and building new objects from it

```
def myMap = [a:1, b:2, c:3]
myMap.clear()
assert myMap.isEmpty()

myMap = [a:1, b:2, c:3]
myMap.remove('a')
assert myMap.size() == 2

assert [a:1] + [b:2] == [a:1, b:2]                    ❶ Creates a
                                                          view onto
myMap = [a:1, b:2, c:3]                                   original map
def abMap = myMap.subMap(['a', 'b'])
assert abMap.size() == 2

abMap = myMap.findAll    { entry -> entry.value < 3 }
assert abMap.size() == 2
assert abMap.a       == 1

def found = myMap.find   { entry -> entry.value < 2 }
assert found.key    == 'a'
assert found.value == 1

def doubled = myMap.collect { entry -> entry.value *= 2 }
assert doubled instanceof List
assert doubled.every     { item -> item % 2 == 0 }

def addTo = []
myMap.collect(addTo)     { entry -> entry.value *= 2 }
assert addTo instanceof List
assert addTo.every       { item -> item % 2 == 0 }
```

The first two examples (`clear` and `remove`) in the listing are from the core JDK; the rest are all GDK methods. Only the `subMap` method ❶ is particularly new here; `collect`, `find`, and `findAll` act as they would with lists, operating on map entries instead of list elements. The `subMap` method is analogous to `subList`, but it specifies a collection of keys as a filter for the view onto the original map.

To assert that the `collect` method works as expected, recall a trick that we discussed about lists: use the `every` method on the list to make sure that every entry is even. The `collect` method comes with a second version that takes an additional collection parameter. It adds all closure results directly to this collection, avoiding the need to create temporary lists.

From the list of available methods that you've seen for other datatypes, you may miss the dearly beloved `isCase` for use with `grep` and `switch`. Don't we want to classify with maps? Well, we need to be more specific: Do we want to classify by the keys or by the values? Either way, an appropriate `isCase` is available when working on Map's key-Set or values.

The GDK introduces two more methods for the map datatype: `asImmutable` and `asSynchronized`. These methods use `Collections.unmodifiableMap` and `Collections.synchronizedMap` to protect the map from unintended content changes and concurrent access. See these methods' Javadocs for more details on the topic.

4.3.3 *Maps in action*

In listing 4.17, we revisit the initial example of counting word frequencies in a text corpus. The strategy is to use a map with each distinct word serving as a key. The mapped value of that word is its frequency in the text corpus. We go through all words in the text and increase the frequency value of that respective word in the map. We need to make sure that we can increase the value when a word is hit the first time and there's no entry yet in the map. Luckily, the `get(key,default)` method does the job.

We then take all keys, put them in a list, and sort it so that it reflects the order of frequency. Finally, we play with the capabilities of lists, ranges, and strings to print a nice statistic.

The text corpus under analysis is Baloo the Bear's anthem on his attitude toward life.

Listing 4.17   Counting word frequency with maps

```
def textCorpus =
"""
Look for the bare necessities
The simple bare necessities
Forget about your worries and your strife
I mean the bare necessities
Old Mother Nature's recipes
That bring the bare necessities of life
"""

def words = textCorpus.tokenize()
def wordFrequency = [:]
words.each { word ->
  wordFrequency[word] = wordFrequency.get(word,0) + 1       ❶ Updates
}                                                              frequency
def wordList = wordFrequency.keySet().toList()                count
wordList.sort { wordFrequency[it] }                          ❷ Sorts by
                                                               frequency
def statistic = "\n"
wordList[-1..-5].each { word ->
  statistic += word.padLeft(12)    + ': '
  statistic += wordFrequency[word] + "\n"
}
assert statistic == """
 necessities: 4
        bare: 4
         the: 3
        your: 2
        life: 1
"""
```

The example nicely combines our knowledge of Groovy's datatypes ❶. Counting the word frequency is essentially a one-liner. It's even shorter than the pseudocode that we used to start this section. Having the `sort` method on the `wordList` accept a closure turns out to be very beneficial ❷, because it's able to implement its comparing logic on the wordFrequency map—on an object totally different from the wordList. Just as an exercise, try to do that in Java, count the lines, and judge the expressiveness of either solution. As an advanced exercise, you could try sorting by frequency and then alphabetically both in Groovy and Java. This will make the expressiveness of Groovy even more obvious.

In listing 4.11, we showed you map/filter/reduce style processing with lists. The same style of processing is frequently used with maps too as shown in this example:

```
def people = [peter: 40, paul: 30, mary: 20]
assert people
    .findAll{ _, age -> age < 35 }
    .collect{ name, _ -> name.toUpperCase() }
    .sort()
    .join(', ') == 'MARY, PAUL'
```

Lists and maps make a powerful duo. There are whole languages that build on just these two datatypes (such as Perl, with lists and hashes) and implement all other datatypes and even objects upon them. Their power comes from the complete and mindfully engineered Java Collections Framework. Thanks to Groovy, this power is now right at our fingertips.

Until now, we carelessly switched back and forth between Groovy and Java collection datatypes. We'll throw more light on this interplay in the next section.

4.4   *Notes on Groovy collections*

The Java Collections API is the basis for all the nice support that Groovy gives you through lists and maps. In fact, Groovy not only uses the same abstractions, it even works on the very same classes that make up the Java Collections API.

This is exceptionally convenient for those who come from Java and already have a good understanding of it. If you haven't, and you're interested in more background information, have a look at your Javadoc starting at java.util.Collection. The JDK documentation also includes a guide and tutorial about Java collections.

One of the typical peculiarities of the Java collections is that you shouldn't try to structurally change one while iterating through it. A *structural* change is one that adds an entry, removes an entry, or changes the sequence of entries when the collection is sequence-aware. This applies even when iterating through a view onto the collection, such as using list[range].

4.4.1   *Understanding concurrent modification*

If you fail to meet this constraint, you'll see a ConcurrentModificationException. For example, you cannot remove all elements from a list by iterating through it and removing the first element at each step:

```
def list = [1, 2, 3, 4]
list.each{ list.remove(0) }
// throws ConcurrentModificationException !!
```

NOTE *Concurrent* in this sense doesn't necessarily mean that a second thread changed the underlying collection. As shown in the example, even a single thread of control can break the structural stability constraint.

In this case, the correct solution is to use the `clear` method. The Java Collections API has lots of such specialized methods. When searching for alternatives, consider `collect`, `addAll`, `removeAll`, `findAll`, and `grep`.

This leads to a second issue: some methods work on a copy of the collection and return it when finished; other methods work directly on the collection object they were called on (we call this the *receiver*[9] object).

4.4.2 *Distinguishing between copy and modify semantics*

Generally, there's no easy way to anticipate whether a method modifies the receiver or returns a copy. Some languages have naming conventions for this. But Groovy couldn't do so because all Java methods are directly visible in Groovy, and Java's method names couldn't be made compliant to such a convention. But Groovy tries to adapt to Java and follow the heuristics that you can spot when looking through the Java Collections API:

- Methods that modify the receiver typically don't return a collection. Examples: `add`, `addAll`, `remove`, `removeAll`, and `retainAll`. Counterexample: `sort`.
- Methods that return a collection typically don't modify the receiver. Examples: `grep`, `findAll`, and `collect`. Counterexample: `sort` (though we recommend using `toSorted` in that case). And yes, `sort` is a counterexample for both, because it returns a collection and modifies the receiver.
- Methods that modify the receiver have *imperative* names. They sound like there could be an exclamation mark behind them. (Indeed, this is Ruby's naming convention for such methods.) Examples: `add`, `addAll`, `remove`, `removeAll`, `retainAll`, and `sort`. Counterexamples: `collect`, `grep`, and `findAll`, which are imperative but don't modify the receiver and return a modified copy.

The preceding rules can be mapped to operators, by applying them to the names of their method counterparts: `<<` `leftShift` is imperative and modifies the receiver (on lists, unfortunately not on strings—doing so would break Java's invariant of strings being immutable); `plus` isn't imperative and returns a copy.

The convention in Groovy is that any method that implements an arithmetic operator (plus, minus, multiply, divide) doesn't modify the receiver but returns a copy.

These aren't clear rules but only heuristics to give you some guidance. Whenever you're in doubt and object identity is important, have a look at the documentation or write a few assertions.

---

[9] From the Smalltalk notion of describing method calls on an object as sending a message to the receiver.

4.5   *Summary*

This has been a long trip through the valley of Groovy's datatypes. There were lots of paths to explore that led to new interesting places.

We introduced ranges as objects that, as opposed to control structures, have their own time and place of creation, can be passed to methods as parameters, and can be returned from method calls. This makes them very flexible, and once the concept of a range is available, many uses beyond simple control structures suggest themselves. The most natural example you've seen is extracting a section of a list using a range as the operand to the list's subscript operator.

Lists and maps are more familiar to Java programmers than ranges but have suffered from a lack of language support in Java itself. Groovy recognizes just how often these datatypes are used, gives them special treatment in terms of literal declarations, and, of course, provides operators and extra methods to make life even easier. The lists and maps used in Groovy are the same ones encountered in Java and come with the same rules and restrictions, although these become less onerous due to some of the additional methods available on the collections.

Throughout our coverage of Groovy's datatypes, you've seen closures used ubiquitously for making functionality available in a simple and unobtrusive manner. In the next chapter, we'll demystify the concept, explain the usual and not-so-usual applications, and show how you can spice up your own code with closures.

Working with closures

5

This chapter covers

- Why you want to have closures
- How to declare and use closures
- How to design methods that make use of closures

I wouldn't like to build a tool that could only do what I had been able to imagine for it.

—Bjarne Stroustrup

Closures are important. Very important. They're arguably one of the most useful features of Groovy. But at the same time they can be a strange concept until you fully understand them. To get the best out of Groovy, or to understand anyone else's Groovy code, you're going to have to be comfortable with closures. Not just "met them once at a wedding" comfortable, but "invite them over for a barbecue on the weekend" comfortable.

Now, we don't want to scare you away. Closures aren't hard—they're just different than anything you might be used to. In a way, this is strange, because one of the chief tenets of object orientation is that objects have behavior as well as data.

Closures are objects of which the main purpose in life is their behavior—that's almost all there is to them.

In previous chapters, you've seen a few uses of closures, so you might already have a good idea of what they're about. Please forgive us if we seem to be going over the same ground again—it's so important, we'd rather repeat ourselves than leave you without a good grasp of the basic principles.

In this chapter, we'll introduce the fundamental concept of closures (again), explain their benefits, and then show you how they can be declared and called. After this basic treatment, we'll look in a bit more depth at other methods available on closures and the *scope* of a closure—that is, the data and members that can be accessed within it—as well as consider what it means to return from a closure. We end the chapter with a discussion of how closures can be used to implement many common design patterns and how they alleviate the need for some others by solving the problem in a different manner.

So, without further ado, let's take a look at what closures really are in the first place.

5.1   *A gentle introduction to closures*

Let's start with a simple definition of closures, and then we'll expand on it with an example. A *closure* is a piece of code wrapped up as an object. It acts like a method in that it can take parameters and return a value. It's a normal object in that you can pass a reference to it just as you can to any other object. Don't forget that the JVM has no idea you're running Groovy code, so there's nothing particularly odd that you could be doing with a closure object. It's just an object. Groovy provides a very easy way of creating closure objects and enables some very smart behavior.

Consider an envelope containing a piece of paper. For other objects, the paper might have the values of variables on it: $x = 5$, $y = 10$, and so on. For a closure, the paper would have a list of instructions. You can give that envelope to someone, and that person might decide to follow the instructions, or they might give the envelope to someone else. That person might decide to follow the instructions lots of times, with a different context each time. For instance, the piece of paper might say, "Send a letter to the person you're thinking of," and the person might flip through the pages of their address book thinking of every person listed in it, following the instructions over and over again, once for each contact in the address book.

The Groovy equivalent of that example would be something like this:

```
Closure envelope = { person -> new Letter(person).send() }
addressBook.each (envelope)
```

That's a fairly long-winded way of going about it, and not idiomatic Groovy, but it shows the distinction between the closure itself (in this case, the value of the `envelope` variable) and its use (as a parameter to the `each` method). Part of what makes closures hard to understand when coming to them for the first time is that they're usually used in an abbreviated form. Groovy makes them very concise because they're so frequently used—but that brevity can be detrimental to the learning process.

Just for comparison, here's the previous code written using the shorthand Groovy provides. When you see this shorthand, it's often worth mentally separating it out into the longer form:

```
addressBook.each { new Letter(it).send() }
```

It's still a method call passing a closure as the single parameter, but that's all hidden—passing a closure to a method is sufficiently common in Groovy that there are special rules for it. Similarly, if the closure needs to take only a single parameter to work on, Groovy provides a default name—it—so that you don't need to declare it specifically. That's how our example ends up so short when we use all the Groovy shortcuts.

Now, we're in danger of getting ahead of ourselves here, so we'll pause and think about why we'd want to have closures in the first palace. Just keep remembering: they're objects that are associated with some code, and Groovy provides neat syntax for them.

5.2　*The case for closures*

Java as a *platform* is great: portable, stable, scalable, and reasonably well performing. Java as a *language* has a lot of advantages but, unfortunately, also some shortcomings.

Some of those deficiencies can be addressed in Groovy through the use of closures. We'll look at two particular areas that benefit from closures: performing everyday tasks with collections, and using resources in a safe manner. In these two common situations, you need to be able to perform some logic that's the same for every case and execute arbitrary code to do the actual work. In the case of collections, that code is the body of the iterator; in the case of resource handling, it's the use of the resource after it's been acquired and before it's been released. In general terms, such a mechanism uses a *callback* to execute the work. Closures are Groovy's way of providing transparent callback targets as first-class citizens.

5.2.1　*Using iterators*

A typical task is to iterate through a collection. Here's how you do it in classic Java:

```
// Java 5
for (ItemType item : list) {
    // do something with item
}
```

With Groovy closures you can do this:

```
// Groovy object iteration
list.each { item -> /* do something with item */ }
```

Since Java 8 there's something similar[1] to Groovy:

```
// Java 8 with lambda
list.stream().forEach( (item) -> {
    // do something with item
} );
```

We don't want to go too much into the differences between closures and lambdas but we'll point out some of them as we go along. Interestingly, Groovy can take full advantage of the JDK additions that have been introduced to support lambdas, especially the streaming API. You can always use closures where lambda expressions are expected, as follows:

```
// Groovy closures with Java 8
list.stream().forEach { println it}
```

Clearly, it's useful to have a for loop that iterates through every item in a collection—otherwise, Groovy wouldn't have it, for starters. (Groovy's for statement is somewhat broader in scope than Java's—see section 6.3 for more details.) It's useful, but it's not everything we could wish for. There are common patterns for *why* we want to iterate through a collection, such as finding whether a particular condition is met by any element, finding *all* the elements met by a condition, or transforming each element into another, thereby creating a new collection.

It'd be madness to have a specialized syntax for all of those patterns. Making a language too smart in a nonextensible way ends up like a road through the jungle—it's fine when you're doing something anticipated by the designers, but as soon as you stray off the path, life is tough. So, without direct language support for all those patterns, what's left? Each of the patterns relies on executing a particular piece of code again and again, once for each element of the collection. Java has no concept of "a particular piece of code" unless it's buried in a method. That method can be part of an interface implementation, but at that point each piece of code needs its own (possibly anonymous) class, and life gets very messy.

Groovy uses closures to specify the code to be executed each time and adds the extra methods (each, find, findAll, collect, and so forth) to the collection classes to make them readily available. Those methods aren't magic—they're simple Groovy, because closures allow the *controlling* logic (the iteration) to be separated from the code to execute for every element. If you find yourself wanting a similar construct that isn't already covered by Groovy, you can add it easily.

Java 8 lambdas address this issue in a similar way as Groovy closures do. The request from the developer community that knew the concept of Groovy closures for years has been so overwhelming that Java saw the need to introduce them.

---

[1] Java 8 works on a *stream* here, not on the collection. This is quite a difference because reading from a stream is *destructive*. You cannot read the same value twice. You most likely never want to share a stream.

Separating iteration logic from what to do on each iteration isn't the only reason for introducing the closure concept. A second reason that may be even more important is the use of closures when handling resources.

5.2.2 *Handling resources with a protocol*

How many times have you seen code that opens a stream but calls `close` at the end of the method, overlooking the fact that the `close` statement may never be reached when an exception occurs while processing? So, it needs to be protected with a `try-catch` block. No—wait—that should be `try-finally`, or should it? And inside the `finally` block, `close` can throw another exception that needs to be handled. There are too many details to remember, and so resource handling is often implemented incorrectly. With Groovy's closure support, you can put that logic in one place and use it like this:

```
new File('myfile.txt').eachLine { println it }
```

The `eachLine` method of `File` now takes care of properly following the *protocol* of opening and closing the file input stream at the appropriate time. This guards you from accidentally producing a resource leak of file handles.

Streams are the most obvious tip of the iceberg of protocol-managed resources. Database connections, statements, transactions, native handles such as graphic resources, network connections, thread pools, and even your GUI are resources that need to be managed—that is, repainted correctly at the right time—and observers and event listeners need to be removed when the time comes, or you end up with a memory leak.

Forgetting to clean up correctly in all situations ought to be a problem that only affects neophyte Java programmers, but because the language provides little help beyond `try-catch-finally`, `try-with-resources`, and the `AutoCloseable` interface, even experienced developers end up making mistakes. It's possible to code around this in an orderly manner, but Java leads inexperienced programmers away from centralized resource handling. Code structures are duplicated, and the probability of not-so-perfect implementations rises with the number of duplicates.

Resource-handling code is often tested poorly. Projects that measure their test coverage typically struggle to fully cover this area. That's because duplicated, widespread resource handling is difficult to test and eats up precious development time. Testing centralized handlers is easy and requires only a single test.

Let's see what resource-handling solutions Java provides and why they're not used often, and then we'll show you the corresponding Groovy solutions.

A COMMON JAVA APPROACH: USE INNER CLASSES

To do centralized resource handling, you need to pass resource-using code to the handler. This should sound familiar by now—it's essentially the same problem we encountered when considering collections: the handler needs to know how to call that code, and therefore it must implement some known interface. In Java, this is frequently implemented by an inner class for two reasons. First, it allows the resource-using code to be close to the calling code (which is often useful for readability). Second, it allows the resource-using code to interact with the context of the calling code, using local variables, calling methods on the relevant object, and so on.

> **NOTE** JUnit, one of the most prominent Java packages outside the JDK, follows this strategy by using the `Runnable` interface with its `runProtected` method.

Anonymous inner classes (and lambdas since Java 8) are mainly used for this kind of pattern—if Java had closures or lambdas from the beginning, it's possible that anonymous inner classes might never have been invented. The rules and limitations that come with them (and with plain inner classes) impose some uncomfortable restrictions. As soon as you have to start typing code like `MyClass.this.doSomething`, you know something is wrong—and that's aside from the amount of distracting clutter required around your code just to create it in the first place. The interaction with the context of the calling code is limited. Rules such as "local variables having to be final to be used" made life so awkward that with Java 8 this restriction was lifted to "essentially final."

Java's limitations get in the way too much to make it an elegant solution. The following example uses a `Resource` that it gets from a `ResourceHandler`, which is responsible for its proper construction and destruction. Only the boldface code is needed for doing the job:

```
// Java
interface ResourceUser { // a @FunctionalInterface in Java 8
  void use(Resource resource)
}

resourceHandler.handle(new ResourceUser(){
    public void use (Resource resource) {
        resource.doSomething()
    }
});
```

The Groovy equivalent of this code reveals all the necessary information without any waste:

```
resourceHandler.handle { resource -> resource.doSomething() }
```

Groovy's scoping is also significantly more flexible and powerful, while removing the "code mess" that inner classes introduce.

AN ALTERNATIVE JAVA APPROACH: THE TEMPLATE METHOD PATTERN

Another strategy to centralize resource handling in Java is to do it in a superclass and let the resource-using code live in a subclass. This is the typical implementation of the Template Method (Gang of Four) pattern.

The downside here is that you either end up with a proliferation of subclasses or use (maybe anonymous) inner subclasses, which brings us back to the drawbacks discussed earlier. It also introduces penalties in terms of code clarity and freedom of implementation, both of which tend to suffer when inheritance is involved. This leads us to take a close look at the dangers of abstraction proliferation.

If there were only *one* interface that could be used for the purpose of passing logic around, like the imaginary `ResourceUser` interface from the previous example, then things wouldn't be too bad. But in Java, there's no such beast—that is, no single `ResourceUser` interface that serves all purposes. The signature of the callback method use needs to adapt to the purpose: the number and type of parameters, the number and type of declared exceptions, and the return type.

A variety of interfaces has evolved over time: `Runnables`, `Observers`, `Listeners`, `Visitors`, `Comparators`, `Strategies`, `Commands`, `Controllers`, and so on.[2] This makes their use more complicated, because with every new interface, there's also a new abstraction or concept that needs to be understood.

In comparison, Groovy closures can handle *any* method signature, and the behavior of the controlling logic may even change depending on the signature of the closure provided to it, as you'll see later.

These two examples of pain-points in Java that can be addressed with closures are just that—examples. If they were the only problems made easier by closures, closures would still be worth having, but reality is much richer. It turns out that closures enable many patterns of programming that would be unthinkable without them.

Before you can live your dreams, however, you need to learn more about the basics of closures. Let's start with how you declare them.

5.3 *Declaring closures*

So far, we've used the simple abbreviated syntax of closures: after a method call, put your code in braces with parameters delimited from the closure body by an arrow.

Let's start by adding to your knowledge about the simple abbreviated syntax, and then we'll look at two more ways to declare a closure: by using them in assignments and by referring to a method.

5.3.1 *Simple declaration*

The next listing shows the simple closure syntax plus a new convenience feature. When there's only one parameter passed into the closure, its declaration is optional. The magic variable `it` can be used instead. See the two equivalent closure declarations in the following listing.

Listing 5.1   Simple abbreviated closure declaration

```
log = ''
(1..10).each{ counter -> log += counter }
assert log == '12345678910'

log = ''
(1..10).each{ log += it }
assert log == '12345678910'
```

---

[2] With Java 8 come new interfaces that are more versatile like `Function`, `Producer`, and `Consumer`. This is nice because we can directly use them in Groovy.

Note that unlike `counter`, the magic variable `it` needs no declaration. This syntax is an abbreviation because the closure object as declared by the braces is the last parameter of the method and would normally appear within the method's parentheses. As you'll see, it's equally valid to put it inside parentheses like any other parameter, although it's hardly ever used this way:

```
log = ''
(1..10).each({ log += it })
assert log == '12345678910'
```

This syntax is simple because it uses only one parameter—the implicit parameter `it`. Multiple parameters can be declared in sequence, delimited by commas. A default value can optionally be assigned to parameters, in case no value is passed from the method to the closure. We'll show examples in section 5.4.

TIP Think of the arrow as an indication that parameters are passed from the method on the left into the closure body on the right.

5.3.2 *Using assignments for declaration*

A second way of declaring a closure is to directly assign it to a variable:

```
def printer = { line -> println line }
```

The closure is declared inside the braces and assigned to the `printer` variable.

TIP Whenever you see the braces of a closure, think: `new Closure(){}`.

There's also a special kind of assignment to the `return` value of a method:

```
def Closure getPrinter() {
    return { line -> println line }
}
```

Again, the braces denote the construction of a new closure object. This object is returned from the method call.

TIP Braces can denote the construction of a new closure object or a Groovy *block*. Blocks can be class, interface, static, or object initializers, or method bodies. Or they can appear with the Groovy keywords `if`, `else`, `synchronized`, `for`, `while`, `switch`, `try`, `catch`, and `finally`. All other occurrences are closures.

As you see, closures are objects. They can be stored in variables, they can be passed around, and, as you probably guessed, you can call methods on them. Being objects, closures can also be returned from a method.[3]

---

[3] This is a key distinction to Java 8 lambdas.

5.3.3 *Referring to methods as closures*

The third way of declaring a closure is to reuse something that's already declared: a method. Methods have a body, may return a value, can take parameters, and can be called. The similarities with closures are obvious, so Groovy lets you reuse the code you already have in methods, but as a closure. Referencing a method as a closure is performed using the `reference.&` operator. The reference is used to specify which instance should be used when the closure is called, just like a normal method call to `reference.someMethod()`. Figure 5.1 shows an assignment using a method closure, breaking up the statement into its constituent parts.

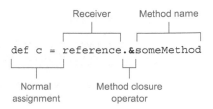

Figure 5.1 Anatomy of a simple method closure assignment statement

Listing 5.2 demonstrates method closures in action, showing two different instances being used to give two different closures, even though the same method is invoked in both cases.

Listing 5.2 Simple method closures in action

```
class SizeFilter {
    Integer limit

    boolean sizeUpTo(String value) {
        return value.size() <= limit
    }
}

SizeFilter filter6 = new SizeFilter(limit:6)        ❶ GroovyBean
SizeFilter filter5 = new SizeFilter(limit:5)            constructor calls

Closure sizeUpTo6 = filter6.&sizeUpTo               ❷ Method closure
                                                        assignment

def words = ['long string', 'medium', 'short', 'tiny']  ❸ Calling with
                                                            closure
assert 'medium' == words.find (sizeUpTo6)
assert 'short'  == words.find (filter5.&sizeUpTo)   ❹ Passing a method
                                                        closure directly
```

First, we create two instances ❶. Each has a separate idea of how long a string it will deem to be valid in the `sizeUpTo` method. We create a reference to that method with `filter6.&sizeUpTo` ❷, showing that the reference can be assigned to a variable, which is then passed at ❸ as a parameter to the `find` method. Alternatively, we can create such a reference directly as a parameter to the find method ❹. We use a sample list of words to check that the closures are doing what we expect them to.

Method closures are limited to instance methods, but they do have another interesting feature—runtime overload resolution, also known as *multimethods*. You'll find out more about multimethods in section 7.3, but the following listing gives a taste.

Listing 5.3   Multimethod, also known as runtime overload resolution, closures

```
class MultiMethodSample {

    int mysteryMethod (String value) {
        return value.length()
    }
    int mysteryMethod (List list) {
        return list.size()
    }
    int mysteryMethod (int x, int y) {
        return x+y
    }
}
MultiMethodSample instance = new MultiMethodSample()
Closure multi = instance.&mysteryMethod

assert 10 == multi ('string arg')
assert  3 == multi (['list', 'of', 'values'])
assert 14 == multi (6, 8)
```

❶ Only a single closure is created

❷ Different implementations are called based on argument types

Here a single instance is used, and indeed a single closure ❶. But each time it's called, a different method implementation is invoked ❷. We don't want to rush ahead of ourselves, but you'll see a lot more of this kind of dynamic behavior in chapter 7.

Now that you've seen all the ways of declaring a closure, it's worth pausing for a moment and seeing them all together, performing the same function, just with different declaration styles.

5.3.4   *Comparing the available options*

Listing 5.4 creates and uses closures in various ways: through simple declaration, assignment to variables, and method closures. In each case, we call the each method on a simple map, providing a closure that doubles a single value. By the time we've finished, we've doubled each value three times.

Listing 5.4   Full closure declaration examples

```
Map map = ['a':1, 'b':2]
map.each{ key, value -> map[key] = value * 2 }
assert map == ['a':2, 'b':4]

Closure doubler = {key, value -> map[key] = value * 2 }
map.each(doubler)
assert map == ['a':4, 'b':8]

def doubleMethod (entry){
    entry.value = entry.value * 2
}
doubler = this.&doubleMethod
map.each(doubler)
assert map == ['a':8, 'b':16]
```

❶ Parameter sequence with commas

❷ Assigns and then calls a closure reference

❸ Usual method declaration

❹ References and calls a method as a closure

In ❶, we pass the closure as the parameter directly. This is the form you've seen most commonly so far.

The declaration of the closure in ❷ is disconnected from its immediate use. The curly braces are Groovy's way of declaring a closure, so we assign a closure object to the variable `doubler`. Some people incorrectly interpret this line as assigning the *result* of a closure call to a variable. Don't fall into that trap! The closure isn't yet called, only declared, until we reach it. There you see that passing the closure as an argument to the `each` method via a reference is exactly the same as declaring the closure *in-place*, the style that we followed in all the previous examples.

The method declared in ❸ is a perfectly ordinary method. There's no trace of our intention to use it as a closure.

In ❹, the `reference.&` operator is used for referencing a method name as a closure. Again, the method isn't immediately called; the execution of the method occurs as part of the next line. This is just like ❷. The closure is passed to the `each` method, which calls it back for each entry in the map.

Typing[4] is optional in Groovy, and consequently it's optional for closure parameters. A special thing about closure parameters with explicit types is that this type isn't checked at compile time but at runtime.

To fully understand how closures work and how to use them within your code, you need to find out how to invoke them. That's the topic of the next section.

5.4 *Using closures*

So far, you've seen how to declare a closure for the purpose of passing it for execution, to the `each` method, for example. But what happens inside the `each` method? How does it call your closure? If you knew this, you could come up with equally smart implementations. We'll first look at how simple calling a closure is and then move on to explore advanced methods that the `Closure` type has to offer.

5.4.1 *Calling a closure*

Suppose you have a reference x pointing to a closure; you can call it with `x.call()` or simply `x()`. You've probably guessed that any arguments to the closure call go between the parentheses.

Let's start with a simple example. The following listing shows the same closure being called both ways.

Listing 5.5 Calling closures

```
def adder = { x, y -> return x+y }

assert adder(4, 3) == 7
assert adder.call(2, 6) == 8
```

---

[4] The word *typing* has two meanings: declaring object types and typing keystrokes. Although Groovy provides optional typing, you still have to key in your program code.

We start off by declaring pretty much the simplest possible closure—a piece of code that returns the sum of the two parameters it's passed. Then we call the closure both directly and using the `call` method. Both ways of calling the closure achieve exactly the same effect.

Now let's try something more involved. In the next listing, we demonstrate calling a closure from within a method body and how the closure gets passed into that method in the first place. The example measures the execution time of the closure.

Listing 5.6   Calling closures

```
def benchmark(int repeat, Closure worker) {        ←──────  ❶ Puts closures last
    def start = System.nanoTime()

    repeat.times { worker(it) }                    ←──────  Calls closure the given
                                                            ❸ number of times
    def stop = System.nanoTime()         ❹ Some
    return stop - start                    postwork
}
def slow = benchmark(10000) { (int) it / 2 }       ❺ Passes different
def fast = benchmark(10000) { it.intdiv(2) }          closures for
assert fast * 2 < slow                                analysis
```

Some prework ❷

Do you remember our performance investigation for regular expression patterns in listing 3.9? We needed to duplicate the benchmarking logic because we had no means to declare how to benchmark something. Now you know how. You can pass a closure into the `benchmark` method, where some pre- and postwork takes control of proper timing.

We put the closure parameter at the end of the parameter list ❶ to allow the simple abbreviated syntax when calling the method. In the example, we declare the type of the closure. This is only to make things more obvious. The `Closure` type is optional.

We effectively start timing the benchmark at ❷. From a general point of view, this is arbitrary prework like opening a file or connecting to a database. It just so happens that our resource is time.

At ❸, we call the given closure as many times as our `repeat` parameter demands. We pass the current count to the closure to make things more interesting. From a general point of view, a resource is passed to the closure.

We stop timing at ❹ and calculate the time taken by the closure. Here's the place for the postwork: closing files, flushing buffers, returning connections to the pool, and so on.

The payoff comes at ❺. We can now pass *logic* to the `benchmark` method. Note that we use the simple abbreviated syntax and use the magic `it` to refer to the current count. As a side effect, we learn that the general number division takes more than two times longer than the optimized `intdiv` method.

> **NOTE**   This kind of benchmarking shouldn't be taken too seriously. There are all kinds of effects that can heavily influence such wall clock–based measurements: the machine characteristics, OS, current machine load, JDK version, just-in-time (JIT) compiler, and HotSpot settings, and so on.

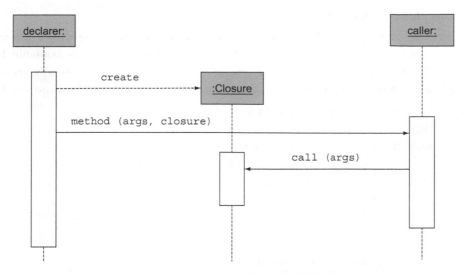

Figure 5.2   UML sequence diagram of the typical sequence of method calls when a declarer creates a closure and attaches it to a `method` invocation on the caller, which in turn calls that closure's `call` method

Figure 5.2 shows the UML sequence diagram for the general calling scheme of the declaring object that creates the closure, the `method` invocation on the caller, and the caller's callback to the given closure.

When calling a closure, you need to pass exactly as many arguments to the closure as it expects to receive, unless the closure defines default values for its parameters. This default value is used when you omit the corresponding argument. The following is a variant of the addition closure as used in listing 5.5, with a default value for the second parameter and two calls—one that passes two arguments, and one that relies on the default:

```
def adder = { x, y=5 -> return x+y }

assert adder(4, 3) == 7
assert adder.call(7) == 12
```

For the use of default parameters in closures, the same rules apply as for default parameters for methods. Also, closures can be used with a parameter list of variable length in the same way that methods can. We'll cover this in chapter 7.

At this point, you should be comfortable with passing closures to methods and have a solid understanding of how the callback is executed (see also the UML diagram in figure 5.2). Whenever you pass a closure to a method, you can be sure that a callback will be executed one way or the other (maybe only conditionally), depending on that method's logic. Closures are capable of more than just being called, though. In the next section, you see what else they have to offer.

5.4.2 *More closure capabilities*

The class `groovy.lang.Closure` is an ordinary class, albeit one with extraordinary power and extra language support. It has a number of methods available beyond `call`. We'll present the most important ones. Even though you'll usually just declare and call closures, it's nice to know there's extra power available when you need it.

REACTING ON THE PARAMETER COUNT OR TYPE

In section 4.3.2 you saw `Map`'s each method. It passes either a `Map.Entry` object or key and value separately into a supplied closure, depending on whether the closure takes one or two arguments. The each method adapts its behavior depending on the number of arguments that the closure that it receives was built with. You can do this in your own methods by retrieving the expected parameter count (and types, if declared) by calling `Closure`'s `getMaximumNumberOfParameters` and `getParameterTypes` methods:

```
def numParams (Closure closure){
   closure.getMaximumNumberOfParameters()
}
assert numParams { one -> }      == 1
assert numParams { one, two -> } == 2

def paramTypes (Closure closure){
   closure.getParameterTypes()
}
assert paramTypes { String s -> } == [String]
assert paramTypes { Number n, Date d -> } == [Number, Date]
```

As in the `Map.each` example, this allows for the luxury of supporting closures with different parameter styles, adapted to the caller's needs.

HOW TO CURRY FAVOR WITH A CLOSURE

Currying is a technique invented by Moses Schönfinkel and Gottlob Frege, and named after the logician Haskell Brooks Curry (1900–1982), a pioneer in *functional programming*. (Unsurprisingly, the functional language Haskell is also named after Curry.) The basic idea is to take a function with multiple parameters and transform it into a function with fewer parameters by fixing some of the values.[5] A classic example is to choose an arbitrary value *n* and transform a function that sums two parameters into a function that takes a single parameter and adds *n* to it.

In Groovy, `Closure`'s curry method returns a clone of the current closure, having bound one or more parameters to a given value. Parameters are bound to `curry`'s arguments from left to right. The following listing gives an implementation.

---

[5] A functional aficionado may point out that currying and partial application are different but related concepts and that Groovy's curry function might better have been named "partial." Perhaps a future version of Groovy will provide alternative names for these methods. In the meantime, we'll give ourselves a bit of poetic license to simplify the jargon in our explanations.

```
def mult    = { x, y -> return x * y }
def twoTimes = mult.curry(2)
assert twoTimes(5) == 10
```

The `twoTimes` closure is a new one that's derived from the `mult` closure by binding the leftmost parameter x. There are also methods to bind the rightmost parameter (rcurry) or the *n*th parameter (ncurry) or do the left binding explicitly (lcurry). But in Groovy it's so easy to literally declare a closure such that currying is used less often than in other functional languages. Here's the literal variant, which is arguably a little less elegant:

```
def twoTimes = { y -> mult 2, y }
```

If you're new to closures or currying, now might be a good time to take a break and re-read the currying discussion. It's a deceptively simple concept to describe mechanically, but it can be quite difficult to internalize. Just take it slowly, and you'll be fine.

The real power of currying comes when the closure's parameters are themselves closures. This is a common construction in functional programming, but it does take a little getting used to.

Suppose you're implementing a logging facility. It should support filtering of log lines, formatting them, and appending them to an output device. Each activity should be configurable. The idea is to provide a single closure for a customized version of each activity, while still allowing you to implement the overall pattern of when to apply a filter, do the formatting, and output the log line in one place. The following listing shows how currying is used to inject the customized activity into that pattern.

```
def configurator = { format, filter, line ->          ❶ Configuration
  filter(line) ?  format(line) : null                     use
}
def appender = { config, append, line ->              ❷ Formatting
  def out = config(line)                                  use
  if (out) append(out)
}
def dateFormatter   = { line -> "${new Date()}: $line" }   ❸ Filter, format,
def debugFilter     = { line -> line.contains('debug') }      and output parts
def consoleAppender = { line -> println line }

def myConf = configurator.curry(dateFormatter, debugFilter)   ❹ Putting it
def myLog  = appender.curry(myConf, consoleAppender)             all together

myLog('here is some debug message')
myLog('this will not be printed')
```

Closures ❶ and ❷ are like recipes: given any filter, output format, destination, and a line to potentially log, they perform the work, delegating appropriately. The short closures in ❸ are the specific ingredients in the recipe. They could be specified every time, but we're always going to use the same ingredients. Currying at ❹ allows us to remember just one object rather than each of the individual parts. To continue the recipe analogy, we've put all the ingredients together, and the result needs to be put in the oven whenever we want to do any logging.

Logging is often dismissed as a dry topic. But, in fact, the few lines in listing 5.8 prove that conception wrong. As a mindful engineer, you know that log statements will be called often, and any logging facility must pay attention to performance. In particular, there should be the least possible performance hit when no log is written.

The time-consuming operations in this example are formatting and printing. Filtering is quick. With the help of closures, we laid out a code pattern that ensures that the expensive operations aren't called for lines that don't need to be printed. The configurator and appender closures implement that pattern.

This pattern is extremely flexible, because the logic of how the filtering works, how the formatting is applied, and how the result is written is fully configurable (even at runtime).

With the help of closures and their curry method, we achieved a solution with the best possible coherence and lowest possible coupling. Note how each of the closures completely addresses exactly *one* concern.

This is the beginning of functional programming. See Andrew Glover's excellent IBM developerWorks online article on functional programming with Groovy closures.[6] It expands on how to use this approach for implementing your own expression language, capturing business rules, and checking your code for holding invariants. Neal Ford's articles at the same site also dive into some more functional thinking concepts using Groovy and other languages.[7]

CLOSURE COMPOSITION

Another cornerstone of functional programming is the ability to work in a compositional way. You may remember from school mathematics that for functions f and g one can write f(g(x)) as the composition of the functions (f . g) (x) where the dot is the composition operator. In Groovy you use the leftShift or the rightShift operator for this purpose, pointing from the inner to the outer closure. You can, for example, compose the twoTimes closure like so:

```
def fourTimes  = twoTimes >> twoTimes
def eightTimes = twoTimes << fourTimes

assert eightTimes(1) == twoTimes(fourTimes(1))
```

[6] "Practically Groovy: Functional programming with curried closures," IBM developerWorks, technical topics, www.ibm.com/developerworks/library/j-pg08235/.
[7] "Functional thinking: Functional features in Groovy, Part 1; Treasures lurking in Groovy, IBM developerWorks, Technical topics, www.ibm.com/developerworks/java/library/j-ft7/.

MEMOIZATION

Closures aren't functions in the mathematical sense. We cannot guarantee[8] that they have no side effects and that they always return the same result when given the same arguments. But programmers may know better and use that knowledge to their advantage.

When you have a closure that's called much too often with the same arguments or the execution of the closure is very expensive, then you may want to cache the results. Groovy closures provide a very simple way to do so with the memoize method. Look how conveniently you can use it for calculating Fibonacci numbers efficiently without interfering with the core logic:

```
def fib
fib = { it < 2 ? 1 : fib(it-1) + fib(it-2) }
fib = fib.memoize()
assert fib(40) == 165_580_141
```

This code takes 0.001 seconds on our machine to execute. Without memoize it takes about 20 seconds!

There are also methods to get more fined-grained control over the cache: memoize-AtMost, memoizeAtLeast, and memoizeBetween. These allow you to set one or both of an upper limit, on the cache size with cache entries ejected on a least recently used (LRU) basis, and a protected minimum limit. Cache entries outside the protected limit are subject to garbage collection, and those below are protected. In section 9.2, you'll also see the @Memoized AST transformation for memoizing *methods*.

JUMPING ON THE TRAMPOLINE

Our fib closure included a recursive call. Such calls can easily lead to a stack overflow, and because the JVM has no tail call elimination, this is difficult to overcome. Groovy offers two approaches. The first follows the trampoline[9] algorithm, and we'll use the respective method for very inefficiently (but *functionally*) finding the last element of anything that has at least a size, a head, and a tail:

```
def last
last = { it.size() == 1 ? it.head() : last.trampoline(it.tail()) }

last = last.trampoline()

assert last(0..10_000) == 10_000
```

Without trampoline, the code goes into a stack overflow before 2,000 iterations. Note that you can use trampoline only for closures that are tail-recursive. For *methods* of that kind you can use Groovy's second weapon against stack overflow, the @TailRecursive AST transformation that we'll encounter in section 9.2.

---

[8] None of the popular JVM languages can give such a guarantee with the notable exception of Frege (www.frege-lang.org). It's a Haskell for the JVM that nicely combines with Groovy.

[9] In computer programming, trampoline has a number of meanings, and is generally associated with jumps (i.e., moving to different code paths); http://en.wikipedia.org/wiki/Trampoline_(computing).

CLASSIFICATION VIA THE ISCASE METHOD

Closures implement the `isCase` method to make them work as classifiers in `grep` and `switch`. In that case, the respective argument is passed into the closure, and calling the closure needs to evaluate to a Groovy Boolean value (see section 6.1) as you see in the following snippet:

```
def odd = { it % 2 == 1 }

assert [1,2,3].grep(odd) == [1, 3]

switch(10) {
    case odd : assert false
}

if (2 in odd) assert false
```

This allows you to classify by arbitrary logic. Again, this is only possible because closures are objects.

REMAINING METHODS

For the sake of completeness, it needs to be said that closures support the `clone` method in the usual Java sense.

The `asWriteable` method returns a clone of the current closure that has an additional `writeTo(Writer)` method to write the result of a closure call directly into the given `Writer`.

Finally, there are a setter and getter for the so-called *delegate*. We'll cross the topic of what a delegate is and how it's used inside a closure when investigating a closure's scoping rules in the next section.

5.5 *Understanding closure scope*

You've seen how to *create* closures when they're needed for a method call and how to work with closures when they're passed to your method. This is very powerful while still simple to use.

This section deepens your understanding of what happens when you use this simple construction. We explore which data and methods you can access from a closure, what difference using the `this` reference makes, and how to put your knowledge to the test with a classic example designed to test any language's expressiveness.

This is a bit of a technical section, and you can safely skip it on first read. But at some point you may want to read it and learn how Groovy can provide all these clever tricks. In fact, knowing the details will enable you to come up with particularly elegant solutions yourself.

By investigating the *scope* of a closure, you'll see

- Which variables are accessible
- When and how variables are bound to a value
- How you can get control over the scoping

We start with an explanation of the behavior that you've seen so far. For that purpose, we revisit a piece of code that does something 10 times:

```
def x = 0
10.times {
    x++
}
assert x == 10
```

It's evident that the closure that's passed into the `times` method can access variable x, which is locally accessible when the closure is declared. Remember: the braces show the *declaration* time of the closure, not the *execution* time. The closure can access x for both reading and writing[10] at declaration time.

This leads to a second thought: the closure surely needs to also access x at execution time. How could it increment it otherwise? But the closure is passed to the `times` method, a method that's called on the `Integer` object with value 10. That method, in turn, calls back to the closure. But the `times` method has no chance of knowing about x. So it cannot pass it to the closure, and it surely has no means of finding out what the closure is doing with it.

The only way in which this can possibly work is if the closure somehow remembers the context of its birth and carries it along throughout its lifetime. That way, it can work on that original context whenever the situation calls for it.

This *birthday context* that the closure remembers needs to be a reference, not a copy. If that context were a copy of the original one, there would be no way of changing the original from inside the closure. But the example clearly changes the value of x—otherwise the assertion would fail. Therefore, the birthday context must be a reference.

5.5.1 Simple variable scope

Figure 5.3 depicts your current understanding of which objects are involved in the `times` example and how they reference each other.

The `Script` creates the `Closure` and is therefore called its *owner*. The closure has a back reference to x, which is in the local scope of its owner. `Script` calls the `times` method on the `Integer` 10 object, passing the declared closure as a parameter. In other words, when `times` is executed, a reference to the closure object lies on the stack. The `times` method uses this reference to execute `Closure`'s call method, passing its local variable count to it. In this specific example, count isn't used within `Closure.call`. Instead, `Closure.call` only works on the x reference that it holds to the local variable x in `Script`.

Through analysis, you see that local variables are bound as *references* to the closure at declaration time.

---

[10] This isn't possible with Java 8 lambdas.

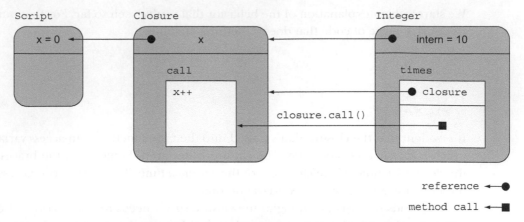

**Figure 5.3 Conceptual view of object references and method calls between a calling script, an
`Integer` object of value `10` that is used in the script, and the closure that is attached to the
`Integer`'s `times` method for defining something that has to be done 10 times**

5.5.2 Inspecting closure scope

It wouldn't be surprising if other scope elements were treated the same as local variables: the value of `this`, fields, methods, and parameters.

This generalization is mostly correct, but the `this` reference is a special case. The Java and Groovy language rule is that any unqualified ("vanilla") `reference` is shorthand for the qualified `this.reference`. Inside a closure, you could legitimately assume `this` would refer to the current object, which is the closure object itself, and thus, all references to the enclosing scope would need to be qualified. This would be very noisy and impractical.

Groovy follows a different strategy, which is quite unique in the landscape of JVM languages: the programmer can control how references are resolved. While you cannot directly set `this` to a different value, you can set a so-called `delegate`, which will be used when resolving free variables. Per default, the `delegate` refers to the `owner`.

If that sounds complicated, don't worry. The effect of this approach is that in the normal case everything works just fine without the need to consider any scoping rules at all, but in special cases, you get an enormous amount of additional flexibility.

Listing 5.9 implements a class `Mother` that should give `birth` to a closure through a method with that name. The class has a property, another method, parameters, and local variables that we can study. The closure should return a list of all elements that are in the current scope. Behind the scenes, these elements will be bound but not evaluated until the closure is called. Let's investigate the result of such a call.

Listing 5.9 Investigating closure scope

```
class Mother {
  def prop = 'prop'
  def method(){ 'method' }
```

```
Closure birth (param) {                          Creation
  def local = 'local'                          ❶ method
  def closure = {
    [ this, prop, method(), local, param ]
  }
  return closure                                    Closure
}                                               ❷ declaration time

Mother julia = new Mother()                         Closure
def closure  = julia.birth('param')            ❸ execution time

def context  = closure.call()                       What "this"
                                               ❹ refers to
assert context[0]    == julia
assert context[1, 2] == ['prop',  'method']         Bound
assert context[3, 4] == ['local', 'param' ]    ❻ variables

assert closure.thisObject == julia
assert closure.owner      == julia             ❼ Read only

assert closure.delegate       == julia
assert closure.resolveStrategy == Closure.OWNER_FIRST  ❽ Scope control
```

Free variables, resolved ❺

We added the optional return type `Closure` to the method declaration ❶ to point out that this method returns a closure object. A method that returns a closure isn't the most common use of closures, but every now and then it comes in handy.

After having constructed a new `Mother`, we call its `birth` method ❷ to retrieve a newly born closure object. Note that we're at *declaration* time of the closure. The list that the closure will return when called doesn't exist yet but local variables are bound as references at this time: `local` and `param`.

Rubber meets the road at ❸. Now we call the closure using the explicit `call` syntax to make it stand out. The closure constructs its list of all resolved references. We store that list in a variable for further inspection.

At ❹ we can see what `this` referred to when the remaining *free* variables `prop` and `method` were resolved such that they have the expected values in ❺. The values of the bound variables `local` and `param` at ❻ should come as no surprise.

At ❼ we ask the closure object itself what it currently uses as `this` and what its `owner` is. While the `thisObject` may change over the lifetime of a closure, the `owner` never does.

While we see at ❽ that the `delegate`, the `owner`, and thus the `thisObject` all refer to the same object, we've finally reached the point where we can exercise control over the scoping. We can, for example, set the delegate to a different object.

The GDK `with` method does exactly that: executing a closure by first setting the delegate to the receiver of the `with` method:

```
def map = [:]
map.with { // delegate is now map
    a = 1  // same as map.a = 1
    b = 2  // same as map.b = 2
}
assert map == [a:1, b:2]
```

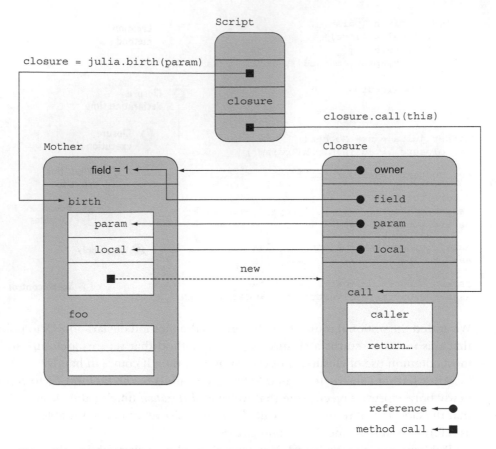

Figure 5.4   Conceptual view of object references and method calls for the general scoping example in listing 5.9, revealing the calls to the `julia` **instance of** `Mother` **for creating a closure that's called in the trailing** `Script` **code to return all values in the current scope.**

The effect is that inside the closure, you don't have to repeat map all the time. This looks like a very small benefit, but it's the mechanism that many other features, such as *Builders* and DSLs, depend on.

Having the local closure scope, the delegate, and the owner raises the question of who is used for resolving references and, in case of conflicts, in which order. This again can be configured by setting the resolveStrategy to OWNER_ONLY, OWNER_FIRST (default), DELEGATE_ONLY, DELEGATE_FIRST, or SELF_ONLY.

Figure 5.4 shows who refers to whom in listing 5.9.

Lectures about scoping rules and closures from other languages such as JavaScript, Lisp, Smalltalk, Perl, Ruby, and Python typically end with mind-boggling examples about variables with identical names, mutually overriding references, and mystic rebirth of supposed-to-be foregone contexts. These examples are like puzzles. They make for an entertaining pastime on a long winter evening, but they have no practical relevance. We'll not provide any of those, because they can easily undermine your carefully built confidence in the scoping rules.

Our intention is to provide a reasonable introduction to Groovy's closures. This should give you the basic understanding that you need when hunting for more complex examples in mailing lists and on the web. Instead of giving a deliberately obscure example, however, we'll provide one that shows how closure scopes can make an otherwise complex task straightforward.

5.5.3 *Scoping at work: the classic accumulator test*

There's a classic example to compare the power of languages by the way they support closures. One of the things it highlights is the power of the scoping rules for those languages as they apply to closures. Paul Graham first proposed this test in his excellent article "Revenge of the Nerds,"[11] which also talks about the difference a language can make. You'll find good arguments in it for switching to Groovy.

In some languages, this test leads to a brain-teasing solution. Not so in Groovy. The Groovy solution is exceptionally obvious and straightforward to achieve.

Here is the original requirement statement:

> We want to write a function that generates accumulators—a function that takes a number n, and returns a function that takes another number i and returns n incremented by i.

The following are proposed solutions for other languages.

In Lisp:

```
(defun foo (n)
   (lambda (i) (incf n i)))
```

In Perl 5:

```
sub foo {
  my ($n) = @_;
  sub {$n += shift}
}
```

In Smalltalk:

```
foo: n
  |s|
  s := n.
  ^[:i| s := s+i. ]
```

---

[11] "The struggle between the pointy-headed academics and the pointy-haired bosses," May 2002; www.paulgraham.com/icad.html.

The following steps lead to a Groovy solution, as shown in listing 5.10:

1   We need a function that returns a closure. In Groovy, we don't have functions, but methods. (Actually, we've not only methods, but also closures. But let's keep it simple.) We use `def` to declare such a method. It has only one line, which after `return` creates a new closure. We'll call this method `foo` to make the solutions comparable in size. The name `createAccumulator` would better reflect the purpose.

2   Our method takes an initial value n as required.

3   Because n is a parameter to the method that *declares* the closure, it gets bound as a reference to the closure scope. We can use it inside the closure body to calculate the incremented value.

4   The incremented value isn't only calculated but also assigned to n as the new value.[12] That way we have a true accumulation.

We add a few assertions to verify our solution and reveal how the accumulator is supposed to be used. The following listing shows the full code.

Listing 5.10   Accumulator problem in Groovy

```
def foo(n) {
    return {n += it}
}

def accumulator =  foo(1)
assert accumulator(2) == 3
assert accumulator(1) == 4
```

All the steps that led to the solution are straightforward applications of what you've learned about closures.

In comparison to the other languages, the Groovy solution is short and surprisingly clear. Groovy has passed this language test exceptionally well.

Is this test of any practical relevance? Maybe not in the sense that we'd ever need an accumulator generator, but it's relevant in a different sense. Passing this test means that the language is able to dynamically put logic in an object and manage the context that this object lives in. This is an indication of how powerful abstractions in that language can be.

5.6   *Returning from closures*

So far, you've seen how to declare closures and how to call them. But there's one crucial topic that we haven't touched yet: how to return from a closure.

---

[12] Remember that n is a reference. Such a construct isn't easily possible with Java 8 lambdas.

In principle, there are two ways of returning:

- The last expression of the closure has been evaluated, and the result of this evaluation is returned. This is called *end return*. Using the `return` keyword in front of the last expression is optional.
- The `return` keyword can also be used to return from the closure prematurely.

This means the following ways of doubling the entries of a list have the very same effect:

```
[1, 2, 3].collect{ it * 2 }
[1, 2, 3].collect{ return it * 2 }
```

A premature return can be used to, for example, double only the even entries:

```
[1, 2, 3].collect{
    if (it%2 == 0) return it * 2
    return it
}
```

This behavior of the `return` keyword inside closures is simple and straightforward. You hardly expect any misconceptions, but there's something to be aware of.

WARNING! There's a difference between using the `return` keyword inside and outside of a closure.

Outside a closure, any occurrence of `return` leaves the current method. When used inside a closure, it only ends the current evaluation of the closure, which is a much more localized effect. For example, when using `List.each`, returning early from the closure doesn't return early from the `each` method—the closure will still be called again with the next element in the list.

While progressing further into the book, we'll hit on this issue again and explore more ways of dealing with it.

5.7　*Support for design patterns*

Design patterns are widely used by developers to enhance the quality of their designs. Each design pattern presents a typical problem that occurs in OOP along with a corresponding well-tested solution. Let's take a closer look at the way the availability of closures affects how, which, and when patterns are used.

If you've never seen design patterns, we suggest you look at the classic *Design Patterns: Elements of Reusable Object-Oriented Software* by Gamma et al. (Addison-Wesley, 1994), or one of the more recent ones such as *Head First Design Patterns* by Freeman et al. (O'Reilly Media, 2004) or *Refactoring to Patterns* by Joshua Kerievsky (Addison-Wesley, 2004). Or, search for "patterns repository" or "patterns catalog" using your favorite search engine.

Although many design patterns are broadly applicable and apply to any language, some are particularly well suited to solving issues that occur when using programming languages like C++ and Java. They most often involve implementing new abstractions and new classes to make the original programs more flexible or maintainable. With Groovy, some of the restrictions that face C++ and Java don't apply, and the design patterns are either of less value or more directly supported using language features rather than introducing new classes. We pick two examples to show the difference: the *Visitor* and *Builder* patterns. As you'll see, closures and dynamic typing are the key differentiators in Groovy that facilitate easier pattern usage.

5.7.1   *Relationship to the Visitor pattern*

The Visitor pattern is particularly useful when you wish to perform complex business functionality on a composite collection (such as a tree or list) of existing simple classes. Rather than altering the existing simple classes to contain the desired business functionality, a `Visitor` class is introduced. `Visitor` knows how to traverse the composite collection and how to perform the business functionality for different kinds of a simple class. If the composite changes or the business functionality changes over time, typically only the `Visitor` class is impacted.

Listing 5.11 shows how simple the Visitor pattern can look in Groovy; the composite traversal code is in the `accept` method of the `Drawing` class, whereas the business functionality (in our case, to perform calculations involving shape area) is contained in two closures that are passed as parameters to the appropriate `accept` methods. There's no need for a separate `Visitor` class in this simple case.

Listing 5.11   Visitor pattern in Groovy

```
class Drawing {
    List shapes
    def accept(Closure yield) { shapes.each{it.accept(yield)} }
}
class Shape {
    def accept(Closure yield) { yield(this) }
}
class Square extends Shape {
    def width
    def area() { width**2 }
}
class Circle extends Shape {
    def radius
    def area() { Math.PI * radius**2 }
}

def picture = new Drawing(shapes:
    [new Square(width:1), new Circle(radius:1)] )

def total = 0
picture.accept { total += it.area() }
println "The shapes in this drawing cover an area of $total units."
println 'The individual contributions are: '
picture.accept { println it.class.name + ":" + it.area() }
```

Running this code will print to the console:

```
The shapes in this drawing cover an area of 4.141592653589793 units.
The individual contributions are:
Square:1
Circle:3.141592653589793
```

5.7.2 *Relationship to the Builder pattern*

The Builder pattern serves to encapsulate the logic associated with constructing a product from its constituent parts. When using the Builder pattern, you normally create a `Builder` class, which contains logic determining which builder methods to call and in which sequence to call them to ensure proper assembly of the product. For each product, you must supply the appropriate logic for each relevant builder method used by the `Builder` class; each builder method typically returns one of the constituent parts.

Coding Java solutions based on the Builder pattern isn't hard, but the Java code tends to be cumbersome and verbose and doesn't highlight the structure of the assembled product. For that reason, the Builder pattern is rarely used in Java; instead, developers use unstructured or replicated builder-type logic mixed in with their other code. This is a shame, because the Builder pattern is so powerful.

Groovy's builders provide a solution using nested closures to conveniently specify even very complex products. Such a specification is easy to read, because the appearance of the code reflects the product structure. Groovy has built-in library classes based on the Builder pattern that allow you to easily build arbitrarily nested node structures, produce markup like HTML or XML, define GUIs in Swing or other widget toolkits, and even access the wide range of functionality in Ant. You'll see lots of examples in chapter 11, and we'll explain how to write your own builders in section 11.9.

5.7.3 *Relationship to other patterns*

Almost all patterns are easier to implement in Groovy than in Java. This is often because Groovy supports more lightweight solutions that make the patterns less of a necessity—mostly because of closures and dynamic typing. In addition, when patterns are required, Groovy often makes expressing them more succinct and simpler to set up.

We discuss a number of patterns elsewhere in this book, such as Strategy (see sections 8.3.3 and 12.1.3), Observer (see section 11.8.2), and Builder (see chapters 11 and 14), which benefit from using closures instead of implementing new classes. Patterns such as Adapter (associated with mixins; see section 8.4.8) and Decorator (see section 13.1.2) benefit from dynamic typing and method lookup. We also briefly discuss patterns such as Template Method (see section 5.2.2) and Value Object (see section 3.3.2), the "incomplete library class" smell (see chapter 8), the Model View Controller pattern (see section 11.6.6), and the Data Transfer Object and Data Access Object patterns (see chapter 13). Just by existing, closures can completely replace the Method Object pattern.

Groovy provides plenty of support for using patterns within your own programs. Its libraries embody pattern practices throughout. Higher-level frameworks such as Grails take it one step further. Grails provides you with a framework built on top of Groovy's libraries and patterns support. Using such frameworks saves you from having to deal with many pattern issues directly by taking advantage of the framework you'll automatically end up using patterns without needing to understand the details in most cases. Even then, it's useful to know about some of the patterns we've touched on so that you can leverage the maximum benefit from whichever frameworks you use.

5.8   *Summary*

You've seen that closures follow our theme of *everything is an object.* They capture a piece of logic, making it possible to pass it around for execution, return it from a method call, or store it for later use.

Closures encourage centralized resource handling, thus making your code more reliable. This doesn't come at any expense. In fact, the codebase is relieved from structural duplication, enhancing expressiveness and maintainability.

Defining and using closures is surprisingly simple because all the difficult tasks, such as keeping track of references and relaying method calls back to the delegating owner, are done transparently. If you don't care about the scoping rules, everything falls into place naturally. If you want to hook into the mechanics and perform tasks such as deviating the calls to the delegate, you can. Of course, such an advanced use needs more care. You also need to be careful when returning from a delegate, particularly when using one in a situation where in other languages you might use a for loop or a similar construct. This has surprised more than one new Groovy developer, although the behavior is logical when examined closely. Re-read section 5.6 when in doubt.

Closures open the door to several ways of doing things that may be new to many developers. Some of these, such as currying, can appear daunting at first sight but allow a great deal of power to be wielded with remarkably little code. Additionally, closures can make familiar design patterns simpler to use or even unnecessary.

Although you now have a good understanding of Groovy's datatypes and closures, you still need a means to control the flow of execution through your program. This is achieved with control structures, which form the topic of the next chapter.

Groovy control structures

The pursuit of truth and beauty is a sphere of activity in which we are permitted to remain children all our lives.

—Albert Einstein

At the hardware level, computer systems use simple arithmetic and logical operations, such as jumping to a new location if a memory value equals zero. Any complex flow of logic that a computer is executing can always be expressed in terms of these simple operations. Fortunately, languages like Java raise the abstraction level available in programs you write so that you can express the flow of logic in terms of higher-level constructs—for example, looping through all of the elements in an array or processing characters until you reach the end of a file.

In this chapter, we explore the constructs Groovy provides to describe logic flow in ways that are even simpler and more expressive than Java. Before we look at the

145

constructs themselves, however, we have to examine Groovy's answer to that age-old philosophical question: What is truth?[1]

6.1   Groovy truth

To understand how Groovy handles control structures such as `if` and `while`, you need to know how it evaluates expressions, which need to have Boolean results. Many of the control structures we examine in this chapter rely on the result of a *Boolean test*—an expression that's first evaluated and then considered as being either `true` or `false`. The outcome of this affects which path is then followed in the code. In Java, the consideration involved is usually trivial, because Java requires the expression to be one resulting in the primitive `boolean` type to start with. Groovy is more relaxed about this, allowing simpler code at the slight expense of language simplicity. We'll examine Groovy's rules for Boolean tests and give some advice to avoid falling into an age-old trap.

6.1.1   Evaluating Boolean tests

The expression of a Boolean test can be of any (nonvoid) type. It can apply to any object. Groovy decides whether to consider the expression as being `true` or `false` by applying the rules shown in table 6.1, based on the result's runtime type. The rules are applied in the order given, and once a rule matches, it completely determines the result.[2]

Table 6.1   Sequence of rules used to evaluate a Boolean test

Runtime type	Evaluation criterion required for truth
Boolean	Corresponding Boolean value is `true`
Matcher	Matcher has a match
Collection	Collection is nonempty
Map	Map is nonempty
String, GString	String is nonempty
Number, Character	Value is nonzero
None of the above	Object reference is non-null

The following listing shows these rules in action, using the Boolean negation operator `!` to assert that expressions that ought to evaluate to `false` really do so.

---

[1] Groovy has no opinion as to what beauty is. We're sure that if it did, however, it would involve expressive minimalism. Closures too, probably.

[2] It would be rare to encounter a situation where more than one rule matched, but you never know when someone will subclass `java.lang.Number` and implement `java.util.Map` at the same time.

Listing 6.1   Example Boolean test evaluations

```
assert true                          Boolean values
assert !false                        are trivial

assert ('a' =~ /./)                  Matchers
assert !('a' =~ /b/)                 must match

assert [1]                           Collections must
assert ![]                           be nonempty

Iterator iter = [1].iterator()
assert iter
iter.next()                          Iterators must have
assert !iter                         next element

assert ['a':1]                       Maps must be
assert ![:]                          nonempty

assert 'a'                           Strings must be
assert !''                           nonempty

assert 1
assert 1.1
assert 1.2f                          Numbers
assert 1.3g                          (any type)
assert 2L                            must be
assert 3G                            nonzero
assert !0

assert ! null                       Objects must
assert new Object()                 be non-null

class AlwaysFalse {
    boolean asBoolean() { false }    ◁── Custom truth
}
assert ! new AlwaysFalse()          ◁── Calls asBoolean()
```

These rules can make testing for "truth" simpler and easier to read. But they come with a price, as you're about to find out.

6.1.2   *Assignments within Boolean tests*

Before we get into the meat of the chapter, we have a warning to point out. Just like Java, Groovy allows the expression used for a Boolean test to be an assignment—and the value of an assignment expression is the value assigned. Unlike Java, the type of a Boolean test isn't restricted to `booleans`, which means that a problem you might have thought was ancient history reappears, albeit in an alleviated manner. Namely, an equality operator == incorrectly entered as an assignment operator = is valid code with a drastically different effect than the intended one. Groovy shields you from falling into this trap for the most common appearance of this error: when it's used as a top-level expression in an `if` statement. But it can still arise in less usual cases.

The following listing leads you through some typical variations of this topic.

Listing 6.2   What happens when == is mistyped as =

```
def x = 1

if (x == 2) {
    assert false
}
/*******************
if (x =  2) {
    println x
}
*******************/
if ((x = 3)) {
    println x
}
assert x == 3

def store = []
while (x = x - 1) {
    store << x
}
assert store == [2, 1]

while (x =  2) {
    println x
    break
}
```

❶ Normal comparison

❷ Not allowed; compiler error

❸ Assigns and tests in nested expression

❹ Deliberate assign and test in while

❺ Ouch—this will print 2

The equality comparison ❶ is fine and would be allowable in Java. In ❷, an equality comparison was intended, but one of the equal signs was left out. This raises a Groovy compiler error, because an assignment isn't allowed as a top-level expression in an if test.

Boolean tests can be nested inside expressions in arbitrary depth; the simplest one is shown at ❸, where extra parentheses around the assignment make it a subexpression, and therefore the assignment becomes compliant with the Groovy language. The value 3 will be assigned to x, and x will be tested for truth. Because 3 is considered true, the value 3 gets printed. This use of parentheses to please the compiler can even be used as a trick to spare an extra line of assignment. The unusual appearance of the extra parentheses then serves as a warning sign for the reader.

The restriction of assignments from being used in top-level Boolean expressions applies only to if and not to other control structures such as while. Doing assignment and testing in one expression are often used with while in the style shown at ❹. This style tends to appear with classic uses like processing tokens retrieved from a parser or reading data from a stream. Although this is convenient, it leaves us with the potential coding pitfall shown at ❺, where x is assigned the value 2 and the loop would never stop if there weren't a break statement.[3]

---

[3] Remember that the code in this book has been executed. If we didn't have the break statement, the book would have taken literally forever to produce.

This potential cause of bugs has given rise to the idiom in other languages (such as C and C++, which suffer from the same problem to a worse degree) of putting constants on the left side of the equality operator when you wish to perform a comparison with one. Such a construct is sometimes called a "Yoda conditional" since in the Star Wars motion picture the Yoda character talks in this swapped fashion like "difficult to see the future is." Following this style the last `while` statement in the previous listing (still with a typo) becomes

```
while (1 =  x) {                    ⟵⟍   Should
    println x                            be ==
}
```

This would raise an error, as you can't assign a value to a constant. We're back to safety—so long as constants are involved. Unfortunately, not only does this fail when both sides of the comparison are variables, it also reduces readability. Whether it's a natural occurrence, a quirk of human languages, or conditioning, most people find `while (x==3)` significantly simpler to read than `while (3==x)`. Although neither is going to cause confusion, the latter tends to slow people down or interrupt their train of thought. In this book, we've favored readability over safety—but our situation is somewhat different than that of normal development. You'll have to decide for yourself which convention suits you and your team better.

Now that we've examined which expressions Groovy will consider to be `true` and `false`, we can start looking at the control structures themselves.

6.2   *Conditional execution structures*

Our first set of control structures deals with conditional execution. They all evaluate a Boolean test and make a choice about what to do next based on whether the result was `true` or `false`. None of these structures should come as a new experience to any Java developer, but, of course, Groovy adds twists of its own. We'll cover `if` statements, the conditional operator, `switch` statements, and assertions.

6.2.1   *The humble if statement*

Our first two structures act *exactly* the same way in Groovy as they do in Java, apart from the evaluation of the Boolean test itself. We start with `if` and `if else` statements.

Just as in Java, the Boolean test expression must be enclosed in parentheses. The conditional block is normally enclosed in curly braces. These braces are optional if the block consists of only one statement.[4]

A special application of the "no braces needed for single statements" rule is the sequential use of `else if`. In this case, the logical indentation of the code is often

---

[4] Even though the braces are optional, many coding conventions insist on them to avoid errors that can occur through careless modification when they're not used.

flattened—that is, all `else` `if` lines have the same indentation although their meaning is nested. The indentation makes no difference to Groovy and is only of aesthetic relevance.

Listing 6.3 gives some examples, using `assert true` to show the blocks of code that will be executed, and `assert false` to show the blocks that won't be.

There should be no surprises in the listing, although it might still look slightly odd to you that non-Boolean expressions such as strings and lists can be used for Boolean tests. Don't worry—it becomes natural over time.

Listing 6.3   The `if` statement in action

```
if (true)      assert true
else           assert false
if (1) {
    assert true
} else {
    assert false
}
if ('nonempty') assert true
else if (['x']) assert false
else            assert false
if (0)          assert false
else if ([])    assert false
else            assert true
```

6.2.2 *The conditional ?: operator and Elvis*

Groovy also supports the ternary conditional operator `?:` for small inline tests, as shown in listing 6.4. This operator returns the object that results from evaluating the expression left or right of the colon, depending on the test before the question mark. If the first expression evaluates to `true`, the middle expression is evaluated. Otherwise, the last expression is evaluated. Just as in Java, whichever of the last two expressions isn't used as the result isn't evaluated.

Listing 6.4   The conditional operator

```
def result = (1==1) ? 'ok' : 'failed'
assert result == 'ok'
result = 'some string' ? 10 : ['x']
assert result == 10
```

Again, notice how the Boolean test (the first expression) can be of any type. Also note that because everything is an object in Groovy, the middle and last expressions can be of radically different types.

Groovy comes with another interesting shortcut for the case that the test expression is to be used as the result value when `true`. Consider this piece of code:

```
def argument = "given"
def standard = "default"
def result   = argument ? argument : standard
```

Groovy allows you to abbreviate the third line as

```
def value = argument ?: standard
```

Not only is this version shorter but it also evaluates the argument only once. When reading the ?: operator like an emoticon you can guess why we call it the *Elvis operator*.

Opinions about the ternary conditional operator vary wildly. Some people find it extremely convenient and use it often. Others find it too Perl-ish. You may well find that you use it less often in Groovy because there are features that make its typical applications obsolete—for example, GStrings (covered in section 3.4.2) allow dynamic creation of strings that would be constructed in Java using the ternary operator.

So far, so Java-like. Things change significantly when we consider switch statements.

6.2.3   *The switch statement and the in operator*

On a recent train ride, I (Dierk) spoke with a teammate about Groovy, mentioning the oh-so-cool switch capabilities. He wouldn't even let me get started, waving his hands and saying, "I never use switch!" I was put off at first, because I lost my momentum in the discussion; but after more thought, I agreed that I don't use it either—*in Java*.

The switch statement in Java is quite restrictive. Originally you could only switch on an int type, with byte, char, and short automatically being promoted to int. As of Java 5, enum types can also be switched on, due to some compiler trickery, and as of Java 7, additional trickery with string hash codes lets you use strings too. But even with these extensions, it's still restrictive. Its applicability is bound to either low-level tasks or some kind of dispatching on a *type code*. In object-oriented languages, the use of type codes is considered smelly.[5]

THE SWITCH STRUCTURE

The general appearance of the switch construct, shown in the following listing, is just like in Java, and its logic is identical in the sense that the handling logic falls through to the next case unless it's exited explicitly. We'll explore exiting options in section 6.4.

> **Listing 6.5   General switch appearance is like Java or C**

```
def a = 1
def log = ''
switch (a) {
    case 0  : log += '0'
    case 1  : log += '1'                     Fall through
    case 2  : log += '2' ; break
    default : log += 'default'
}
assert log == '12'
```

---

[5]   See "Replace Conditional with Polymorphism" in chapter 9 of *Refactoring* by Martin Fowler (Addison-Wesley, 2000).

Although the *fall through* is supported in Groovy, there are few cases where this feature really enhances the readability of the code. It usually does more harm than good (this applies to Java, too). As a general rule, putting a break at the end of each case is good style.

SWITCH WITH CLASSIFIERS

You've seen the Groovy `switch` used for classification in section 3.5.5 and when working through the datatypes. A *classifier* is eligible as a `switch` case if it implements the `isCase` method. In other words, a Groovy `switch` like

```
switch (candidate) {
    case classifier1   : handle1()        ; break
    case classifier2   : handle2()        ; break
    default            : handleDefault()
}
```

is roughly equivalent (besides the fall through and exit handling) to

```
if       (classifier1.isCase(candidate)) handle1()
else if (classifier2.isCase(candidate)) handle2()
else      handleDefault()
```

This allows expressive classifications and even some unconventional uses with mixed classifiers. Unlike Java's constant cases, the candidate may match more than one classifier. This means that the order of cases is important in Groovy, whereas it doesn't affect behavior in Java. The next listing gives an example of multiple types of classifiers. After having checked that our number 10 isn't zero, isn't in range 0..9, isn't in list [8,9,11], isn't of type `Float`, and isn't an integral multiple of 3, we finally find it to be made of two characters.

Listing 6.6   Advanced `switch` and mixed classifiers

```
switch (10) {
    case 0            : assert false ; break
    case 0..9         : assert false ; break        ❶ Type case
    case [8,9,11]     : assert false ; break
    case Float        : assert false ; break        ❷ Closure case
    case {it%3 == 0}: assert false ; break
    case ~/../        : assert true  ; break         ❸ Regular
    default           : assert false ; break            expression case
}
```

The new feature ❶ is that we can classify by type. `Float` is of type `java.lang.Class`, and the GDK enhances `Class` by adding an `isCase` method that tests the candidate with `isInstance`.

The `isCase` method on closures ❷ passes the candidate into the closure and returns the result of the closure call coerced to a `Boolean`.

The final classification ❸ as a two-digit number works because `~/../` is a `Pattern` and the `isCase` method on patterns applies its test to the `toString` value of the argument.

To leverage the power of the `switch` construct, it's essential to know the available `isCase` implementations. It's not possible to provide an exhaustive list, because any custom type in your code or in a library can implement it. Table 6.2 has the list of known implementations in the GDK.

Table 6.2 Standard implementations of `isCase` **for** `switch`, `grep`, **and** `in`

Class	`a.isCase(b)` implemented as
Object	`a.equals(b)`
Class	`a.isInstance(b)`
Collection	`a.contains(b)`
Range	`a.contains(b)`
Pattern	`a.matcher(b.toString()).matches()`
String	`(a==null && b==null) || a.equals(b)`
Closure	`a.call(b)`

NOTE The `isCase` method is also used with `grep` on collections such that *collection*.grep(*classifier*) returns a collection of all items that are a case of that classifier.

THE IN OPERATOR

The `isCase` logic is actually used three times: for `switch` cases for `grep` classification and for the `in` operator as used for conditionals like the following assertion:

```
def okValues = [1, 2, 3]
def value    = 2
assert value in okValues
```

Using the Groovy `switch` in the sense of a classifier is a big step forward. It adds much to the readability of the code. The reader sees a simple classification instead of a tangled, nested construction of `if` statements. Again, you're able to reveal *what* the code does rather than *how* it does it.

As pointed out in section 4.1.2, the `switch` classification on ranges is particularly convenient for modeling business rules that tend to prefer discrete classification to continuous functions. The resulting code reads almost like a specification.

Look actively through your code for places to implement `isCase`. A characteristic sign of looming classifiers is lengthy `else if` constructions.

> **Advanced topic**
>
> It's possible to overload the `isCase` method to support different kinds of classification logic depending on the candidate type. If you provide both methods, `isCase(String candidate)` and `isCase(Integer candidate)`, then `switch('1')` can behave differently than `switch(1)` with your object as the classifier.

Our next topic, *assertions,* may not look particularly important at first glance. But although assertions don't change the business capabilities of the code, they do make the code more robust in production. Moreover, they do something even better: enhance the development team's confidence in their code, as well as their ability to remain agile during additional enhancements and ongoing maintenance.

6.2.4 Sanity checking with assertions

This book contains several hundred assertion statements—and indeed, you've already seen a number of them. Now it's time to go into extra detail. We'll look at producing meaningful error messages from failed assertions, reflect over reasonable uses of this keyword, and show how to use it for inline unit tests. We'll also quickly compare the Groovy solution to Java's `assert` keyword and assertions as used in unit test cases.

PRODUCING INFORMATIVE FAILURE MESSAGES

When an assertion fails, it produces a stack trace and a message. Put the code

```
a = 1
assert a==2
```

in a file called FailingAssert.groovy, and let it run via

```
> groovy FailingAssert.groovy
```

It's expected to fail, and it does so with the message

```
Assertion failed:

assert a==2
       ||
       |false
       1
       at FailingAssert.run(FailingAssert.groovy:2)
       at FailingAssert.main(FailingAssert.groovy)
```

You see that on failure, the assertion prints out the failed expression and the value of all subexpressions plus the stack trace.

This is a lot of information, and it's sufficient to locate and understand the error in most cases, but not always. Let's try another example that tries to protect a file reading code from being executed if the file doesn't exist or cannot be read (Perl programmers will see the analogy to `or die`):

```
input = new File('no such file')
assert  input.exists()
assert  input.canRead()
println input.text
```

This produces the output

```
Caught: java.lang.AssertionError: Expression: input.exists()
   ...
```

which isn't very informative. The missing information here is what the bad filename was. To this end, assertions can be instrumented with a trailing message:

```
input = new File('no such file')
assert input.exists()  , "cannot find '$input.name'"
assert input.canRead() , "cannot read '$input.canonicalPath'"
println input.text
```

This produces the following:

```
... cannot find 'no such file'. Expression: input.exists()
```

which is the information we need. But this special case also reveals the sometimes unnecessary use of assertions, because in this case we could easily leave the assertions out:

```
input = new File('no such file')
println input.text
```

The result is the following sufficient error message:

```
FileNotFoundException: no such file (The system cannot find the file
specified)
```

This leads to the following best practices with assertions:

- Before writing an assertion, let your code fail, and see whether any other thrown exception is good enough.
- When writing an assertion, let it fail the first time, and see whether the failure message is sufficient. If not, add a message. Let it fail again to verify that the message is now good enough.
- If you feel you need an assertion to clarify or protect your code, add it regardless of the previous rules.
- If you feel you need a message to clarify the meaning or purpose of your assertion, add it regardless of the previous rules.

ENSURE CODE WITH INLINE UNIT TESTS

Finally, there's a potentially controversial use of assertions as unit tests that lives right inside production code and gets executed with it. The following listing shows this strategy with a nontrivial regular expression that extracts a hostname from a URL. The pattern is first constructed and then applied to some assertions before being put to action. We also implement a simple method `assertHost` for easy asserting of a match grouping.[6]

---

[6] Please note that we use regexes here only to show the value of assertions. If we really set out to find the hostname of a URL, we'd use `candidate.toURL().host`.

Listing 6.7　Using assertions for inline unit tests

```
def host = /\/\/([a-zA-Z0-9-]+(\.[a-zA-Z0-9-])*?)(:|\/)/          ◁┐ Regular
                                                                     │ expression
assertHost 'http://a.b.c:8080/bla',     host, 'a.b.c'                │ matching host
assertHost 'http://a.b.c/bla',          host, 'a.b.c'
assertHost 'http://127.0.0.1:8080/bla', host, '127.0.0.1'
assertHost 'http://t-online.de/bla',    host, 't-online.de'
assertHost 'http://T-online.de/bla',    host, 'T-online.de'

def assertHost (candidate, regex, expected){
    candidate.eachMatch(regex){ assert it[1] == expected
}
                                                            ┌ Trailing code
// ... use host regex ...                               ◁──┘ goes here
```

Imagine finding a Groovy script such as this sitting on a production filesystem and let's assume you want to understand it. If you're very lucky, the script might be under version control and have a test harness that's run against it regularly. But if that isn't the case, or if the preceding example assertions were perhaps included as comments, then a reader of the script cannot *really* be sure that it works as expected. In such circumstances, the value of inline assertions becomes obvious.

Some may fear a bad impact on performance when doing this style of inline unit tests. The best answer is to use a profiler and investigate where performance is really relevant. Our assertions in listing 6.7 run in a few milliseconds and shouldn't normally be an issue. When performance is important, one possibility would be to put inline unit tests where they're executed only once per loaded class: in a static initializer. You'll need to decide for yourself whether inline unit tests suit your scenarios, but we strongly recommend them as a technique to keep in mind and apply on a case-by-case basis.

RELATIONSHIPS TO OTHER ASSERTIONS

Java has had an `assert` keyword since JDK 1.4. It differs from Groovy assertions in that it has a slightly different syntax (a colon instead of a comma to separate the Boolean test from the message) and it can be enabled and disabled. Java's assertion feature isn't as powerful, because it works only on a Java Boolean test, whereas the Groovy `assert` keyword takes a full Groovy conditional (see section 6.1).

The JDK documentation has a long chapter on assertions that discusses the disabling feature for assertions and its impact on compiling, starting the virtual machine, and resulting design issues. Although this is fine and the design rationale behind Java assertions is clear, we feel the disabling feature is the biggest stumbling block for using assertions in Java. You can never be sure that your assertions are really executed.

Some people claim that for performance reasons, assertions should be disabled in production, after the code has been tested with assertions enabled. On this issue, Bertrand Meyer,[7] the father of *design by contract*, pointed out that it's like learning to

---

[7]　See *Object-Oriented Software Construction*, 2nd ed., by Bertrand Meyer (Prentice-Hall, 1997).

swim with a swimming belt and taking it off when leaving the pool and getting in the ocean. In Groovy, your assertions are always executed.

Assertions also play a central role in unit tests. Groovy comes with a bundled version of JUnit, the leading unit test framework for Java. JUnit makes a lot of specialized assertions available to its `TestCases`. Groovy adds even more of them, as you'll see in chapter 17. The information that Groovy provides when assertions fail makes them very convenient when writing unit tests, because it relieves the tester from writing lots of messages.

Assertions can make a big difference to your personal programming style and even more to the culture of a development team, regardless of whether they're used inline or in separate unit tests. Asserting your assumptions not only makes your code more reliable, it also makes it easier to understand and easier to work with.

That's it for conditional execution structures. They're the basis for any kind of logical branching and a prerequisite to allow looping—the language feature that makes your computer do all the repetitive work for you. The next two sections cover the looping structures `while` and `for`.

6.3 Looping

The structures you've seen so far have evaluated a Boolean test *once* and changed the path of execution once based on the result of the condition. Looping, on the other hand, repeats the execution of a block of code multiple times. The loops available in Groovy are `while` and `for`, both of which we cover here.

6.3.1 Looping with while

The `while` construct is like its Java counterpart. The only difference is the one you've seen already—the power of Groovy Boolean test expressions. To summarize, the Boolean test is evaluated, and if it's `true`, the body of the loop is then executed. The test is then reevaluated, and so forth. Only when the test becomes `false` does control proceed past the `while` loop. The next listing shows an example that removes all entries from a list. We visited this problem in chapter 3, where you discovered that you can't use each for that purpose. The second example adds the values again in a one-liner body without the optional braces.

Listing 6.8 Example `while` loops

```
def list = [1,2,3]
while (list) {
    list.remove(0)
}
assert list == []

while (list.size() < 3) list << list.size()+1
assert list == [1,2,3]
```

Again, there should be no surprises in this code, with the exception of using just `list` as the Boolean test in the first loop.

Note that there are no do {} while (condition) or repeat {} until (condition) loops in Groovy. Of course with closures you could write your own *do-while* or *repeat-until* control structures with only some minor restrictions and differences compared to a language-supported equivalent. We discuss some of these differences in the next section. In chapter 19, we look at a WhenUntilTransform which even removes some of the limitations.

6.3.2 *Looping with for*

Considering it's probably the most commonly used type of loop, the traditional for loop in Java is relatively hard to use, when you examine it closely. Through familiarity, people who have used a language with a similar structure (and there are many such languages) grow to find it easy to use, but that is solely due to frequent use, not to good design. Although the nature of the traditional for loop is powerful, it's rarely used in a way that can't be more simply expressed in terms of iterating through a collection-like data structure. Although supporting most forms of the for loop that Java supports, Groovy embraces this simplicity and strongly encourages for loops following this structure:

```
for (variable in iterable) { body }
```

where variable may optionally have a declared type. The Groovy for loop iterates over iterable. Frequently used iterables are ranges, collections, maps, arrays, iterators, and enumerations. In fact, any object can be an iterable. Groovy applies the same logic as for *object iteration*, described in chapter 12.

Braces around the *body* are optional if it consists of only one statement. The following listing shows some of the possible combinations.

Listing 6.9 Multiple for loop examples

```
def store = ''
for (String s in 'a'..'c') store += s          ❶ Explicit typing,
assert store == 'abc'                             over string range,
                                                  no braces

store = ''
for (i in [1, 2, 3]) {                         ❷ Implicit typing,
    store += i                                    over list as
}                                                 collection, braces
assert store == '123'

def myString = 'Old school Java'
store = ''                                     ❸ Explicit typing,
for (int i=0; i < myString.size(); i++) {         Java-style
    store += myString[i]                          traditional for
}                                                 loop, braces
assert store == myString

myString = 'Java range index'
store = ''                                     ❹ Explicit typing,
for (int i : 0 ..< myString.size()) {             Java-style
    store += myString[i]                          iterable index,
}                                                 braces
assert store == myString
```

```
myString = 'Groovy range index'
store = ''
for (i in 0 ..< myString.size()) {
    store += myString[i]
}
assert store == myString
```

5 **Implicit typing, over half-exclusive IntRange, braces**

```
myString = 'Java string Iterable'
store = ''
for (String s : myString) {
    store += s
}
assert store == myString
```

6 **Explicit typing, Java-style iterable value, braces**

```
myString = 'Groovy iterator'
store = ''
for (s in myString) {
    store += s
}
assert store == myString
```

7 **Implicit typing, over string as collection, braces**

The first example ❶ uses explicit typing for s and no braces with a loop body of a single statement. The looping is done on a range of strings.

   The usual for loop appearance when working on a collection is shown in ❷. Recall that thanks to *autoboxing*, this also works for arrays.

   Groovy also supports Java for loops style ❸ and the more recent iterable variants either on the index ❹ or the string value itself ❻.

   Looping on a half-exclusive integer range ❺ is a slight improvement over the traditional Java for loop style ❸ or an equivalent to the Java iterable index style ❹.

   The final example ❼ illustrates the typical Groovy style recommended when working on strings. It's more Groovy to treat a string as a collection of characters.

   Using the for loop with object iteration as described in section 12.1.3 provides some very powerful combinations. You can use it to print a file line-by-line via

```
def file = new File('myFileName.txt')
for (line in file) println line
```

or to print all one-digit matches of a regular expression:

```
def matcher = '12xy3'=~/\d/
for (match in matcher) println match
```

If the container object is null, no iteration will occur:

```
for (x in null) println 'This will not be printed!'
```

If Groovy cannot make the container object iterable by any means, the fallback solution is to do an iteration that contains only the container object itself:

```
for (x in new Object()) println "Printed once for object $x"
```

Object iteration makes the Groovy for loop a sophisticated control structure. It's a valid counterpart to using methods that iterate over an object with closures, such as using Collection's each method.

The main difference is that the body of a for loop isn't a closure! That means this body is a block:

```
for (x in 0..9) { println x }
```

whereas this body is a closure:

```
(0..9).each { println it }
```

Even though they look similar, they're very different in construction.

A closure is an object of its own and has all the features that you saw in chapter 5. It can be constructed in a different place and passed to the each method. The body of the for loop, in contrast, is directly generated as bytecode at its point of appearance. No special scoping rules apply.

This distinction is even more important when it comes to managing exit handling from the body. The next section shows why.

6.4   Exiting blocks and methods

Although it's nice to have code that reads as a simple list of instructions with no jumping around, it's often vital that control is passed from the current block or method to the enclosing block or calling method—or sometimes even further up the call stack. Just like in Java, Groovy allows this to happen in an expected, orderly fashion with return, break, and continue statements, and in emergency situations with exceptions. Let's take a closer look.

6.4.1   Normal termination: return/break/continue

The general logic of return, break, and continue is similar to Java. One difference is the return keyword is optional for the last expression in a method or closure. If it's omitted, the return value is that of the last expression. Methods with explicit return type void don't return a value; closures always return a value.[8]

The following listing shows how the current loop is cut short with continue and prematurely ended with break. Like Java, there's an optional label.

> **Listing 6.10   Simple break and continue**

```
def a = 1
while (true) {          ⟵──── Do forever
    a++
    break               ⟵─┐  Forever is
}                         │  over now
assert a == 2
```

---

[8]   But what if the last evaluated expression of a closure is a void method call? In this case, the closure returns null.

```
for (i in 0..10) {
    if (i == 0)  continue    ◄──── Proceed with 1
    a++
    if (i > 0) break        ◄─┐ Premature
}                             │ loop end
assert a == 3
```

In classic programming style, the use of break and continue is sometimes considered smelly. But it can be useful for controlling the workflow in services that run in an endless loop. Similarly, returning from multiple points in the method is frowned upon in some circles, but other people find it can greatly increase the readability of methods that might be able to return a result early. We encourage you to figure out what you find most readable and discuss it with whoever else is going to be reading your code—consistency is as important as anything else.

As a final note on return handling, remember that closures, when used with iteration methods like each, have a different meaning of return than the control structures while and for, as explained in section 5.6.

6.4.2 Exceptions: throw/try-catch-finally

Exception handling in Groovy is similar to Java and follows the same logic. Just as in Java, you can specify a complete try-catch-finally sequence of blocks, or just try-catch, or just try-finally. Note that unlike various other control structures, braces are required around the block bodies whether or not they contain more than one statement. The main difference between Java and Groovy in terms of exceptions is that declarations of exceptions in the method signature are optional, even for checked exceptions. The next listing shows the usual behavior.

Listing 6.11   Exception handling in Groovy

```
def myMethod() {
    throw new IllegalArgumentException()
}

def log = []
try {
    myMethod()
} catch (Exception e) {
    log << e.toString()
} finally {
    log << 'finally'
}
assert log.size() == 2
```

There are no compile-time or runtime warnings from Groovy when checked exceptions aren't declared. When a checked exception isn't handled, it's propagated up the execution stack like a RuntimeException.

Java 7 introduced a multi-catch syntax. Groovy also supports this as this code shows:

```
try {
  if (Math.random() < 0.5) 1 / 0
  else null.hashCode()
} catch (ArithmeticException | NullPointerException exception) {
  println exception.class.name
}
```

> **NOTE** Java 7 introduced a try-with-resources mechanism. At the time of writing, Groovy doesn't support that syntax. try-with-resources isn't needed in Groovy, where we have full closure support. A future version of Groovy may support the Java 7 notation to ease cut-and-paste compatibility between the two languages, but even if it does, we'd encourage you to consider the closure variants for managing resources, which are cleaner and more powerful.

We cover integration between Java and Groovy in more detail in chapter 16; but it's worthwhile noting an issue relating to exceptions here. When using a Groovy class from Java, you need to be careful. The Groovy methods will not declare that they throw any checked exceptions unless you've explicitly added the declaration, even though they might throw checked exceptions at runtime. Unfortunately, the Java compiler attempts to be clever and will complain if you try to catch a checked exception in Java when it believes there's no way that the exception can be thrown. If you run into this and need to explicitly catch a checked exception generated in Groovy code, you may need to add a throws declaration to the Groovy code, just to keep javac happy.

6.5   *Summary*

This was our tour through Groovy's control structures: conditionally executing code, looping, and exiting blocks and methods early. It wasn't too surprising because everything turned out to be like Java, enriched with a bit of Groovy flavor. The only structural difference was the for loop. Exception handling is very similar to Java, except without the requirement to declare checked exceptions.[9]

Groovy's handling of Boolean tests is consistently available both in conditional execution structures and in loops. We examined the differences between Java and Groovy in determining when a Boolean test is considered to be true. This is a crucial area to understand, because idiomatic Groovy will often use tests that aren't simple Boolean expressions.

The switch keyword and its use as a general classifier bring a new object-oriented quality to conditionals. The interplay with the isCase method allows objects to control how they're treated not only inside switch but also for the grep method on lists and the in operator in Boolean expressions. You get three for one. Although the use

---

[9] Checked exceptions are regarded by many as an experiment that was worth performing but that proved not to be as useful as had been hoped.

of switch is often discouraged in object-oriented languages, the new power given to it by Groovy gives it a new sense of purpose.

In the overall picture, *assertions* find their place as the bread-and-butter tool for the mindful developer. They belong in the toolbox of every programmer who cares about their craft.

With what you learned in the tour, you have all the means to do any kind of procedural programming. But certainly, you have higher goals and want to master object-oriented programming. The next chapter will teach you how.

Object orientation,
Groovy style

7

Any intelligent fool can make things bigger, more complex, and more violent. It takes a touch of genius—and a lot of courage—to move in the opposite direction.

—Albert Einstein

There's a common misconception about scripting languages. Because a scripting language might support a less rigid approach to typing and provide some initially surprising syntax shorthands, it may be perceived as a nice new toy for hackers rather than a language suitable for serious OOP. This reputation stems from the time when scripting was done in terms of shell scripts or early versions of Perl, where the lack of encapsulation and other object-oriented features sometimes led to poor code management, frequent code duplication, and obscure hidden bugs. It

164

wasn't helped by languages that combined notations from several existing sources as part of their heritage.

Over time, the scripting landscape has changed dramatically. Perl has added support for object orientation, Python has extended its object-oriented support, and, more recently, even JavaScript can be generated from more strictly typed languages like TypeScript and PureScript.

Groovy extends the reach of Java by making it scriptable, but it also provides new language constructs to better reveal the intent of the developer. You've already seen that Groovy provides reference types in cases where Java uses nonobject primitive types, introduces ranges and closures as first-class objects, and has many shorthand notations for working with collections of objects. But these enhancements are just scratching the surface. Groovy allows you to not just *write* code but to *design* it and keep this design visible.

In this chapter, we'll take you on a journey. We begin in familiar territory, with classes, objects, constructors, references, and so forth. Every so often, there's something a bit different, a little tweak of Grooviness. By the end of the chapter, you'll see code that reads so much like plain English that it could have been mistaken for a comment. Welcome to the Groovy world.

7.1 Defining classes and scripts

Class definition in Groovy is almost identical to Java; classes are declared using the class keyword and may contain *fields, constructors, initializers,* and *methods.*[1] Methods and constructors may themselves use *local variables* as part of their implementation code. Scripts are different—offering additional flexibility but with some restrictions too. They may contain code, variable definitions, and method definitions, as well as class definitions. We'll describe how all of these members are declared and cover a previously unseen operator on the way.

7.1.1 Defining fields and local variables

In its simplest terms, a variable is a name associated with a slot of memory that can hold a value. Just as in Java, Groovy has *local variables*, which are scoped within the method they're part of, and *fields*, which are associated with classes or instances of those classes. Fields and local variables are declared in much the same way, so we cover them together.

DECLARING VARIABLES

Fields and local variables must be declared before first use (except for a special case involving scripts, which we discuss later). This helps to enforce scoping rules and protects the programmer from accidental misspellings. The declaration always involves specifying a name, and may optionally include a type, modifiers, and assignment of an initial value. Once declared, variables are referenced by their name.

---

[1] *Interfaces* are also like their Java counterparts, but we'll hold off discussing those further until section 7.3.2.

Scripts allow the use of undeclared variables, in which case these variables are assumed to come from the script's *binding* and are added to the binding if they're not yet there. The binding is a data store that enables transfer of variables to and from the caller of a script. Section 16.2.2 has more details about this mechanism.

Groovy uses Java's *modifiers*—the keywords `private`, `protected`, and `public` for modifying visibility[2]; `final` for disallowing reassignment; and `static` to denote *class variables*. A nonstatic field is also known as an *instance variable*. These modifiers all have the same meaning as in Java.

The default visibility for fields has a special meaning in Groovy. When no visibility modifier is attached to a field declaration, a *property* is generated for the respective name. You'll learn more about properties in section 7.4 when we present GroovyBeans.

Defining the type of a variable is optional. But the identifier must not stand alone in the declaration. When no type and modifier are given, the `def` keyword must be used as a replacement, effectively indicating that the field or variable can be assigned an object of any type at runtime.

The following listing depicts the general appearance of field and variable declarations with optional assignment and using a comma-separated list of identifiers to declare multiple references at once.

Listing 7.1   Variable declaration examples

```
class ClassWithTypedAndUntypedFieldsAndProperties {

    public    fieldWithModifier
    String    typedField
    def       untypedField
    protected field1, field2, field3
    private   assignedField = new Date()

    static    classField
    public static final String CONSTA = 'a', CONSTB = 'b'

    def someMethod(){
        def localUntypedMethodVar = 1
        int localTypedMethodVar = 1
        def localVarWithoutAssignment, andAnotherOne
    }
}

def localvar = 1        ⟵  Local variable to script
boundvar1 = 1           ⟵  From the binding

def someMethod(){
    def localMethodVar = 1    Local method to script
    boundvar2 = 1
}

someMethod()
```

2 Java's default *package-wide* visibility is supported via the `@PackageScope` annotation.

Assignments to typed references must conform to the type. You saw in chapter 3 that Groovy provides autoboxing and coercion when it makes sense. All other cases are type-breaking assignments and lead to a `ClassCastException` at runtime, as can be seen in the following listing.[3]

Listing 7.2 Variable declaration examples

```
final String PI = '3.14'
assert PI.class.name == 'java.lang.String'
assert PI.size() == 4
GroovyAssert.shouldFail(ClassCastException){
    Float areaOfCircleRadiusOne = PI
}
```

As previously discussed, variables can be referred to by name in the same way as in Java—but Groovy provides a few more interesting possibilities.

REFERENCING AND DEREFERENCING FIELDS

In addition to referring to fields by name with the *obj.fieldname*[4] syntax, they can also be referenced with the subscript operator, as shown in the next listing. This allows you to access fields using a dynamically determined name.

Listing 7.3 Referencing fields with the subscript operator

```
class Counter {
    public count = 0
}
def counter = new Counter()

counter.count = 1
assert counter.count == 1

def fieldName = 'count'
counter[fieldName] = 2
assert counter['count'] == 2
```

Accessing fields in such a dynamic way is part of the bigger picture of dynamic execution that we'll analyze in the course of this chapter.

If you worked through the Groovy datatype descriptions, your next question will probably be: Can I override the subscript operator? Sure you can, and you'll *extend* but not *override* the general field-access mechanism that way. But you can do even better and extend the field-access operator!

Listing 7.4 shows how to do that. To extend both `set` and `get` access, provide the following methods

```
Object get (String name)
void    set (String name, Object value)
```

---

[3] The `shouldFail` method as used in this example checks that a `ClassCastException` occurs. More details can be found in section 17.3.

[4] This notation can also appear in the form of *obj.@fieldname*, as you'll see in section 7.4.2.

There's no restriction on what you do inside these methods; get can return artificial values, effectively *pretending* that your class has the requested field. In listing 7.4, the same value is always returned, regardless of which field value is requested. The set method is used for counting the write attempts.

Listing 7.4   Extending the general field-access mechanism

```
class PretendFieldCounter {
    public count = 0

    Object get (String name) {
        return 'pretend value'
    }
    void set (String name, Object value) {
        count++
    }
}

def pretender = new PretendFieldCounter()

assert pretender.isNoField == 'pretend value'
assert pretender.count      == 0

pretender.isNoFieldEither  = 'just to increase counter'

assert pretender.count      == 1
```

With the count field, you can see that it looks like the get/set methods aren't used if the requested field is present. This is true for our special case. In section 7.4 you'll see the full set of rules that produces this effect.

Generally speaking, overriding the get method means to override the *dot-fieldname* operator. Overriding the set method overrides the *field-assignment* operator.

> **FOR THE GEEKS**   What about a statement of the form *x.y.z=something*? This is equivalent to getX().getY().setZ(something).

Referencing fields is also connected to the topic of *properties,* which we'll explore in section 7.4, where we'll discuss the need for the additional *obj.@fieldname* syntax.

7.1.2   *Methods and parameters*

Method declarations follow the same concepts you've seen for variables: the usual Java modifiers can be used; declaring a return type is optional; and, if no modifiers or return type are supplied, the def keyword fills the hole. When the def keyword is used, the return type is deemed to be unrestricted (although it can still have no return type, the equivalent of a void method). In this case, under the covers, the return type will be java.lang.Object. The default visibility of methods is public.

The following listing shows the typical cases in a self-describing manner.

Listing 7.5   Declaring methods

```
class ClassWithTypedAndUntypedMethods {

  static void main(args) {
    def some = new ClassWithTypedAndUntypedMethods()
    some.publicVoidMethod()
    assert 'hi' == some.publicUntypedMethod()
    assert 'ho' == some.publicTypedMethod()
    combinedMethod()
  }

  void publicVoidMethod() { }

  def publicUntypedMethod() {
    return 'hi'
  }

  String publicTypedMethod() {
    return 'ho'
  }

  private static final void combinedMethod() { }
}
```

1 Implicit public

Calls static method of current class

The `main` method **1** has interesting twists. First, the `public` modifier can be omitted because it's the default. Second, `args` usually has to be of type `String[]` to make the `main` method the one to start the class execution. Thanks to Groovy's method dispatch, it works anyway, although `args` is now implicitly of static type `java.lang.Object`. Third, because return types aren't used for the dispatch, we can further omit the `void` declaration.

So, the Java declaration

```
public static void main (String[] args)
```

boils down to this in Groovy:

```
static main (args)
```

> **NOTE**   The Java compiler fails on missing return statements when a return type is declared for the method. In Groovy, return statements are optional, therefore it's impossible for the compiler to detect "accidentally" missing returns.

The `main(args)` example illustrates that declaring explicit parameter types is optional. When type declarations are omitted, `Object` is used. Multiple parameters can be used in sequence, delimited by commas. The following listing shows that explicit and omitted parameter types can also be mixed.

Listing 7.6   Declaring parameter lists

```
class ClassWithTypedAndUntypedMethodParams {
  static void main(args) {
    assert 'untyped' == method(1)
    assert 'typed' == method('whatever')
    assert 'two args' == method(1, 2)
  }
```

```
static method(arg) {
  return 'untyped'
}
static method(String arg) {
  return 'typed'
}
static method(arg1, Number arg2) {
  return 'two args'
}
}
```

In the examples so far, all method calls have involved *positional* parameters, where the meaning of each argument is determined from its position in the parameter list. This is easy to understand and convenient for the simple cases you've seen, but suffers from a number of drawbacks for more complex scenarios:

- You must remember the exact sequence of the parameters, which gets increasingly difficult with the length of the parameter list. We recommend a coding style that encourages small numbers of parameters, but this isn't always possible.
- If it makes sense to call the method with different information for alternative use scenarios, different methods must be constructed to handle these alternatives. This can quickly become cumbersome and lead to a proliferation of methods, especially where some parameters are optional. It's especially difficult if many of the optional parameters have the same type. Fortunately, Groovy comes to the rescue with using maps as *named* parameters.

NOTE Whenever we talk about named parameters, we mean keys of a map that are used as an argument in method or constructor calls. From a programmer's perspective, this looks pretty much like native support for named parameters, but it isn't. This trick is needed because the JVM doesn't support storing parameter names in the bytecode.[5]

The following listing illustrates Groovy method definitions and calls supporting positional and named parameters, parameter lists of variable length, and optional parameters with default values. The example provides four alternative summing mechanisms, each highlighting different approaches for defining the method call parameters.

Listing 7.7 Advanced parameter uses

```
class Summer {
    def sumWithDefaults(a, b, c=0){         Explicit arguments
        return a + b + c              ❶    and default value
    }
    def sumWithList(List args){            Defines
        return args.inject(0){sum,i -> sum += i}  ❷ arguments as list
    }
```

5 This isn't strictly true. Some APIs define their own @ParameterName annotations to store such information and Java 8 can optionally do so. It would be more accurate to say there is no universally adopted approach that is guaranteed to be enabled.

```
    def sumWithOptionals(a, b, Object[] optionals){
        return a + b + sumWithList(optionals.toList())
    }
    def sumNamed(Map args){
        ['a','b','c'].each{args.get(it,0)}
        return args.a + args.b + args.c
    }
}

def summer = new Summer()

assert 2 == summer.sumWithDefaults(1,1)
assert 3 == summer.sumWithDefaults(1,1,1)

assert 2 == summer.sumWithList([1,1])
assert 3 == summer.sumWithList([1,1,1])

assert 2 == summer.sumWithOptionals(1,1)
assert 3 == summer.sumWithOptionals(1,1,1)

assert 2 == summer.sumNamed(a:1, b:1)
assert 3 == summer.sumNamed(a:1, b:1, c:1)
assert 1 == summer.sumNamed(c:1)
```

❸ Optional arguments as array

❹ Defines arguments as map

All four alternatives have their pros and cons. In ❶, sumWithDefaults, we have the most obvious declaration of the arguments expected for the method call. It meets the needs of the sample script—being able to add two or three numbers together—but we're limited to as many arguments as we have declared parameters.

Using lists as shown in ❷ is easy in Groovy, because in the method call, the arguments only have to be placed in brackets. We can also support argument lists of arbitrary length. But it's not as obvious what the individual list entries should mean. Therefore, this alternative is best suited when all arguments have the same meaning, as they do here where they're used for adding. Refer to section 4.2.3 for details about the List.inject method.

The sumWithOptionals method ❸ can be called with two or more parameters. To declare such a method, define the last argument as an array. Groovy's dynamic method dispatch bundles excessive arguments into that array.

Named arguments can be supported by using a map as in ❹. It's good practice to reset any missing values to a default before working with them. This also better reveals what keys will be used in the method body, because this isn't obvious from the method declaration.

When designing your methods, you have to choose one of the alternatives. You may wish to formalize your choice within a project or incorporate the Groovy coding style.

NOTE There are more ways of implementing parameter lists of variable length. You can use *varargs* with the method(args...) or method(Type[] args) notation or even hook into Groovy's method dispatch by overriding the invoke-Method(name, params[]) that every GroovyObject provides. You'll learn more about these hooks in section 7.6.2.

ADVANCED NAMING

When calling a method on an object reference, you should usually follow this format:

```
objectReference.methodName()
```

This format imposes the Java restrictions for method names; for example, they may not contain special characters such as minus (-) or dot (.). But Groovy allows you to use these characters in method names if you put quotes around the name:

```
objectReference.'my.methodName'()
```

This feature supports scenarios where the method name of a call becomes part of the functionality. You won't normally use this feature directly, but it is used under the covers by other parts of Groovy. You'll see this in action in chapters 8 and 10.

> **FOR THE GEEKS**   Where there's a string, you can generally also use a GString. So how about obj."${var}"()? Yes, this is also possible, and the GString will be resolved to determine the name of the method that's called on the object!

That's it for the basics of class members. Before we leave this topic, though, there's one convenient operator we should introduce while we're thinking about referring to members via references.

7.1.3   *Safe dereferencing with the ?. operator*

When a reference doesn't point to any specific object, its value is null. When calling a method or accessing a field on a null reference, a NullPointerException (NPE) is thrown. This is useful to protect code from working on undefined preconditions, but it can easily get in the way of "best-effort" code that should be executed for valid references and just be silent otherwise.

Listing 7.8 shows several alternative approaches to protect code from NPEs. As an example, we wish to access a deeply nested entry within a hierarchy of maps, which results in a *path expression*—a dotted concatenation of references that's typically cumbersome to protect from NPEs. We can use explicit if checks or use the try-catch mechanism. Groovy provides the additional ?. operator for safe dereferencing. When the reference before that operator is a null reference, the evaluation of the current expression stops, and null is returned.

Listing 7.8   Protecting from NullPointerExceptions using the ?. operator

```
def map = [a:[b:[c:1]]]

assert map.a.b.c == 1

if (map && map.a && map.a.x){          ❶ Protects with if:
    assert map.a.x.c == null              short-circuit
}                                         evaluation

try {                                  ❷ Protects with
    assert map.a.x.c == null              try-catch
} catch (NullPointerException ignore){
}
                                       ❸ Safe
assert map?.a?.x?.c == null               dereferencing
```

In comparison, using the safe dereferencing operator in ❸ is the most elegant and expressive solution.

Note that ❶ is more compact than its Java equivalent, which would need three additional nullity checks. It works because the expression is evaluated from left to right, and the `&&` operator stops evaluation with the first operand that evaluates to `false`. This is known as *short-circuit evaluation*.

Alternative ❷ is a bit verbose and doesn't allow fine-grained control to protect only selective parts of the path expression. It also abuses the exception-handling mechanism. Exceptions weren't designed for this kind of situation, which is easily avoided by verifying that the references are non-`null` before dereferencing them. Causing an exception and then catching it is the equivalent of steering a car by installing big bumpers and bouncing off buildings.

Some software engineers like to think about code in terms of *cyclomatic complexity* (http://en.wikipedia.org/wiki/Cyclomatic_complexity), which in short describes code complexity by analyzing alternative pathways through the code. The safe dereferencing operator merges alternative pathways and therefore reduces complexity when compared to its alternatives; essentially, the metric indicates that the code will be easier to understand and simpler to verify as correct.

7.1.4 Constructors

Objects are instantiated from their classes via *constructors*. If no constructor is given, an implicit constructor without arguments is supplied by the compiler. This appears to be exactly like in Java, but because this is Groovy, it should not be surprising that additional features are available.

In section 7.1.2, we examined the merits of *named* parameters versus *positional* ones, as well as the need for *optional* parameters. The same arguments applicable to method calls are relevant for constructors, too, so Groovy provides the same convenience mechanisms. We'll first look at constructors with positional parameters, and then we'll examine named parameters.

POSITIONAL PARAMETERS

Until now, we've only used implicit constructors. The following listing introduces the first explicit one. Notice that just like all other methods, the constructor is `public` by default. We can call the constructor in three different ways: the usual Java way, with enforced type coercion by using the as keyword, or with implicit type coercion.

Listing 7.9   Calling constructors with positional parameters

```
class VendorWithCtor {
    String name, product

    VendorWithCtor(name, product) {          ← Constructor
        this.name    = name                     definition
        this.product = product
    }
}
```

```
def first = new VendorWithCtor('Canoo','ULC')
```
← Normal constructor use

```
def second = ['Canoo','ULC'] as VendorWithCtor
```
← ❶ Coercion with as

```
VendorWithCtor third = ['Canoo','ULC']
```
← ❷ Coercion in assignment

The coercion in ❶ and ❷ may be surprising. When Groovy sees the need to coerce a list to some other type, it tries to call the type's constructor with all arguments supplied by the list, in list order. This need for coercion can be enforced with the as keyword or arise from assignments to explicitly typed references. The latter of these is called *implicit construction*, which we'll cover shortly.

NAMED PARAMETERS

Named parameters in constructors are handy. One use case that crops up frequently is creating *immutable* classes that have some parameters that are optional. Using positional parameters would quickly become cumbersome because you'd need to have constructors allowing for all combinations of the optional parameters.

As an example, suppose in listing 7.9 that VendorWithCtor should be immutable and name and product can be optional. We'd need four[6] constructors: an empty one, one to set name, one to set product, and one to set both attributes. To make things worse, we couldn't have a constructor with only one argument, because we couldn't distinguish whether to set the name or the product attribute (they're both strings). We'd need an artificial extra argument for distinction, or we'd need to strongly type the parameters.

But don't panic: Groovy's special way of supporting named parameters comes to the rescue again.

The following listing shows how to use named parameters with a simplified version of the VendorWithCtor class. It relies on the implicit default constructor. Could that be any easier?

Listing 7.10 Calling constructors with named parameters

```
class SimpleVendor {
    String name, product
}

new SimpleVendor()
new SimpleVendor(name: 'Canoo')
new SimpleVendor(product: 'ULC')
new SimpleVendor(name: 'Canoo', product: 'ULC')

def vendor = new SimpleVendor(name: 'Canoo')
assert 'Canoo' == vendor.name
```

---

[6] In general, 2^n constructors are needed, where *n* is the number of optional attributes.

The listing illustrates how flexible named parameters are for your constructors. In cases where you don't want this flexibility and want to lock down all of your parameters, define your desired constructor explicitly; the implicit constructor with named parameters will no longer be available.

Coming back to how we started this section, the *empty* default constructor invocation new SimpleVendor() appears in a new light. Although it looks exactly like its Java equivalent, it's a special case of the default constructor with *named* parameters that happen to be called without any being supplied.

IMPLICIT CONSTRUCTORS

Finally, there's a way to call a constructor implicitly by simply providing the constructor arguments as a list. That means that instead of calling the Dimension(width, height) constructor explicitly, for example, you can use

```
java.awt.Dimension area

area = [200, 100]

assert area.width  == 200
assert area.height == 100
```

Of course, Groovy must know which constructor to call, and therefore implicit constructors are solely available for assignment to statically typed references where the type provides the respective constructor. They don't work for abstract classes or even interfaces.

Implicit constructors are often used with builders, as you'll see in the SwingBuilder example in section 11.6.

That's it for the usual class members. This is a solid basis we can build upon. But we're not yet in the penthouse; we've four more levels to go. Next, we'll walk through the topic of how to organize classes and scripts before reaching the level of advanced object-oriented features. The next floor after that is named GroovyBeans and deals with simple object-oriented information *about* objects. At this level, we can play with Groovy's *power features*. Finally, we'll visit the highest level, where we look at advanced syntax features.

7.2 *Organizing classes and scripts*

In section 2.4.1, you saw that Groovy classes are Java classes at the bytecode level, and consequently, Groovy objects are Java objects in memory. At the source-code level, Groovy class and object handling is for all practical purposes a superset of the Java syntax. We'll examine the organization of classes and source files, and the relationships between the two. We'll also consider Groovy's use of packages and type aliasing, as well as demystify where Groovy can load classes from its classpath.

7.2.1   *File to class relationship*

The relationship between files and class declarations isn't as fixed as in Java. Groovy files can contain any number of public class declarations according to the following rules:

- If a Groovy file contains *no* class declaration, it's handled as a script; that is, it's transparently wrapped into a class of type `Script`. This automatically generated class has the same name as the source script filename[7] (without the extension). The content of the file is wrapped into a `run` method, and an additional `main` method is constructed for easily starting the script.
- If a Groovy file contains exactly *one* class declaration with the same name as the file (without the extension), then there's the same one-to-one relationship as in Java.
- A Groovy file may contain *multiple* class declarations of any visibility, and there's no enforced rule that any of them must match the filename. The `groovyc` compiler happily creates *.class files for all declared classes in such a file. If you wish to invoke your script directly—for example, using `groovy` on the command line or within an IDE—then the first class within your file should have a `main` method.[8]
- A Groovy file may *mix* class declarations and scripting code. In this case, the scripting code will become the main class to be executed, so don't declare a class yourself having the same name as the source filename.

When not compiling explicitly, Groovy finds a class by matching its name to a corresponding *.groovy source file. At this point, naming becomes important. Groovy only finds classes where the class name matches the source filename. When such a file is found, all declared classes in that file are parsed and become known to Groovy.

The following listing shows a sample script with two simple classes, `Vendor` and `Address`. For the moment, they have no methods, only public fields.

Listing 7.11   Multiple class declarations in one file

```
class Vendor {
    public String      name
    public String      product
    public Address      address = new Address()
}

class Address  {
    public String      street, town, state
    public int      zip
}

def canoo = new Vendor()
canoo.name                 = 'Canoo Engineering AG'
canoo.product              = 'UltraLightClient (ULC)'
```

---

[7] Because the class has no package name, it's implicitly placed in the default package.

[8] Strictly speaking, you can alternatively extend `GroovyTestCase` or implement the `Runnable` interface.

```
canoo.address.street  = 'Kirschgartenst. 7'
canoo.address.zip     =  4051
canoo.address.town    = 'Basel'
canoo.address.state   = 'Switzerland'

assert canoo.dump()          =~ /ULC/
assert canoo.address.dump()  =~ /Basel/
```

`Vendor` and `Address` are simple data storage classes. They're roughly equivalent to `struct` in C or `record` in Pascal. We'll soon explore more elegant ways of defining such classes.

The previous example illustrates a convenient convention supported by Groovy's source file to class mapping rules, which we discussed earlier. This convention allows small helper classes that are used only with the current main class or current script to be declared within the same source file. Compare this with Java, which allows you to use nested classes to introduce locally used classes without cluttering up your public class namespace or making navigation of the codebase more difficult by requiring a proliferation of source-code files. Although it isn't exactly the same, this convention has similar benefits for Groovy developers.

7.2.2 *Organizing classes in packages*

Groovy follows Java's approach of organizing files in packages of hierarchical structure. The package structure is used to find the corresponding class files in the filesystem's directories.

Because *.groovy source files aren't necessarily compiled to *.class files, there's also a need to look up *.groovy files. When doing so, the same strategy is used: the compiler looks for a Groovy class `Vendor` in the `business` package in the file `business/Vendor.groovy`.

In listing 7.12, we separate the `Vendor` and `Address` classes from the script code, as shown in listing 7.11, and move them to the `business` package.

CLASSPATH

The lookup has to start somewhere, and Java uses its *classpath* for this purpose. The classpath is a list of possible starting points for the lookup of *.class files. Groovy reuses the classpath for looking up *.groovy files.

When looking for a given class, if Groovy finds both a *.class and a *.groovy file, it uses whichever is newer; that is, it'll recompile source files into *.class files if they've changed since the previous class file was compiled.[9]

PACKAGES

Exactly like in Java, Groovy classes must specify their package before the class definition. When no package declaration is given, the default package is assumed.

The following listing shows the file `business/Vendor.groovy`, which has a package statement as its first line.

---

[9]　Whether classes are checked for runtime updates can be controlled by the `CompilerConfiguration`, which obeys the system property `groovy.recompile` by default. See the API documentation for details.

Listing 7.12 **Vendor** and **Address** classes moved to the **business** package

```
package business

class Vendor {
    public String  name
    public String  product
    public Address address = new Address()
}
class Address {
    public String  street, town, state
    public int     zip
}
```

To reference `Vendor` in the business package, you can either use `business.Vendor` within the code or use `import` statements for abbreviation.

IMPORTS

Groovy follows Java's notion of allowing `import` statements before any class declaration to abbreviate class references.

> **NOTE** Please keep in mind that unlike in some other scripting languages, an `import` statement has nothing to do with literal inclusion of the imported class or file. It merely informs the compiler how to resolve references.

The following listing shows the use of an `import` statement, with the `.*` notation advising the compiler to try resolving all unknown class references against all classes in the business package.

Listing 7.13 Using **import** to access **Vendor** in the business package

```
import business.*

def canoo = new Vendor()
canoo.name          = 'Canoo Engineering AG'
canoo.product       = 'UltraLightClient (ULC)'

assert canoo.dump() =~ /ULC/
```

Default import statements

By default, Groovy imports six packages and two classes, making it seem like every Groovy code program contains the following initial statements:

```
import java.lang.*
import java.util.*
import java.io.*
import java.net.*
import groovy.lang.*
import groovy.util.*
import java.math.BigInteger
import java.math.BigDecimal
```

TYPE ALIASING

An import statement has another nice twist: together with the as keyword, it can be used for *type aliasing*. Whereas a normal import statement allows a fully qualified class to be referred to by its base name, a type alias allows a fully qualified class to be referred to by a name of your choosing. This feature resolves naming conflicts and supports local changes or bug fixes to a third-party library.

Consider the following library class:

```
package thirdparty

class MathLib {
  Integer twice(Integer value) {
    return value * 3          // intentionally wrong!
  }
  Integer half(Integer value) {
    return value / 2
  }
}
```

Note its obvious error[10] (although in general it might not be an error but just a locally desired modification). Suppose now that we have existing code that uses that library:

```
assert 10 == new MathLib().twice(5)
```

We can use a type alias to rename the old library and then use an inheritance to make a fix. No change is required to the original code that was using the library, as you can see in the following listing.

Listing 7.14 Using import as for local library modifications

```
import thirdparty.MathLib as OrigMathLib

class MathLib extends OrigMathLib {
    Integer twice(Integer value) {         Use code for
        return value * 2                   library remains
    }                                      unchanged
}
// nothing changes below here              Invokes fixed
def mathlib = new MathLib()                method

assert 10 == mathlib.twice(5)              Invokes original
assert 2 == mathlib.half(5)                method
```

Now, suppose that we have the following additional math library that we need to use:

```
package thirdparty2

class MathLib {
    Integer increment(Integer value) {
        return value + 1
    }
}
```

---

[10] Where are the library author's unit tests?

Although it has a different package, it has the same name as the previous library. Without aliasing, we have to fully qualify one or both of the libraries within our code. With aliasing, we can avoid this in an elegant way and improve communication by better indicating intent within our program about the role of the third-party library's code, as shown in the next listing.

Listing 7.15　Using `import as` for avoiding name clashes

```
import thirdparty.MathLib as TwiceHalfMathLib
import thirdparty2.MathLib as IncMathLib
def math1 = new TwiceHalfMathLib()
def math2 = new IncMathLib()
assert 3 == math1.half(math2.increment(5))
```

If we later find a math package with both increment and twice/half functionality, we can refer to that new library twice and keep our more meaningful names.

You should consider using aliases within your own program, even when using simple built-in types. If you're developing an adventure game, for example, you might alias `Map` to `SatchelContents`. (Here we mean `java.util.Map` and not `TreasureMap`, which our adventure game might allow us to place within the satchel!) This doesn't provide the strong typing that defining a separate `SatchelContents` class would give, but it does greatly improve the human understandability of the code.

7.2.3　*Further classpath considerations*

Finding classes in *.class and *.groovy files is an important part of working with Groovy, and unfortunately a likely source of problems.

If you installed the JDK including the documentation, you'll find the classpath explanation under `%JAVA_HOME%/docs/technotes/tools/windows/classpath.html` under Windows, or under a similar directory for Linux and Solaris. Everything the documentation says equally applies to Groovy.

A number of contributors can influence the effective classpath in use. The overview in table 7.1 may serve as a reference when you're looking for a possible "bad guy" that's messing up your classpath.

Table 7.1　Forming the classpath

Origin	Definition	Purpose and Use
JDK/JRE	`%JAVA_HOME%/lib` `%JAVA_HOME%/lib/ext`	Boot classpath for the Java runtime environment and its extensions
OS setting	`CLASSPATH variable`	Provides general default settings
Command shell	`CLASSPATH variable`	Provides more specialized settings

Java	`-cp`
	`--classpath`
	`option`
		Settings per runtime invocation

Table 7.1 Forming the classpath

Origin	Definition	Purpose and Use
Groovy	`%GROOVY_HOME%/lib`	Groovy runtime environment
Groovy	`-cp`	Settings per groovy execution call
Groovy	`.`	Groovy classpath defaults to the current directory

Groovy defines its classpath in a special configuration file under `%GROOVY_HOME%/conf`. Looking at the file `groovy-starter.conf` reveals the following lines (beside others):

```
# Load required libraries
load ${groovy.home}/lib/*.jar
# load user specific libraries
# load ${user.home}/.groovy/lib/*
```

Uncommenting the last line by removing the leading hash sign enables a cool feature. In your personal home directory user.home, you can use a subdirectory .groovy/lib (note the leading dot!), where you can store any *.class or *.jar files that you want to have accessible whenever you work with Groovy.

If you have problems finding your user.home, open a command shell and execute

```
groovy -e "println System.properties.'user.home'"
```

Chances are, you're in this directory by default anyway.

Chapter 16 goes through more advanced classpath issues that need to be respected when embedding Groovy in environments that manage their own class-loading infrastructure—for example, an *application server.*

You're now able to use constructors in a number of different ways to make new instances of a class. Classes may reside in packages, and you've seen how to make them known via `import` statements. This wraps up our exploration of object basics. The next step is to explore more advanced object-oriented features.

7.3 Advanced object-oriented features

Before beginning to embrace further parts of the Groovy libraries that make fundamental use of the object-oriented features we've been discussing, we first stop to briefly explore other object-oriented concepts that change once you enter the Groovy world. We'll cover inheritance and interfaces, which will be familiar from Java, and multimethods, which will give you a taste of the dynamic object orientation coming later. Finally, we'll look at Groovy's support for traits that offer incredible flexibility when composing functionality.

7.3.1 Using inheritance

You've seen how to explicitly add your own fields, methods, and constructors into your class definitions. Inheritance allows you to implicitly add fields and methods from a base class. The mechanism is useful in a range of use cases. We leave it up to others[11] to describe its benefits and warn you about the potential overuse of this feature. We simply let you know that all the inheritance features of Java (including abstract classes) are available in Groovy and also work (almost seamlessly[12]) between Groovy and Java.

Groovy classes can extend Groovy and Java classes and interfaces alike. Java classes can also extend Groovy classes and interfaces. You need to compile your Java and Groovy classes in a particular order for this to work (see section 16.4.2 for more details). The only other thing you need to be aware of is that Groovy is more dynamic than Java when it selects which methods to invoke for you. This feature is known as *multimethods* and is discussed further in section 7.3.3.

7.3.2   *Using interfaces*

A frequently advocated style of Java programming involves using Java's interface mechanism. Code written using this style refers to the dependent classes that it uses solely by interface. The dependent classes can be safely changed later without requiring changes to the original program. If a developer accidentally tries to change one of the classes for another that doesn't comply with the interface, this discrepancy is detected at compile time. Groovy fully supports the Java interface mechanism.

Some[13] argue that interfaces alone aren't strong enough, and design-by-contract is more important for achieving safe object substitution and allowing nonbreaking changes to your libraries. Judicious use of abstract methods and inheritance becomes just as important as using interfaces. Groovy's support for Java's abstract methods, its automatically enabled `assert` statement, and its built-in ready access to test methods mean that it's ideally suited to also support this stricter approach.

Still others argue that dynamic typing is the best approach, leading to much less typing and less scaffolding code without much reduced safety—which should be covered by tests in any case. The good news is that Groovy supports this style as well. To give you a flavor of how this would impact you in everyday coding, consider how you'd build a plug-in mechanism in Java and Groovy.

In Java, you'd normally write an interface for the plug-in mechanism and then an implementation class for each plug-in that implements that interface. In Groovy, dynamic typing allows you to more easily create and use implementations that meet a certain need. You're likely to be able to create just two classes as part of developing two plug-in implementations. In general, you have a lot less scaffolding code and a lot less typing.

---

[11] Rebecca Wirfs-Brock et al., *Designing Object-Oriented Software* (Prentice-Hall, 1990) is a good place to begin.

[12] The only limitation that we're aware of has to do with map-based constructors, which Groovy provides by default. These aren't available directly in Java if you extend a Groovy class. They're provided by Groovy as a runtime trick.

[13] See Bertrand Meyer, *Object-oriented Software Construction*, 2nd ed. (Prentice-Hall, 1997) and http://cafe.elharo .com/java/the-three-reasons-for-data-encapsulation/.

> **Implementing interfaces and SAM types**
>
> If you decide to make heavy use of interfaces, Groovy provides ways to make them more dynamic. If you have an interface, `MyInterface`, with a single method and a closure, `myClosure`, you can use the `as` keyword to coerce the closure to be of type `MyInterface`. In fact from Groovy 2.2, you don't even need the `as` keyword. Groovy does implicit closure coercion into single abstract method types as shown in this example, where the `addListener` method would normally require an `ActionListener`:
>
> ```
> import java.awt.event.ActionListener
> listeners = []
> def addListener(ActionListener al) { listeners << al }
> addListener { println "I heard that!" }
> listeners*.actionPerformed()
> ```
>
> Alternatively, if you have an interface with several methods, you can create a map of closures keyed on the method names and coerce the map to your interface type. See the Groovy documentation for more details: http://docs.groovy-lang.org/latest/html/documentation/core-semantics.html#closure-coercion.

In summary, if you've come from the Java world, you may be used to following a strict style of coding that strongly encourages interfaces. When using Groovy, you're not compelled to stick with any one style. In many situations, you can minimize the amount of typing by making use of dynamic typing; and if you really need it, the full use of interfaces is available.

7.3.3 Multimethods

Remember that Groovy's mechanics of method lookup take the dynamic type of method arguments into account, whereas Java relies on the static type. This Groovy feature is called multimethods.

The following listing shows two methods, both called `oracle`, that are distinguishable only by their argument types. They're called two times with arguments of the same static type but different dynamic types.

Listing 7.16   Multimethods: method dispatch on runtime type

```
def oracle(Object o) { return 'object' }
def oracle(String o) { return 'string' }

Object x = 1
Object y = 'foo'

assert 'object' == oracle(x)          Returns object
assert 'string' == oracle(y)      ◁── in Java
```

The x argument is of static type `Object` and of runtime type `Integer`. The y argument is of static type `Object` but of runtime type `String`. Both arguments are of the same *static* type, which would make the equivalent Java program dispatch both to `oracle(Object)`.

Because Groovy dispatches by the *runtime* type, the specialized implementation of oracle(String) is used in the second case.

With this capability in place, you can better avoid duplicated code by being able to override behavior more selectively. Consider the equals implementation in the following listing that overrides Object's default equals method only for the argument type Equalizer.

Listing 7.17 Multimethods to selectively override equals

```
class Equalizer {
    boolean equals(Equalizer e){
        return true
    }
}

Object same  = new Equalizer()
Object other = new Object()

assert   new Equalizer().equals( same  )
assert ! new Equalizer().equals( other )
```

When an object of type Equalizer is passed to the equals method, the specialized implementation is chosen. When an arbitrary object is passed, the default implementation of its superclass Object.equals is called, which implements the equality check as a reference identity check.

The net effect is that the caller of the equals method can be fully unaware of the difference. From a caller's perspective, it looks like equals(Equalizer) would override equals(Object), which would be impossible to do in Java. Instead, a Java programmer has to write it like this:

```
public class Equalizer {                // Java
    public boolean equals(Object obj)
    {
        if (obj == null)                return false;
        if (!(obj instanceof Equalizer)) return false;
        Equalizer w = (Equalizer) obj;
        return true;                    // custom logic here
    }
}
```

This is unfortunate, because the logic of how to correctly override equals needs to be duplicated for every custom type in Java. This is another example where Java uses the static type Object and leaves the work of dynamic type resolution to the programmer.

NOTE Wherever there's a Java API that uses the static type Object, this code effectively loses the strength of static typing. You'll inevitably find it used with typecasts, compromising compile-time type safety. This is why the Java type concept is called *weak* static typing: you lose the merits of static typing without getting the benefits of a dynamically typed language such as multimethods.

Groovy, in contrast, comes with a single and consistent implementation of dispatching methods by the dynamic types of their arguments.

That's it for multimethods, but in terms of advanced object-oriented features, we've saved the best for last. One of the benefits of object-oriented languages is the flexibility in designing systems through composition and subtyping. Java's decision to adopt single inheritance of implementation greatly simplified the language at the expense of making it more difficult to support certain kinds of reuse. We've all heard the mantra "prefer delegation over inheritance." It's arguable that this is a direct consequence of Java's restrictions. A programmer might have the desire to share code capabilities within their classes without duplication, but given Java's restrictions, they create inappropriate subtype relationships. Default methods in Java 8 interfaces lift this restriction somewhat but still don't allow a full "design by capability" that includes state. Groovy introduces traits to support composition of capabilities in a very flexible way. We'll cover traits next.

7.3.4 Using traits

Groovy traits support composition of capabilities. Capabilities that are designed to be shared are implemented in traits. Your classes can then implement those traits to indicate that they provide that capability.[14] They "inherit" the implementation from the trait but can override it if they wish. If this sounds like Java 8 default methods, you're on the right track, but Groovy traits also support state. Let's look at some examples.

Assume we have to model a `Book` class. Books have an ISBN number. Books also have a title just like other types of publications but not all publications have an ISBN. So our domain is books that are subclasses of publications:

```
class Publication {
    String title
}

class Book extends Publication {
    String isbn
}
```

But in our application, we also need to save `Book` instances to a database. Saving has nothing to do with books or publications but is an independent capability that applies to all persistent entities.

The following listing solves this design task with Groovy traits in a very fine-grained manner such that one can mix-and-match the capabilities of having identifiers and versions for persistent entities.

---

[14] Before Groovy 2.3 the way to share capabilities among classes was through the `@Mixin` annotation, which is now deprecated in favor of more powerful traits.

Listing 7.18   Traits with inheritance

```
trait HasId {                           ←── Defines a trait
    long id                                  with state
}

trait HasVersion {
    long version
}

trait Persistent {
    boolean save() { println "saving ${this.dump()}" }
}
                                                    ←── Traits can use
trait Entity implements Persistent, HasId, HasVersion {  subtyping
    boolean save() {
        version++
        Persistent.super.save()         ←── Uses specific
    }                                        methods
}

class Publication implements Entity {   ←──     ❶ Implements
    String title                                   the trait
}

class Book extends Publication {
    String isbn
}

Entity gina = new Book(id:1, version:1, title:"gina", isbn:"111111")
gina.save()
assert gina.version == 2
```

At ❶ we make Publication an Entity. This is what we call the *intrusive* way of applying traits. There's an even more flexible one: applying them *nonintrusively* at runtime. Publications stay totally agnostic of persistency:

```
class Publication {
    String title
}
```

We apply the trait later when needed with the enforced coercion through the as keyword:

```
Entity gina = new Book(title:"gina", isbn:"111111") as Entity
gina.id = 1
gina.version = 1
```

Note that gina is no longer of type Book as it was before. That's the price we pay for flexibility. But this nonintrusive way of extending a class independent from its inheritance in a type-safe manner is a great way of developing incrementally.

That's all you need to know to get started using traits. There are some more advanced details such as rules for dealing with conflicts when two or more traits define the same method, and rules for chaining traits and restrictions when combining traits with AST transformations. See the Groovy documentation on traits for more details.[15]

7.4 *Working with GroovyBeans*

The JavaBeans specification[16] was introduced with Java 1.1 to define a lightweight and generic software component model for Java. The component model builds on naming conventions and APIs that allow Java classes to expose their properties to other classes and tools. This greatly enhanced the ability to define and use reusable components and opened up the possibility of developing component-aware tools.

The first tools were mainly visually oriented, such as visual builders that retrieved and manipulated properties of visual components. Over time, the JavaBeans concept has been widely used and extended to a range of use cases including server-side components (in JavaServer Pages [JSP]), transactional behavior and persistence (Enterprise JavaBeans [EJB]), object-relational mapping (ORM) frameworks, and countless other frameworks and tools.

Groovy makes using JavaBeans (and therefore most of these other JavaBean-related frameworks) easier with special language support. This support covers three aspects: special Groovy syntax for creating JavaBean classes; mechanisms for easily accessing beans, regardless of whether they were declared in Groovy or Java; and support for JavaBean event handling. This section will examine each part of this language-level support, as well as cover the library support provided by the Expando class.

7.4.1 *Declaring beans*

JavaBeans are normal classes that follow certain naming conventions. For example, to make a String property myProp available in a JavaBean, the bean's class must have public methods declared as String getMyProp and void setMyProp (String value). The JavaBean specification also strongly recommends that beans should be *serializable* so they can be persistent and provide a parameterless constructor to allow easy construction of objects from within tools. A typical Java implementation is

```
// Java
public class MyBean implements java.io.Serializable {
  private String myprop;
  public String getMyprop(){
    return myprop;
  }
  public void setMyprop(String value){
    myprop = value;
  }
}
```

---

[15] Groovy Language Documentation, 1.4.2, "Traits," http://docs.groovy-lang.org/docs/groovy-latest/html/documentation/#_traits.

[16] The JavaBeans spec, www.oracle.com/technetwork/java/javase/overview/spec-136004.html.

The Groovy equivalent is

```
class MyBean implements Serializable {
  String myprop
}
```

The most obvious difference is size. One line of Groovy replaces seven lines of Java. But it's not only about less typing, it's also about self-documentation. In Groovy, it's easier to assess which fields are considered exposed properties: all fields that are declared with default visibility. The three related pieces of information—the field and the two accessor methods—are kept together in one declaration. Changing the type or name of the property requires changing the code in only a single place.

> **NOTE** Older versions of Groovy used an @Property syntax for denoting properties. This was considered ugly and was removed in favor of handling properties as a "default visibility."

Underneath the covers, Groovy provides public accessor methods similar to this Java code equivalent, but you don't have to type them. Moreover, they're generated only if they don't already exist in the class. This allows you to *override* the standard accessors with either customized logic or constrained visibility. Groovy also provides a private backing field (again similar to the Java equivalent code). Note that the JavaBean specification cares only about the available accessor methods and doesn't even require a backing field, but having one is an intuitive and simple way to implement the methods—so that's what Groovy does.

> **NOTE** It's important that Groovy constructs the accessor methods and adds them to the bytecode. This ensures that when using a MyBean in the Java world, the Groovy MyBean class is recognized as a proper JavaBean.

The following listing shows the declaration options for properties with optional typing and assignment. The rules are equivalent to those for fields (see section 7.2.1).

Listing 7.19   Declaring properties in GroovyBeans

```
class MyBean implements Serializable {
    def untyped
    String typed
    def item1, item2
    def assigned = 'default value'
}
def bean = new MyBean()
assert 'default value' == bean.getAssigned()
bean.setUntyped('some value')
assert 'some value' == bean.getUntyped()
bean = new MyBean(typed:'another value')
assert 'another value' == bean.getTyped()
```

Properties are sometimes called *readable* or *writeable* depending on whether the corresponding getter or setter method is available. Groovy properties are both readable and writeable, but you can always roll your own if you have special requirements. When the `final` keyword is used with a property declaration, the property will only be readable (no setter method is created and the backing field is final).

Writing GroovyBeans is a simple and elegant solution for fully compliant JavaBean support, with the option of specifying types as required.

7.4.2 Working with beans

The wide adoption of the JavaBeans concept in the world of Java has led to a common programming style where bean-style accessor methods are limited to simple access (costly operations are strictly avoided in these methods). These are the types of accessors generated for you by Groovy. If you have complex additional logic related to a property, you can always override the relevant getter or setter method, but you're usually better off writing a separate business method for your advanced logic.

ACCESSOR METHODS

Even for classes that don't fully comply with the JavaBeans standard, you can usually assume that such an accessor method can be called without a big performance penalty or other harmful side effects. The characteristics of an accessor method are much like those of a direct field access (without breaking the *uniform access principle*[17]).

Groovy supports this style at the language level according to the mapping of method calls shown in table 7.2.

Table 7.2 Groovy accessor method to property mappings

Java	Groovy
`getPropertyname()`	`propertyname`
`setPropertyname(value)`	`propertyname = value`

This mapping works regardless of whether it's applied to a Groovy or *plain old Java object* (POJO), and it works for beans as well as for all other classes. The next listing shows this in a combination of bean-style and derived properties.

Listing 7.20 Calling accessors the Groovy way

```
class MrBean {
    String firstname, lastname        ◁─┤ Groovy style
                                           properties
    String getName(){                  ◁─┐ Getter for derived
        return "$firstname $lastname"   ❶   property
    }
}
```

---

[17] "Uniform Access Principle," http://en.wikipedia.org/wiki/Uniform_access_principle.

Generic
constructor

```
def bean = new MrBean(firstname: 'Rowan')
bean.lastname = 'Atkinson'                          ← ❷ Calls setter

assert 'Rowan Atkinson' == bean.name                ← ❸ Calls getter
```

Note how much the Groovy-style property access in ❷ and ❸ looks like direct field access, whereas ❶ makes clear that there's no field but only some derived value. From a caller's point of view, the access is truly *uniform*.

Because field access and the accessor method shortcut have an identical syntax, it takes rules to choose one or the other.

> **NOTE** When both a field and the corresponding accessor method are accessible to the caller, the property reference is resolved as an accessor method call. If only one is accessible, that option is chosen.

That looks straightforward, and it is in the majority of cases. But there are some points to consider, as you'll see next.

FIELD ACCESS WITH .@

Before we leave the topic of properties, we have one more example to explore. The following listing illustrates how you can provide your own accessor methods and also how to bypass the accessor mechanism. You can get directly to the field using the `.@` (*dot-at*) operator when the need arises.

Listing 7.21   Advanced accessors with Groovy

```
class DoublerBean {
    public value                      ← Visible field

    void setValue(value){
        this.value = value            ← ❶ Inner field access
    }

    def getValue(){
        value * 2                     ← ❷ Inner field access
    }
}

def bean = new DoublerBean(value: 100)
                                      ❸ Property access          Outer field access
assert 200 == bean.value             ←
assert 100 == bean.@value            ←
```

Let's start with what's familiar: `bean.value` at ❸ calls `getValue` and thus returns the doubled value. But wait—`getValue` calculates the result at ❷ as `value * 2`. If `value` at this point was interpreted as a bean shortcut for `getValue`, we'd have an endless recursion.

A similar situation arises at ❶, where the assignment `this.value =` would in bean terms be interpreted as `this.setValue`, which would also let us fall into endless looping. Therefore, the following rules have been set up.

RULES Inside the lexical scope of a field, references to `fieldname` or `this.fieldname` are resolved as field access, not as property access. The same effect can be achieved from outside the scope using the *reference.@fieldname* syntax.

It needs to be mentioned that these rules can produce pathological corner cases with logical but surprising behavior, such as when using @ from a static context or with def x=this; x.@fieldname, and so on. We'll not go into more details here, because such a design is discouraged. Decide whether to expose the state as a field, as a property, or via explicit accessor methods, but don't mix these approaches. Keep the access uniform.

BEAN-STYLE EVENT HANDLING

Besides properties, JavaBeans can also be *event sources* that feed *event listeners.*[18] An event listener is an object with a *callback method* that gets called to notify the listener that an event was *fired.* An *event object* that further qualifies the event is passed as a parameter to the callback method.

The JDK is full of different types of event listeners. A simple event listener is the `ActionListener` on a button, which calls an `actionPerformed(ActionEvent)` method whenever the button is clicked. A more complex example is the `VetoableChangeListener` that allows listeners to throw a `PropertyVetoException` inside their `vetoableChange(PropertyChangeEvent)` method to roll back a change to a bean's property. Other uses are multifold, and it's impossible to provide an exhaustive list.

Groovy supports event listeners in a simple but powerful way. Suppose you need to create a Swing JButton with the label "Push me!" that prints the label to the console when it's clicked. A Java implementation can use an anonymous inner class in the following way:

```
// Java
final JButton button = new JButton("Push me!");
button.addActionListener(new IActionListener(){
    public void actionPerformed(ActionEvent event){
        System.out.println(button.getText());
    }
});
```

The developer needs to know about the respective listener and event types (or interfaces), as well as about the registration and callback methods.

A Groovy programmer only has to attach a closure to the button as if it were a field named by the respective callback method:

```
button = new JButton('Push me!')
button.actionPerformed = { event ->
    println button.text
}
```

---

[18] See the JavaBeans Specification: http://www.oracle.com/technetwork/java/javase/overview/spec-136004.html.

The event parameter is added only to show how we could get it when needed. In this example, it could have been omitted, because it's not used inside the closure.

> **NOTE**   Groovy uses *bean introspection* to determine whether a field setter refers to a callback method of a listener that's supported by the bean. If so, a Closure-Listener is transparently added that calls the closure when notified. A ClosureListener is a proxy implementation of the required listener interface.

Event handling is conceived as a JavaBeans standard. But you don't need to somehow declare your object to be a bean before you can do any event handling. The dependency is the other way around: as soon as your object supports this style of event handling, it's called a bean.

Although Groovy adds the ability to register event listeners easily as closures, the Java style of bean event handling remains fully intact. That means you can still use all available Java methods to get a list of all registered listeners, adding more of them, or removing them when they're no longer needed.

7.4.3   Using bean methods for any object

Groovy doesn't distinguish between beans and other kinds of object. It solely relies on the accessibility of the respective getter and setter methods.

The following listing shows how to use the getProperties method and thus the properties property (sorry for the tricky wording) to get a map of a bean's properties. You can do so with any object you fancy.

Listing 7.22   GDK methods for bean properties

```
class ClassWithProperties {
    def        someProperty
    public     someField
    private    somePrivateField
}

def obj = new ClassWithProperties()

def store = []
obj.properties.each { property ->
    store += property.key
    store += property.value
}
assert store.contains('someProperty')
assert store.contains('someField')          == false
assert store.contains('somePrivateField')   == false
assert store.contains('class')

assert obj.properties.size() == 2
```

In addition to the property that's explicitly declared, you also see *class* and *metaClass* references. These are artifacts of the Groovy class generation.[19]

---

[19] The class property stems from Java. But tools that use Java's bean introspection often hide this property.

This was a taste of what will be explained in more detail in section 12.1.

7.4.4 *Fields, accessors, maps, and Expando*

In Groovy code, you'll often find expressions such as `object.name`. Here's what happens when Groovy resolves this reference:

- If `object` refers to a map, `object.name` refers to the value corresponding to the name key that's stored in the map. Otherwise, if `name` is a property of `object`, the property is referenced (with precedence of accessor methods over fields, as you saw in section 7.4.2).
- Every Groovy object has the opportunity to implement its own `getProperty (name)` and `setProperty(name, value)` methods. When it does, these implementations are used to control the property access. Maps, for example, use this mechanism to expose keys as properties.
- Field access can be intercepted by providing the `object.get(name)` method, as shown in section 7.1.1. This is a last resort as far as the Groovy runtime is concerned: it's used only when there's no appropriate JavaBeans property available and when `getProperty` isn't implemented.

It's worth noting that when `name` contains special characters that wouldn't be valid for an identifier, it can be supplied in string delimiters—for example, `object.'my-name'`. You can also use a GString: `def name = 'my-name'; object."$name"`. As you saw in section 7.1.1 and we'll further explore in section 12.1.1, there's also a `getAt` implementation on `Object` that delegates to the property access so that you can access a property via `object[name]`.

The rationale behind the admittedly nontrivial reference resolution is to allow dynamic state and behavior for Groovy objects. Groovy comes with an example of how useful this feature is: *Expando*. An Expando can be thought of as an *expandable* alternative to a bean, albeit one that can be used only within Groovy and not directly in Java. It supports the Groovy style of property access with a few extensions. Listing 7.23 shows how an Expando object can be expanded with properties by assignment, analogous to maps. The difference comes with assigning closures to a property. Those are executed when accessing the property, optionally taking parameters. In the example, the boxer fights back by returning multiple times what he has taken before.

Listing 7.23 An example using Expando

```
def boxer = new Expando()
assert null == boxer.takeThis

boxer.takeThis = 'ouch!'
assert 'ouch!' == boxer.takeThis

boxer.fightBack = {times -> delegate.takeThis * times  }
assert 'ouch!ouch!ouch!' == boxer.fightBack(3)
```

In a way, Expando's ability to assign closures to properties and have property access calling the stored closures is like dynamically attaching methods to an object.

Maps and Expandos are extreme solutions when it comes to avoiding writing simple data structures as classes, because they don't require *any* extra class to be written. In Groovy, accessing the keys of a map or the properties of an Expando doesn't look different from accessing the properties of a full-blown JavaBean. This comes at a price: Expandos cannot be used as beans in the Java world and don't support any kind of typing.

7.5   *Using advanced syntax features*

This section presents three power features that Groovy supports at the language level: GPath, the spread operator, and command chains.

We start by looking at GPaths. A *GPath* is a construction in Groovy code that powers object navigation. The name is chosen as an analogy to XPath, which is a standard for describing traversal of XML (and equivalent) documents. Just like an XPath, a GPath is aimed at expressiveness: realizing short, compact expressions that are still easy to read.

GPaths are almost entirely built on concepts that you've already seen: field access, shortened method calls, and the GDK methods added to `Collection`. They introduce only one new operator: the `*.` (*spread-dot*) operator. Let's start working with it right away.

7.5.1   *Querying objects with GPaths*

We'll explore Groovy by paving a path through the Reflection API. The goal is to get a sorted list of all getter methods for the current object. We'll do so step by step, so please open a `groovyConsole` and follow along. You'll try to get information about your current object, so type

```
this
```

and run the script (by pressing Ctrl-Enter). In the output pane, you'll see something like

```
Script1@e7e8eb
```

which is the string representation of the current object. To get information about the class of this object, you could use `this.getClass`, but in Groovy you can type

```
this.class
```

which displays (after you run the script again)

```
class Script2
```

The class object reveals available methods with `getMethods`, so type

```
this.class.methods
```

which prints a long list of method object descriptions. This is too much information for the moment. You're only interested in the method names. Each method object has a `getName` method, so call

```
this.class.methods.name
```

and get a list of method names, returned as a list of string objects. You can easily work on it, applying what you learned about strings, regular expressions, and lists. Because you're only interested in getter methods and want to have them sorted, type

```
this.class.methods.name.grep(~/get.*/).sort()
```

and voilà, you'll get the result

```
["getBinding", "getClass", "getMetaClass", "getProperty"]
```

Such an expression is called a GPath. One special thing about it is that you can call the name property on a list of method objects and receive a list of string objects—that is, the *names*.

The rule behind this is that

```
list.property
```

is equal to

```
list.collect{ item -> item?.property }
```

This is an abbreviation of the special case when properties are accessed on lists. The general case reads like

```
list*.member
```

where `*.` is the spread-dot operator and `member` can be a field access, a property access, or a method call. The spread-dot operator is needed whenever a method should be applied to all elements of the list rather than to the list itself. It is equivalent to

```
list.collect{ item -> item?.member }
```

To see GPath in action, we step into an example that's reasonably close to reality. Suppose you're processing invoices that consist of line items, where each line refers to the sold product and a multiplicity. A product has a price in dollars and a name. An invoice could look like table 7.3.

Table 7.3 Sample invoice

Name	Price in $	Count	Total
ULC	1,499	5	7,495
Visual editor	499	1	499

Figure 7.1 depicts the corresponding software model in a UML class diagram. The `Invoice` class aggregates multiple `LineItems` that in turn refer to a `Product`.

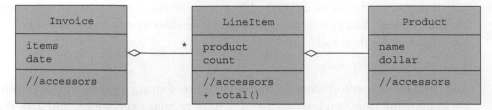

Figure 7.1   UML class diagram of an `Invoice` class that aggregates multiple instances of a `LineItem` class, which in turn aggregates exactly one instance of a `Product` class

The following listing is the Groovy implementation of this design. It defines the classes as GroovyBeans, constructs sample invoices with this structure, and uses GPath expressions to query the object graph in multiple ways.

Listing 7.24   Invoice example for GPath

```
class Invoice {
    List    items
    Date    date
}
class LineItem {
    Product product
    int     count
    int total() {
        return product.dollar * count
    }
}
class Product {
    String  name
    def     dollar
}

def ulcDate = Date.parse('yyyy-MM-dd', '2015-01-01')
def otherDate = Date.parse('yyyy-MM-dd', '2015-02-02')
def ulc = new Product(dollar:1499, name:'ULC')
def ve  = new Product(dollar:499,  name:'Visual Editor')

def invoices = [
    new Invoice(date:ulcDate, items: [
        new LineItem(count:5, product:ulc),
        new LineItem(count:1, product:ve)
    ]),
    new Invoice(date:otherDate, items: [
        new LineItem(count:4, product:ve)
    ])
]

def allItems = invoices.items.flatten()

assert [5*1499, 499, 4*499] == allItems*.total()

assert ['ULC'] == allItems.grep{it.total() > 7000}.product.name
```

Sets up data structures

Fills with sample data

❶ Total for each line item

❷ Query of product names

```
def searchDates = invoices.grep{
    it.items.any{it.product == ulc}
}.date*.toString()
assert [ulcDate.toString()] == searchDates
```

❸ Query of invoice date

The queries in the listing are fairly involved. The first ❶ finds the total for each invoice, adding up all the line items. We then run a query ❷ which finds all the names of products that have a line item with a total of over $7,000. The next query ❸ finds the date of each invoice containing a purchase of the ULC product and turns it into a string.

Printing the full Java equivalent here would cover several pages and would not be a very exciting read. Java 8 improves the Java comparison to some degree, but the metrics still very much favor Groovy whether you measure lines of code (LOC), number of statements, or complexity in the sense of nesting depth.

Writing less code isn't just an exercise for its own sake. It also means lower chances of making errors and thus less testing effort. Whereas some new developers think of a good day as one in which they've *added* lots of lines to the codebase, we consider a really good day as one in which we've added functionality but *removed* lines from the codebase.

In a lot of languages, less code comes at the expense of clarity. Not so in Groovy. The GPath example is the best proof. It's much easier to read and understand than its Java counterpart. Even the complexity metrics are superior.

As a final observation, consider maintainability. Suppose your customer refines their requirements, and you need to change the lookup logic. How much effort does that take in Groovy as opposed to Java?

7.5.2 *Injecting the spread operator*

Groovy provides a * (*spread*) operator that's connected to the spread-dot operator in that it deals with tearing a list apart. It can be seen as the reverse counterpart of the subscript operator that creates a list from a sequence of comma-separated objects. The spread operator distributes all items of a list to a receiver that can take this sequence. Such a receiver can be a method that takes a sequence of arguments or a list constructor.

What is this good for? Suppose you've a method that returns multiple results in a list, and your code needs to pass these results to a second method. The spread operator distributes the result values over the second method's parameters:

```
def getList(){
    return [1,2,3]
}
def sum(a,b,c){
    return a + b + c
}
assert 6 == sum(*list)
```

This allows clever meshing of methods that return and receive multiple values while allowing the receiving method to declare each parameter separately.

The distribution with the spread operator also works on ranges and when distributing all items of a list into a second list:

```
def range = (1..3)
assert [0,1,2,3] == [0,*range]
```

The same trick can be applied to maps:

```
def map = [a:1,b:2]
assert [a:1, b:2, c:3] == [c:3, *:map]
```

The spread operator eliminates the need for boilerplate code that would otherwise be necessary to merge lists, ranges, and maps into the expected format. You'll see this in action in section 10.3, where this operator helps implement a user command language for database access.

As shown in the previous assertions, the spread operator is used inside expressions, supporting a functional style of programming as opposed to a procedural style. In a procedural style, you'd introduce statements like `list.addAll(otherlist)`.

Now comes a Groovy's syntax feature that makes reading Groovy code like plain English.

7.5.3   *Concise syntax with command chains*

Much of the Groovy goodness comes from the combination of simple language features. Command chains are such a feature that's based on a very simple idea: one can omit dots and parentheses in chain-of-method calls.

When a chain-of-method call looks like

```
link(producer).to(consumer)
```

then Groovy allows you to write this as

```
link producer to consumer
```

which reads like an English sentence and is immensely useful in DSLs.

Command chains are also possible with methods that have multiple arguments or that take an argument map. The following lines are equivalent:

```
move(10, forward).painting(color:blue)
move 10, forward painting color:blue
```

Note that this is a pure syntax feature and doesn't require any special provision when defining the methods. It works with all methods that have at least one argument. Without an argument, the syntax would be ambiguous. A method without parentheses and not at least one argument is indistinguishable from property access. If that were allowed, the sequencing of method names and arguments would be destroyed with one exception: in the very last position of a method chain. And, in fact, this is the one and only position where a property access is allowed.

Groovy is often perceived as a scripting language for the JVM, and it is. Scripts cannot impose lots of ceremonial syntax to please the compiler. That would be too cumbersome for the script author. But making Java scriptable isn't the most distinctive feature. Groovy syntax is made so that the programmer can always clearly reveal his intent.

7.6 Summary

Congratulations on making it to the end of this chapter. If you're new to dynamic languages, your head may be spinning right now—it's been quite a journey!

The chapter started without too many surprises, showing the similarities between Java and Groovy in terms of defining and organizing classes. As we introduced named parameters for constructors and methods, optional parameters for methods, and dynamic field lookup with the subscript operator, as well as Groovy's "load at runtime" abilities, it became obvious that Groovy has more spring in its step than Java.

Groovy's handling of the JavaBeans conventions reinforced this, as we showed Groovy classes with JavaBean-style properties that were simpler and more expressive to both create and use than their Java equivalents. By the time you saw Groovy's power features such as GPath, command chains, and traits, you could value the clarity of the syntax.

In retrospect, the dependencies and mutual support between these different aspects of the language become obvious: using the map datatype with default constructors, using the range datatype with the subscript operator, using operator overriding with the switch control structure, using closures for grepping through a list, using the list datatype in generic constructors, using bean properties with a fieldlike syntax, and so on. This seamless interplay not only gives Groovy its power but also makes it fun to use.

What's perhaps most striking is the compactness of the Groovy code, while the readability is preserved if not enhanced. It has been reported[20] that developer productivity hasn't improved much since the 1970s in terms of lines of code written per day. The boost in productivity comes from the fact that a single line of code nowadays expresses much more than in previous eras. Now, if a single line of Groovy can replace multiple lines of Java, we could start to see the next major boost in developer productivity.

Descriptions of static languages can stop at this point. You learned the syntax and that's it. Not so for Groovy. You've only swallowed the blue pill of the static parts of the language. Next comes the red pill for you: Groovy's dynamic language features.

---

[20] The *Journal of Defense Software Engineering*, 8/2000, www.crosstalkonline.org/storage/issue-archives/2000/200008/200008-0-Issue.pdf, based on the work of Gerald M. Weinberg.

Dynamic programming
with Groovy

8

> **This chapter covers**
> - How Groovy supports dynamic programming
> - An explanation of the Meta Object Protocol (MOP)
> - How to utilize the MOP for your own purposes

> *Until real software engineering is developed, the next best practice is to develop with a dynamic system that has extreme late binding in all aspects.*
>
> —Alan Kay

We're going to start our journey with a few general considerations about dynamic programming, how it differs from conventional object-oriented approaches, and why you want to have it in your toolbox. We'll show how the MOP serves as the central hub that provides you with dynamic programming capabilities. Groovy comes with dynamic features out-of-the-box but you can also add your own. There are various ways of achieving this and we'll start with the simpler ones and slowly move on to the more advanced use cases. As you'll see, there's no reason to be scared about words like "dynamic" or "meta." If by the end of this chapter you say, "Well, it isn't so magical after all," then we've achieved our goal.

If you seek perfection in completeness, designing and implementing an object-oriented system becomes hard. It may well be impossible.

Imagine you're responsible for `java.lang.Integer`. You're of course aware that this class will be used for counting, indexing, calculations, and so on, but you cannot possibly anticipate all use cases.

Before not too long, somebody will come along and would like to use it with a `times` method like in `3.times { println it }`, which you haven't foreseen, or calculate dates as in `2.weeks.from.today`, but you haven't provided a `getWeeks()` method on `Integer` that would be needed to make this possible.

On another occasion, another user of your class may prefer having an exception being thrown on `Integer.MAX_VALUE + 1` rather than returning a negative number.

A third user would like to optimize an algorithm and count the number of modulo operations on any integer that happen when the algorithm is executed. You're very unlikely to have anticipated such a requirement.

The good news is dynamic programming allows adding such *features* later—without even touching the original! And the original can even be a Java class as long as it's called from Groovy.

Changes to such a ubiquitously used class as `Integer` are better only applied to the scope where you need them or you risk interference with seemingly unrelated parts of your codebase. Therefore, dynamic programming allows using such a feature only temporarily: adding and removing it at runtime; limiting its use to a given piece of code, a class, or only single instances; or even confining it to the current thread of execution.

Dynamic programming has a wide range of applicability, including

- Designing DSLs (see chapter 18)
- Implementing builders (see chapter 11)
- Advanced logging, tracing, debugging, and profiling
- Automated testing even where testing seems impossible (see chapter 17)
- Putting lipstick on existing APIs—for example, by eliminating the "incomplete library class" smell[1]—to make them more complete, coherent, and accessible
- Organizing the codebase so that features are kept in one place even if their behavior involves the collaboration of multiple classes; for example, you need abstractions for date, time, and duration working together to provide the date-calculation feature.

The last point is particularly interesting. You can observe it in Grails where the *persistency feature* is dynamically available in all domain classes. On a domain class like `Person` you can call `Person.findAllByFirstName('Dierk')` to find all people in the database that share the first name Dierk, even though this method doesn't exist!

---

[1] See chapter 3 of *Refactoring*, by Martin Fowler and Kent Beck (Addison-Wesley, 1999).

Note that such an approach has one quality that static code generation never achieves: because the code isn't materialized anywhere, you cannot introduce errors in it! Also, your code is kept as clean as possible and you never have to read through code that was generated!

In this chapter, we'll go through the various means of dynamic programming in Groovy and provide examples of use cases. Now, let's start with looking at what mechanics make programming *dynamic*.

8.1   What is dynamic programming?

In classic object-oriented systems, every class has a well-known set of states, captured in the fields of that class, and well-known behavior, defined by its methods. Neither the set of states nor the behavior ever changes after compilation, and it's identical for all instances of a class.

Dynamic programming breaks this limitation by allowing the introduction of a new state, or even more importantly, allowing the addition of a new behavior or modification of an existing one.

What is "meta"?

Meta means applying a concept onto itself—for example, metainformation is information about information. Likewise, because programming is "writing code," metaprogramming means writing code that writes code. This includes source-code generation (for example, producing a long string that's then evaluated as a script), bytecode generation as explained in the next chapter, and pretending or synthesizing methods. The latter is part of dynamic programming and we'll encounter it later in this chapter.

The use of "meta" as a qualifier in the Groovy runtime system is in many places debatable. Anyway, it isn't only there for historical reasons; it also suggests that we're working on an elevated abstraction level whenever this word is used.

How can you possibly add a new state and behavior at runtime, when you're working on the JVM and the Java object model provides no such means? As the saying goes, "Every problem in computer science can be solved with a layer of indirection (besides the problem of too many layers of indirection)."[2] Enter the Meta Object Protocol.

8.2   Meta Object Protocol

The approach is actually rather straightforward. Whenever Groovy calls a method, it doesn't call it directly but asks an intermediate layer to do so on its behalf. The intermediate layer provides hooks that allow you to influence its inner workings.

---

[2] For a brief biography of David Wheeler, said to have invented the subroutine, see http://en.wikipedia.org/wiki/David_Wheeler_%28British_computer_scientist%29.

A protocol is a collection of rules and formats. The MOP is the collection of rules of how a request for a method call is handled by the Groovy runtime system and how to control the intermediate layer. The format of the protocol is defined by the respective APIs, which we'll walk through in the course of this chapter.

An important part of understanding the mechanics is knowing what it means when we say that Groovy calls a method. When writing Groovy source code, the Groovy compiler generates bytecode that calls into the MOP.

As an illustration, assume that your Groovy source code contains the statement

```
println 'Hello' // Groovy
```

Then the resulting bytecode that Groovy produces is roughly equivalent to the following Java code:

```
InvokerHelper.invokeMethod(this, "println", {"Hello"}); // Java
```

When executed, the `InvokerHelper` as part of the MOP looks for the method named `"println"` with a `String` argument, finds that the Groovy runtime has registered such a method for `java.lang.Object`, and calls that implementation. This is a slightly simplified description of what actually happens, but one that explains the principle and one that we can start with.

> **NOTE** Every innocent method call that you write in Groovy is really a call into the MOP, regardless of whether the call target has been compiled with Groovy or Java. This applies equally to static and instance method calls, constructor calls, and property access, even if the target is the same object as the caller.

Figure 8.1 shows how the MOP works like a filter for all method calls that originate from code that was compiled by Groovy. The MOP is like a pair of rainbow-colored glasses that makes all objects appear rich and powerful.

Figure 8.1 shows what happens by default. Of course, you can also call into the MOP from Java but this requires calling `InvokerHelper.invokeMethod()` explicitly. By default, Java classes only see what's in the bytecode of a class and not what the MOP adds to it, even if the target class was compiled by Groovy.

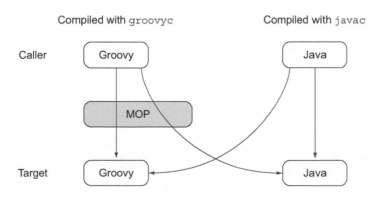

Figure 8.1 Every method call from a Groovy class or object into either Groovy or Java automatically goes through the MOP. Method calls from Java to both Groovy and Java targets don't use the MOP per default.

There's no spoon

Relating to the *Matrix* motion picture,[3] there's no such thing as a Groovy class. You may have noticed that we avoid the wording of Java class versus Groovy class. That's because classes are classes, regardless of who compiled them. They have the same format and constraints. Of course, they differ in content, but so do all classes anyway.

The MOP needs a lot of information to find the right call target for each method call that it serves. This information is stored in so-called metaclasses. These metaclasses aren't fixed. One part of dynamic programming is changing the content of metaclasses and replacing one metaclass with another. We'll explore this in section 8.4.

But even with the default metaclass being in place, which does nothing fancy besides providing the GDK methods and doing some very advanced performance optimizations, the MOP knows about some special methods that allow the first degree of dynamic behavior. They're called *hook methods*.

8.3   *Customizing the MOP with hook methods*

The core of the MOP responsibilities is finding and selecting the right target method and handling the case when the requested method cannot be found. The first hook method that we'll look at allows customizing the "missing method" case. A second one covers the case that a property access fails to find a property of the requested name. Then we'll explore the effects of combining hook methods with closure properties to allow instance-specific hooks that can even change at runtime. We finish up with custom logic for methods that objects need to provide if they implement the Groovy-Object interface.

8.3.1   *Customizing methodMissing*

Whenever a method cannot be found in the target object, the MOP looks for the hook method

```
Object methodMissing(String name, Object arguments)
```

and invokes it with the requested method name and arguments.

The next listing uses this hook in a Pretender class to merely return a string that shows what had been requested. The Pretender only *pretends*[4] to have the method hello(String), but in the bytecode of the class there's no such method.

---

[3]   The main character sees a child playing with a dynamic spoon object and realizes that it isn't a truly physical object. Dynamic programming is kind of like that.

[4]   Some call this a synthesized method, but we feel this suggests that it somehow materializes, which it doesn't.

Listing 8.1 Bouncing when a missing method is called

```
class Pretender {
    def methodMissing(String name, Object args) {
        "called $name with $args"
    }
}
def bounce = new Pretender()
assert bounce.hello('world') == 'called hello with [world]'
```

The target is absolutely free in what it does inside `methodMissing`. It may provide a
more sophisticated error handling than merely throwing a `MissingMethodException`
(which is the default), delegate all calls to a collaborating object, or inspect the
method name and arguments to derive what needs to be done.

The use case in listing 8.1 goes into the direction that Grails provides with its
dynamic finder methods in the Groovy object-relational mapping (GORM). The following listing outlines the approach. A method name like `findByXXX` is analyzed to
select the search criterion.

Listing 8.2 Using `methodMissing` to simulate a miniature GORM

```
class MiniGorm {
    def db = []
    def methodMissing(String name, Object args) {
        db.find { it[name.toLowerCase()-'findby'] == args[0] }    ← Extracts
    }                                                                criterion from
}                                                                    method name

def people = new MiniGorm()                          ← Sets up
def dierk  = [first: 'Dierk', last:'Koenig']           test data
def paul   = [first: 'Paul',  last:'King']
people.db << dierk << paul                           ← Calls with
                                                       pretended
assert people.findByFirst('Dierk') == dierk          ← methods
assert people.findByLast('King')   == paul
```

Of course, a full implementation of GORM dynamic finder methods is more complex,
but the principle and the mechanics are the same.

> **FOR THE GEEKS** You can share the implementation of `methodMissing` by vari-
> ous means. One is to put it in a base superclass. In section 8.4 we'll see how
> methods can be injected into a class without even pretending to have access
> to the code of that class! You can even pretend to have hook methods.

The `methodMissing` hook is quite simple to understand and use. Yet, it's very versatile
and covers the vast majority of use cases for dynamic programming with DSLs. It's a
very good entry point into dynamic programming and a good default choice when
deciding upon which means of dynamic programming to apply. It comes with a counterpart that does to property access what `methodMissing` does to method calls.

8.3.2 *Customizing propertyMissing*

What `methodMissing` is for method calls, `propertyMissing` is for property access. You implement

```
Object propertyMissing(String name)
```

to catch all access to nonexisting properties. All the rest is exactly analogous to `methodMissing` such that the following listing should be rather self-explanatory. We try to access the `hello` property, which isn't in the bytecode.

Listing 8.3 Bouncing when a missing property is accessed

```
class PropPretender {
    def propertyMissing(String name) {
        "accessed $name"
    }
}
def bounce = new PropPretender()
assert bounce.hello == 'accessed hello'
```

This hook is a specialization of `methodMissing`: if you pretend the respective getter method, you achieve the same effect. Anyway, having this more specialized hook is sometimes convenient. In listing 8.4 we use this hook as a method of the `Script` class to implement an easy way to calculate with binary numbers. This actually feels like a DSL.

The idea is quite simple. We'd like to use symbols like `IOOI` to specify a positive integer of value 9 in its binary form. Now, simply using this symbol would throw us a `MissingPropertyException`. By providing a `propertyMissing` hook we can do the translation from a string into an integer.

Listing 8.4 Using `propertyMissing` to calculate with binary numbers in DSL style

```
def propertyMissing(String name) {
    int result = 0
    name.each {
        result <<= 1
        if (it == 'I') result++
    }
    return result
}
assert IIOI +
       IOI ==
    IOOIO
```

In case you have difficulties with the string-to-integer translation logic here, don't worry, it's an implementation detail. The main point to take away is how to use the hook method.

Where there's specialization, there may also be generalization and, actually, there is. But before we come to that in section 8.3.4, we'll enter a new dimension of dynamicity.

8.3.3   Using closures for dynamic hooks

By now, you may have the impression that MOP hook methods are very conventional. And in a way they are. They're just ordinary methods.

But if you think that this means that their behavior is guaranteed to be identical for all instances of your class, then this isn't quite so in Groovy. In fact, if you wish so, you can even change the hook logic during the lifetime of an object!

Hook methods aren't static. They're instance methods. Being that, they can work with the object's state. This state can include parameters for the hook logic. If these properties are of type `Closure`, then we have another example of parameterization with logic (see chapter 5).

The next listing maintains a `whatToDo` property of type `Closure` that's called from inside a hook method. This allows changing the hook logic at runtime, and (not shown) having multiple instances of `DynamicPretender` using different closures.

Listing 8.5   Using the closure property to change hook logic at runtime

```
class DynamicPretender {
    Closure whatToDo = { name -> "accessed $name"}      ◁─┤  Closure property
    def propertyMissing(String name) {                        with default logic
        whatToDo(name)                     ◁─┐  Delegates to
    }                                         the closure
}
def one = new DynamicPretender()
assert one.hello == 'accessed hello'
one.whatToDo     = { name -> name.size() }   ◁─┐  Changes hook
assert one.hello == 5                            behavior at runtime
```

In classic Java programming, the behavior of a class never changes and the behavior is the same for all objects of the class. At best, you can use a Strategy pattern[5] to switch between objects that behave differently. The previous pattern of using a closure property to customize behavior of an object has a dynamic touch in itself, even though it's totally independent of the MOP. But in combination with the MOP, it adds a new dimension to the solution space.

> **NOTE** All features of dynamic programming that are explained in this chapter can be combined with closure properties to open another dimension of versatility.

The hook methods that we've talked about so far apply regardless whether the call target is compiled by Groovy or Java. The next section will be about more specific handling that the MOP applies to Groovy targets.

---

[5] *Design Patterns: Elements of Reusable Object-Oriented Software*, by Gamma et al. (Addison-Wesley, 1994).

8.3.4 *Customizing GroovyObject methods*

All classes that are compiled by Groovy implement the GroovyObject interface, which looks like this:

```
public interface GroovyObject {
    Object    invokeMethod(String methodName, Object args);
    Object    getProperty(String propertyName);
    void      setProperty(String propertyName, Object newValue);
    MetaClass getMetaClass();
    void      setMetaClass(MetaClass metaClass);
}
```

Again, you're free to implement any such methods in your Groovy class to your liking. If you don't, then the Groovy compiler will insert a default implementation for you. This default implementation is the same as if you'd inherit from GroovyObjectSupport, which basically relays all calls to the metaclass. It roughly looks like this (excerpt):

```
public abstract class GroovyObjectSupport implements GroovyObject {

    public Object invokeMethod(String name, Object args) {
        return getMetaClass().invokeMethod(this, name, args);
    }
    public Object getProperty(String property) {
        return getMetaClass().getProperty(this, property);
    }
    public void setProperty(String property, Object newValue) {
        getMetaClass().setProperty(this, property, newValue);
    }
    // more here...
}
```

We defer the explanation of the metaclass handling to the next section. For the moment, it's just a device that we can use for calling into the MOP.

> **NOTE** You can fool the MOP into thinking that a class that was actually compiled by Java was compiled by Groovy. You only need to implement the Groovy-Object interface or, more conveniently, extend GroovyObjectSupport.

As soon as a class implements GroovyObject, the following rules apply:

- Every access to a property calls the getProperty() method.[6]
- Every modification of a property calls the setProperty() method.
- Every call to an unknown method calls invokeMethod(). If the method is known, invokeMethod() is only called if the class implements GroovyObject and the marker interface GroovyInterceptable.

Let's use this newly acquired knowledge to play with the Groovy language rules. In Groovy, parentheses for method calls are optional for top-level statements, but only if

---

[6] There is a special handling for maps in the default metaclass that makes sure that even though Map isn't a GroovyObject, every property access on a map is relayed to the respective MapEntry.

there's at least one argument. This is needed to distinguish method calls from property access. We cannot call `toString()` without the parentheses because `toString` would refer to the property of the name `toString`. The next listing allows us to go around this limitation. We implement `getProperty()` such that if the property exists, we return its value; if not, we assume that the parameterless method will be executed. Such a feature can be interesting when designing DSLs.

> **Listing 8.6 Using `getProperty` to call parameterless methods without parentheses**

```
class NoParens {
    def getProperty(String propertyName) {                      ❶ Properties
        if (metaClass.hasProperty(this, propertyName)) {           have priority
            return metaClass.getProperty(this, propertyName)
        }
        invokeMethod propertyName, null        ❷ Dynamic
    }                                             invocation
}

class PropUser extends NoParens {              ❸ Subclass for
    boolean existingProperty = true               feature sharing
}

def user = new PropUser()
assert user.existingProperty                   ❹ Look, Ma, no
assert user.toString() == user.toString           parentheses!
```

This example uses the metaclass and so leads us slowly into the topic of the next section where we'll explore this concept in more detail.

When we ❶ check whether a known property is requested, we ask the `metaClass` (that is, we call the `getMetaClass()` method) if it has such a property. In case it has, we ask the `metaClass` for its value. Note that we cannot simply use `this."$propertyName"` because this would call `getProperty()` again, leading to endless recursion.

To eventually execute the method ❷, we call the default implementation of the `invokeMethod()` hook, which relays the call to the metaclass.

We see in ❸ that subclasses can share this `NoParens` feature. Subclassing is generally not a good way of sharing features but it works. We'll discuss this further and provide better alternatives at a later time.

We assert ❹ that omitting parentheses really works with selecting the ubiquitously available `toString()` method as our test candidate. Existing properties remain untouched.

Implementing `get/setProperty` can often improve the elegance of an API. Just consider Groovy maps. They relay property access like `map.a` to map content access like `map['a']` and you can do the equivalent with your own objects.

> **NOTE** Once you've implemented `getProperty()`, every property will be found and thus `propertyMissing()` will no longer be called.

So far, you've seen various means of dynamic programming that require access to the source code of the target class and the possibility to apply modifications to it. We call this approach *intrusive.* You may be glad to hear that there's also a *nonintrusive* approach, which is the topic of our next section.

8.4   *Modifying behavior through the metaclass*

By now you should feel at ease with the situation that all method calls that originate from Groovy code are routed through the MOP. If the last sentence still sounds odd to you, consider rereading section 8.2 and doing more experiments around the provided examples until you've gained enough confidence to proceed.

With `methodMissing` and `propertyMissing` you've seen examples of hook methods that the MOP invokes when it cannot find the requested method or property. In this section, we'll explore how Groovy tries to locate those and how you can use the lookup mechanism for the purposes of customizing the object's behavior.

8.4.1   *MetaClass knows it all*

For every class `A` in the class loader, Groovy maintains a metaclass—an object of type `MetaClass`. This metaclass maintains the collection of all methods and properties of `A`, starting with the bytecode information of `A` and adding additional methods that Groovy knows about per default (`DefaultGroovyMethods`).

Generally, all instances of class `A` share the same metaclass. But Groovy also supports having per-instance metaclasses—that is, different instances of `A` may refer to different metaclasses. We'll revisit this situation later.

You can easily ask any metaclass for its metainformation (recall seeing the information in figure 1.6, which displayed the Groovy Object Browser).

Listing 8.7 inspects the capabilities of `MetaClass` by asking `String` for its metaclass and calling various methods on it. We inspect the availability of methods with `respondsTo`, list all `properties`, list all `methods` from the bytecode, list all `meta-Methods` that Groovy added dynamically, and call `invokeMethod`, `invokeStaticMethod`, and `invokeConstructor` to show dynamic invocation.

> **Listing 8.7 `MetaClass` is key to Groovy reflection and dynamic method invocation**

```
MetaClass mc = String.metaClass
final Object[] NO_ARGS = []
assert   1   == mc.respondsTo("toString", NO_ARGS).size()
assert   3   == mc.properties.size()
assert  74   == mc.methods.size()                          ⟵  Numbers may vary
assert 176   == mc.metaMethods.size()                           depending on Java
assert ""    == mc.invokeMethod("","toString", NO_ARGS)         version.
assert null  == mc.invokeStaticMethod(String, "println", NO_ARGS)
assert ""    == mc.invokeConstructor(NO_ARGS)
```

There are more methods and more variants in `MetaClass`, but those in the previous listing give a good overview of what it does in general: providing means of *reflection* and *dynamic invocation.*

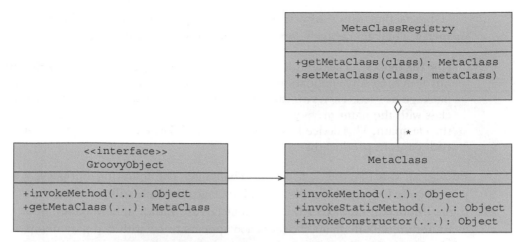

Figure 8.2   A UML class diagram of the `GroovyObject` **interface that refers to an instance of class** `MetaClass`, **where** `MetaClass` **objects are also aggregated by the** `MetaClassRegistry` **to allow class-based retrieval of metaclasses in addition to** `GroovyObject`**'s optional object-based retrieval.**

Calling a method means calling the metaclass

You can assume that Groovy never calls methods directly in the bytecode but always through the object's metaclass. At least, this is how it looks to you as a programmer.

Behind the scenes there are optimizations going on that technically circumvent the metaclass, but only when it's safe to do so.

Even the MOP hook methods that you've seen in earlier sections make no exception. If you provide your own implementation of let's say `invokeMethod`, then this method is added to your object's metaclass at class loading time and later invoked from there.[7]

All this should look to you as a pretty simple rule and you may ask what's so special about it. The trick is that a metaclass can change at runtime and that an object may also change its metaclass. Let's first investigate how Groovy finds metaclasses.

8.4.2   How to find the metaclass and invoke methods

You've seen that all `GroovyObjects` have a `metaClass` property (`setMetaClass` and `getMetaClass` methods). That makes it easy to find the metaclass for them. You simply ask the object with `obj.metaClass`.

If you don't provide a custom implementation of the `metaClass` property accessor methods, the default implementation looks up the metaclass in the so-called `Meta-ClassRegistry`. The registry maintains a map of classes and their metaclasses. Figure 8.2 displays the connection among `GroovyObject`, `MetaClass`, and `MetaClassRegistry`.

---

[7] If you add hook methods like `invokeMethod` to a superclass or interface, you need to previously call `Expando-MetaClass.enableGlobally()` if you want that hook method to apply further down the inheritance hierarchy.

Objects that don't inherit from GroovyObject aren't asked for the metaClass property. Their metaclass is retrieved from the MetaClassRegistry.

FOR THE GEEKS   The default metaclass can be changed from the outside without touching any application code. Let's assume you have a class Custom in package custom. Then you can change its default metaclass by putting a metaclass with the name groovy.runtime.metaclass.custom.CustomMetaClass on the classpath. This device has been proven useful when inspecting large Groovy codebases in production.

Putting all this together is a bit of a challenge. The following snippet is a sketch in pseudocode to keep the level of detail manageable while still revealing the core of the logic. Important methods from the metaclass are shown in bold italics, hook methods as underlined. Note that invokeMethod appears twice: with two parameters as a hook method and with three parameters in MetaClass.

At the very beginning, you decide whether you have a GroovyObject and, if not, look for the metaclass in the registry and use it to invoke the requested method:

```
// MOP pseudo code
def mopInvoke(Object obj, String method, Object args) {
    if (obj instanceof GroovyObject) {
        return groovyObjectInvoke(obj, method, args)
    }
    registry.getMetaClass(obj.class).invokeMethod(obj, method, args)
}
```

If you have a GroovyObject, you use the metaClass property to find the metaclass but you also have to care for the special handling around GroovyInterceptable and unknown methods (see section 8.2):

```
def groovyObjectInvoke(Object obj, String method, Object args){
    if (obj instanceof GroovyInterceptable) {
        return obj.metaClass.invokeMethod(method, args)
    }
    if (! obj.metaClass.respondsTo(method, args)) {
        return obj.metaClass.invokeMethod(method, args)
    }
    obj.metaClass.invokeMethod(obj, method, args)
}
```

You may ask why methodMissing doesn't appear in the preceding code. This case is handled in the default metaclass:

```
// Default meta class pseudo code
def invokeMethod(Object obj, String method, Object args) {
    if (obj.metaClass.respondsTo(method, args)) {
        return methodCall(obj, method, args)
    }
```

```
    if (methodMissingAvailable(obj)) {
        return obj.metaClass.methodMissing(method, args)
    }
    throw new MissingMethodException()
}
```

Don't forget that all the previous is pseudocode, that actual implementation differs quite a bit, mostly for performance reasons. Also, the code is supposed to have Java semantics; that is, all method calls and property access are direct and don't go through the MOP itself. Otherwise, you'd run into endless recursion.

The mechanics of the MOP may appear complex but for usual cases you can assume that all method calls go through the metaclass and the default metaclass is in place. This raises the question what other metaclasses are available and why you'd want to use them.

8.4.3 Setting other metaclasses

Groovy comes with a number of metaclasses:

- The default metaclass `MetaClassImpl`, which is used in the vast majority of cases
- The `ExpandoMetaClass`, which can expand the state and behavior
- A `ProxyMetaClass`, which can decorate a metaclass with interception capabilities
- Additional metaclasses that are used internally and for testing purposes

Let's look at `ProxyMetaClass` as an example of how to use a customized metaclass. A `ProxyMetaClass` wraps an existing metaclass that it relays all method calls to. When doing so, it provides the ability to execute customized logic before and after each method call. That customized logic is captured in a so-called `Interceptor`. With Groovy comes a `TracingInterceptor` that simply logs all method access to a `writer`, effectively providing a trace of all method calls. The following listing configures such a `ProxyMetaClass` with a `TracingInterceptor` and assigns this metaclass to an arbitrary Groovy object that should be subject to tracing.

> **Listing 8.8   Assigning a `ProxyMetaClass` to a `GroovyObject` for tracing method calls**

```
class InspectMe {
    int outer(){
        return inner()
    }
    private int inner(){
        return 1
    }
}

def tracer = new TracingInterceptor(writer: new StringWriter())    ◁——❶ Setup
def proxyMetaClass = ProxyMetaClass.getInstance(InspectMe)
proxyMetaClass.interceptor = tracer

InspectMe inspectMe = new InspectMe()                        ❷ Assigning a
inspectMe.metaClass = proxyMetaClass                            metaclass
```

```
assert 1 == inspectMe.outer()                           ┌───  ❸  Normal
                                                        ◄─┘        method call
assert "\n" + tracer.writer.toString() == """
before InspectMe.outer()
  before InspectMe.inner()
  after  InspectMe.inner()
after  InspectMe.outer()
"""
```

Our self-testing code requires a small change to the default. In ❶ we set up the Tracing-Interceptor to not print to System.out but to use a StringWriter that we can later inspect for its content.

In ❷ we assign our metaclass to the object under inspection. We do have a per-instance metaclass this way.

When we call any method on our object under inspection as in ❸, then all method calls and returns are traced, even in private methods. Note that this doesn't require any change in InspectMe nor is that class in any way aware of the tracing. It's all controlled from the outside. This is what we call *nonintrusive*.

> **Interceptors are more than aspects**
>
> Interceptors may remind one or the other reader of aspect-oriented programming (AOP) and the TracingInterceptor suggests this connotation. But interceptors can do much more: they can redirect to a different method, change the arguments, suppress the method call, and even change the return value!

Oftentimes, you may want to use the proxy metaclass only temporarily and set the metaclass back to the original afterwards. In such a case you can put the proxy-using code inside a closure and give it to the use method like this:

```
proxyMetaClass.use(inspectMe){
    inspectMe.outer() // proxy in use
}
// proxy is no longer in use
```

Manually setting the metaclass of a Groovy object works as expected and working through the example has confirmed your understanding of the MOP. But Groovy wouldn't be Groovy if it would leave you behind with only the low-level devices.

In the next sections you'll see ways of working with the MOP on a higher level of abstraction to make it more accessible, more flexible, and more convenient to work with for specialized use cases.

8.4.4 *Expanding the metaclass*

Groovy has, since its early days, a class called Expando. It's a tiny class with few methods but one interesting characteristic: it can expand its state and behavior. The following listing uses an Expando as a boxer who can take some hits but will eventually fight back.

Listing 8.9   An `Expando` can extend the state and behavior at runtime

```
def boxer = new Expando()

boxer.takeThis  = 'ouch!'
boxer.fightBack = { times -> takeThis * times  }

assert boxer.fightBack(3) == 'ouch!ouch!ouch!'
```

A new state is assigned to not-yet-existing properties, analogous to what you've seen for maps.

A new behavior is assigned to not-yet-existing properties as closures. After the assignment, it can be called as if it was a method.

The reason for explaining the `Expando` class here is that there's an `ExpandoMetaClass` in Groovy that, as you may have guessed, is a metaclass that works like an `Expando`. You can register a new state (properties) and new behavior (methods) in the metaclass by using property assignments.

Listing 8.10 introduces the concept with an example that adds a new method called `low()` to `java.lang.String`. It does the same as `toLowerCase()` but is shorter and the spelling is easier to remember. We don't need to set the `ExpandoMetaClass` explicitly. Groovy automatically replaces the default metaclass with an `ExpandoMetaClass` when we apply any modification to it.

Listing 8.10   Adding `low()` to `java.lang.String` via `ExpandoMetaClass`

```
assert String.metaClass =~ /MetaClassImpl/
String.metaClass.low   = {-> delegate.toLowerCase() }
assert String.metaClass =~ /ExpandoMetaClass/

assert "DiErK".low() == "dierk"
```

Note that our closure uses the `delegate` reference to refer to the actual `String` instance that the closure is called upon. The closure must also have the right number of parameters. The usual rules for closure parameters apply—type markers are optional, and you can use default values, varargs, and so forth. Because our method will not have any parameters we use an empty parameter list `{-> ...}`.

The next listing adds a new property (`myProp`) and a new method (`test`) to the metaclass of `MyGroovy1`—a class that's written in Groovy. Note that the dynamic `test` method refers to the dynamic property `myProp`. These dynamic features are only available for objects of type `MyGroovy1` that have been constructed *after* the metaclass modification.

Listing 8.11   Modifying the metaclass of a class (Groovy and Java)

```
class MyGroovy1 { }

def before = new MyGroovy1()

MyGroovy1.metaClass.myProp = "MyGroovy prop"
MyGroovy1.metaClass.test = {-> myProp }
```

```
try {
    before.test()
    assert false, "should throw MME"
} catch(mme) { }

assert new MyGroovy1().test() == "MyGroovy prop"
```

Not available

Here we've changed the metaclass of a class and thus for all instances of that class. In the following listing we do the very same but only on a single instance. Only the myGroovy instance gets the new dynamic features because we only modify a per-instance metaclass.

Listing 8.12 Modifying the metaclass of a Groovy instance

```
class MyGroovy2 { }

def myGroovy = new MyGroovy2()

myGroovy.metaClass.myProp = "MyGroovy prop"
myGroovy.metaClass.test = {-> myProp }

try {
    new MyGroovy2().test()
    assert false, "should throw MME"
} catch(mme) { }

assert myGroovy.test() == "MyGroovy prop"
```

Not available

Per-instance metaclasses are very valuable because they allow fine-grained control over where and how dynamic features are added.

Imagine a large development team where accidentally two developers modify the same metaclass with the same method names for different reasons. The last modification wins and may compromise the logic of the developer who did the first change.[8]

With per-instance metaclasses such clashes are easier to avoid. The next listing uses per-instance metaclasses even for such a ubiquitous Java object as a String while avoiding clashes.

Listing 8.13 Modifying the metaclass of a Java instance

```
def myJava = new String()

myJava.metaClass.myProp = "MyJava prop"
myJava.metaClass.test = {-> myProp }

try {
    new String().test()
    assert false, "should throw MME"
} catch(mme) { }

assert myJava.test() == "MyJava prop"
```

Not available

---

[8] This situation is often called "monkey patching," referring to programmers who use programming constructs that they've seen elsewhere without fully understanding what they do: "monkey see, monkey do."

So far, we've asked classes and objects for their metaclass every single time when we did a modification. Listing 8.14 introduces a new so-called *builder* style for doing multiple changes at once. We use it to encode and decode strings by moving every character up and down the alphabet with the respective methods, a metaclass property to capture how many characters to shift up or down, and property accessor methods to work more conveniently with the code and the original.

If you've ever seen Stanley Kubrick's motion picture *A Space Odyssey*, you may remember the super-intelligent computer HAL. It turns out that this is an encoded version of IBM. Well, things could have been worse for that company if the writer Arthur C. Clarke had chosen a different shift distance for the encoding...

Listing 8.14 Decoding *A Space Odyssey* with a metaclass builder

```
def move(string, distance) {
    string.collect { (it as char) + distance as char }.join()
}

String.metaClass {
    shift = -1
    encode  {-> move delegate, shift  }
    decode  {-> move delegate, -shift }
    getCode {-> encode() }
    getOrig {-> decode() }
}

assert "IBM".encode() == "HAL"
assert "HAL".orig     == "IBM"

def ibm = "IBM"
ibm.shift = 7
assert ibm.code == "PIT"
```

Note that we can change the shift distance on a per-instance basis by setting the respective property.

NOTE Modifying the metaclass of the String class will affect all future String instances.

In all the preceding examples, we've added new instance methods to all instances of a class or to only a specific instance of a class. The following listing adds a static method to java.lang.Integer by using the static keyword. We can now ask the Integer class (as opposed to an Integer object) for the answer to "life, the universe, and everything."

Listing 8.15 Adding a static method to a class

```
Integer.metaClass.static.answer = {-> 42}

assert Integer.answer() == 42
```

When talking about objects, we also have to consider inheritance. Listing 8.16 adds a new method `toTable()` dynamically to a superclass and asserts that it's transparently available in its subclass.

We can even modify the metaclass of interfaces and all classes that implement this interface share the new behavior.

Listing 8.16   Metaclass changes for superclasses and interfaces

```
class MySuperGroovy { }
class MySubGroovy extends MySuperGroovy { }

MySuperGroovy.metaClass.added = {-> true }

assert new MySubGroovy().added()

Map.metaClass.toTable = {->
    delegate.collect{ [it.key, it.value] }
}

assert [a:1, b:2].toTable() == [
    ['a', 1],
    ['b', 2]
]
```

Note that we call `toTable()` on a literally declared map, which is of type `LinkedHash-Map`. Even though we've added the new method to the metaclass of the `java.util.Map` interface, it's available for all instances of its subtypes.

We mop[9] up the metaclass topic with an example that should illustrate that we can add any kind of method dynamically, even operator methods and MOP hook methods.

Listing 8.17 adds the `>>>` operator to strings with the `rightShiftUnsigned` operator method to split the string by words and push them to the right. It then replaces names with nicknames by calling a method of the to-be-replaced name with the replacement as the argument. To make this possible for every conceivable name, it adds the `methodMissing` hook to `String`.

Listing 8.17   Metaclass injection of operator and MOP hook methods

```
String.metaClass {
    rightShiftUnsigned = { prefix ->
        delegate.replaceAll(~/\w+/) { prefix + it }
    }
    methodMissing = { String name, args->
        delegate.replaceAll name, args[0]
    }
}

def people = "Dierk,Guillaume,Paul,Hamlet,Jon"
people  >>>= "\n    "
people     =   people.Dierk('Mittie').Guillaume('Mr.G')
```

---

[9] Pun intended but we'll try not to wring out the analogy too far.

```
assert people == '''
    Mittie,
    Mr.G,
    Paul,
    Hamlet,
    Jon'''
```

Some takeaways and rules of thumb for metaclasses:

- All method calls from Groovy code go through a metaclass.
- Metaclasses can change for all instances of a class or per a single instance.
- Metaclass changes affect all future instances in all running threads.
- Metaclasses allow nonintrusive changes to both Groovy and Java code as long as the caller is Groovy. We can even change access to final classes like `java.lang.String`.
- Metaclass changes can take the form of property accessors (pretending property access), operator methods, `GroovyObject` methods, or MOP hook methods.
- `ExpandoMetaClass` makes metaclass modifications more convenient.
- Metaclass changes are best applied only once, preferably at application startup time.

The last point directly leads us to another concept of dynamic programming in Groovy. `ExpandoMetaClass` isn't designed for easily removing a once dynamically added method or undoing any other change. For such temporary changes, Groovy provides category classes.

8.4.5 Temporary MOP modifications using category classes

Metaclasses are the main workhorses for dynamic programming in Groovy but sometimes you don't need their full power and would prefer an alternative that's small and focused and confined to the current thread and a small piece of code. This is exactly what category classes are. We'll look into how you use existing category classes, what benefits they bring, and how to write your own ones.

Using a category class is trivial. Groovy adds a `use` method to `java.lang.Object` that takes two parameters: a category class (or any number thereof) and a closure:

```
use CategoryClass, {
    // new methods are available
}
// new methods are no longer available
```

While the closure is executed, the MOP is modified as defined by the category. After the closure execution is finished, the MOP is reset to its old state.

Listing 8.18 leads us through two examples of using a category: a `TimeCategory` that's part of Groovy and the `java.util.Collections` class.

`TimeCategory` allows simplified working with date, time, and duration for both, easier definition and easier calculation. If you have an appointment in two weeks, you can find the date with `2.weeks.from.today`.

`Collections` is the unmodified class from the JDK. It contains a number of static helper methods.

Listing 8.18 How to use existing categories like `TimeCategory` and `Collections`

```
import groovy.time.TimeCategory

def janFirst1970 = new Date(0)
use TimeCategory, {
    Date   xmas = janFirst1970 + 1.year - 7.days
    assert xmas.month == Calendar.DECEMBER
    assert xmas.date  == 25
}

use Collections, {
    def list     = [0, 1, 2, 3]
    list.rotate 1
    assert list == [3, 0, 1, 2]
}
```

Inside the closures, we have new properties on numbers (1.year), new operator methods for calculating dates, and a new `rotate` method on lists. Outside the closures, no such feature is visible. Note that `janFirst1970` was constructed before the use closure.

Category classes are by no means special. Neither do they implement a certain interface nor do they inherit from a certain class. They aren't configured or registered anywhere! They just happen to contain static methods with at least one parameter.

When a class is used as an argument to the use method, it becomes a category class and every static method like

```
static ReturnType methodName(Receiver self, optionalArgs) {...}
```

becomes available on the receiver as if the `Receiver` had an instance method like

```
ReturnType methodName(optionalArgs) {...}
```

As always, an example says it better than any explanation. Listing 8.19 defines a class `Marshal` with static methods to `marshal` and `unMarshal` an integer to and from a string. The string version may be used for sending the integer to a remote machine. When we use the `Marshal` category class, we can call `marshal()` on an integer and `unMarshal()` on a string.

Listing 8.19 Running a category to `marshal` and `unMarshal` integers to/from strings

```
class Marshal {
    static String marshal(Integer self) {
        self.toString()
    }
    static Integer unMarshal(String self) {
        self.toInteger()
    }
}
```

```
use Marshal, {
    assert   1.marshal()   == "1"
    assert "1".unMarshal() == 1
    [Integer.MIN_VALUE, -1, 0, Integer.MAX_VALUE].each {
        assert it.marshal().unMarshal() == it
    }
}
```

Naming the receiver object self is just a convention. You can use any name you want. Groovy's design decision of using static methods to implement category behavior has a few beneficial effects.

- You're much less likely to run into concurrency issues, because there's less shared state.
- You can use a plethora of classes as categories even if they've been implemented without knowing about Groovy. Collections was just an example of many classes with static methods that reside in widely used helper libraries.
- They can easily be created in Groovy, Java, or any other JVM language that produces classes and static methods.

Category classes are a good place to collect methods that work conjointly on different types, such as Integer and String, to accomplish a feature like marshaling.

Key characteristics of using category classes are:

- The use method applies categories to the runtime scope of the closure (as opposed to the lexical scope). That means you can extract code from the closure into a method and call the method from inside the closure.
- Category use is confined to the current thread.
- Category use is nonintrusive.
- If the receiver type refers to a superclass or even an interface, then the method will be available in all subclasses/implementors without further configuration.
- Category method names can well take the form of property accessors (pretending property access), operator methods, and GroovyObject methods. MOP hook methods cannot be added through a category class.[10]
- Category methods can override method definitions in the metaclass.
- Where performance is crucial, use categories with care and measure their influence.
- Categories cannot introduce a new state in the receiver object; they cannot add new properties with a backing field.

The last point reveals that even though categories are a great tool for combining behavior into reusable features they do have their limitations when it comes to sharing state.

---

[10] This is a restriction as of Groovy 2.4. The feature may become available in later versions.

In addition to the way that you've seen here, there are two more ways to bring in category methods: as extension methods and through the @Category annotation.

8.4.6 *Writing extension modules*

Extension modules can be seen as categories that are always visible: you don't need to call use to enable the methods. Just like Groovy enriches the JDK classes with custom methods, you can make your categories globally visible and make them behave like methods from the GDK. One of the most interesting use cases for this is that you can bundle such extension modules into their own JAR file and make them available to other programs just by adding the JAR file to your classpath.

Converting a category into an extension module is straightforward. Imagine that you want to use the Marshal category defined in listing 8.19 without having to explicitly use the category. To achieve that, you only need two steps:

1 Write the Marshal class into its own source file (we'll place it in regina/Marshal.groovy).

2 Write an extension module descriptor and make it available on a classpath.

The first step is straightforward, but what is the descriptor file? You need to create a file named org.codehaus.groovy.runtime.ExtensionModule and ensure it's found in the META-INF/services folder of your JAR. This file is used internally by Groovy to load your extension module and make the category transparently available. The descriptor file consists of four entries:

```
moduleName=regina-marshal
moduleVersion=1.0
extensionClasses=regina.Marshal
staticExtensionClasses=
```

The moduleName and moduleVersion entries are used by Groovy when the runtime is initialized. If two versions of a module of the same name are found on the classpath, the module will not be loaded and an error will be thrown. The extensionClasses entry is a comma-separated list of category-like classes. This means that you can define multiple categories in a single extension module. Here there's only one extension class, so the line only contains the fully qualified name of the category class.

Interestingly, extension modules allow you to define static extension methods (add static methods to existing classes). In that case, the static methods must be defined in a separate class, but are written in the same way.

As you can see, bundling extension modules is very easy: the minimum that's required is a descriptor file. One could decide, for example, to write an extension module for the very famous StringUtils class from Apache Commons.[11] In that case, you wouldn't need to put the StringUtils class into your JAR file. All that's needed is a descriptor file, which makes the StringUtils class available as an extension module!

---

[11] Commons Lang provides helper utilities for the java.lang API, including String manipulation methods missing from java.lang.String. See http://commons.apache.org/proper/commons-lang/.

```
moduleName=apache-commons-stringutils
moduleVersion=3.2
extensionClasses=org.apache.commons.lang3.StringUtils
```

The use of the category format makes extension modules very appealing because it's a common pattern to find utility classes in the form of static methods. Commons Lang is just one example. Extension modules have an interesting advantage compared to categories: while the latter are totally dynamic, the former are statically bound (they're known when Groovy initializes), making them compatible with type checking and static compilation (see chapter 10 for details).

8.4.7   Using the @Category annotation

With `@Category`, you write your class as if it were an instance class but the annotation adjusts it to have the required format needed for categories, meaning, methods are made static and the `self` parameter, such as you saw in listing 18.9, is automatically added. The following listing shows how we might rewrite listing 18.9 to use the category annotation.

Listing 8.20   Using @Category to create your own category

```
@Category(Integer)
class IntegerMarshal {              ◁─┐   Specifies the
  String marshal() {                  ❶  type of self
    toString()            ◁─┐
  }                         │ ❷  Implicit
}                           ❷  this

@Category(String)
class StringMarshal {
  Integer unMarshal() {
    this.toInteger()        ◁─┐  Explicit
  }                         ❸  this
}
use ([IntegerMarshal, StringMarshal]) {   ◁─┐  List variant
  assert   1.marshal()    == "1"          ❹  of use
  assert "1".unMarshal() == 1
}
```

The `@Category` annotation can only be used for creating categories associated with a single class; therefore we split our category into two. First up is our category methods for `Integer`, though in this case there's only one. We place that method in an `IntegerMarshal` class and annotate it with `@Category(Integer)` ❶. Methods aren't written as static methods but in instance form with no `self` parameter required. Implicit ❷ and explicit ❸ references to `this` are automatically changed into `self` reference. Using our category class is the same as before, though in this case we now have two category classes so we use the list variant of the method ❹.

That finishes our discussion of categories. Next up are Mixins, which are the final topic in our dynamic programming tour.

8.4.8   *Merging classes with Mixins*

Have you ever noticed that in Java many interface names (`Appendable`, `Adjustable`, `Activatable`, `Callable`, `Cloneable`, `Closeable`, and many more) end with "-able"?. That's because they refer to an *ability*.

An object may have many abilities and so its class may implement many interfaces, but reusing implementations of any such ability is restricted to only one superclass. In Java and Groovy alike, you can only inherit once even though you can implement many interfaces.

> **NOTE** Using inheritance for reuse of an ability implementation is often frowned upon. Instead of implementation reuse, it's considered good object-oriented design to only use inheritance if there's a true is-a relationship between the subclass and superclass.

If you have a superclass A with a subclass B then any object of class B isn't only a B, it also *is* an A! The definitions of A and B typically reside in different files.[12] The situation looks as if A and B would be merged when constructing an instance of B. They share both state and behavior.

This class merging by inheritance is pretty restricted in Java.

- You cannot use it when inheritance has already been used for other purposes.
- You cannot merge (inherit from) more than one class.
- It's intrusive. You have to change the class definition.
- You cannot do it with final classes.

Groovy provides a feature called Mixin that addresses exactly these limitations. This feature comes in two flavors. The first flavor is the `@Mixin` class annotation. This feature is now deprecated because the more powerful trait mechanism (see section 7.3.4) provides a better alternative, but we'll describe it anyway for users of older versions of Groovy where traits didn't exist. The second flavor is the `mixin` method, which is available on any class or metaclass. We'll discuss this after `@Mixin`.

The following listing uses the `@Mixin` class annotation to mix reusable state and behavior into a test case that uses inheritance to be recognized by the testing framework.

Listing 8.21   Mixing a feature into a test case by using the `@Mixin` annotation

```
@Mixin(MessageFeature)
class FirstTest extends GroovyTestCase {
    void testWithMixinUsage() {
        message = "Called from Test"
        assertMessage "Called from Test"
    }
}
```

[12] Because of Java's late binding, you cannot even be sure that the A that was available at compile time is the same A that's used at runtime. Java is much more dynamic than many might assume.

```
class MessageFeature {
    def message
    void assertMessage(String msg) {
        assertEquals msg, message
    }
}
```

Note that you can execute listing 8.21 as a script and it will run the test case with the bundled JUnit. Test frameworks for both unit and functional tests tend to use inheritance a lot even though this is no longer considered good framework design. Inheritance makes it more difficult to nicely factor out common state and behavior. With Mixins, you can circumvent this restriction. They make a good companion for unit tests with JUnit and functional tests with Canoo WebTest.

Using the `@Mixin` annotation is intrusive. You have to change the code of the class that receives the new features. Listing 8.22, in contrast, works nonintrusively. It calls the `mixin` method on the `ArrayList` type to mix in two different features that "sieve" factors of 2 or any other number from a list of numbers. Such a feature is helpful when implementing the Sieve of Erastothenes[13] to efficiently find prime numbers.

Listing 8.22 Mixing in multiple sieve features nonintrusively

```
class EvenSieve {
    def getNo2() {
        removeAll { it % 2 == 0}
        return this
    }
}
class MinusSieve {
    def minus(int num) {
        removeAll { it % num == 0}
        return this
    }
}

ArrayList.mixin EvenSieve, MinusSieve

assert (0..10).toList().no2 - 3 - 5 == [1, 7]
```

You see that we can mix in multiple classes (`EvenSieve`, `MinusSieve`) with property accessor methods (`getNo2`) and operator methods (`minus`).

The surprising part is how easily the sieve classes implement their feature methods as if they were of type `ArrayList` themselves, which they aren't. Even the return value `this` refers to the actual `ArrayList` instance when the method is called from the `ArrayList`, but not when you're looking at `this` from inside the feature method.

Mixins are often compared with multiple inheritance but they're of a different nature. In the first place, our `ArrayList` doesn't become a subtype of `MinusSieve`.

---

[13] The Sieve of Eratosthenes is an ancient algorithm for finding all prime numbers up to any given limit. See http://en.wikipedia.org/wiki/Sieve_of_Eratosthenes.

Any `instanceof` test will fail. There's no is-a relationship and no polymorphism. You can use enforced type coercion with the as operator, though.

Unlike many models of multiple inheritance, the mixing in of new features always happens in traceable sequence and, in case of conflicts, the latest addition wins. Mixins work like metaclass changes in that respect.

To sum it up, here are the important characteristics of Mixins:

- You can instantiate objects from a blend of many classes. The object's state and behavior encompasses all properties and methods of all mixed classes.
- There's an intrusive use with the `@Mixin` class annotation and a nonintrusive use with the `mixin` method on classes. Both alternatives happen at runtime (as opposed to compile time). `@Mixin` happens at class construction time in a static initializer.
- Mixins are visible in all threads.
- There are no restrictions on what methods to mix in. Property accessors, operator methods, `GroovyObject` methods, and even MOP hook methods all work fine.
- You can mix into superclasses and interfaces.
- A Mixin can override a method of a previous Mixin but not methods in the metaclass.
- There's no per-instance Mixin. You can only mix into classes and metaclasses. To achieve the effect of a per-instance Mixin, you can mix into a per-instance metaclass.
- Mixins cannot easily be undone.

In general, Mixins are designed for sharing features while not modifying any existing behavior of the receiver. Features can build on top of each other and merge and blend with the receiver. And remember traits from section 7.3.4, which provide an alternative approach to some of the problems which Mixins solve.

MOP priorities

It's always good advice to keep things simple. With dynamic programming one can easily go overboard by doing too much, such as using category classes, metaclass changes, and Mixins in combination. If you do anyway, then categories are looked at first, then the metaclass, and finally the Mixins:

```
category class > meta class > mixin
```

But this only applies to methods that are defined for the same class and have the same parameter types. Otherwise, the rules for method dispatch by class/super-class/interface take precedence.

NOTE In case of multiple method definitions, a category class shadows a previously applied category class. Changes to an `ExpandoMetaClass` override previously added methods in that metaclass. Later applied Mixins shadow previously applied Mixins.

That's it for the technical description of Groovy's dynamic programming devices. We discussed quite a number of different concepts for you to understand and remember. Their real value will become apparent when you use them in practice and the following use cases may give you some inspiration for when and how to try dynamic programming yourself.

8.5 *Real-world dynamic programming in action*

After having seen the various means of dynamic programming in Groovy you may ask yourself how this applies to real-world projects. If you haven't seen much dynamic programming in your career so far, you may even ask whether it's valuable at all because, apparently, you've been able to live without it so far.

This section presents five scenarios that we've derived from working experience with Groovy. They're taken from real codebases with minor modifications. We'll always start with explaining the task so that you can take it as an exercise to come up with your own solution. Then we'll present a solution and talk about the design rationale. We start simple and proceed to the more complex.

8.5.1 *Calculating with metrics*

We always do silly mistakes when calculating with measurements that have a different order of magnitude. How many nanoseconds are there in a second? Hmm, we must concede that we'd rather look it up than guessing.

But Groovy can help us. Let's take meters, centimeters, and millimeters as a simple example. If we could simply write "1.m + 20.cm - 8.mm", that would be much easier than calculating with 1,192 millimeters.

The task is to make this possible. Calculations will be done in millimeters. The feature will be ubiquitously available.

The following listing addresses the requirements by adding the respective property accessor methods.

Listing 8.23 Metric calculations that avoid common magnitude mistakes

```
Number.metaClass {
    getMm = { delegate           }
    getCm = { delegate *  10.mm }
    getM  = { delegate * 100.cm }
}

assert 1.m + 20.cm - 8.mm == 1.192.m
```

We chose a metaclass modification as the vehicle to introduce the new getters for the remainder of the program. We add them to the Number interface to not only accommodate Integers but also Doubles, Floats, and so on.

Note that from inside one new feature method we can call the others. Specifying that one meter is 100 cm is more obvious than trying to specify a meter in terms of millimeters.

A solution like the example can be found in many DSLs. You'll find more examples in chapter 18.

8.5.2 *Replacing constructors with factory methods*

New objects are usually constructed by using the new keyword and a constructor as in new Integer(42). Many question this language design and you often hear the advice to favor factory methods over direct constructor calls.

The task is to change the Groovy language so that every class can be constructed by a static factory method called make with the same parameters as the respective constructor (for example, Integer.make(42) will replace new Integer(42)).

The next listing goes for a solution that's essentially a one-liner, even though it's typeset on three lines for better reading. It tests itself with factory methods that take zero, one, and two parameters.

Listing 8.24   Introducing static factory methods to all classes

```
import java.awt.Dimension

Class.metaClass.make = { Object[] args ->
    delegate.metaClass.invokeConstructor(*args)
}

assert new HashMap()         ==  HashMap.make()
assert new Integer(42)       ==  Integer.make(42)
assert new Dimension(2, 3)   ==  Dimension.make(2, 3)
```

Quite obviously, we have to introduce the make method on some metaclass. But which one? It will be available on every class—on every instance of java.lang.Class. Therefore, we add it to the metaclass of the Class class.[14]

Invoking the constructor is done dynamically; that is, on the metaclass of the current Class object, which we refer to as the delegate. To allow any number of parameters we use varargs (Object[]) in the closure parameter list and spread all arguments over the invokeConstructor argument list with the spread operator (*args).

This has been a tiny change and we've seemingly changed all classes in the system! That's the true power of dynamic programming. Try this with a static language.

Our example has a number of real-world uses. The Ruby language, for example, solely relies on this approach to constructing objects. Tammo Freese first explored the solution when he, Johannes Link, and I (Dierk) designed our "Groovy in a Day" workshop.

8.5.3 *Fooling IDEs for fun and profit*

Imagine you had a set of components that you have to connect. One component's output channel will be connected to another component's input channel. Let's call the process of defining the connections *wiring*.

---

[14] If you've gone cross-eyed by now, don't worry. That's a healthy reaction. Rereading and understanding the last paragraph will improve your nerd level at the possible risk of compromising your common sense.

You could do the wiring by maintaining a list of pairs where every pair reflects one connection between a source and a target component. But you don't get much IDE support when you create such pairs.

The task is to allow an approach to wiring that gives you IDE support and checks for assignable types such that only channels of assignable types are wired. All components should remain untouched in the wiring process.

The next listing comes up with a solution that fools your IDE into thinking that there would be property assignments while you actually intercept the assignment and only register the call for the wiring. Depending on the quality of your IDE support, it will check the assignment statements for assignable types and will suggest only those.

Listing 8.25 Temporarily faking property assignments for configuration purposes

```
interface ChannelComponent {}
class Producer implements ChannelComponent {
    List<Integer> outChannel
}
class Adaptor implements ChannelComponent {
    List<Integer> inChannel
    List<String>  outChannel
}
class Printer implements ChannelComponent {
    List<String> inChannel
}

class WiringCategory {
    static connections = []                                         Intercepts
    static setInChannel(ChannelComponent self, value){       <──┐   assignments
        connections << [target:self, source:value]
    }
    static getOutChannel(ChannelComponent self){
        self
    }
}

Producer producer = new Producer()
Adaptor  adaptor  = new Adaptor()
Printer  printer  = new Printer()

use WiringCategory, {
    adaptor.inChannel = producer.outChannel      Fakes
    printer.inChannel = adaptor.outChannel        assignments
}

assert WiringCategory.connections == [
        [source: producer, target: adaptor],
        [source: adaptor,  target: printer]
]
```

Because the components will remain untouched, you use a category class for the scope of the wiring. The assignments are intercepted by overriding the respective property getter and setter methods nonintrusively on the common interface of all components.

The solution is a simplified version of the wiring in the PillarOne project (www.pillarone.org). PillarOne is an open source project for risk calculation in the insurance industry. It makes heavy use of Groovy for specifying risk models made from wired components.

8.5.4 *Undoing metaclass modifications*

Modifying a metaclass is simple. Undoing such a modification can be a bit involved, though. The task is to try various approaches and to start with an experiment that modifies the `size()` method of `String` such that it returns twice the actual value by referring to the old implementation. Later you want to set the `size()` method back to the original behavior.

The next listing searches the metaclass of `String` for the `MetaMethod` of `size()` and stores it for later reference. A `MetaMethod` has an `invoke` method that takes the receiver object as the first parameter.

Listing 8.26 Method aliasing and undoing metaclass modifications

```
MetaClass oldMetaClass = String.metaClass                    ❶ Stores old
                                                                 metaclass
MetaMethod alias = String.metaClass.metaMethods
                   .find { it.name == 'size' }
String.metaClass {                                           ❷ Stores
    oldSize = { -> alias.invoke delegate  }                      MetaMethod
    size    = { -> oldSize() * 2 }
}

assert "abc".size()    == 6
assert "abc".oldSize() == 3

if (oldMetaClass.is(String.metaClass)){                      ❸ Reverses
    String.metaClass {                                           modification
        size    = { -> alias.invoke delegate }
        oldSize = { -> throw new UnsupportedOperationException() }
    }
} else {
    String.metaClass = oldMetaClass                          ❹ Resets
}                                                                metaclass

assert "abc".size() == 3
```

When overriding a method on the metaclass, there's nothing like "super" that we'd have used in subclasses to refer to an original implementation in a superclass. As a replacement, we introduce a new method `oldSize()` as an alias for the ❷ old method so that we can refer to it.

Undoing that modification comes in two flavors: doing a ❸ reverse modification or ❹ setting the metaclass instance back to the original instance ❶ in case the instance has changed. If before the modification the default metaclass was in use, then it was changed into an `ExpandoMetaClass` with the first modification and we can reset to the old metaclass. Otherwise, we've already started with an `ExpandoMetaClass` and only modified that instance.

Resetting the metaclass instance is the cleaner way but it's only available if there were no changes to the metaclass of `String` before we started. The code in listing 8.26 is again a simplified version of metaclass handling in the PillarOne project.

8.5.5 *The Intercept/Cache/Invoke pattern*

The `methodMissing` hook method is a cornerstone of the MOP. Some people even define dynamic programming by the availability of such a method. But it comes at a cost. Because Groovy first tries all other possibilities of finding a suitable method before it finally calls `methodMissing`, this requires some time. It's also very common that a method that has been called once will be called again.

The task is to step into `methodMissing` at most once for every distinct method call. For example, we want to support methods of the form `findBy<propertyName>(value)` that searches any collective datatype for items that have a property of that name with the given value. We seek an optimized and nonintrusive version of listing 8.2.

The following listing searches a list of maps for planets with a given name or average distance from Earth in astronomical units (rounded).

Listing 8.27   The Intercept/Cache/Invoke pattern for finding by property value

```
ArrayList.metaClass.methodMissing = { String name, Object args ->
    assert name.startsWith("findBy")
    assert args.size() == 1                                        ❶ Caches
    Object.metaClass."$name" = { value ->                            the
        delegate.find { it[name.toLowerCase()-'findby'] == value }   method
    }
    delegate."$name"(args[0])        ┌── Invokes the
}                                    ❷   method

def data = [
    [name:'moon',    au: 0.0025],
    [name:'sun',     au: 1    ],
    [name:'neptune', au:30    ],
]
                                     ┌── Intercepted
                                         call
assert data.findByName('moon')   ◄──
assert data.findByName('sun')    ◄──
assert data.findByAu(1)              ── Cached call
```

We add the `methodMissing` hook to the metaclass of `ArrayList`. Whenever we enter the hook method we add a new method of the requested name to our metaclass ❶. For this new method, the missing hook method will never be called again, because it's no longer missing. We've *synthesized* a new method.

We also need to execute the synthesized method, which we do in ❷.

The Intercept/Cache/Invoke pattern was invented by Graeme Rocher, the project lead of the Grails web platform. It's a core part of the Grails infrastructure. The productive version is a bit more elaborate than our example, mainly to work nicely in highly concurrent environments, but the general approach is the same.

8.6   *Summary*

We hope that by now you've gained a good overview of the concepts that allow dynamic programming with Groovy. These language capabilities may have been new to you and thus unfamiliar and maybe even daunting.

But even if they appear like magic, they're all easily explained by the fact that Groovy sees the world through the glasses of the MOP. The MOP itself offers many alternatives for adapting it to new necessities.

We can use the MOP hook methods intrusively or apply nonintrusive changes by switching metaclasses, modifying metaclasses, using categories, or mixing in a new state and behavior. All these devices come in combination with the Groovy method dispatch, property handling, operator methods, GroovyObject methods, and inheritance. The pervasive use of closures adds another dimension of dynamically changing behavior at runtime.

Once you've experienced the merits of dynamic programming, you'll find it unwieldy to go back to a static language.

You may be surprised to hear that the topic of dynamic programming isn't over, yet. What we've covered so far is the runtime aspect of it. But there are also compile-time aspects that we'll explore in the next chapter.

Compile-time metaprogramming and AST transformations

This chapter covers

- Removing redundancy and verbosity with Groovy's metaprogramming annotations
- Writing your own compiler extensions using the AST transformations feature
- Compile-time metaprogramming testing, tools, and pitfalls

It is my firm belief that all successful languages are grown and not merely designed from first principles.

—Bjarne Stroustrup,
The Design and Evolution of C++

The previous chapter covered dynamic programming with Groovy, where the behavior of a type or even an individual object can change while the program is executing. You don't always need the behavior to vary that dynamically though—sometimes you want only to be able to apply common patterns in an expressive and efficient manner once and for all when the class is compiled.

This chapter covers compile-time metaprogramming or AST transformations. You'll learn a bit about the concept and its importance. Then we'll explore most of the transformations Groovy ships with, such as @ToString, @EqualsAndHashCode, and @Lazy, and show you how these keep your code lean and clean. Next, we'll dive into more details about how AST transformations work and ways to create AST data structures. Then you'll write your own *local* and *global* AST transformations before we look at tools available for viewing and testing AST data structures. As a final step, you'll see some of the common mistakes and limitations encountered with compile-time metaprogramming.

9.1   *A brief history*

The term *compile-time metaprogramming* has only recently entered the vocabulary of mainstream Groovy developers and some of the more daring Java developers. But Java has had a long history of code generation: tools and frameworks that automatically create code in the hopes of reducing development time. In the good-old days, when CORBA services were the standard remoting technology, it was common to have Java source code automatically generated as part of your build process. More modern applications still do similar things. The common wsdl2java and wsimport applications read WSDL (Web Service Definition Language) interface documents and produce source code for projects using web services. This approach is so common that Maven even has a convention for dealing with the files: put them all in a folder called generated.

9.1.1   *Generating bytecode, not source code*

The technologies listed so far share a common trait: they all generate source code as part of the build process. Like many other modern languages, Groovy takes a different approach to code generation. Instead of writing out source code that the standard compiler can later read and convert to bytecode, Groovy lets you, the programmer, get involved in the compilation process.

> ### How are getters and setters generated?
> In Groovy there's no need to write getters and setters for fields: they'll be generated for you. This occurs without a separate source-code file listing these getters and setters hidden on the disk somewhere. The Groovy compiler is smart enough to just read your source and write out the correct class definition in the .class file. These changes are all visible from Java or other languages calling your code, because they're part of the compilation process. As far as anything looking at the class is concerned, the getters and setters exist as if they'd been handwritten.

From the very beginning, Groovy has made life easier for programmers by manipulating what gets written into the final JVM .class file. The difficulty was that if you wanted a new feature in the language, then you needed to download the Groovy source code and write the feature yourself. But this all changed with the 1.6 release and has evolved further in later releases.

9.1.2 *Putting the power of code generation in the hands of developers*

AST transformations have been part of Groovy since version 1.6. The AST part of this is an *abstract syntax tree*—a representation of code as data. This feature allows you to modify the code being generated without ever needing a source-code representation. For example, you can add new methods and fields to a class, or add code into the method bodies. Although no source code is generated, the bytecode is present in the final class file in an entirely ordinary way. This is important because it means Java objects calling your Groovy objects will see the new code, which isn't the case for changes made through runtime metaprogramming.

Compile-time metaprogramming is an exciting area of the language. There are many new libraries and frameworks for Groovy that generate verbose, boilerplate code directly into the .class files instead of forcing all the users to write extra source code. Code generation is no longer limited to those brave developers willing to download and build the source code for the Groovy compiler: it's available to anyone using Groovy. If you have a great idea for a new language feature then it's possible to write it today as a library. This powerful technique creates a living language, where you're allowed to extend the language in the direction best suited to your project. Many of Groovy's features are implemented on top of the AST transformation framework. For example, the @Delegate, @Immutable, and @Log annotations all hook into the compiler and affect the final .class file. @Bindable is the secret to UI property binding in the Griffon framework (or writing Groovy Swing in general). The Spock and GContracts libraries both leverage AST transforms, providing useful and productivity-boosting results. Compile-time metaprogramming is used by these libraries to produce more readable tests and more correct runtime behavior.

Before you start writing your own transformations, we'll look at a few annotations that ship with Groovy, so you can get a feel for what's possible. It's worth bearing in mind any repetitive coding tasks you've recently had to perform; if they sound like the kind of work that these annotations help with, you may well be able to eliminate them soon.

9.2 *Making Groovy cleaner and leaner*

Groovy ships with many AST transformations that you can use today to get rid of those annoying bits of repetitive code in your classes. When applied properly, the annotations described here make your code less verbose, so that the bulk of the code expresses meaningful business logic to the *reader* instead of meaningful code templates to the *compiler*. AST transformations cover a wide range of functionality, from generating standard toString() methods, to easing object delegation, to cleaning up Java synchronization constructs, and more. You don't need to know anything about compilers or Groovy internals before using the annotations described in this section: just annotate a class or method and watch your standard code templates disappear.

For the purposes of this section, we've divided the existing AST transformations into six categories:

- Code-generation transformations
- Class design and design pattern annotations
- Logging improvements
- Declarative concurrency
- Easier cloning and externalizing
- Scripting support

Let's start by looking at some annotations that write code into your class so that you don't have to.

9.2.1   *Code-generation transformations*

AST transformations often focus on automating the repetitive task of writing common methods like `equals(Object)`, `hashCode()`, and constructors that generate the code for you so that you don't have to write it yourself. The built-in annotations in this category are `@ToString`, `@EqualsAndHashCode`, `@TupleConstructor`, `@Lazy`, `@Indexed-Property`, `@InheritConstructors`, `@Builder`, and `@Sortable`. See also `@Newify` in section 19.8.

@GROOVY.TRANSFORM.TOSTRING

Annotating a class with the `@ToString` annotation gives that class a standard `toString()` method. `@ToString` prints out the class name and, by default, all of the field values, as you can see in the simple example in the following listing.

Listing 9.1   Using `@ToString` to generate a `toString()` method

```
import groovy.transform.ToString

@ToString
class Detective {
    String firstName, lastName
}

def sherlock = new Detective(firstName: 'Sherlock', lastName: 'Holmes')
assert sherlock.toString() == 'Detective(Sherlock, Holmes)'
```

You can also control the information that `toString()` displays with various annotation parameters. An example including property names and eliding `null` values is shown in the following listing.

Listing 9.2   Using `@ToString` with annotation parameters

```
import groovy.transform.ToString

@ToString(includeNames = true, ignoreNulls = true)
class Sleuth {
    String firstName, lastName
}
```

```
def nancy = new Sleuth(firstName: 'Nancy', lastName: 'Drew')
assert nancy.toString() == 'Sleuth(firstName:Nancy, lastName:Drew)'
nancy.lastName = null
assert nancy.toString() == 'Sleuth(firstName:Nancy)'
```

Other annotation parameters let you exclude certain properties, include fields, exclude the package name from the class name, include properties from superclasses, and cache the produced value (useful for immutable objects) if you wish. A full description of the available parameters for @ToString appears in appendix E.

You might wonder what the generated toString() method looks like. Remember we said that no source code is produced, so there's no code to show you directly, but we can show you the equivalent code (and later you'll see the tools that allow you to do this yourself) for the Sleuth class's toString() method, which would look something like this:

```
String toString() {
  def _result = new StringBuilder()
  def $toStringFirst = true
  _result.append('Sleuth(')

  def firstName = InvokerHelper.getProperty(this, 'firstName')
  if (firstName != null) {
    if ($toStringFirst) {
      $toStringFirst = false
    } else {
      _result.append(', ')
    }
    _result.append('firstName:')
    if (firstName.is(this)) {
      _result.append('(this)')
    } else {
      _result.append(InvokerHelper.toString(firstName))
    }
  }

  def lastName = InvokerHelper.getProperty(this, 'lastName')
  // ... ditto of above if statement but for lastName

  _result.append(')')
  return _result.toString()
}
```

Don't be too concerned about the details in this equivalent code listing. After our tour of Groovy's built-in transformations, you'll get to see more details about such generated code. Most of the code should look similar to what you might write by hand, but for the curious, we'll point out that there are some calls of InvokerHelper utility methods that you can safely ignore if you haven't come across them before. They ensure that the property values printed will be correct even if dynamic changes have been made, and these values will be output using Groovy's standard formatting mechanisms.

That's it for the @ToString transform. Next we'll look at another boilerplate-saving transformation for some of the other methods from Java's Object class.

@GROOVY.TRANSFORM.EQUALSANDHASHCODE

Implementing the `equals()` and `hashCode()` methods correctly is repetitive and error-prone. Luckily the `@EqualsAndHashCode` annotation does it for you. The generated `equals()` method obeys the contract of `Object.equals()`, and the generated `hashCode()` produces an appropriate hash value using a standard algorithm factoring in the constituent fields. The following listing shows using `@EqualsAndHashCode` in action on an `Actor` class.

Listing 9.3   @EqualsAndHashCode generates equals() and hashCode() methods

```
import groovy.transform.EqualsAndHashCode

@EqualsAndHashCode
class Actor {
    String firstName, lastName
}
def magneto = new Actor(firstName:'Ian', lastName: 'McKellen')
def gandalf = new Actor(firstName:'Ian', lastName: 'McKellen')
assert magneto == gandalf
```

You can customize the `equals()` and `hashCode()` methods created using annotation parameters. With these, you can easily exclude certain properties from the calculation, include fields in the calculation, or cache the calculated values (appropriate if you have an immutable class). A full description of the available parameters for `@EqualsAndHashCode` appears in appendix E.

@GROOVY.TRANSFORM.TUPLECONSTRUCTOR

Groovy has a flexible syntax for creating objects, such as named arguments and with blocks. But sometimes you want the object constructor to take all of the fields explicitly, especially when you're creating the Groovy object from Java code. The `@Tuple-Constructor` annotation adds this constructor onto the object, as you can see in the following listing.

Listing 9.4   Using @TupleConstructor to generate Java-style constructors

```
import groovy.transform.TupleConstructor

@TupleConstructor
class Athlete {
    String firstName, lastName
}
def a1 = new Athlete('Michael', 'Jordan')
def a2 = new Athlete('Michael')
assert a1.firstName == a2.firstName
```

By default, the overloaded constructors use the declaration order of the properties to determine the order of the parameters (and if the `includeFields` annotation parameter is enabled, then the fields will follow the properties, again in declaration order). In addition, each constructor argument is defined with Java's default value for the argument type, allowing you to leave off parameters from the right if you plan to set those values later or you're coding a scenario where the default suffices. There are numerous other ways to fine-tune the exact behavior in a very flexible way using annotation parameters. These parameters let you include or exclude certain properties, include fields, or interact with the superclass properties in various ways. Appendix E provides a full explanation of the available annotation parameters.

The @ToString, @EqualsAndHashCode, and @TupleConstructor annotations are so useful that in many cases you may want to use all three annotations together. In section 9.2.2 we'll review @Canonical and @Immutable, which allow you to do just that. But first, let's look at other very handy boilerplate-saving annotations.

@GROOVY.TRANSFORM.LAZY

Lazy instantiation is a common idiom in Java. If a field is expensive to create, such as a database connection, then the field is initialized to null, and the actual connection is created only the first time that field is used. Typical in this idiom is a null check and instantiation within a getter method. But not only is this boilerplate code, there are numerous tricky scenarios, such as correctly handling creation in a multi-threaded environment, which are error-prone. The @Lazy field annotation correctly delays field instantiation until the time when that field is first used and correctly handles numerous tricky special cases. An example illustrating this concept is shown in the following listing.

Listing 9.5 Using @Lazy to delay property instantiation

```
class Resource {
    private static alive = 0
    private static used = 0
    Resource() { alive++ }
    def use() { used++ }
    static stats() { "$alive alive, $used used" }
}

class ResourceMain {
    def res1 = new Resource()
    @Lazy res2 = new Resource()
    @Lazy static res3 = { new Resource() }()
    @Lazy(soft=true) volatile Resource res4
}

new ResourceMain().with {
    assert Resource.stats() == '1 alive, 0 used'
    res2.use()
    res3.use()
    res4.use()
    assert Resource.stats() == '4 alive, 3 used'
    assert res4 instanceof Resource
    def expected = 'res4=java.lang.ref.SoftReference'
    assert it.dump().contains(expected)
}
```

- ① Defines Resource class with inbuilt statistics
- ② Declares normal resource
- ③ Declares @Lazy resource
- ④ Declares static @Lazy resource
- ⑤ Thread-safe and compatible with garbage collection
- ⑥ After ResourceMain creation only res1 is alive
- ⑦ Using res2, res3, res4 creates instances lazily
- ⑧ Verifies res4 class
- ⑨ Verifies soft reference used internally

We first create a `Resource` class with inbuilt instance-tracking counters **❶**. This class and the counters are simply to help us understand what `@Lazy` is doing for us. In practice, this would be your database (or other expensive) resource. We now declare a `ResourceMain` class with four `Resource` properties. Normally you might have just one resource property but we want to illustrate available options.

The first property, `res1` **❷**, is a normal Groovy property. The backing field for that property will point to an eagerly created `Resource` instance created when the `ResourceMain` instance is created. The second property, `res2` **❸**, is lazily created. When the `ResourceMain` instance is created, the backing field for `res2` will remain `null`. In the getter method for `res2`, a check is made to see if the backing field is `null`, and if so, a new `Resource` is created.

For the third property, `res3` **❹**, we indicate that we want a static singleton `Resource`. The `static` modifier on the field denotes this case and the compiler knows to adopt the thread-safe *lazy initialization holder class idiom*.[1] This property also illustrates special syntax supported by the `@Lazy` annotation. If you have complex initialization logic where you can't use the normal syntax for defining an initial value (for example, you might need `try-catch` logic), then you declare that logic as if it were a `Closure` but follow it by a matching pair of round brackets, as if you were following Groovy's normal convention for calling a closure. We didn't strictly need anything complex for our example but it does illustrate the idea.

For an efficient thread-safe lazy instance field in Java, we might be tempted to use the *double-checked locking idiom*.[2] A correct implementation of double-checked locking would have a `volatile` private field and a `synchronized` getter. We use the `volatile` modifier to indicate this case as shown for `res4` **❺**. Groovy automatically provides a correct implementation of the idiom. There are two other salient points to note about the declaration for `res4`.

First, no initial value is given. In this case, the default no-arg constructor for the property's type will be called. If the type of the field is abstract or it doesn't have a no-arg constructor, you'll receive a runtime error. For clarity, and to avoid a missing constructor exception, you might consider always supplying an initial value.

Second, we made use of the optional `soft` parameter annotation. This determines if the field should be a `SoftReference`, and therefore eligible for garbage collection. By default, the field isn't a soft reference. A typical use case for making a soft reference would be if a resource was only rarely used but consumed significant memory. Allowing it to be garbage collected and recreated if needed again might be a prudent use of the memory footprint. We'd recommend avoiding premature optimization and only using this option if performance tests indicated a memory issue.

The remainder of the example checks `Resource` statistics to confirm the expected behavior. We first check **❻** that creating our `ResourceMain` instance causes only one

---

[1] Described in item 71 of *Effective Java*, 2nd ed., by Joshua Bloch (Addison-Wesley, 2008).

[2] Explained in section 16.2 of *Java Concurrency in Practice*, by Brian Goetz et al. (Addison-Wesley, 2006).

Resource to be created (the eager one). After attempting to use all of our resources, we note they're all created ❼. As a final check, we can see that when using the soft reference, a Resource is returned from the res4 getter ❽ but the internal backing field is a soft reference to the Resource instance ❾. We're using Groovy's dump() method to display some of the Resource internals but we don't need to worry about the details here.

The use of lazy idioms and soft references are advanced topics and the code to do them correctly is notoriously error-prone. Using @Lazy with its optional parameters and modifier keywords is an easy way to leverage the advantages of deferred initialization but also make sure your code is correct.

@GROOVY.TRANSFORM.INDEXEDPROPERTY

Groovy automatically provides getters and setters for properties. This follows Java's conventions for JavaBeans. What you may not know is that additional JavaBean conventions exist for dealing with array properties. In addition to providing setters and getters for the whole array, there are extra getter and setter methods that take an index value and work on just one member of the array. As you can see in listing 9.6, Groovy doesn't automatically provide these extra methods because Groovy's array-like notation is even easier to use ❶. But if you're creating classes that need to be accessed from Java or by JavaBean-aware tools, then you can use the @IndexedProperty annotation to have these methods added automatically. This works for both arrays and lists (and anything else supporting Groovy's subscript (getAt/putAt) operator). You can see @IndexedProperty in use in the following listing.

Listing 9.6 Using @IndexedProperty to generate index-based setters and getters

```
import groovy.transform.IndexedProperty

class Author {
    String name
    @IndexedProperty List<String> books
}

def books = ['The Mysterious Affair at Styles',
             'The Murder at the Vicarage']

new Author(name: 'Agatha Christie', books: books).with {
    books[0] = 'Murder on the Orient Express'
    setBooks(0, 'Death on the Nile')
    assert getBooks(0) == 'Death on the Nile'
}
```

❶ Groovy idiom for setting first property

❷ JavaBean approach to setting a single element

❸ JavaBean approach to reading a single element

The generated indexed setter and getter can be used to set a specific element ❷ and read it ❸ respectively.

@GROOVY.TRANSFORM.INHERITCONSTRUCTORS

The @InheritConstructors annotation removes the boilerplate of writing matching constructors for a superclass. Suppose you wanted to write your own custom PrintWriter-like class. The java.io.PrintWriter class has eight constructors, and your subclass should probably provide the same set of creation options. @Inherit-Constructors to the rescue. The annotation creates matching constructors for every superclass constructor. You can see two of them in use in the following listing.

Listing 9.7   Using `@InheritConstructors` to automatically generate constructors

```
import groovy.transform.InheritConstructors

@InheritConstructors
class MyPrintWriter extends PrintWriter { }           File f
                                                      variant
def pw1 = new MyPrintWriter(new File('out1.txt'))
def pw2 = new MyPrintWriter('out2.txt', 'US-ASCII')   String filename,
[pw1, pw2].each {                                     String charset
  it << 'foo'                                          variant
  it.close()
}
assert new File('out1.txt').text == new File('out2.txt').text
['out1.txt', 'out2.txt'].each{ new File(it).delete() }
```

The important code as far as this annotation is concerned happens when we use the two constructors, but for completeness, the remainder of the example uses the custom print writers to write content to the two output files that are then compared and deleted.

You can still write your own constructors, of course. If there's a conflict with a superclass constructor then @InheritConstructors is smart enough to back off and not overwrite your implementation. A word of warning, however: think about your subclass when using this annotation. If your subclass introduces required properties, then it's often best to make those properties required in a constructor and not implement too many of the superclass constructors. Plus, some Groovy features rely on the availability of a constructor without parameters, so having one on your class is typically a good idea; bear this in mind if you inherit constructors from a class without a no-arg constructor.

You can fine-tune whether annotations on a parent constructor are copied into your constructors using annotation parameters. A full description of the available parameters for @InheritConstructors appears in appendix E.

@GROOVY.TRANSFORM.SORTABLE

The @Sortable annotation, shown in the following listing, removes the boilerplate of writing the implementation code for the methods of the Comparable and Comparator interfaces.

Listing 9.8   Using `@Sortable` to generate `Comparable`/`Comparator` methods

```
import groovy.transform.Sortable

@Sortable(includes = 'last,initial')          Sorts by last
class Politician {                          ❶ then by initial
    String first
    Character initial
    String last
```

```
    String initials() { first[0] + initial + last[0] }
}

def politicians = [
    new Politician(first: 'Margaret', initial: 'H', last: 'Thatcher'),
    new Politician(first: 'George', initial: 'W', last: 'Bush')
]

def sorted = politicians.toSorted()
assert sorted*.initials() == ['GWB', 'MHT']
def byInitial = Politician.comparatorByInitial()
sorted = politicians.toSorted(byInitial)
assert sorted*.initials() == ['MHT', 'GWB']
```

2 Performs default sort

3 Autogenerates comparator based on initial

4 Sorts by initial

Using `@Sortable` is easy. Just include the annotation on your class definition. In this example we chose to make sorting based on the `last` name and, if those are equal, then based on the `initial`. We used the optional `includes` annotation parameter **1** to achieve that behavior. `@Sortable` adds `Comparable<Politician>` to the list of implemented interfaces of our `Politician` class and adds a `compareTo` method containing the appropriate comparison logic. Calling `sort()` is enough to invoke that logic. In our example, we then take the politician's initials as our final result **2**. In addition, `@Sortable` adds comparators for each of our included properties. Under the covers it creates an appropriate `Comparator` class containing a `compare` method but we don't need to worry about the details because it also provides a method to gain access to singleton instances of those classes. In our example, we access the comparator for the `initial` property **3** and use one of the sort methods available for comparators **4**.

In addition to the optional `includes` annotation parameter, there's an `excludes` parameter. This is handy if you have many properties and want to exclude one or two from affecting the sort behavior. Appendix E provides a full explanation of the available annotation parameters.

@GROOVY.TRANSFORM.BUILDER

The `@Builder` annotation removes the boilerplate of writing instance-building code. Given Groovy's built-in support for compact instance creation, you might ask why such code is needed. Consider the following `Chemist` class:

```
class Chemist {
    String first, last
    int born
}
```

You can create a new instance easily, like this:

```
def c = new Chemist(first: "Marie", last: "Curie", born: 1867)
```

But what if you misspell one of the properties or supply the wrong type? You might have an IDE that's powerful enough to give you a warning, but otherwise, the first indication you'll have that something is wrong is when you receive a `MissingProperty-Exception` or some kind of `CastException` at runtime. Similarly, if you need to create instances from Java, Groovy's conventions don't make things easier for you. In these scenarios, you might find the `@Builder` annotation exactly meets your needs. Here's an example of the `@Builder` annotation in use.

Listing 9.9 Using `@Builder` to make building classes easier

```
import groovy.transform.builder.Builder

@Builder
class Chemist {
  String first
  String last
  int born
}
def builder = Chemist.builder()
def c = builder.first("Marie").last("Curie").born(1867).build()
assert c.first == "Marie"
assert c.last == "Curie"
assert c.born == 1867
```

❶ Accessing a builder instance

❷ Fluent API style instance creation

We access a builder **❶** and use it to create our `Chemist` instance **❷**. Each of the methods has a typed parameter that allows better Java integration and the potential for increased IDE completion and checking.

Because one size doesn't fit all when building, the `@Builder` annotation allows the building process to be customized by supplying alternative strategy classes. Groovy comes with four built-in strategies (in the `groovy.transform.builder` package) to cover some fairly common scenarios, but feel free to provide your own if you have different requirements. Table 9.1 summarizes the built-in `@Builder` strategies. If, like in listing 9.9, no strategy is specified, the `DefaultStrategy` is used. Consult the GroovyDoc (http://docs.groovy-lang.org/latest/html/gapi/groovy/transform/builder/Builder.html) for these annotations for more details.

Table 9.1 Built-in `@Builder` strategies

Strategy	Description
DefaultStrategy	Creates a nested helper class for instance creation. Each method in the helper class returns the helper until finally a `build()` method is called, which returns a created instance.
SimpleStrategy	Creates chainable setters, where each setter returns the object itself after updating the appropriate property.
ExternalStrategy	Allows you to annotate an explicit builder class while leaving some builder class being built untouched. This is appropriate when you want to create a builder for a class you don't have control over such as from a library or another team in your organization.
InitializerStrategy	Creates a nested helper class for instance creation that when used with `@CompileStatic` allows type-safe object creation. Compatible with `@Immutable`.

The @Builder annotation provides numerous annotation parameters to allow further customization. In addition to specifying the strategy, you can include or exclude properties as well as rename various generated methods or classes. Note that not all strategies support all annotation parameters; consult the GroovyDoc for each strategy for further details. Appendix E provides a full explanation of the available annotation parameters.

That's the last of the code-generation annotations in Groovy. Next up on the tour are annotations that help you maintain a better designed and more object-oriented system.

9.2.2 Class design and design pattern annotations

Some transformations focus on implementing common design patterns or best-practice idioms. The goal is to make the right design decisions also the easiest ones to implement. The annotations in this category are @Canonical, @Immutable, @Delegate, @Singleton, @Memoized, and @TailRecursive, and their goal is to bring clarity of design intent and correctness of implementation when using these design patterns. See also @Category in section 8.4.7.

@GROOVY.TRANSFORM.CANONICAL

@ToString, @EqualsAndHashCode, and @TupleConstructor are commonly used together to create standard, or canonical, objects. Groovy provides @Canonical to make this a little easier. @Canonical is the combination of all three of these transformations. As you can see in the following listing, a canonical object has tuple constructors, equals() and hashCode() implementations, and a standard toString() representation.

> **Listing 9.10 @Canonical generates equals(), hashCode(), toString(), and constructors**

```
import groovy.transform.Canonical

@Canonical
class Inventor {
    String firstName, lastName
}                                                            Automatic
                                                             tuple
def i1 = new Inventor('Thomas', 'Edison')    ◁───┘          constructor
def i2 = new Inventor('Thomas')
assert i1 != i2                                              Objects not equal despite
assert i1.firstName == i2.firstName                         equal firstName property
assert i1.toString() == 'Inventor(Thomas, Edison)'
```

Automatic toString method ↳ (pointing to last assert line)

The @Canonical annotation takes optional parameters to include or exclude properties from the constructor and method implementations that it creates. If you wish to have more fine-grained control over the transformation's behavior, you can override its defaults by using one of the constituent annotations in conjunction with @Canonical. If you want to use @Canonical but customize the @ToString behavior, then annotate the class with both @Canonical and @ToString. The @ToString definition and parameters takes precedence over @Canonical. And just what exactly is a sensible default? A complete listing of the default values for @Canonical is given in appendix E.

@GROOVY.TRANSFORM.IMMUTABLE

Immutable types (such as `String`) permit no changes in state: when an instance has been created it can never be altered. The main advantage of immutability is that the object is side-effect free and thread safe. There's almost no way to change an immutable object from within a method or any way to abuse an immutable object across threads (without resorting to using reflection, that is). Also, there's never a need to make a defensive copy of an immutable object, or worry about what other objects may have references to your internal state. Working with immutable objects is highly recommended on the Java platform. Groovy provides the `groovy.transform.Immutable` transformation to help you easily create immutable objects, as shown in the following listing.

Listing 9.11 Using `@Immutable` to mark fields final and suppress setter methods

```
import groovy.transform.Immutable
import static groovy.test.GroovyAssert.shouldFail

@Immutable
class Genius {
    String firstName, lastName
}
def g1 = new Genius(firstName: 'Albert', lastName: "Einstein")    ◀──❶  Map-based
assert g1.toString() == 'Genius(Albert, Einstein)'                       constructor

def g2 = new Genius('Leonardo', "da Vinci")    ◀── ❸ Tuple
assert g2.firstName == 'Leonardo'              ◀── constructor
assert g1 != g2    ◀──           ❹ Property getter

shouldFail(ReadOnlyPropertyException) {
    g2.lastName = 'DiCaprio'          ❺ Appropriate equals
}                                       and hashCode
```

toString method ❷

The `Genius` class has quite a lot of generated code. It's absent from the source but we can see it once we start using the class:

- A `Map`-based constructor ❶
- A tuple constructor ❸
- A getter for each property, for example ❹
- An appropriate `toString` method ❷
- Appropriate `equals` and `hashCode` methods ❺

The `@Immutable` annotation is very intelligent about which properties to handle. All properties in an `@Immutable` class must also be marked `Immutable`, or be of a known immutable type such as a primitive type, `String`, `Color`, or `URI`. Known "effectively immutable" fields are also handled. Dates, arrays, and other cloneable objects are defensively copied in the constructor and getters so that state cannot be changed, and `List`, `Map`, and `Collection` classes are converted to `Immutable` objects in the constructor. Also, the `@Immutable` annotation shares similar behavior to `@ToString` and `@Equals-AndHashCode`: your class receives a nicely formatted `toString()` method and correct equals(Object) and hashCode() implementations. @Immutable uses sensible defaults for generating the toString(), equals(Object), and hashCode() methods, and they are fully described in appendix E.

> **WARNING!** Earlier versions of the Groovy codebase contained two @Immutable annotations: groovy.lang.Immutable and groovy.transform.Immutable. The one in the groovy.lang package is deprecated. Please only use the new one in groovy.transform.

@GROOVY.LANG.DELEGATE

In Java, one of easiest ways to reuse existing code is with a parent class, but just because it's easy doesn't mean that it's the best approach. If you genuinely have a pure is-a relationship between two classes, then inheritance might be appropriate, but in many cases when constructing the new class you want to make modifications to the behavior of some of the methods. In those cases, consider delegation. A delegate is a has-a relationship between two classes. Typically, one class will contain a reference to another and then also share some of the API with that class. The following example might illustrate this better. First, let's look at how we might be tempted to use inheritance to create a NoisySet class that prints some output whenever an item is added to the set. A naïve attempt might assume that a NoisySet *is-a* HashSet and might look something like this:

```
class NoisySet extends HashSet {
    @Override
    boolean add(item) {
        println "adding $item"
        super.add(item)
    }
    @Override
    boolean addAll(Collection items) {
        items.each { println "adding $it" }
        super.addAll(items)
    }
}
```

This approach is broken. Any items added using addAll will be printed out twice because under the covers addAll calls add within HashSet. For this simple case, we could remove the println statements in addAll but it would be a brittle solution—if the HashSet implementation changed in the future, we might no longer be printing out all the items! The solution is to use delegation. It's a well-known and relatively straightforward design pattern but involves quite a bit of boilerplate code. For our example, it would look something like this:

```
class NoisySet implements Set {
    private Set delegate = new HashSet()

    @Override
    boolean add(item) {
        println "adding $item"
        delegate.add(item)
    }
```

```
    @Override
    boolean addAll(Collection items) {
        items.each { println "adding $it" }
        delegate.addAll(items)
    }

    @Override
    boolean isEmpty() {
        return delegate.isEmpty()
    }

    @Override
    boolean contains(Object o) {
        return delegate.contains(o)
    }

    // ... ditto for size, iterator, toArray, remove,
    // containsAll, retainAll, removeAll, clear ...
}
```

In this approach, our `NoisySet` *has-a* `HashSet`. We simply define a private delegate field. Then for each method in `HashSet` (or more accurately for each method in the `Set` interface) we provide an implementation that calls through to the delegate. The `add` and `addAll` methods will also contain the `println` statements required by our noisy set.

What is wrong with this implementation? Strictly speaking nothing, but it does suffer from the problem that if the base class ever changed, we'd need to add delegate methods. Also, the intent isn't very clear. Intermixed with the two methods we actually changed are another 10 boilerplate methods that increase the maintenance footprint of the class and provide noise when trying to understand what the class is doing. Okay, we're implementing a noisy set but we want its design to be noise free! Let's consider an alternative implementation of `NoisySet` using the `@Delegate` annotation as shown in the following listing.

Listing 9.12   Using `@Delegate`

```
class NoisySet {
  @Delegate
  Set delegate = new HashSet()

  @Override
  boolean add(item) {
    println "adding $item"
    delegate.add(item)
  }

  @Override
  boolean addAll(Collection items) {
    items.each { println "adding $it" }
    delegate.addAll(items)
  }
}
```

```
Set ns = new NoisySet()
ns.add(1)
ns.addAll([2, 3])
assert ns.size() == 3
```

This example has a much clearer intent. We're using delegation but changing two of
the methods. The @Delegate transformation adds *all* of the public instance methods
from the delegate onto your class, and automatically calls the delegate when those
methods are invoked. This is how NoisySet can implement Set yet only declare two
methods instead of every method on the Set interface. By default, the owning class is
also made to implement all of the interfaces defined by the delegate as well, so you
don't even need to explicitly implement the Set interface if you don't want.

There could be a conflict between the owner class and one of the delegate methods, or if multiple delegates are in use, between two methods with the same signature
coming from different delegates. In that case, the first existing method is used. The
delegate fields are processed in the order they appear in the class. If any method signature matches an existing signature, that method is skipped. If that isn't what you
require, you can fine-tune the behavior using annotation parameters that are described
in appendix E.

@GROOVY.LANG.SINGLETON

The Singleton pattern is intended to ensure that only one instance of a class exists
within your system at a time. A standard way to achieve this behavior is for a class to
have a private static reference to this instance, a private constructor so that it cannot
be instantiated outside the class, and a public static method to access the single
instance. If you were to manually implement a singleton in Groovy it would look something like this:

```
class Zeus {
    static final Zeus instance = new Zeus()
    private Zeus() { }
}

assert Zeus.instance
```

This isn't too much code to write, particularly as the code generation in Groovy
already supplies the accessor method, but it can be simplified using the @Singleton
annotation. The obvious advantage is less code, but it also means that invoking the
private constructor results in an exception, as shown in the following listing.

Listing 9.13 Using @Singleton to enforce a single instance of an object

```
import static groovy.test.GroovyAssert.shouldFail

@Singleton class Zeus { }

assert Zeus.instance
def ex = shouldFail(RuntimeException) { new Zeus() }
assert ex.message ==
    "Can't instantiate singleton Zeus. Use Zeus.instance"
```

An additional advantage is that you can use the @Lazy annotation parameter to properly generate a lazily instantiated instance, which marks the instance variable as volatile and correctly performs double-checked locking in the instantiation method. Appendix E describes the available annotation parameters for @Singleton.

> **NOTE**   The Singleton pattern can be useful, but it's considered by some to be an anti-pattern. Certainly in Java, a singleton offers no layers of abstraction: it's a concrete type and cannot be extended or easily mocked or changed. The story is a little better in Groovy but there are often better approaches. Also, when using singletons, improper serialization or multiple classloaders can result in two instances of the singleton object, and there are also thread safety complications. Singletons are useful, but be aware of the downsides.

@GROOVY.TRANSFORM.MEMOIZED

For pure functional methods that always return the same result given the same inputs it can be efficient to cache the results, especially if calculating the result is quite complex or time-consuming. You could do this manually yourself but the groovy .transform.Memoized transformation can do it automatically for you, as shown in the following listing.

Listing 9.14   Using @Memoized to cache method results

```
import groovy.transform.Memoized

class Calc {
  def log = []

  @Memoized                          ❶ Enables
  int sum(int a, int b) {              memoization by
    log << "$a+$b"                     annotating a method
    a + b                            ❷ Logs all
  }                                    calculations
}
new Calc().with {
  assert sum(3, 4) == 7            ❸ Calculation
  assert sum(4, 4) == 8              performed first time
  assert sum(3, 4) == 7           ❹ Results returned
  assert log.join(' ') == '3+4 4+4'  from cache
}                                  ❺ Logging shows calculations
                                     performed once each
```

All you need to do is annotate the method or methods you want to enable. In our case that's the sum method ❶. To show that caching is actually taking place we'll also log the parameters each time a calculation occurs ❷. We'll call the sum with the parameters 3 and 4 twice ❸, ❹ but those parameters will appear in the log only once ❺.

The annotation has a few parameters for tweaking the caching behavior. See appendix E for details. Also, remember that if it's a closure you want to memoize and not a class method, then see Closure's memoize method discussed in chapter 5.

@GROOVY.TRANSFORM.TAILRECURSIVE

When implementing algorithms in a functional style, recursion is often used in preference to imperative loops. If you were implementing a utility class with a function that returns the items from a list in reverse order (and ignoring that such a function already exists), you might use code such as this:

```
class ListUtil {
    static List reverse(List list) {
        if (list.isEmpty()) list
        else reverse(list.tail()) + list.head()
    }
}

assert ListUtil.reverse(['a', 'b', 'c']) == ['c', 'b', 'a']
```

This code works as it should and is reasonably elegant, though it could possibly be slower than its imperative equivalent. (We value correctness and clarity ahead of speed but sometimes need a little bit of speed too.) More importantly, for large lists, the code is subject to a stack overflow error. Some languages might try to automatically optimize such code to make it as fast as equivalent imperative code or to unravel the recursion to potentially avoid the stack overflow problem. Current versions of Groovy don't promise such optimizations but do put you in control of optimizing a subset of recursive functions known as tail-recursive functions.

The previous example, while recursive, wasn't tail-recursive. When calling back to itself, the last thing a tail-recursive function must do is call itself and nothing else. In our reverse code we reverse the tail (recursively) but then append the head. So, the first thing we need to do is rewrite the code to be tail-recursive. For our case, we introduce an additional parameter that stores the reversed list so far. Once we have a tail-recursive function we can then add the @TailRecursive annotation. Groovy will unravel the code and replace it with equivalent iterative code. Let's look at this in more detail in the following listing.

Listing 9.15   Using `@TailRecursive` to optimize tail calls

```
import groovy.transform.TailRecursive

class ListUtil {
    static reverse(List list) {
        doReverse(list, [])
    }

    @TailRecursive
    private static doReverse(List todo, List done) {      ←┐ Rewritten
        if (todo.isEmpty()) done                            │ function with
        else doReverse(todo.tail(), [todo.head()] + done)   ┘ tail recursion
    }
}

assert ListUtil.reverse(['a', 'b', 'c']) == ['c', 'b', 'a']
```

NOTE Before Groovy 2.3 introduced the `@TailRecursive` annotation, the way to avoid stack overflow when using recursion with closures was to use the `Closure.trampoline()` method (available since Groovy 1.8). This method wraps the closure into a `TrampolineClosure`, which, instead of doing a recursive call to the closure, returns a new closure, which is called during the next step of the computation. This turns a recursive execution into a sequential one, thus helping avoiding the stack overflow, albeit at some performance cost.

That's the end of the discussion of the class design and design pattern annotations. Before moving on to concurrency and scripting annotations, let's see some of the annotation-based logging improvements in Groovy.

9.2.3 *Logging improvements*

There's still a surprising amount of debate about the best way of logging errors and informative messages from Java, and new logging frameworks are still in development. The `@Log` family of annotations exists to simplify correct logging idioms from Groovy code. The family includes `@Log`, `@Log4j`, `@Log4j2`, `@Slf4j`, and `@Commons`.

The annotation does more than just create a logger for you. To understand the power of `@Log`, consider the following listing and ask yourself if the `runLongDatabaseQuery()` method will be executed.

> **Listing 9.16   Using `@Log` to inject a `Logger` object into an object**

```
import groovy.util.logging.Log

@Log
class Database {
    def search() {
        log.fine(runLongDatabaseQuery())
    }

    def runLongDatabaseQuery() {
        println 'Calling database'            ◁─── Calling
        /* ... */                                  database
        return 'query result'
    }
}

new Database().search()
```

From a Java background, the obvious answer would be yes, the `runLongDatabaseQuery()` method will be executed, because in Java, method arguments are always evaluated before the method is called. There's no way to avoid this. In Groovy, the answer is maybe: it depends on whether the `FINE` log level is enabled.

The `@Log` annotation first creates a logger based on the name of your class. It then wraps any logging method with a conditional checking whether that level is enabled before trying to execute the logging line. The result is equivalent to wrapping the logging call in a `if (logger.isEnabled(LogLevel.FINE))` condition. The arguments to the method may never be evaluated depending on the logging configuration. The transformation is smart too; no check is made if the parameter is a constant such as a simple string or integer. This improves the readability significantly—there's no more need to include manual checks everywhere for the sake of performance. Groovy does the correct thing by default.

The `@Log` family of annotations takes one optional parameter: the name of the log variable. By default the log variable is called `log`, but you can change it to whatever you want. If you don't like how Groovy initializes the `Logger` object based on the current class name, then add your own logger field and update the annotation to refer to the field name. Five major logging frameworks are covered by Groovy, and each has its own annotation. The five annotations are detailed in table 9.2 (they're all in the `groovy.util.logging` package).

Table 9.2   Five `@Log` annotations

Name	Description
`@Log`	Injects a static final `java.util.logging.Logger` into your class and initializes it using `Logger.getLogger(class.name)`.
`@Commons`	Injects an Apache Commons logger as a static final `org.apache.commons.logging.Log` into your class and initializes it using `LogFactory.getLog(class)`.
`@Log4j`	Injects a Log4j logger as a static final `org.apache.log4j.Logger` into your class and initializes it using `Logger.getLogger(class)`.
`@Log4j2`	Injects a Log4j2 logger as a static final `org.apache.log4j.Logger` into your class and initializes it using `Logger.getLogger(class)`.
`@Slf4j`	Injects an Slf4j logger as a static final `org.slf4j.Logger` into your class and initializes it using `org.slf4j.LoggerFactory.getLogger(class)`. The LogBack framework uses SLF4J as the underlying logger, so LogBack users should use `@Slf4j`.

It doesn't stop there though, because the `@Log` feature is extensible. You can use your own company's logger as well, as long as you implement one interface to define your new annotation. This extension mechanism is how the standard five `@Log` annotations are implemented, so there are five good examples in the Groovy codebase. To implement the interface you need to define a new `Logger` object and instantiate it, determine if a method should be wrapped in a conditional check, and then wrap the log call in a guard. Writing the AST for this isn't hard, but you'll need to understand the rest of the chapter before tackling the problem.

Next we'll look at declarative concurrency. Groovy provides annotations to declare how your code is locked during multithreaded access instead of writing the code that performs low-level locking.

9.2.4 Declarative concurrency

Synchronization and access to a mutable state is hard to get right. Proper synchronization can leave your little branch of business logic hidden, surrounded by a forest of lock acquire and lock release code. The concurrency-related annotations aim to remedy this problem: @Synchronized, @WithReadLock, and @WithWriteLock.

@GROOVY.TRANSFORM.SYNCHRONIZED

Code that's accessed from several threads at once often needs to be synchronized to avoid common concurrency problems. One problem with this is that correct concurrent code is hard: it's all too easy to introduce one problem when trying to solve another. The easiest solution for Java developers is to add the synchronized keyword to the method declaration. This is another instance where the *easiest* solution isn't the *best* solution.

> ### Avoid low-level synchronization
>
> Java contains many fine primitives for working with concurrent code, such as the synchronized keyword and the contents of the java.util.concurrent package. But these are mostly primitives and not abstractions. The tools are low level and meant to serve as a foundation. GPars is a framework for parallelization that's built on top of these primitives. It provides many abstractions that shield you from low-level coordination tasks. GPars is described fully in chapter 18.

The problem with method-level synchronization is that it's very coarse-grained and it's also part of the public API of the object. You're effectively locking on a publicly accessible reference: the this reference. Some secure coding standards ban method-level synchronization or synchronization on the this reference because an attacker who has a reference to your object can interfere with your synchronization by synchronizing on it. It's best to declare a local, private lock and expose that lock to subclasses if classes need to coordinate locking. Doing this correctly is easy with the @Synchronized annotation, as seen in the following listing.

Listing 9.17 Declarative synchronization with @Synchronized

```
import groovy.transform.Synchronized

class PhoneBook1 {
    private final phoneNumbers = [:]

    @Synchronized
    def getNumber(key) {
        phoneNumbers[key]
    }

    @Synchronized
    void addNumber(key, value) {
        phoneNumbers[key] = value
    }
}
```

```
                    def p1 = new PhoneBook1()
                    (0..99).collect { num ->                              Each thread adds a
                        Thread.start {                                    dummy phonebook
                            p1.addNumber('Number' + num, '98765' + num)   entry
                        }
 Check a            }*.join()                                         Await completion of
 sample             assert p1.getNumber('Number43') == '9876543'     100 parallel threads
 number
```

This annotation injects a lock object into your class. The object is a zero-length
`Object` array so that your class remains serializable (which an `Object` instance
isn't). And any method marked with the annotation has a synchronized block
around it but without method synchronization. If you want to limit the scope of
your synchronized block, then provide a name for the lock using the default annotation parameter and write the synchronized block yourself when needed, as shown
in the following listing.

Listing 9.18 Mixing `@Synchronized` with custom synchronized block

```
import groovy.transform.Synchronized
import groovy.util.logging.Log

@Log
class PhoneBook2 {
    private final phoneNumbers = [:]
    private final lock = new Object[0]             Manually
                                                    created lock

    @Synchronized('lock')                          Specifies lock
    def getNumber(key) {                           name
            phoneNumbers[key]
    }

    def addNumber(key, value) {
        log.info("Adding phone number $value")
        synchronized (lock) {                      Manually
            phoneNumbers[key] = value              synchronized
        }                                          block
    }
}

def p2 = new PhoneBook2()
(0..99).collect { num ->
    Thread.start {
        p2.addNumber('Number' + num, '98765' + num)
    }
}*.join()
assert p2.getNumber('Number43') == '9876543'
```

Synchronization is a low-level, primitive operation. Java has higher-level locking mechanisms as well, and the following two annotations help make them easy to use.

@GROOVY.TRANSFORM.WITHREADLOCK AND @GROOVY.TRANSFORM.WITHWRITELOCK
Java 5 included the `java.util.concurrent.locks.ReentrantReadWriteLock` class as
a tool to use when you need more control over locking than simply using synchronized blocks. A `ReentrantReadWriteLock` can guard against either read access or

write access, where many readers are allowed concurrently, but only one writer is allowed. Although this is a very useful concurrency abstraction, acquiring and releasing a lock correctly is cumbersome, as you can see in this code snippet:

```
import java.util.concurrent.locks.ReentrantReadWriteLock

class PhoneBook3 {
    private final phoneNumbers = [:]
    final private lock = new ReentrantReadWriteLock()

    def getNumber(key) {
        lock.readLock().lock()
        try {
            phoneNumbers[key]
        } finally {
            lock.readLock().unlock()
        }
    }

    def addNumber(key, value) {
        lock.writeLock().lock()
        try {
            phoneNumbers[key] = value
        } finally {
            lock.writeLock().unlock()
        }
    }
}
```

Phew, that's quite a bit of code. It *does* do the right thing: reading data is guarded with a read lock and writing data is guarded with a write lock. But the code is much simpler when you use the @WithReadLock and @WithWriteLock annotations instead as shown here:

```
import groovy.transform.*

class PhoneBook3 {
    private final phoneNumbers = [:]

    @WithReadLock
    def getNumber(key) {
        phoneNumbers[key]
    }

    @WithWriteLock
    def addNumber(key, value) {
        phoneNumbers[key] = value
    }
}
```

This time the logic of the class stands out instead of being drowned in a sea of try-finally blocks, and you'll never forget to release a lock. Similar to @Synchronized, these annotations take a parameter for the lock name, and that lock will be used if it exists in the class. You might wonder how to test this class. It isn't that hard, but if you want to actually ensure that the read and write locks are working correctly, it can be a bit of work. What we'll do is add some `println` debugging lines[3] and `sleep` calls[4] into the preceding example and then start off a bunch of interleaving threads that will read and write phone numbers concurrently. The complete example is shown in the following listing.

Listing 9.19   Using `@WithReadLock` and `@WithWriteLock` for efficient concurrency

```
import groovy.transform.*

class PhoneBook3 {
    private final phoneNumbers = dummyNums()          ← Fills phonebook
                                                         with dummy
    private dummyNums() {                                 numbers
        (1..8).collectEntries {
            ['Number' + it, '765432' + it]
        }
    }

    @WithReadLock
    def getNumber(key) {
        println "Reading started for $key"
        phoneNumbers[key]
        sleep 80
        println "Reading done for $key"
    }

    @WithWriteLock
    def addNumber(key, value) {
        println "Writing started for $key"
        phoneNumbers[key] = value
        sleep 100
        println "Writing done for $key"
    }
}

def p3 = new PhoneBook3()

(3..4).each{ count ->                          Starts writer
    Thread.start {                             threads
        sleep 100 * count
        p3.addNumber('Number' + count, '9876543')
    }
}
(2..6).collect{ count ->
    Thread.start {                             Starts interleaved
        sleep 100 * count                      reader threads
        p3.getNumber('Number' + count)
    }
}*.join()
```

---

[3] We don't recommend using `println` statements in multithreaded code as a general rule, but we'll get away with it in this simple example.

[4] If we didn't add some `sleep` calls, things would happen so quickly that you'll likely not get any concurrency.

The exact output will vary depending on your machine speed and language versions, but you should see something like this:

```
Reading started for Number2
Reading started for Number3
Reading done for Number2
Reading done for Number3
Writing started for Number3
Writing done for Number3
Reading started for Number4
Reading done for Number4
Writing started for Number4
Writing done for Number4
Reading started for Number5
Reading started for Number6
Reading done for Number6
Reading done for Number5
```

The important thing should be that multiple reads should be happening concurrently, but when any thread is writing, no other reading or writing should be taking place.

These examples all show how annotations for AST transformations work. There are other ways to be thread-safe as well. You could use an appropriate collection type from the `java.util.concurrent` package such as `CopyOnWriteArrayList` or `Concurrent-HashMap`, or you could use immutable objects or persistent data structures. The value in the Groovy annotation approach is that synchronization and safety are declarative. You don't explain how the synchronization works, you just declare that it exists and let Groovy do the rest.

In general, declarative solutions offer good abstractions, where you don't need to see the details and can focus on the more important parts of the code instead of the low-level mechanics. The same is true for other areas where you traditionally end up with a lot of boilerplate code to write. Each *individual* bit of boilerplate is simple enough, but after you've written it enough times you're bound to make a subtle mistake—and it really impacts the readability of the class. The same idea extends to other operations you might wish to perform on your objects, too.

9.2.5   *Easier cloning and externalizing*

Implementing `Cloneable` and `Externalizable` correctly isn't always simple. The `@Auto-Clone` annotation can give you a reasonable and configurable cloning strategy by adding just the annotation. In a similar vein, `@AutoExternalize` makes implementing `Externalizable` simpler by correctly creating default read and write methods.

@GROOVY.TRANSFORM.AUTOCLONE

Classes that implement `Cloneable` should provide a public clone method that creates a copy of the class. At its simplest, the `@AutoClone` annotation causes your class to implement `Cloneable` and provides a default and simple clone method implementation. But because one size doesn't fit all when it comes to cloning, the `@Auto-Clone` annotation supports several slightly different styles of cloning. We'll look at these styles shortly, but let's first look at the annotation in action as shown in the following listing.

Listing 9.20 `@AutoClone` **provides cloning capability**

```
import groovy.transform.AutoClone

@AutoClone
class Chef1 {
    String name
    List<String> recipes
    Date born
}

def name = 'Heston Blumenthal'
def recipes = ['Snail porridge', 'Bacon & egg ice cream']
def born = Date.parse('yyyy-MM-dd', '1966-05-27')
def c1 = new Chef1(name: name, recipes: recipes, born: born)
def c2 = c1.clone()
assert c2.recipes == recipes
```

Under the covers, your class will be augmented to look something like this:

```
class Chef1 implements Cloneable {
    ...
    Chef1 clone() throws CloneNotSupportedException {
        Chef1 _result = (Chef1) super.clone()
        if (recipes instanceof Cloneable) {
            _result.recipes = (List<String>) recipes.clone()
        }
        _result.born = (Date) born.clone()
        return _result
    }
}
```

The superclass `clone()` method is invoked, followed by invoking `clone()` on each `Cloneable` field or property in the class. If a field or property isn't `Cloneable` then it's simply copied in a bitwise fashion. If some properties don't support cloning, then a `CloneNotSupportedException` is thrown. You might wonder about the check for cloning recipes. Its type is `List`, which isn't `Cloneable` though many list implementations including Groovy's default list type (`ArrayList`) are, and so in our case recipes will be (shallow) cloned. Deep copies are left to the end user (you) to implement. That was simple but doesn't cover a range of cloning scenarios. For a wider range of scenarios you need to select the appropriate cloning style. The available options are listed in table 9.3.

Table 9.3   Four @AutoClone styles

Name	Description
CLONE	Adds a clone() method to your class. The clone() method will call super.clone() before calling clone() on each Cloneable property of the class. Doesn't provide deep cloning. Not suitable if you have final properties. This is the default cloning style if no style attribute is provided.
SIMPLE	Adds a clone() method to your class that calls the no-arg constructor then copies each property calling clone() for each Cloneable property. Handles inheritance hierarchies. Not suitable if you have final properties. Doesn't provide deep cloning.
COPY_CONSTRUCTOR	Adds a copy constructor, which takes your class as its parameter, and a clone() method to your class. The copy constructor method copies each property calling clone() for each Cloneable property. The clone() method creates a new instance making use of the copy constructor. Suitable if you have final properties. Handles inheritance hierarchies. Doesn't provide deep cloning.
SERIALIZATION	Adds a clone() method to your class that uses serialization to copy your class. Suitable if your class already implements the Serializable or Externalizable interface. Automatically performs deep cloning. Not as time or memory efficient. Not suitable if you have final properties.

So, using the SIMPLE style, your augmented class will have this form:

```
class Chef1 implements Cloneable {
    ...
    protected void cloneOrCopyMembers(Chef1 other) {
        other.name = name
        if (recipes instanceof Cloneable) {
            other.recipes = (List<String>) recipes.clone()
        } else {
            other.recipes = recipes
        }
        other.born = (Date) born.clone()
    }

    Chef1 clone() throws CloneNotSupportedException {
        Chef1 _result = new Chef1()
        this.cloneOrCopyMembers(_result)
        return _result
    }
}
```

And, with the SERIALIZATION style, your class would need to implement Serializable (or Externalizable) and the generated method would look like this:

```
Object clone() throws CloneNotSupportedException {
    def baos = new ByteArrayOutputStream()
    baos.withObjectOutputStream{ it.writeObject(this) }
    def bais = new ByteArrayInputStream(baos.toByteArray())
    bais.withObjectInputStream(getClass().classLoader){ it.readObject() }
}
```

Another popular cloning approach is to use the COPY_CONSTRUCTOR style. As shown in table 9.3, it handles both final properties and inheritance hierarchies. The following listing illustrates these features.

Listing 9.21 Using the COPY_CONSTRUCTOR style with @AutoClone

```groovy
import groovy.transform.*
import static groovy.transform.AutoCloneStyle.*

@TupleConstructor
@AutoClone(style=COPY_CONSTRUCTOR)
class Person {
    final String name
    final Date born
}

@TupleConstructor(includeSuperProperties=true,
        callSuper=true)
@AutoClone(style=COPY_CONSTRUCTOR)
class Chef2 extends Person {
    final List<String> recipes
}

def name = 'Jamie Oliver'
def recipes = ['Lentil Soup', 'Crispy Duck']
def born = Date.parse('yyyy-MM-dd', '1975-05-27')
def c1 = new Chef2(name, born, recipes)
def c2 = c1.clone()
assert c2.name == name
assert c2.born == born
assert c2.recipes == recipes
```

The added methods generated for the Chef2 class look roughly like this:

```groovy
protected Chef2(Chef2 other) {
    super(other)
    if (other.recipes instanceof Cloneable) {
        this.recipes = (List<String>) other.recipes.clone()
    } else {
        this.recipes = other.recipes
    }
}

public Chef2 clone() throws CloneNotSupportedException {
    new Chef2(this)
}
```

You can use several annotation parameters to fine tune @AutoClone, and these parameters are described in appendix E. With these annotation parameters and @AutoClone's supported styles, many of your cloning scenarios should be covered. But for more complex objects, it's often best to write your own clone method so that you can have complete control.

@GROOVY.TRANSFORM.AUTOEXTERNALIZE

The `Externalizable` interface is similar to Serializable in that it's used to persist objects into a binary form. `Externalizable` was added to the JDK after Serializable. The new interface gives you more control over the persisted form than Serializable does, and it doesn't use reflection, which at one time was a performance bottleneck. Some performance-sensitive applications prefer using `Externalizable`.

A class marked `@AutoExternalize` automatically implements the Externalizable interface, gaining two new method implementations: `readExternal(ObjectInput)` and `writeExternal(ObjectOutput)`. An example of its usage is in the following listing.

Listing 9.22   Using `@AutoExternalize` for easier serialization

```
import groovy.transform.*

@AutoExternalize
@ToString
class Composer {
    String name
    int born
    boolean married
}

def c = new Composer(name: 'Wolfgang Amadeus Mozart',
        born: 1756, married: true)

def baos = new ByteArrayOutputStream()
baos.withObjectOutputStream{ os -> os.writeObject(c) }
def bais = new ByteArrayInputStream(baos.toByteArray())
def loader = getClass().classLoader
def result
bais.withObjectInputStream(loader) {
    result = it.readObject().toString()
}
assert result == 'Composer(Wolfgang Amadeus Mozart, 1756, true)'
```

The generated methods look something like this:

```
class Composer implements Externalizable {
    ...
    void writeExternal(ObjectOutput out) throws IOException {
        out.writeObject(name)
        out.writeInt(born)
        out.writeBoolean(married)
    }

    void readExternal(ObjectInput oin) {
        name = (String) oin.readObject()
        born = oin.readInt()
        married = oin.readBoolean()
    }
}
```

You can fine-tune the @AutoExternalize behavior using the annotation parameters described in appendix E. Note that if you look into the source code for @Auto-Externalize it's defined as an annotation alias combining the @ExternalizeMethods and @ExternalizeVerifier annotations. This split of functionality into two places can be considered an internal implementation detail. It does, however, allow the two bits of functionality to be run at different compiler phases. You might consider this technique when writing your own AST transformations.

That's all for the cloning and externalizing annotations. The next set of annotations we'll discuss exist to make using Groovy as a scripting language safe and secure.

9.2.6 Scripting support

You saw in section 2.3 that scripting is an integral part of the Groovy language. It should come as no surprise that some AST transforms have been developed to make your scripting even more productive. These range from transforms that give you some control over the created script class or its components to ones designed to assist with security and robustness. The transforms that fall into this category include @Field, @BaseScript, @TimedInterrupt, @ThreadInterrupt, and @ConditionalInterrupt. You should also check out the GroovyDoc for @SourceURI, which gives you a hook back to a script's source.

Security and robustness are important aspects of modern software. Groovy makes it easy to run scripts submitted by your users (as well as your own scripts), but this can be a security hole that needs to be shielded not only against unauthorized access but also against accidental programming errors. No one wants a set of long-running scripts to cause a denial of service. These scripting annotations automatically add safety hooks into scripts so that they time out, respect a thread interrupt, or otherwise behave correctly. They're designed to be added automatically to scripts executing in GroovyShell or another evaluator, but you can also use them yourself on your own scripts and classes.

@GROOVY.TRANSFORM.TIMEDINTERRUPT

Annotating a class with @TimedInterrupt sets a maximum time the script or instances of the class are allowed to exist. If the maximum time is exceeded then a Timeout-Exception is thrown. This annotation is designed to guard against runaway processes, infinite loops, or a maliciously long-running user script.

When annotated, the object instance marks the instantiation time in the constructor. If this instance later detects that the maximum runtime is exceeded then it throws an exception. Checks are made at the beginning of every method call, the first line of every closure, and within every iteration of a for or while loop. If the object sits idle and is never invoked, then no exception is thrown regardless of how much time passes. The following listing is a simple example of its use.

Listing 9.23 **Using `@TimedInterrupt` to guard against slow scripts**

```
import groovy.transform.TimedInterrupt
import java.util.concurrent.TimeoutException
import static java.util.concurrent.TimeUnit.MILLISECONDS

@TimedInterrupt(value = 480L, unit = MILLISECONDS)        ◁─┐ Just a little
class BlastOff1 {                                           │ less than 500
    def log = []                                            │ milliseconds

    def countdown(n) {
        sleep 100
        log << n
        if (n == 0) log << 'ignition'
        else countdown(n - 1)
    }
}

def b = new BlastOff1()
Thread.start {
    try {
        b.countdown(10)
    } catch (TimeoutException ignore) {
        b.log << 'aborted'
    }
}.join()
assert b.log.join(' ') == '10 9 8 7 6 aborted'
```

Annotation parameters you can use to fine-tune the behavior are described in appendix E.

@GROOVY.TRANSFORM.THREADINTERRUPT

For timely responsiveness, long-running user scripts *should* periodically check the `Thread.currentThread().isInterrupted()` status and throw an `Interrupted-Exception` when an interrupt is detected. But in practice, scripts are almost never written this way. An easy way to properly respect the interrupted flag is to use the `@ThreadInterrupt` annotation. When this annotation is present, your script or class will automatically check the `isInterrupted()` flag and throw an `Interrupted-Exception` if the thread is interrupted. These checks occur at the start of every method call, at the start of every closure, and within every iteration of a loop. An example is shown in the following listing.

Listing 9.24 **Using `@ThreadInterrupt` to detect interruptions**

```
import groovy.transform.ThreadInterrupt

@ThreadInterrupt
class BlastOff2 {
    def log = []

    def countdown(n) {
        Thread.sleep 100
        log << n
```

```
        if (n == 0) log << 'ignition'
        else countdown(n - 1)
    }
}

def b = new BlastOff2()
def t1 = Thread.start {
    try {
        b.countdown(10)
    } catch(InterruptedException ignore) {
        b.log << 'aborted'
    }
}
sleep 590
t1.interrupt()
t1.join()
assert b.log.join(' ') == '10 9 8 7 6 aborted'
```

Just a little less than 600 milliseconds ←┤ *(pointing to `sleep 590`)*

Similar to `@TimedInterrupt`, there are some parameters you can use to tweak the behavior of `@ThreadInterrupt` that are detailed in appendix E.

@GROOVY.TRANSFORM.CONDITIONALINTERRUPT

The last annotation in the `Interrupt` family is `@ConditionalInterrupt`. This annotation allows you to specify your own custom interrupt logic to be woven into a class. Like the others, the interrupt check occurs at the start of every method, the start of every closure, and each loop iteration.

The way you specify the conditional interrupt is within a closure annotation parameter. You can reference any variable that's in scope within this closure. For scripts, general script variables are in scope, and for classes, instance fields are in scope. The following listing shows a script that executes some work 1,000 times or until 10 exceptions have been thrown, whichever comes sooner.

Listing 9.25   Using `@ConditionalInterrupt` to set an automatic error threshold

```
import groovy.transform.ConditionalInterrupt

@ConditionalInterrupt({ count <= 5 })
class BlastOff3 {
    def log = []
    def count = 10

    def countdown() {
        while (count != 0) {
            log << count
            count--
        }
        log << 'ignition'
    }
}

def b = new BlastOff3()
try {
    b.countdown()
```

```
} catch (InterruptedException ignore) {
    b.log << 'aborted'
}
assert b.log.join(' ') == '10 9 8 7 6 aborted'
```

Parameters you can use to tweak the functionality of @ConditionalInterrupt are described in appendix E.

@GROOVY.TRANSFORM.FIELD

Section 7.2 gave details about how Groovy "wraps" script files into a script class and automatically provides main and run methods. The code inside your script ends up being placed inside the run method, which makes it a local variable declaration. Suppose you have a script containing the lines

```
def x = 4
println x
```

then the generated script file looks like this:

```
class ScriptXXXXX extends Script {
  public static void main(String[] args) {
    new ScriptXXXXX().run()          ◁────  Slightly simplified,
  }                                          ignoring some
                                             unimportant
  public run() {                             details
    def x = 4
    println x
  }
}
```

As you can see, the variable x is a local variable definition within the run method. It wouldn't be visible to other methods or be available across multiple calls of the run method. For most scripts this is exactly what you want. Annotating a variable with @Field promotes it to a field within your script class. Let's look at this in action in the following listing.

Listing 9.26   Using @Field for class-level instance variables in a script

```
import groovy.transform.Field

@Field List awe = [1, 2, 3]        | Variable awe is an
def awesum() { awe.sum() }      ◁──┘ instance field of script
assert awesum() == 6
```

The equivalent generated code would look like this:

```
class ScriptYYYYY extends Script {
  List awe = [1, 2, 3]

  public static void main(String[] args) {
    new ScriptYYYYY().run()          ◁────  Again, slightly
  }                                          simplified

  public awesum() {
    awe.sum()
  }
```

```
  public run() {
    assert awesum() == 6
  }
}
```

@GROOVY.TRANSFORM.BASESCRIPT

Annotating a script with `@BaseScript` lets you customize a script's parent class. Suppose you wanted all your scripts to save all printed lines to a log. You could add boilerplate code into each script to achieve this. But imagine you later wanted to alter your logging approach. Your maintenance burden would be quite high as you'd need to refactor each script. Let's look at an alternative approach using `@BaseScript`. For the purposes of this example, we'll use a very simple logging mechanism; we'll keep only a list of printed strings.

Listing 9.27   Using `@BaseScript` to customize a script's parent class

```
@BaseScript(LoggingScript)
import groovy.transform.BaseScript

abstract class LoggingScript extends Script {
  def log = []
  void println(args) {
    log << args
    System.out.println args
  }
}

println 'hello'
println 3 * 5

assert log.join(' ') == 'hello 15'
```

For this example, we placed the `LoggingScript` base class right into our script, but obviously to share this across scripts you'd normally want to place that into its own separate source file. Now, our generated script will extend from `LoggingScript` instead of the normal `Script` class and so it will contain the `log` field and augmented `println` method. You can see another example of `@BaseScript` in section 19.2.2.

9.2.7   *More transformations*

There are other transformations as well, but they're covered elsewhere in the book. `@PackageScope` is discussed in chapter 7 and `@Category` and `@Mixin` are covered in chapter 8. See chapter 11 for a discussion of `@Bindable`, `@Vetoable`, and `@Listener-List`. `@Newify` is covered in section 19.8.

That's the end of our tour of the AST transformations that come with Groovy. You can use these annotations today without knowing much more. But you don't have to be satisfied with just what Groovy gives you. You're free to write your own annotations as well. The rest of this chapter delves into the task of implementing your own annotations using AST transformations. We're going to discuss local and global transformations, writing your own AST, testing your work, and the known limitations.

So why exactly would you want to write your own AST transformation? There are some good reasons to use compile-time metaprogramming instead of runtime. If you want Java to see the changes you make to a Groovy class, then use an AST transformation to write your changes directly into the produced class file. The code-generation transformations are good examples of doing this. If you need to avoid evaluating a method parameter before a method is invoked, then use an AST transform to avoid or wrap the call, as the @Log transformation does. And as we'll see later, you may also find compile-time metaprogramming a good fit for advanced or fine-grained control over DSLs. Lastly, if you want to do something wildly different, like change the semantics of the language, then your best approach is an AST transform. Let's get into deeper explanations and in-depth examples.

Throughout this chapter, you've heard the term *abstract syntax tree* several times, usually abbreviated as AST, but we haven't looked at what it really means. It's time to take a deep dive into AST and the Groovy compiler.

9.3   *Exploring AST*

To use AST transformations, you don't necessarily need to understand all the details of their inner workings, but to write your own transformations, it's important to have at least a little bit of knowledge about how the compiler works and which data structures it uses. In this section you'll learn about ASTs, see some of the AST visualization tools available for the platform, and understand the basics of the Groovy compiler.

An AST is a representation of your program in tree form. The tree has nodes that can have leaves and branches, and there's a single root node. Many compilers, not just Groovy, create an AST as a step toward a compiled program. In general and simplified terms, running a Groovy script is a multistep process, as shown in figure 9.1.

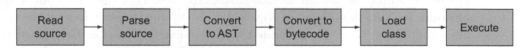

Figure 9.1   General process of compiling and running a Groovy script

First, the Groovy compiler reads the source file and checks it for basic forms of validity. Then the source code is converted into an AST, which is eventually converted to bytecode. Finally, the JVM loads the class and executes it. The AST is where all of the interesting language stuff happens. For example, adding getters and setters for properties happens in AST, and giving a script a main() method happens there. If you want to write a language feature, then you'll quite possibly be working with the AST. Let's look at simple AST examples to help you understand it better. Figure 9.2 shows the tree representing the expression 1 + 1, the simplest nontrivial example.

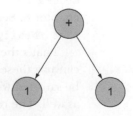

Figure 9.2   An AST for the expression 1 + 1

The plus operation is a *binary* one: it has two operands, a left and a right. When this program is executed, a plus operation is executed and (hopefully) the result is 2. Figure 9.3 shows a slightly more advanced example: the expression $1 + 2 + 3$.

It's no accident that the branch $1 + 2$ forms the leftmost branch. Addition is associated left to right, and to compute the answer to $1 + 2 + 3$ you must first compute $1 + 2$. Only then will you be able to evaluate $3 + 3$ and see the result as 6. Figure 9.4 shows a more realistic example, the groovy script assert $1 + 1 == 2$.

In Groovy terms, this script creates an `AssertStatement`, which has a `BooleanExpression`, which in turn has a `BinaryExpression`. It's this `BinaryExpression` that holds the == equals operator. Entire programs are

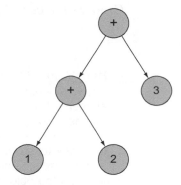

Figure 9.3   An AST for the expression 1 + 2 + 3

easily represented in tree form, and the tree can be analyzed, navigated, and transformed as part of the compilation.

Each language (or compiler, really) has its own tree structure, and it's up to the AST implementors to determine the exact structure. In Groovy, each element of the tree is an instance of the class `ASTNode`, and there's a subclass for everything in the language: `BooleanExpression`, `ForStatement`, `WhileStatement`, `ClosureExpression`, to name a few. There are over 75 subclasses of `ASTNode`, and having a good IDE to help you navigate the class hierarchy is highly recommended. Point your IDE to the

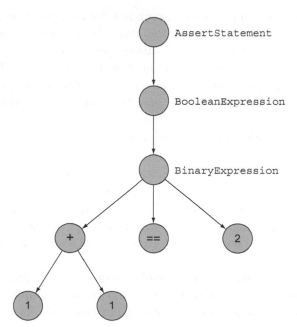

Figure 9.4   An AST for the expression assert 1 + 1 == 2

Groovy sources and you should be fine; some IDEs will automatically download them for you.

> **Homogeneous versus heterogeneous AST**
>
> *Heterogeneous AST* is the term for having one subclass of ASTNode for each language element. The tree is populated with many different types, and analyzing the tree means reading the type of the tree leaves, not just reading the leaf properties. The javac compiler from Oracle also uses a heterogeneous AST. The advantage is that it's easy to store and retrieve node-specific data from the AST leaves. Other languages use a *homogeneous* AST, where every node in the tree is the same type. Imagine if all the objects in the entire tree were of the concrete type ASTNode. The main advantage in this approach is that tree visitors are trivial to write, but static analysis is more difficult. The book *Language Implementation Patterns* by Terence Parr (Pragmatic Bookshelf, 2010) offers excellent in-depth coverage of ASTs.

9.3.1 *Tools of the trade*

At this point you no doubt have many questions about Groovy, ASTs, and class files. Groovy compiles to Java class files, so to analyze bytecode of a .class file you can always use the javap application from the JDK. But that's a very low-level approach, which can be time-consuming and frustrating, particularly if you're trying to examine code of any significant size. Luckily, there are many tools at your disposal if you're interested in digging a little deeper into how things work. If you plan on working with compile-time metaprogramming then each of the tools listed here will be an invaluable asset in your toolbox.

Groovy Console's AST browser and source viewer is GroovyConsole, which is included in the Groovy installation and contains a tool that lets you view and analyze the AST of a Groovy script. Once you have GroovyConsole open, you can analyze any script using the menu item Script> View AST or the Ctrl-T shortcut (Cmd-T on Macs). The window that opens is called the AST browser. The AST browser has three parts: the tree view, the property table, and the decompiled source view, as shown in figure 9.5.

The tree view displays the AST of your script using a standard tree widget. You can expand and navigate nodes, and otherwise explore the AST. As you click a tree node, the property table on the right lists all of the properties of the node, and the main GroovyConsole window highlights the source code corresponding to that AST node. The decompiled source view, along the bottom of the window, displays the AST rendered as Groovy source code. The generated source code is perhaps the easiest way to understand what the AST contains because it's much easier to read source code than a tree component.

Throughout this chapter we've shown snippets of equivalent generated source code for several of the transforms. Now would be a great time to try examples within the GroovyConsole's AST browser and see the equivalent generated code for yourself.

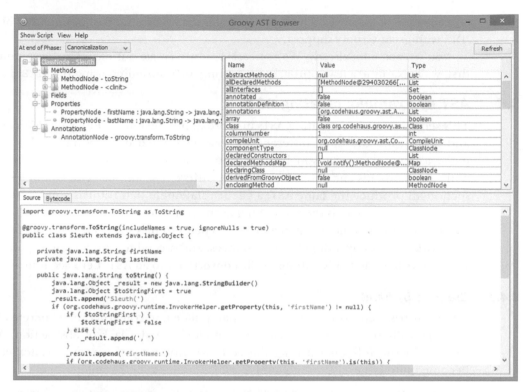

Figure 9.5 Groovy's standard AST browser showing the AST data structures (top left), the properties (top right), and the equivalent source code (bottom)

You should change the Phase dropdown list between the various phases and refresh the generated code to see how the output changes during the compilation process. Setting the phase to Canonicalization is often useful, because most of the transforms have been invoked by then but other details added later don't clutter up the class file.

The decompiled source viewer is one of the best features to learn and understand how Groovy works. Even if you're not attempting to write AST transformations, it can be a real learning experience to see how different pieces of Groovy source code get transformed into the final output.

9.3.2 Other tools

The last important tools are a good decompiler and debugger. A decompiler will reverse-engineer the source code out of a class file, and the results can be quite amazing. Any Java decompiler should work perfectly well with Groovy, and there are many open source and free ones to choose from. JD-GUI is also nice. It's free for noncommercial use but isn't open source. Also a good IDE and debugger aid greatly when exploring the large ASTNode class hierarchy. When there are over 75 subclasses to navigate, it's important to be able to quickly find the source code you need and view the current state of instances. There are several open source and free options available for IDEs with great Groovy support.

You've seen a lot already. We're nearly ready to create our own transformations. But first, we'll examine a few approaches to writing ASTs, including using the AstBuilder.

9.4   *AST by example: creating ASTs*

This section examines creating ASTs in more depth, first by building an AST manually, and then using the three different approaches offered by AstBuilder. It's hard to make a general comparison between the options. Each approach has advantages and disadvantages and should be used in different scenarios. The examples in this section all produce the same AST: a return statement that returns a new instance of java.util.Date. This is the same thing as the source code return new Date(), except that it's the AST and not the actual source. The examples start at the lowest level possible, working directly with ASTNode instances, and ascend toward a higher level, where you can write code that's automatically converted into an AST. Let's see it in action.

9.4.1   *Creating by hand*

The most basic approach is to directly manipulate and construct the concrete classes. The main disadvantages are verbosity, complexity, and a lack of abstraction. As you can see in the following listing, the code to produce just a return statement can become quite large.

Listing 9.28   Creating AST objects by hand

```
import org.codehaus.groovy.ast.ClassHelper
import org.codehaus.groovy.ast.expr.*
import org.codehaus.groovy.ast.stmt.ReturnStatement

def ast = new ReturnStatement(
    new ConstructorCallExpression(
        ClassHelper.make(Date),
        ArgumentListExpression.EMPTY_ARGUMENTS
    )
)

assert ast instanceof ReturnStatement
```

For simple problems that approach suffices. An IDE gives you code completion and some type checking, and should allow you to navigate to the source code of the ASTNode class hierarchy, which helps a lot with the learning process. Also, there are no limitations on the AST you can produce. Any tree whatsoever can be created by directly using the classes like this, which isn't the case for some of the other approaches. Also, it's quite easy to merge in information from the calling context.

There are some disadvantages to this approach, and for larger, more real-world examples this technique becomes a burden. First, the code to create an AST quickly becomes large and doesn't really resemble the source code it's trying to model. For big examples it's difficult to read the source code you write and mentally map it into the code it's meant to produce. Second, you need to manage things like Variable-Scope and tying the nodes together yourself. For example, many tasks involve two steps, such as creating a MethodNode and then adding it to the parent class. To be effective you'll need to learn a large part of the API. Third, this approach offers no abstraction layer over the raw AST.

The lack of abstraction can be seen in the example. For example, a Constructor-CallExpression accepts a ClassNode and an Expression as arguments (they're used as the constructor type and arguments). To write this AST by hand you need to know that an empty argument list is ArgumentListExpression.EMPTY_ARGUMENTS and not null. Also, you need to know that the best type to use for the constructor arguments is an ArgumentListExpression object. You *can* use other types but they probably aren't what you intend. Lastly and most importantly, a ClassNode should be made by calling the ClassHelper.make() method.

Creating a ClassNode with ClassHelper
The ClassHelper class contains logic for creating and caching a ClassNode correctly, which isn't exactly a simple process. If you need a ClassNode object, then always create it through ClassHelper, passing either a Class reference or a String representing a fully qualified class name. The String parameter is useful when you don't want a compile-time dependency on the target class.

Before looking at alternatives, it's worth pointing out that there are some utility classes that reduce the burden of using the AST nodes directly. The main class is General-Utils in the org.codehaus.groovy.ast.tools package. Using static imports from this class allows you to improve the previous listing to look like the following.

Listing 9.29 Using the GeneralUtils helper class

```
import org.codehaus.groovy.ast.stmt.ReturnStatement
import static org.codehaus.groovy.ast.ClassHelper.make
import static org.codehaus.groovy.ast.tools.GeneralUtils.*

def ast = returnS(ctorX(make(Date)))
assert ast instanceof ReturnStatement
```

This is an improvement but this helper class doesn't cover all of the ASTNode classes and you still need to know most of the implementation details of the ASTNode classes. A good abstraction should allow you to create ASTNode types without knowing all of this low-level information. Luckily, Groovy provides the AstBuilder.

9.4.2 AstBuilder.buildFromSpec

This approach provides a light DSL over the ASTNode class hierarchy. It should look similar to listing 9.28 but it's slightly cleaner as can be seen in the following listing.

Listing 9.30   Creating AST objects using `buildFromSpec`

```
import org.codehaus.groovy.ast.builder.AstBuilder
import org.codehaus.groovy.ast.stmt.ReturnStatement

def ast = new AstBuilder().buildFromSpec {
    returnStatement {
        constructorCall(Date) {
            argumentList {}
        }
    }
}

assert ast[0] instanceof ReturnStatement
```

The `AstBuilder` is a convenient shortcut for writing shorter, more concise AST. A shorthand notation exists for every `ASTNode` type, and much of the API is simplified. For instance, you can work directly with `Class` objects instead of `ClassNode` objects, and scopes are largely handled for you. Similar to the by-hand approach, there are no limitations on the AST you create and it's easy to merge in code and parameters from the surrounding context. The best documentation for `buildFromSpec` is the unit test, which shows the correct use of every single node type.

`AstBuilder.buildFromSpec` helps eliminate verbosity and some complexity. It *almost* matches the flexibility of calling the constructors by hand, suffering only from the fact that passing and referencing `Class` literals means that `Class` must be present at compile time (a limitation the manual approach doesn't share). The `buildFromSpec` API currently doesn't allow you to use `ClassHelper` in all cases—class literals are sometimes required. But the main disadvantage is that the DSL offers little in terms of abstraction. To effectively write a new AST you'll still need to know a lot about what AST you want to produce. You don't need to worry about scopes, but you'll need to know that a `ReturnStatement` requires an `Expression` and a `ConstructorCallExpression` requires an `ArgumentListExpression`. The next two alternatives offer better abstraction but with some loss in flexibility.

9.4.3   *AstBuilder.buildFromString*

The `AstBuilder` object has a `buildFromString` method that converts Groovy source code into the corresponding AST. By default it compiles the code to the class-generation phase and returns only the AST for the enclosed script, not any classes defined within the script. Of course, both of these behaviors can be changed by passing different arguments to the method. This approach allows you to create an AST without knowing anything about the underlying object hierarchy: at this point we have a genuine abstraction over the AST classes. The following listing shows the `buildFromString` approach in action.

Listing 9.31   Creating AST objects using `buildFromString`

```
import org.codehaus.groovy.ast.builder.AstBuilder
import org.codehaus.groovy.ast.stmt.BlockStatement
import org.codehaus.groovy.ast.stmt.ReturnStatement
```

```
def ast = new AstBuilder().buildFromString('new Date()')
assert ast[0] instanceof BlockStatement
assert ast[0].statements[0] instanceof ReturnStatement
```

The only knowledge required is that a script is a `BlockStatement` and that `Block-Statement` has a `ReturnStatement` in its statement list. As you can see, this is a terse mechanism for AST creation, and the intent of the produced code is clear. This is the preferred approach when accepting and compiling user input, because it can usually be converted into a `String`.

The main limitation is flexibility. How exactly do you merge in code or variables from the calling context? You need to resort to `String` concatenation as shown in the following listing, which creates a method returning twice π.

Listing 9.32 Trying to mix dynamic code with `buildFromString`

```
import org.codehaus.groovy.ast.builder.AstBuilder
import org.codehaus.groovy.control.CompilePhase
import org.codehaus.groovy.ast.*

def approxPI = 3.14G
def ast = new AstBuilder().buildFromString(
    CompilePhase.CLASS_GENERATION,
    false,
    'static double getTwoPI() { def pi = ' + approxPI + '; pi * 2 }'
)

assert ast[1] instanceof ClassNode
def method = ast[1].methods.find { it.name == 'getTwoPI' }
assert method instanceof MethodNode
```

That's a little complicated! Pushing compile-time data, such as the approximate value of π in the preceding example, into the AST requires `String` concatenation and potentially escaping, and getting the `MethodNode` requires searching through all the methods defined on the class and pulling it out by name. And we haven't even looked into how you might access other `ASTNode` implementation details such as `VariableScope` objects.

For more advanced examples it might be too difficult to manage this complexity. You can use the `buildFromString` method for this type of task, but it's fraught with difficulties. This is an abstraction over `ASTNodes` that doesn't easily allow you to dive deeper into the code when the need arises. Finally, synthesizing some types of structural nodes is difficult.

The `buildFromString` method and the next approach are great for creating method bodies, expressions, or statements. But if you're dealing with structures like `ClassNodes`, `MethodNodes`, or `FieldNodes`, then it's easier to use `buildFromSpec` or create the nodes by hand.

9.4.4 *AstBuilder.buildFromCode*

The last approach is possibly the most interesting. Using the `buildFromCode` method you can specify your source code directly as source code, and the builder turns it into

AST. This is similar to the `buildFromString` approach except that the input isn't a `String`, it's just code.

Listing 9.33 Creating AST objects using `buildFromCode`

```
import org.codehaus.groovy.ast.builder.AstBuilder
import org.codehaus.groovy.ast.stmt.ReturnStatement

def ast = new AstBuilder().buildFromCode {
  new Date()
}
assert ast[0].statements[0] instanceof ReturnStatement
```

This is quite simple, and it reads like code because it *is* code! The advantage is that the Groovy compiler and IDEs will highlight syntax correctly, do code completion, and generally validate your input. But its strength is also its weakness. The main disadvantage is that the Groovy compiler will validate your input. For instance, you cannot declare a new class within a closure body, so declaring a new class (or method) using `buildFromCode` isn't allowed. Also, there's no way to bind in data from the enclosing context. The `new Date()` expression here is only executed at runtime. The scope at compile time is different from the scope at runtime, so any variables in scope at compile time won't be available when the code is executed. There's no way to write the `getTwoPI()` method using this approach. When it's appropriate, this is the most elegant solution, and offers the best abstraction level—but there's a price to pay in flexibility.

There are many different scenarios where ASTs can be useful, and there are several APIs to help you build them. There's no one right way to create an AST. In general, our advice is the same for most things in life: start simple, stay simple. If you think the `AstBuilder` simplifies your implementation, then by all means use it. But if you find yourself fighting against it, or spending too much time figuring out how it works, then just go the simple route and write the AST by hand. There's a lot to learn with compile-time metaprogramming, and your time is probably better spent writing a few more tests than trimming down your AST generation by a few more lines of code.

If the caveats on `AstBuilder` use leave you feeling a little underwhelmed, stay tuned for Groovy macros that aim to remove some of the limitations of `AstBuilder`. Groovy macros are scheduled in Groovy's roadmap for version 2.5.

You've seen plenty of built-in AST transforms and you now understand a lot more about the AST data structures. Let's put your newfound knowledge to use and let you create some of your own AST transforms!

9.5   *AST by example: local transformations*

All of the examples presented so far, such as `@ToString` and `@Canonical`, are known as *local transformations*. A local transformation relies on annotations to rewrite Groovy code. There are other forms of transformations as well; however a local transformation has the advantage of being the easiest to write: Groovy takes care of instantiating and invoking your transformation correctly, as well as making sure to *avoid* calling it when it's not needed. Features written as local transformations modify the class generated by Groovy and are activated by annotating existing code structures, such as a method or a class.

Let's start your exploration with a simple example of a local transformation. To demonstrate a local transformation, you're going to create a method annotation that marks a method as being a Java `main` method. The transformation will add a `main` method that can be a public entry point to run the class, and that `main` method will create an instance of your class and call its annotated method. What you want to end up with is the ability to write code that looks like this:

```
class Greeter {
    @Main
    def greet() {
        println "Hello from the greet() method!"
    }
}
```

There's no point in running this code at this point, because the `@Main` annotation doesn't exist yet, but after just a few more steps, you'll have written this annotation and also a transformation that creates a `main` method on the `Greeter` class. This `main` method will create an instance of the `Greeter` class and then invoke the `greet()` method on it. After your transformation runs, the source equivalent of the modified AST tree will be

```
class Greeter {
  def greet() {
    println "Hello from the greet() method!"
  }
  public static void main(String[] args) {
    new Greeter().greet()
  }
}
```

and the output from invoking this class as a console application will be

```
Hello from the greet() method!
```

From the sample use you can glean some information about the objects involved. You need to define an annotation called `@Main`, and that must trigger the AST transformation to create the `main` method. There isn't much more to it than that. Creating and invoking the object is all done internally by Groovy. Figure 9.6 shows the classes involved with a local AST transformation.

You could define the `@Main` annotation using Groovy or as a standard Java annotation; there's no Groovy magic involved. If you chose Groovy you'd follow normal conventions and place it in a file called Main.groovy. Here's what it would look like (a full listing is coming shortly):

```
@Retention(RetentionPolicy.SOURCE)
@Target([ElementType.METHOD])
@GroovyASTTransformationClass(classes = [MainTransformation])
@interface Main {}
```

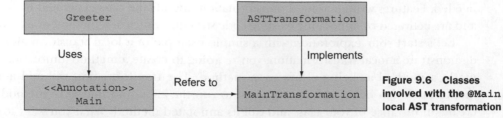

Figure 9.6 Classes involved with the @Main local AST transformation

The retention policy should be SOURCE, meaning that the compiler doesn't carry the presence of this annotation through to the final class file. The target element type specifies what the annotation can be applied to—so in this case, you're going to use METHOD. If you've written normal Java annotations before you'll have come across these concepts.

The use of the GroovyASTTransformationClass annotation is special to the Groovy compiler. It specifies the class (or classes) implementing the logic of the AST transformation, and is how the compiler binds the pieces together. In this case, that's the MainTransformation class, which you'll write next. Before seeing all of the details though, let's have a look at a class skeleton and sketch out what the transformation should do.

Following normal naming conventions, you'd place your code in a file called Main-Transformation.groovy and that file would have the following form:

```
@GroovyASTTransformation(phase = CompilePhase.INSTRUCTION_SELECTION)
class MainTransformation implements ASTTransformation {
  void visit(ASTNode[] astNodes, SourceUnit sourceUnit) {
    // perform any checks
    // construct appropriate main method
    // add main method to class
  }
}
```

There are two important things to note about this example:

- The class is annotated with @GroovyASTTransformation, which informs the Groovy compiler of the phase in which you want the transformation to be invoked. This is a required annotation for a transformation and must be Semantic Analysis or later. It can't be any earlier than that because your original annotation wouldn't be loaded at that point. There's a bit of a chicken and egg problem with trying to go earlier.
- Your transformation class must implement the ASTTransformation interface, which has a single method, called visit. The visit method takes two parameters. For simple transformations, you only need to use the ASTNode[] parameter. Element 0 contains the annotation that triggered the transformation and element 1 contains the ASTNode that was annotated.

Your `MainTransformation` class will be instantiated and invoked by Groovy when the `@Main` annotation is encountered. The code inside the `visit` method must accomplish these steps:

1 Perform any checks.
2 Find the method that was annotated with `@Main` (in this case `greet()`).
3 Get a reference to the enclosing class (`Greeter`).
4 Create a synthetic public static void `main` method and instantiate the `Greeter` instance within it.
5 Invoke the `greet()` method on the `Greeter` instance.
6 Add the new method onto the `Greeter` class.

There's one more requirement that we haven't mentioned until now. Before compiling your `Greeter` class, compiled versions of the classes for `@Main` and `MainTransformation` must be on the classpath. There are several ways to achieve this. If you're compiling by hand from the command line or using your IDE, ensure that those files are compiled first. If you have a build tool like Gradle you can configure your build file so that compilation of your transformation classes occurs before compilation of classes that use those transformations. For the purposes of this chapter, place everything in the one source file but use a new `GroovyShell` to compile your `Greeter` class after everything else has been compiled.

The complete example is shown in the following listing.

Listing 9.34 Implementing the `ASTTransformation` for the `@Main` annotation

```
import org.codehaus.groovy.ast.*
import org.codehaus.groovy.transform.*
import java.lang.annotation.*
import org.codehaus.groovy.control.*

@Retention(RetentionPolicy.SOURCE)
@Target([ElementType.METHOD])
@GroovyASTTransformationClass(classes = [MainTransformation])
@interface Main {}

import static groovyjarjarasm.asm.Opcodes.*
import static org.codehaus.groovy.ast.ClassHelper.VOID_TYPE
import static org.codehaus.groovy.ast.tools.GeneralUtils.*

@GroovyASTTransformation(phase = CompilePhase.INSTRUCTION_SELECTION)
class MainTransformation implements ASTTransformation {
  private NO_EXCEPTIONS = ClassNode.EMPTY_ARRAY
  private STRING_ARRAY = ClassHelper.STRING_TYPE.makeArray()

  void visit(ASTNode[] astNodes, SourceUnit sourceUnit) {
    if (astNodes?.size() != 2) return
    if (!(astNodes[0] instanceof AnnotationNode)) return
    if (astNodes[0].classNode.name != Main.name) return
    if (!(astNodes[1] instanceof MethodNode)) return
```

Annotation class definition

Defensive programming via guard clauses

```
        def targetMethod = astNodes[1]
        def targetClass = targetMethod.declaringClass
        def targetInstance = ctorX(targetClass)
        def callTarget = callX(targetInstance, targetMethod.name)
        def mainBody = block(stmt(callTarget))
        def visibility = ACC_STATIC | ACC_PUBLIC
        def parameters = params(param(STRING_ARRAY, 'args'))
        targetClass.addMethod('main', visibility,
            VOID_TYPE, parameters, NO_EXCEPTIONS, mainBody)
    }
}

new GroovyShell(getClass().classLoader).evaluate '''
class Greeter {
  @Main
  def greet() {
    println "Hello from the greet() method!"
  }
}
'''
```

New
Greeter().greet()

Adds public static
void main method

The visit method is where the interesting action happens. It shows how to create
ASTNode objects. You can call constructors directly, or use the GeneralUtils helper
class as shown here, or you're also free to use the AstBuilder as discussed in section 9.4.
The code sample does *some* error checking on the input, because in production code
it's often best to state your assumptions with a few assertions or guard clauses.

It may not be obvious, but there are a few assumptions made even in this small
example. The enclosing class must have a no-argument constructor (because you call
new Greeter()) that creates the object in a usable state. The example also doesn't
cater to annotating multiple methods, or annotating a static method, or handling an
existing main method. You can obviously extend this example in numerous ways if
you're feeling adventurous. Let's look at a few extensions now.

Listing 9.35   Implementing an enhanced @Main2 transformation

```
import org.codehaus.groovy.ast.*
import org.codehaus.groovy.ast.stmt.BlockStatement
import org.codehaus.groovy.transform.*
import java.lang.annotation.*
import org.codehaus.groovy.control.*

@Retention(RetentionPolicy.SOURCE)
@Target([ElementType.METHOD])
@GroovyASTTransformationClass(classes = [MainTransformation2])
@interface Main2 {
  boolean merge() default false
}

import static org.codehaus.groovy.ast.ClassHelper.VOID_TYPE
import static org.codehaus.groovy.ast.tools.GeneralUtils.*

@GroovyASTTransformation(phase = CompilePhase.INSTRUCTION_SELECTION)
class MainTransformation2 extends AbstractASTTransformation {
  private MSG1 = "@Main2 annotation use requires no-arg constructor!"
```

Defines an
annotation
attribute

```
    private MSG2 = "@Main2 annotation used but main already exists!"
    private NO_EXCEPTIONS = ClassNode.EMPTY_ARRAY
    private NO_PARAMS = Parameter.EMPTY_ARRAY
    private STRING_ARRAY = ClassHelper.STRING_TYPE.makeArray()

    void visit(ASTNode[] astNodes, SourceUnit sourceUnit) {
      init(astNodes, sourceUnit)
      def (anno, mainMethod) = astNodes

      boolean merge = getMemberValue(anno, 'merge')        ◁─┤ Reads
      def mainClass = mainMethod.declaringClass                 annotation
      def callTarget                                            attribute value
      if (mainMethod.isStatic()) {
        callTarget = mainClass
      } else {
        if (!hasNoArgConstructor(mainClass)) {             ┐ Indicates error if
          addError(MSG1, mainMethod)            ◁───        missing no-arg
          return                                           ┘ constructor
        }
        callTarget = ctorX(mainClass)
      }
      def callStatement = stmt(callX(callTarget, mainMethod.name))
      def parameters = params(param(STRING_ARRAY, 'args'))
      def existingMain = mainClass.getDeclaredMethod('main', parameters)
      if (existingMain && !merge) {
        addError(MSG2, mainMethod)              ◁─┐ Indicates error
        return                                      unless explicit
      }                                           ┘ merging

      if (existingMain) {
        if (existingMain.code instanceof BlockStatement) {  ┐ Handles block
          existingMain.code.addStatement(callStatement)  ◁─┘ statement case
        } else {
          block(existingMain.code).addStatement(callStatement)  ◁─┐ Handles single
        }                                                          statement case
      } else {
        mainClass.addMethod('main', ACC_STATIC | ACC_PUBLIC,
            VOID_TYPE, parameters, NO_EXCEPTIONS, block(callStatement))
      }
    }

  private hasNoArgConstructor(mainClass) {
    def constructors = mainClass.declaredConstructors
    def explicitNoArg = constructors.find { it.parameters == NO_PARAMS }
    def implicitNoArg = constructors.size() == 0
    implicitNoArg || explicitNoArg
  }
}

new GroovyShell(getClass().classLoader).evaluate '''
class Greeter {
    public static void main(String[] args) {
        println 'Hello from main()'
    }
```

```
    @Main2(merge=true)
    def greet() {
        println "Hello from the greet() instance method!"
    }

    @Main2(merge=true)
    static greet2() {
        println "Hello from the greet2() static method!"
    }
}
'''
```

Several edge cases are now handled. We now check for two types of error. First, if the class containing the method being annotated (the `Greeter` class in this example) doesn't have a no-arg constructor we stop compilation with an error message. Second, if an existing main method is found we'll also treat that as an error unless the annotation's `merge` attribute has been set to `true`, in which case we'll add the calling code to the existing `main` method. We'll also cater to static methods annotated with `@Main2` calling that static method from inside the `main` method instead of creating a new instance. Finally, there's an implementation detail we need to handle. For the case of adding code to an existing `main` method, we'll account for `main` methods containing just a single statement as well as ones that contain a block of statements.

The edge cases of writing transformations can sometimes be challenging. Writing an AST transformation forces you to sit and think about just what *could* happen in the language, and you'll come away from the experience with a much better understanding of Groovy.

When you write an AST transformation, you'll need to decide which compiler phase to target. The choice depends on what you're trying to do to the AST. A full description of the different compiler phases, as well as some hints for choosing which phase to target, appears in appendix F.

Local transformations require an annotation, which isn't particularly limiting when you consider that Groovy annotations are more flexible than Java's. They can appear in more places within a source file than in Java, including `import` statements. When in doubt choose a local transformation because it's the easiest to write. You can always refactor to a global transformation or hard-code a transformation into a class-loader later.

9.6   *AST by example: global transformations*

Global transformations are similar to local transformations except that no annotation is required to wire-in a visitor. Instead of having the end user specify when your transformation is applied, global transformations are simply applied to every single source unit in the compilation. Global transformations can also be applied to any phase in the compilation, even those before semantic analysis. With this flexibility comes a performance penalty. All compilations will take longer, even if your transformation isn't used. For this reason you should use global transformations with reticence and consider implementing global transformations in Java or using @CompileStatic for the performance benefits.

Global transformations are specified in JAR file metadata. To deploy a global transformation it must be packaged into a JAR file, and the META-INF metadata must specify the fully qualified path of your transformation class. Let's see this in action with an example. Imagine a transformation that adds a static method to every class that returns the date and time of the compilation as a String. You could use it from any class or script as follows:

```
println 'script compiled at: ' + compiledTime
class MyClass { }
println 'script class compiled at: ' + MyClass.compiledTime
```

Don't try to run this as is just yet because we haven't created the global transformation yet. We'll have a test coming up shortly that will give you a proper chance to see this transform in action. Also, remember that free-standing scripts without classes still get generated into a Script subclass during compilation, so adding a getCompiledTime() method to every Class in the SourceUnit should be enough to accomplish this feature. For this transformation we're going to add a public static method called getCompiledTime to every class in the SourceUnit, and it will simply return the date of compilation as a String.

In local transformations we manipulated the supplied ASTNode[] to find the context in which we were invoked. For global transformations this array holds little of interest. Instead we need to query the SourceUnit to find our source AST. It contains all the classes that were defined in the file along with the script, which itself is a class of type Script.

The following listing shows the implementation of our global transformation.

Listing 9.36 Adding a new method to a class using a global AST transformation

```
package regina

import org.codehaus.groovy.ast.*
import org.codehaus.groovy.transform.*
import org.codehaus.groovy.control.*
import org.codehaus.groovy.ast.builder.AstBuilder
import static groovyjarjarasm.asm.Opcodes.*

@GroovyASTTransformation(phase=CompilePhase.CONVERSION)
class CompiledAtASTTransformation implements ASTTransformation {

  private static final compileTime = new Date().toString()

  void visit(ASTNode[] astNodes, SourceUnit sourceUnit) {
    List classes = sourceUnit.ast?.classes
    classes.each { ClassNode clazz ->
      clazz.addMethod(makeMethod())
    }
  }
```

```
MethodNode makeMethod() {
  def ast = new AstBuilder().buildFromSpec {
    method('getCompiledTime', ACC_PUBLIC | ACC_STATIC, String) {
      parameters {}
      exceptions {}
      block {
        returnStatement {
          constant(compileTime)
        }
      }
      annotations {}
    }
  }
  ast[0]
}
}
```

For simplicity, the error checking was left out of the example; in a real transformation you'd apply similar guard clauses to the ones we used in the @Main example from listing 9.34. Now all we need to do is tell the compiler about our transformation so it can be applied appropriately.

The first requirement is that the transformation class or classes plus a particularly named metadata configuration file must be on the classpath. A common way to do this is to create a JAR file containing all of the necessary pieces. The JAR file must contain your AST transformation classes as well as a special file named org.codehaus.groovy .transform.ASTTransformation in the META-INF/services directory. By convention, the services directory is the standard place for putting configuration metadata files like the one we need to create. The configuration file is a simple text file, and each line is a fully qualified class name of an AST transformation. So, for our case we need the single-line regina.CompiledAtASTTransformation.

The full contents of our JAR file, including classes and services, can be seen in figure 9.7.

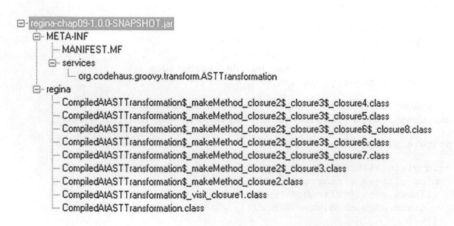

Figure 9.7 Contents of JAR file containing `CompiledAtASTTransformation`

The name of the JAR file doesn't matter. As long as it's on the classpath during compilation, the Groovy compiler will read the configuration file and apply any transformations listed within it. To make things easy, the sample code for this book has a little Gradle build file to generate the JAR for you. Just run `gradlew jar` at the command line to create the JAR in your build/libs folder. Feel free to create the JAR manually or using your own tool of choice.

Once we have our global transform on our Groovy classpath, we can test it by compiling any class or script. The following listing shows how.

Listing 9.37 Example showing use of `getCompiledTime()` on a class

```
package regina

class CompiledAtASTTransformationTest extends GroovyTestCase {
  // matches format: EEE MMM dd HH:mm:ss zzz yyyy
  static DATE_FMT = /\w{3} \w{3} \d\d \d\d:\d\d:\d\d \S{3,9} \d{4}/

  @Override
  protected void setUp() throws Exception {
    super.setUp()
  }

  void testShouldApplyToThisTest() {
    assert compiledTime.toString() =~ DATE_FMT
  }

  void testShouldApplyToScriptAndScriptClasses() {
    assertScript '''
      import static regina.CompiledAtASTTransformationTest.*
      assert compiledTime.toString() =~ DATE_FMT
      class MyClass { }
      assert MyClass.compiledTime.toString() =~ DATE_FMT
    '''
  }
}
```

The fact that the global transformation will typically be packaged in a JAR file has an effect on your project structure. If you want to use the transformation within your project, then the transformation JAR must be built before the compilation of the rest of your project. For most build tools and IDEs this means creating a separate project for the transformation, possibly along with a separate build script. Again, to make your life simple, the sample source code uses Gradle to make it easy for you to run the preceding test without you having to go to such trouble and without the global transform impacting any other Groovy work you might be doing. Simply run `gradlew test` from the command line to run the test.

There's one more feature of global AST transformations that DSL writers find useful. You can specify a file extension to which the Groovy compiler will automatically apply your transformation. The mechanism to define a file extension is similar to defining the transformation. Simply write the file extensions (without any wildcards) into a file called org.codehaus.groovy.source.Extensions and include it in your JAR

Error reporting

Errors can be reported using the `addError` and `addException` methods on `Source-Unit`; however, it's much better to use an `ErrorHandler`, which can be retrieved from the `SourceUnit` with the `getErrorHandler()` method. This object collects all of the error messages during the compile and has a broader API. There are methods to add an error and fail the build, add an error but continue, add warnings, and more. And please, for the sake of your users, always add error messages that contain a good description of what happened, the conditions that caused the error, and the line number where the error occurred. If your users really wanted cryptic or bizarre compilation failures, they'd be using C++.

next to the org.codehaus.groovy.transform.ASTTransformation file. Each line of the file should list a file extension without any sort of wildcards attached. Your final JAR file needs to contain both the ASTTransformation file and the extensions configuration file, plus any required .class files.

There's a lot to learn with compile-time metaprogramming, and your time is probably better spent writing a few more tests than trimming down your AST generation by a few more lines of code. That brings us to our next topic: testing.

9.7   *Testing AST transformations*

Test, test, test. It's hard to overtest an AST transformation because source code can come in a dizzying array of variations, each exposing unique edge cases. Also, during upgrades between Groovy versions you need a good regression test. Luckily, transformations are easy to test. Local transformations are the most testable. Typically, you create a nested class within your test case that contains your annotation and then test against that class. Consider the test for `@WithReadLock` in the following listing.

Listing 9.38   Possible unit test for the `@WithReadLock` transformation

```
import groovy.transform.WithReadLock
import java.util.concurrent.locks.ReentrantReadWriteLock
import static java.lang.reflect.Modifier.*

class ReadWriteLockTestWithNestedClass extends GroovyTestCase {

  static class MyClass {                          ⟵—┐ Nested
    @WithReadLock                                    │ class
    void readerMethod1() {}
  }

  void testLockFieldDefaultsForReadLock() {
    def field = MyClass.getDeclaredField('$reentrantlock')
    assert isPrivate(field.modifiers)
    assert !isTransient(field.modifiers)
    assert isFinal(field.modifiers)
    assert !isStatic(field.modifiers)
    assert field.type == ReentrantReadWriteLock
  }
}
```

This test case asserts that `WithReadLock` on a method creates a private final instance field called `$reentrantlock` with type `ReentrantReadWriteLock`. This is a simple and readable approach, and it works especially well within an IDE where the class can be verified and easily seen in searches. But there are two disadvantages. One, with a lot of tests come a lot of nested classes, and this can clutter up your namespace. Your build will create many, many extra classes that don't have meaning outside of a specific test method. And two, there's no way to debug the AST transformation in an IDE because by the time the test runs the class is already compiled. To work around these issues you can use a `GroovyClassLoader` to compile the class. The same test is presented in the following listing but this time using a `GroovyClassLoader`.

Listing 9.39   Improved unit test for the `@WithReadLock` transformation

```
import java.util.concurrent.locks.ReentrantReadWriteLock
import static java.lang.reflect.Modifier.*

class ReadWriteLockTestClassLoader extends GroovyTestCase {

  public void testLockFieldDefaultsForReadLock() {
    def tester = new GroovyClassLoader().parseClass('''
      class MyClass {
        @groovy.transform.WithReadLock
        public void readerMethod1() { }
      }
    ''')

    def field = tester.getDeclaredField('$reentrantlock')
    assert isPrivate(field.modifiers)
    assert !isTransient(field.modifiers)
    assert isFinal(field.modifiers)
    assert !isStatic(field.modifiers)
    assert field.type == ReentrantReadWriteLock
  }
}
```

With this approach debugger breakpoints should be hit when compiling `MyClass`, making development and troubleshooting much easier. Also, all class definitions are local to the test method, so the test isn't polluted with dozens of private classes and there are never naming conflicts. But the class definition within a string makes it more difficult to find uses of your annotation. If you need to create instances or run a script as setup, you may want to use `GroovyShell` instead of `GroovyClassLoader`, as shown in the following listing.

Listing 9.40   An AST transformation unit test based on `GroovyShell`

```
import java.lang.reflect.Modifier

class ReadWriteLockTestGroovyShell extends GroovyTestCase {

  public void testLockFieldDefaultsForReadLock() {
    def tester = new GroovyShell().evaluate('''
      import groovy.transform.WithReadLock
```

```
  class MyClass {
    @WithReadLock
    public void readerMethod1() { }
  }
  new MyClass()
''')

  def field = tester.getClass().getDeclaredField('$reentrantlock')
  assert Modifier.isPrivate(field.modifiers)
  // and more assertions...
  }
}
```

Notice how this script returns a new instance of MyClass. GroovyClassLoader and GroovyShell are similar, and which you use is largely a matter of preference. One tip: try to leave your assertions out of the string script. The more you can leave out of the string the better, because tools will have a much easier time understanding and supporting your code.

Global transformations are a little harder to test because they must generally be packaged and on the classpath before your test is compiled. To make testing global transformations easier, Groovy contains a class created specifically for testing called TransformTestHelper. You configure the object with a transformation and a compiler phase in which the transform should run, and then ask it to compile a file or string into a class you can test against. The following listing shows an example of Transform-TestHelper.

Listing 9.41   Using `TransformTestHelper` for testing transformations

```
import org.codehaus.groovy.tools.ast.TransformTestHelper
import static groovy.test.GroovyAssert.shouldFail
import static org.codehaus.groovy.control.CompilePhase.*

def DATE_FMT = /\w{3} \w{3} \d\d \d\d:\d\d:\d\d \S{3,9} \d{4}/

def folder = new File('src/main/groovy/regina')
def source = new File(folder, 'CompiledAtASTTransformation.groovy')
def transform = getClass().classLoader.parseClass(source).newInstance()

def helper = new TransformTestHelper(transform, PARSING)
def clazz = helper.parse(' class MyClass {} ')
shouldFail(MissingMethodException) {
  clazz.getCompileTime()
}

helper = new TransformTestHelper(transform, CONVERSION)
clazz = helper.parse(' class MyClass {} ')
assert clazz.getCompiledTime()
assert clazz.getCompiledTime() =~ DATE_FMT
```

Finally, Groovy comes with an AST transformation aimed at testing other AST transformations: @groovy.transform.ASTTest. While the tests we've shown you so far are testing the behavior of the AST transformation once it's been applied, testing an AST transformation properly requires you to perform assertions on the AST itself. For example, each AST node contains a map of custom metadata, called `nodeMetaData`, where the writer of an AST transformation is allowed to store information. This feature is also used internally by the compiler. The type checker, written in the form of an AST transformation, also stores inferred types in the form of node metadata. The problem is that this information isn't available in the class file or at runtime. This means that `TransformTestHelper` wouldn't be able to access it because the information is lost.

This means that when using `TransformTestHelper`, you're testing the result of the AST transformation, but you're not testing the transformation itself. `@ASTTest` will let you do that. It's an annotation that you can put on any AST node that accepts annotations, and that requires two arguments: a compile phase and a code block. For example, you can write:

```
@ASTTest(phase=CompilePhase.SEMANTIC_ANALYSIS, value={
    assert node instanceof DeclarationExpression
})
def name = 'Testing an AST transformation'
```

As you can see, the code block, in the form of a closure, has access to a special variable called `node`, which corresponds to the annotated node. This allows you to write custom assertions on the AST itself! Writing `CompilePhase.SEMANTIC_ANALYSIS` means that the assertion will be executed after the semantic analysis phase has completed.

Because not all AST nodes accept annotations, in addition to the `node` variable, the code block gives access to a helper method called `lookup`. The role of this method is to search for a specific AST node starting from the annotated node. Let's imagine that you want to perform an assertion on a `for` loop. As you cannot annotate the `for` loop directly, we'll use the `lookup` method to find it, as shown in the following listing.

> **Listing 9.42   Using `@ASTTest` with a `lookup` function**

```
import groovy.transform.ASTTest
import org.codehaus.groovy.ast.stmt.ForStatement
import org.codehaus.groovy.control.CompilePhase

@ASTTest(phase=CompilePhase.SEMANTIC_ANALYSIS, value={
    lookup('anchor').each { n ->
        assert n instanceof ForStatement
    }
})
void doSomething() {
    println 'Hello, Groovy!'
    anchor: for (int i=0; i<10;i++) { println "Iteration $i" }
}
```

Annotates an enclosing node →

Calls lookup to find a node labeled with 'anchor' ←

Performs assertion on each matching node ←

Uses a label on the node ←

This technique, which uses a label as a marker, allows you to reach any AST node that is inside the scope of a node that can be annotated. Using `@ASTTest`, you're now capable of testing the transformation during the compilation itself, which is a big plus over runtime checks.

Between `GroovyShell`, `GroovyClassLoader`, `@ASTTest`, and `TransformTestHelper`, there are quite a few options for testing. The hard part of testing isn't overall test coverage, but covering the edge cases. For instance, do your tests cover code that's written as a script *and* code that's written as a class? How about a mixture of both? Does it cover inner classes and anonymous classes? Have you considered what happens with internal naming conflicts? How does it run when other transformations are present? Properly testing transformations is a fun challenge. There are many opportunities to learn from your own experience but also the experience of others. The Groovy source code contains many unit tests for transformations. Doing a little code archeology now is time well spent, especially if it avoids a future late-night support call.

9.8   Limitations

Congratulations! You've almost finished your training in compile-time metaprogramming. Consider yourself armed and dangerous, both to others and yourself. It may be tempting to write a new language feature, but be careful. There are limitations and drawbacks to mucking about with the Groovy compiler. This section contains the bare minimum set of limitations you should know before embarking on your journey.

9.8.1   It's early binding

Groovy's power comes from late binding. Methods can be added to classes at runtime. Method overloading is resolved at runtime. Missing method exceptions can be caught and handled at runtime. In contrast, all the AST transformation work occurs at compile time, making it less flexible than dynamic metaprogramming. It can be very useful, but in general runs against the spirit of the dynamic parts of Groovy. If you can find a runtime solution then use it. Sometimes the best answer to the question "When should I use compile-time metaprogramming?" is "Only when you have to."

9.8.2   It's fragile

The syntax of Groovy and the GDK classes (anything in the `groovy.*` package) forms a public contract that's guaranteed to be backwards compatible between releases. You may have noticed from the `import` statements in the code examples that most of the AST-related code is in the `org.codehaus.groovy` packages. The backwards compatibility promises are weaker here. As new features are added to the language, there may be instances where breaking changes are introduced to the AST node hierarchy.

9.8.3   It adds complexity

When you use compile-time metaprogramming you're basically adding a feature to the language. If you add too many features, your users will drown in complexity. If you provide too many similar features, users may be confused about the best way to use an object. Language designers talk about orthogonality and composition: features should be independent of one another and be able to be used together without conflicts. Complexity lies at the intersection of overlapping language features. Consider how

Java generics, autoboxing, and primitive types intersect. There are many edge cases where unboxing a `Boolean` into a `boolean` throws a `NullPointerException`. Or a `List` can hold all objects except primitives. When several features come together edge cases occur, and sharp edges are dangerous. Be sparing in your cleverness.

9.8.4 Its syntax is fixed

AST transformations can change the *meaning*, or semantics, of code. For instance, Spock repurposes the logical OR operator (|) and the break/continue label to have a special meaning in test specifications. But Spock doesn't introduce any new syntax. The syntax of Groovy is fixed by the parser. Invalid Groovy won't parse, and AST transformations will not be invoked for it. You can change the semantics of the language, but you cannot change the syntax…except that you actually can if you're determined enough. Under the covers, Groovy uses ANTLR as a parser, and it's possible to write an ANTLR plugin for Groovy. That's a topic that deserves its own book, but information about how to do it can be found online.

9.8.5 It's not typed

Most interesting AST transformations rely on knowing the type of a variable. To Groovy, almost everything is an object. It's surprisingly difficult to determine the type of an instance and impossible to determine at compile time exactly where a method call will dispatch. For instance, metaclass additions are rarely known at compile time yet affect method dispatch. You can try to keep track of this information yourself, but as soon as a closure is declared, or a second thread is run, then the variable may no longer be what you think it is. This is acceptable for some tools like IDE integration or static analysis that read and make suggestions based on AST. But if you're rewriting AST and generating new bytecode, then guessing the type of an instance and getting it wrong can have disastrous effects on a program, especially if it fails to compile because of your mistake. Be careful what you think you know about types. It's easy to make a guess, and it's easy to be wrong.

9.8.6 It's unhygienic

It's possible, using an AST transformation, to introduce a field, class, method, or variable that conflicts with an existing one. If you add a method called `getCompiled-Time()`, you need to consider the possibility that the target class already has that method. The term for a compile-time metaprogramming system that allows naming conflicts is *unhygienic*. It's not really a term of derision, but it's obvious that the term was coined by users with a hygienic language. It's not an insurmountable problem, and you should carefully select names for synthetic variables and private fields and methods. The $ symbol is typically used in the identifier name because this symbol is rarely used in user-written code. For example, `@WithReadLock` generates a field called `$reentrantlock`. You can still have a conflict, but it should be rare. Choose your names carefully.

And with that the compile-time metaprogramming training is complete. It's time to go out into the world and write some interesting code.

9.9   *Next steps*

If you have an idea you want to implement, then the next steps are fairly obvious. Take a look at the templates in the Groovy source distribution, set up a project, and write some code. But before going too far we recommend talking about the idea on the Groovy mailing list. The community takes an active role helping people refine their ideas and make decisions about implementation. You may find you're talked into using runtime metaprogramming instead.

If you don't have a specific idea but want to learn more, then writing a static analysis rule for CodeNarc is an excellent way to get started. It's a small and well-contained project, the community is friendly, and you should be able to make a contribution within an hour or two. There's a `create-rule` script that comes with the project that creates all the needed files and unit test templates for new rules. CodeNarc is based on AST visitors, and the various types of visitors are fully described in appendix G.

For bookworms, there are other resources available. One of the authors keeps an active blog that includes several articles related to Groovy and compile-time metaprogramming. But other languages are worth investigating as well. Java, C#, Clojure, and JRuby also expose their ASTs to programmers or allow you to work directly with expression trees, and their documentation is easily found with a search engine. Of the languages listed, Clojure has the best support with a feature called Macros, which is arguably a more advanced and powerful form of the AST transformations described in this chapter. For an overview of language implementation in general, we definitely recommend *Language Implementation Patterns* by Terence Parr (Pragmatic Brookshelf, 2010). For an overview and classic reference for compile-time metaprogramming in Lisp, read Paul Graham's *On Lisp*, which is freely available for download at www.paulgraham.com/onlisp.html.

9.10   *Summary*

Compile-time metaprogramming is a new, exciting, and growing area of the Groovy ecosystem. Many of the new Groovy features use compile-time metaprogramming to eliminate redundant or verbose code. Use annotations like `@Canonical`, `@Lazy`, and `@InheritConstructors` to remove this unnecessary code from your source files yet still have it visible from Java. Use `@Delegate`, `@Immutable`, and `@Singleton` for an easy path to correct object design. The annotations `@Log`, `@Commons`, `@Log4j`, and `@Slf4j` streamline declaring and using loggers. Declarative concurrency constructs like `@Synchronized` clean up multithreaded code considerably, `@AutoClone` and `@Auto-Externalize` help make externalizing and cloning simple, and scripting has become much safer with `@TimedInterrupt`, `@ThreadInterrupt`, and `@ConditionalInterrupt`.

Writing your own transformation involves either a local AST transformation, which manipulates the AST when a certain annotation is discovered, or a global AST transformation, which is run for every compiled class. If your transformation needs to know information about the tree, then you'll probably need a code visitor to walk the entire AST, visiting nodes as they're found in the source code. If neither local nor global transformation is suitable for your scenario then you can always weave a visitor directly into a classloader without too much effort.

Groovy contains several alternatives for generating ASTs. Writing them by hand using the class constructors is always an option, but it's worth learning the `AstBuilder` API as well. The `buildFromSpec` method offers a useful DSL over the constructors; `buildFromString` offers a useful abstraction over all the classes, and `buildFromCode` provides an intuitive and elegant way to convert source into an AST.

There are several standard tools for working with ASTs. The javap application displays the raw .class file output. Groovy Console's AST browser is much more advanced, and shows the AST in tree form and also generated source-code form. A good Java decompiler is always a useful view of transformation results too, but perhaps the best tool is a large suite of unit tests. `GroovyClassLoader`, `GroovyShell`, and `TransformTestHelper` can all be used to test drive (or regression test) AST transformations.

Compile-time metaprogramming isn't suitable for every scenario. In general, we prefer late binding and flexibility. But there are concrete advantages: Java integration, easy embedded language development, delayed evaluation, and the ability to change the semantics of the language. AST transformations are opening a whole new world of what's possible with Groovy. After reading this chapter you should be better prepared to go into that world and see what new and useful tools you can create.

10

Groovy as
a static language

This chapter covers

- Incorporating static typing in a dynamic language
- Using the `@TypeChecked` annotation
- Type inference and flow typing
- Static compilation and the `@CompileStatic` annotation
- Type checking extensions

We shall not cease from exploration, and the end of all our exploring will be to arrive where we started and know the place for the first time.

—T. S. Eliot

There are endless debates in computer programming. *vi* or *emacs?* Tabs or spaces? Interfaces or abstract classes? Likewise, the debate over the benefits of static versus dynamic languages is never ending. You'll find people telling you that static languages are the best because you can find errors at compile time, while on the other side, people will empathize how powerful and concise dynamic code can be. In most languages, you have to choose one or the other. Not so in Groovy.

Groovy gives you the best of both worlds: it's dynamic, yet able to apply type checks just like static languages. It can optionally provide the runtime characteristics of a static language. It's your choice.

Groovy has a very interesting history with regards to typing, because it's derived from a strongly typed, *static* language, Java, but itself is a strongly typed *dynamic* language. A lot of the power of the language comes from its dynamic nature: MOP methods, metaprogramming, and all the other advanced features that we've introduced in the preceding chapters. These features heavily rely on the fact that the Groovy language defines a dynamic execution model, which supports, for example, defining and extending types *at runtime*. Yet at the same time, static typing is widely understood and cherished by many JVM developers who might be looking at other languages beyond Java.

In this chapter, you'll learn

- Why optional static type checking and static compilation were introduced into Groovy
- In what situations you can use these features
- What the limits are
- How you can extend the static type system of Groovy to provide even more type safety than Java

In a way, we started with static Java, added more and more dynamic features, made them statically verifiable, even produced optional static runtime characteristics, but reentered the static world with many more options and a better language than before.

Buckle up! It's an in-depth and fast-paced journey. Let's start with a look at why you might want static typing in the first place.

10.1 Motivation for optional static typing

It's clear that Groovy's success is related to its powerful runtime metaprogramming capabilities. When the Groovy team announced that Groovy 2 would support static typing, a lot of people were wondering why we did so. Groovy is, and will remain, a dynamic language, but it now offers *optional* static typing. This is in line with a general agnostic stance Groovy takes on style. Functional or imperative, static or dynamic, Groovy lets you decide. The objective of the language isn't to force you into a particular style or paradigm but to give you options. It won't lock you into a particular mindset, that dynamic languages are generally better than static ones, or vice versa.

Groovy has been designed recognizing that both static and dynamic language features have their place. The individual programmer can weigh the advantages and drawbacks and should be smart enough to choose the best approach for the task at hand. With Groovy, no one will ever tell you that you must use static typing, but if you want to, you can. Since version 2, Groovy gives you the best of both worlds, and more importantly, lets you mix and match approaches as needed.

10.1.1   *The role of types in Groovy*

Often programmers are confused when they have to describe the various type systems. If you ask someone if a dynamic language implies weak typing, the answer will likely be "of course." The truth is more complex. Despite being a dynamic language, Groovy is a strongly typed language. And it was strongly typed even before the release of Groovy 2. In fact, Groovy is a dynamic, *optionally typed* language. The difference is that types in Groovy are very important and are in the heart of the dynamic dispatch system. Types are used at runtime for the method dispatch. The fact that types are mainly used at runtime allows a lot of flexibility, but often creates the misconception that types aren't used at all.

The following methods aren't equivalent:

```
def greet(message)        { println "1: $message" }
def greet(String message) { println "2: $message" }
```

The fact that the first one omits the type is a convenience for accepting any type, but the type is important. If no `println` method exists at runtime accepting the actual type of message, then Groovy would report an error. In the second case, one would only be able to call the `greet` method if the actual argument is of type `String`. So imagine that we're calling the code like this:

```
greet 'Hello'
greet ((Object)'World')
```

The actual output would be:

```
2: Hello
1: World
```

Someone not used to Groovy may find the output surprising, but it illustrates the concept that optional typing doesn't mean that the language is untyped. On the contrary, types are very important, and the explicit cast to `Object` on the second line is a way, in Groovy, to bypass the dynamic method selection and force a specific overload of a method to be chosen. Don't worry if you don't fully understand the method dispatch concept at this point—we'll cover this in detail in this chapter. What's important to understand is that Groovy always had a strongly typed system, but it was mainly used at runtime, not at compile time.

A typical argument against runtime method dispatch is that if a method doesn't exist, you'll only have an error at runtime, although you could have caught the problem at compile time. That's exactly where Groovy 2's static type checker comes into action. It can perform static analysis of your code at compile time and report errors like missing methods and more.

10.1.2   *Type checking a dynamic language?*

At first, the idea may appear strange. Because Groovy is a dynamic language, there's absolutely no reason why a method not discoverable at compile time couldn't, in practice, exist at runtime. So performing type checking of dynamic code is, in theory, walking upside down. The following listing defines and uses a dynamic method that's perfectly available at runtime but not at compile time.

Listing 10.1   A method may exist only at runtime

```
class Duck {
  def methodMissing(String name, args) {        ◀── ❶ Dynamic method
    println "$name!"                                     missing behavior
  }                                             ◀──┐
}                                                   │  Prints name of
                                                  ❷ method being called
def duck = new Duck()            │  Calls a dynamic
duck.quack()                   ◀─┘  method
```

The class Duck doesn't define any method named quack, yet the code compiles fine and, at runtime, it's still working. It works because we define a handler ❶ for calls to methods that don't exist. In our case, it just prints the name of the method being called ❷. Groovy supports many tricks like this one as you've seen in chapter 8.

So in short: the dynamic capabilities of Groovy disallow type checking. But type checking can be very useful to spot typos like in the following listing.

Listing 10.2   Can you spot the typo?

```
class Detective {
  String firstName
  String lastName
}

def sherlock = new Detective(firstname: 'Sherlock', lastname: 'Holmes')
assert sherlock.lastName == 'Holmes'
```

If you compile this code, no error will occur. If you don't spot the error (a syntax highlighting editor can warn you here; see figure 10.1) and correct it, then only at runtime when you execute the code will you be faced with a MissingPropertyException. It works this way because Groovy is a dynamic language and it's possible that at runtime, the perceived error is handled (for example, we might have a metaclass that makes property access case-insensitive).

Despite the IDE warnings and the quite reasonable error message at runtime, it would be nice to catch the typo in cases where dynamic features aren't used anyway.

This is the main reason why static type checking was introduced in Groovy 2: it gives you the familiar compile-time type checking through an optional annotation by which you declare that you don't expect any dynamic features to be used in that part of the code.

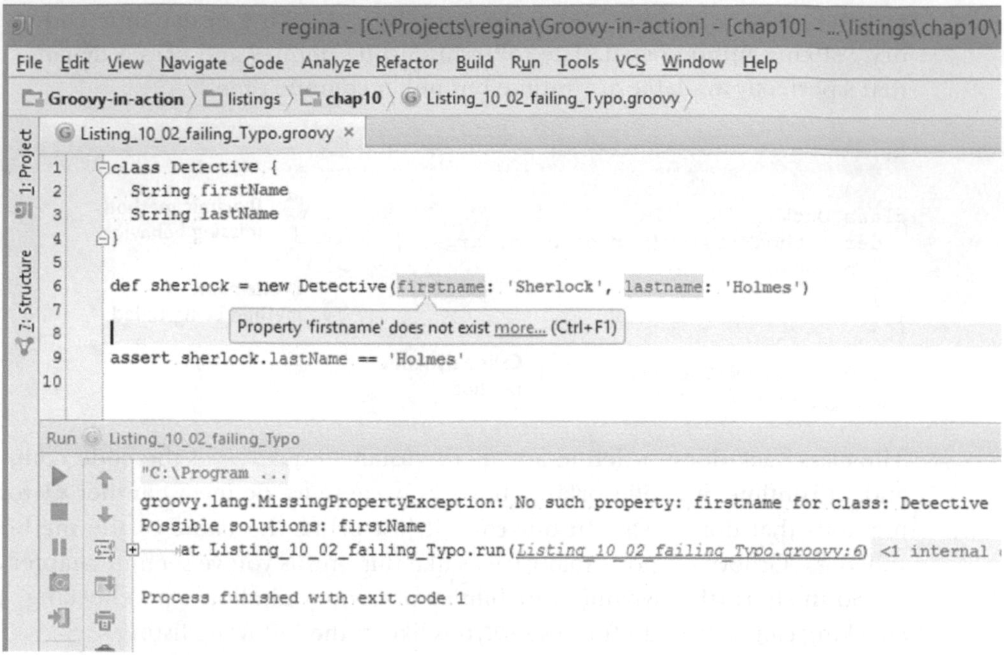

Figure 10.1   An IDE will warn you of suspect naming even with dynamic code

10.2   *Using @TypeChecked*

Performing additional static type checking is as easy as annotating it with `@groovy`
`.transform.TypeChecked`. The `@TypeChecked` annotation can be applied on classes or
methods. In the following listing, the whole class will be type checked, including fields,
properties, inner classes, and closures.

Listing 10.3   Type checking a full class

```
import groovy.transform.TypeChecked

@TypeChecked
class Sleuth {
  String firstName
  String lastName

  String getFullName() { "$firstName $lastName" }
}

def nancy = new Sleuth(firstName: 'Nancy', lastName: 'Drew')
assert nancy.fullName == 'Nancy Drew'
```

The checking process includes verifying that fields and properties exist at compile
time. If you want more fine-grained control, you can choose to instead annotate one
or more methods of a class. In the following listing, type checking is only applied to

the getFullName method ❶, which would allow other methods such as makePeace ❷ to use the dynamic features of the language.

Listing 10.4 Type checking a single method

```
import groovy.transform.TypeChecked

class Actor {
  String firstName, lastName

  @TypeChecked
  String getFullName() { "$firstName $lastName" }          ❶ Checked

  void makePeace() {
    new AntBuilder().echo('Peace was never an option')      ❷ Dynamic
  }                                                            features
}                                                              allowed
```
```
def magneto = new Actor(firstName: 'Ian', lastName: 'McKellen')
assert magneto.fullName == 'Ian McKellen'
magneto.makePeace()
```

For this example, we could have also chosen to annotate at the class level and then turn off checking just for the makePeace method. You'll see what's involved later when we discuss in more detail mixing static and dynamic code. We'll also discuss Ant-Builder in more detail in chapter 11. For now you need only know that it's indeed a dynamic feature; the AntBuilder class has no echo method but the builder instead calls Ant's echo task.

Listings 10.3 and 10.4 would both compile fine without the TypeChecked annotation, because there's actually no error in the code. It's also worth understanding that adding the annotation *won't change the behavior of the application at runtime!*

> **NOTE** Some of the upcoming listings are designed not to compile. So, if you get an error, don't be too surprised, that's exactly what's supposed to happen. But remember that all of our listings are like a giant suite of tests. How do we make a listing pass that doesn't even compile? We make it a script and wrap it into a shouldFail call. If you're interested in what's going on behind the scenes, chapters 16 and 17 discuss more about integrating and testing scripts, respectively.

Next, let's make a few errors and let @TypeChecked catch them.

10.2.1 Finding typos

Perhaps the most frequent complaint against dynamic languages is the lack of compile-time recognition of typos. By adding @TypeChecked, you're allowing the Groovy compiler to catch such errors in much the same way the Java compiler does for a Java source file. Let's make sure the Groovy compiler recognizes such errors by amending listing 10.3 as follows to introduce a small typo.

Listing 10.5   Catching a typo at compile time

```
import groovy.transform.TypeChecked

@TypeChecked                                              Uppercase N
class Sleuth {
  String firstName
  String lastName
  String getFullName() { "$firstName $lastname" }        Incorrect
}                                                          lowercase n
```

In listing 10.5, the getFullName method is supposed to return a string that combines the first and last names. But there's a typo inside the GString: lastname is used instead of lastName (note the uppercase N). It's quite obvious that this is an error, but without @TypeChecked, it's absolutely impossible for the compiler to report it, and you have to rely on the fact of calling getFullName to find the bug, which is often too late. Now if you compile listing 10.5, you'll see that the compilation fails with the following message:

```
[Static type checking] - The variable [lastname] is undeclared.
at line: 7, column: 39
```

As you can see, adding @TypeChecked allowed the compiler to check the class, but more importantly, features like interpolated strings are also checked. What happens here is that the compiler analyzed the GString, found the use of a variable named lastname, but couldn't find any local variable, field, or property of which the name matched. Instead of letting this pass, the compiler now reports an error and fails compilation.

Finding typos is obviously not limited to variables, fields, and properties: it works the same for methods, as you're going to see.

10.2.2 *Resolving method calls*

Resolving method calls is a key concept that differentiates a dynamic language from a static one. As you've seen, Groovy is a dynamic language, so method calls are normally resolved at runtime. Java resolves method calls at compile time.

Activating type checking in Groovy means that you'd like the compiler to report errors at compile time if a method doesn't exist. For that, you need to be able to resolve its name, but you also need to check for the existence of a method that matches the parameters. To simplify slightly, you're expecting Groovy to give error messages like the Java compiler would.[1] In the following listing, the compiler will report an error because a misspelled method doesn't exist.

---

[1]   In fact, Groovy has a few special cases and doesn't behave exactly like Java; it follows these rules: http://docs.groovy-lang.org/latest/html/documentation/#_method_resolution.

Listing 10.6   Find a typo in a method name

```
@groovy.transform.TypeChecked
class Person {
  String name
  String getFullName() { name.toUppercase() }
}
```

> Incorrect lowercase c

Compiling listing 10.6 would trigger the following compilation error:

```
[Static type checking] - Cannot find matching method
java.lang.String#toUppercase()
```

The reason is that we wanted to call the `toUpperCase` method but we misspelled the method name. The situation isn't always that simple. You might not have made a spelling error, but you might have mixed up the order of the parameters or supplied the wrong type to one of the parameters. As an example, it's easy to switch two arguments, as shown in the next listing.

Listing 10.7   The method doesn't exist with the provided arguments

```
@groovy.transform.TypeChecked
class Repeat {
    static void repeat(int n, String message) {
        n.times{ println message }
    }
    static void main(String... args) {
        repeat('Hello', 4)
    }
}
```

When compiling this example, the compiler fails with

```
[Static type checking] - Cannot find matching method
Repeat#repeat(java.lang.String, int)
```

Since `@TypeChecked` works at compile time it cannot always know what the runtime method dispatch will do. It needs to make assumptions. There's a remaining risk that it chooses the "wrong" method. This will later become more important when we introduce `@CompileStatic`, which additionally has an effect on the generated code.

Luckily, using `@TypeChecked` provides a lot of very interesting compile-time errors that justify its use and, as we've discussed before, you're in control of when to turn it on and off.

10.2.3   *Checking assignments*

While nicely supporting a functional programming style that emphasizes immutability, Groovy is first and foremost an imperative language that uses assignments. So it should come as no surprise that `@TypeChecked` checks assignments at compile time. The following listing contains invalid assignments that `@TypeChecked` would complain about.

Listing 10.8   Type checking assignments

```
@groovy.transform.TypeChecked
void testAssignmentsShouldThrowCompilationErrors() {
  Set set = new Object()
  byte b = 200L
  List<Integer> list = ['Richard', 'Mary']
  int prim = null
}
```

Cannot cast Object into Set

Possible loss of precision

Wrong generics

Primitives cannot be null

The relevant parts from the compiler errors are:

```
Cannot assign value of type java.lang.Object to variable
  of type java.util.Set
Possible loss of precision from long to byte
Incompatible generic argument types. Cannot assign
  java.util.List <java.lang.String> to: java.util.List <Integer>
Cannot assign value of type java.lang.Object to variable of type int
```

It's worth noting that there are four exceptions to the assignment rules that are covered by the type checker, corresponding to five cases where Groovy wouldn't throw any errors at runtime: assignments to `String`, `Boolean`, `boolean`, `Class`, and `String` assignments to `enum` values. There are special coercion rules for these special cases. For example, the following assignment is something totally valid in Groovy (independently of type checking):

```
String person = new Person(name: 'Philip')
```

Groovy transparently calls the `toString` method on the `Person` class in this case.

We've explained in chapter 6 that you can also assign any object to a `boolean` (or `Boolean`) when discussing the Groovy truth:

```
boolean flag = person
```

But it's little known that Groovy also allows anything to be converted to a `Class`! You can write

```
Class personClass = 'com.acme.Person'
```

Groovy converts an object to a `Class` by calling its `toString` method to get the class name and then loading that class.

If you attempt to assign a `String` value to an `enum`, Groovy will use the `enum`'s implicit `valueOf(String)` method when performing the assignment.

You can use all of these techniques together with `@TypeChecked` as shown in the following listing.

Listing 10.9   Type checking assignment coercion

```
enum MyEnum {
    var, val
}
```

```
@groovy.transform.TypeChecked
void testAssignmentsWithCoercion() {
    MyEnum val = 'val'
    assert val == MyEnum.val

    String blue = java.awt.Color.BLUE
    assert blue == 'java.awt.Color[r=0,g=0,b=255]'

    boolean nonEmpty = new Date()
    Boolean empty = ''
    assert nonEmpty
    assert !empty

    Class stringClass = 'java.lang.String'
    assert stringClass.interfaces.size() == 3
}
```

Strings coerced to enum values

Anything coerced to String

Anything coerced to boolean/Boolean

Strings coerced to classes

```
testAssignmentsWithCoercion()
```

Automatic coercion of any object to a `String`, `Boolean`, `boolean`, or `Class`, and `String` assignments to enum values is a useful feature. You wouldn't like to lose that feature just because of the use of a type checker. For that reason, the Groovy type checker is aware of those features and will let those cases pass, even if the left-hand side and the right-hand side of assignments otherwise appear invalid.[2]

As you'll see in the following examples, this is a general rule that the type checker tries to follow whenever possible: if a "dynamic Groovy" feature exists, try to be aware of it and let it pass. Of course, there are some cases where it's not possible, but obviously, using a type checker isn't a reason to make the Groovy language more verbose and turn it back into Java!

For the very same reason, the type checker embeds a smart type inference engine that makes the code elegant while keeping it concise.

10.2.4 *Type inference*

A type inference engine is a component that's capable of determining the type of expressions even when there's no explicit type declaration. Take the following declaration in Java:

```
String text = "Type is explicit";
```

The type of the text variable is explicit, so the compiler doesn't have to make any computation to determine it. If a method is called on the text variable, it has to be declared on the type `String`.

Groovy has the `def` keyword, which allows you to declare a type in a very short manner, so the equivalent code is shorter:

```
def text = 'Type is implicit'
```

[2] For the complete rules see http://docs.groovy-lang.org/latest/html/documentation/#_type_checking _assignments.

Here, def is equivalent to declaring it as Object, but because Groovy resolves method calls at runtime, the compiler doesn't need to know the explicit type at compile time. But if you want to do type checking, you face a problem because the compiler wouldn't know that the text variable is in fact of type String. Groovy has to infer it. This not only includes information on how text was declared but also all assignments made on it.

DEF VERSUS EXPLICIT TYPE
The fact that Groovy has a type inference engine doesn't mean that you can use def everywhere and still pass the type checker. Sometimes you need to give Groovy more hints about your intentions.

Likewise, it's definitely not advisable to declare a field or a property with def, especially because we're living in a multithreaded world. Let's take a look at the following listing, which exhibits a bad coding style in the context of type checking.

Listing 10.10 Properties shouldn't be declared with def for type checking

```
class Holder {
  def value = 'My value'                              Property
}                                              ① declaration

@groovy.transform.TypeChecked
void testNoCompileTimeErrorDueToDef() {        ② Creates Holder
  def holder = new Holder()                        instance
  holder.value = 5                             Holder value
}                                              ③ type changes!

testNoCompileTimeErrorDueToDef()
```

If you look solely at the Holder class definition, in particular the declaration of the value property ①, you might think that the type of the value field is String, because of the default value that's assigned to it. The truth is more complex, because def is equivalent to Object, so while a String is used as the default value, any variable of any type inheriting from Object can be assigned to it. In particular, in our example, the type of value changes from String (its initial default value set when we create the instance at ②) to Integer when we explicitly set the value property ③! While the type changes of local references can be predicted (because the scope is well defined and we know exactly what methods are called), it's not the case for an "external" reference. Worse than that, such a reference can change at any time from any thread. For that reason, the type checker won't do any type inference in these cases, but instead relies on the declared type, so it's important to use an explicit type in that case.

> **TIP** Using explicit types is considered good style for documentation reasons, especially in method signatures and properties. Using def is okay for local variables or to signal "I really don't care," in which case you probably won't make use of @TypeChecked anyway.

Groovy 1.8 introduced the notion of primitive type optimizations. With `def`, you'll never get an optimized primitive type like `int` but an `Integer` object.

Last but not least, using an explicit type also causes additional type checks. The assignment case that we've explained earlier is one use case. If you want to make sure that one doesn't assign just anything to a variable, you can declare the type explicitly and the type checker will guarantee that all future assignments will be valid.

GENERICS

You may be surprised to hear that Java also has a type inference engine. In fact, Java 7 has one due to the introduction of the diamond operator. In the following code, the type of the generic type argument on the right-hand side of the assignment is determined by the type inference engine:

```
List<String> list = new ArrayList<>(); // Java
```

Java 8 has a much smarter type inference engine, made necessary by the introduction of lambdas to the language, but it makes it clear that generics are one of the pain points of a static language. On one side, they made it very powerful, but on the other side, they're often very difficult to write or awfully verbose.

Without type checking, we can almost say that Groovy only makes use of generics for decorative reasons. This isn't totally true because they're used for compatibility with Java, but internally, Groovy makes minimal use of generics. You'll be aware that Java's type erasure throws away generics information at runtime. You could consider that dynamic Groovy is more aggressive at throwing away that kind of information.

With type checking, the game is very different because generics dramatically improve the expressiveness of the type system. Declaring a list with a generic type will remove the need for explicit casts of arguments. For those reasons, Groovy's type checker needs to understand generics, but it also needs to be more powerful than Java's. Let's consider the following listing, which shows a typical list declaration.

Listing 10.11 In-place list declaration

```
def authors = ['Dierk', 'Guillaume']
authors.each { println it }
```

List iteration   ❶ Declaration of a list

In the first line ❶ we use a very idiomatic way to declare the list. Under the hood, Groovy will create an `ArrayList` of strings, but the fact that it contains strings is arbitrary. But as soon as you start using type checking, determining the type of the components is very important, so the type inference engine cannot limit itself to determine that the type of authors is `List`. Instead, it's smart enough to tell that it's a `List<String>`. To understand why it's important, let's update listing 10.11 to make it use `@TypeChecked` as shown in the following listing.

Listing 10.12 Type checking generics

```
import groovy.transform.TypeChecked

@TypeChecked
void printAuthors() {
  def authors = ['Dierk', 'Guillaume']
  printToUpperCase(authors)
}

void printToUpperCase(List<String> authors) {
  authors.each { println it.toUpperCase() }
}

printAuthors()
```

In this example, the `printAuthors` method calls another method internally that's named `printToUpperCase`, but only accepts a `List<String>`. If the type checker wasn't able to perform type inference of generic type arguments, then the type information on the `authors` variable won't be sufficient to call the `printToUpperCase` method.

Fortunately, the type inference engine of Groovy is smart enough to resolve this case and even capable to deal with types that you can't even express in Groovy (or Java), like we'll discuss later (see section 10.3.1). Of course, using generics explicitly isn't something that programmers of dynamic languages are used to, so here again, you'll have the choice to use implicit or explicit generic type declarations, but in case you choose implicit types, then you're relying on a type inference system, which may behave differently from what you expect.[3]

10.2.5 *Type-checked Grooviness*

Type checking shouldn't make your code more verbose nor let it lose its groove. This section shows idiomatic Groovy code that's out-of-the-box compatible with type checking.

LIST AND MAP CONSTRUCTORS

There are several ways to create objects in Groovy. The most widely used (and also best performing) approach comes from Java and consists in calling a constructor:

```
Dimension d = new Dimension(800, 600)
```

But Groovy also provides a short notation equivalent to the above, using a list:

```
Dimension d = [800, 600]
```

In this case, Groovy makes use of the declaration type of the variable (`Dimension`), then takes the list and tries to find a constructor of which the argument types match the types of the elements of the list. So here, Groovy would try to find a constructor to `Dimension` that takes two integers as arguments.

---

[3] As Groovy derives from Java, it uses the same generics model. It has both advantages and drawbacks, but you must be aware that the type checker can be fragile with regards to generics.

Let's see what would happen with dynamic Groovy if you made an error when using this shortcut. Instead of supplying the two required integer values, suppose you supplied only one as shown in the following listing.

```
import static groovy.test.GroovyAssert.shouldFail

void oneDimensional() {
    java.awt.Dimension d = [100]          Two parameters
}                                         required! Runtime
                                          error here!
shouldFail(ClassCastException) {
    oneDimensional()
}
```

When you execute this example, you'll get a cast exception at runtime. We confirm that behavior with the shouldFail clause.

The nice thing is that this list-style constructor shortcut is compatible with type checking, and when used together you'll benefit from additional checks at compile time, as the following listing shows.

```
@groovy.transform.TypeChecked
void alsoOneDimensional() {            Two parameters
    java.awt.Dimension d = [100]       required.
}                                      Compilation fails!
```

When the compiler analyzes the list-style constructor call, it fails to find a Dimension (int) constructor and complains with:

```
No matching constructor found: java.awt.Dimension<init>(int)
```

This is an illustration of how you can benefit from type checking in a situation where you know you don't use the dynamic features of Groovy. The error is there, but the only way for the compiler to be certain that it's an error is by using @TypeChecked.

Another interesting constructor call shortcut in Groovy is the map-style constructor. In that case, the right-hand side of the declaration isn't a list but a map, which gives the advantage of being able to use named arguments, as seen in the following listing.

```
import groovy.transform.TypeChecked

class Athlete {
  String first, last
  int age
}
```

```
@TypeChecked
void ageInteger() {
  Athlete ok = [first: 'Michael', last: 'Jordan', age: 52]      ◀──❶ Passes
}

@TypeChecked
void ageString() {
  Athlete bad = [first: 'Michael', last: 'Jordan', age: '52']   ◀──❷ Fails
}
```

For this example, first use of the shortcut syntax for map-style constructors ❶ is correct. What Groovy does in that case is equivalent to the following:

```
Athlete ok = new Athlete()
ok.first = 'Michael'
ok.last = 'Jordan'
ok.age = 52
```

The problem is that on our second usage ❷ we made a mistake and used a String for the age property instead of an int. Without type checking, you'd have to run that code to find the error and, unless you have good test coverage, running it might mean it's in production and perhaps that's too late. Activating type checking gives you the advantage of catching the problem earlier, during compilation. The type checker would fail with the following error:

```
Cannot assign value of type java.lang.String to variable of type int
```

Of course, the verifications that the type checker performs here are also available if you use the long variant of the map-style constructor, which is:

```
new Athlete(first: 'Michael', last: 'Jordan', age: '52')             ◀── Fails
```

While being compatible with list- and map-style constructors, there are some limitations to what you can do if you activate type checking. In listing 10.16, we're trying to use the list-style constructor with a list that's provided externally, as the parameter of a method call. While this would work at runtime, it's not compatible with type checking, because unless you analyze every call site to the method, you cannot determine statically what will be the types of the elements of the list.

> **Listing 10.16   Type checking error with list-style constructor**

```
import groovy.transform.*

@TupleConstructor
class Author {
    String first
    String last
    int born
}
```

```
@TypeChecked
Author createAuthor(List params) {          Compile-
    Author a = params                        time error!
    a
}
createAuthor(['Agatha', 'Christie', 1890])
```

It's possible to make this pass statically, but you're facing the same problem as the one you'd have in Java: you'd have to add a lot of code to ensure type safety, as the following listing tries to achieve.

Listing 10.17   Fixing type safety

```
import groovy.transform.*

@TupleConstructor
class Author {
  String first
  String last
  int born
}

@TypeChecked
Author createAuthor(List params) {
  if (params.size() != 3) {
    throw new IllegalArgumentException('Incorrect number of arguments')
  }
  String first = params[0]
  String last = params[1]               No need to cast
  Integer age = (Integer) params[2]     as String on LHS
  Author a = [first, last, age]         Cast required
  a
}                                       Passes

assert createAuthor(['Agatha', 'Christie', 1890]).born == 1890
```

Please note that compile-time type safety isn't fully guaranteed here, because we have to check that the list contains at least three elements and that can only be done at runtime.[4] While, in general, Groovy constructs are compatible with type checking, there might be situations like this one where you'd have to rewrite your code to ensure type safety. One may argue that this is exactly what you're trying to achieve by annotating your code with @TypeChecked, so limitations are acceptable. From a language point of view, Groovy's static checking capabilities were designed to reduce as much as possible the cases where you'd need to change your code to work in the static and dynamic "modes."

In that context, one of the interesting cases to study is closures: they're one of the most appealing features of the language, and making them compatible with type checking is a challenge.

---

[4] There's more that we could do here with typed tuples but that's beyond the scope of what we want to discuss in this book.

10.2.6 *Type checking closures*

Closures are very similar to methods: they're blocks of code that can accept parameters and return values. When it comes to type checking, however, there's a big difference between a method and a closure: while in the first one the signature is declared explicitly, for closures, the return type is implicit and arguments are optional. Moreover, what gives the closures their name is the fact that they're able to capture local variables and references from the enclosing scope. Let's examine these differences in more detail.

CLOSURE RETURN TYPES

The following listing compares two equivalent operations: one defined as a method, the other defined as a closure.

Listing 10.18   Comparing methods and closures

```
def sum1(int x, int y) { x + y }
def sum2 = { int x, int y -> x + y }
assert sum1(3, 4) == 7
assert sum2(4, 5) == 9
```

❶ sum function defined using a closure

sum function defined using a method

The difference is that the closure can be manipulated as data, making it ideal to be passed as an arguments to a method. It's the most elegant solution to the Gang of Four Strategy design pattern. This means that at ❶, the type of the sum2 variable is a Closure. As closures are Callable, it's possible to call them using the same syntax as a regular method call.

By using @TypeChecked, Groovy can infer the return type of a closure. In listing 10.18, because the closure body only depends on its parameters, which are of type int, the return type of the closure can be inferred as int, so the type of the sum2 variable is, in the end, inferred as Closure<Integer>. This means that if you try to assign it to a Closure<String>, for example, it would fail as shown in the following listing.

Listing 10.19   Checking closure return types

```
import groovy.transform.TypeChecked

class Logger {
  static void print(Closure<String> messageProvider) {
    println "Received message : ${messageProvider()}"
  }
}

@TypeChecked
void testMessage() {
  def returnsString = { 'Hello, Groovy!' }
  def returnsInt = { int x, int y -> x + y }
  Logger.print(returnsString)
  Logger.print(returnsInt)
}
```

❶ Passes

❷ Compilation fails

Because the `print` method in the `Logger` class accepts a closure that returns a `String`, calling it with `returnsString` ❶ is correct because the body of that closure only returns a `String` (a constant one). But when trying to call `print` with the `returnsInt` closure ❷, which returns an `int`, the type checker will complain and you'll see a compile-time error:

```
Cannot call Logger#print(groovy.lang.Closure <java.lang.String>)
with arguments [groovy.lang.Closure <java.lang.Integer>]
```

CLOSURE ARGUMENT TYPES

Handling closure argument types can be a little tricky. As you've seen in chapter 5, closures can have an implicit "it" parameter corresponding to the first argument of a closure call. The type of this parameter is `Object`. That doesn't give much help to the type checker. So, in general, if you want to use type checking with closures in Groovy you might need to declare the types of the closure parameters explicitly. The good news is that there are cases where the argument types can be inferred. We'll look at the various cases in the remainder of this section.

Suppose you're entering information about users on your site and have created the following domain class to capture their username and password:

```
class User {
  String name
  String password
}
```

And now suppose you wish to run some validation rules to check various characteristics of a user instance. You might create some code such as shown in the following listing.

Listing 10.20   Dynamic validation of a user instance

```
void validate(User u, Closure<Boolean> rule) {
  if (!rule.call(u)) {
    println "User $u.name $u.password rejected"        ❶ Apply rule
  }
}

void validateAll(user) {
                                                        ❷ Example passing rule
  validate(user) { !it.name.isEmpty() }
  validate(user) { it.password.size() > 7 }            ❸ Example failing rule
  // other rules ...
}

def bob = new User(name: 'Bob', password: 'secr3t')
validateAll(bob)
```

Here we evaluate each validation rule, passing it the user instance ❶, and reject the user if he or she fails the rule. In our case, user Bob doesn't have an empty name, so our first example rule ❷ will pass but Bob's password is too short and the second rule will fail ❸. What can we say about the nature of these rules? They're likely to be very simple, perhaps not needing any fancy dynamic capabilities, and most certainly will make heavy use of properties from our `User` domain class. They seem like a good candidate for additional type checking.

We can naively try to apply type checking to our `validateAll` method; however, there will be three things that the static compiler won't like, as shown in the following listing.

Listing 10.21   Type checker will get grumpy if it sees too many `Object` types

```
import groovy.transform.TypeChecked

void validate(User u, Closure<Boolean> rule) {
  if (!rule.call(u)) {
    println "User $u.name $u.password rejected"
  }
}

@TypeChecked
void validateAll(user) {                              ←  Error: type of
  validate(user) { !it.name.isEmpty() }        ←          user is Object
  validate(user) { it.password.size() > 7 }    ←  Error: no property
}                                                        name for Object

                                                   ←  Error: no property
def bob = new User(name: 'Bob', password: 'secr3t')   password for Object
validateAll(bob)
```

The first thing we can do is explicitly add the necessary type declarations as shown in the next listing.

Listing 10.22   User validation with explicit parameter types

```
import groovy.transform.TypeChecked

void validate(User u, Closure<Boolean> rule) {
  if (!rule.call(u)) {
    println "User $u.name $u.password rejected"
  }
}

@TypeChecked
void validateAll(User user) {                              User type in
  validate(user) { User u -> !u.name.isEmpty() }      method and closure
  validate(user) { User u -> u.password.size() > 7 }  declarations
}

def bob = new User(name: 'Bob', password: 'secr3t')
validateAll(bob)
```

While being a bit more verbose, adding explicit type information isn't necessarily a bad option, but we do have a few other possibilities available to us. First, it might be possible to leverage Groovy's ability to automatically convert a closure to a single abstract method (SAM) type (see chapter 7). Let's consider that next.

SAM TYPE CONVERSION

If we have an appropriate SAM type available that already has type information expressed in its parameter declarations, the type checker can use that information to derive the argument type information for the closure arguments. We can incorporate that approach into our user validation example as the following listing shows.

Listing 10.23   User validation harnessing a SAM method

```
import groovy.transform.TypeChecked

interface Predicate<On> { boolean apply(On e) }        ❶ SAM type
                                                           definition

void validate(User u, Predicate<User> rule) {          ❷ SAM type
  if (!rule.apply(u)) {                                     argument
    println "User $u.name $u.password rejected"
  }
}

@TypeChecked
void validateAll(User user) {
  validate(user) { !it.name.isEmpty() }                ❸ Implicit type
  validate(user) { it.password.size() > 7 }               inferred
}

def bob = new User(name: 'Bob', password: 'secr3t')
validateAll(bob)
```

Because the method of our SAM type uses a generic type for its argument ❶ and our `validate` method supplies `User` for the type parameter ❷, the necessary type information can be inferred by the type checker. Therefore, our closure rules ❸ don't need the explicit `User` type that was required in listing 10.22.

Another alternative that the type checker can possibly use to determine argument type information is API metadata. Groovy has several annotations that add metadata to the API. Let's look at those next.

@CLOSUREPARAMS

Another alternative that the type checker can use to determine argument type information is API metadata, if it's available. Groovy provides the `@ClosureParams` annotation as used in the following listing to give type hints for the expected parameter types of the validation closure.

Listing 10.24   User validation leveraging `ClosureParams`

```
import groovy.transform.TypeChecked       First parameter to
import groovy.transform.stc.*             validate method is
                                          of type User
void validate(User u,
          @ClosureParams(FirstParam) Closure<Boolean> rule) {   Type hint
  if (!rule.call(u)) {                                           FirstParam
    println "User $u.name $u.password rejected"                 refers to
  }                                                           ❶ User type
}
```

```
@TypeChecked
void validateAll(User user) {
  validate(user) { !it.name.isEmpty() }
  validate(user) { it.password.size() > 7 }
}

def bob = new User(name: 'Bob', password: 'secr3t')
validateAll(bob)
```

The `@ClosureParams` annotation is added to the closure parameter, in our case the rule parameter ❶. The `@ClosureParams` annotation minimally accepts one argument, a *type hint*. The type hint is a class that's responsible for completing type information at compile time for the closure. In this example, the type hint being used is `groovy.transform.stc.FirstParam`, which indicates to the type checker that the closure will accept one parameter of which the type is the type of the first parameter of the method. In our case, the first parameter of the method is `User`, so it indicates to the type checker that the first parameter of the closure is in fact a `User`.

Numerous type hint classes are provided. As an example, if a closure has one `User` argument and the method you're annotating is passed a `List<User>` in its second argument, you can use `SecondParam.FirstGenericType` like this:

```
void validateUsers(Date when,                                    Second
    List<User> users,                                  ←─────── parameter
    @ClosureParams(SecondParam.FirstGenericType) Closure c) {  ←──── User is
    /* method body omitted */                                         generic type
}                                                                     from second
                                                                      parameter
```

Some hint type classes support optional information; for example, if you have a closure that takes two arguments, a `String` and an `int`, you could use:

```
@ClosureParams(value=SimpleType,options=['java.lang.String','int'])
Closure c
```

See the Groovy documentation for a complete list of available type hint classes.[5] You should also be aware that much of the Groovy-GDK has these annotations included. So, for the most part, when you're using any Groovy library methods, you'll have type-checking support.

Now let's move on to another annotation that also augments your API with metadata and see if we can put it to good use for our user validation example.

@DELEGATESTO

There's another trick for giving information to the type checker that can often be used when writing DSLs. You can use the `@DelegatesTo` annotation. We'll have a brief look at it here and come back to it in more detail in the last section of this chapter when we look at tricks for extending the type checker for scenarios such as type checking your own DSLs.

---

[5] Groovy Language Documentation, version 2.4.3, http://docs.groovy-lang.org/latest/html/documentation/#_the_code_closureparams_code_annotation.

First, let's relook at our validation rules. All of our rules so far have expressions of the form `u.name.isEmpty()` or `it.password.size()`. Perhaps the person writing the rules isn't an IT guru but some business expert. We might want to allow him or her to just write `name.isEmpty()` and `password.size()`.[6] So, let's look at revising our validation code to support this capability.

An interesting feature of Groovy closures is that they have delegates, as explained in chapter 5. Delegates can be considered as the message receiver when none is specified. So, to implement our revised validation rules, we just need to ensure that the user is set as the `delegate`. The following listing does exactly that.

Listing 10.25   Toward a user validation DSL

```
def validate(User u, Closure rule) {        ❶ Sets user
  rule.delegate = u                              as delegate
  rule()                                       ❷ Calls
}                                                  validation rule

Simplified  ❸  void validateAll(User u) {
rule            validate(u) { if (name.isEmpty()) println 'Empty name' }
syntax          validate(u) { if (password.size() < 8) println 'Password too short' }
            }

def bob = new User(name: 'Bob', password: 'secr3t')
validateAll(bob)
```

The differences from our earlier solutions are minimal. We set the `delegate` before calling the rule ❶. Because the `delegate` is set, we can now call the rule without a parameter ❷. And, finally, our rules can use the slightly simplified syntax we were hoping to achieve ❸. The solution works but so far it's dynamic. The type checker can't know in general that the delegate has been set at runtime, there are no explicit types for the closure, and on top of that there are now properties like `name` and `password` that aren't declared anywhere. Again, API metadata comes to the rescue. This time with the `@DelegatesTo` annotation that specifically covers this case.

To use this approach, simply annotate the `rule` closure and indicate the type of the `Closure` delegate. For our case, we declare that the delegate will be of type `User` as the following listing shows.

Listing 10.26   Type-checked user validation DSL using `DelegatesTo`

```
import groovy.transform.TypeChecked

def validate(User u, @DelegatesTo(User) Closure rule) {    ← Annotation
  rule.delegate = u                                            on Closure
  rule()                                                       parameter
}
```

---

[6]   See chapter 19 if you want to see tricks for even further simplifications.

```
@TypeChecked
void validateAll(User u) {
    validate(u) { if (name.isEmpty()) println 'Empty name' }
    validate(u) { if (password.size() < 8) println 'Password too short' }
}

def bob = new User(name: 'Bob', password: 'secr3t')
validateAll(bob)
```

There's a slight variation to the approach. You still need to annotate the closure parameter with @DelegatesTo but instead of explicitly setting the delegate type (User in our example), you use the @DelegateTo.Target annotation on another parameter and let the compiler determine the type. The following listing uses that variant.

Listing 10.27   **Type-checked user validation DSL using** DelegatesTo.Target

```
import groovy.transform.TypeChecked

def validate(@DelegatesTo.Target User u, @DelegatesTo Closure rule) {    ⟵ Annotates Closure and User
    rule.delegate = u
    rule()
}

@TypeChecked
void validateAll(User u) {
    validate(u) { if (name.isEmpty()) println 'Empty name' }
    validate(u) { if (password.size() < 8) println 'Password too short' }
}

def bob = new User(name: 'Bob', password: 'secr3t')
validateAll(bob)
```

This approach becomes particularly interesting in conjunction with flow typing, which we cover in more detail in section 10.5.

10.2.7 *Revisiting dynamic features in light of type checking*

While some people may want to perform static type analysis on their full codebase, it's in practice very unlikely that all your Groovy code can be statically checked. There's a very good reason for that. You saw in chapter 8 that a lot of the Groovy features are dynamic: categories, metaclasses, builders, and mixins to name a few. Let's examine a few of these and consider the implications of trying to statically check some of these use scenarios.

CATEGORIES

As an example, take this use of Groovy's TimeCategory class:

```
use (TimeCategory) {
    duration = 1.week - 1.day
}
```

Here, TimeCategory adds methods at runtime that are difficult to examine for the type checker. The following listing uses the category out of its lexical scope to point out the issue.

Listing 10.28   Valid dynamic code that cannot be type checked

```
import groovy.time.TimeCategory

class VacationHelper {
    static duration() {
        use(TimeCategory) {
            doCompute()
        }
    }

    static doCompute() { 1.week - 1.day }
}

assert VacationHelper.duration().toString() == '6 days'
```

This code is totally valid even if the doCompute method itself doesn't explicitly use
TimeCategory, because it's called from the duration method that has "opened" the
category. If one calls doCompute directly, it would fail, so the code validity depends on
the entry point, which is beyond the scope of static analysis. For that reason, you cannot use categories with the type checker. See chapter 19 if you want to see tricks for
even further simplifications.

   You might think this is a very contrived example and perhaps we should be forced
to refactor code like in listing 10.28 to require any dynamic code to "live" inside the
use block. But as you'll see in chapter 11, we definitely don't want to do that. There
we'll see that the same building logic can be used with multiple builders: NodeBuilder
and MarkupBuilder.

METACLASSES

Another dynamic Groovy feature that isn't amenable to static analysis is runtime
metaprogramming through metaclasses. The following listing uses Groovy's Expando-
MetaClass with the Intercept-Cache-Invoke pattern as seen in chapter 8 to add new
methods at runtime.

Listing 10.29   Using ExpandoMetaClass

```
class Spy {
    static {
        def mc = new ExpandoMetaClass(Spy, false, true)      ◁─┐ Creates an
        mc.initialize()                                           ExpandoMetaClass
        Spy.metaClass = mc                                        for Spy class
    }
    String name = "James"

    void methodMissing(String name, args) {              ❶ If method not
        if (name.startsWith('changeNameTo')) {             found, defines
            println "Adding method $name"                  new one
            String newName = name.substring(12)
            def newMethod = { delegate.name = newName }    ◁─┐
Call new     Spy.metaClass."$name" = newMethod            ◁─── ❷ Cache
method  └─▷  newMethod()                                          method
```

```
            } else {
                throw new MissingMethodException(name, this.class, args)
            }
        }
    }
}

def spy = new Spy()
assert "James" == spy.name
spy.changeNameToAustin()
assert "Austin" == spy.name
spy.changeNameToMaxwell()
assert "Maxwell" == spy.name
spy.changeNameToAustin()
```

Calling this code will produce the following output:

```
Adding method changeNameToAustin
Adding method changeNameToMaxwell
```

This is a typical use of `ExpandoMetaClass` as a tool to create DSLs. Here, instead of having the user call the `setName` method on a person, we allow them to use `change-NameTo<PersonName>`. At ❶, we're creating a new method if none is found, which delegates to the setter and caches the newly created method in ❷. This explains why the last call to `changeNameToAustin` doesn't trigger a call to `methodMissing`, because this time the method is known and cached.

Obviously, there's no way for a static analysis tool to determine all possible method calls because the behavior is defined at runtime, when `methodMissing` actually gets called. For that reason, you cannot use metaclasses in combination with `@TypeChecked`.

Categories and metaclasses aren't the only features of Groovy that aren't compatible with type checking and also why we don't believe applying `@TypeChecked` on your whole Groovy codebase makes much sense: if you do, this means that you explicitly decide not to use half of the features of the language, including some that are in particular very powerful: builders.

BUILDERS

Builders are a central feature of many DSLs written in Groovy and we'll cover them in detail in chapter 11. They make dealing with hierarchical data incredibly easy and provide an elegant and concise syntax. While Groovy makes it easy to write builders, it also provides some builders for common use cases, such as the `MarkupBuilder` to generate XML markup, or the `JsonBuilder` to output JSON. Builders often use many dynamic features, including closure delegates, method missing, and property missing, making the code often impossible to check statically. (Section 10.5 explains how you can help the type checker in such situations, making it in many cases possible to perform static type checking of even purely dynamic code!) Let's see the issue firsthand in the following listing that emits proper HTML code.

Listing 10.30 Using `MarkupBuilder` and unresolved methods

```
import groovy.xml.MarkupBuilder

def writer = new StringWriter()
def xml = new MarkupBuilder(writer)        ◁  Instantiate
                                              MarkupBuilder
xml.html {
    head {                                 ❶ Method calls that
        title('An XHTML Page')                @TypeChecked
    }                                         would reject
}

println writer
```

This example says it all: the `MarkupBuilder` class doesn't define any `html`, `head`, or `title` methods ❶, so if you tried to apply `@TypeChecked` on this example, the compiler would report them as compilation errors. But you can see that this works at runtime. If you're anything like us, you want both: dynamic features *and* type checks for your code. Groovy allows you to mix both approaches.

10.2.8 *Mixing type-checked code with dynamic code*

The first solution relies on annotating individual methods with `@TypeChecked` instead of annotating a whole class. The following listing calls dynamic builder code from a statically type-checked method.

Listing 10.31 Mixing `@TypeChecked` and dynamic code in a single class

```
import groovy.xml.MarkupBuilder
import groovy.transform.TypeChecked

class HTMLExample {
    private static String buildPage(String pageTitle) {
        def writer - new StringWriter()
        def xml = new MarkupBuilder(writer)

        xml.html {
            head { title(pageTitle) }
        }
        writer
    }                                     Type check only
                                     ◁    this method
    @TypeChecked
    static String page404() {
        buildPage '404 - Not Found'
    }
}

HTMLExample.page404()
```

While being an easy solution, this technique has drawbacks:

- You have to annotate each method that you want to be type checked with `@TypeChecked`.
- Static initializers blocks, instance initializer blocks, and fields cannot be annotated, so they'll never be type checked.

It's also worth noting that the method level is the finest granularity for type checking: you cannot mix type-checked and not-type-checked code in a single method body. This implies that if a method defines an anonymous inner class or a closure inside, then the anonymous inner class (respectively the closure) will only be type checked if the method or the class is itself annotated.

SKIPPING TYPE CHECKING

Fortunately, the type checker provides a way to enable type checking on a full class but skip some methods. This should be used, for example, if a class mostly consists of statically checkable code and has only a few methods that use dynamic features. We can modify listing 10.31 to use the `TypeCheckingMode` option as shown in the following listing.

Listing 10.32 Using `TypeCheckingMode.SKIP`

```
import groovy.xml.MarkupBuilder
import groovy.transform.TypeChecked
import groovy.transform.TypeCheckingMode       Type-checked
                                               class...
@TypeChecked
class HTMLExample {
    @TypeChecked(TypeCheckingMode.SKIP)         ...but exclude
    private static String buildPage(String pageTitle) {   this method
        def writer = new StringWriter()
        def xml = new MarkupBuilder(writer)

        xml.html {
            head { title(pageTitle) }
        }
        writer
    }

    static String page404() {
        buildPage '404 - Not Found'
    }
}

HTMLExample.page404()
```

Depending on your needs, you might want to use one option or the other.

> **TIP** If you like the benefits of type checking and only use dynamic features in quite specific places, then we'd recommend using `TypeCheckingMode.SKIP` because it more clearly clarifies the exact portions of the code that are "dynamic."

10.3 *Flow typing*

In the previous sections, we've spent time explaining what `@TypeChecked` would offer you, and what it would prohibit, but we also explained why it was difficult to perform static analysis of a dynamic language. The semantics of a dynamic program are difficult, if not impossible, to determine at compile time, meaning that the type checker might think that one method will be called, but in reality, another one would be. To reduce the gap between the dynamic and the static behavior, the type inference engine uses the principle of *flow typing*.

Flow typing is the ability to determine the type of a variable at some point in the code, depending on the previous assignments. The next listing contains a series of assignments that change the runtime type.

Listing 10.33   Flow typing and subsequent assignments

```
import groovy.transform.TypeChecked

@TypeChecked
def flowTyping() {
    def var = 'A string'
    var = var.toUpperCase()
    var = var.length()
    var = String.valueOf(var)
    var = 2*var
    var
}
```

1 Assigns String to var

2 Assigns another String to var

3 Assigns int to var

4 Assigns String to var

5 Fails! Trying to call (int*String)

This example makes use of a single variable (var) to which different objects are stored at different lines. The type of var, at any particular point, depends on the execution flow. It means that the type of the variable that is inferred **1**—that is, a String—is used **2** to determine what method can be called on var. The result of the method call is a String, so the inferred type of var after the assignment will remain a String. But we're calling the length() method, which is known to return an int **3**. The type checker is aware of that, so it knows the method that is called is in fact String#valueOf(int) **4**, which returns a String. This is why the only compilation error that will appear is at **5**, because we're trying to call the multiply method on an integer **2**, and that method doesn't accept a String as a second argument. Because no such method exists, the compiler reports an error.

The alternative, for the type checker, would've been to take all assignments into consideration and determine a single inferred type for var that would be used everywhere. Here, because we're assigning both a String and an Integer, the only type that would match is Object. One could consider this the right thing to do; however, it has a major problem: it would make the code much more verbose because you'd have to use explicit casts everywhere! The code would be equivalent to what you have to do in Java:

```
Object var = "A string";
var = ((String)var).toUpperCase();
var = ((String)var).length();
var = String.valueOf((Integer)var);
```

This code wouldn't feel like Groovy!

> **NOTE** Listing 10.33 is using bad style. It stores objects of different types in a single variable. Groovy makes it easy to write much less imperative equivalent versions of the preceding code but doesn't prevent you from using bad style: its goal is to help you to write effective, readable, and concise code. In any language, you can write bad code and Groovy isn't an exception to that rule.

Though we showed you an admittedly contrived example above to introduce you to the idea of flow typing, it really makes a lot of sense for more complex code and is particularly useful if you consider type hierarchies like in the following listing.

Listing 10.34   Type hierarchies and flow typing

```
import groovy.transform.TypeChecked

interface Flying {
  void fly()
}

class Bird implements Flying {
  void fly() { println "I'm flying!" }
}

class Canary extends Bird {
  void sing() { println "Tweet!" }
}

@TypeChecked
void aviary() {
  def o = new Bird()
  o.fly()                    ❶ A bird
                                can fly
  o = new Canary()
  o.fly()                    ❷ A canary can fly
  o.sing()                     and also sing
}

aviary()
```

The big difference with Java is that here, you can have type-checked code that's written in an idiomatic Groovy way (`def`, no semicolons, no `instanceof`) but still doesn't require any cast! In particular, you don't have to tell the compiler it's a bird ❶ or a canary ❷, when calling the respective methods. Of course, if you add the following lines:

```
o = new Bird()             Would fail
o.sing()                   compilation
```

then the type checker would report a compilation error, because it realizes that the `sing` method isn't defined on an object of type `Bird`. Flow typing, which is part of the type inference engine, is quite easy to understand for "linear" flows like this one. But real-life code isn't as simple and we have to introduce a new concept, the *least upper bound*, to understand the behavior of the type checker in more advanced circumstances.

10.3.1 *Least upper bound*

The type inference engine of Groovy has proven to be pretty smart. In reality, it's even smarter than you might think, which can lead to results that are surprising at first. For example, the type checker is able to represent types that you can't define. To illustrate the concept, let's look at the following code:

```
def list = [23, 3.14]
```

Could you at first glance determine what the type of the list is? Several answers are possible, but if you take a close look at the elements, you'd see that the first one is an `Integer`, while the second one is a `BigDecimal` (in Groovy, decimal numbers are Big-Decimal by default, not double like in Java). So the type checker has to compute the common supertype of those two elements. From memory, you'd probably guess `Number`, which is an interface. That is correct, but both `Integer` and `BigDecimal` implement `Serializable`, so why would you prefer `Number` over `Serializable`? Why not choose the lowest concrete common superclass (which in this case, would be `Object`).

To solve the problem, Groovy introduces the concept of *least upper bound*, which is some kind of virtual type that the user cannot define[7] but that the compiler knows about. In this case, the least upper bound is something that is a `Number`, `Comparable`, and `Serializable`.[8]

Another option for the type inference engine would have to say that the list is a list of `Integer` *or* `BigDecimal` (a union type). But this causes problems, as shown in the following listing.

Listing 10.35   Least upper bound versus union type

```
import groovy.transform.TypeChecked

interface Polite {
    void greet()
    void thank()
}

class Person implements Polite {
    String name
    void greet() { println "Hello, I'm $name!" }
    void thank() { println 'Thanks!' }
}

class Owl implements Polite {
    void greet() { hoot() }
    void thank() { hoot() }
    void hoot() { println 'Hoot' }
}
```

---

[7]   Neither Java nor Groovy support the notion of union types or higher-rank type classes at the syntax level. Given Groovy's excellent extensibility, there have been some interesting type class experiments for Groovy but details are beyond the scope of this book.

[8]   A limit to the current implementation is that this virtual type isn't fully aware of the fact that `Comparable` only applies to the same types (`Integer` with `Integer`, `BigDecimal` with `BigDecimal`).

```
@TypeChecked
void main() {
    def list = [new Person(name: 'Bill'), new Owl()]   ←   Creates list with
    Polite p1 = list[0]                                      Person and Owl
    Polite o1 = list[1]                                 ←   Assigns either element to
    Owl o2    = list[0]                                 ←   variable of type Polite
    Person p2 = list[1]   ←
}                               Tries to assign         ❶ Tries to assign first
                                second element             element to Owl
main()                        ❷ to Person
```

If the type of the list was inferred as a union type, then the assignments at ❶ and ❷ would have been valid, because the type checker can't determine, in general, what will be the type of the *n*th element of the list. This would trigger a runtime error that we want to avoid. Using the least upper bound, Groovy only allows assignments to the common supertype or any of the interfaces implemented by all the elements of the list. This means that even if potentially an assignment would work at runtime (if we assign the first element of the list to a Person, for example), the type checker will report a compile-time error because type safety isn't guaranteed.

Lists are far from being the only place where a least upper bound is computed. The following listing poses another challenge to the type checker by putting an assignment inside a conditional branch.

Listing 10.36   Conditionals trigger least upper bound computation

```
import groovy.transform.TypeChecked

@TypeChecked                                         ❶ Variable
void leastUpperBoundOnConditional() {                   initialized
    def o = new Date()              ←                    with Date
    if (Math.random()) {            ←                 Random
        o = 'Hello'       ←                           condition
    }                       Assigns
    o.time   ←            ❷ a String
}            Tries to
             call o.time
```

Without @TypeChecked the code may succeed or fail depending on a random factor! But a type checker doesn't play dice; it has to make some guarantees on your code. Therefore, if an assignment to a variable is made inside a conditional branch, then after the conditional, the only type that can be guaranteed is the least upper bound of the variable type before the conditional ❶ and all assignments inside the conditional ❷; that is, here a Date and a String. So if you compile listing 10.36, the compiler will fail with the following error:

```
No such property: time for class: java.io.Serializable
```

Internally, the least upper bound is also used to compute the inferred return type of a method or a closure. For that, the type checker collects all return expressions (both explicit, using the return keyword, and implicit, without return) and compares their inferred type to the declared method return type. If any of the return statement isn't compatible with the return type, an error is thrown. If, as expected, all returns are compatible, the inferred return type of the method is computed as the least upper bound of all returns.

DECLARING THE RETURN TYPE

In Groovy, people often declare methods using def as the return type and sometimes (implicitly or explicitly) for argument types. In general, this isn't a problem; however, when the method belongs to a public API, it's preferable to declare an explicit return type and explicit method parameters. This is a good idea for interoperability with Java and for documenting your API's contract and, as you've just seen, it helps the type checker perform additional checks too.

10.3.2 Smart instanceof inference

How many times have you written code like this in Java?

```
if (obj instanceof Person) {
    value = ((Person)obj).getName();
}
```

And then you may have wondered why you have to perform an explicit cast although you've just indicated that obj was an instance of Person. This is typical boilerplate code. In dynamic Groovy, you don't have the problem. You can write:

```
if (obj instanceof Person) {
    value = obj.name
}
```

What about type-checked Groovy code? The good news is that it's exactly the same! Even if you use type checking, the compiler won't force you to add an explicit cast.

COMPATIBILITY WITH AST TRANSFORMATIONS

AST transformations, as explained in chapter 9, are compile-time metaprogramming features that allow code generation. With that, one could wonder if they're compatible with type checking. There are two answers. The first one is yes, of course. If you use @Log, the type checker will recognize the added log field. The second answer is maybe. The main reason is that for an AST transformation to work, it has to be designed to provide type information. Because AST transformations are aimed at code generation, the generated code may be written in a dynamic fashion, which doesn't allow it to be type checked. In general, the AST transformations that Groovy comes with are compatible with type checking, but it's not mandatory: should you find an AST transformation that doesn't work in combination with @TypeChecked, we strongly recommend that you raise a ticket on the Groovy project bug tracker.

Before we jump on the static compilation subject, let's study one last issue you may face with type-checked code, regarding closures.

10.3.3 Closure-shared variables

You've seen previously that the type checker is aware of closures and their enclosing context. It's possible, for a closure, to capture local variables, and a difference with anonymous inner classes in Java, for example, is that those variables don't have to be final to be used inside the closure body. The following listing illustrates this by modifying a variable that's bound from the enclosing scope.

Listing 10.37 Writing to a closure-shared variable

```
import groovy.transform.TypeChecked

@TypeChecked
def captureOfALocalVariable() {
  def msg = 'Hello'              // Variable msg is closure-shared variable
  def cl = { msg = 'Hi!' }       // Closure can write to msg
  assert msg == 'Hello'
  cl()                           // Closure is called ❶
  assert msg == 'Hi!'
}

captureOfALocalVariable()
```

A closure-shared variable doesn't have to be explicitly declared as shared: as the example shows, it's shared because it's used inside a closure, and nothing prevents the closure from overwriting the variable. Actually, we see that it's only when the closure is called ❶ that the value changes. This is very important to understand, because as closures are code as data, they can be manipulated and executed at any time. A slight change at ❶ may totally change the result:

```
Thread.start { cl() }
```

In this case, the closure is called asynchronously. This is only an example of a deferred call, but you can imagine many others (executors, thread pools, and so on), so in general, it's not because a closure is defined that you know at compile time when it'll be executed. For that reason, closure-shared variables cannot participate in flow typing as other regular variables. Instead, the compiler uses the least upper bound once again to tell you what you're allowed to do.

In particular, method calls on closure-shared variables are only possible on methods that exist on the least upper bound of all assignments. Attempts to use other methods will fail compilation as shown in the following listing.

Listing 10.38 toUpperCase isn't defined on the least upper bound

```
@TypeChecked
void notAllowed() {
    def var = "String"
    def cl = { var = new Date() }
    cl()
    var = var.toUpperCase()
}
```

Even if in this example it's clear that when the closure is called, in general, we cannot make specific assumptions, so the least upper bound of String and Date is computed. Because the toUpperCase method isn't defined on this least upper bound, the compiler will report an explicit error:

```
A closure shared variable [var] has been assigned with various types and the
method [toUpperCase()] does not exist in the lowest upper bound of those
types: [java.io.Serializable <? extends java.lang.Object>]. In general, this
is a bad practice (variable reuse) because the compiler cannot determine
safely what is the type of the variable at the moment of the call in a
multithreaded context.
```

The error message is a bit long, but gives you a chance to understand what's happening. In particular, it describes why it's not a good idea to use a closure-shared variable to store objects of different types. In contrast, the following listing won't trigger any compilation error, even though the closure is assigned values of different types.

> **Listing 10.39 Valid assignment of closure-shared variables**

```
class A { void foo() {} }
class B extends A { void bar() {} }

@TypeChecked
void main() {
    def var = new A()
    def cl = { var = new B() }
    cl()
    var.foo()
}

main()
```

The difference is that the method foo, which is called at the end of the main method, *is* defined in the least upper bound of A and B. Because the compiler can ensure that the method exists, it has no reason to report an error. There's a lesson to be learned here. If you're facing obscure error messages because your code exhibits complex least upper bound types, it's probably a sign that your design is too complex and needs to be refactored.

We've now completed our tour of @TypeChecked features and it's time to go a little further in the static world by describing its cousin annotation, @CompileStatic.

10.4 *Static compilation*

Having seen the benefits of @TypeChecked raises the question whether we can profit from even more static features like precalculated method dispatch for better performance and restricted static call semantics. You guessed it right: we can.

Many programmers live under the misconception that dynamic languages are always slower than statically-compiled languages. This isn't always true. Groovy is generally almost as fast as Java. But there are situations where the cost of dynamic method selection becomes relevant like when optimizing a tight inner loop on the performance-critical path. (Remember: always measure before optimizing!) In other situations, you may want to selectively disable the method object protocol and thus all dynamic features of Groovy.

Before Groovy 2, the only choice was to write parts of your application in Java. Do you remember the rainbow-colored glasses in figure 8.1 that Groovy wears when looking at Java code? Here's how you can take them off and still write nice Groovy code that now has all the static characteristics of Java.

10.4.1 @CompileStatic

Static compilation in Groovy can be achieved by annotating a class or a method with @CompileStatic. The rules for @CompileStatic are exactly the same as they are for @TypeChecked: you can annotate a class or a method, and if you do so, all the code within the scope of the annotation becomes statically compiled. The annotation also accepts the optional type checking mode attribute (TypeCheckingMode.SKIP), which allows skipping a method or a class from static compilation.

The question is now to tell what actually changes when you switch from @Type-Checked to @CompileStatic. To prove the difference, we'll use an example in listing 10.40 that's often used to "prove" the superiority of any language against any other: the Fibonacci suite. While we doubt that a lot of production code relies on the generation of Fibonacci numbers, the example is particularly challenging because it's a micro-benchmark that focuses on recursive calls and primitive computations, where Java used to be much faster than Groovy.

Listing 10.40 Fibonacci in action

```
@Grab('org.gperfutils:gbench:0.4.3-groovy-2.4')
import groovy.transform.CompileStatic

def dynamicFib(n)     { n<1 ? 1 : dynamicFib(n-1) + dynamicFib(n-2) }

int primFib(int n)    { n<1 ? 1 : primFib(n-1)    + primFib(n-2)    }

@CompileStatic
int staticFib(int n) { n<1 ? 1 : staticFib(n-1)   + staticFib(n-2)  }

def r = benchmark {
  'Dynamic Groovy'            { dynamicFib(10) }
  'Primitive optimized Groovy' { primFib(10)    }
  'Statically compiled Groovy' { staticFib(10)  }
}
r.prettyPrint()
```

The listing makes use of GBench (https://code.google.com/p/gbench/), a benchmarking library for Groovy, to make measurements of performance. Here the output of this script tells us which methods are faster than others. The following figures were obtained on a laptop, but what's interesting is the relative difference between them:

```
                              user   system    cpu    real
Dynamic Groovy                6662      0      6662    6662
Primitive optimized Groovy    1383      0      1383    1383
Statically compiled Groovy     581      0       581     603
```

As you can see, if you don't use any explicit type, Fibonacci can be really slow. But as soon as you tell Groovy that the method will only work for primitive integers, the compiler is able to generate optimized bytecode and reach performance that's close to Java. But adding `@CompileStatic` to the code makes it even better: it becomes twice as fast as the version with primitive type optimization on par with Java.[9]

Let's examine what makes such a performance boost possible.

10.4.2 Method dispatch

To understand how method dispatch works in Groovy, we'll start by explaining how it works in Java. The following listing shows a simple greeting class that demonstrates what a static language like Java does at compile time:

Listing 10.41 Statically compiled greeting in Java

```
public class Greeter {                  // Java!
    static void greet(Object o) {
        System.out.println("Hello, object "+o);
    }
    static void greet(String s) {
        System.out.println("Hello, string " + s);
    }
    public static void main(String...args) {
        Object o = "Bob";
        String s = "Bob";
        greet(o);
        greet(s);
    }
}
```

If you run this program in Java, it will output the following:

```
Hello, object Bob
Hello, string Bob
```

Now if you copy and paste the very same code in Groovy and execute again, you'll see a difference:

```
Hello, string Bob
Hello, string Bob
```

The same string appears twice! In fact, a lot of programmers ignore how Java dispatches method calls, but this example shows that the target methods are selected at compile time, based on the declaration type of the arguments. It's very important to understand that it's based on the declaration type, so here, even if both o and s contain the same string, because one is declared as `Object` and the second one is declared as a `String`, the compiler will choose the `Object` variant of the overloaded `greet` method for the first case, and the `String` variant for the second case.

---

[9] The benchmark doesn't call any native Java method here, but it would be easy to do so and verify the claim.

Groovy is the opposite, using the runtime argument types. Runtime dispatch often looks more natural to new programmers, because it's using the type that we actually have.

But method dispatch requires some logic and, when done at runtime, it adds a little to the cost of method invocation, which explains why Groovy is in general a little bit slower than Java. Groovy is quite intelligent about the dispatch logic, though, and keeps a cache to avoid recalculation when it can be sure that it can safely jump to the same call site.

@COMPILESTATIC METHOD DISPATCH

By annotating your code with `@CompileStatic`, not only are you activating type checking, but you're also asking the compiler to generate statically compiled code. In short, the generated code follows the same rules as in Java, with some differences.

Statically compiled Groovy code will have bytecode that's close, if not equal, to what the Java compiler generates. Therefore, using `@CompileStatic` provides the same level of performance as Java!

But there's now an issue that Groovy has to solve: when using `@CompileStatic` how should the method selection operate given that the runtime types aren't available at compile time?

The solution is that statically compiled Groovy selects methods like Java does, with a twist.

INFERRED TYPE METHOD DISPATCH

As opposed to Java, Groovy doesn't use the *declared* types of the arguments for the static method dispatch but the *inferred* types! The following listing motivates this decision by being able to find the method we expect where Java cannot.

Listing 10.42 Static method dispatch in Groovy

```
import groovy.transform.CompileStatic
static String prettify(String s) { "String: $s" }
static String prettify(Date d)   { "Date: ${d.time}" }

@CompileStatic
void test() {
    def var = "I'm a String"          ❶  Using def, which is
    println prettify(var)                 equivalent to Object
}
test()                       ❷  Calls
                                prettify(String)
```

The test method declares a variable using `def` ❶. It's not final (it doesn't have to be, because we're using flow typing), yet the compiler is able to infer that the type of `var` is `String` when we reach ❷. So instead of calling `prettify(Object)` like Java would do, we'll call `prettify(String)`, which is also what dynamic Groovy would have done!

STATIC COMPILATION BY DEFAULT?

While static compilation for Groovy was being developed, some people feared that the semantics of the language would change and that Groovy would move from a dynamic language to a static one. Let's make it very clear: that isn't the case. Groovy is and remains a primarily dynamic language that offers an optional static compilation mode. The Groovy development team considers that there are so many advantages to using dynamic (legacy) Groovy that there's absolutely no reason to switch to static compilation by default.

But the introduction of this feature in Groovy 2 also attracted people from the Java (and other statically compiled languages) world who wanted to activate static compilation by default. We don't encourage this, but if you really want to do it, take a look at chapter 16.

So what's static compilation good for in Groovy? We think there are a few valid use cases for statically compiled code:

- *Optimizing hotspots*—This is the first obvious reason, but it's important to double check with facts. Never optimize without measuring first! Remember: premature performance optimization is evil.

- *Frameworks*—Grails (www.grails.org) is an example of a full-stack framework written in Groovy to build web applications. Since frameworks are used as foundations to real applications, it's good to have the smallest footprint and best performance possible. Instead of writing parts of the framework in Java, framework writers now have the ability to keep using Groovy as their development language.

- *Immunity to monkey patching*—This use case is interesting, because statically compiled Groovy classes behave like Java classes. They're immune to runtime metaprogramming. The following listing demonstrates how to make Groovy code immune to metaprogramming changes.

Listing 10.43   Immunity to monkey patching

```groovy
import groovy.transform.CompileStatic

class MyFramework {
  static int sizeOf(String s) { s.size() }       ①

  @CompileStatic
  static int staticSizeOf(String s) { s.size() }  ②
}

String s = 'a happy new year!'
s.metaClass.size = { -> 5 }                        ③
assert s.size() == 5                               ④
assert MyFramework.sizeOf(s) == 5                  ⑤
assert MyFramework.staticSizeOf(s) == 17          ⑥
```

① sizeOf method uses dynamic dispatch

② staticSizeOf method uses static dispatch

③ Changes metaclass so that size always returns 5

④ Checks that size returns 5

⑤ Checks that calling size from framework returns 5

⑥ Checks that from statically compiled method returns original size

---

In this example, we simulate the use of the `size` method on `String` by a framework. The first case ① isn't statically compiled, while in the other ② we're using `@CompileStatic`. To be safe, it's better if the framework uses the real method, but here, on line ❸, we're defining a custom metaclass that makes `size` return 5, so calling `size` on s like on line ❹ returns 5 as expected. It's also the case when we call the framework method, which itself calls the `size` method ❺, making it clear that the framework inherited a behavior that's defined externally. But at ❻ we're using the statically compiled method, and the result is different: it calls the original method, instead of the stubbed one. That's what we call immunity to monkey patching: by using `@Compile-Static`, the method makes a direct call to `size`, instead of going through the meta-object protocol.

If you ever choose to make use of static compilation intensively in your framework, it's interesting to notice that Groovy provides a shortcut for `@CompileStatic(Type-CheckingMode.SKIP)`, named `@CompileDynamic`. You may find this useful if you only want to exclude one or two methods from static compilation in a class.

In this section, we've explained how you could use `@CompileStatic` instead of `@TypeChecked` to enforce static semantics, but we didn't show why you should prefer one over the other. There's one good reason to prefer `@TypeChecked` over `@Compile-Static` when it comes to type checking DSLs, as you'll see in the next section.

10.5 *Static type checking extensions*

One of the most important use cases for Groovy is implementation of internal DSLs, which we'll cover in chapter 19. Groovy makes it very easy thanks to both advanced syntax features and metaprogramming. DSLs are aimed toward experts of a domain. It's easy to design a DSL that's aimed, for example, toward the person responsible for schedules at school:

```
book meeting room 'Honolulu' between 9.am and 12.am to 'B2'
```

The following listing defines a DSL for such bookings.

Listing 10.44 Booking DSL

```
import groovy.transform.Canonical

@Canonical
class Booking {
    String meetingRoom
    String className
    Date start, end
}

def book(meeting) {
    [room: { name ->
        [between: { sd ->
            [and: { ed ->
                [to: { to ->
                    def b = new Booking(meetingRoom: name,
                        className: to, start: sd, end: ed)
                    println b
                    b
                }]
            }]
        }]
}
```

```
                }]
            }]
        }]
}

def meeting
@Category(Integer)
class TimeCategory {
    static Date getAm(Integer self) {
        def d = Calendar.instance
        d.set(Calendar.MINUTE, 0)
        d.set(Calendar.SECOND, 0)
        d.set(Calendar.HOUR_OF_DAY, self)
        d.time
    }
}
use(TimeCategory) {
    book meeting room 'Honolulu' between 9.am and 12.am to 'B2'
}
```

The details of the implementation are unimportant here, but please note that it's heavily making use of maps and closures. If we tried to apply @TypeChecked to the user script, it would fail with lots of errors, because in the script context, nothing is known in advance: book is an unknown method, meeting is an undefined variable, room is an unknown property, and so forth. There's no information that the type checker could use to help. But you, as a DSL designer, know a lot about the context, as well as you know much about the implementation details. This means that there are chances that if you give hints to the type checker, it will be able to help you in return.

WHY TYPE CHECKING DSLS?
Why would you want to perform type checking on a user script? The first reason is that people writing those scripts aren't necessarily developers. They don't know what a unit test is and they certainly don't want to write unit tests for everything they write. Knowing that and the fact that the scripts will directly go in production, you'd certainly want to avoid bad scripts being uploaded. On the contrary, it's better to catch errors earlier and report them to the user before the script gets executed.

In fact, you'll do the best you can to perform static analysis of dynamic code and, just like type checking, report errors to the user. In this section, you'll see how to make this possible and what Groovy has to offer to make the language even more type-safe than what you can find in lots of statically compiled languages!

Last but not least, Groovy doesn't make it mandatory for a DSL to be type-safe. It's up to you, and the language designers won't force you to use a particular implementation of the DSL to make it type-safe. The design of the type checking extensions, for example, makes it easy to add type checking afterwards. This means that you can focus on the implementation of your DSL on a first step, then write extensions to make it type-safe on a second step. The fact that you'll want to use static analysis later should never drive the implementation of the DSL.

10.5.1 *@DelegatesTo revisited*

We discussed `@DelegatesTo` and `@DelegatesTo.Target` in section 10.2.6 when implementing a user validation script. We didn't go into details about when `@DelegatesTo.Target` would be particularly useful. Well, it turns out to be very useful when building DSLs. Let's consider a very slight extension to our user validation script to allow it to validate multiple domain classes.

Listing 10.45 Using `@DelegatesTo.Target`

```
import groovy.transform.TypeChecked

class Address { String country }                          Compiler will      ❶
class WishList { List<String> items }                     determine type.

def validate(@DelegatesTo.Target def o, @DelegatesTo Closure rule) {  ⬅
  rule.delegate = o
  rule()
}
                                                          First parameter   ❷
@TypeChecked                                              is Address.
void validateAll() {
  def a = new Address(country: 'Australia')               Address inferred  ❸
  validate(a) {                                    ⬅      so country will
    if (country[0] == 'X')                         ⬅      be found.
      println 'No countries start with that'
  }
  def wl = new WishList(items: ['iphone', 'iphone'])      First parameter   ❹
  validate(wl) {                                   ⬅      is WishList.
    if (items != items.toUnique())                 ⬅
      println 'Item appeared twice'                       WishList inferred
  }                                                       so items will be
}                                                  ❺      found.

validateAll()
```

At ❶, we're using `@DelegatesTo.Target`, which tells the compiler that when our `rule` closure is used, then the delegate type will be the type of the first argument of the method call. So when we're calling the method ❷, the flow type for `o`, inferred by the compiler, is `Address`, and the `country` property is recognized ❸. Afterwards, the type of `o` changes, but thanks to flow typing, it's still recognized that the `validate` method will be called with a `WishList` as first argument ❹, so `items` will be resolved ❺.

As you can see, `@DelegatesTo` is a very powerful tool that dramatically improves the intelligence of the type checker. It's especially useful for builder-like DSLs. It's also worth noting that even if you don't use `@TypeChecked`, it's recommended to document your API using `@DelegatesTo`, because it gives more information to the users of your API on one side, but it also helps IDEs, which will be capable of proposing improved code completion.

Table 10.1 summarizes the optional parameters accepted by `@DelegatesTo`.

Table 10.1 Parameters of `@DelegatesTo`

Parameter	Description	Example

`type` (optional)	Type name to be used when neither value nor target can represent the delegate type	`public <T,U extends`
		`Configurable<T>> U`
		`configure(Class<U> clazz,`
		`@DelegatesTo(type="T") Closure`
		`configSpec)`

`value` (optional)	Explicit type of delegate	`@DelegatesTo(Person)`
`strategy` (optional)	The closure resolve strategy; defaults to `OWNER_FIRST`	`@DelegatesTo(value=Person,` `strategy=Closure.DELEGATE_ONLY)`

`target` (optional, in combination with `@DelegatesTo.Target`)	ID of the target parameter that determines the delegate type	`void`
		`validate(@DelegatesTo.Target(`
		`'delegate') target,`
		`@DelegatesTo(target='delegate')`
		`action) { … }`

While `@DelegatesTo` is very helpful, it's still not enough to solve all type checking issues that you can face with DSLs. For those, Groovy provides an advanced mechanism called type checking extensions.

10.5.2 *Type checking extension scripts*

At the core of type checking extensions sits an event-based API. The type checker, internally, throws events to which you, as a type checking extension designer, can react. For example, when it starts visiting a method, an event is sent. Likewise, when a method is selected (in the sense of type checking, meaning that a method with the correct name and argument types exists), a method selection event is sent. There are multiple events to which you can react, making it possible to extend the behavior of the type checker.

The goal of this chapter isn't to tell you how you should implement a DSL in Groovy. For that, we refer you to chapter 19. The idea is rather to take a look at snippets of code that can be considered DSLs, and make them type-safe. Consider the following code:

```
robot.move 100.meters
```

It's a single line of code that can be written by a robot expert. This line of code doesn't define any robot variable, nor does it define a `move` method or a `meters` method on an integer. Groovy can compile this without problems, and there are ways to make it statically checked without having to explicitly add `@TypeChecked` to the code. See chapter 16, in particular `ASTTransformationCustomizer` for a more in-depth explanation. What would happen if you did so? The compiler would fail with

```
[Static type checking] - The variable [robot] is undeclared.
[Static type checking] - No such property: meters for class: int
```

It fails because it doesn't know how the code is supposed to be executed. With more context, it would be able to find out what the type of the `robot` variable is. So let's imagine that the script is executed inside a `GroovyShell` and the `robot` variable resides in its binding:

```
def binding = new Binding()
binding.robot = new Robot()
def shell = new GroovyShell(binding,config)
shell.evaluate(script)
```

Even though the `robot` object is now available, its type is still unknown. Likewise, the `meters` property for `100` looks spurious. The following listing comes to the rescue with the help of a type checking extension.

Listing 10.46   Robot type checking extension

```
unresolvedVariable { var ->
  if (var.name == 'robot') {
    storeType(var, lookupClassNodeFor('Robot'))
    handled = true
  }
}

unresolvedProperty { pexp ->
  if (getType(pexp.objectExpression) == int_TYPE &&
      pexp.propertyAsString == 'meters') {
    storeType(pexp, long_TYPE)
    handled = true
  }
}
```

❶ An unresolved 'robot' variable has type Robot.

❷ An unresolved 'meters' property on an int has type long.

What we see here is that the type checking extension is itself a DSL! In fact, it's a DSL aimed at type checking DSLs. Listing 10.46 defines two handlers, reacting to two different events, which are in fact the errors that the type checker has thrown: one handler will allow us to react to the fact that the `robot` variable is unknown and will inform the type checker that the type is `Robot` ❶, and the second one will let us explain that `100.meters` returns a `long` ❷. Both handlers follow a common formula. They typically have a guard to be very specific about their purpose. They typically make adjustments to the typing information. Finally, the `handled` property is usually set to tell the compiler whether the extension has resolved the missing information so the type checker knows whether further handling, like reporting a type error, is required.

KNOW YOUR AST
At this point, you should be warned: writing a type checking extension requires knowledge about the Groovy's AST. If you're used to writing AST transformations as described in chapter 9, writing type checking extensions should be a piece of cake.

EVENT TYPES
Table 10.2 summarizes the available event types and their purposes. For a full description, see appendix H.

Table 10.2 Type checking events

Event	Called when
setup	Once the type checker finishes initialization
finish	After the type checker completes type checking
unresolvedVariable	A variable cannot be resolved (typed)
unresolvedProperty	A property cannot be resolved (x.property)
unresolvedAttribute	An attribute cannot be resolved (x.@attr)
beforeMethodCall	Before the type checker tries to resolve a method call
afterMethodCall	After the type checker tried to resolve a method call
onMethodSelection	The type checker finds the target method of a call
methodNotFound	The type checker cannot find a matching method for the call
beforeVisitMethod	Before the type checker starts analyzing a method body
afterVisitMethod	After the type checker completes the analysis of a method body
beforeVisitClass	Before the type checker starts analyzing a class
afterVisitClass	After the type checker completes the analysis of a class
incompatibleAssignment	If an assignment is invalid
ambiguousMethods	If the type checker cannot choose among several methods
incompatibleReturnType	If the inferred return type isn't compatible with the declared return type

Generally, type checking extensions fall into two categories:

- *Extensions that react to errors of the type checker*—In this case, what you want is to give hints and provide context information.
- *Extensions that perform additional checks*—In this case, type checking passes without an extension, but you want to leverage the type checking architecture to perform additional static analysis.

The second category makes type checking extensions an advanced tool that many other languages can only dream of no matter how type-safe they claim to be.

IMPROVED TYPE CHECKING
In chapter 13 you'll learn how to do database programming in Groovy and use statements like

```
sql.eachRow('SELECT * FROM Person') { … }
```

This eachRow method takes a string as an argument that corresponds to a SQL query. The cool news is, with type check extensions, you can even type-check the literal string for being a syntactically correct SQL statement!

The logical steps to perform SQL syntax checking are simple:

- Whenever the type checker finds that you call `eachRow` on a `sql` object, and that the first argument is a `String`, parse the SQL query, check the syntax, and throw compilation errors if the syntax is invalid.

Such an extension has already been written[10] and can be found in the following listing. It's impressively short compared to the importance of the feature that we implement.

Listing 10.47   Syntax checking of SQL queries

```
@Grab('com.github.jsqlparser:jsqlparser:0.9.2')
import net.sf.jsqlparser.parser.CCJSqlParserManager

afterMethodCall { mc ->
  def receiver = mc.receiver
  if (!isVariableExpression(receiver)) return
  def method = getTargetMethod(mc)
  if (classNodeFor(groovy.sql.Sql) == getType(receiver)      ❶ Info extraction
     && method.name == 'eachRow') {                             and guards
    def argList = getArguments(mc)
    if (argList && isConstantExpression(argList[0])) {

      def pm = new CCJSqlParserManager()
      def sqlQuery = argList[0].text                         ❷ Validate SQL
      try {                                                     using library
        pm.parse(new StringReader(sqlQuery))
      } catch (e) {
        addStaticTypeError("SQL query is not valid: $e", argList[0])   ◁──
      }
    }                                                        Flag an error
  }                                                          if invalid ❸
}
```

The first part of the extension follows the formula we saw in the previous extension in listing 10.46: some information extraction and some guards ❶. We make use of a third-party library during the processing part of the extension ❷, showing that even if you plug into the compilation process, you can use external libraries (here, the library is fetched using `@Grab`). The type checking architecture gives access to the actual string value that represents the SQL query, so the third-party library can be used to parse it.

The final part ❸ is a little different. The earlier handlers were called in the case of errors and had to indicate if they "fixed" the error. The `afterMethodCall` event is called for every method. Our goal should be to do nothing unless an error is found. In our case, if an error is detected, `addStaticTypeError` is called to add an error to

---

[10] This example is courtesy of André Steingress; see this blog post for details: http://blog.andresteingress.com/2013/01/25/groovy-2-1-type-checking-extensions/.

the compilation unit. This means that if the user calls `eachRow` with a syntactically incorrect SQL query, the compilation now fails.

So for listing 10.47:

```
@TypeChecked(extensions = 'Listing_10_47_SQLExtension.groovy')
findAthletes(Sql sql) {
  sql.eachRow('select * frm Athlete') { row -> println row }    <─┐  Typo 'frm'
}                                                                    not 'from'
```

you'd receive an error like this:

```
Sql.groovy: 7: [Static type checking] - SQL query is not valid:
net.sf.jsqlparser.JSQLParserException
 @ line 7, column 15.
    sql.eachRow('select * frm Athlete') { row -> println row }
                ^

1 error
```

You might wonder what the `extensions` attribute on the `TypeChecked` annotation is all about. It points to the extension we want. We'll cover the details next. But before we move on, we should point out that you're not limited to only parsing the query. You have access to the closure too, so you could perform type checking of the closure with regards to what the query is supposed to return. In that case, the type checker would require additional metadata, in particular the database schema that you can read from the database and check against your types at hand. This should give you a glimpse at the vast possibilities.

APPLYING EXTENSIONS

Once you've written a type checking extension, you still need to get them applied. It's in fact very easy: both `@TypeChecked` and `@CompileStatic` accept an optional parameter named `extensions`. It accepts a list of strings corresponding to paths to type checking extension scripts that need to reside on the classpath or fully qualified class names in the case of precompiled extension classes. For example:

```
@TypeChecked(extensions_['/regina/RobotExtension.groovy',
                         'regina.SQLExtension'])
void usesExtensions() { … }
```

This implies that the `RobotExtension.groovy` script and `SQLExtension` class file are on the classpath. If not, compilation would fail. Chapter 16 describes numerous elegant ways to transparently apply type checking as well as extensions. We recommend that you use annotations explicitly during the design of an extension, then make it transparently applied. The advantage is that it makes the fact that a DSL is statically analyzed totally transparent to the user.

10.5.3 Limits

In listing 10.47, we've shown how you could analyze a SQL query passed as an argument to `eachRow`. But a limit to this extension is that the SQL query must be a constant string directly used as an argument. If the string is stored in a variable, for example, it should be obvious that no analysis can be performed.[11]

You may be tempted to alter the AST from inside a type checking extension. Never even try!

> **WARNING!**   You cannot alter the AST from inside a type checking extension. You need to use the mechanics of AST transformations for that purpose.

Otherwise, your imagination is the only limit.

10.6 Summary

This has been a long and challenging chapter. Congratulations that you followed it through! Core language topics such as method dispatch and type systems are sometimes considered dry but we hope to have given you something valuable in return: the ability to fully understand what's going on and to use the power of Groovy's internals to your advantage.

You've seen how to leverage the `@TypeChecking` annotation to achieve the same level of type safety that static languages offer while retaining the feel of Groovy. Type checking is well suited to make developers who come from Java perfectly at ease with Groovy.

On that basis, we made Groovy produce bytecode as if it were a static language. The `@CompileStatic` annotation gives compiled Groovy code the same characteristics as plain Java with respect to performance and unmodifiable behavior. Groovy makes no concessions, though, when it comes to keeping the code free of nonessentials. Type inference and flow typing have proven to be our friends.

But the absolutely stunning feature is the ability to extend the type checker so easily. Who had ever envisioned that Groovy wouldn't even type-check itself, but even embedded languages like SQL or self-made DSLs? We wonder what *you* will do with type checking extensions. Checking against web service schemata, HTML doctypes, ECMAScript standards, or including code quality checks? Please post to the forum about your experiences!

---

[11] Even if you track assignments, in the end an SQL query can be composed or come from a method parameter, so there'll always be cases that are impossible to solve.

Part 2

Around
the Groovy library

Civilization advances by extending the number of important operations which we can perform without thinking of them.

—Alfred North Whitehead

Part 1 has lifted you to the level where you can confidently work with the Groovy language. You've also seen a glimpse of some of the fundamental parts of the Groovy library. Part 2 builds upon this knowledge, diving into other pieces of the Groovy library and exploring how Groovy extends the Java Runtime Environment. You've already seen how Groovy tries to make commonly performed tasks as easy as possible in the language—this part of the book shows how the same principle is applied in Groovy's libraries, using many of the advanced language features available to let you do more work with less code.

Chapter 11 introduces the builder concept, which is one of Groovy's distinctive capabilities, because it can only be implemented in a general library class with a truly dynamic language. We'll examine the builders that come as part of the Groovy distribution and show you how to implement your own builders.

Chapter 12 covers, at the object/method level, pure GDK library capabilities that weren't presented in part 1, because they aren't directly related to language features.

Chapter 13 goes through Groovy's library support for dealing with relational and other database systems, providing total flexibility where necessary and significant shortcuts where simple solutions suffice.

Chapter 14 dives into the special topic of XML and JSON support in Groovy: reading and writing documents with ultimate performance, transforming them into other representations, and using XML or JSON for interoperation between heterogeneous systems.

Chapter 15 guides you through the world of web services and how to use the Groovy library and language features to take advantage of this cornucopia of information.

Chapter 16 shows how to seamlessly integrate Groovy with Java projects and other JVM languages.

Part 3 will lead you to new places where Groovy is applied for testing, concurrent programming, DSLs, and the whole ecosystem around it.

11

Working with builders

This chapter covers
- The builder concept
- Using common builders bundled with the Groovy distribution
- Writing your own builders

Art is the imposing of a pattern on experience, and our aesthetic enjoyment is recognition of the pattern.

—Alfred North Whitehead

As software developers, everything we do day in and day out is building: we build graphical applications, command-line tools, data stores, and a lot of other, often invisible products. To this end we make use of components and frameworks as building blocks assembled on a fundamental base. We build by following the rules of the architecture and the best practices of our trade.

Not surprisingly, the general task of building faces us with recurring activities and structures. Over time, developer experience has led to proven standard solutions for repetitive building tasks captured in terms of patterns. One such pattern is the Builder pattern. In this pattern, a *builder* object is used to help build a complex object, called the Product. It encapsulates the logic of how to assemble the product from given pieces.

Products can be complex because they maintain a tricky internal state (think of a parser object) or because they're built of numerous objects with interdependencies. The latter case is frequently seen when there are treelike structures that you find everywhere in the world of software:

- Most obviously, a filesystem is a tree of directories and files.
- This book is a tree of parts, chapters, sections, subsections, and paragraphs.
- HTML and XML documents have a treelike document object model.
- Test cases are bundled into suites and suites are bundled into higher-level suites such that a tree of tests is constructed.
- GUIs are built from components that are assembled into containers. A Swing JFrame may include multiple JPanels that again include multiple JPanels, etc. A JavaFX scene graph is a tree of nodes.
- Less obviously, business objects often form a tree at runtime: invoice objects that refer to multiple line items that refer to products, and so on.

Surprisingly, most programming languages have a hard time modeling this oh-so-common structure, especially *building* a treelike structure in program code. Most of the time the programmer is left with the task of calling several addChild and setParent methods.

This has two major drawbacks:

- The logic of how to properly build the tree structure is often subject to massive duplication.
- When reading the code, it's hard to get an overview picture of the nesting structure.

To overcome the latter drawback there are many approaches that store the nesting structure in some external format, possibly XML or JSON, and construct runtime objects from there. This, of course, has other limitations, because you lose all the merits of your programming language when defining the structure. This leads to a lack of flexibility and is likely to produce a lot of duplication.

Groovy offers an alternative approach. Its builder support allows you to define nested, treelike structures right inside the code, being descriptive and flexible at the same time. When viewing the code, at least in reasonably simple situations, the resulting hierarchy is easily visible on the screen. Groovy enables this style of coding through the use of closures, the MOP (usually), and simple map declarations.

Understanding the sample code doesn't require a deep understanding of these helper classes or of the MOP, but if you feel uncertain about closures and map literals, you might want to have a look back to chapters 4 (for maps) and 5 (for closures), or at least have them earmarked for quick reference.

In this chapter, you'll try out representative builders that come bundled with Groovy, including NodeBuilder, MarkupBuilder, StreamingMarkupBuilder, AntBuilder,

SwingBuilder, and SceneGraphBuilder from GroovyFX. You should also consult the API documentation for other builders such as CliBuilder, JmxBuilder, Namespace-Builder, ObjectGraphBuilder, DOMBuilder, SAXBuilder, StaxBuilder, and Compiler-CustomizationBuilder. Each of these builder implementations has specific uses and details, but they all follow the same general pattern of building some kind of nested data or product using nested (but otherwise standard) Groovy code.

Special *library* support comes in the form of helper classes BuilderSupport and FactoryBuilderSupport. It isn't universally true (and is certainly not a requirement), but many of the builders that come with Groovy subclass one of these two support classes. The final thing you'll learn in this chapter is how to implement your own builder with or without the helper classes.

11.1 Learning by example: Using a builder

Builders are easier to understand with concrete examples, so we'll look at sample code and compare it with how we'd achieve the same result without builders. At this point we're not going to present the *details* of builders, just the *feeling* of using them. We happen to use MarkupBuilder, but the general principle is the same for all of the builders.

Builders provide a convenient way of building hierarchical data models. They don't allow you to create anything you couldn't have created before, but the convenience they add is enormous, giving a direct correlation between hierarchy in the code and the hierarchy of the generated data. We demonstrate this by building the short XML[1] document shown in listing 11.1. The XML contains information about the numbers 10–15: their square values and their factors.[2] Obviously this isn't a terribly useful document in real-world terms, but it means we can focus on the code for generating the XML instead of the code required to gather more interesting data. There's nothing in the example that wouldn't apply just as much in a more complex case.

Listing 11.1   XML example data: Squares and factors of 10–15

```
<?xml version="1.0"?>
<numbers>
  <description>Squares and factors of 10..15</description>
  <number value="10" square="100">
    <factor value="2" />
    <factor value="5" />
  </number>
  <number value="11" square="121" />
  <number value="12" square="144">
    <factor value="2" />
    <factor value="3" />
    <factor value="4" />
    <factor value="6" />
  </number>
```

---

[1] For more information about XML processing in Groovy see chapter 14.
[2] For any given x the factors are all numbers y such that x % y == 0.

```
<number value="13" square="169" />
<number value="14" square="196">
  <factor value="2" />
  <factor value="7" />
</number>
<number value="15" square="225">
  <factor value="3" />
  <factor value="5" />
</number>
</numbers>
```

Before we show the Groovy way of generating this, let's look at how we'd do it in Java using the W3C DOM API. Don't worry if you haven't used DOM before—the idea isn't to understand the details of the code, it's more to get an idea of the shape and complexity of the code required. To keep the example in listing 11.2 short, we'll assume we've already constructed an empty Document, and we won't do anything with it when we've finished. All we're interested in is creating the data.

Listing 11.2   Java snippet for producing the example XML

```
// Java!
// … doc made available here …
Element numbers     = doc.createElement("numbers");
Element description = doc.createElement("description");
doc.appendChild(numbers);
numbers.appendChild(description);
description.setTextContent("Squares and factors of 10..15");

for (int i=10; i <= 15; i++)
{
    Element number = doc.createElement("number");
    numbers.appendChild(number);
    number.setAttribute("value",  String.valueOf(i));
    number.setAttribute("square", String.valueOf(i*i));
    for (int j=2; j < i; j++)
    {
        if (i % j == 0)
        {
            Element factor = doc.createElement("factor");
            factor.setAttribute("value", String.valueOf(j));
            number.appendChild(factor);
        }
    }
}
```

Note how there's a lot of text in listing 11.2 that isn't directly related to the data itself—all the calls to methods, and explicitly stating the hierarchy using variables. This is remarkably error-prone—just in creating this simple example, we accidentally appended two elements to the wrong place. The hierarchy isn't at all evident, either. The numbers element appears at the same indentation level as the description element, despite one being a parent of the other. The loops create a feeling of hierarchy, but it's only incidental. In a different example they could be setting attributes on another element, without adding to the depth of the tree at all.

Now let's look at the Groovy equivalent in the next listing. In fact, this is a complete script that writes the XML out to the console when it's run. You'll see later on how simple it is to write the content elsewhere, but for the moment the default behavior makes testing the example very easy.

Listing 11.3 Using `MarkupBuilder` to produce the sample XML

```
def builder = new groovy.xml.MarkupBuilder()
builder.numbers {

    description 'Squares and factors of 10..15'

    for (i in 10..15) {                              ⟵  Emit number
        number (value: i, square: i*i) {                 elements 10–15
            for (j in 2..<i) {
                if (i % j == 0) {
                    factor (value: j)                ⟵  Emit each
                }                                        factor element
            }
        }
    }
}
```

This time, there's very little to the program apart from the data. There's no need for variables to hold elements while we build up the data for them—the data is constructed "inline," with method parameters specifying attributes and closures specifying nested elements. The hierarchy is much clearer, too: every child element is indented further than the parent element. The exact amount of indentation depends on other control structures such as the `if` and `for` statements, but there's no danger of accidentally having, say, `factor` elements show up as siblings of `number` elements.

The example may feel slightly like magic at the moment. That's a natural first reaction to builders, as we appear to be getting something almost for nothing. We generally view anything magical as somewhat suspicious—if it appears too good to be true, it usually is. As you shall see, however, builders are clever but not miraculous. They use the language features provided by Groovy, particularly closures and metaprogramming, and combine them to form a very elegant coding pattern.

Now that you've got a first impression of what using a builder looks like and what they're good for, let's go into a bit more detail and see how they work, as you learn how to create hierarchies of straightforward objects instead of XML elements.

11.2 *Building object trees with NodeBuilder*

We start the more detailed explanation of builders with the same example we used in section 7.5 to demonstrate GPath: modeling invoices with line items and products. We'll build a runtime structure of *nodes* rather than specialized business objects and watch the building process closely. Along the way, you'll learn not only about how

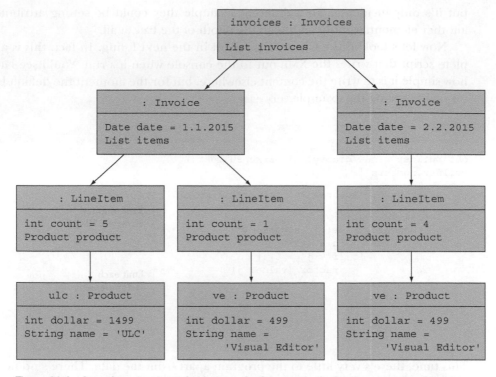

Figure 11.1 A runtime structure of objects and references in the invoice example where an invoices node refers to multiple instances of the Invoice class that in turn holds one or more LineItem objects that further refer to a single Product object each.

NodeBuilder works, but how the general principle of builders is applied in Groovy. We'll then consider how the declarative style of builder use can be freely mixed in with normal logic.

Builders can be used without any special knowledge, but to understand how they work, it's a prerequisite to know about *pretended* and *relayed methods* (see section 7.6) and closure scoping (see section 5.5.2).

Based on our invoice example from section 7.5.1, we set out to build a runtime object structure as depicted in figure 11.1.

In listing 7.24 we constructed this runtime structure with three defined classes, Invoice, LineItem, and Product, and through calling their default constructors in a nested manner.

11.2.1 NodeBuilder in action: a closer look at builder code

Listing 11.4 shows the equivalent using a NodeBuilder. The NodeBuilder can replace all three of the classes (Invoice, LineItem, and Product), assuming that we're treating them as data storage types (that is, we don't need to add methods for business logic or other behavior). Also added is a final GPath expression to prove that we can still walk conveniently through the object graph. This is the same query we used in section 7.5.1. Note how the tree structure from figure 11.1 is reflected in the code!

Listing 11.4 Invoice example with `NodeBuilder`

```
def builder = new NodeBuilder()                                         ❶ Builder
def ulcDate = Date.parse('yyyy-MM-dd', "2015-01-01")                      creation
def otherDate = Date.parse('yyyy-MM-dd', '2015-02-02')
def invoices = builder.invoices {                                       ❷ Root node
  invoice(date: ulcDate) {                                                creation
    item(count: 5) {
      product(name: 'ULC', dollar: 1499)                               ❸ Invoice
    }                                                                     creation
    item(count: 1) {
      product(name: 'Visual Editor', dollar: 499)
    }
  }
  invoice(date: otherDate) {
    item(count: 4) {
      product(name: 'Visual Editor', dollar: 499)
    }
  }
}

soldAt = invoices.grep {                                                ❹ GPath
  it.item.product.any { it.'@name' == 'ULC' }                            query
}.'@date'
assert soldAt == [ulcDate]
```

We make a new instance of the `NodeBuilder` for later use ❶, and then call the `invoices` method on the `NodeBuilder` instance ❷. This is a *pretended* method—the `NodeBuilder` intercepts the method call. It constructs a node based on the name of the intercepted method name and returns it into the `invoices` variable.[3] Before the node is constructed, the trailing closure is called to construct its nested nodes. To make this possible, the `BuilderSupport` that `NodeBuilder` inherits from sets the closure's delegate to the `NodeBuilder` instance.

The `invoice` method call is relayed to the `NodeBuilder` instance ❸, because it's the current closure's delegate. This method also takes a map as a parameter. The content of this map describes the attributes of the constructed node.

As a last step, we need to adapt the GPath to use it in ❹. First, we've broken it into multiple lines to allow proper typesetting in the book. Second, node attributes are no longer accessible as properties but like map entries. Therefore, `product.name` now becomes `product['@name']` or, even shorter, `product.'@name'`. The additional `@` is used for denoting attributes in analogy to XPath attribute conventions. A third change

---

[3] Because `invoices` is the root node, the method name makes no difference in how we use the node in the example. Listing 11.4 also works if you replace `builder.invoice` with `builder.whatever`.

is that through the general handling mechanism of nodes, `item.product` is now a list of products, not a single one.

11.2.2 *Understanding the builder concept*

From the preceding example we extract the following general rules:

- Nodes are constructed from *pretended* method calls on the builder.
- Method names determine node names.
- When a map is passed as a method argument, it determines the node's attributes. Generally speaking, each key–value pair in the map is used to call the field's setter method named by the *key* with the *value*. This refinement will later be used with `SwingBuilder` to register `EventListeners`.
- Nesting of nodes is done with closures. Closures *relay* method calls to the builder.

This concept is an implementation of the Builder pattern. Instead of programming *how* some treelike structure is built, only the result, the *what,* is specified. The *how* is left to the builder.

Note that only simple attribute names can be declared in the attribute map without enclosing the name in single or double quotes. Similarly, node names are constructed from method names, so if you need names that wouldn't be valid Groovy identifiers, such as "x.y" or "x-y", you'll again need to use quotes.

So far, we've done pretty much the same as we did with handmade classes but without writing the extra code. This is already a useful advantage but there's more to come.

11.2.3 *Smart building with logic*

With builders you can mix declarative style and Groovy logic as listing 11.5 shows. We create nested invoices in a loop for three consecutive days, with sales of the product growing each day. To assess the result, we use a pretty-printing facility available for nodes.

Listing 11.5   Using Logic inside the `NodeBuilder`

```
TimeZone.default = TimeZone.getTimeZone("CET")          ◁——  Sets TimeZone for
                                                              consistent Date
def builder = new NodeBuilder()                               toString() values in test
def invoices = builder.invoices {
  for (day in 1..3) {                                    ◁——  Loops over
    def invDate = Date.parse('yyyy-MM-dd', "2015-01-0$day")   three days
    invoice(date: invDate) {
      item(count: day) {                                 ❶  Code for
        product(name: 'ULC', dollar: 1499)                  building a
      }                                                      single invoice
    }
  }
}
```

```
def writer = new StringWriter()
invoices.print(new PrintWriter(writer))          ◁─┐  Prints to a
                                                     StringWriter
assert writer.toString() == """\                     for testing
invoices() {
  invoice(date:Thu Jan 01 00:00:00 CET 2015) {
    item(count:1) {
      product(name:'ULC', dollar:1499)
    }
  }
  invoice(date:Fri Jan 02 00:00:00 CET 2015) {
    item(count:2) {
      product(name:'ULC', dollar:1499)
    }
  }
  invoice(date:Sat Jan 03 00:00:00 CET 2015) {
    item(count:3) {
      product(name:'ULC', dollar:1499)
    }
  }
}
"""
```

The code for building a single invoice ❶ calls the NodeBuilder's *pretended* methods directly. This is fine for loops like for and while, but when looping with closures like in a [1..3].each{} loop, you have to call the NodeBuilder like builder.invoice, because it wouldn't be known otherwise. The closure passed to each will have a delegate of the calling context (that is, the script), whereas the rest of the method calls appear within closures that have had their delegates set to the instance of Node-Builder. It's very important to understand what the delegate of each closure is. Just remember that the first thing a method call to NodeBuilder does is set the closure of the delegate parameter to the builder itself.

Of course, there are more options available than just for and while. The closure is just normal code. You can use other control structures such as if and switch as well.

Nodes as constructed with the NodeBuilder have some interesting methods as listed in table 11.1. Note that these methods being present on the nodes doesn't prevent you from having nodes of the same name (for example, a node called iterator). You build child nodes by calling methods on the NodeBuilder, not on the nodes themselves. For a complete and up-to-date description have a look at its GroovyDoc API documentation. Nodes are used throughout the Groovy library for transparently storing treelike structures. You'll see further uses of nodes when we explore XmlParser in chapter 14.

Table 11.1 Public node methods (excerpt)

Return type	Method name	Purpose
Object	name()	The name of the node, for instance invoice
Object	value()	The node itself

Table 11.1 Public node methods (excerpt) *(continued)*

Return type	Method name	Purpose
Map	`attributes()`	All attributes in a map
Node	`parent()`	The back reference to the parent
List	`children()`	The list of all children
Iterator	`iterator()`	The Iterator over all children
List	`depthFirst()`	Provides a collection of all the nodes in the tree using a depth-first traversal
List	`breadthFirst()`	Provides a collection of all the nodes in the tree using a breadth-first traversal
void	`print(PrintWriter out)`	Pretty-printing as nested structure

With this in mind you may want to have some fun by typing

```
println invoices.depthFirst()*.name()
```

That's all there is to `NodeBuilder`. It makes a representative example for all builders in the sense that whenever using a builder, you create a builder instance, and call methods on it with attached nested closures that result in an object tree.

11.3 Working with MarkupBuilder

In listing 11.5 you saw the structured, pretty-printed output from a tree of nodes. This can be very useful when debugging object structures, but you frequently want to exchange that information with non-Groovy programs or store it in a standard format for later retrieval. XML is one obvious candidate format, so of course Groovy makes it easy to generate. You've already encountered `MarkupBuilder` in our quick introduction, and now you're going to have a closer look at its capabilities, both with XML and HTML.

11.3.1 Building XML

Listing 11.6 shows how simple that is: replace the `NodeBuilder` with a `MarkupBuilder` and, voilà, you're done. The only other difference is the way you obtain the results. Because markup is usually generated for formatted output, the printing is done implicitly as soon as the construction is finished. To make testing possible, a `Writer` is passed into `MarkupBuilder`'s constructor.

Listing 11.6 Invoice example with `MarkupBuilder`

```
import groovy.xml.MarkupBuilder

TimeZone.default = TimeZone.getTimeZone("CET")

def writer = new StringWriter()              New: MarkupBuilder
def builder = new MarkupBuilder(writer)      replaces NodeBuilder
```

```
builder.invoices {
  for (day in 1..3) {
    def invDate = Date.parse('yyyy-MM-dd', "2015-01-0$day")
    invoice(date: invDate) {
      item(count: day) {
        product(name: 'ULC', dollar: 1499)
      }
    }
  }
}

assert "\n" + writer.toString() == """
<invoices>
  <invoice date='Thu Jan 01 00:00:00 CET 2015'>
    <item count='1'>
      <product name='ULC' dollar='1499' />
    </item>
  </invoice>
  <invoice date='Fri Jan 02 00:00:00 CET 2015'>
    <item count='2'>
      <product name='ULC' dollar='1499' />
    </item>
  </invoice>
  <invoice date='Sat Jan 03 00:00:00 CET 2015'>
    <item count='3'>
      <product name='ULC' dollar='1499' />
    </item>
  </invoice>
</invoices>"""
```

There is no change whatsoever in the two listings as far as the nested builder calls are concerned. That means we can extract that code in a method and pass it different builders for different purposes. This is an inherent benefit of the Builder pattern.

Just as with `NodeBuilder`, you need to be careful about node and attribute names containing "special" characters. This frequently occurs when using `MarkupBuilder`, as multiword names often appear with hyphens in XML. Suppose you want to generate a J2EE `web.xml` descriptor with a `MarkupBuilder`. You'd need to construct markup like `<web-app>` but you cannot have a minus sign in a method name, so you need quotes, like this:

```
def writer = new StringWriter()
def builder = new groovy.xml.MarkupBuilder(writer)

def web = builder.'web-app' {
    builder.'display-name'('Groovy WebApp')
}

def result = writer.toString().replaceAll("\r","")

assert "\n"+result == """
<web-app>
  <display-name>Groovy WebApp</display-name>
</web-app>"""
```

Note that a method name in quotes also needs an object reference to be called upon like `this` or `builder` in the preceding example.

11.3.2 *Building HTML*

XML and HTML follow the common strategy of bringing structure to a text by using markup with *tags*. Rules for HTML are a bit more special, but for the sole purpose of building a *well-formed* serialized format the same rules apply.

It should come as no surprise that `MarkupBuilder` can also produce HTML to realize web pages as shown in figure 11.2.

This web page is created from the following HTML source code:

```html
<html>
 <head>
  <title>Constructed by MarkupBuilder</title>
 </head>
 <body>
  <h1>What can I do with MarkupBuilder?</h1>
  <form action='whatever'>
   <input checked='checked' type='checkbox' id='Produce HTML'/>
   <label for='Produce HTML'>Produce HTML</label>
   <br/>
   <input checked='checked' type='checkbox' id='Produce XML'/>
   <label for='Produce XML'>Produce XML</label>
   <br/>
   <input checked='checked' type='checkbox' id='Have some fun'/>
   <label for='Have some fun'>Have some fun</label>
   <br/>
  </form>
 </body>
</html>
```

The following listing shows how this HTML source code is built with a `MarkupBuilder`. It's all straightforward. For building the checkboxes, we use a list of labels and do the iterations with the `for` loop.

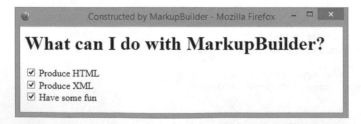

Figure 11.2   Web page that's rendered by the browser from HTML source code that was built from `MarkupBuilder` to show a level-one heading and three checkboxes with labels

Listing 11.7   HTML GUI with `MarkupBuilder`

```
def writer = new FileWriter('markup.html')
def html   = new groovy.xml.MarkupBuilder(writer)
html.html {
  head {
    title 'Constructed by MarkupBuilder'
  }
  body {
    h1 'What can I do with MarkupBuilder?'
    form (action:'whatever') {
      for (line in ['Produce HTML','Produce XML','Have some fun']){
        input(type:'checkbox',checked:'checked', id:line, '')
        label(for:line, line)
        br()
} } } }
```

HTML source code as produced by the `MarkupBuilder` is always properly built with respect to balancing and nesting tags. It also deals with a number of character-encoding issues like replacing the < character with the < entity. See the GroovyDoc API documentation for details.

`MarkupBuilder` expects that the last argument to each method call is either a closure for further nesting or a string that makes the text content.

NOTE If you need to create mixed elements (that is, elements with intermingled text and child elements, such as `<parent>Some text<child>Child text</child>More text</parent>`) then you can use a special `mkp` notation.[4] Use `mkp.yield` normally and `mkp.yieldUnescaped` if you want to bypass escaping of special symbols like the ampersand, less-than, and greater-than characters, which are normally escaped and replaced with their equivalent HTML encoding.

That's it for `MarkupBuilder`. It's often used whenever XML processing is to be done and when developing web applications. `MarkupBuilder` also works nicely in combination with Groovy's templating engines that are the topic of section 12.4. There's another markup builder class that comes bundled with Groovy: `StreamingMarkupBuilder`. It's especially designed for handling streaming scenarios. Let's look at that next.

11.4   *Working with StreamingMarkupBuilder*

In streaming scenarios (for example, when creating large markup files) you might consider using `StreamingMarkupBuilder`. It's almost a drop-in replacement for `MarkupBuilder` but there are a few differences you should be aware of. First let's take our invoices example and tweak it to use `StreamingMarkupBuilder` as shown in the following listing.

---

[4] mkp is short for markup but the abbreviation isn't likely to conflict with a name you might want to use in your created content.

Listing 11.8 Invoice example with `StreamingMarkupBuilder`

```
def builder = new groovy.xml.StreamingMarkupBuilder()
def writable = builder.bind {
  invoices {
    for (day in 1..3) {
      def invDate = Date.parse('yyyy-MM-dd', "2015-01-0$day")
      invoice(date: invDate) {
        item(count: day) {
          product(name: 'ULC', dollar: 1499)
        }
      }
    }
  }
}
def result = writable.toString()
assert result.startsWith("<invoices><invoice date='Thu Jan 01")
assert result.endsWith('</invoice></invoices>')
```

> The bind method introduces markup closure

> Root node must be included in markup...

> ...or writable.writeTo(file)

> Checking start and end of long single line

One difference you might notice straightaway is that instead of calling `build.invoices` you call `builder.bind` and `invoices` becomes the first method called within the markup closure. From that point on, the closure contents are identical. Another difference you may have spotted is that the output isn't indented and will be just one long line. For simplicity and ease of typesetting, we won't check the whole generated line, just its start and end. The decision to not indent aligns with the goals of this streaming builder. It keeps just the minimal amount of information in memory at any time and spits out characters to its output stream as quickly as it can.

If XML isn't your thing and you prefer JSON, Groovy comes with builders for that too (covered in chapter 14).

That's quite a few options you have for creating structured data. Let's consider now some alternative applications of the builder concept.

11.5 Task automation with AntBuilder

Ant (http://ant.apache.org/) is a *build* automation tool. If you've never worked with Ant you should give it a try. It's a great tool for any kind of automation task and works nicely in combination with Groovy. For the remainder of this section it's assumed that you have some basic understanding of Ant.

As a build tool on its own, Ant has lost ground in recent years. But more popular build toolkits like Gradle (www.gradle.org) still make heavy use of Ant and allow accessing the underlying Ant tasks with the help of `AntBuilder`. See section 20.4 for more on Gradle.

`AntBuilder` is a Groovy builder that's used to build and execute Ant datatypes and tasks. This allows you to harness the power of Ant directly within Groovy scripts and classes. Representing interactions with the outside world—manipulating the filesystem, compiling code, running unit tests, fetching the contents of websites—is often more easily expressed in Ant than with the standard Java libraries. Using Ant within normal Java programs is a little clumsy at times, but Groovy makes it straightforward with `AntBuilder`. This section shows how Ant scripts can be represented in Groovy, examines how `AntBuilder` works, and demonstrates what a powerful combination the two technologies can form.

Ant uses the notion of a *build* for describing its work. Unfortunately, this naming sometimes clashes with what we do in this book in a builder. For distinction in the text, *build* is always set in italics when referring to the Ant meaning of the word.

11.5.1 *From Ant scripts to Groovy scripts*

Ant *build* scripts are typically used for automating tasks that need to be done as part of the process of transforming source files and other resources into project deliverables (executables and other artifacts). *Build* scripts often involve a range of tasks: cleaning directories, compiling code, running unit tests, producing documentation, moving and copying files, bundling archive files, deploying the application, and much more.

A first example of an Ant *build* script was shown in the introductory sections of this book in listing 1.2. Listing 11.9 provides another tiny example to show the XML-based syntax of Ant *build* scripts. It achieves one of the tasks that *build* this book: cleaning the target directory and copying the raw documents to it excluding any temporary word documents.

Listing 11.9 Tiny Ant script for file manipulation

```
<project name="prepareBookDirs" default="copy">

  <property name="target.dir"   value="target"/>
  <property name="chapters.dir" value="chapters"/>

  <target name="copy">
    <delete dir="${target.dir}" />
    <copy todir="${target.dir}">
      <fileset dir="${chapters.dir}"
        includes="*.doc"
        excludes="~*"    />
    </copy>
  </target>
</project>
```

After saving such a script to build.xml it can be started from the command line via the ant command and produces an output like this:

```
C:\groovy-book> ant
Buildfile: build.xml

copy:
    [delete] Deleting directory C:\safe\subversion\groovy-book\target
      [copy] Copying 10 files to C:\safe\subversion\groovy-book\target

BUILD SUCCESSFUL
Total time: 0 seconds
```

The real production process doesn't use this build.xml file but an `AntBuilder` in a Groovy script:

```
TARGET_DIR   = 'target'
CHAPTERS_DIR = 'chapters'
ant          = new AntBuilder()

ant.delete(dir:TARGET_DIR)
ant.copy(todir:TARGET_DIR){
    fileset(dir:CHAPTERS_DIR, includes:'*.doc', excludes:'~*')
}
```

When transferring Ant *build* scripts to Groovy scripts by using the `AntBuilder`, the following rules apply:

- Ant *task names* map to `AntBuilder` method names.
- Ant *attributes* are passed as a map to `AntBuilder` methods.
- Where traditional Ant uses strings for other datatypes (for example, `boolean` and `int`), Groovy code can directly pass data of the correct type (for example, `ant.copy(…, overwrite:true)`).
- Nested Ant tasks or elements map to method calls in the attached closure.

Ant comes with a cornucopia of useful tasks, far more than we could possibly describe here. Please refer to the Ant documentation at http://ant.apache.org/manual.

Groovy comes with a bundled version of Ant that's used automatically (without any further setup) whenever you use `AntBuilder`.

11.5.2 *How AntBuilder works*

Looking at the similarity of the build.xml and the corresponding Groovy script one could easily assume that `AntBuilder` builds this XML like a `MarkupBuilder` and passes it to Ant for execution. This isn't the case.

The Groovy `AntBuilder` works directly on the Java classes that Ant uses for doing its work. We need to take a quick detour into the internals of Ant to build a better picture of `AntBuilder`'s approach.

When Ant has parsed the build.xml it iterates through the XML nodes and builds Java objects from it. When it sees the `copy` element it looks into a `taskdef` and finds that it must construct an `org.apache.tools.ant.taskdefs.Copy` object. Similarly, the nested `fileset` element results in a `FileSet` object that's *added* to the `Copy` object. When all the task objects are created, their `perform` method is called that finally executes the task logic. Figure 11.3 shows the resulting object dependencies in a UML class diagram.

`AntBuilder` follows the same approach but without the need to work on the XML structure. When the `copy` method is called on `AntBuilder`, it uses Ant's helper methods to construct an instance of Ant's `Copy` object. The nested `fileset` call is handled equivalently. As a result, the very same object structure as depicted in figure 11.3 is created.

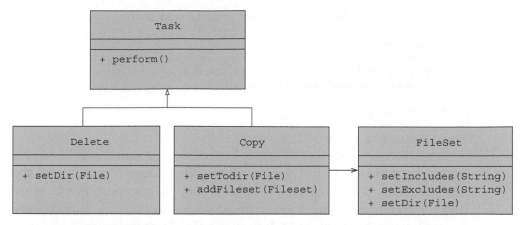

Figure 11.3 **UML class diagram of Ant's** `Delete` **and** `Copy` **tasks that both inherit from the** `Task` **class, where** `Copy` **also refers to a** `FileSet` **object that was added at** *build* **construction time via** `Copy`**'s** `addFileset()` **method.**

When the construction of a *top-level* element is finished, `AntBuilder` automatically calls its `perform` method to start task execution.

11.5.3 Smart automation scripts with logic

`AntBuilder` shines when it comes to using Ant functionality mixed with logic. In Ant, even the simplest conditional logic is very cumbersome to use.

Suppose your *build* should fail with an error message when you try to run it on an unsupported version of Java. Look at a possible build.xml that implements this feature,[5] just to get an impression of the complexity, not to go through all details:

```
<project name="AntIf" default="main" >

    <target name="check.java.version">
        <condition property="java.version.ok">
            <contains string="${java.version}" substring="1.7"/>
        </condition>
        <fail unless="java.version.ok">
            This build script requires JDK 1.7.x.
        </fail>
    </target>

    <target name="main"
        depends="check.java.version"
        if="java.version.ok">

        <!-- further action -->

    </target>

</project>
```

---

[5] It may seem odd to think of failure as a feature, but if you've ever fought against a build that just didn't quite work, you'll understand that a failure with an explanation can save hours of frustration!

The same can be achieved with the following Groovy script:

```
ant = new AntBuilder()
if ( ! System.properties.'java.version'.contains('1.7')) {
    ant.fail 'This build script requires JDK 1.7.x but was ' +
        System.properties.'java.version'
}
// further action
```

The advantage is obvious.

When it comes to even putting any kind of looping logic inside an Ant *build*, plain Ant cannot offer anything. There are additional packages like `Jelly` and `AntContrib` that enhance Ant with logic, but then you end up programming in XML syntax, which isn't for everybody. Using `AntBuilder` allows you to smoothly integrate any kind of Groovy looping logic with Ant's declarative style of task definitions.

For all the usual automation tasks that one encounters in software development projects, the combination of Groovy and `AntBuilder` is the one-two punch. `AntBuilder` gives you simple access to a huge amount of Ant's functionality, while Groovy allows setting this functionality into action in the most flexible ways. Whenever you find yourself struggling with Ant's XML approach, check whether you can use Groovy to make things easier. Whenever struggling with an automation task in Groovy, have a look at the Ant documentation and search for a task that does the trick. One powerful trick is to use Ant-in-Groovy-in-Ant. The `<groovy>` task allows you to run Groovy code within an Ant script, and sets up an `AntBuilder` attached to the project containing the script. This allows you to express sophisticated logic within your build, and reference the results elsewhere in the Ant script.

`AntBuilder` is a prominent example of providing an intuitive API to a Java framework by using Groovy builders, but it's not the only one. The next section presents `SwingBuilder`, which simplifies implementing GUIs with the Java Swing framework.

11.6   *Easy GUIs with SwingBuilder*

Even in the era of web applications it's profitable to know how to build interactive desktop applications with a user-friendly GUI in terms of presentation and responsiveness. For this purpose, Java provides three frameworks: the Abstract Window Toolkit (AWT), Swing, and since recently JavaFX.

Groovy's `SwingBuilder` is a simplified API to the Swing framework allowing quicker development and easier maintenance through a lot of shortcut expressions and by revealing the GUI's containment structure in the structure of the code.

We'll start our presentation of `SwingBuilder` with a simple initial example that reads a password from user input for further processing in a script. With this example in mind, the main concept, the range of features, and the rationale of the implementation will be explained. Finally, we'll apply this knowledge on a complete Swing application.

For the remainder of this section it's assumed that you have some basic understanding of how to program with Swing. If you're new to Swing, you may want to first work through the Swing tutorial at http://java.sun.com/docs/books/tutorial/uiswing/index.html.

11.6.1 *Reading a password with SwingBuilder*

In a recent project we used a little Groovy automation script to connect to a secure website. We needed to give it a password but certainly we didn't want to hardwire it in the code. The script was used for a corporate client so we couldn't just read it from a file, the command line, or the standard input stream because the password would then possibly be visible to others.

Luckily, we remembered that Swing provides a JPasswordField that shields user input from accidental over-the-shoulder readers with an echo character (* by default). Placed inside a JFrame the simple-most solution looks like that shown in figure 11.4.

Figure 11.4 JPasswordField **to read a password from user input**

Using SwingBuilder, it was easy to integrate that dialog in a script. Listing 11.10 contains the snippet that achieves this. It follows the same strategy that you've already seen for other builders: it creates a builder instance and calls methods on it with attached closures that make up the nesting structure and argument maps that further define properties of the product.

For the case of the password dialog, the nesting structure is simple: there's only one container—the outermost JFrame—containing one simple component—the JPasswordField.

Because we're working with Swing widgets, we need to add an ActionListener to the password field whose actionPerformed method is called as soon as the users have finished their input. In Groovy, we can do that with a simple closure.

We need to call JFrame's layout manager via the pack method and make it visible and start the main loop via show, as shown next.

Listing 11.10 Simple password dialog with SwingBuilder

```
import groovy.swing.SwingBuilder

swing = new SwingBuilder()
frame = swing.frame(title:'Password') {
    passwordField(columns:10, actionPerformed: { event ->
        println event.source.text
        // any further processing is called here
        System.exit(0)
        }
    )
}
frame.pack()
frame.visible = true
```

The example shows two idiosyncrasies of `SwingBuilder`:

- For constructing a `JFrame` the according method name is `frame`, *not* `jFrame` as one may expect. This allows reusing code with builders for other widget sets like `AWTBuilder` (not yet available), `SWTBuilder`, or `ULCBuilder`.[6]

- Adding the `ActionListener` to the password field follows the style that you've seen in section 7.4.2; that is, we define a closure that's executed when the field notifies its listener's `actionPerformed` method. In this closure, we print the current content of the field and exit the application. It's important to spot that the closure is specified as a value in the map, *not* a closure to be one level down from the password field itself.

Note that the flow of execution is different from normal console-based scripts but similar to normal Swing applications. The flow doesn't wait for the user input but runs right until the end where Swing's main loop is started implicitly. When the users have committed their input with the Enter key, the flow proceeds in the `actionPerformed` closure. This is where any trailing activities must reside.

The initial example was very basic. For more elaborate uses we need more information about `SwingBuilder`'s access to Swing's views and models, as well as guidance on how to use layout managers and Swing's `Action` concept. The next sections are about those features.

If you'd rather like to look at some advanced examples at this point, you can do so within your Groovy distribution and online. Table 11.2 gives directions, where `GROOVY_SOURCES` refers to the Groovy source tree in the project's version control.

Table 11.2 `SwingBuilder` **uses within the Groovy distribution and online source repository**

Example	Location	Purpose/features
groovyConsole	GROOVY_HOME /lib/groovy-*.jar groovy/ui/Console.groovy	Interactive Groovy shell, using MenuBar, Menu, MenuItem, Accelerator, CaretListener, Action, TextArea, TextPane, StyledDocument, Look&Feel, FileChooser, and Dialog
ObjectBrowser	GROOVY_HOME /lib/groovy-*.jar groovy/inspect/swingui/ ObjectBrowser.groovy	Inspecting objects, using Label, TabbedPane, Table, Table-Model, ClosureColumn, Mouse-Listener, BorderLayout, FlowLayout, Look&Feel, ScrollPane, and Dialog

---

[6] ULC is a server-side widget set that allows writing web applications on the server in a Swing-equivalent manner. The UI is presented on the client through an application-independent UI engine. ULCBuilder enables you to write Groovy ULC applications analogous to writing Swing applications with SwingBuilder. See www.canoo.com/ulc.

Table 11.2   `SwingBuilder` **uses within the Groovy distribution and online source repository**

Example	Location	Purpose/features

`paintingByNumbers`	`GROOVY_SOURCES`
	`/examples/groovy2d/`
	`paintingByNumbers.groovy`
		Random patchwork graphics,
		using simple Java2D API graphics

`BloglinesClient`	`GROOVY_SOURCES`
	`/examples/swing/`
	`BloglinesClient.groovy`
		RSS reader, using `Lists`,
		`ListModels`, `ScrollPanes`,
		`ValueChangedListeners`, and
		a define-before-layout approach

`Widgets`	`GROOVY_SOURCES`
	`/examples/swing/`
	`Widgets.groovy`
		Swing Widget demonstrator, using
		various `Dialogs`, `MenuBar`,
		`Menu`, `MenuItem`, `Action`,
		`TabbedPane`, `Panel`, `Grid-`
		`Layout`, `GridBagLayout`,
		`Constraints`, `BorderLayout`,
		`FormattedTextField`,
		`Slider`, and `Spinner`
		(with model)

`SwingDemo`	`GROOVY_TEST_SOURCES`
	`/groovy/swing/`
	`SwingDemo.groovy`
		`SwingBuilder` demonstrator
		giving access to
		`groovy.model.MvcDemo`,
		`TableDemo`, and `TableLayout-`
		`Demo`, additionally featuring `VBox`,
		`ComboBox`, `Table`, `TableModel`,
		`TableLayout (td, tr)`,
		`PropertyColumn`, and
		`ClosureColumn`

11.6.2 *Creating Swing widgets*

`SwingBuilder` is simple in appearance but very elaborate inside. Its methods don't only create and connect the plain Swing widgets that represent views but also give access to those objects that Swing uses for gluing together the final GUI-like actions, models, layout managers, and constraints.

This section lists the factory method calls for building views. Trailing sections go into detail about building supporting objects.

`SwingBuilder` knows about the Swing widgets that are listed in table 11.3. If no other indication is given, the factory methods in the table return the product object, optionally setting properties from a supplied map.

`SwingBuilder` cares about proper containment of widgets by following the closure's nesting structure. Only *standalone* containers are to be used without a parent. See the Swing API documentation for full coverage of the product classes and their properties.

Table 11.3 SwingBuilder's widget factory methods

SwingBuilder method	Product	Notes
button	JButton	
buttonGroup	ButtonGroup	Invisible; used to group radio buttons and checkboxes.
checkBox	JCheckBox	
checkBoxMenuItem	JCheckBoxMenuItem	
colorChooser	JColorChooser	
comboBox	JComboBox	Obeys optional argument items.
desktopPane	JDesktopPane	
dialog	JDialog	Can be used inside a parent container as well as standalone.
editorPane	JEditorPane	
fileChooser	JFileChooser	
formattedTextField	JFormattedTextField	Obeys either *format* or *value* properties (in that order)
frame	JFrame	Standalone container.
internalFrame	JInternalFrame	
label	JLabel	
layeredPane	JLayeredPane	
list	JList	
menu	JMenu	
menuBar	JMenuBar	
menuItem	JMenuItem	
optionPane	JOptionPane	
panel	JPanel	
passwordField	JPasswordField	
popupMenu	JPopupMenu	
progressBar	JProgressBar	
radioButton	JRadioButton	
radioButtonMenuItem	JRadioButtonMenuItem	
scrollBar	JScrollBar	

Table 11.3   `SwingBuilder`'s widget factory methods

SwingBuilder method	Product	Notes
scrollPane	JScrollPane	Initializes its subcomponents.
separator	JSeparator	
slider	JSlider	
spinner	JSpinner	
splitPane	JSplitPane	
tabbedPane	JTabbedPane	
table	JTable	
textArea	JTextArea	
textField	JTextField	
textPane	JTextPane	
toggleButton	JToggleButton	
toolBar	JToolBar	
tree	JTree	
viewport	JViewport	
window	JWindow	Can be used inside a parent container as well as standalone. Obeys the owner argument to override containment.

What's missing in `SwingBuilder` is `JToolTip`, which cannot be set as a nested element but only via the `toolTipText` attribute. Also missing is `JApplet`, which is not implemented at the time of this writing.

With the information from table 11.3 we can construct a first little GUI that looks like figure 11.5. The outermost container is a `JFrame` that contains two top-level elements: a `JMenuBar` and a `JPanel`. The `JMenuBar` in turn contains a `JMenu` with `JMenu-Items`. The `JPanel` contains three `JComponents`: a `JLabel`, a `JSlider`, and a `JComboBox` with a simple list.

We were tempted to show this simple containment structure in a diagram and we would have done so if we were programming in Java. But because we use Groovy's

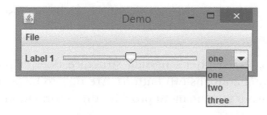

Figure 11.5 Swing GUI with multiple contained widgets

`SwingBuilder` the containment structure is nicely reflected in the code itself, as you can see in the following listing. The code is its own documentation.

Listing 11.11 Simple widget containment demo with `SwingBuilder`

```
import groovy.swing.SwingBuilder

swing = new SwingBuilder()
frame = swing.frame(title:'Demo') {
    menuBar {
        menu('File') {
            menuItem 'New'
            menuItem 'Open'
        }
    }
    panel {
        label 'Label 1'
        slider()
        comboBox(items:['one','two','three'])
    }
}
frame.pack()
frame.visible = true
```

The Java equivalent isn't only three to four times longer (and thus too long to print here), but, perhaps more importantly, it fails to reveal the widget containment in the code layout. If you've ever written Swing GUIs in Java, the code in listing 11.11 will probably feel like a big improvement.

IMPLEMENTATION DETAIL We made use of `SwingBuilder`'s default `text` key in the attribute map, so `menu(text:'File')` can be abbreviated as `menu('File')`. Where parentheses are optional, even `menuItem 'New'` is possible, as demonstrated in listing 11.11.

The label, slider, and combo box need to be contained in a panel because a frame's root pane can contain at most only one element. The panel serves as this single element.

NOTE `SwingBuilder` is an ideal place to make use of the *implicit constructor* as introduced in section 7.1.4. Say you want to set a frame's `size` attribute. In Java, you need to create a `Dimension` object for that purpose. With Groovy's general constructor you write `frame(size:[100,100])`.

The panel in listing 11.11 somehow needs to visually arrange its contained widget. For that purpose, it uses its default `LayoutManager`, which is `FlowLayout` for `JPanel`s. `SwingBuilder` also gives access to Swing's other `LayoutManager`s as shown in the next section.

11.6.3 Arranging your widgets

For visual arrangement of widgets, the builder's nesting structure doesn't provide enough information. Suppose a panel contains two buttons. Are they to be arranged horizontally or vertically? Swing's layout management provides this information.

Layout management with `SwingBuilder` can be achieved in two ways: by setting the according properties on the widgets themselves or by using nested method calls.

We begin with the first option, which works without any layout-specific treatment in Swing-Builder. This is shown with an example that uses Swing's `BorderLayout` with `JButtons` in figure 11.6.

Figure 11.6 Swing `BorderLayout` defined through `SwingBuilder`

The next listing (it produces the layout of figure 11.6) shows that no special methods need to be called. It's sufficient to set the according properties on the Swing widgets: `layout` and `constraints`. We use Groovy's import as feature for convenience to ease access to `BorderLayout` with the `BL` abbreviation.

Listing 11.12 Laying out widgets the common Swing way

```
import groovy.swing.SwingBuilder
import java.awt.BorderLayout as BL

swing = new SwingBuilder()
frame = swing.frame(title:'Layout Demo') {
    panel(layout: new BL()) {
        button(constraints: BL.NORTH,  'North' )
        button(constraints: BL.CENTER, 'Center')
        button(constraints: BL.SOUTH,  'South' )
        button(constraints: BL.EAST,   'East'  )
        button(constraints: BL.WEST,   'West'  )
    }
}
frame.pack()
frame.visible = true
```

The second option for laying out widgets is using method calls as listed in table 11.4 that work inside the nesting structure. In addition to Swing's standard layout options, `SwingBuilder` also provides simplified access to supporting objects like constraints, glues, and struts. See the Swing API documentation for full coverage of the several layout managers, a description of their "layouting" strategy, their properties together with predefined constant values, and the constraints they rely upon.

Table 11.4 `SwingBuilder`'s methods for laying out components within a UI

SwingBuilder method	Swing class/method	Notes
borderLayout	BorderLayout	Layout manager
boxLayout	BoxLayout	Layout manager; obeys *axis*, default: `X_AXIS`
cardLayout	CardLayout	Layout manager

Table 11.4 `SwingBuilder`'s methods for laying out components within a UI *(continued)*

SwingBuilder method	Swing class/method	Notes
flowLayout	FlowLayout	Layout manager
gridBagLayout	GridBagLayout	Layout manager
gridBagConstraints	GridBagConstraints	Constraints to be used with GridBagLayout
gbc	GridBagConstraints	Abbreviation for gridBagConstraints
gridLayout	GridLayout	Layout manager
overlayLayout	OverlayLayout	Layout manager
springLayout	SpringLayout	Layout manager
tableLayout	n/a	Container; needs nested tr()/td() calls
hbox	Box.createHorizontalBox	Container
hglue	Box.createHorizontalGlue	Widget
hstrut	Box.createHorizontalStrut	Widget; obeys *width*, default: 6
vbox	Box.createVerticalBox	Container
vglue	Box.createVerticalGlue	Widget
vstrut	Box.createVerticalStrut	Widget; obeys *height*, default: 6
glue	Box.createGlue	Widget
rigidArea	Box.createRigidArea	Widget; obeys *size* or *(width, height)*, default: 6

All layout management methods in table 11.4 can be used as a nested element of the laid out container as shown in the following code snippet, which arranges two buttons horizontally:

```
panel {
    boxLayout()
    button 'one'
    button 'two'
}
```

In contrast, container methods as marked in table 11.4 start their own nesting structure to lay out their nested widgets like this, which arranges two buttons vertically:

```
vbox {
    button 'one'
    button 'two'
}
```

In HTML-based web applications, tables are often used to control the page layout. SwingBuilder allows following the same approach with a genuine TableLayout that almost looks like HTML made by MarkupBuilder:

```
tableLayout{
    tr {
        td { button 'one' }
        td { button 'two' }
    }
    tr {
        td(colspan:2) { button 'three' }
    }
}
```

Note td's colspan attribute. The table layout can be adjusted with such cell attributes. The available cell attributes is listed in table 11.5 or can be derived from the API documentation of groovy.swing.impl.TableLayoutCell.

Table 11.5 Cell attributes in table layout

Attribute	Type	Range/default
align	String	'LEFT', 'CENTER', 'RIGHT'
valign	String	'TOP', 'MIDDLE', 'BOTTOM'
colspan	int	Default: 1
rowspan	int	Default: 1
colfill	boolean	Default: false
rowfill	boolean	Default: false

Still left to explain from table 11.4 are the invisible horizontal and vertical glues, struts, and the rigid area. Within SwingBuilder they're used like any other widget in the containment structure. They fill excessive space in the layout. Struts are of fixed size while glues grow and shrink with the available space. A rigid area simply is a two-dimensional strut.

A simple example of a vertical glue between two buttons is shown next. It fills vertical space, effectively forcing button 'one' to flow to the left and button 'two' to flow to the right of the surrounding panel.

```
panel {
    button 'one'
    glue()
    button 'two'
}
```

More precisely, a *glue* is an invisible widget that has an indefinite maximum size and minimum size of [0,0]. The effect of adding a glue to a container depends on that container's layout management and the (preferred, minimum, maximum) size of other contained widgets.

So far you've seen how to create and compose widgets and how to arrange them. For setting them into action, widgets and their according event listeners need some way to refer to each other. The next sections show how to do that.

11.6.4 *Referring to widgets*

Suppose you have an application with a text field and a button. When pushing the button, the current content of the text field is to be printed to the console. This simple application could look like figure 11.7.

Figure 11.7 A simple application that prints the content of the text field to the console.

The corresponding code would contain a snippet like this (which is incomplete):

```
textField(columns:10)
button(text:'Print', actionPerformed: { event ->
    println 'the entered text is ... ???'
})
```

To print the content of the text field, the `actionPerformed` closure would need some reference to it. This section is about ways of obtaining such a reference:

- By traversing the containment structure
- By ID
- By variables

The first option makes use of the `event` object that gets passed to the closure. It has a `source` property that refers to the source of the event: the button. So, at least, you have a reference to the button.

The button and text field are nested in the same parent container, available via button's `parent` property. That `parent` property in turn reveals its nested `components` and the text field happens to be the first one of those. The final traversal looks like the following:

```
panel {
    textField(columns:10)
    button(text:'Print', actionPerformed: { event ->
        println event.source.parent.components[0].text
    })
}
```

This works, but is ugly for a number of reasons. First, the path expression doesn't nicely reveal that you're referring to the text field at all. Second, when rearranging the containment structure, the code will break. Third, the purpose of the text field remains unexplained.

The second option of referencing addresses these concerns. An `id` attribute can be attached to the text field. It's successively available as a property on the `Swing-Builder` itself.

```
swing = new SwingBuilder()
frame = swing.frame(title:'Printer') {
    panel {
        textField(id:'message', columns:10)
        button(text:'Print', actionPerformed: {
            println swing.message.text
        })
    }
}
```

This is much better but raises the question why this special handling is needed at all. Why not simply use variables for referencing an object? In fact, you can do so and the following code snippet works as well:

```
message = textField(columns:10)
button(text:'Print', actionPerformed: {
    println message.text
})
```

This looks very appealing at first sight but you need to be careful when things aren't as simple as in this example. Variables need to be known in the scope of the referrer and they must have been properly assigned before use. SwingBuilder's simple appearance can easily lead to overlooking this. Remember that you're in a closure and thus in a closed block. You cannot simply introduce a variable to the enclosing scope.

Suppose you set out to print not the text field content, but the frame title. You already have a variable called frame. A first (unsuccessful) try could be

```
button(text:'Print', actionPerformed: {
    println frame.title                  // fails !!!
})
```

But this fails because you're still in the process of frame construction when trying to reference it. It isn't even declared, yet!

Obviously, when going the "reference by variable" route it makes sense to first fully construct your widgets and take care of nesting, layout, and referencing afterwards.

This can look like the following code snippet where you first construct the frame and hold a reference to it. When defining the containment structure, you can use this reference at two places: where the frame widget is needed for containment and in the actionPerformed closure. SwingBuilder's widget method allows placing a predefined widget in the containment structure.

```
swing = new SwingBuilder()
frame = swing.frame(title:'Printer')

swing.widget(frame) {
    panel {
        textField(columns:10)
        button(text:'Print', actionPerformed: {
            println frame.title
        })
    }
}
```

You can do the same with the button and attach the listener after the frame construction is finished:

```
swing = new SwingBuilder()
button = swing.button('Print')

frame = swing.frame(title:'Printer') {
    panel {
        textField(columns:10)
        widget(button)
    }
}

button.actionPerformed = {
    println frame.title
}
```

The latter is particularly handy when constructing views or attaching listeners gets more complex such that it would hamper understanding the containment structure if done inline.

A further Swing abstraction that helps code readability is the `Action` concept. The next section shows how it's supported in `SwingBuilder`.

11.6.5 *Using Swing actions*

The full description of Swing's `Action` concept is in the API documentation of `javax.swing.Action`, but in short, an `Action` is an `ActionListener` that can be used from multiple widgets. In addition to a shared `actionPerformed` method it stores common properties and broadcasts property changes to its widgets.

This is particularly helpful when a menu item and a toolbar button should do the same thing. With a shared `Action`, they share, for instance, the enabled state such that disabling the `Action` instantly disables both the menu item and the toolbar button.

Table 11.6 lists the predefined `Action` properties with a short description.

Table 11.6 Predefined `Action` properties

Property	Type	Note
closure	Closure	Introduced by `SwingBuilder`; the closure to be called for `actionPerformed()`
accelerator	String	Keystroke to invoke a `JMenuItem`, even if not visible
mnemonic	single char String	Character in the *name* used for quick navigation to the widget
name	String	Default text for widgets
shortDescription	String	Used for tooltip text

Table 11.6 Predefined `Action` properties

Property	Type	Note
longDescription	String	Can be used for context help
enabled	Boolean	Shared enabled state
smallIcon	javax.swing.Icon	Shared icon for widgets (toolbar buttons), typically javax.swing.ImageIcon
keyStroke	String	General keystroke to invoke the action

The accelerator and keyStroke properties both take String representations of a keystroke as described with javax.swing.KeyStroke.getKeyStroke(String)—you don't have to bother with the keystroke abstractions but can simply use 'ctrl ENTER' and the like.

As expected, SwingBuilder uses the action method to create an action object, like this:

```
swing = new SwingBuilder()

printAction = swing.action(name:'Print', closure: {
    println swing.message.text
})
```

Such a reference can be used with the action property of its widgets.

```
frame = swing.frame(title:'Printer') {
    panel {
        textField(action: printAction, id:'message',columns:10)
        button    (action: printAction)
    }
}
```

We added the action method to both widgets so the action closure gets called when pressing the Enter key in the text field.

The button no longer needs a text property. Instead, it retrieves its label from the action name.

There's a second option of referring to an action that's equally valid but a bit less intuitive: an action can be nested. For this purpose there's a second flavor of the action method that makes the given action known to the parent (similar to the widget() method):

```
frame = swing.frame(title:'Printer') {
    panel {
        textField(id:'message',columns:10) { action(printAction) }
        button                             { action(printAction) }
    }
}
```

Using `SwingBuilder`'s action support is usually a good choice. It helps in terms of structuring the code, achieving consistent action behavior, and providing user-friendly GUIs that can be controlled by keyboard or mouse alike.

11.6.6 *Using models*

Swing follows the Model-View-Controller (MVC) pattern and, thus, models are used to provide widgets with data. All the usual Swing models can be used with `SwingBuilder`. In addition, `SwingBuilder` provides convenience factory methods for models as listed in table 11.7.

Table 11.7   Factory methods for models

Method	Model	Note
boundedRangeModel	DefaultBoundedRangeModel	For JSlider and JProgressBar
spinnerDateModel	SpinnerDateModel	For JSpinner
spinnerListModel	SpinnerListModel	For JSpinner
spinnerNumberModel	SpinnerNumberModel	For JSpinner
tableModel	groovy.model.DefaultTableModel	For JTable; obeys the *model* or *list* properties as ValueModel (in that order); supports nested TableColumns
propertyColumn	TableColumn	Supports header, propertyName, type(Class)
closureColumn	TableColumn	Supports header, read(Closure), write(Closure), type(Class)

NOTE   At the time of this writing, there's no special `SwingBuilder` support for `TreeModel` to be used with `JTree` or `ListModel` to be used with `JList` and `JComboBox`.

From table 11.7 the `tableModel` is most special. We start its presentation with a small example table that lists the names and favorite colors of some members of a famous Australian children's band. It produces the GUI shown in figure 11.8.

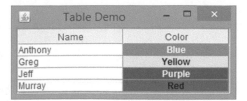

Figure 11.8 Table backed by
`tableModel` **and** `propertyColumns`

The next listing contains the code that makes up the GUI of figure 11.8. The `table-Model` method uses nested `TableColumn` objects, `propertyColumn` in this example. Note the containment of `scrollPane` – `table` – `tableModel` – `propertyColumn` is reflected in the code layout.

Listing 11.13 Example of a table backed by `tableModel` **and** `propertyColumns`

```
import groovy.swing.SwingBuilder
import groovy.transform.Canonical
import javax.swing.JLabel
import javax.swing.JTable
import javax.swing.table.TableCellRenderer
import java.awt.Color
import java.awt.Component

import static java.awt.Color.*

@Canonical
class NamedColor {
  String name
  Color foreground, background
}

purple = new NamedColor('Purple', WHITE, new Color(127, 0, 255))
mediumBlue = new NamedColor('Blue', WHITE, new Color(64, 128, 255))
brightYellow = new NamedColor('Yellow', BLACK, YELLOW)
brightRed = new NamedColor('Red', BLACK, RED)

data = [
    [name: 'Anthony', color: mediumBlue],
    [name: 'Greg', color: brightYellow],
    [name: 'Jeff', color: purple],
    [name: 'Murray', color: brightRed]
]

swing = new SwingBuilder()
frame = swing.frame(title: 'Table Demo') {
  scrollPane {
    table(id: 'table') {
      tableModel(list: data) {
        propertyColumn(header: 'Name', propertyName: 'name')
```

```
        propertyColumn(
            header: 'Color', propertyName: 'color', type: NamedColor  ◁──  ❶ Model can
        )                                                                      have rich
    }                                                                          types
}
}
}
frame.pack()                                                               ❷ Registering a
swing.table.setDefaultRenderer(NamedColor, new ColorRenderer())  ◁──┐        renderer for
frame.visible = true                                                        a rich type

class ColorRenderer extends JLabel implements TableCellRenderer {  ◁──┐  ❸ Implementing
  ColorRenderer() { opaque = true }                                          a renderer

  Component getTableCellRendererComponent(JTable table, color,
      boolean selected, boolean focus, int row, int col) {
    background = color.background
    foreground = color.foreground
    text = color.name
    horizontalAlignment = CENTER
    this
  }
}
```

When using propertyColumn the data must be a list of objects that can be asked for the propertyName. By default the returned property value is assumed to be a String value but other types like Integer are also handled and converted as you'd expect. (You'll see an example using integers in listing 11.14.) You can also specify your own custom types, in our case NamedColor ❶. We defined our own renderer for Named-Color instances ❸ that sets foreground and background colors and sets an appropriate alignment. We register our renderer with the table ❷.

If the data isn't exactly in the format that should be displayed in the table, closure-Column allows you to funnel all read and write access to the data through a read or write closure. For example, if you didn't want to use the custom renderer in listing 11.3, you could replace the propertyColumn line with a closureColumn:

```
closureColumn(header: 'Color', read: {it.color.name})
```

When your table is editable for the user or you change the table content programmatically, consider providing an additional write closure. It's used for converting the external format of a value back to the table's internal format. Think about it as the *reverse* operation of the read closure.

SwingBuilder's special support for TableColumns makes using TableModels much easier. Normally there's no more need to implement extra TableModel classes on your own, but you can certainly still do so when the need arises and use them with the JTable model property. Nested tableModel methods can also take a custom model argument to allow this.

11.6.7 *Binding made easy*

In earlier examples in this section, you've seen actions, events, and listeners as the low-level glue that binds together our widgets and other logic. The conventions around how we glue things together are well understood but often involve significant boilerplate code. Wouldn't it be nice if Groovy could support ways to remove such boilerplate? Doesn't that sound like the kind of problem that AST transformations from chapter 9 were designed to solve? Indeed, Groovy provides the @Bindable, @Vetoable, and @ListenerList AST transformations to solve this exact problem.

Consider a Person domain object with name and age properties. If other components in our application have an interest in when those properties change, the standard conventions would require us to add methods for adding and removing property change listeners and firing property change events to our class. The Groovy code would look like this:

```
import groovy.beans.*

class Person {
  @Bindable String name
  @Vetoable int age
}
```

The equivalent generated code would look like this (excerpt):

```
import java.beans.*

class Person { // truncated to save some trees. Original is 88 such lines.
  private String name
  private int age
  final private PropertyChangeSupport this$propChangeSupport =
      new PropertyChangeSupport(this)
  void addPropertyChangeListener(PropertyChangeListener listener) {
    this$propChangeSupport.addPropertyChangeListener(listener)
  }
  void removePropertyChangeListener(String name,
                                    PropertyChangeListener listener) {
    this$propChangeSupport.removePropertyChangeListener(name, listener)
  }
  void firePropertyChange(String name, oldValue, newValue) {
    this$propChangeSupport.firePropertyChange(name, oldValue, newValue)
  }
  void setName(String value) {
    this.firePropertyChange('name', name, name = value )
  }
  String getName() {
    name
  }
}
```

The annotated code is much more readable and maintainable. It's a similar story for @ListenerList, so we won't bother you with the details. Instead, it's time to dive right in and create an application that uses all three AST transforms.

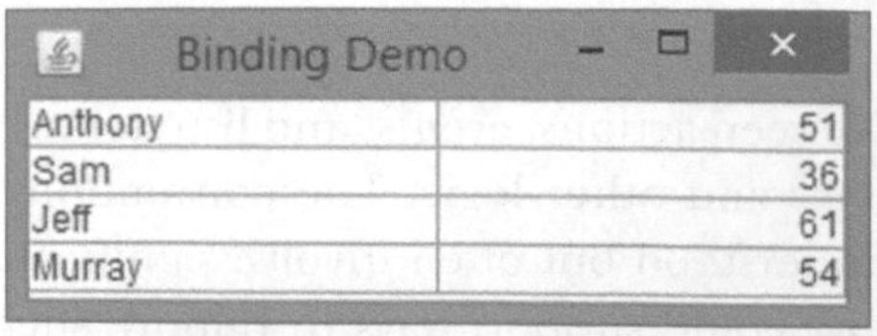

Figure 11.9   An application
with bindable components

We'll create a variation of our Wiggle's application from the last section.[7] This time
we'll record the name and age of the original band members. We'll use a similar table
model as we did in our previous example but with an age property instead of color.
We'll also make the columns editable. The UI will look like that shown in figure 11.9.

Our data for the table model will now be a list of Person domain objects but otherwise the table model shouldn't look unfamiliar. Our Person objects will also be designed
to listen for birthday events. We'll also create a BirthdayNotifier domain object that
notifies Person instances when they have a birthday so that they can increment their
age. Putting this altogether gives us the following listing.

Listing 11.14   Example of an application with bindable components

```
import groovy.beans.*
import groovy.swing.SwingBuilder

import java.awt.event.ActionEvent
import java.awt.event.ActionListener
import java.beans.PropertyVetoException

class Person implements ActionListener {
  @Bindable String name
  @Vetoable int age

  void actionPerformed(ActionEvent e) {
    if (e.actionCommand == name) setAge(age + 1)
  }
}

class BirthdayNotifier {
  @ListenerList List<ActionListener> listeners

  def triggerBirthday(name) {
    def event = new ActionEvent(this, 0, name)
    fireActionPerformed(event)
  }
}
data = [
    new Person(name: 'Anthony', age: 51),
    new Person(name: 'Greg', age: 42),
    new Person(name: 'Jeff', age: 60),
    new Person(name: 'Murray', age: 54)
]
```

---

[7] You did guess that was the band (www.thewiggles.com) we were talking about didn't you?

```
swing = new SwingBuilder()
frame = swing.frame(title: 'Binding Demo') {
  table {
    tableModel(list: data, id: 'tableModel') {
      propertyColumn(header: 'Name', propertyName: 'name',
          editable: true)
      propertyColumn(header: 'Age', propertyName: 'age',
          type: Integer, editable: true)
    }
  }
}
frame.pack()
frame.visible = true

notifier = new BirthdayNotifier()
data.each {
  it.addPropertyChangeListener { evt ->
    println "$evt.newValue has replaced $evt.oldValue"    ◁——  ❶ Logs when
  }                                                                  name changes
  it.addVetoableChangeListener { evt ->
    if (evt.newValue < 0)
      throw new PropertyVetoException("Can't have -ve age", evt)  ❷ Logs when age
    else                                                            changes but
      println "$evt.source.name now has age $evt.newValue"         vetoes -ve ages
  }
  notifier.addActionListener(it)                ◁——   Listens for birthday
}                                               ❸    notifications
try {
  data[0].age = -99
} catch (e) {                                   ◁——   Attempts to
  println "Change ignored: $e.message"          ❹    trigger invalid age
}
data[1].name = 'Sam'                            ❺   Sam replaces
data[1].age = 36                                    Greg

notifier.triggerBirthday(data[2].name)          ◁——   Jeff has a
                                                ❻    birthday
swing.tableModel.fireTableDataChanged()
```

After creating our UI, we glue our pieces together. For each Person instance, we:

- Add a logging closure that tracks name changes ❶.
- Add a logging closure that tracks age changes but vetoes the change if a negative age change is attempted ❷.
- Register the instance as a listener for birthday events ❸.

Finally, we start changing properties. We first attempt to set a negative age value ❹. Then we alter wiggle at index value 1 to change the name and age ❺. Then we trigger a birthday event for the wiggle at index value 2 ❻.

When you run this example you'll see sample output as follows:

```
Change ignored: Can't have -ve age
Sam has replaced Greg
Sam now has age 36
Jeff now has age 61
```

If you start editing the table cells, you'll start to see additional log output produced. Play around now and convince yourself that you understand how all the components are interacting.

So far, you've seen only relatively small examples and snippets that discuss possible variations. We still owe you a comprehensive example of a Swing application built with `SwingBuilder`. We'll keep that promise in the next section.

11.6.8 *Putting it all together*

It's time to implement a complete application using `SwingBuilder`. The idea is to create something that shows how all the pieces we've gone through fit together and that also reveals the benefit that Groovy's dynamic nature brings to application development.

GATHERING REQUIREMENTS

The application should plot arbitrary mathematical functions with one free variable, $f(x)$ in mathematical terms. The user enters the function in the format of a Groovy expression on x.

The application, as displayed in figure 11.10, will provide the user with the following features:

- Defining the function.
- Plotting the graph by pressing Enter in any input field, by clicking the Paint button, by choosing from a menu, or by pressing Ctrl-P.
- Defining domain and range upper and lower bounds either by typing in a new value or by increasing or decreasing the current value with mouse or arrow keys. A repaint should be triggered immediately when any of these values changes.
- Resizing the window to resize the plotting canvas.
- Supporting quick navigation by means of all menus and buttons.

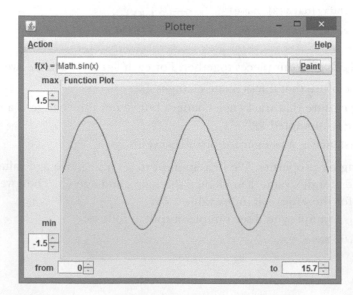

Figure 11.10   A general function plotter built with `SwingBuilder`

A Help/About as shown in figure 11.11 will be provided via menu and via the F1 function key

GETTING PREPARED

SwingBuilder makes it possible to start with a minimal design and refine and extend the containment structure and layout management as the application grows. This is a big improvement over ordinary Swing programming in Java and competitive to using visual builders.[8]

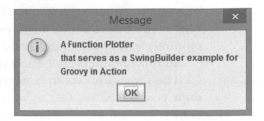

Figure 11.11 A Help/About message made by `SwingBuilder`

But sketching the design in advance prevents it from getting lost. Figure 11.12 splits the expected GUI in pieces, gives hints about the general layout management, and notes some ideas about the components.

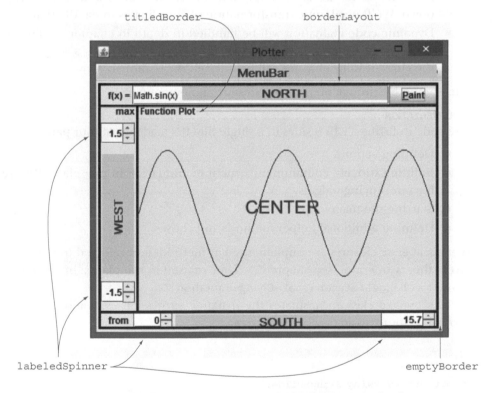

Figure 11.12   Design sketch of components and layout for the plotter application

---

[8] In fact, since many visual builders create source code that's effectively only usable within the builder, and effectively unreadable on its own, SwingBuilder could be said to have the edge over them.

The requirements suggest a `BorderLayout`. All function-specific controls can float to `NORTH`, and dimension controls can be placed `WEST` and `SOUTH`. Most important, the plotting canvas can be `CENTER`ed and will thus expand when resized.

All subcontainers can be arranged as horizontal or vertical boxes.

The dimension controls `max/min/from/to` that are placed at the corners share some commonalities: they're built from a label, a small space, a spinner, and a spinner model. It would be nice to avoid code duplication and have something like a `labeled-Spinner` concept.

Two questions are still open: how to plot a graph using Swing and how to dynamically evaluate the function text. This isn't explained in too much detail because our current focus is on `SwingBuilder`. In brief:

- Any Swing widget can be asked for its `Graphics` object (and thus, we can use a simple panel). This in turn has a number of painting methods. See the API documentation of `java.awt.Graphics`. The main point to consider is the system of coordinates. It starts at the upper-left corner with `[0, 0]` and expands right and down. We'll need some transformation of coordinates to handle that.
- Dynamic code evaluation will be handled in depth in chapter 16. For our simple purpose we can ask a GroovyShell to *parse* the text into a script. We pass it the current value of x and calling `script.run()` returns $f(x)$.

This should be enough preparation to start implementing.

IMPLEMENTATION

The code in listing 11.15 resides in a single file. It's made up of four parts:

- Defining actions.
- Building widgets, containment structure, and layout in one place; IDs are used for referencing widgets.
- Starting the main loop.
- Defining additional helper methods and classes.

`EventListener` closures are implemented as methods and referred to as method closures (the `.&` operator, see chapter 5). They're used in two places: in actions and the spinner's `ChangeListener` (`stateChanged` method).

The `Dynamo` class encapsulates the dynamic expression evaluation. It caches the current script to avoid excessive reparsing.

Listing 11.15   Mathematical function plotter application

```
import groovy.swing.SwingBuilder
import java.awt.Color
import java.awt.BorderLayout        as BL
import javax.swing.WindowConstants  as WC        Type aliases as
import javax.swing.BorderFactory    as BF        shortcuts
import javax.swing.JOptionPane

swing = new SwingBuilder()
```

```
paint = swing.action(
    name:         'Paint',
    closure:      this.&paintGraph,          ◁─┐  Refers to
    mnemonic:     'P',                             method closure
    accelerator: 'ctrl P'
)
about = swing.action(
    name:         'About',
    closure:      this.&showAbout,
    mnemonic:     'A',
    accelerator: 'F1'
)

frame = swing.frame(title:'Plotter',                  General
    location:[100,100], size:[500,500],        ◁─┐    constructor
    defaultCloseOperation:WC.EXIT_ON_CLOSE) {
    menuBar (){
        menu(mnemonic:'A','Action'){
            menuItem(action:paint)
        }                                       Separates
        glue()                            ◁─┐   help menu
        menu(mnemonic:'H','Help'){
            menuItem(action:about)
        }
    }
    panel (border:BF.createEmptyBorder(6,6,6,6)) {
        borderLayout()
        vbox (constraints: BL.NORTH){
            hbox {
                hstrut(width:10)
                label 'f(x) = '
                textField(id:'function',action:paint,'Math.sin(x)')
                button(action:paint)
            }
        }
        vbox (constraints: BL.WEST){             Uses factory
            labeledSpinner('max',1d)      ◁─┐    method
            20.times { swing.vglue() }
            labeledSpinner('min',-1d)
        }
        vbox(constraints: BL.CENTER,
            border:BF.createTitledBorder('Function Plot')) {
            panel(id:'canvas')
        }
        hbox (constraints: BL.SOUTH){
            hstrut(width:10)
            labeledSpinner('from',0d)       ❶ Builds
            10.times { swing.hglue() }  ◁─┐    with logic
            labeledSpinner('to',6.3d)
        }
    }
}
frame.visible = true

// implementation methods
```

```
def labeledSpinner(label, value){                          Factory
    swing.label(label)                              ❷      method
    swing.hstrut()
    swing.spinner(id:label, stateChanged:this.&paintGraph,
        model:swing.spinnerNumberModel(value:value)
    )
}
def paintGraph(event) {                                    Method used
    calc = new Dynamo(swing.function.text)          ❸      as closure
    gfx  = swing.canvas.graphics
    int width  = swing.canvas.size.width
    int height = swing.canvas.size.height
    gfx.color  = new Color(255, 255, 150)
    gfx.fillRect(0, 0, width, height)
    gfx.color  = Color.blue
    xFactor    = (swing.to.value - swing.from.value) / width
    yFactor    = height / (swing.max.value - swing.min.value)
    int ceiling = height + swing.min.value * yFactor              Main
    int lastY   = calc.f(swing.from.value) * yFactor             plotting
    for (x in (1..width)) {                                      loop
        int y = calc.f(swing.from.value + x * xFactor) * yFactor
        gfx.drawLine(x-1, ceiling-lastY, x, ceiling-y)
        lastY = y
    }
}
void showAbout(event) {                                    Shows
    JOptionPane.showMessageDialog(frame,                   message
'''A Function Plotter                                      dialog
that serves as a SwingBuilder example for
Groovy in Action''')
}
// Keep all dynamic invocation handling in one place.
class Dynamo {
    static final GroovyShell SHELL = new GroovyShell()
    Script functionScript
    Dynamo(String function){
        functionScript = SHELL.parse(function)             Once per
    }                                                      paint
    Object f(x) {
        functionScript.x = x
        return functionScript.run()      ◄───── For each x
    }
}
```

It doesn't happen too often, but sometimes *building with logic* that you've seen with other builders is also useful with SwingBuilder, like in ❶. At this point the rationale is that adding a single glue isn't enough to push the labeled spinners into their corners because box layout tries to distribute component sizes evenly. The same effect could have been achieved by using a more complex layout manager.

The labeledSpinner method ❷ is perfect for putting your builder and closure knowledge to the test: Why is the extra 'swing.' prefix needed? The answer is because labeledSpinner is a callback from the closure's delegate (swing) to the enclosing scope (our main Script). But this raises a second question: How can swing then ever add the parent; for example, the label to the parent hbox? Builders keep track of the current parent in their internal state. So swing still knows that we're adding something to that box.

There's no point in going into too much detail about the actual plotting performed in ❸. We figure out the current dimension because the user may resize the panel, fill it with the background color to erase any old function plot, calculate scaling factors, and finally draw in an upside-down manner to cope with Swing's way of handling coordinates.

ASSESSMENT

Even though we set out to produce a complete application example and we achieved a lot within a hundred lines of code, I'm afraid it isn't production-ready. We should have included exception handling for invalid scripts and those that don't return a number, together with warnings and failure indications, in a dialog or a status bar, for example.

Allowing users to provide executable code can also be a security issue. This topic will be examined in chapter 16.

Performance could be improved by a number of means, such as:

- Double buffering (plotting on an invisible canvas and toggle canvases afterwards)
- Sweeping through the domain with a step size > 1 when plotting
- Reparsing function text only when changed

If you liked this example and aim to improve your SwingBuilder skills, why not extend the example with new features? Some useful additions could be:

- Coordinate lines, tick marks, and labels
- History of plotted functions
- Table of *x*/*y* values
- Immediate repaint on focusGained, resized

Finally, we'd like to add that there's much more about Swing that we haven't yet mentioned: *drag and drop, look and feel,* all kinds of *ModelListeners, renderers, editors,* and so on. Even so, we hope we've refreshed your curiosity about Swing and shown how Groovy's SwingBuilder provides a smooth introduction into the world of desktop applications.

One thing that we particularly like about SwingBuilder is that it's instantly available wherever there's Groovy. Other scripting languages often require additionally installing a special GUI toolkit (tk, Gtk, Fox, and others) and you can bet that when downloading a program, it requires the one toolkit that you haven't installed on your current machine. SwingBuilder only relies on Swing and that comes with your Java installation.

But this isn't yet the end of the story. The next section will lead us to even fancier user interfaces.

Figure 11.13 "Hello FX World" as generated with the GroovyFX
`SceneGraphBuilder` using gradients, fonts, images, and effects

11.7 *Modern UIs with GroovyFX SceneGraphBuilder*

`SwingBuilder` makes creating desktop applications fun and worthwhile, but it can
only build Swing applications and has been recently superseded by JavaFX. JavaFX 2 is
included in all Java 7 distributions since update 10 and JavaFX 8 comes bundled with
Java 8. So JavaFX is "the new Swing," and you guessed right that Groovy is by your side
when it comes to building JavaFX applications.

At the time of this writing, the Groovy support for JavaFX isn't included in the standard distribution of Groovy but in an extra project called GroovyFX that you'll find at
http://groovyfx.org. It's easy to use because you can directly refer to it with a `@Grab`
annotation as you'll see soon.

JavaFX introduces the notion of a scene graph as opposed to the canvas-based
graphics system of Swing. All widgets in the UI are nodes in that scene graph and creating a JavaFX view means that you're building that graph. It should come as no surprise that GroovyFX offers you a `SceneGraphBuilder` to simplify this work.

Listing 11.16 makes use of the `SceneGraphBuilder` for saying "Hello" to the FX
world, resulting in the display of figure 11.13. The `start` method automatically instantiates the builder and sets it as the delegate such that the builder is totally hidden
behind the scenes (no pun implied).

Listing 11.16 GroovyFX greets the world

```
@Grab('org.codehaus.groovyfx:groovyfx:0.3.1')

import static groovyx.javafx.GroovyFX.start

start {
  stage title: 'GroovyFX Hello World', visible: true, {
    scene fill: BLACK, width: 600, height: 300, {
      hbox padding: 40, alignment:'center', {
```

```
      text 'Hello', font: '80pt sanserif', {
        fill linearGradient(endX: 0, stops: [PALEGREEN, SEAGREEN])
      }
      text ' FX ', font: '80pt sanserif', {
        fill   linearGradient(endX: 0, stops: [CYAN, DODGERBLUE])
        effect dropShadow(color: DODGERBLUE, radius: 25, spread: 0.35)
      }
      imageView 'file:World.png', effect:reflection()
    }
  }
 }
}
```

The general approach of `SceneGraphBuilder` isn't much different from `Swing-Builder`, and for the typical widgets and layouts, you can reuse what you learned in the previous section. There are a few specialties, though. JavaFX calls a frame a *stage* and the root component a *scene.*

Describing all the details of JavaFX and how GroovyFX maps onto them is, of course, far beyond the scope of this book, but we encourage you to explore the awesome capabilities of that technology. A very good starting point is the demo folder of the GroovyFX project.

The mapping between `SceneGraphBuilder` methods and `SceneGraph` nodes is usually pretty straightforward:

- `arc` maps to `javafx.scene.shape.Arc`
- `boxBlur` maps to `javafx.scene.effect.BoxBlur`
- `circle` maps to `javafx.scene.shape.Circle`

And so on. With the help of your IDE you'll easily find your way around.

Java-style JavaFX builders

JavaFX has seen many versions. Version 2 introduced builders in a Java-style with nested method calls and vararg parameter lists. This was widely seen as an improvement because it was a step in the direction of the ease of use that Groovy provides. This feature was deprecated in version 8 for reasons that remain unclear. The speculation is that generating these builder classes became too costly because in Java you cannot do it dynamically as in Groovy. The best way to use JavaFX with builders is again GroovyFX.

Here are some features of JavaFX that might be of particular interest:

- Layout definitions in FXML created by visual tools
- Styling via CSS, including gradients and effects
- Translations, transitions, and animations
- Properties and binding
- 3D worlds

For some of those there's special GroovyFX support that we'd like to point you to. Let's start with FXML.

11.7.1 *Application design with FXML*

Oracle offers a free tool called `SceneBuilder` as displayed in figure 11.14 that can be used to visually compose a JavaFX application. The result of the design process is stored in FXML.

From an application, you can read that file and get hold of the JavaFX node that's the root of all elements that you've created in `SceneBuilder`. GroovyFX has a very simple way to achieve this:

```
fxml resource("/SceneBuilderOutput.fxml")
```

As a special bonus comes the `resource()` method that finds the FXML file on the classpath. But having the root of all your components isn't the end of the story. You also need a way to refer to special components in the graph, let's say a button. There's an easy way to achieve this: inside `SceneBuilder` you assign an ID like `myButton` to that button (in some versions of the tool called CSS ID). In your GroovyFX code, you can then refer to that button as if you had assigned that ID in the code. So Groovy understands `myButton` as a direct reference to that button object!

From our experience we've come to the conclusion that the best way to use the visual builder is to have the general structure in FXML and use the visual builder to create and maintain it. All details should be under programmatic control, though. That means that the tool only creates layouts and containers with a fixed ID. What goes into the containers is then managed through code.

This leaves us with the question of how to bind data and logic to components.

Figure 11.14 `SceneBuilder` when creating the "Hello FX World" JavaFX application

11.7.2 *Properties and binding*

JavaFX makes Properties (the capitalization is on purpose) first-class citizens that are far more powerful than plain-old JavaBean properties. They're themselves objects with added capabilities. First and foremost, they're *observable*. Second, and as a direct consequence, they're *bindable*.

This is extremely powerful—much more than we first expected—but it comes at the expense of lots of additional boilerplate code when creating a class with JavaFX Properties in plain Java. But Groovy comes to the rescue with all its language sophistication.

Let's assume the greeting of our "Hello FX World" should come from a model. That model would have the greeting as a JavaFX property, like so:

```
import groovyx.javafx.beans.FXBindable
class GreetingModel {
    @FXBindable String hi = "Hello"
}
```

Then our application can create an instance of that model:

```
def model = new GreetingModel()
```

and the `SceneGraphBuilder` can bind the text node to the `hi` Property:

```
text bind(model.hi())
```

Note that we aren't setting the value of `hi`, we're binding the `hi` Property! The difference is that whenever the value of that Property changes the view will automatically update, without any `ValueChangeListeners` or other controllers being in the play.

Let's end with a few considerations about desktop applications that you build with `SwingBuilder` or `SceneGraphBuilder`.

11.7.3 *Groovy desktop applications*

No matter whether or not you have Swing or JavaFX as your toolkit for your desktop application, you'll profit from structuring your code properly. All toolkits support a separation of responsibilities in MVC but this still leaves important questions unanswered:

- May a view refer to other views?
- May controllers refer to views? To all or only to selected ones?
- Which code has to run in which thread? What if there are exceptions?

Independent of your UI toolkit of choice you have to find answers to these questions for any project of reasonable size and importance. For any such project you need more support than plain Groovy can provide and I (Dierk) suggest that you have a serious look at OpenDolphin (http://open-dolphin.org) as it leads to the highest degree of decoupling between views and between views and controllers, and provides an easy-to-use threading model.

OpenDolphin provides special support for Groovy and many interesting Open-Dolphin demos use GroovyFX for the views.

If you're looking for an MVC framework with event, lifecycle, and resource management; build automation; testing; packaging; and much more, then Griffon[9] should be on your list.

Having seen the merits of `NodeBuilder`, `MarkupBuilder`, `StreamingMarkup-Builder`, `AntBuilder`, `SwingBuilder`, and `SceneGraphBuilder`, it's reasonable to ask whether you can use that concept for your own kind of builder. You know the answer already, right? Of course you can—and of course Groovy makes it easy. The next section gives the details.

11.8 Creating your own builder

The built-in builders are very useful, but of course they aren't tailored for your specific needs. Given how frequently hierarchies are used within software development, it wouldn't be at all surprising to find that you had a domain-specific use for builders that isn't quite covered with `NodeBuilder` and its colleagues. Fortunately, Groovy makes it easy to build your own builder (which isn't as recursive as it sounds). Let's plunge ahead with an example.

Suppose you're creating an application that helps you keep track of dietary information about the food you're consuming. You're about to have lunch and being so enthralled by writing new Groovy examples, you haven't been getting as much exercise as you'd like. You'd like to know if you should be having that extra slice of pizza, but can you really tell if you haven't added up the calories, carbs, protein, and so forth. So, you'd like to have some help in tracking this sort of information. You'd like to enter something like this:

```
lunch.count {
  pizza(size: 'large') {
    crust('thin')
    topping('pepperoni')
    topping('veggies')
  }
  appetizer {
    wings(quantity: 2)
    'garlic-bread'()
  }
}
```

And let the computer give you the good (or bad) news about that extra slice!

We'll keep the example simple and only count calories. The nested structure allows you to track calorie information for whole meals if you know it or for individual

---

[9] Griffon is a desktop application development platform for the JVM. Inspired by Grails, Griffon leverages the use of the Groovy language and concepts like convention over configuration. See http://new.griffon-framework.org. Another source is *Griffon in Action* by Andres Almiray et al. (Manning Publications, 2012).

ingredients that might make up a meal. For simplicity we'll keep a map of ingredient-to-calorie values in an in-memory map. Obviously, you could extend the example to use a proper database and you might want to track more than calories.

There are three ways to go about writing a calorie builder in Groovy:

- Subclass `BuilderSupport`
- Subclass `FactoryBuilderSupport`
- Roll your own dynamic behavior

Let's examine each of these in turn.

11.8.1 Subclassing BuilderSupport

Many builders in the Groovy library subclass `groovy.util.BuilderSupport`. This class implements the general builder strategy features including the ability to *pretend* your builder methods, to recursively process any attached closures, to *relay* method calls in closures back to your builder, and call your builder's *template* methods.

For implementing you own builder, you subclass `BuilderSupport` and implement the template methods as listed in table 11.8. There is no need to do anything more.

Table 11.8 Template methods for builders

Info	Returns	Name	Parameters	Call triggered by
abstract	Object	createNode	Object name	foo()
abstract	Object	createNode	Object name, Object value	foo('x')
abstract	Object	createNode	Object name, Map attributes	foo(a:1)
abstract	Object	createNode	Object name, Map attributes, Object value	foo(a:1, 'x')
abstract	void	setParent	Object parent, Object child	createNode finished
empty	void	nodeCompleted	Object parent, Object node	recursive closure call finished

`BuilderSupport` follows this construction algorithm:

- When hitting a builder method, call the appropriate `createNode` method.
- Call `setParent` with the current parent and the node you've just created (unless it's a root node, because that has no parent).
- Process any attached closure. (This is where recursion happens.)
- Call `nodeCompleted` with the current parent and the created node (even if parent is `null`).

That means that a code fragment like

```
builder = new MyBuilder()
builder.foo() {
    bar(a:1)
}
```

will result in method calls similar to those shown in the following pseudocode (indentation indicates recursion depth):

```
builder = new MyBuilder()
foo = builder.createNode('foo')
// no setParent() call because we are a root node
    bar = builder.createNode('bar',[a:1])
    builder.setParent(foo, bar)
        // no closure to process for bar
    builder.nodeCompleted(foo, bar)
builder.nodeCompleted(null, foo)
```

Note that the foo and bar variables aren't used inside the *real* builder. They're used in this pseudocode only for illustrating identities.

In terms of the implementation, nodeCompleted isn't a template method in the strict meaning of the word because it's not declared abstract in BuilderSupport but has an empty default implementation. It's added to table 11.8 because most builders need to override it anyway.

Further methods of BuilderSupport are listed in table 11.9. See their API documentation for more details.

Table 11.9   More BuilderSupport methods

Returns	Name	Parameters	Use
Object	getCurrent		The node under construction; the *parent* when processing a closure
Object	getName	String methodName	Override to allow builder-specific name conversions; default obeys nameMappingClosure
void	setClosureDelegate	Closure closure, Object node	Override to allow mix of builders

The next section puts all this together in a complete example.

THE CALORIE BUILDER EXAMPLE

Let's create a first version of the calorie builder with the help of the BuilderSupport class as shown in the following listing. Our example will override the four createNode methods as well as the setParent and nodeCompleted methods.

Listing 11.17 Using `BuilderSupport` for calorie builder

```
class CalorieBuilder1 extends BuilderSupport {
  def calories = 0.0
  def name = 'root'
  def calorieDatabase = [
      crust    : [thin: 169, classic: 212, deepdish: 259, stuffed: 360],
      topping  : [pepperoni: 24, veggies: 10, cheese: 50],
      appetizer: [wings: 60, 'garlic-bread': 180]
  ]

  def createNode(name) {
    [name: name, calories: 0.0]
  }

  def createNode(name, value) {
    def result = createNode(name) + [value: value]
    findCalories(result, name, value)
    result
  }

  def createNode(name, Map attributes) {
    createNode(name) + [*: attributes]
  }

  def createNode(name, Map attributes, value) {
    createNode(name, value) + [*: attributes]
  }

  void setParent(parent, child) {
    if (child.size && parent.size && child.size != parent.size)
      throw new IllegalStateException("Conflicting sizes found")
    if (child.size) {
      child.scale = (child.size == 'large') ? 1.5 : 1.0
    }
  }

  void nodeCompleted(parentOrNull, node) {
    def parent = parentOrNull ?: this
    def qty = node.quantity ?: 1
    def scale = node.scale ?: 1.0
    findCalories(node, parent.name, node.name)
    parent.calories += node.calories * qty * scale
  }

  private void findCalories(Map map, name, value) {
    if (calorieDatabase.containsKey(name)) {
      map.calories = calorieDatabase[name][value].toInteger()
    }
  }

}

def lunch = new CalorieBuilder1()

lunch.count {
  pizza(size: 'large') {
    crust('thin')
    topping('pepperoni')
```

❶ Handles cases like crust('thin')

❷ Checks consistency between child and parent

❸ Handles cases like appetizer { wings() }

```
        topping('veggies')
    }
    appetizer {
      wings(quantity: 2)
      'garlic-bread'()
    }
}
```

```
assert lunch.calories == 604.5
```

The approach we'll use is to collect all the information we're given at any level in our builder tree within a map. This is done in the createNode methods. The attributes go straight into the map and the name and value also go in using name and value as the keys. We'll also try to populate calorie information if we can; for example, given crust('thin'), we can look for a "thin crust" item in our calorie database ❶ and, having found one, we can add [calories: 169] into our map.

Next up we have the setParent method. Here we could link our maps together if we wanted to, perhaps with parent and children keys in our maps. Such linking isn't required for something as simple as calorie counting, so instead we'll crosscheck sizes ❷ between parent and child nodes; if you tell us you're having a large pizza but with only a regular-sized crust, it sounds as if you might be cheating on your counting, so we'll flag that as an error. We'll also set up a scaling factor if we find a large-size item. This doesn't require access to both child and parent maps, and so could have been done in various other places, but it's convenient to set it here while processing size information.

Finally, we have the nodeCompleted method. At this point, we'll either be at a leaf node or a parent node. As an example leaf node, we might have completed the wings node in this fragment:

```
appetizer {
    wings()
}
```

and at this point we'll find the "wings appetizer" item in our calorie database ❸. We save the calories information in our map for the wings node but also bump up the parent appetizer calorie value. If we find ourselves completing an aggregate node like appetizer, then we won't find it in the calorie database, but the appetizer node will already have the correct calorie value because we can be sure that, by this point, all of its child nodes have been processed. So, we can bump up our parent's calorie value. When bumping the parent's calorie value, we multiply by any quantity or scaling factors for the current node.

There's also one special case. For the root node, the parent will have a null value. In that case, we treat the builder itself as if it were the parent and bump up its calorie value, which is the value our test will later check.

So we ended up having to do a bit of work, but by using BuilderSupport, we could make our changes in a very structured and consistent way. Much of the behind-the-scenes work was taken care of for us and we could focus on the logic of our application.

Suppose we now wish to beef up[10] our application's functionality. We might want to start tracking carbs, proteins, gluten-free status, and other information for our ingredients and meals. The first thing we might want to do is introduce a whole set of richer domain types. We can support such a change and keep our `BuilderSupport` approach, but more than likely we'll end up funneling creation of our nodes through one of the `createNode` methods and it would have an unwieldy mess of `if-then-else` or switch logic that created all of our types. Surely there's a better way? Enter the `FactoryBuilderSupport` class.

11.8.2 Subclassing FactoryBuilderSupport

This support class has similar goals to builder support but makes use of the Factory pattern to greatly simplify domain class construction. To use this approach, you must associate a factory with each node type that you want to support. The factory must implement the `Factory` interface that's described in table 11.10. A common trick is to override the `AbstractFactory` class and then just implement the required methods.

Table 11.10   Methods from `groovy.util.Factory`

Returns	Name	Parameters	Use
Object	newInstance, isHandlesNodeChildren(), onFactoryRegistration(), onNodeChildren()	FactoryBuilder-Support builder, Object name, Object value, Map properties	Responsible for creating the appropriate object for a given node
boolean	onHandleNodeAttributes()	FactoryBuilder-Support builder, Object node, Map attributes	Sets properties on the node
void	onNodeCompleted	FactoryBuilder-Support builder, Object parent, Object child	Responsible for any cleanup
void	setParent	FactoryBuilder-Support builder, Object parent, Object child	Responsible for establishing parent–child relationships
void	setChild	FactoryBuilder-Support builder, Object parent, Object child	May be useful to make adjustments to parent–child relationships
boolean	isLeaf		Prohibits any further nested method calls

---

[10] We'll try not to dine out too much on the food puns.

When creating our builder we extend the `FactoryBuilderSupport` class and before using the builder we must register all of our relevant factories. Let's see this in action in an example.

THE CALORIE BUILDER EXAMPLE

Let's create a second version of our calorie builder with the help of the `Factory-BuilderSupport` class as shown in listing 11.18. Our example will create just a single factory, the `CalorieBeanFactory`, which will be responsible for creating all of our domain classes. Its strategy for creating the classes will be simple. It will attempt to create a new instance using an uppercased version of the node name; so for instance, when finding the `pizza` node, we'll create an instance of the `Pizza` class. Let's see this altogether in the following listing.

Listing 11.18   Using `FactoryBuilderSupport` for calorie builder

```
class CalorieBuilder2 extends FactoryBuilderSupport {
  def calories = 0.0
  def factory = new CalorieBeanFactory(getClass().classLoader)

  protected void postInstantiate(name, Map attrs, node) {
    super.postInstantiate(name, attrs, node)
    attrs.each { k, v -> node[k] = v }
  }

  protected Factory resolveFactory(name, Map attrs, value) {
    return factory
  }

  void setParent(parent, child) {
    if (child.hasProperty("size")) {
      child.scale = child.size == 'large' ? 1.5 : 1.0
    }
  }

  void nodeCompleted(parentOrNull, node) {
    def parent = parentOrNull ?: this
    def qty = node.quantity ?: 1
    def scale = node.scale ?: 1.0
    parent.calories += node.calories * qty * scale
  }
}

class CalorieBeanFactory extends AbstractFactory {
  private ClassLoader loader

  CalorieBeanFactory(ClassLoader loader) {
    this.loader = loader
  }

  def newInstance(FactoryBuilderSupport fbs, name, value, Map attrs) {
    def className = name[0].toUpperCase() +
        name[1..-1].replaceAll(/-(.)/) { it[1].toUpperCase() }
    def clazz = loader.loadClass(className)
    return value ? clazz.newInstance(value: value) : clazz.newInstance()
  }
}
```

```
class Countable {
  int quantity
  def scale
  def calories = 0.0
}

class Count extends Countable {}

class Pizza extends Countable {
  def size
}

abstract class CountableGroup extends Countable {
  String value

  abstract getCalorieDB()

  def getCalories() { calorieDB[value] }
}

class Crust extends CountableGroup {
  def calorieDB = [thin: 169, classic: 212, deepdish: 259, stuffed: 360]
}

class Topping extends CountableGroup {
  def calorieDB = [pepperoni: 24, veggies: 10, cheese: 50]
}

class Appetizer extends Countable {}

class Wings extends Countable {
  def calories = 60
}

class GarlicBread extends Countable {
  def calories = 180
}

def lunch = new CalorieBuilder2()

lunch.count {
  pizza(size: 'large') {
    crust('thin')
    topping('pepperoni')
    topping('veggies')
  }
  appetizer {
    wings(quantity: 2)
    'garlic-bread'()
  }
}

assert lunch.calories == 604.5
```

Our calories database has been pushed down into the domain classes and we've used a few intermediate parent classes to reduce some duplication. There are only a few lines of business logic within the nodeCompleted method of our builder.

For our application, having rich domain classes might add more complexity to the solution than we need but it's easy to see how extensible this approach can be.

11.8.3 *Rolling your own*

The final approach we have available to use is to go directly to Groovy's low-level method interception hooks. This provides us with the ultimate flexibility but may require a fair bit of work. Depending on your scenario, though, it might be the best approach.

THE CALORIE BUILDER EXAMPLE

Let's create a third version of our calorie builder as shown in the following listing.

Listing 11.19 By-hand calorie builder

```
class CalorieBuilder3 {
  def calorieDatabase = [
      crust    : [thin: 169, classic: 212, deepdish: 259, stuffed: 360],
      topping  : [pepperoni: 24, veggies: 10, cheese: 50],
      appetizer: [wings: 60, 'garlic-bread': 180]
  ]
  def parent = new Stack()
  def getCalories() { parent.peek().calories }

  CalorieBuilder3() {
    parent.push([calories:0.0])
  }

  def invokeMethod(String methodName, args) {
    def current = [name: methodName, calories:0.0]
    if (args && args[0] instanceof Map) {
      current << args[0]
    }
    countCalories(current, parent.peek().name, methodName)
    if (args && args[0] instanceof String) {
      countCalories(current, methodName, args[0])
    }
    if (args && args.size() > 1 && args[1] instanceof String) {
      countCalories(current, methodName, args[1])
    }
    current.scale = current.size == 'large' ? 1.5 : 1.0

    if (args && args[-1] instanceof Closure) {
      parent.push(current)
      Closure nested = args[-1]
      nested.delegate = this
      nested.call()
      parent.pop()
    }
    def qty = current.quantity ?: 1
    def scale = current.scale ?: 1.0
    parent.peek().calories += current.calories * qty * scale
  }

  private void countCalories(Map current, String key, String value) {
    if (calorieDatabase.containsKey(key)) {
      current.calories = calorieDatabase[key][value].toInteger()
    }
  }
}
```

```
def lunch = new CalorieBuilder3()

lunch.count {
  pizza(size: 'large') {
    crust('thin')
    topping('pepperoni')
    topping('veggies')
  }
  appetizer {
    wings(quantity: 2)
    'garlic-bread'()
  }
}

assert lunch.calories == 604.5
```

In this version, we intercept all method calls using the standard `invokeMethod` hook. We look up the names of the methods that are called in our calorie database and store away any calorie values if they were found. For aggregate nodes we dive down and process child nodes setting the appropriate delegates for the nested closures as we go. Upon returning we add up the calorie values found for our child nodes. We again use a `Map` to store relevant information and to handle nesting we use a stack to keep track of the current `Map` to store information in. It turns out not to be too difficult for this simple example but, in general, this approach can quickly become unwieldy if the number of types of nodes that need to be supported grows large.

That wraps up our roll your own version of the calorie builder. You can see that you have quite a few options for creating builders, each with its own strengths and weaknesses.

That's all there is to implementing your own builder. We hope we've convinced you about the simplicity of that task. At least, the core steps of making your code working as a builder are simple. It goes without saying that any specific builder can still be as complex as any piece of code.

11.9   Summary

The way that Groovy works with builders and the simplicity that it brings to defining your own ones is one of Groovy's genuine contributions to the open source community. In fact, it's so appealing that other well-established languages copied the concept. This is fair enough, because Groovy has adopted so many great features from other languages as well.

What makes builders special is their *descriptive* nature while still being ordinary executable code. Together with Groovy's feature of executing code dynamically, this combination comes close to the ambition of LISP: working as an *executable specification*.

Builders can be seen as a way of implementing DSLs. You've seen many domains in this chapter, from runtime structures (`NodeBuilder`) through text structures (`MarkupBuilder` and friends), task automation (`AntBuilder`) and desktop UIs (`SwingBuilder` and `SceneGraphBuilder`), to ones we've only just dreamed up—our calorie-counting builders. These are distinct domains, and making them easy to work with is the job of a DSL. Chapter 19 covers the whole range of Groovy features that make it our first choice for implementing DSLs.

With DSLs it should be possible to express domain facts in a way that's more flexible, powerful, and easier to read than XML but not as demanding as full-blown programming languages. Groovy builders are an ideal vehicle to achieve this. We look forward to seeing which domains will have Groovy builders created for them. How about a workflow engine, for example? Animation? A new way of considering threading, built from parallel pieces of logic? Who knows—perhaps you'll be the one to bring the next big thing to Groovy. Whatever domain you may choose to tackle, Groovy's support for builders is likely to be able to help you.

Now that we've examined builders, it's time to revisit a topic we've frequently mentioned in passing: the GDK, or Groovy's way of extending the JDK.

Working with the GDK

12

This chapter covers

- How Groovy extends the JVM
- GDK extensions
- Working with objects

> *Einstein argued that there must be simplified explanations of nature, because*
> *God is not capricious or arbitrary. No such faith comforts the software engineer.*
>
> —Fred Brooks

Learning a new programming language is a twofold task: learning the syntax and learning the standard library. Learning the syntax is a matter of days and getting proficient with new language idioms may require a few weeks, but working through a new library can easily take several months.

Luckily, no Java programmer needs to go through this time-consuming activity when learning Groovy. They already know most of the Groovy Standard Library, because that's the set of APIs that the Java Runtime provides. You can work with Groovy by solely using objects and methods as provided by the Java platform, although this approach doesn't fully leverage the power of Groovy.

Groovy extends this foundation by providing an extension to the core Java classes, called the GDK. The GDK includes some new classes and utility libraries, but for the most part, it seamlessly integrates with existing core Java classes like `String`, `Numbers`, `Collections`, and `Object`, offering a superset of functionality for each class. Groovy does this in a way that's normally not possible for Java applications. Figure 12.1 provides an architectural overview.

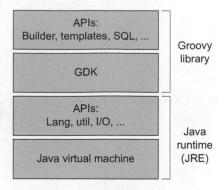

Figure 12.1   GDK's place in the Groovy architecture

This chapter will give you an overview of how Groovy extends the JVM, what functionality is provided, and how to use these extensions to increase your productivity. You'll find that the GDK extensions make Groovy more convenient to work with, make scripting easier, provide new dynamic features, offer a more consistent way of handling objects, and adapt the Java APIs to the Groovy language idioms.

Let's start with `Object`, the most general and most important class in the JDK, and see how Groovy further extends the GDK with features for exploration and control.

12.1   Working with objects

Java comes with a narrow API of 11 methods for its central abstraction `java.lang.Object`. These methods deal with the object lifecycle (`clone`, `finalize`), object equality (`equals`, `hashCode`), information (`toString`), self-reflection (`getClass`), and multithreading support (`notify`, `notifyAll`, three versions of `wait`).

Groovy adds much to the self-reflective and informational aspects of the API to better support live exploration of objects. It handles identity/equality differently and therefore needs to extend the respective API. It adds convenience methods to `Object` for the purpose of making these methods available anywhere in the code. It also adds collection-aware methods to `Object` that are useful when the object can be seen as some kind of collection even though it's not necessarily of static type `java.util.Collection`. This last category also includes the handling of object arrays.

We'll go through these categories one by one, starting with self-reflective and informational methods.

12.1.1   Interactive objects

When working on a program, you often need to inspect your objects, whether for debugging, logging, or tracing purposes. In dynamic languages such as Groovy, this need is even greater, because you may work with your programming language in an interactive fashion, asking your objects about their state and capabilities to subsequently send them messages.

OBJECT INFORMATION IN STRINGS

Often, the first task is to ask an object for some general information about itself: toString() in Java parlance. Groovy adds two more methods of this kind:

- dump returns a description of the object's state, namely its fields and their values.
- inspect makes a best effort to return the object as it could appear in Groovy source code, with lists and maps in the format of their literal declaration. If it cannot do better, it falls back to toString.

You can call these methods on a string that contains a single newline character as shown in the following listing.[1]

Listing 12.1 Using dump and inspect

```
def newline = "\n"

assert newline.toString() == "\n"

assert newline.dump() ==
'''<java.lang.String@a value=
 hash=10 hash32=0>'''

assert newline.inspect() == /'\n'/
```

Note how inspect returns a string that's equivalent to newline's literal declaration: the characters backslash and n are enclosed in double quotes (four characters total), whereas toString returns only the newline character (one character). The dump of a string object may yield different results in other JVMs.

If these methods aren't sufficient when working with Groovy interactively, remember that you can fire up the graphical ObjectBrowser via

```
groovy.inspect.swingui.ObjectBrowser.inspect(obj)
```

You've seen the dump method reveal the object's fields and their values. The same and more can be done with the object's properties.

ACCESSING PROPERTIES

Remember that any Groovy object can be seen as a JavaBean, as you saw in section 7.4. You've already seen that its properties can be inspected with the getProperties method or the properties property. The getProperties method returns a read-only map of property names and their current values. During inspection, printing the whole map of properties is as easy as

```
println properties
```

or

```
println someObj.properties
```

---

[1] The exact information returned by dump differs slightly between JDK versions.

When doing so, you may see more properties than you expected, because Groovy's class-generation mechanism introduces accessors for that object's `class` and `Meta-Class` properties behind the scenes.

Listing 12.2 shows property reflection in use. The example uses a class with a `first` property and a `second` read-only property that returns a derived value and isn't backed by a field. We also define a public field, `third`, without accessor methods. The listing shows how to list all keys of that object's properties.

Of course, you can ask the map of properties for the value of a property either with the subscript operator or with the dot-propertyname syntax. This last option looks exactly the same as directly asking the object for the value of a property if its name is known at coding time. This raises the question of whether you can ask an object directly for a property value if its name is only known at runtime and resides in a variable. Listing 12.2 shows that you can do so by using the subscript operator directly on the object without the need for redirection over the `properties` map.

Because we know that the subscript operator is implemented via the `getAt` method, it would be surprising if the `putAt` method for subscript-assignment weren't implemented in the same manner. Again, the following listing shows that this works and allows us to assign a value to a property the name of which is derived dynamically.

Listing 12.2   Reflecting on properties

```
class MyClass {
    def first = 1                // read-write property
    def getSecond() { first * 2 }    // read-only property
    public third = 3             // public field
    def myMethod() { }           // public method
}
def obj = new MyClass()

assert obj.hasProperty('first')          ① Property check
assert obj.respondsTo('myMethod')        ② Method check

def keys = ['first', 'second', 'class']
assert obj.properties.keySet() == new HashSet(keys)

assert 1 == obj.properties['first']      ③ Properties map
assert 1 == obj.properties.first

assert 1 == obj.first                    ④ Direct access
assert 1 == obj['first']    // getAt('first')

def one = 'first'
def two = 'second'
obj[one] = obj[two]         // putAt(one)     ⑤ Dynamic assignment
assert obj.dump() =~ 'first=2'           ⑥ Field introspection
```

Using the `hasProperty` ① and `respondsTo` ② methods you can check if the object has the specified property or method, respectively. This works for public as well as for private fields and methods.

At ❸ and ❹, you see that objects implement the getAt and putAt methods by default, such that the code appears to be accessing a map of properties as far as the subscript operator is concerned.

The code at ❺ shows a simple way of introspecting an object via the dump method. Because the first property is backed by a field of the same name, this field and its current value appear in the dump. Note that this field is private and wouldn't be visible otherwise. This trick is useful, especially in test cases.

> **NOTE** When working with Groovy code, you may also come across Object's method getMetaPropertyValues. It's used internally with an object's meta-information and returns a list of PropertyValue objects that encapsulate the *name, type,* and *value* of a property.

Working with properties means working on a higher level of abstraction than working with methods or even fields directly. We'll now take one step down and look at dynamic method invocation.

12.1.2 *Convenient Object methods*

How often have you typed System.out.println when programming Java? In Groovy, you can achieve the same result with println, which is an abbreviation for this.println; and because the GDK makes println available on Object, you can use this anywhere in the code. This is what we call a *convenience method*.

This section walks through the available convenience methods and their uses, as listed in table 12.1.

Table 12.1 Object **convenience methods**

Introduced Object method	Meaning
addShutdownHook {closure}	Add a shutdown hook via the Runtime; see the Neo4J listings in chapter 13 for an example
is(other)	Compare Object identities (references)
isCase(caseValue, switchValue)	Default implementation: equality
print(), print(value), println(), println(value)	System.out.print…
printf(formatStr, value) printf(formatStr, value[])	Java 5 System.out.printf()
sprintf(formatStr, value) sprintf(formatStr, value[])	Java 5 String.format(), which returns a formatted String
sleep(millis) sleep(millis) {onInterrupt}	static Thread.currentThread(). sleep(millis)
use(categoryClass) {closure} use(categoryClassList) {closure}	Use metamethods as defined in categoryClass for the scope of the closure

Table 12.1 `Object` **convenience methods** *(continued)*

Introduced `Object` method	Meaning
`with {closure}`	Any method invoked inside the closure will first be invoked on the self-reference; more formally the `Closure` delegate is the self-reference; there's also an alias for with: `identity`.

Let's go through the methods.

Because Groovy uses the `==` operator for equality instead of identity checking, you need a replacement for the Java meaning of `==`. That's what the `is` method provides. In Java:

```
if ( a == b ) { /* more code here */}
```

In Groovy:

```
if ( a.is(b)) { /* more code here */}
```

The `is` method saves you the work of comparing the `System.identityHashCode(obj)` of a and b manually.

The `isCase` method occurred often in the Groovy language description in part 1. For `Object`, the GDK provides a default implementation that checks for object equality. Note that this means you can use any (Java) object in a Groovy `grep` or `switch`:

```
switch(new Date(0)){
    case new Date(0) : println 'dates are equal'
}
```

The `identity` or `with` method, which are synonyms, calls the attached closure with the receiver object as the closure's delegate. Use it when a piece of code deals primarily with only one object, like the following:

```
new Date().identity {
    println "$date.$month.$year"
}
```

The properties `date`, `month`, and `year` will now be resolved against the current date. The same can be done with the `with` method, which can be used to simplify object creation:

```
def address = new Address()
address.with {
    streetName = 'Mainstreet'
    houseNumber = '42'
}
```

For this simple example, Groovy's named argument constructor syntax would have worked even more simply, but you might need `try-catch` blocks or other more complicated logic when setting the properties.

The versions of print and println print to System.out by default, whereas println emits an additional line feed. Of course, you can still call these methods on any kind of PrintStream or PrintWriter to send your output in other directions.

The same is true for the printf method. It's based on Java's formatted print support, which has been available since Java 5 and works only if you run Groovy under Java 5 or higher. A RuntimeException is thrown otherwise. In terms of supported formatting features, we cannot present the full list here. Have a look at the Javadoc for class java.util.Formatter. The full description covers about 1,800 lines.

In Groovy, printf isn't as crucial as in other languages, because GStrings already provide excellent support at the language level and the String datatype provides the most common features of left and right padding and centering text. But there are times when formatted output is more convenient to achieve with a *format* string, especially when the user should be able to configure the output format to their preferences. The line

```
printf('PI=%2.5f and E=%2.5f', Math.PI, Math.E)
```

prints

```
PI=3.14159 and E=2.71828
```

Note that we've used printf with three arguments, but because a format string may contain an arbitrary number of placeholders, printf supports an argument list of arbitrary length. It goes without saying that the number of additional arguments must match the number of placeholders in the format string, unless you explicitly specify the argument number to use in the format string. You can also provide a single argument of type list—for example, [Math.PI, Math.E].

When working through the Formatter API documentation, you'll notice some advanced topics around printf:

- Conversions apply when a placeholder and the corresponding argument are of different types.
- Placeholders can be prefixed with n$ to map the placeholder to the *n*th argument in the list. This may get you in conflict with the GString meaning of $. Therefore, it's wise to use only single-quoted string literals as printf format strings.

The sprintf method works similar to the printf method, with the difference that instead of printing to System.out, this method will return the formatted String instead. This method is identical to the String.format method.

The use method allows you to use a list of categories to extend the functionality provided in classes. This is done by creating a category, and using that category in the use method. Any method not found in the object the method is used on will be searched for in the applied category. For example:

```
class StringCasingCategory {
  static String lower(String string) {
    return string.toLowerCase()
```

```
    }
}
use(StringCasingCategory) {
  assert "groovy" == "GroOvy".lower()
}
```

The last convenience method in our list is `sleep`, which suspends the current thread for a given number of milliseconds. It enhances the JDK method `Thread.sleep` by automatically handling interruptions such that sleep is called again until the given time has elapsed (as closely as the machine timer can tell). This makes the effective sleep time more predictable.

If you want to handle interruptions differently, you can attach a closure that's called when `sleep` encounters an `InterruptedException`.

With the `sleep` method, you can have fun, as with the following example. Run it from the Groovy shell or command-line console after predicting its output. Did you guess correctly what it does?

```
text = """
This text appears
slowly on the screen
as if someone was
typing it.
"""
for (c in text) {
    sleep 100
    print c
}
```

These are all methods that the GDK adds to every object for convenience. But objects frequently come in a crowd. For such cases, the GDK provides methods to select them one-by-one, as shown in the next section.

12.1.3 *Iterative Object methods*

In the Java world, any *collection* (in the general meaning of the word) of objects can support inspection of its contained items by providing an `Iterator`, a separate object that knows how to walk through that collection. Oh, wait—sometimes an `Enumeration` is used instead. As a further inconsistency, `Iterators` aren't directly available on arrays and a lot of other common types.

With the introduction of Java 5, the `Iterable<T>` interface was created so that the object can be used in the `for-each` statement, which makes iterations in Java a bit easier. For example:

```
for (MyClass obj : collection ){
    // do something with obj
}
```

While Groovy supports the preceding syntax, Groovy provides a simpler and more consistent way of doing this:

```
collection.each { /* do something with it */}
```

Besides the simple `each` method, you can use any of the iterative methods that are listed in table 12.2.

Table 12.2 Iterative `Object` methods

Return value	Method
boolean	any {closure}
Collection	List collect {closure}
Object	each {closure}
Object	eachWithIndex {closure}
boolean	every {closure}
Object	find {closure}
Collection	findAll {closure}
int	findIndexOf {closure}
List	findIndexValues {closure}
int	findLastIndexOf {closure}
Object	findResult
List	grep(Object filter)
Object	inject {closure}
Collection	split {closure}

What's so useful about the methods in table 12.2 is that you can use them on *any* object you fancy. The GDK makes these methods available on `Object` and yields the respective items. As we described in section 6.3.2, this iteration strategy is also used in Groovy's `for` loop.

Getting the items is done with a best-effort strategy for the candidate types in table 12.3, where the first matching possibility is chosen.

Table 12.3 Priority of `Object`'s iteration strategy

No.	Candidate	Use with
1.	java.util.Iterator	Itself
2.	org.w3c.dom.NodeList	Iterator over Nodes
3.	java.util.Enumeration	Convert to iterator
4.	java.util.regex.Matcher	Iterator over matches
5.	java.lang.Iterable	Iterable.iterator()
6.	Responds to iterator method	Call it

Table 12.3   Priority of `Object`'s iteration strategy (*continued*)

No.	Candidate	Use with
7.	Collectable	`Collection.iterator()`
8.	`java.util.Map`	Iterator over `Map.Entry` objects
9.	Array	Iterator over array items
10.	`MethodClosure`	Iterator over calls
11.	`java.lang.String`	Iterator over characters
12.	`java.io.File`	Iterator over lines
13.	`null`	Empty iterator
13.	Otherwise	Iterator that only contains the candidate

This allows for flexible uses of Groovy's iteration-aware methods. There's no need to care whether you work with an iterator, an enumeration, a collection, or whatever, for example, within a GPath expression.

The possible candidates in table 12.3 are fairly straightforward, but some background information certainly helps:

- *Candidate 2*—A `NodeList` is used with a document object model (DOM). Such a DOM can be constructed from, for example, XML or HTML documents. We'll revisit this topic in chapter 14.
- *Candidate 6*—A candidate object may provide its `Iterator` with the `iterator` method. Instead of a single static interface, the availability of the `iterator` method is used in the sense of duck-typing. An example is `groovy.util.Node`.
- *Candidate 7*—A candidate object is *collectable* if it can be coerced into an object of type `java.util.Collection`.
- *Candidate 10*—This is an unconventional way of providing an `Iterator`, but it's interesting because it puts our Groovy knowledge to the test.

Suppose you have a method that takes a closure as a parameter and calls the closure back with a single argument, multiple times, using a different argument each time. This could be seen as successively passing arguments to a closure. *Successively passing arguments* is exactly what an `Iterator` does. To make this method work as an iterator, refer to it as a `MethodClosure`, as described in section 5.3.3.

As an example, imagine calculating $sin(x)$ for sample domain values of x between 0 and 2π. A `domain` method can feed an arbitrary `yield` closure with these x samples:

```
samples = 4
def domain(yield) {
    step = Math.PI * 2 / samples
    (0..samples).each { yield it*step }
}
```

Printing the *x* values would be as simple as invoking

```
domain { println it}
```

As the `domain` method successively passes objects to the given closure, it can be used with the object-iteration methods such as with `collect` to get a list of sine values for all samples from the domain. Use a reference to the `domain` method: `this.&domain`, which makes it a `MethodClosure`:

```
this.&domain.collect { Math.sin(it) }
```

Using a `MethodClosure` as an `Iterator` doesn't seem to provide much advantage other than reusing a method that possibly already exists. Our `domain` method could have returned a list of *x* values. Things would have been easier to understand that way. There also isn't a performance or memory consumption gain, because this list is constructed behind the scenes anyway when converting the closure.

But it may be handy when the method does more than our simple example. For statistical purposes it could produce side-effects. It could get data from a live data feed or some expensive resource with an elaborate caching strategy. Because references to `MethodClosures` can be held in variables, you could change this strategy at runtime (Strategy pattern).[2]

Those were the GDK methods for `Object`. There are more methods in the GDK for arrays of objects. They make arrays usable as lists such that Groovy programmers can use them interchangeably. These methods were described in section 4.2.

Not surprisingly, GDK's `Object` methods are about all-purpose functionality such as revealing information about an object's state and dynamically accessing properties and invoking methods. Iterating over objects can be done regardless of each object's behavior.

The next sections will cover GDK methods for more specialized but frequently used JDK classes used for I/O, such as `File`.

12.2 Working with files and I/O

Many scripts (and perhaps most large applications) make heavy use of files and other sources of data from remote systems. The JDK addresses this need with its `java.io` and `java.net` packages. It provides elaborate support with the `File` and `URL` classes and numerous versions of streams, readers, and writers. Since Java 7, there is also a `java.nio.file` package which provides more advanced access to files, file attributes, and filesystems. We won't discuss that package here, but Groovy extends those classes too. See table C.9 for more details.

But the programmer is left with the repetitive, tedious, and error-prone task of managing I/O resources, such as properly closing an opened file even if exceptions occur while processing.

---

[2] Gamma et al., *Design Patterns* (Addison-Wesley, 1995).

This is where the GDK steps in and provides numerous methods that let you focus on the task at hand rather than thinking about I/O boilerplate code. This results in faster development, better readability of your code, and more stable solutions, because resource leaks are less likely with centralized error-handling. Having read chapter 5, you may correctly surmise that this is a job for closures.

In table 12.3, you saw that `File` objects work with `Object`'s iteration methods. The next listing uses this approach to print itself to the console: the output is exactly what you see. Assertions are used to show the use of `any`, `findAll`, and `grep`. Note that `file.grep{it}` returns only nonempty lines, because empty strings evaluate to `false`.

Listing 12.3 File's object iteration method examples

```
file = new File('Listing_12_03_File_Iteration.groovy')
file.each { println it }
assert file.any { it =~ /File/ }
assert 3 == file.findAll { it =~ /File/ }.size()

assert 5 == file.grep { it }.size()
```

Additionally, the GDK defines many methods with overloaded variants for `File`, `URL`, `Reader`, `Writer`, `InputStream`, `OutputStream`, and others. Table 12.4 lists just the `File` methods added by the GDK. The full list of all methods is in appendix C. We'll present explanations and examples for some of the main variants of these methods. The use of the remaining methods/variants is analogous.

Obviously, some of the methods in table 12.4 are concerned with reading, others with writing; we'll explain them separately. There are also methods that are specifically concerned with conversions. Their method names start with `transform` or `new`. We'll illustrate their use in a separate section. Finally, we'll cover the serialization support provided.

The `eachDir`, `eachDirMatch`, `eachDirRecurse`, and `eachFile` methods stand out as dealing with aspects of the filesystem rather than I/O operations. We'll cover them first, followed by the `traverse` method, which provides the same functionality as the methods mentioned before, but provides a much more flexible way of handling files and directories. We'll dive into the `traverse` method after handling the other four methods.

12.2.1 *Traversing the filesystem*

Groovy follows the Java approach of using the `File` class for both files and directories, where a `File` object represents a location (not *content*, contrary to a common misconception).

Using a `File` object from Groovy often includes calling its JDK methods in a property-style manner. To display information about the current directory, you can use

```
file = new File('.')
println file.name
println file.absolutePath
println file.canonicalPath
println file.directory
```

Table 12.4   GDK methods for `java.io.File`

`append(InputStream)`	`eachLine(int, Closure)`	`renameTo(String)`
`append(Object, String)`	`eachObject(Closure)`	`setBytes(byte[])`
`append(Writer, String)`	`filterLine(Writer,`	`setText(String)`
`append(Reader, String)`	`    Closure)`	`setText(String, String)`
`append(Object)`	`filterLine(String,`	`size()`
`append(Reader)`	`    Closure)`	`splitEachLine(String,`
`append(Writer)`	`filterLine(Closure)`	`    String, Closure)`
`append(byte[])`	`filterLine(Writer, String,`	`splitEachLine(String,`
`asType(Class)`	`    Closure)`	`    Closure)`
`asWritable()`	`getBytes()`	`splitEachLine(Pattern,`
`asWritable(String)`	`getText(String)`	`    Closure)`
`static createTempDir(`	`getText()`	`splitEachLine(Pattern,`
`    String, String)`	`leftShift(Object)`	`    String, Closure)`
`static createTempDir()`	`leftShift(byte[])`	`traverse(Closure)`
`deleteDir()`	`leftShift(InputStream)`	`traverse(Map)`
`directorySize()`	`newDataInputStream()`	`traverse(Map, Closure)`
`eachByte(int, Closure)`	`newDataOutputStream()`	`withDataInputStream(`
`eachByte(Closure)`	`newInputStream()`	`    Closure)`
`eachDir(Closure)`	`newObjectInputStream()`	`withDataOutputStream(`
`eachDirMatch(Object,`	`newObjectInputStream(`	`    Closure)`
`    Closure)`	`    ClassLoader)`	`withInputStream(Closure)`
`eachDirRecurse(Closure)`	`newObjectOutputStream()`	`withObjectInputStream(`
`eachFile(Closure)`	`newOutputStream()`	`    Closure)`
`eachFile(FileType, Closure)`	`newPrintWriter(String)`	`withObjectInputStream(`
`eachFileMatch(Object,`	`newPrintWriter()`	`    ClassLoader, Closure)`
`    Closure)`	`newReader(String)`	`withObjectOutputStream(`
`eachFileMatch(FileType,`	`newReader()`	`    Closure)`
`    Object, Closure)`	`newWriter(boolean)`	`withOutputStream(Closure)`
`eachFileRecurse(Closure)`	`newWriter(String, boolean)`	`withPrintWriter(Closure)`
`eachFileRecurseFileType(`	`newWriter()`	`withPrintWriter(String,`
`    Closure)`	`newWriter(String)`	`    Closure)`
`eachLine(String, Closure)`	`readBytes()`	`withReader(Closure)`
`eachLine(Closure)`	`readLines(String)`	`withReader(String,`
`eachLine(String, int,`	`readLines()`	`    Closure)`
`    Closure)`		`withWriter(Closure)`
		`withWriter(String,`
		`    Closure)`
		`withWriterAppend(String,`
		`    Closure)`
		`withWriterAppend(Closure)`
		`write(String, String)`
		`write(String)`

Listing 12.4 shows this in conjunction with the GDK methods `eachDir`, `eachDir-Match`, `eachDirRecurse`, `eachFile`, `eachFileMatch`, and `eachFileRecurse`. They all work with a closure that gets a `File` object passed into it, disregarding the filesystem entries that represent the current and parent directories (".” and “..”). While `each-File` yields `File` objects that may represent files or directories, `eachDir` yields only the latter.

Filtering can be achieved with `eachFileMatch`, which applies the `isCase` method of its filter argument on each filename. As the name suggests, `eachFileRecurse` runs recursively through all subdirectories.

In listing 12.4, we investigate a directory tree. The source listings for this chapter are in a single flat directory, so it's not very interesting to traverse. Instead we'll look at chapter 9. In addition to numerous top-level files, it contains a mini-Gradle build structure as shown here:

```
chap09
│   build.gradle
│   Listing_09_01_ToStringDetective.groovy
│   // other top level files not shown
│
├──.gradle
│   └──// contents not shown
│
├──build
│   └──// contents not shown
│
├──gradle
│   └──wrapper
│          // contents not shown
│
└──src
    ├──main
    │   ├──groovy
    │   │   └──regina
    │   │          CompiledAtASTTransformation.groovy
    │   │
    │   └──resources
    │       └──META-INF
    │           └──services
    │                  org.codehaus.groovy.transform.ASTTransformation
    │
    └──test
        └──groovy
            └──regina
                   CompiledAtASTTransformationTest.groovy
```

Let's now use the additional GDK `File` methods to record and count files and directories underneath our top-level directory as shown in the following listing.

Listing 12.4   `File` methods for traversing the filesystem

```
import static groovy.io.FileType.DIRECTORIES
import static groovy.io.FileType.FILES

def topDir = new File('../chap09')
def srcDir = new File(topDir, 'src')

dirs = []                                          ⟵┐ Closure recording
srcDir.eachDir { dirs << it.name }                 ⟵┘ directory names
assert  ['main', 'test'] == dirs

dirs = []                                          ⟵┐ Recursively records
topDir.eachDirRecurse { dirs << it.name }          ⟵┘ directory names
assert dirs.containsAll(['gradle', 'src', 'main'])
assert dirs.containsAll(['groovy', 'services', 'wrapper'])
```

```
dirs = []
topDir.eachDirMatch(~/[^l]*/) { dirs << it.name }
assert dirs == ['src']
```
◁─┤ **Records directory names matching a pattern (.gradle is excluded here)**

```
files = []
topDir.eachFile { files << it.name }
assert files.contains('Listing_09_01_ToStringDetective.groovy')
assert files.contains('src')
```
◁─┤ **Records filenames and directory names**

```
files = []
topDir.eachFile(FILES) { files << it.name }
assert files.contains('Listing_09_01_ToStringDetective.groovy')
```
◁─┤ **Records filenames**

```
count = 0
srcDir.eachFileRecurse { if (it.directory) count++ }
assert 9 == count
```
◁─┤ **Counts directory names recursively**

```
count = 0
srcDir.eachFileRecurse(DIRECTORIES) { count++ }
assert 9 == count
```
◁─┤ **Counts directory names recursively, alternative solution**

```
files = []
topDir.eachFileMatch(~/Listing_09_01.*/) { files << it.name }
assert ['Listing_09_01_ToStringDetective.groovy'] == files
```
◁─┤ **Records filenames and directory names matching a pattern**

Inside the preceding closures, we get access to a reference of type File. We'll further explore what we can do with such a reference.

Alternatively, it's also possible to use the traverse method on File. The traverse method is an adaptable method providing many options to traverse a filesystem. Table 12.5 describes the traverse options.

Table 12.5   traverse options

Option	Description
type	An enum of type FileType to determine if normal files, directories, or both are processed.
preDir	A closure run before each directory is processed and optionally returning a FileVisitResult[a] that can be used to control subsequent processing.
preRoot	A boolean indicating that the preDir closure should be applied at the root level.
postDir	A closure run after each directory is processed and optionally returning a FileVisitResult that can be used to control subsequent processing.
postRoot	A boolean indicating that the postDir closure should be applied at the root level.
visitRoot	A boolean indicating that the given closure should be applied for the root directory (not applicable if type is set to FileType#FILES).

Table 12.5   traverse options *(continued)*

Option	Description
maxDepth	The maximum number of directory levels when recursing (default is –1, which means infinite, set to 0 for no recursion).
filter	A filter to perform on traversed files/directories (using the `DefaultGroovyMethods#isCase` method). If set, only files/directories that match are candidates for visiting.
nameFilter	A filter to perform on the name of traversed files/directories (using the `DefaultGroovyMethods#isCase` method). If set, only files/directories that match are candidates for visiting (must not be set if `filter` is set).
excludeFilter	A filter to perform on the name of traversed files/directories (using the `DefaultGroovyMethods#isCase` method). If set, only files/directories that match are candidates for visiting (must not be set if `filter` is set).
excludeNameFilter	A filter to perform on the names of traversed files/directories (using the `DefaultGroovyMethods#isCase` method). If set, any candidates that match won't be visited (must not be set if `excludeFilter` is set).
sort	A closure that if set causes the files and subdirectories for each directory to be processed in sorted order. Note that even when processing only files, the order of visited subdirectories will be affected by this parameter.

a. CONTINUE, SKIP_SIBLINGS, SKIP_SUBTREE, or TERMINATE.

An example of the `traverse` method based on the file structure listed before can be seen in the following listing.

Listing 12.5   File methods for traversing the filesystem

```
import static groovy.io.FileType.ANY
import static groovy.io.FileVisitResult.SKIP_SUBTREE

def totalSize = 0
def count = 0
def sortByTypeThenName = { a, b ->
  a.isFile() != b.isFile() ?
      a.isFile() <=> b.isFile() :
      a.name <=> b.name
}
def log = []

inputDir = new File('../chap09/')

inputDir.traverse(
    type             : ANY,
    nameFilter       : ~/.*groovy.*/,
    excludeNameFilter : ~/.*Test.*/,
```

```
    preDir        : {
      if (it.name =~ '.?gradle|build') return SKIP_SUBTREE
      count = 0
      totalSize = 0
    },
    postDir       : {
      if (count) {
        log << "Found $count files in $it.name : $totalSize bytes"
        count = 0
        totalSize = 0
      }
    },
    postRoot      : true,
    sort          : sortByTypeThenName
) {it -> totalSize += it.size(); count++ }
println log.join('\n')
assert log.size() == 3
assert log*.replaceAll(/\d+/, '*').join('\n') == '''
Found * files in regina : * bytes
Found * files in services : * bytes
Found * files in chap* : * bytes
'''.trim()
```

Here, we again choose to explore the chapter 9 directory structure. That directory is traversed using the `traverse` method that's supplied with an options map. The options indicate that any file or directory will be matched. Only Groovy files will be matched, but any test classes will be excluded, and so will some Gradle-related directories. Any items found will be counted, and their file size will be summed per directory. The sorting here doesn't have any effect on totals or counts, but might be handy when processing files in a certain order, say by date, might be required. After printing the result to standard output, we assert that the result satisfies an expected value that has digits replaced by a star to avoid slight differences in file sizes across various machines.

12.2.2 *Reading from input sources*

Suppose we have a file example.txt in the data directory below our current one. It contains

```
line one
line two
line three
```

One of the most common operations with such small text files is to read them at once into a single string. Doing so and printing the contents to the console is as easy as calling the file's `text` property (similar to the `getText` method):

```
println new File('data/example.txt').text
```

What's particularly nice about the `text` property is that it's available not only on `File`, but also on `Reader`, `InputStream`, and even `URL`. Where applicable, you can pass a `Charset` to the `getText` method. See the API documentation of `java.nio.charset` `.Charset` for details of how to obtain a reference to a `Charset`.

> **NOTE** Groovy comes with a class `groovy.util.CharsetToolkit` that can be used to guess the encoding. See its API documentation for details.

The following listing goes through examples of file reading with more fine-grained control. The `readLines` method returns a list of strings, each representing one line in the input source with newline characters chopped.

Listing 12.6 File-reading examples

```
example = new File('data/example.txt')

lines = ['line one', 'line two', 'line three']
assert lines == example.readLines()

example.eachLine {
  assert it.startsWith('line')
}

hex = []
example.eachByte { hex << it }
assert hex.size() == example.length()

example.splitEachLine(/\s/) {
  assert 'line' == it[0]
}

example.withReader { reader ->
  assert 'line one' == reader.readLine()
}
```

The `eachLine` method works on files exactly like the iteration method `each` does. The method is also available on `Reader`, `InputStream`, and `URL`. Input sources can be read a byte at a time with `eachByte`, where an object of type `java.lang.Byte` gets passed into the closure.

 When the input source is made of formatted lines, `splitEachLine` can be handy. For every line, it yields a list of items to its closure determined by splitting the line with the given regular expression.

 Generally, the `with<Resource>` method passes the `<Resource>` into the closure, handling resource management appropriately. The same applies to the `withReader` method. The `readLine` method can then be used on such a given `Reader`.

 This file-reading code reads nicely because Groovy relieves us of all the resource handling. You'd be disappointed if writing weren't equally straightforward.

12.2.3 *Writing to output destinations*

Just as the previous paragraph showed how easy it is to read a file using a one liner, you can do the same when writing the file. One of the easiest ways of writing to a file is by calling the `text` property of `File` (similar to calling the `setText` method):

```
new File("/tmp/example.txt").text = "line one"
```

That will create the example.txt file in the /tmp directory if the file doesn't exist yet, and replace the contents by the `String` value passed to the `text` property.

Listing 12.7 shows more methods for writing to an output destination. Writing a whole file at once can be achieved with `File`'s `write` method; appending is done with `append`. The `with<Resource>` method works exactly as you'd expect. The use of `withWriter` and `withWriterAppend` is shown in the listing; `withPrintWriter` and `withOutputStream` are analogous. The left-shift operator on `File` has the meaning of *append*.

Listing 12.7 File-writing examples

```
def outFile = new File('data/example.txt')

def lines = ['line one','line two','line three']

outFile.write(lines[0..1].join("\n"))          Writing/appending with
outFile.append("\n"+lines[2])                  simple method calls

assert lines == outFile.readLines()

outFile.withWriter { writer ->
  writer.writeLine(lines[0])                   Writing/
}                                              appending
outFile.withWriterAppend('ISO8859-1') { writer -> with closures
  writer << lines[1] << "\n"
}
outFile << lines[2]        ⟵    Appending with
                                left-shift operator
```

The example file has been opened and closed eight times: six times for writing, two times for reading. You see no error-handling code for properly closing the file in case of exceptions. `File`'s GDK methods handle that on our behalf.

Note the use of the `writeLine` and `<<` (left-shift) methods. Other classes that are enhanced by the GDK with the left-shift operator with the exact same meaning are `Process` and `Socket`.

The left-shift operator on `Writer` objects is a clever beast. It relays to `Writer`'s write method, which in the GDK makes a best effort to write the argument. The idea is to write a string representation with special support for arrays, maps, and collections. For general objects, `toString` is used.

If the argument is of type `InputStream` or `Reader`, its content is pumped into the `Writer`. The following listing shows this in action.

Listing 12.8 Using `Writer`'s smart left-shift operator

```
TimeZone.default = TimeZone.getTimeZone("CET")
reader = new StringReader('abc')
writer = new StringWriter()

writer << "\nsome String"    << "\n"
writer << [a:1, b:2]         << "\n"
writer << [3,4]              << "\n"
```

```
writer << new Date(0)        << "\n"
writer << reader             << "\n"

assert writer.toString() == '''
some String
[a:1, b:2]
[3, 4]
Thu Jan 01 01:00:00 CET 1970
abc
'''
```

Note that connecting a reader with a writer is as simple as

```
writer << reader
```

It may seem like magic, but it's a straightforward application of operator overriding done by the GDK.

The left-shift operator on `Writer` objects has special support for arguments of type `Writable`. In general, a `Writable` is an object with a `write` method: it knows how to write something. This makes a `Writable` applicable to

```
writer << writable
```

The `Writable` interface is newly introduced by the GDK and used with Groovy's template engines, as you'll see in section 12.4. It's also used with filtering, as shown in the next section.

12.2.4 *Filters and conversions*

There are times when ready-made resource handling as implemented by the with<Resource> method isn't what you want. This is when you can use the methods `newReader`, `newInputStream`, `newDataInputStream`, `newDataOutputStream`, `newObject-OutputStream`, `newOutputStream`, `newWriter`, and `newPrintWriter` to convert from a `File` object to the type of resource you need.

A second kind of conversion is transformation of the content, either character by character or line by line. Listing 12.9 shows how you can use `transformChar` and `transformLine` for this task. They both take a closure argument that determines the transformation result. Whatever that closure returns gets written to the `writer` argument.

Also shown is filtering with the `filterLine` method. Here, each line is relayed to the writer if the closure returns `true` (see section 6.1).

Listing 12.9 Transforming and filtering examples

```
def n = System.lineSeparator()          ◄─┐  System-dependent
                                        ❶  line separator
reader = new StringReader('abc')
writer = new StringWriter()

reader.transformChar(writer) { it.next() }   ◄─┐  Transforms
assert 'bcd' == writer.toString()               'abc' to 'bcd'
```

```
reader = new File('../data/example.txt').newReader()
writer = new StringWriter()

reader.transformLine(writer) { it - 'line' }
assert " one${n} two${n} three${n}" == writer.toString()

input  = new File('../data/example.txt')
writer = new StringWriter()

input.filterLine(writer) { it =~ /one/ }
assert "line one${n}" == writer.toString()

writer = new StringWriter()
writer << input.filterLine { it.size() > 8 }
assert "line three${n}"  == writer.toString()
```

Chops 'line' from each line of the example file

Reads only lines containing 'one'

❷ Reads only long lines

We define a system-dependent line separator (using a JDK 7 method[3]) ❶ so that the test passes across all OSs. Also, note that the last example of filterLine ❷ doesn't take a writer argument but returns a Writable that's then written to the writer with the left-shift operator.

NOTE The *Line methods use the newLine method of the according writer, thus producing system-dependent line feeds. They also produce a line feed after the last line, even if a source stream didn't end with it.

A frequently used conversion is from binary data to strings with base-64 encoding, where binary data is represented only in printable characters, as specified in RFC 2045. This can be useful for sending binary-coded data in an email, for example. The name of this codec comes from it having 64 symbols in its "alphabet,"[4] just as the decimal system is base 10 (10 symbols: 0–9) and binary is base 2 (2 symbols: 0 and 1):

```
byte[] data = new byte[256]
for (i in 0..255) { data[i] = i }

store = data.encodeBase64().toString()

assert store.startsWith('AAECAwQFBg')
assert store.endsWith  ('r7/P3+/w==')

restored = store.decodeBase64()

assert data.toList() == restored.toList()
```

An interesting feature of the encodeBase64 method is that it returns a Writable and can thus be used with writers; the returned object also implements toString conveniently. This has saved us the work of pushing the Writable into a StringWriter.

Base-64 encoding works with arbitrary binary data with no meaning attached to it. To encode objects instead, we need to venture into the world of serialization, which is the topic of the next section.

---

[3] You can get the "line separator" property yourself on earlier JDKs.

[4] One extra character is used for padding at the end of a block of data, but that isn't relevant when considering the effective base of the codec.

12.2.5 *Streaming serialized objects*

Java comes with a serialization protocol that allows objects of type `Serializable` to be stored in a format so that they can be restored in VM instances that are disconnected in either space or time.[5] Serialized objects can be written to `ObjectOutputStreams` and read from `ObjectInputStreams`. These streams allow making deep copies of objects (with `ByteArrayIn/OutputStream`), sending objects across networks, and storing objects in files or databases.

Listing 12.10 shows the special GDK support for reading serialized objects from a file. First, an `Integer`, a `String`, and a `Date` are written to a file. They're then restored with `File`'s new `eachObject` method. A final assertion checks whether the restored objects are equal to the original.

Listing 12.10   Reading serialized objects from files

```
file = new File('objects.dat')
file.deleteOnExit()                                     ◁──┐  Cleans up after
                                                           │  ourselves
objects = [1, "Hello Groovy!", new Date()]
file.withObjectOutputStream { outstream ->
  objects.each {
    outstream << it                          ◁──┐  Serializes each
  }                                             │  object in the
}                                               │  list in turn

retrieved = []
file.withObjectInputStream { instream ->
  instream.eachObject {
    retrieved << it                          ◁──┐  Deserializes each
  }                                             │  object in turn
}

assert retrieved == objects
```

As a variant, instead of using `withObjectInputStream` we could have used

```
file.eachObject
```

or

```
file.newObjectInputStream().eachObject
```

and obtained similar results, but the version in the listing automatically cleans up stream resources as soon as they're no longer in use and is the recommended approach.

12.2.6 *Temporary data and file copying*

Groovy makes it very easy to work with temporary files and folders. The GDK provides methods for creating and removing temporary files and directories, and getting the size of directory contents. Besides that, Groovy makes it easy to copy file

---

[5] See "Interface Serializable," which also lists all known subinterfaces, http://docs.oracle.com/javase/8/docs/api/java/io/Serializable.html.

contents using the `DataOutputStream` and `DataInputStream`. This is best illustrated by the following listing that creates a temporary directory with a file, which is copied and later removed.

Listing 12.11   File copy in temporary directory

```
File tempDir = File.createTempDir()          ◁──┐  Creates a temporary
                                                 │  directory
assert tempDir.directorySize() == 0

File source = new File(tempDir, 'input.dat')  ◁──┤  Creates a file and
source.bytes = "hello world".bytes                  sets file contents

assert tempDir.directorySize() == 11         ◁──┐  Checks that directory
                                                 │  size increased
File destination = new File(tempDir, 'output.dat')

destination.withDataOutputStream { os->      ◁──┐  Copies file and checks
    source.withDataInputStream { is->            │  that directory size
        os << is                                 │  doubled
    }
}

assert tempDir.directorySize() == 22          ──┐  Deletes
                                                 │  directory
tempDir.deleteDir()                          ◁──┘
```

Checks that directory is empty (annotation for `assert tempDir.directorySize() == 0`)

That's it for file access and I/O as far as the GDK is concerned. Daily work with files and streams is a combination of using JDK, GDK, and often `AntBuilder` functionality. Thanks to Groovy's seamless integration, it still looks like a single library, as you'll see in the code examples in part 3.

12.3   *Working with threads and processes*

> *The only reason for time is so that everything doesn't happen at once.*
>
> —Albert Einstein

One of Java's merits is its great support for multithreading. The Java platform provides various means for scheduling and executing threads of control efficiently, whereas the Java language allows easy definition of `Runnable` objects for multithreaded execution and control by `wait`/`notify` schemes and the `synchronized` keyword.

Threads are useful for organizing execution flow inside an application. Processes, in contrast, deal with functionality outside your Java or Groovy application. They cannot share objects but need to communicate via streams or other external means. They often appear in Groovy automation scripts, because by nature, such scripts trigger machine-dependent functionality.

The GDK supports working with threads and processes by introducing new Groovy-friendly methods for these classes, as you'll see in the following sections. For the remainder of this section, it's assumed that you have some basic understanding of Java's multithreading. It's useful to look at the API documentation of `java.lang.Thread` and `java.lang.Process`.

12.3.1 *Groovy multithreading*

The first and foremost Groovy feature for multithreading support is that `Closure` implements `Runnable`. This allows simple thread definitions like

```
t = new Thread() { /* Closure body */ }
t.start()
```

This can even be simplified with two new static methods on the `Thread` class, each with two variants:

```
Thread.start { /* Closure body */ }
```

or

```
Thread.start('threadName') { /* Closure body */ }
```

Java has the concept of a *daemon thread*; therefore so does Groovy. The runtime system handles such a thread differently than a non-daemon thread. Usually, a Java or Groovy application doesn't exit as long as one of its threads is still alive. This doesn't apply to daemon threads—they don't prevent the application from exiting. A daemon thread can be started via

```
Thread.startDaemon { /* Closure body */ }
```

or

```
Thread.startDaemon('threadName') { /* Closure body */ }
```

For a deferred start of a closure in its own thread, there's a new method `runAfter (milliseconds)` on `java.util.Timer`. To start after a one-second delay, use it like

```
new Timer().runAfter(1000){ /* Closure body */}
```

Let's look at a listing showing the Groovy solution for the classical producer–consumer problem. The producer pushes integer values on a stack, and the consumer pops them when available. The push/pop actions are reported; the report might look like the leftmost column of the listing. Additional columns (not generated by the code) show how over time the producer refills the storage that the consumer has emptied:

```
                 Producer    Storage   Consumer
push: 0             0 ->     0
push: 1             1 ->     01
push: 2             2 ->     012
pop : 2                      01          -> 2
push: 3             3 ->     013
push: 4             4 ->     0134
pop : 4                      013         -> 4
push: 5             5 ->     0135
```

```
push: 6          6 ->      01356
pop : 6                    0135          -> 6
push: 7          7 ->      01357
push: 8          8 ->      013578
pop : 8                    01357         -> 8
push: 9          9 ->      013579
pop : 9                    01357         -> 9
pop : 7                    0135          -> 7
pop : 5                    013           -> 5
pop : 3                    01            -> 3
pop : 1                    0             -> 1
pop : 0                                  -> 0
```

The actual sequence isn't predictable (that's part of the fun). We use closures for running something (producing and consuming) in a separate thread and `sleep` to slow down the consumer. We introduce a `Storage` class that holds our stack and synchronizes access to it. If we try to `pop` from an empty stack, we'll `wait` until the producer has caught up.

The following listing shows the code.

Listing 12.12 Using threads with synchronization for the producer–consumer problem

```
import java.util.concurrent.BlockingQueue;
import java.util.concurrent.LinkedBlockingQueue;              Creates
                                                              a new
Thread.metaClass.'static'.getName = { Thread.currentThread().name }  ◁  method to
                                                                          get thread
BlockingQueue sharedQueue = [] as LinkedBlockingQueue    ◁──┐   name
                                                            Creates
Thread.start('push') {                              ◁──┐    shared
    10.times {                                          │    queue
        try {
            println("${Thread.name}\t: ${it}")
            sharedQueue << it                      Starts thread
            sleep 100                              producing 10 items
        } catch (InterruptedException ignore) {}
    }
}
Thread.start('pop') {              ◁──┤  Starts thread
    for (i in 0..9) {                    consuming 10 items
        sleep 200
        println("${Thread.name}\t: ${sharedQueue.take()}")

    }
}
```

Try to run this code multiple times and you'll see varying output depending on your system's scheduler. It's also fun to play with different `sleep` values.

Groovy makes concurrent programming syntactically easy, although the issue is inherently tricky and can lead to subtle errors. If you set out to dive deeply into this topic, ensure you read up on the subject.[6]

---

[6] One excellent book is Brian Goetz's, *Java Concurrency in Practice* (Addison Wesley, 2006).

12.3.2 *Integrating external processes*

A *process* is an abstraction for concurrent execution that happens outside your JVM. Control is relayed from the VM to the system's runtime, the OS that also runs your VM. Such functionality provides access to your machine, which can be both a blessing and a source of problems. It's a blessing because you can leverage the power of your machine; for example, reformatting a hard disk programmatically or doing something less intrusive such as calling shell scripts. Problems occur when you try to use processes across platforms or when the need for synchronization arises.

To create a process, you need to work with a string the value of which is the command to execute. The GDK allows this with the execute method on strings that return the corresponding `Process` object:

```
Process proc = myCommandString.execute()
```

Instead of a string, the command can also be a list (or array) of strings. This is useful when the command is made up of multiple entries that would require putting arguments in quotes, which may also require character escaping (when the argument contains quotes). The full list of related GDK methods is shown in table 12.6.

Table 12.6 Process-related GDK methods

List	Process (cont'd)
execute(List, File)	getText()
execute()	leftShift(byte[])
execute(String[], File)	leftShift(Object)
Process	or(Process)
closeStreams()	pipeTo(Process)
consumeProcessErrorStream(	waitForOrKill(long)
Appendable)	waitForProcessOutput(
consumeProcessErrorStream(	OutputStream, OutputStream)
OutputStream)	waitForProcessOutput()
consumeProcessOutput(	waitForProcessOutput(
OutputStream, OutputStream)	Appendable, Appendable)
consumeProcessOutput(	withOutputStream(Closure)
Appendable, Appendable)	withWriter(Closure)
consumeProcessOutput()	**String**
consumeProcessOutputStream(	execute(List, File)
OutputStream)	execute(String[], File)
consumeProcessOutputStream(	execute()
Appendable)	**String[]**
getErr()	execute()
getIn()	execute(String[], File)
getOut()	execute(List, File)

Suppose you create a method that creates a process from Windows's `dir` command. You may get passed a directory name that contains backslashes or whitespace characters. The simplest way to deal with this is something like

```
def dircmd = ['cmd','/c','dir']
def dir    = /\Program Files/
def proc   = (dircmd + dir).execute()
```

NOTE Depending on your system, you need a command processor to execute console commands. On Windows, that's `cmd.exe` (`command.com` on Win98). The `/c` option closes the console shell when the command has finished.

When creating a process, you can further define environment settings: use the so-called environment variables as a list (or array) of key–value strings and a `File` object to specify the directory where the process is executed (`null` stays in the current directory).

You can list the Windows settings for your process with the `set` command:

```
def env = ['USERNAME=mittie']
def proc = 'cmd /c set'.execute(env, new File('/'))
```

You'll notice that providing your own environment parameters also suppresses the inheritance of current environment parameters to your *child* process (with the possible exception of default parameters).

Now that we've obtained a `Process` object, we'd like to see the produced output. The GDK adds the `getText` method to achieve this. In other words, the `text` property gives you the output as a `String`:

```
println proc.text
```

More fine-grained control can be achieved by using the input, output, and error streams of the process as available in the respective properties:

```
InputStream  in  = proc.in
InputStream  err = proc.err
OutputStream out = proc.out
```

Note that the naming is from the Groovy/Java point of view as opposed to the point of view of the external process. The `stdin` for the external process is `proc.out` on the Groovy/Java side. Figure 12.2 depicts the mapping.

Instead of appending to `proc.out`, you can also append to the process itself with the same effect:

```
proc.out << "one\n"
proc     << "two\n"
```

Figure 12.2 How `java.lang.Process` streams map to the streams from an external process

You never know whether your process might possibly hang forever. The common way of dealing with this problem is to start a watchdog thread that waits for a maximum time and destroys the process if it hasn't finished by then. The GDK provides the method `waitForOrKill(millis)` on `Process`:

```
proc.waitForOrKill(1000)
```

This gives us enough to start a little experiment.

Let's say that we want to get a listing of some of our files, and we want to case-insensitive reverse sort them, for reasons well beyond the scope of this book. Just assume there's a good reason to do so. There are many ways to accomplish this using Unix commands, and the next example is just that; it gives a demonstration of how processes can be piped together and how the output of such a process chain can be used.

Listing 12.13   Finding the earliest listing via command-line processing

```
def listFiles = 'ls'.execute()
def ignoreCase = "tr '[A-Z]' '[a-z]'".execute()
def reverseSort = 'sort -r'.execute()

listFiles | ignoreCase | reverseSort

reverseSort.waitForOrKill(1000)
if(reverseSort.exitValue()) {
    print reverseSort.err.text
} else {
    print reverseSort.text
}
```

We're using the `pipeTo` method of `Process`, which is invoked by using the overridden or (`|`) operator. Then we wait for the process to finish with a safe time to wait, and print the result.

The observant reader (yes, that's all of you!) will have recognized that although the code is a slick solution, there's also a pure Groovy solution that's platform independent. Coming up with a pure Groovy solution is left as an exercise to you. This chapter should have given you all the necessary means to do so.

Instead of only handling output, it's of course also possible to combine input and output of processes and link them together. The next example listing will dive a bit into that.

Listing 12.14   Finding the earliest listing via command-line processing

```
def outputBuffer = new StringBuffer()
def errorBuffer  = new StringBuffer()

zipProcess   = 'gzip -c'.execute()
unzipProcess = 'gunzip -c'.execute()

unzipProcess.consumeProcessOutput(outputBuffer, errorBuffer)
zipProcess.consumeProcessErrorStream(errorBuffer)
```

```
zipProcess | unzipProcess
zipProcess.withWriter { writer ->
    writer << 'Hello World'
}
unzipProcess.waitForOrKill(1000)

println 'Output: ' + outputBuffer
println 'Error : ' + errorBuffer
```

The preceding code is quite simple and easy to understand. If you're feeling masochistic, you may want to try writing the equivalent code in Java. We don't recommend it.

Working with external processes is inherently platform-dependent. The difference isn't only in what capabilities each platform provides, but also in how to call such processes correctly from Java. For cross-platform scripting, things can get really hairy.

Luckily, we can follow the footsteps of pioneers. The Ant developers did all the grunt work and captured it in the exec task. For example, to call the CVS[7] executable on Windows and capture the command output for later analysis, we can use `AntBuilder`:

```
ant = new AntBuilder()

ant.exec(
    dir            : '.'          ,
    executable     : 'cvs.exe' ,
    outputproperty : 'cvsout'   ,
    errorproperty  : 'cvserror',
    resultproperty : 'cvsresult')
    {
        arg(line  : ' checkout MyModule')
    }

println ant.project.properties.cvsresult
```

In trailing code, refer to `ant.project.properties.cvsout` as a simple string.

Traditionally, scripts have often been associated with running other processes to perform the bulk of their work. Although Groovy brings the full power of the Java platform (and then some!) to scripting, it doesn't shy away from this situation. Another common use of scripting languages is for processing text. Again, Groovy is up to the task, as we show in the next section.

12.4 *Working with templates*

Groovy is a pragmatic language. Rather than following any dogma in language and library design, it focuses on getting recurring tasks done. Working with templates is such a task.

---

[7] There's also a specialized CVS task for Ant that we'd use if the example was about connecting to CVS rather than showing different means of talking to external processes.

A template is essentially text. Unlike fixed literal text, a template allows predefined modifications. These modifications follow some structure; they don't occur wildly.

If you think about a web application, literal text would be a static HTML page. At the other end of the continuum are web application frameworks that create such HTML solely by programming logic, such as *JavaServer Faces* (JSF). In between are approaches like *JavaServer Pages* (JSP) and others that create the final HTML from a template.

The use of templating isn't limited to web applications. It's equally useful for

- Organizing database queries
- Helping to connect to web services
- Generating code
- Transforming XML
- Predefining PostScript documents
- Standard emails

and much more, as you'll see in the remainder of the book.

We briefly describe what templates look like before launching into a full example. We also examine some of the more advanced uses of templates. Understanding the content of this section is also important when we come to the next topic, Groovlets.

12.4.1 *Understanding the template format*

The format of templates is inspired by the JSP syntax, the JSP *Expression Language* (EL), the Velocity framework, and GStrings. The idea is to use placeholders inside the running text. Table 12.7 lists the supported placeholders and their purpose. If you've ever worked with JSP or a similar technology, it will feel familiar.

Table 12.7   Template placeholders

Marker	Purpose
`$variable`	Insert the value of the `variable` into the text
`${groovycode}`	Evaluate single-line `groovycode`, and insert the result into the text
`<%=groovycode%>`	Evaluate the `groovycode`, and insert the result into the text
`<%groovycode%>`	Evaluate the `groovycode`

The `groovy.text` package defines multiple template engines. These engines (the name *factory* would better reveal their purpose) have `createTemplate` methods that read the template's raw text from an input source (`String`, `Reader`, `File`, or `URL`) and return a `Template` object.

`Template` objects can make a final text by replacing all the placeholders with their respective values. A map of variable names and their respective values (the *binding*) is

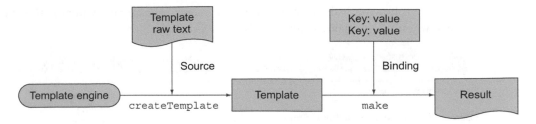

Figure 12.3 **Templates are created from a template engine and called with a binding to make the final result.**

therefore passed to the template's `make` method, which returns the final text in terms of a `Writable`. Figure 12.3 shows how all this fits together.

Different `Template` classes provide different runtime characteristics. One implementation might fully read the raw text and cache it for the later *make* step; other implementations might only store a reference to the source and merge it with the binding at *make* time. The latter *streaming* scenario can use source `Readers` and result `Writers` for optimized performance and scalability.

12.4.2 *Templates in action*

Suppose you've been asked to write a tool that sends out monthly email reminders, and your boss wants it to support mail-merge functionality (in other words, personalized content). A sample mail may look like this with variable items in bold:

```
Dear Mrs. Davis,
another month has passed and it's time for these
2 tasks:
- visit the Groovy in Action Second Edition (ReGinA) page
- chat with ReGinA readers

your collaboration is very much appreciated.
```

First, we need to think about placeholders.

`Davis` seems to be a last name, so we need a variable for that; we refer to it as `$lastname`.

`Mrs.` should get extra handling, because not all people have a salutation and we don't want to have that extra space character when there's none. This leads to a simple Groovy expression that we enclose in braces. The placeholder becomes `${salutation?salutation+' ':''}`

For the tasks, we use a simple list of strings and ask for the list's `<%=tasks.size()%>`. Iteration is trickier, but listing 12.15 shows how to use `<% %>` to solve that. Note that we can open the `each` closure in one placeholder and close it in a second one. The text that's between these two is processed for each task. We can even use the closure's `it` reference.

In the following listing, we use the `SimpleTemplateEngine`, which is the standard choice when no specialized behavior is required.

Listing 12.15   Using a simple template engine for email text

```
mailReminder =
'''
Dear ${salutation?salutation+' ':''}$lastname,          ← Text of template
another month has passed and it's time for these           containing
<%=tasks.size()%> tasks:                                   placeholders
<% tasks.each { %>- $it
<% } %>
your collaboration is very much appreciated
'''

def engine   = new groovy.text.SimpleTemplateEngine()
def template = engine.createTemplate(mailReminder)
def binding  = [
    salutation: 'Mrs.',                                    Variables to
    lastname  : 'Davis',                                   substitute in
    tasks     : ['visit the Groovy in Action (GinA) page', the template
                 'chat with GinA readers']
]

assert template.make(binding).toString() ==    ← Evaluates the
'''                                                template against
Dear Mrs. Davis,                                   the binding
another month has passed and it's time for these
2 tasks:
- visit the Groovy in Action (GinA) page
- chat with GinA readers

your collaboration is very much appreciated
'''
```

If you'd prefer, you can construct the engine via `SimpleTemplateEngine(true)` to make it print additional information on how it works inside. You'll see the following output:

```
-- script source --
/* Generated by SimpleTemplateEngine */
out.print("\n");
out.print("Dear ${salutation?salutation+' ':''}$lastname,\n");
out.print("another month has passed and it's time for these\n");
out.print("");out.print("${tasks.size()}");
out.print(" tasks:\n");
out.print(""); tasks.each { ;
out.print("- $it \n");
out.print(""); } ;
out.print(" \n");
out.print("your collaboration is very much appreciated\n");
out.print("");

-- script end --
```

That means the template is a Groovy script, generated from the template source and invoked dynamically. All the $ and ${} placeholders work because they're placed inside double quotes. The iteration logic (in bold) is literally inserted in the script as it appears between <% %>.

The log output is also useful in case of errors in the script. Error messages with line and column indications relate to that generated script.

12.4.3 *Advanced template issues*

Also interesting is the `out` variable in the preceding output. It refers to a `Writer` that's placed into the binding by default and is thus also available in template placeholders. You can use it like

```
<%
    tasks.each { out.println('- '+it) }
%>
```

When working with templates, here are some points to consider:

- If you choose to declare the template's raw text in a string (as in listing 12.15), you should use single-quoted string literals, rather than double-quoted ones, which may be transformed into GStrings. Using GStrings would result in resolving $ and ${} placeholders at the time you call `createTemplate`,[8] not at make time. Sometimes this may be what you want, but most of the time probably not.
- Templates have no defined escaping. For the rare case when you need to include %> in your template literally, you need a trick to make the engine accept it. One way is to put the offending text in a variable, pass that into the binding, and refer to it in the text via $variable.

The `groovy.text` and `groovy.text.markup` packages currently provide five template engines that all obey the same format of placeholders but have different characteristics:

- `SimpleTemplateEngine` produces the template in terms of a script as discussed previously. At make time that script writes line by line to the output destination. The script is cached.
- `StreamingTemplateEngine` has equivalent functionality to the `SimpleTemplate-Engine` but creates the template using writable closures making it more scalable for large templates. In particular, this template engine can handle strings larger than 64,000, which causes problems for the other Groovy template engines.
- `GStringTemplateEngine` holds the template in terms of a writable closure, possibly providing better performance and scalability for large templates and for stateless streaming scenarios. See section 12.2.2.

---

[8] Maybe even earlier; see section 13.2.5.

- `XmlTemplateEngine` is optimized when the template's raw text and the resulting text are both valid XML. It operates on nodes in the DOM and can thus provide a pretty-printed result. Unlike other engines, it produces system-dependent line feeds.
- `MarkupTemplateEngine` compiles the template for better performance and optionally provides type checking on model attributes used in the template. It has many benefits and we recommend it highly. For further details, consult the Groovy documentation.[9]

For more details on these engines, see the respective API documentation pages.

So far you've seen four ways to generate text dynamically: GStrings, `Formatter` (with `printf` calls, for example), `MarkupBuilder`, and templates. Each has its own sweet spot of applicability. GStrings and `Formatter` work best for simple in-code purposes, `MarkupBuilder` for producing structured text with mostly dynamic content, and templates for mostly static text with few dynamic parts injected. Of course, combinations aren't only possible but normal in real-world applications.

One obvious application where templates and markup go together is for web applications. Our next section introduces Groovlets, Groovy's built-in support for simple yet powerful web applications.

12.5   *Working with Groovlets*

The Java platform is available in a standard edition (Java SE) and an enterprise edition (Java EE). So far, we've only worked with features of the standard edition; we'll now look at a special capability that Groovy adds to the enterprise edition. In particular, we'll look at the Java EE Servlet technology[10] for implementing web applications. For the remainder of this chapter, it's assumed that you have some basic understanding of servlets.

Groovlets are to Groovy what servlets are to Java: a basic, standardized way of writing web applications. The pure use of Groovlets is good for small and simple applications, whereas more demanding applications benefit from frameworks such as Grails (see chapter 20) or Ratpack (www.ratpack.io/).

We're going to start with a simple "Hello world" program, which we use to demonstrate installation. We'll briefly look at an inspection Groovlet that illustrates some of the kinds of information available to the Groovlet environment before moving on to a guessing game that lets us examine how data flows in Groovlets. Finally, we'll rewrite the guessing game using the templating technology you saw in section 12.4.

---

[9] Groovy Language Documentation, section 3.11.7: The `MarkupTemplateEngine` is primarily aimed at generating XML-like markup, but that can be used to generate any text-based content. It relies on a DSL that uses the builder syntax. See http://docs.groovy-lang.org/latest/html/documentation/#_the_markuptemplateengine.

[10] A description of Java Servlet technology can be found at www.oracle.com/technetwork/java/index-jsp-135475.html.

Figure 12.4 "Hello world"
as done with Groovlets

12.5.1 Starting with "Hello world"

We'd like to write a "Hello world" Groovlet that displays a welcome message in the browser. It should look something like the screenshot shown in figure 12.4. What's the bare minimum that we have to do to get this Groovlet working?

First, we need a Java EE–compliant web server. There are lots of open source pure Java servers available for free, ranging from Jetty (lightweight, in-process capabilities) to Tomcat (feature rich) to JBoss (application server). The easiest way of installing a web server is by using Grape. You can do so using the following listing.

Listing 12.16 Simple Groovy web server

```
@Grab('org.eclipse.jetty.aggregate:jetty-server:8.1.16.v20140903')
@Grab('org.eclipse.jetty.aggregate:jetty-servlet:8.1.16.v20140903')
@Grab('javax.servlet:javax.servlet-api:3.0.1')

import org.eclipse.jetty.server.Server
import org.eclipse.jetty.servlet.*
import groovy.servlet.*
import static org.eclipse.jetty.servlet.ServletContextHandler.*

def server = new Server(1234)
def context = new ServletContextHandler(server, "/", SESSIONS)
context.resourceBase = "."
context.addServlet(GroovyServlet, "*.groovy")
server.start()
```

Use the supplied listing file in the book's sample code, and you can start this server from the command line with the following command:

```
groovy Listing_12_16_GroovletExample.groovy
```

The name of the file isn't important—for example, you could type the previous listing in a file named something like `webserver.groovy`, and start it using the following command:

```
groovy -Dgroovy.grape.report.downloads=true webserver.groovy
```

Here we chose to also add a useful debugging option. The `-D` option makes Grape log verbose output when resolving and downloading dependencies. Depending on your Grape repository and internet speed, the script might seem to otherwise hang the first time you invoke it. When everything goes right, you should see a similar output as the following:

```
Resolving dependency: javax.servlet#javax.servlet-api;3.0.1
{default=[default]}
Resolving dependency: org.eclipse.jetty.aggregate#jetty-
servlet;8.1.9.v20130131 {default=[default]}
Resolving dependency: org.eclipse.jetty.aggregate#jetty-
server;8.1.9.v20130131 {default=[default]}
Preparing to download artifact javax.servlet#javax.servlet-
api;3.0.1!javax.servlet-api.jar
Preparing to download artifact org.eclipse.jetty.aggregate#jetty-
servlet;8.1.9.v20130131!jetty-servlet.jar
Preparing to download artifact org.eclipse.jetty.aggregate#jetty-
server;8.1.9.v20130131!jetty-server.jar
2013-03-04 23:01:36.710:INFO:oejs.Server:jetty-8.1.9.v20130131
2013-03-04 23:01:36.820:INFO:oejs.AbstractConnector:Started
SelectChannelConnector@0.0.0.0:1234
```

If you look carefully you'll see that the last line mentions that Jetty has started successfully and is now listing on port 1234, ready to serve Groovlets.

With this configuration in place, we can start writing our first Groovlet. Listing 12.17 implements it by using the default builder available under the name html in the Groovlets binding. You should save it next to the webserver.groovy as hello.groovy.

Listing 12.17   The "Hello world" Groovlet using the HTML builder

```
html.html{
    head {
        title 'Groovlet Demonstrator'
    }
    body { h1 'Welcome to the World of Groovlets' }
}
```

Pretty slick, eh? You can see its output by starting your web server and pointing your browser to http://localhost:1234/Listing_12_17_HelloWorldGroovlet.groovy (or if you typed the listing into a file called, say hello.groovy, change the URL to http://localhost:1234/hello.groovy and make sure it's in the same directory as the *.groovy file with your running servlet engine).

At this point, it's fun to play around with changing the Groovlet, saving the file, and reloading the page in the browser.

NOTE   No server restart or application reload is needed to see changed output. This makes for rapid application development!

A Groovlet is essentially an ordinary Groovy script that sends its output to your browser. To understand what's achievable with Groovlets, you need to know what information they can work on.

Now we've got a web server up and running that's capable of serving Groovy pages. If, however, you're not able to use Grape, or want to deploy in a Java EE container, you must make the web server aware of this capability. In the usual Java EE manner, you can achieve this via the standard web.xml file. The following listing contains a sample. The symbolic name `Groovy` is mapped to the class `GroovyServlet`. This class is able to load *.groovy scripts to handle them as Groovlets.

Listing 12.18   Sample web.xml file for configuring a web application for Groovlet use

```
<web-app xmlns="http://java.sun.com/xml/ns/javaee"
  xmlns:xsi="http://www.w3.org/2001/XMLSchema-instance"
  xsi:schemaLocation="http://java.sun.com/xml/ns/javaee http://java.sun.com/
    xml/ns/javaee/web-app_3_0.xsd" version="3.0">
    <servlet>
      <servlet-name>Groovlet</servlet-name>
      <servlet-class>groovy.servlet.GroovyServlet</servlet-class>
    </servlet>
    <servlet>
        <servlet-name>Template</servlet-name>
        <servlet-class>groovy.servlet.TemplateServlet</servlet-class>
    </servlet>

    <servlet-mapping>
        <servlet-name>Groovlet</servlet-name>
        <url-pattern>*.groovy</url-pattern>
    </servlet-mapping>
    <servlet-mapping>
        <servlet-name>Template</servlet-name>
        <url-pattern>*.html</url-pattern>
    </servlet-mapping>
    <servlet-mapping>
        <servlet-name>Template</servlet-name>
        <url-pattern>*.gsp</url-pattern>
    </servlet-mapping>

</web-app>
```

All requests (the URL pattern *) are dispatched to `Groovy`. All other entries, such as `display-name` and `description`, are for documentation purposes only.

12.5.2   Groovlet binding

Like all other Groovy scripts, Groovlets have a binding that contains information, which can be accessed with the `binding` property. For Groovlets, this information is

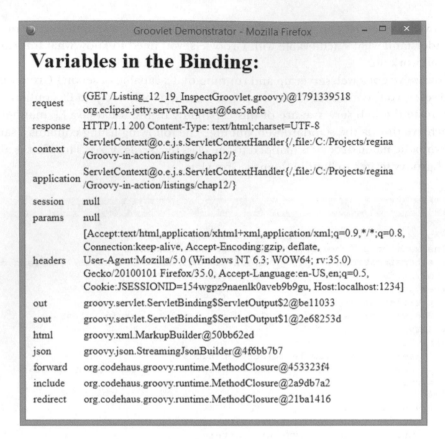

Figure 12.5   Inspecting the Groovlet binding

provided by the `GroovyServlet` that handles the request. Listing 12.19 asks the binding what's inside and puts it on your browser screen if you request the following:

http://localhost:1234/Listing_12_19_InspectGroovlet.groovy

When displayed in your browser. It should look something like the screenshot shown in Figure 12.5.

Listing 12.19   Inspect.groovy Groovlet reveals what's in the Groovlet binding

```
html.html{
    head {
        title 'Groovlet Demonstrator'
    }
    body {
        h1 'Variables in the Binding:'
        table(summary:'binding') {
            tbody {
                binding.variables.each { key, value ->
```

```
                        tr {
                            td key.toString()
                            td(value ? value.toString() : 'null')
}  }  }  }  }  }
```

This little Groovlet gives us a valid HTML table. Note the summary attribute of the table element and the nested tbody element. They're often forgotten because browsers don't complain if they're missing. But without them, the HTML will not be fully compliant with recent HTML standards.

Table 12.8 lists the output as produced by listing 12.19 and additional use information.

Table 12.8   Information available to Groovlets

Name	Note	Example use
headers	Map of HTTP request headers	headers.host
params	Map of HTTP request parameters	params.myParam
session	ServletSession, can be null	session?.myParam
request	HttpServletRequest	request.remoteHost
response	HttpServletResponse	response.contentType='text/xml'
context	ServletContext	context.myParam
application	ServletContext (same as context)	application.myParam
out	response.writer	Lazy init, not in binding
sout	response.outputStream	Lazy init, not in binding
html	Builder initialized as new MarkupBuilder(out)	Lazy init, not in binding
json	Builder initialized as new StreamingJsonBuilder(out)	Lazy init, not in binding

The variables out, sout, html, and json are initialized lazily; they're null until the Groovlet uses them the first time. This allows us to work on the response object before the output stream is opened. This can be necessary to set response properties such as the contentType.

The session variable is null unless there's session information for the current conversation. This allows optimization for stateless Groovlets that don't need session information. To use session information in Groovlets, you typically start like so:

```
if (!session) // error handling here if needed
session = request.session
```

NOTE Session-related error handling may be needed if the Groovlet is to be used only after some prework has been done that should have initialized the session already. Think about an online shop where the user has put a product in their shopping cart. This information is stored in the session. When the user tries to check out but the session has expired, there will be no item to pay for because the session is `null`.

A Groovlet is also evaluated with the use of the `ServletCategory` that adds the methods `get/set` and `getAt/putAt` to the classes `ServletContext`, `HttpSession`, `ServletRequest`, and `PageContext`.

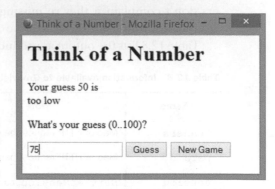

A small example will show how all this works together. Figure 12.6 shows the UI of a little web game. It takes a random number between 0 and 100 and lets the user guess it, giving indications whether the guess was too high or too low.

Figure 12.6 HTML UI of the High/Low game

Listing 12.20 shows the Groovlet code that implements the game. To view it, you should point your browser to http://localhost:1234/Listing_12_20_HiLowGame.groovy.

The game needs to handle session data and request parameters. The target number is stored as an `Integer` value in the session under the symbolic name `goal`. It's initialized to a random number on first use as well as when a new game is requested.

The request parameter `guess` carries the last input value; `restart` is submitted if the user clicks the New Game button. When dealing with request parameters, you need to be aware that they can be `null` (if not submitted) or an empty string (when submitted without value).

Listing 12.20 Groovlet code of the High/Low game

```
def session = request.session
def guess   = params.guess
guess = guess ? guess.toInteger() : null
if (params.restart) guess = null

if (!session.goal || params.restart) {          Generates a
    session.goal = (Math.random()*100).toInteger()   number to guess,
}                                                 if necessary
def goal = session.goal

html.html{ head { title 'Think of a Number'  }   ⟵  Starts a builder to
    body {                                           generate HTML
        h1 'Think of a Number'
        if (goal && guess) {
            div "Your guess $guess is "   ⟵  Uses a GString as a
            switch (guess) {                  simple template for text
```

```
                            case goal       : div 'correct!'; break     |  Classifies
                            case {it < goal} : div 'too low' ; break     |  the guess
                            case {it > goal} : div 'too high'; break     |  appropriately
                        }
                    }
                    p "What's your guess (0..100)?"
                    form(action:'Listing_12_20_HiLowGame.groovy'){   <—|  Displays a form
                        input(type:'text', name:'guess', '')          |  posting to the
                        button(type:'submit', 'Guess')                 |  same page again
                        button(type:'submit', name:'restart', value:'true',
                            'New Game')
        }   }   }
```

The code is divided into two pieces. It starts with a controller part that cares about the current state (the session) and requested actions (the parameters). The second part is the HTML builder, which plays the role of the view, visualizing the current state.

So far, our Groovlets have built the view only through the HTML builder, but there are more options.

12.5.3 *Templating Groovlets*

With the out writer available in the Groovlet binding, you can write directly to the response object. That means you can do things like

```
out << '<HTML>'
                // more output here …
out << '</HTML>'
```

or output the current date and time as GStrings like

```
out << "<HTML><BODY>${new Date().toGMTString()}</BODY></HTML>"
```

In section 12.4, you found that Groovy templates almost read like JSPs, so using them in this scenario is an obvious choice. The following listing stores an HTML template for the High/Low game that works with the goal and guess parameters.

Listing 12.21   Number.template.html as a view for the High/Low game

```
<html>
  <head>
    <title>Think of a Number</title>
  </head>
  <body>
    <h1>Think of a Number</h1>
<% if (bind.hasProperty('guess') { %>
    Your guess $guess is <%
    switch (guess) {
      case goal : out << 'correct!'; break
      case {it < goal} : out << 'too low' ; break
      case {it > goal} : out << 'too high'; break
    }
    %>
    <p>What&quot;s your guess (0..100)?</p>
```

```
  <form action='Listing_12_22_TemplateGroovlet.groovy'>
    <input type='text' name='guess'>
    <button type='submit'>Guess</button>
    <button type='submit' name='restart' value='true'>New Game
    </button>
  </form>
</body>
</html>
```

Notice how the template contains a GString (the guess) and Groovy code inside <%...%>. This template can be used from a controlling Groovlet with the same initial logic as listing 12.20 but with the rendering logic replaced with some template rendering code ❶ as the following listing shows.

Listing 12.22   A template-based Groovlet

```
def session = request.session
def guess   = params.guess
guess = guess ? guess.toInteger() : null
if (params.restart) guess = null

if (!session.goal || params.restart) {
  session.goal = (Math.random()*100).toInteger()
}

def engine   = new groovy.text.SimpleTemplateEngine()
def source   = getClass().classLoader.
    getResource('Number.template.html')
def template = engine.createTemplate(source)
out << template.make(guess: guess, goal: session.goal)
```

❶ Template rendering code

The template is evaluated appropriately, with the GString placeholder being replaced and the embedded code being executed.

A specialty of this approach is that the controlling Groovlet needs to read the template source as a resource from the classpath, because it cannot know where the respective file would be located. For our embedded Jetty example, it's easy; again just place it next to the *.groovy file running your servlet engine. To make this possible in Tomcat or any other Java EE container, the template file must be stored in the classes directory of your web application.

The organizational style of having a controller Groovlet and a view template allows a practical division of concerns, and keeps templating nicely separated from business logic or database access.

When the emphasis of the web application is on the templates rather than on the controlling logic, Groovy also supports a full JSP-like approach sometimes dubbed Groovy Server Pages (GSP). It works exactly like the preceding templates with the same binding as for Groovlets.

A special TemplateServlet acts in the role of the controlling Groovlet. Configure it webservice.groovy by adding the following line:

```
context.addServlet(TemplateServlet, "*.html")
```

Or, alternatively, in your web.xml by adding this code snippet:

```
<servlet>
    <servlet-name>template</servlet-name>
    <servlet-class>groovy.servlet.TemplateServlet</servlet-class>
</servlet>
<servlet-mapping>
    <servlet-name>template</servlet-name>
    <url-pattern>*.html</url-pattern>
</servlet-mapping>
```

All *.html requests will then be relayed to the appropriate template. You can test this by placing the following code snippet (demo.html) into the directory containing your servlet engine script and access it by going to http://localhost:1234/demo.html:

```
<html>
  <body>
    <% 3.times { %>
      Hello Groovy!
    <% } %>
  </body>
</html>
```

`TemplateServlet` will also care for properly caching each template. This gives better performance than reconstructing the template for every request.

Of course, there's more to implementing web applications than mastering the basic technology. But our focus here is only on the Groovy aspects, leaving much room for more books to be written about how to implement full web applications with Groovy.

For further pointers to Groovy-related web technologies, see http://freshmeat .net/projects/gvtags, http://groovestry.sourceforge.net, and http://biscuit.javanicus .com/biscuit/.

12.6 Summary

The GDK—the way that Groovy augments and enhances the JDK—provides key devices for a wide range of programming tasks.

The GDK makes I/O handling a breeze. It takes away low-level considerations in common situations, dealing with resource management automatically. The difference isn't only in terms of development speed when writing the program code initially. You may even be a little slower in the beginning, because you need some time to adapt, and typing time is rarely the bottleneck of programming. The real benefit comes from working on a slightly higher level of abstraction.

Similarly, instead of teasing the programmer with *how* to properly walk through an enumeration/iteration/collection/array, the GDK lets you focus on *what* to achieve; for example, to find something using col.find{} regardless of what col is.

Working with threads and processes is equally easy in Groovy. Multithreading is a tricky topic at the best of times, and again Groovy reduces the amount of scaffolding code required, making it easier to see what's going on. Process handling can be vital in a scripting language, and Groovy not only makes working with the plain Java `Process` class straightforward, but also facilitates the executable handling semantics from Ant using `AntBuilder`.

Dynamically filling in templates can be important in a variety of applications, and Groovy comes with an easy-to-grasp templating technology, using a syntax that's familiar to most Java programmers.

Although the standard JDK is important, the importance of Java EE cannot be overstated. Groovy participates in this arena, too, providing Groovlets as yet another web application framework. You'll learn more about web applications when we consider Grails in chapter 16.

It may look like the Groovy *language* made much of this possible, but this is only one side of the story. The Groovy language—and its MOP in particular—provides the means that the GDK employs. What the GDK does with the JDK can be done with any library or API. That's what some people call *language-oriented programming*: lifting your code up to a level where it directly expresses your concerns.

Database programming with Groovy

13

This chapter covers

- Using the low-level Groovy API for interacting with relational databases
- Transactions, batching operations, and retrieving database metadata
- `DataSet`s for performing CRUD operations
- Architectural and design of a data access layer
- Groovy and NoSQL databases

As far as the laws of mathematics refer to reality, they are not certain, and as far as they are certain, they do not refer to reality.

—Albert Einstein

Databases are stores of structured data. If your Groovy application needs persistent data, you most likely will need to talk to one. There are many different kinds, each with particular advantages, disadvantages, and characteristics; luckily Groovy makes it easy to talk to whichever kind you need. Perhaps the most well-known kind of database is the family of relational[1] databases, but other kinds include object-oriented,

---

[1] *An Introduction to Database Systems*, by C. J. Date (Addison-Wesley, 2003).

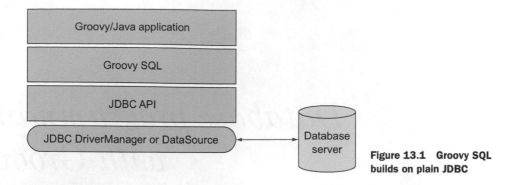

Figure 13.1   Groovy SQL builds on plain JDBC

key–value stores, document-centric, and graph. We'll concentrate on relational databases first and briefly cover some of the NoSQL[2] forms later in the chapter.

13.1   *Groovy SQL: a better JDBC*

Relational databases are data stores that are based on a *relational model*. It's this model that makes them so powerful. Its mathematical foundation allows you to reason about the results of operations and lets database engines perform appropriate optimizations.

Database access is also highly standardized, allowing multiple applications to coordinate by sharing their data even if these applications are built with different technologies. The standard that incorporates the relational algebra is SQL.

Because using SQL and connecting to relational databases is such an important task, any programming language worth talking about provides a way of doing it. Scripting languages—notably PHP, Python, and Ruby—provide simple and immediate access, whereas Java comes with the JDBC API, which isn't as simple but comes with some levels of improved consistency across different database systems and improved integration with Java objects.

Now comes Groovy. The Groovy database connectivity support (Groovy SQL for short) is plain JDBC with sugar from Groovy's `groovy.sql` library package. It takes only a handful of classes (the main four being `Sql`, `DataSet`, `GroovyResultSet`, and `GroovyRowResult`) to make database work short and sweet. Figure 13.1 shows where Groovy SQL fits into the API stack.

> **NOTE FOR MODULE USERS**   Groovy 2 introduced modularization (see section B.3 of appendix B) and groovy-sql is one of the available modules. If you're using the groovy-all JAR file or using one of the Groovy distributions, you'll automatically have the groovy-sql module available to you. If you're integrating directly with the core module groovy.jar file, then you might need to `@Grab` the groovy-sql module (contained in a groovy-sql.jar/) or place the JAR file on your classpath. The listings for this chapter have the necessary module `@Grab` statements in them but they're commented out and not needed for most users.

---

[2]   *Seven Databases in Seven Weeks: A Guide to Modern Databases and the NoSQL Movement,* by E. Redmond and J. R. Wilson (Pragmatic Programmers, 2012).

Groovy SQL lifts JDBC to a level of user-friendliness that's comparable to, and in some respects better than, that offered by other scripting languages. But it also plays nicely at the object level. JDBC is often used with database-related design patterns that evolved around it. In this chapter, you'll see some of them in the form of *data transfer objects* (DTOs) and *data access objects* (DAOs). You'll witness how Groovy SQL reduces the need for creating such extra classes, sometimes eliminating the extra work.

Database systems and SQL make a topic of their own, and many books have been written about them. You need this knowledge for our examples, but explaining it here would exceed the scope of this book.[3] In return for your understanding, we keep the SQL examples reasonably basic.

For the remainder of this section, it's assumed that you have some basic knowledge about SQL and how to work with relational databases in Java.

When you've finished this section, you'll be able to work on your databases through Groovy for any kind of administration task, automated or ad hoc reporting, persisting your business objects, and leveraging the power of the relational data model—all in a simple yet organized manner.

13.1.1 *Setting up for database access*

It's fairly obvious that you cannot do anything before you have a database system that you can use. Groovy has no database in its distribution. If you have a database system that comes with a JDBC driver, you can go with it. You might want to check if one was installed along with your JDK installation (many distributions bundle Java DB[4]). Otherwise, you'll need to install one, where *install* can mean totally different things for different database products.

INSTALLING A DATABASE

The examples in this chapter should work with most vendor and open source databases that support JDBC. We used the popular HyperSQL Database (HSQLDB), which you can download from http://hsqldb.org. We used version 2.3.2 but any recent version should work. HSQLDB is an easily embeddable, Java-only database engine with a small footprint but is still fairly feature complete. Installing HSQLDB means putting the hsqldb.jar file on your classpath when executing this chapter's examples, or using the appropriate @Grab statement as per the sample listings. See section 7.2.3 for details of how to add JAR files to the classpath. Remember that you can drop a JAR file into your <user.home>/.groovy/lib directory to have it on your classpath whenever you start any of Groovy's built-in tools.

If you decide to use a different database system, follow its installation instructions. Typically, you'll also have a JAR file that needs to be added to the classpath, because at

---

[3] See *An Introduction to Database Systems*, by C. J. Date (Addison Wesley, 2003) for a good introduction.

[4] Java DB is Oracle's supported distribution of the Apache Derby open source database. It is included in the JDK. See www.oracle.com/technetwork/java/javadb/.

least the implementation-specific driver or data source class needs to be found there. You'll also need to adjust the URL to suit your selected database engine.

> **NOTE FOR WINDOWS USERS**   The JdbcOdbcDriver is on the classpath by default because it ships with the JDK. It allows connections to database systems that implement the Open Database Connectivity (ODBC) standard over the so-called JDBC–ODBC bridge. Popular ODBC data sources are Microsoft Excel and Microsoft Access. This driver isn't intended for production use, however. It's an easy way to explore a database exposed by ODBC, but a dedicated JDBC driver is usually a more stable and better-performing long-term solution.

Database products also differ in the SQL they accept. Every system has its own *dialect*.[5] Because our examples use HSQLDB, the SQL that you'll see in the examples is in HSQLDB dialect. Should you choose to use a different database, the examples should be very similar, but see the manual of your database product for possible deviations.

Basic relational database operations are supported in Groovy according to the design guideline that simple tasks should be easy and advanced tasks should be possible. This section is solely about simple tasks. That means you can expect an easy introduction into the topic. We'll go through:

- Connecting to the database
- Creating the database schema
- Working with sample data

Working with data is done through four operations: *create*, *read*, *update*, and *delete*, together called CRUD operations.

At the end of this section, you'll be able to do standard database work with Groovy. The knowledge in this section will be sufficient to write whole applications that utilize databases. The remainder of the section will expand your design choices to more elaborate solutions.

FIRST CONTACT

Regardless of your technology, you must provide four pieces of information to access a database:

- The database URL
- Username
- Password
- Driver class name (which can sometimes be derived automatically)

The database URL needs a short explanation. A database URL (a JDBC URL in our context) is a platform-independent way of addressing a database. It always starts with jdbc: followed by a vendor-specific subprotocol. You need to refer to your database system's documentation for possible subprotocols.

---

[5] "The wonderful thing about standards is: there are so many to choose from."—Prof. Andrew Tennenbaum.

HSQLDB supports several subprotocols, and the main ones are listed in table 13.1.[6]

Table 13.1 HSQLDB subprotocols

URL pattern	Purpose
`jdbc:hsqldb:hsql://server/dbname`	Connects to a HSQLDB server process; use when multiple clients or processes need to share the database
`jdbc:hsqldb:file:/path/dbname`	Connects to a single-client HSQLDB instance with file-based persistence; multiple files starting with *dbname* will be created if the database doesn't yet exist
`jdbc:hsqldb:mem:dbname`	Connects to a nonpersistent in-memory database

When using the HSQLDB in-memory database, for example, our database URL will be `jdbc:hsqldb:mem:GinA`. Changing to the server or file-based version is as easy as changing the URL accordingly.

We'll use standard username/password settings: `sa` for sysadmin and an empty password string. It goes without saying that this is acceptable only for experimental purposes.

The driver class name will be `org.hsqldb.jdbcDriver`. If you use a different vendor, this name will also be different.

Where do you put this information? In Groovy, you access the database through an object of type `groovy.sql.Sql`.[7] There are a few ways to get such an object. The most common is through `Sql`'s `newInstance` factory method, passing the preceding information as parameters. The following listing shows typical use.

Listing 13.1 Connecting to a database

```
import groovy.sql.Sql

def url = 'jdbc:hsqldb:mem:GinA'
def user = 'sa'
def password = ''
def driver = 'org.hsqldb.jdbcDriver'
def sql = Sql.newInstance(url, user, password, driver)

// use 'sql' instance ...

sql.close()
```

Congratulations; you've successfully connected to the database!

When you look into `Sql`'s API documentation, you'll find more variants of the `newInstance` factory method. It might seem like there are many variants to choose

---

[6] But see the relevant documentation (http://hsqldb.org/doc/2.0/guide/dbproperties-chapt.html) for reading from read-only resource databases, turning on security, or a whole host of other database properties that can be set as part of the URL.

[7] If you think this naming is questionable, we wouldn't disagree. If it helps, you can think of it as a database API that for the most part exposes SQL statements to the programmer.

from, but you'll quickly find that there are typically only one or two that are appropriate for any given scenario. We'll cover some of the common scenarios to make it a bit easier for you.

Listing 13.1 assumes that the JAR file containing the required JDBC driver is on the classpath as we alluded to earlier in this section. That typically involves declaring or defining a dependency to the required JAR file in your IDE or build system. To support the creation of self-contained scripts, Groovy's @Grab annotation can be used. For our example we could tweak the earlier listing as follows:

```
@Grab('org.hsqldb:hsqldb:2.3.2')
@GrabConfig(systemClassLoader=true)
import groovy.sql.Sql
// ... as before ...
```

This adds the required JAR file (downloading if needed) to the classpath on the fly. You'd need to change the artifact reference if you aren't using the particular version of HSQLDB that we used in our examples. Don't worry too much about the @Grab-Config statement. Groovy has some simple class-loading infrastructure under the covers that you normally don't need to even know about; here we're telling that infrastructure to load the driver in a way that allows the JDK's DriverManager class to see your driver class.

The map variant of the newInstance method allows Groovy's named-parameter convention to be applied and also makes it easy to set additional parameters when needed. Our call to newInstance using that variant could look as follows:

```
def sql = Sql.newInstance(
    url: 'jdbc:hsqldb:mem:GinA',
    user: 'sa',
    password: '',
    driver: 'org.hsqldb.jdbcDriver',
    cacheStatements: true,
    resultSetConcurrency: CONCUR_READ_ONLY)
```

While discussing variants, we should also cover the alternative withInstance method. It has the same variants as the newInstance method and automatically calls the close method. Using it would look like this:

```
Sql.withInstance(url, user, password, driver) { sql ->
  // use 'sql' instance ...
}
```

The other scenario, which is quite common, is using a DataSource. We cover that next.

DRIVERMANAGER VS. DATASOURCE
If you look back to figure 13.1, you'll notice two concepts below the JDBC API: Driver-Manager and DataSource. The Sql.newInstance methods always go through the DriverManager facility, which can be seen as the classic low-level way of connecting. Since JDK 1.4, there has been a second way that uses the DataSource concept.

Although the `DriverManager` facility is still supported for backward compatibility, using `DataSource` is generally preferable. In addition to providing a connection to the database, it may optionally manage a *connection pool* and support *distributed transactions* (not explained here). Because obtaining connections to a database is a time-consuming operation, it's common to reuse them. The pool is the storage facility that provides you with a connection. You have to pass the connection back after use so that others can reuse it. If you forget to return it, the pool becomes pointless. To avoid that, Groovy SQL transparently returns the connection for you.

`DataSources` become even more important when running in a managed environment such as within an application server. A managed environment provides its applications with `DataSource` objects to make its special features (such as connection pooling) available. In this scenario, `DataSource` objects are often retrieved through the Java Naming and Directory Interface (JNDI).

Now that you've heard about the merits of `DataSources`, how do you use them in Groovy? Your database vendor provides its own implementation of the `javax.sql.DataSource` interface. HSQLDB, for example, provides the class `org.hsqldb.jdbc.JDBCDataSource` for that purpose. To obtain a `Sql` instance for a `DataSource`, you need to create it, optionally set its properties, and pass it to the `Sql` constructor, as can be seen in the following listing.

> **Listing 13.2 Connecting using a `DataSource`**

```
import groovy.sql.Sql
import org.hsqldb.jdbc.JDBCDataSource

def dataSource = new JDBCDataSource(
    database: 'jdbc:hsqldb:mem:marathon', user: 'sa', password: '')
def sql = new Sql(dataSource)

// use 'sql' instance ...

sql.close()
```

> **NOTE FOR ENTERPRISE DEVELOPERS** If you're using an application server, you might retrieve the `DataSource` using JNDI as previously mentioned. The advantage of this approach is that it allows administration of the database to be more independent from your program. Your program doesn't need to mention specific database drivers or `DataSource` classes, and you could migrate from one database to another with reduced effort. But we did mention the dialect differences, didn't we?

No matter whether you use a `DataSource` in the `Sql` constructor or the `DriverManager` facility through `Sql.newInstance`, in the end you have a reference to a `Sql` instance (as the value of the `sql` variable). You can work with this reference regardless of how it was constructed.

These are the recommended ways of connecting to the database in Groovy. In situations when you already have a database connection and you'd like to work on it through Groovy, you can use new Sql(connection). But beware that in this case, Groovy SQL cannot manage that connection and you have to take care of properly closing it yourself.

If you have a Sql instance and you need a second one with the same characteristics (a clone), you can use new Sql(sql).

Now that you have a Sql instance that represents your connection to the database, you'll use it to execute SQL statements.

13.1.2 Executing SQL

Once you have a Sql instance in the sql reference, executing an SQL statement on the database is as easy as

```
sql.execute(statement)
```

Groovy SQL carries out all the management work around that call: getting a connection (possibly from the DataSource connection pool), constructing and configuring the statement, sending it, logging encountered exceptions, and closing resources (statement and connection) properly even if exceptions have been thrown. It even does a bit more, as you'll see in the course of this chapter.

CREATING THE DATABASE SCHEMA

The first thing you can use the execute method for is creating the database schema. Let's assume we're going to store data about marathon athletes and their performances. To identify an athlete, we need the first name, last name, and date of birth. A first attempt might be

```
sql.execute '''
  CREATE TABLE Athlete (
    firstname    VARCHAR(64),
    lastname     VARCHAR(64),
    dateOfBirth DATE
  );
'''
```

This does the job but isn't very realistic because we'll need a primary key to look up athletes and we didn't define one. It's obvious that none of these fields listed is unique in itself. A combination of all three is unlikely to have duplicates, but such a compound key is always tricky to deal with and is still not guaranteed to be unique.

It's conventional to use an artificial key (also known as a *surrogate key*) in such cases, so we'll introduce one. Because we're lazy, we'll let the database figure out how to create one as shown in the following listing.

Listing 13.3 Creating a table in a database

```
import groovy.sql.Sql

def url = 'jdbc:hsqldb:mem:GinA'
def user = 'sa'
def password = ''
```

```
def driver = 'org.hsqldb.jdbcDriver'
def sql = Sql.newInstance(url, user, password, driver)

sql.execute '''
  CREATE TABLE Athlete (
    athleteId    INTEGER GENERATED BY DEFAULT AS IDENTITY,  ⟵┐  Column
    firstname    VARCHAR(64),                                  │  value will be
    lastname     VARCHAR(64),                                  │  automatically
    dateOfBirth DATE                                           │  generated
  );
'''

sql.close()
```

That's the minimal schema we'll start with. We'll work with it in an agile way; the schema will grow over time. Reconstructing the schema programmatically every time we need it makes this agile database programming possible. But wait. If we issue the preceding statement to a database instance that already has an `Athlete` table (maybe from our last run), it will throw a `SqlException`. We need to drop the old one, but only if an old one exists:

```
sql.execute '''
    DROP    TABLE Athlete    IF EXISTS;
'''
```

As the SQL boilerplate code grows, it starts to bury the interesting information. For our purposes, in the following listing we'll refactor this boilerplate code into a static helper method, `create()`, within a utility class, `DbUtil`, and call that in future examples.[8]

> **Listing 13.4   A static helper method, `create()`, within a utility class, `DbUtil`**

```
import groovy.sql.Sql

class DbUtil {
    static Sql create() {
        def url = 'jdbc:hsqldb:mem:GinA'
        def user = 'sa'
        def password = ''
        def driver = 'org.hsqldb.jdbcDriver'
        def sql = Sql.newInstance(url, user, password, driver)

        sql.execute """
            DROP TABLE Athlete IF EXISTS cascade;
            DROP TABLE Record IF EXISTS;
        """

        sql.execute """
            CREATE TABLE Athlete (
                athleteId    INTEGER GENERATED BY DEFAULT AS IDENTITY,
                firstname    VARCHAR(64),
```

---

[8] See the book's sample code for the full listing.

```
              lastname     VARCHAR(64),
              dateOfBirth DATE,
              UNIQUE(athleteId)
          );
      """

      // additional set up will be added in future examples

      sql
  }

    // additional utility methods will be added in future examples
}
```

Note that this could be refactored into a template if you find yourself writing repeated code for multiple tables.

INSERTING DATA

With the schema defined, you can start entering data. You can use the execute method for this purpose. Let's add a marathon runner:

```
sql.execute '''
  INSERT INTO Athlete (firstname, lastname, dateOfBirth)
            VALUES ('Paul',     'Tergat', '1969-06-17');
'''
```

We were once in a project where we used this approach to insert a thousand records of carefully hand-managed test data. But this approach is difficult to read and manage, because it contains a lot of duplication. You can make the execute method produce what is called a *prepared statement*, a SQL statement with occurrences of values replaced by placeholders (question marks).

You can reuse the same statement for a possibly large sequence of calls with different values per call. The JDBC driver has to do its per-statement work only once instead of numerous times. The work per statement includes parsing the SQL, validating, optimizing access paths, and constructing an execution plan. The more complex the statement, the more time-consuming this work becomes. In other words, using a prepared statement is always a good move. In Java, prepared statements are represented using the java.sql.PreparedStatement interface.

The following example separates the SQL from the data used:

```
def athleteInsert = '''
    INSERT INTO Athlete (firstname, lastname, dateOfBirth)
            VALUES  (?, ?, ?);
'''
sql.execute athleteInsert, ['Khalid',  'Khannouchi', '1971-12-22']
```

The execute method is smart enough to know when it needs to work with a prepared statement. The preceding construction also better supports reading the list of fields from an external source such as a file and populating the database with it. The approach also avoids a nasty security vulnerability known as *SQL injection*.

NOTE In SQL, string values are placed in single quotes like `'Paul'`. But with a prepared statement, these single quotes must not be used. They aren't present in the prepared statement, nor are they part of the string data passed in the list of values. (In other words, the single quotes in those values are for Groovy, not for SQL.) Similarly, even though dates have been represented here as strings, they really are dates in the database. You could have passed an instance of `java.util.Date` to the `execute` method, and in production code this would be more likely, but the sample code in this chapter is clearer using simple string representations.

When the statement gets more complicated, the mapping between each question mark and the corresponding list entry can become difficult to follow. In the course of development, the statement or the list may change, and the task of keeping both in sync is a likely source of errors.

It would be nicer if you could use a placeholder that better reveals its purpose and goes around the rigid sequence constraint. Toward that end, `execute` can also produce a prepared statement from a GString. We show this with a map for the athlete's data but you could just as easily use a full-blown `Athlete` object instead—with the additional work of creating an `Athlete` class to start with, of course:

```
def data = [first: 'Ronaldo', last: 'da Costa',  birth: '1970-06-07']
sql.execute """
   INSERT INTO Athlete (firstname, lastname, dateOfBirth)
     VALUES (${data.first}, ${data.last}, ${data.birth});
"""
```

Pay attention to the tripled double quotes around the statement, and remember that this construction produces a prepared statement and will therefore be just as efficient and safe on the database as the question-mark version (indeed that's what it's turned into under the covers).

This might sound like magic to you and might leave you with some doubts, because after all you cannot *see* whether we're telling the truth. But we can enable logging and assess our claim. Use the following lines to see what happens behind the curtain:

```
import java.util.logging.*

Logger.getLogger('groovy.sql').level = Level.FINE
// your execute(GString)
```

For the previous example this produces:[9]

```
19/04/2015 7:23:28 PM groovy.sql.Sql getStatement
FINE: SELECT * FROM Athlete
```

---

[9] If you have trouble, see troubleshooting comments in the sample code for the book.

```
19/04/2015 7:23:28 PM groovy.sql.Sql getPreparedStatement
FINE:
        INSERT INTO Athlete (firstname, lastname, dateOfBirth)
                    VALUES (?,?,?);
    | [Ronaldo, da Costa, 1970-06-07]
```

It goes without saying that logging the SQL that's eventually executed is always a good practice during development. Also note that because we have a real prepared statement, the SQL expression uses no single quotes around the placeholder. The special use of GStrings as SQL statements limits the use of placeholders to places where a question mark would otherwise be allowed in a prepared statement.[10]

Before moving on, we should summarize options for execute that we've discussed so far. There are three main variants of the execute statement as shown in table 13.2.

Table 13.2 Main versions of the `execute` method

Returns	Method name	Parameters
boolean	execute	String statement
boolean	execute	String prepStmt, List values
boolean	execute	GString prepStmt

If you look at the GroovyDoc for the `Sql` class you'll note a number of other variants of the execute method. These variants support less common calling scenarios such as using varargs-style parameters instead of a list, using named parameters (discussed in section 13.2), and variants taking an additional closure to support SQL statements that might return zero or more results. See the GroovyDoc for additional details and examples of these other variants.

Before completing our discussion of inserting data, we should mention the closely related executeInsert method. It supports similar parameter variants as execute but expects the provided SQL to represent an INSERT statement and can provide additional information via the return value. The normal execute statement returns a Boolean (which is frequently ignored) indicating whether the statement returned a ResultSet. The executeInsert statement instead returns a list of any autogenerated key values. So in the example you could find out what athleteId was automatically assigned for any inserted row. There are also variants of executeInsert that take a list of key column names of interest, allowing you more control over which autogenerated keys might interest you. Let's put together the execute and executeInsert examples into a complete listing.

---

[10] There's an escape mechanism. See the GroovyDoc for `Sql#expand` for more details.

> **Listing 13.5   Inserting athletes into our table**

```
import util.DbUtil

def sql = DbUtil.create()

sql.execute '''
  INSERT INTO Athlete (firstname, lastname, dateOfBirth)
  VALUES ('Paul', 'Tergat', '1969-06-17')
'''

def data = [first: 'Khalid', last: 'Khannouchi', birth: '1971-12-22']
def keys = sql.executeInsert """
  INSERT INTO Athlete (firstname, lastname, dateOfBirth)
  VALUES (${data.first}, ${data.last}, ${data.birth})
"""
assert keys[0] == [1]

def insertSql = '''
  INSERT INTO Athlete (firstname, lastname, dateOfBirth)
  VALUES (?,?,?)
'''
def params = ['Ronaldo', 'da Costa', '1970-06-07']
def keyColumnNames = ['ATHLETEID']
keys = sql.executeInsert insertSql, params, keyColumnNames
assert keys[0] == [ATHLETEID: 2]

sql.close()
```

- Inserts using plain statement
- GString variant
- Checks generated keys for second row ❶
- Lists of params variant
- Checks generated athleteId key for third row ❷

HSQLDB starts autogenerated values from zero and increments by one, so the second row will have value 1 ❶ and the third row 2 ❷. If you're using a different database, these values may be different so the related assertions may need to change.

You now have three rows in your Athlete table. Because you're using an in-memory database, it will turn out to be handy to populate some rows like this for many of the future examples. For convenience in future examples, we'll move this logic into two helper methods: the insertAthlete method will insert one athlete, the populate method will call insertAthlete for three sample athletes. Both methods are added to our DbUtil class.[11]

The first important steps have been done: you connected to the database, created the schema, and inserted data. In other words, you've covered the C in CRUD. Still to come are *read*, *update*, and *delete*. Let's look at *read* next.

READING DATA

Usually the most frequently used operation is reading data.[12] Reading has different aspects, depending on whether you look for a single row or multiple rows, what query

---

[11] See the book's sample code for the full listing.
[12] This isn't necessarily true in all databases—when a database is used essentially for audit logging, for instance, it may be read very rarely. But *most* databases are more frequently read than changed.

information is available, and how you intend to process the retrieved data. The `Sql` class provides a range of methods, as listed in table 13.3, to cover these cases. The variants for handling of plain and prepared statements are the same as for execute.

Table 13.3   Main methods for reading data from the database

Returns	Method	Parameters
void	eachRow	`String   statement                  { row -> code }`
void	eachRow	`String   prepStmt, List values { row -> code }`
void	eachRow	`GString prepStmt                  { row -> code }`
void	query	`String   statement                  { resultSet -> code }`
void	query	`String   prepStmt, List values { resultSet -> code }`
void	query	`GString prepStmt                  { resultSet -> code }`
List	rows	`String   statement`
List	rows	`String   prepStmt, List values`
List	rows	`GString prepStmt`
Object	firstRow	`String   statement`
Object	firstRow	`String   prepStmt, List values`
Object	firstRow	`GString prepStmt`

You'll again find additional variants when looking at the GroovyDoc. Some of these extra variants are needed for paging and named parameters which we'll cover in section 13.2. See the GroovyDoc for further details and examples if the standard variants don't meet your needs.

The methods `eachRow` and `query` use a closure for processing the result. `query` calls the given closure once and passes the full `java.sql.ResultSet` into it; `eachRow` calls the closure for each row of the result, thus relieving the programmer from the usual iteration work.

FETCHING A ROW AT A TIME WITH EACHROW
Suppose you'd like to print a report about all known athletes that should look like this:

```
----- Athlete Info ------
Paul Tergat
born on 17. Jun 1969 (Tue)
------------------------
Khalid Khannouchi
born on 22. Dec 1971 (Wed)
------------------------
Ronaldo da Costa
born on 07. Jun 1970 (Sun)
------------------------
```

You can achieve this by using eachRow and a simple selection statement. The row that's passed into the closure is an interesting object. You can use the column names as if they were property names of that object:

```
println ' Athlete Info '.center(25,'-')
def fmt = new java.text.SimpleDateFormat('dd. MMM yyyy (E)',
                                         Locale.US)
db.eachRow('SELECT * FROM Athlete'){ athlete ->
    println athlete.firstname + ' ' + athlete.lastname
    println 'born on '+ fmt.format(athlete.dateOfBirth)
    println '-' * 25
}
```

Note how you're using the row as if it were an Athlete object, which it isn't. But you can also use the row as if it were a list (which it isn't either) and call the subscript operator on it. To print

```
Paul Tergat
Khalid Khannouchi
Ronaldo da Costa
```

you could call

```
db.eachRow('SELECT firstname, lastname FROM Athlete'){ row ->
    println row[0] + ' ' + row[1]
}
```

> **NOTE** When working with column indexes, it's always safer to explicitly specify the sequence of column names in the select statement. 'SELECT *' may sometimes return the columns in an expected order (for example, the order they were defined in CREATE TABLE), but this isn't guaranteed for all database management systems.

So what's that row object, after all? It's of type groovy.sql.GroovyResultSet, which is a decorator around the underlying java.sql.ResultSet. Being a Groovy object, it can pretend to have properties and provide Groovy-friendly indexing (starting from zero, allowing negative indexes that count from the end).

FETCHING A RESULTSET WITH QUERY

The query method allows you to customize the iteration over the query results at the expense of convenience, because you can only work with the good-old java.sql.Result-Set. Suppose you're only interested in the first athlete, and don't want to go through all results for that purpose. You can use query like this:

```
db.query('SELECT firstname, lastname FROM Athlete'){ resultSet ->
    if (resultSet.next()){
        print    resultSet.getString(1)
        print    ' '
        println resultSet.getString('lastname')
    }
}
```

Just like the eachRow method, the query method manages your resources (the connection and the statement). The downside is that the ResultSet that gets passed into the closure is less convenient to work with. You need to call next to move the cursor forward, you need to call type-specific getters (getString, getDate, and so on), and—most annoyingly—indexes start at *one* instead of *zero*.

FETCHING ALL ROWS AT ONCE

As shown in table 13.3, it's also possible to fetch all rows at once into a (possibly long) list with the rows method. Each list item can be used with an index or a property name (just like in eachRow). Suppose you have a simple requirement, like printing the following:

```
There are 3 Athletes:
Paul Tergat, Khalid Khannouchi, Ronaldo da Costa
```

You can use a simple database call like

```
List athletes = db.rows('SELECT firstname, lastname FROM Athlete')
println "There are ${athletes.size()} Athletes:"
println athletes.collect{"${it[0]} ${it.lastname}"}.join(", ")
```

Having the selection results in a list makes them eligible to be put in GPath expressions. The example shows this with the collect method, but you can imagine find, findAll, grep, any, every, and so forth in its place.

> **NOTE** The list items are implemented as GroovyRowResult objects, the equivalent of GroovyResultSet object as used with eachRow.

The firstRow(stmt) method returns the equivalent of rows(stmt)[0] but, if your database supports it, only requests the first row (see section 13.2.3 for more details on how this trick is supported). Let's put all of this together in a complete listing.

Listing 13.6   Reading athlete information from our table

```
import util.DbUtil

def sql = DbUtil.create()
DbUtil.populate(sql)

def expected = ['Paul Tergat', 'Khalid Khannouchi', 'Ronaldo da Costa']

def rowNum = 0
sql.query('SELECT firstname, lastname FROM Athlete') { resultSet ->
  while (resultSet.next()) {
    def first = resultSet.getString(1)
    def last = resultSet.getString('lastname')
    assert expected[rowNum++] == "$first $last"
  }
}
```

① Reads using query

② External iteration on the ResultSet

③ Accesses properties via JDBC API calls

```
                   rowNum = 0
Reads        ┌─▷ sql.eachRow('SELECT firstname, lastname FROM Athlete') { row ->
using rows ④        def first = row[0]
                    def last = row.lastname
Reads      ⑥        assert expected[rowNum++] == "$first $last"
using      └─  }                                                              ⑤
firstRow   └─▷ def first = sql.firstRow('SELECT lastname, dateOfBirth FROM Athlete')   Accesses
                assert first.values().sort().join(',') == 'Tergat,1969-06-17'          properties
Reads      ⑦                                                                           via map or
using rows └─▷ List athletes = sql.rows('SELECT firstname, lastname FROM Athlete')     list styles
                assert athletes.size() == 3
More       ⑧   assert athletes.collect { "$it.FIRSTNAME ${it[-1]}" } == expected
efficient
size       ┌─▷ assert sql.firstRow('SELECT COUNT(*) AS num FROM Athlete').num == 3
calculation
```

This listing provides an excellent summary of your options for reading data. You can use the query method ❶, in which case you need to handle iteration of the result set yourself ❷ and use JDBC API calls to access column values ❸. You can use the internal iterator style eachRow method ❹, in which case a closure is called with a GroovyRow-Result for each row returned by the query. GroovyRowResult supports accessing column values ❺ using 0-based ordinal syntax (with Groovy's normal conventions around negative index values) or (case-insensitive) named property syntax. You can use firstRow ❻ for efficient access to a single row or rows ❼ for all rows. Both methods also use a GroovyRowResult to represent a row. These methods provide many options for reading and manipulating database information. You'll soon be working with database data with the same ease and efficiency that Groovy offers for Java's collection structures. Do remember, though, to make the database do work when appropriate (for example, ❽).

That's it for reading data. The next CRUD operation is *updating*.

UPDATING DATA

The update operation works with the execute method in the same way you've seen so far. Suppose we initially insert only the last name of a marathon runner:

```
sql.execute '''
  INSERT INTO Athlete (lastname) VALUES ('da Costa')
'''
```

Now suppose we want to update the row to also include the athlete's first name:

```
sql.execute '''
  UPDATE Athlete SET firstname='Ronaldo' where lastname='da Costa'
'''
```

Our update here used a plain statement but, just like for inserting, we could have provided a list of parameters or used a GString to enforce the use of a prepared statement.

As you saw for inserting, there's a closely related method for updating with some special features. The executeUpdate method works the same way as execute but provides a different return value. execute returns a Boolean indicating whether the statement returned a ResultSet and executeUpdate returns the number of rows that were changed by the update. So, to change the athlete again, this time entering the date of birth you'd use:

```
def updateCount = sql.executeUpdate '''
  UPDATE Athlete SET dateOfBirth='1970-06-07' where lastname='da Costa'
'''
assert updateCount == 1
```

Putting that altogether gives you the following complete listing.

Listing 13.7   Updating a table row

```
import util.DbUtil

def sql = DbUtil.create()

sql.execute '''
  INSERT INTO Athlete (lastname) VALUES ('da Costa')
'''

sql.execute '''
  UPDATE Athlete SET firstname='Ronaldo' where lastname='da Costa'
'''

def updateCount = sql.executeUpdate '''
  UPDATE Athlete SET dateOfBirth='1970-06-07' where lastname='da Costa'
'''
assert updateCount == 1                    ◁─┐ Checks one row
                                               was updated
def row = sql.firstRow '''
  SELECT * FROM Athlete where lastname = 'da Costa'
'''
assert "${row.firstname} ${row.lastname} ${row.dateofbirth}" ==
    'Ronaldo da Costa 1970-06-07'

sql.close()
```

DELETING DATA

So far, you've created tables and inserted, read, and updated. The last CRUD operation you need to examine is *delete*. You'll use the execute method and pass in the appropriate SQL statement. A complete listing follows.

Listing 13.8   Deleting a table row

```
import util.DbUtil

def sql = DbUtil.create()        ┌ Populates using                            Checks
DbUtil.populate(sql)          ◁─┘ helper method                              initially
                                                                             three
                                                                             rows
assert sql.firstRow('SELECT COUNT(*) as num FROM Athlete').num == 3   ◁─┘
```

```
sql.execute "DELETE FROM Athlete WHERE lastname = 'Tergat'"

assert sql.firstRow('SELECT COUNT(*) as num FROM Athlete').num == 2
```

Two rows left after delete

You've seen how easy it is to execute SQL with Groovy to perform basic CRUD operations, but many applications need more advanced processing. That's the topic of our next section.

13.2 Advanced Groovy SQL

Groovy's SQL features provide a higher-level API above JDBC. But that doesn't mean when you need to do something a little out of the ordinary that Groovy's SQL libraries get in your way. You can always start working directly at the JDBC level if you need to, but what you'll discover in the rest of this section is that many other common database tasks also have special support from Groovy SQL. We'll start by looking at database transactions.

13.2.1 Performing transactional updates

In many scenarios, for data integrity reasons, it's important to update multiple pieces of information all at the same time or, if that isn't possible, change none of the information. Such systems are said to support transactions and preserve ACID properties. When using a single database, JDBC provides such functionality out of the box, presuming, of course, your database supports this feature.

By default, every JDBC update is treated as a transaction. If you want to perform multiple updates, that normally involves turning off the *autocommit* behavior, performing your changes, and either committing, if everything went according to plan, or rolling back the transaction if there was a problem and then resetting the autocommit status (if needed). Thankfully Groovy SQL provides a nice little shortcut for these steps.

Suppose you wanted to add two new athletes to the database and suppose it's important that they both are added in one transaction. It would be as simple as including the operations within a `withTransaction` block as shown in the following listing.

Listing 13.9 Invoking a transaction

```
import static util.DbUtil.*

def sql = create()
populate(sql)

sql.withTransaction {
    insertAthlete(sql, 'Haile', 'Gebrselassie', '1973-04-18')
    insertAthlete(sql, 'Patrick', 'Makau', '1985-03-02')
}

assert sql.firstRow('SELECT COUNT(*) as num FROM Athlete').num == 5
```

This isn't only significantly shorter but much less error-prone.

There are times when data integrity isn't your primary concern, instead efficiency is. That's where batch processing comes into play. We cover that next.

13.2.2 *Working with batches*

Whenever you send commands or queries to a database server, there will be some communication overhead. When large volumes of information must be sent, this overhead can become significant. Batch processing is a standard mechanism to minimize this overhead and it comes in two flavors.

The first variant allows arbitrary commands to be sent to the database. An optional parameter (not used here) allows you to set a batch size. If you don't set a batch size, then all commands will be in the one batch unless you manually call `stmt.execute-Batch()`, which allows you to chunk the batch into arbitrary-sized pieces. If you wanted to combine an insert into the `Athlete` table and one for a related `Record` table as a batch, you'd execute the following `withBatch` statement:

```
sql.withBatch { stmt ->
    stmt.addBatch '''
    INSERT INTO Athlete (firstname, lastname, dateOfBirth)
    VALUES ('Paula', 'Radcliffe', '1973-12-17')'''
    stmt.addBatch """
    INSERT INTO Record (time, venue, whenRun, fkAthlete)
        SELECT ${2*60*60+15*60+25}, 'London', '2003-04-13',
        athleteId FROM Athlete WHERE lastname='Radcliffe'"""
}
```

If logging is turned on, this produces:

```
22/04/2013 6:34:59 AM groovy.sql.BatchingStatementWrapper processResult
FINE: Successfully executed batch with 2 command(s)
```

Before proceeding further, we should dive under the covers and see what this `Record` table looks like. It's created with the following SQL:

```
CREATE TABLE Record (
    runId       INTEGER GENERATED BY DEFAULT AS IDENTITY,
    time        INTEGER,    -- in seconds
    venue       VARCHAR(64),
    whenRun     DATE,
    fkAthlete   INTEGER,
    CONSTRAINT fk FOREIGN KEY (fkAthlete)
      REFERENCES Athlete (athleteId) ON DELETE CASCADE
);
```

We modify our `DbUtil` create and populate methods to create and fill in four sample `Record` rows respectively.[13]

---

[13] It follows the same pattern as we saw earlier for the Athlete table. Full details can be seen in the DbUtil class within the sample code.

The second batch variant uses prepared statements and is used when all the commands in the batch involve the same kind of operation. For example, if we want to enter multiple athletes as a batch operation, and we wanted to chunk the batch into pieces of size 3, we'd use the following code:

```
def qry = '''
  INSERT INTO Athlete (firstname, lastname, dateOfBirth)
  VALUES (?,?,?)
'''
sql.withBatch(3, qry) { ps ->
  ps.addBatch('Paula',     'Radcliffe',   '1973-12-17')
  ps.addBatch('Catherine', 'Ndereba',     '1972-07-21')
  ps.addBatch('Naoko',     'Takahashi',   '1972-05-06')
  ps.addBatch('Tegla',     'Loroupe',     '1973-05-09')
  ps.addBatch('Ingrid',    'Kristiansen', '1956-03-21')
}
```

If logging is turned on, this produces:

```
20/04/2015 2:18:10 AM groovy.sql.BatchingStatementWrapper processResult
FINE: Successfully executed batch with 3 command(s)
20/04/2015 2:18:10 AM groovy.sql.BatchingStatementWrapper processResult
FINE: Successfully executed batch with 2 command(s)
```

Let's see the complete listing (including some assertions that our additional rows were added).

Listing 13.10 Batching operations

```
import util.DbUtil

def sql = DbUtil.create()
DbUtil.populate(sql)
DbUtil.enableLogging()

sql.withBatch { stmt ->
    stmt.addBatch '''
    INSERT INTO Athlete (firstname, lastname, dateOfBirth)
    VALUES ('Paula', 'Radcliffe', '1973-12-17')'''
    stmt.addBatch """
    INSERT INTO Record (time, venue, whenRun, fkAthlete)
      SELECT ${2*60*60+15*60+25}, 'London', '2003-04-13',
      athleteId FROM Athlete WHERE lastname='Radcliffe'"""
}

assert sql.firstRow('SELECT COUNT(*) as num FROM Athlete').num == 4
assert sql.firstRow('SELECT COUNT(*) as num FROM Record').num == 5

def qry = '''
  INSERT INTO Athlete (firstname, lastname, dateOfBirth)
  VALUES (?,?,?)
'''
```

```
sql.withBatch(3, qry) { ps ->
    ps.addBatch('Catherine', 'Ndereba', '1972-07-21')
    ps.addBatch('Naoko', 'Takahashi', '1972-05-06')
    ps.addBatch('Tegla', 'Loroupe', '1973-05-09')
    ps.addBatch('Ingrid', 'Kristiansen', '1956-03-21')
}

assert sql.firstRow('SELECT COUNT(*) as num FROM Athlete').num == 8
```

Sometimes you might have a different kind of performance problem. Your queries may produce too much data. To combat this problem let's look at pagination.

13.2.3   *Working with pagination*

When working with large databases, it's sometimes useful to only work with a subset of the returned information. This can be useful when you need a small subset of sample data or when working with the information in chunks (for example, displaying a page of information at a time on a website). Many Groovy SQL commands contain variants that allow subsets to be worked with; for example, the rows method takes an optional offset and size parameter as shown in the following listing, which returns athletes in chunks of two.

Listing 13.11   Pagination operations

```
import util.DbUtil

def sql = DbUtil.create()
DbUtil.populate(sql)

def qry = 'SELECT * FROM Athlete'
assert sql.rows(qry, 1, 2)*.lastname == ['Tergat', 'Khannouchi']
assert sql.rows(qry, 3, 2)*.lastname == ['da Costa']
```

Relational database systems reveal information about themselves in so-called *metadata*. This is "data about the data"—in its simplest terms, information like the types and names of columns, tables, and so forth. A look at accessing such information is next.

13.2.4   *Fetching metadata*

Earlier we looked at methods to print out parts of our Athlete table. Let's now consider writing a helper method that should dump the content of any given table. The table name is provided as a method parameter. If you call the method as dump(sql, 'Athlete'), it should print

```
------- CONTENT OF TABLE Athlete -------
0: ATHLETEID        0
1: FIRSTNAME        Paul
2: LASTNAME         Tergat
3: DATEOFBIRTH      1969-06-17
----------------------------------------
    ... other rows ...
```

For proper display, you need additional questions answered:

- How many columns should we display?
- What are the column names?

Luckily, `ResultSet` (and thus also the `GroovyResultSet`) provides a method called `getMetaData` that returns a `ResultSetMetaData` object. This contains all the necessary information. See its API documentation in the following listing for details.

Listing 13.12   Accessing metadata

```
import util.DbUtil

def sql = DbUtil.create()
DbUtil.populate(sql)

def dump(sql, tablename) {
  println " CONTENT OF TABLE ${tablename} ".center(32, '-')
  sql.eachRow('SELECT * FROM ' + tablename) { rs ->
    def meta = rs.getMetaData()
    if (meta.columnCount <= 0) return
    for (i in 0..<meta.columnCount) {
      print "${i}: ${meta.getColumnLabel(i + 1)}".padRight(20)      ➊ Counts from 1
      println rs[i]?.toString()                                     ➋ Counts from 0
    }                                                                   and possibly null
    println '-' * 32
  }
}

def baos = new ByteArrayOutputStream()                              ➌ Captures
System.setOut(new PrintStream(baos))                                  standard out

dump(sql, 'Athlete')
assert baos.toString().readLines()*.trim().join('\n') == '''\
--- CONTENT OF TABLE Athlete ---
0: ATHLETEID        0
1: FIRSTNAME        Paul
2: LASTNAME         Tergat
3: DATEOFBIRTH      1969-06-17
--------------------------------
0: ATHLETEID        1
1: FIRSTNAME        Khalid
2: LASTNAME         Khannouchi
3: DATEOFBIRTH      1971-12-22
--------------------------------
0: ATHLETEID        2
1: FIRSTNAME        Ronaldo
2: LASTNAME         da Costa
3: DATEOFBIRTH      1970-06-07
--------------------------------\
'''
```

Like all the classes from the `java.sql` package, `ResultSetMetaData` works with indexes starting at 1. Therefore, you need to call `getColumnLabel` ➊ with `(i+1)`. You also use the safe dereferencing operator (see section 7.1.3) in case the value at the given index is null ❷. You'll override standard output and capture it into a byte array so you can check that the method is printing the correct value ❸.

Making use of metadata is so common that Groovy SQL provides additional variants of some of its methods that take a Closure that works exclusively with the metadata. You saw earlier that an eachRow method was available that took an SQL query and a closure:

```
eachRow(String sql, Closure rowClosure)
```

which would normally be called using the normal trailing Closure syntax. The metadata variant has an extra parameter:

```
eachRow(String sql, Closure metaClosure, Closure rowClosure)
```

The metaClosure is called once and passed the ResultSetMetaData object from the query result. The rowClosure is then called once for each row. Here's how you might use it to rework the dump method:

```
def dump2(sql, tablename) {
  def printColNames = { meta ->
    (1..meta.columnCount).each {
      print meta.getColumnLabel(it).padRight(12)
    }
    println()
  }
  def printRow = { row ->
    row.toRowResult().values().each {
      print it.toString().padRight(12) }
    println()
  }
  sql.eachRow('SELECT * FROM ' + tablename, printColNames, printRow)
}
```

One thing you might notice here is that we didn't use the trailing closure syntax. We certainly could have chosen to do so, though we often avoid that style when calling methods with multiple closure parameters. Let's add formatting characters and checks that we produce the correct output (for both the Athlete and Record tables) as shown in the following complete listing.

Listing 13.13 Using a metadata closure

```
import util.DbUtil

def sql = DbUtil.create()
DbUtil.populate(sql)
```

```
def dump2(sql, tablename) {
  def printColNames = { meta ->
    def width = meta.columnCount * 12
    println " CONTENT OF TABLE ${tablename} ".center(width, '-')
    (1..meta.columnCount).each {
      print meta.getColumnLabel(it).padRight(12)
    }
    println()
    println '-' * width
  }
  def printRow = { row ->
    row.toRowResult().values().each {
      print it.toString().padRight(12)
    }
    println()
  }
  sql.eachRow('SELECT * FROM ' + tablename, printColNames, printRow)
}

def baos = new ByteArrayOutputStream()
System.setOut(new PrintStream(baos))

dump2(sql, 'Athlete')
assert baos.toString().readLines()*.trim().join('\n') == '''\
----------- CONTENT OF TABLE Athlete -----------
ATHLETEID   FIRSTNAME   LASTNAME    DATEOFBIRTH
------------------------------------------------
0           Paul        Tergat      1969-06-17
1           Khalid      Khannouchi  1971-12-22
2           Ronaldo     da Costa    1970-06-07\
'''

baos.reset()
dump2(sql, 'Record')
assert baos.toString().readLines()*.trim().join('\n') == '''\
---------------- CONTENT OF TABLE Record ------------------
RUNID       TIME        VENUE       WHENRUN     FKATHLETE
------------------------------------------------------------
0           7495        Berlin      2003-09-28  0
1           7538        London      2002-04-14  1
2           7542        Chicago     1999-10-24  1
3           7565        Berlin      1998-09-20  2\
'''
```

You've seen that using GStrings provides for succinct and clear expression of our SQL commands, but there's an alternative syntax using named and named-ordinal parameters. We'll look at that next.

13.2.5 Working with named and named-ordinal parameters

You saw earlier that many Groovy SQL methods have multiple variants—String, String plus a list of parameters, and GString variants, to name three. For most users, these variants will be quite sufficient but there are a few scenarios where an alternate syntax is useful. In particular, when integrating with Java, where GStrings might be less convenient to use, or when handling multiple objects containing properties to be fed into the SQL. Sometimes also, you might wish to mix your queries with some templating solution where GStrings may not be convenient. In such circumstances, named and named-ordinal parameters are useful.

NAMED PARAMETERS

With this style, you use placeholders similar to what we showed earlier for Prepared-Statements; however, instead of a series of question marks and a list of parameters, you have one parameter that could be a domain object or a map and each placeholder references the relevant property from the parameter. Two placeholder syntax styles are supported: using either a colon (:) before the property name or a question mark–dot (?.) before the property name.

First, let's assume you have the following SQL insert fragment that will begin your SQL examples in this section:

```
def insertPrefix = '''
  INSERT INTO Athlete (firstname, lastname, dateOfBirth)
  VALUES '''
```

and the following map:

```
def loroupe = [first: 'Tegla', last: 'Loroupe', dob: '1973-05-09']
```

Then you can insert runner Loroupe into the database as follows using the colon form:

```
db.execute insertPrefix + '(:first,:last,:dob)', loroupe
```

Alternatively, you can use Groovy's named parameter style method call to include the map inline (for runner Kristiansen):

```
db.execute insertPrefix + '(:first,:last,:dob)',
    first: 'Ingrid', last: 'Kristiansen', dob: '1956-03-21'
```

If you wanted to use domain objects, you might declare one like so:

```
@Canonical class Athlete { String first, last, dob }
def ndereba = new Athlete('Catherine', 'Ndereba', '1972-07-21')
```

You could add this athlete as follows using the question mark form:

```
db.execute insertPrefix + '(?.first,?.last,?.dob)', ndereba
```

NAMED-ORDINAL PARAMETERS

As a final example, perhaps the information you have is in multiple objects (in this case one domain object and one map). In that case, use an alternative to the question mark–dot form that also includes the numeric index of which parameter is referred to. Here's an example:

```
def takahashi = new Athlete('Naoko', 'Takahashi')
def takahashiExtra = [dob: '1972-05-06']

db.execute insertPrefix + '(?1.first,?1.last,?2.dob)',
    takahashi, takahashiExtra
```

Putting these snippets together gives us the following listing.

Listing 13.14 Using named and named-ordinal parameters

```
import groovy.transform.Canonical
import util.DbUtil

def sql = DbUtil.create()
DbUtil.populate(sql)

def insertPrefix = '''
INSERT INTO Athlete (firstname, lastname, dateOfBirth) VALUES
'''

sql.execute insertPrefix + '(:first,:last,:dob)', first: 'Ingrid',
        last: 'Kristiansen', dob: '1956-03-21'

def loroupe = [first: 'Tegla', last: 'Loroupe', dob: '1973-05-09']
sql.execute insertPrefix + '(:first,:last,:dob)', loroupe

@Canonical class Athlete { String first, last, dob }

def ndereba = new Athlete('Catherine', 'Ndereba', '1972-07-21')
sql.execute insertPrefix + '(?.first,?.last,?.dob)', ndereba

def takahashi = new Athlete('Naoko', 'Takahashi')
def takahashiExtra = [dob: '1972-05-06']
def namedOrdinalSuffix = '(?1.first,?1.last,?2.dob)'
sql.execute insertPrefix + namedOrdinalSuffix, takahashi, takahashiExtra

assert sql.firstRow('SELECT COUNT(*) as num FROM Athlete').num == 7
```

That wraps up our discussion on this special parameter syntax. Next we'll look at Groovy's special support for stored procedures.

13.2.6 *Using stored procedures*

One feature that many databases support is the ability to store code or functions in the database itself. We won't argue whether this is always an ideal practice but we acknowledge that there are times when we've needed to support use of such procedures. JDBC has support for such scenarios, but it can be a little cumbersome. Groovy SQL streamlines the process a little bit for you. We'll also note that the details of defining stored procedures and functions may vary slightly depending on your database[14] but how you call equivalent procedures across varying databases should remain the same.

---

[14] And to be honest there isn't much Groovy SQL can do to assist you with these differences!

We'll look at creating and then using stored procedures. First you'll create a SELECT_ATHLETE_RECORD stored function, which returns a table of data. Then you'll process the returned table using eachRow as shown in the following listing.

Listing 13.15   Working with a stored procedure

```
import util.DbUtil

def sql = DbUtil.create()
DbUtil.populate(sql)

sql.execute '''
  CREATE FUNCTION SELECT_ATHLETE_RECORD ()
  RETURNS TABLE (lastname VARCHAR(64), venue VARCHAR(64), whenRun DATE)
  READS SQL DATA
  RETURN TABLE (
    SELECT Athlete.lastname, Record.venue, Record.whenRun
    FROM Athlete, Record
    WHERE Athlete.athleteId = Record.fkAthlete
    ORDER BY whenRun
  )
'''
def result = []
sql.eachRow('CALL SELECT_ATHLETE_RECORD()') {
  result << "$it.lastname $it.venue $it.whenRun"
}
assert result == [
    'da Costa Berlin 1998-09-20',
    'Khannouchi Chicago 1999-10-24',
    'Khannouchi London 2002-04-14',
    'Tergat Berlin 2003-09-28'
]
```

Creating the stored function involved executing the appropriate SQL. The stored function joins information from the Athlete and Record tables and returns the resulting rows. You used eachRow to process those rows but could have used any of the methods for processing rows.

Consider now a FULL_NAME stored function that takes a parameter. If you give it an athlete's last name, it will return the full name. The following listing shows how you could create and then use such a function.

Listing 13.16   Working with a stored procedure with simple parameters

```
import util.DbUtil

def sql = DbUtil.create()
DbUtil.populate(sql)

sql.execute '''
  CREATE FUNCTION FULL_NAME (p_lastname VARCHAR(64))
  RETURNS VARCHAR(100)
  READS SQL DATA
```

```
  BEGIN ATOMIC
    DECLARE ans VARCHAR(100);
    SELECT CONCAT(firstname, ' ', lastname) INTO ans
    FROM Athlete WHERE lastname = p_lastname;
    RETURN ans;
  END
'''

assert sql.firstRow("{? = CALL FULL_NAME(?)}",
    ['Tergat'])[0] == 'Paul Tergat'
```

The creation of the stored function is again a simple execute statement. You can again use any of the reading methods. It makes most sense to use firstRow here because you'll always get back only one row. As before, our SQL statement will involve using the SQL call method but we'll also use a placeholder to indicate that a parameter is required and another to indicate that a result is returned.

So far our stored functions have returned single or multiple rows. JDBC also supports what are known as IN, OUT, and INOUT parameters for stored procedures. This mechanism allows multiple unrelated return values. We'll illustrate this mechanism by creating a stored procedure to concatenate two strings. Groovy and Java both support native string concatenation but we'll ignore that fact for the purposes of this example. We'll start by defining our procedure in the following listing.

Listing 13.17   A stored procedure with IN and OUT parameters

```
import groovy.sql.Sql
import util.DbUtil

def sql = DbUtil.create()
DbUtil.populate(sql)

sql.execute '''
  CREATE PROCEDURE CONCAT_NAME (OUT fullname VARCHAR(100),
    IN first VARCHAR(50), IN last VARCHAR(50))
  BEGIN ATOMIC
    SET fullname = CONCAT(first, ' ', last);
  END
'''

sql.call("{call CONCAT_NAME(?, ?, ?)}",
    [Sql.VARCHAR, 'Paul', 'Tergat']) {
  fullname -> assert fullname == 'Paul Tergat'
}
```

When defining the stored procedure we use two input parameters (first and last) and one output parameter (fullname), but we could have any combination of IN, OUT, and INOUT parameters if needed. To invoke our stored procedure we use Groovy's special call method. This method supports a number of special conventions. The first and last names are passed in the normal way, but for the OUT parameter we instead pass in the type that the stored procedure will produce, which for us is a VARCHAR. Because we have an OUT parameter, we'll use the Closure variant of the method. It calls our closure passing in the OUT parameter from the stored procedure, and for this example we'll check its value with an assertion.

You've seen how easy it is to execute SQL with Groovy including advanced use techniques. Wouldn't it be nice not to have to worry about the SQL at all? Unlikely as that concept sounds, it's the topic of our next section.

13.3   *DataSets for SQL without SQL*

We demanded that simple tasks should be easy. So far, you've seen simple SQL and easy ways for sending it to the database. It's hard to believe that database programming can be any simpler, but it can.

Groovy provides a basic way of working with the database that doesn't even work with SQL. This approach is based on the concept of a DataSet, and we'll look at each of the operations it supports:

- Adding a row to a table
- Working through all rows of a table or a view
- Selecting rows of a table or a view by simple expressions

You cannot define a schema that way or use delete or update operations. But you can mix the use of DataSets with other Groovy SQL operations and use whatever seems most appropriate for the task at hand.

A groovy.sql.DataSet is a subclass of and a decorator around groovy.sql.Sql. Figure 13.2 shows the UML class diagram.

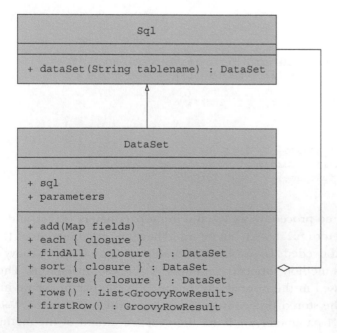

Figure 13.2   UML class diagram of groovy.sql.DataSet decorating groovy.sql.Sql

The conventional way of retrieving a DataSet instance is to call Sql's factory method dataSet. You pass it the name of the table that this DataSet should work with. For more alternatives, see the API documentation of Sql and DataSet:

```
// assuming sql refers to an instance of Sql
athletes = sql.dataSet('Athlete')
```

Let's explore what you can do with such an instance.

13.3.1 Using DataSet operations

With an instance of a DataSet, you can call its methods, as listed in figure 13.2. We can add a new row to the Athlete table with

```
athletes.add(
    firstname:   'Paula',
    lastname:    'Radcliffe',
    dateOfBirth: '1973-12-17')
```

That's all we need to do. A SQL insert statement will be created behind the scenes and executed immediately. If we omit any of the fields, a null value will be inserted instead.

We can also use the athletes to work with what's currently in the table. The code

```
athletes.each {
    println it.firstname
}
```

would print

```
Paul
Khalid
Ronaldo
Paula
```

Let's see this in action in a complete listing.

Listing 13.18 Using DataSets for SQL-free code

```
import util.DbUtil

def sql = DbUtil.create()
DbUtil.populate(sql)

def athletes = sql.dataSet('Athlete')          ❶ Treats an SQL
                                                 table like a list
def result = []                                  of maplike rows
athletes.each { result << it.firstname }
assert result == ['Paul', 'Khalid', 'Ronaldo']  Initially we have our
                                                 three sample athletes
athletes.add(
    firstname: 'Paula',
    lastname: 'Radcliffe',
    dateOfBirth: '1973-12-17'
)
```

```
result = athletes.rows().collect { it.firstname }
assert result == ['Paul', 'Khalid', 'Ronaldo', 'Paula']
```

Uses rows followed by collect ❷

Confirm we now have four athletes

When processing each athlete (note the use of the implicit `it` variable), it works analogously to the `GroovyResultSet` you saw before: you can use fieldnames as if they were properties and use positive or negative indexes. The goal of the abstraction provided by the `DataSet` methods (`each`, `add`, and `findAll`) is that a `DataSet` can be used in much the same way as any other collection and no SQL needs to appear in your code (for example, ❶). The abstraction has been kept simple, so other methods you might expect to find on collections (for example, `collect`) aren't currently found within the `DataSet` class. Instead there are two hooks, via the `firstRow` and `rows` methods, which then allow you to call `collect` if required ❷.

Now comes the `findAll` method, which looks simple at first but turns out to be *very* sophisticated. Let's start with trying

```
athletes.findAll{ it.dateOfBirth > '1970-1-1' }
```

This method call returns a new `DataSet`, which can in turn be used with the `each` method to work over the filtered result:

```
youngsters = athletes.findAll{ it.dateOfBirth > '1970-1-1' }
youngsters.each { println it.firstname }
```

What's behind this construction? At first sight, you might guess that the `findAll` method fetches all the rows from the table, applying the closure and adding rows that pass the filter to a list internally. This would be far too time-consuming for large tables. Instead, `findAll` produces a SQL statement that reflects the expression within the closure. This generated statement is encapsulated in the returned `youngsters` `DataSet`.

It's hard to believe that Groovy can do that,[15] but proof is available. Any `DataSet` encapsulates a statement in its `sql` property, and because that's the SQL of a prepared statement, it also needs parameters, which are stored in the `parameters` property. Let's find out what these properties are for our sample code:

```
youngsters = athletes.findAll{ it.dateOfBirth > '1970-1-1' }
println youngsters.sql
println youngsters.parameters
youngsters.each { println it.firstname }
```

These lines print

```
select * from Athlete where dateOfBirth > ?
["1970-1-1"]
Khalid
Ronaldo
Paula
```

---

[15] It may be slightly easier to believe if you've looked at Microsoft's LINQ project or similar projects. Groovy has had this feature since before LINQ was generally available but now the technique is widely used.

So take note:

- `findAll` only creates a new `DataSet` (with the enclosed prepared statement).
- `findAll` doesn't even access the database.
- Only the trailing `each` triggers the database call.

To prove this to yourself, you can add logging to the program in the same way we did in section 10.1.2. Logging is useful during development to see *when* the database is accessed, as well as *how* it's accessed.

But the buck doesn't stop here. Because the `findAll` method returns a `DataSet` that can be interpreted as a filtered selection of the original `DataSet` (which was the whole `Athlete` table in our example), it would be surprising if it weren't possible to combine filters. And yes, you can. The lines

```
youngsters = athletes.findAll{ it.dateOfBirth > '1970-1-1' }
paula      = youngsters.findAll{ it.firstname == 'Paula' }
println paula.sql
println paula.parameters
```

print

```
select * from Athlete where dateOfBirth > ? and firstname = ?
[1970-1-1, Paula]
```

Interestingly enough, we can achieve the same effect by providing a combined filter expression in the `findAll` closure:

```
youngsters = athletes.findAll{
    it.dateOfBirth > '1970-1-1' && it.firstname == 'Paula'
}
```

You can legitimately ask how this could possibly work. Here is the answer: the expression in the `findAll` closure *is never executed!* Instead, the `DataSet` implementation fetches Groovy's internal representation of the closure's code. This internal representation is the AST and was generated by the Groovy parser. By walking over the AST (with a Visitor pattern), the `DataSet` implementation emits the SQL equivalent of each AST node. The mapping is listed in table 13.4.

Table 13.4 Mapping of Groovy AST nodes to their SQL equivalents

AST node	SQL equivalent
`&&`	`And`
`||`	`Or`
`==`	`=`
Other operators	Themselves, literally
`it.`*propertyname*	`propertyname`
Constant expression	`?` (Expression is added to the parameters list)

This also means that the following restrictions apply for expressions inside the find-All closure:

- They must be legal Groovy code (otherwise, the Groovy parser fails).
- They must contain only expressions as listed in table 13.4, excluding variables and method calls.

These restrictions limit the possibilities of filtering DataSets. Conversely, this approach brings a new quality to database programming: using the parser of your programming language for checking your selection expression at *compile* time.

If you put syntactically invalid SQL into a string and pass it to Sql's execute method, you won't notice the error until the database is accessed and throws a SqlException.

If you put a syntactically invalid expression into a findAll closure and choose to compile your code, the compiler fails without accessing the database. You also get better error messages that way, because the compiler can point you to the offending code. With good IDE support, your IDE can open the editor on such failing code or even highlight the error while editing.

That's quite a lot to absorb. Let's look at what we've discussed in a complete listing.

Listing 13.19   Using DataSets with filtering

```
import util.DbUtil

def sql = DbUtil.create()
DbUtil.populate(sql)
DbUtil.enableLogging()

def athletes = sql.dataSet('Athlete')

athletes.add(
    firstname: 'Paula',
    lastname: 'Radcliffe',
    dateOfBirth: '1973-12-17'
)

def query = athletes.findAll { it.firstname >= 'P' }
query = query.findAll { it.dateOfBirth > '1970-01-01' }
query = query.sort { it.dateOfBirth }
query = query.reverse()
assert query.sql == 'select * from Athlete where firstname >= ? and ' +
    'dateOfBirth > ? order by dateOfBirth DESC'
assert query.parameters == ['P', '1970-01-01']
assert query.rows()*.firstname == ['Paula', 'Ronaldo']
```

Now might be a good time to have a cup of coffee. Let the last couple of pages sink in. Read them again. Try a few example queries for yourself. This ability to view the code within the closure as data and transform it into another type of code (SQL) rather than a block to be executed may be one of the most important concepts in ushering in a new era of database application development.

So far you've seen DataSets working on a single table only. We'll next explore how to use this concept more generally.

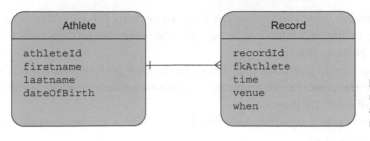

Figure 13.3 Entity-relationship diagram of athletes and multiple records

13.3.2 *DataSets on database views*

DataSets are a convenient way to work on a single table. But working on a single table is usually not of much value in a relational model.

You saw earlier that we stored the marathon world records for our athletes in a separate table. Each row in the Record table captures how many seconds a particular marathoner took, and when and where it happened. For relating such a row with the according athlete, we refer to the athlete's unique ID, the athleteId, by the foreign key fkAthlete. Figure 13.3 shows the relationship. Note that we also introduce a recordId[16] to give this performance a unique handle.

For filling the Record table with example data, we unfortunately cannot easily use a DataSet; we'd need to know the corresponding athleteId, which we cannot foresee because it's dynamically generated by the database. The next best solution is to use a helper method that executes an insert statement to retrieve the athleteId from a subselect. Here's some sample code, which uses parameters for most values but has a hard-coded distance for demonstration purposes. Likewise, it assumes there will be only one athlete with a given last name—something we wouldn't do in real life code:

```
def insertRecord(h, m, s, venue, date, lastname){
    def time = h*60*60 + m*60 + s
    db.execute """
        INSERT INTO Record (time, venue, when, fkAthlete)
            SELECT $time, $venue, $date,
                athleteId FROM Athlete WHERE lastname=$lastname;
    """
}
```

We can now call the insertRecord method with example data:

```
insertRecord(2,4,55, 'Berlin',  '2003-09-28', 'Tergat')
insertRecord(2,5,38, 'London',  '2002-04-14', 'Khannouchi')
insertRecord(2,5,42, 'Chicago', '1999-10-24', 'Khannouchi')
insertRecord(2,6,05, 'Berlin',  '1998-09-20', 'da Costa')
```

---

[16] There's no pressing need for the recordId. We introduce it because that's our usual working pattern when creating tables.

After this preparation, how can we use DataSets to list runs for an athlete name? We need to join the information from that Record table with the information from the Athlete table to retrieve the names.

Of course, we could read both tables and do the join programmatically, but that wouldn't leverage the power of the relational model and wouldn't perform well because of the overhead of each database call.

The trick is to create a database *view* that behaves like a read-only table made up from an arbitrary selection.

Here's how to create a view named AthleteRecord that combines athletes with their records as if we have a combined table that contains both tables but only for athletes for whom we have record information:

```
DROP   VIEW AthleteRecord IF EXISTS;
CREATE VIEW AthleteRecord AS
    SELECT * FROM Athlete INNER JOIN Run
        ON fkAthlete=athleteId;
```

With this view, we can create a DataSet and work with it as if it were one big table.[17] To find where Khalid Khannouchi performed his records, we can use

```
record = db.dataSet('AthleteRecord').findAll{ it.firstname=='Khalid' }
record.each{ println it.lastname + ' ' + it.venue }
```

which prints

```
Khannouchi London
Khannouchi Chicago
```

Let's have a look at these snippets as a complete listing.

Listing 13.20   Using DataSets with views

```
import util.DbUtil

def sql = DbUtil.create()
DbUtil.populate(sql)

sql.execute '''
    DROP   VIEW AthleteRecord IF EXISTS;
    CREATE VIEW AthleteRecord AS
      SELECT * FROM Athlete LEFT OUTER JOIN Record
        ON fkAthlete=athleteId;
'''

def records = sql.dataSet('AthleteRecord').findAll {
  it.firstname == 'Khalid'
}
def result = records.rows().collect { "$it.lastname $it.venue" }
assert ['Khannouchi London', 'Khannouchi Chicago'] == result
```

---

[17] You may wish to compare this approach with the SELECT_ATHLETE_RUN stored procedure earlier in this chapter.

What you've done here is remove SQL-specific knowledge, such as how to join two tables, from the application. This makes the code more portable across database vendors, as well as making it readable to developers who may not be particularly skilled in SQL. This comes at the expense of putting it into the infrastructure (the database setup code). This requires the database structure to be under your control. In large organizations, where the database is maintained by an entirely different set of people, the challenge is to get these administrators on board for efficient collaboration and for leveraging their database knowledge in your project.

You now have the tools you need to access a database. Giving someone a chisel doesn't make them a carpenter. How the tools are used is as important as the tools themselves.

13.4 Organizing database work

Knowing the technical details of database programming is one thing, but organizing a whole application for database use takes more than that. You have to take care of design considerations such as separation of concerns, assigning responsibility, and keeping the codebase manageable and maintainable—free from duplication.

This section will give you insight into how Groovy SQL fits into the overall architecture of a database application. We'll plan the architecture, define what the application has to be capable of, and then implement the application in a layered fashion, examining how Groovy makes things easier at every level. No single and authoritative solution fits all needs. Instead, you need to use your imagination and creativity to find out how to relate the presented rules, structures, and patterns to the situation at hand.

13.4.1 Architectural overview

Today's architectural patterns usually call for a layered architecture, as depicted in figure 13.4. The lowest layer is the *infrastructure* that shields all upper layers

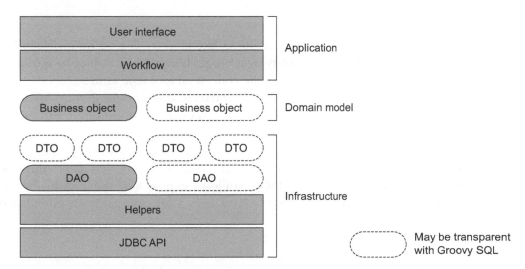

Figure 13.4 Layered architecture for database programming

from SQL specifics. It presents DAOs to the *domain model* layer above it. There often is a one-to-one relationship between *business objects* in the domain model layer and DAOs. Classically, DAOs and business objects pass DTOs back and forth for communication.

Above the domain model layer is the *application* layer, which makes use of the business objects in its workflow and presents them within the UI.

Layering also means that any layer may call the layer below it, but never the one above. *Strict* layering also forbids calling layers deeper than the one directly below; for example, calls from the application layer to the infrastructure layer would be forbidden.

With the advent of Groovy SQL, things can be done more easily. First, custom-built DTOs become obsolete, due to the dynamic nature of Groovy's classes. There's no more need to create special classes for each DTO type. A DAO can exchange information with *transparent* types—types that are independent of any DAO or business object specifics. Good candidates for transparent DTOs are `GroovyRowResult`, `Map`, `List`, and `Expando`. For DTOs that should encapsulate a collection of business objects, a list of these DTOs or a `DataSet` may be used.

> **NOTE** With layering as in figure 13.4, DAOs aren't allowed to directly return business objects, because calling their constructor would mean calling into the upper domain model layer. As a trick, they can pass back a map of properties and let the caller object do the construction, such as `new MyBusiness-Object(map)`.

For simple read-only data, business objects can also be replaced by transparently using a `GroovyRowResult`, a `Map`, or an `Expando`. Suppose the following line exists in the application code:

```
out << athlete.firstname
```

To a reader of this code, everything looks like `athlete` is a business object. But you cannot tell whether it's really of type `Athlete`. It could just as well be a `GroovyRow-Result`, a `Map`, or an `Expando`. From the code, it all looks the same.

Of course, this works only in simple scenarios. If you go for *domain-driven design*,[18] you'll want to implement your business objects explicitly (most often with the help of GroovyBeans).

DAOs can sometimes be replaced by transparently using a `DataSet`, as you saw in the previous section. There's a crucial point about `DataSet`s that makes this possible: the way they handle `findAll`. DAOs shouldn't expose SQL specifics to their caller, because that makes the infrastructure layer *leaky*. Conventional DAOs often break this

---

[18] *Domain-Driven Design: Tackling Complexity in the Heart of Software*, by Eric Evans (Addison Wesley, 2003).

constraint by allowing the caller to pass parts of the WHERE clause; or they end up with a plethora of methods like

```
findByFirstName(firstname)
findByLastName(lastname)
findByFirstAndLastName(firstname, lastname)
findByBirthdateBefore(date)
...
```

You've also seen that DataSets can replace DAOs, which represent sophisticated relations by providing the appropriate view in the database schema.

All this is interesting in theory, but it's what it looks like in practice that counts. In the next section, we'll examine some real code.

13.4.2 *Specifying the application behavior*

Thinking through the architecture is nice, but only the code tells the truth. So let's go for a full example of managing our athletes.

We'll use a layered architecture similar to figure 13.4, albeit not a strict version. Our general approach is bottom-up. We begin at the infrastructure layer, starting with helpers and deciding what DAOs we're going to provide. DTOs will all be transparent. From our decisions about DAOs, the business objects will fall into place almost automatically. Finally, we have to implement the application. Because our current focus is on database programming, we'll keep the UI and workflow basic and provide a small command-line interface.

Here is how the application should work. The application should start by creating the database schema. With logging enabled, we should see the following output when the application starts:

```
DROP   TABLE Athlete   IF EXISTS;
CREATE TABLE Athlete (
    athleteId   INTEGER GENERATED BY DEFAULT AS IDENTITY,
    dateOfBirth DATE,
    firstname   VARCHAR(64),
    lastname    VARCHAR(64)
);
```

Entering athletes should be like in this transcript (input in bold):

```
create Paul Tergat 1969-06-17
1 Athlete(s) in DB:
id firstname   lastname      dateOfBirth
0: Paul        Tergat        1969-06-17
create Khalid Khannouchi
2 Athlete(s) in DB:
id firstname   lastname      dateOfBirth
0: Paul        Tergat        1969-06-17
1: Khalid      Khannouchi    null
```

Note that we use the create operation and pass parameters in a well-known sequence. Missing parameters result in null values. The current list of athletes is displayed after the operation, sorted by the automatically generated ID.

The update operation should work for a given ID, fieldname, and new value:

```
update 1 dateOfBirth 1971-12-22
1 row(s) updated
2 Athlete(s) in DB:
id firstname  lastname    dateOfBirth
0: Paul       Tergat      1969-06-17
1: Khalid     Khannouchi  1971-12-22
```

The list of athletes should be sortable, where the sort is performed by the database, not in the application code. It needs to support multiple-column sorts:

```
sort firstname
2 Athlete(s) in DB:
id firstname  lastname    dateOfBirth
1: Khalid     Khannouchi  1971-12-22
0: Paul       Tergat      1969-06-17
```

The delete operation should accept an ID and delete the corresponding row:

```
delete 1
1 row(s) deleted
1 Athlete(s) in DB:
id firstname  lastname    dateOfBirth
0: Paul       Tergat      1969-06-17
```

The application is to be terminated with the exit operation.

No validation of user input needs to be implemented; we also don't need to gracefully handle database errors resulting from bad user input.

Let's see how to design and implement the infrastructure, domain model, and application layer to make this functionality work.

13.4.3 *Implementing the infrastructure*

The infrastructure contains helpers and DAOs. For our example, we have a single helper class DbHelper, an AthleteDAO, and a general abstract DataAccessObject as depicted in figure 13.5.

The DbHelper is responsible for providing access to an instance of groovy.sql.Sql through its db property and setting it to a default value. The second responsibility is to support automatic schema creation by executing the DDL for a given Data-AccessObject.

The DataAccessObject is a general implementation of the basic CRUD operations. The AthleteDAO is a specialization of a DataAccessObject providing the least possible information for accessing an Athlete table: the fieldnames and their types.

We'll next go through the classes to see how they implement their responsibilities.

IMPLEMENTING DBHELPER

The implementation of DbHelper as in listing 13.21 yields no surprises. It contains the code for a database connection via the Sql class and the SQL template for creating a table. Unlike in previously presented variants, we now use a SimpleTemplateEngine for separation of concerns.

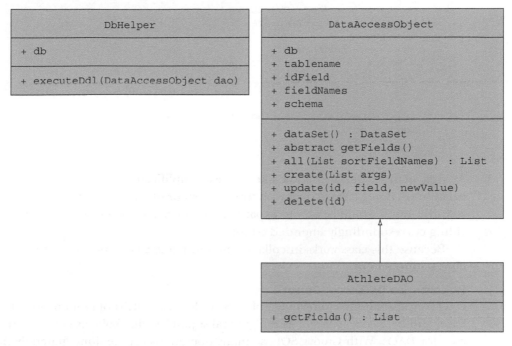

Figure 13.5 UML class diagram of the athlete example's infrastructure layer

The template contains the *structure* of a simple table definition in SQL; the Data-AccessObject as passed into executeDdl is used for getting *details* about the table name and other schema details, such as fieldnames and their SQL types.

Listing 13.21 Athlete example infrastructure: DbHelper

```
package layering

import groovy.sql.Sql
import groovy.text.SimpleTemplateEngine as STE

import org.hsqldb.jdbc.JDBCDataSource

class DbHelper {
  Sql db

  DbHelper() {
    db = new Sql(new JDBCDataSource(
        database: 'jdbc:hsqldb:mem:GinA', user: 'sa', password: ''))
  }
  def simpleTemplate = new STE().createTemplate('''
DROP   TABLE $name   IF EXISTS;
CREATE TABLE $name (
    ${lowname}Id   INTEGER GENERATED BY DEFAULT AS IDENTITY,
$fields
);
''')
```

```
    def executeDdl(DataAccessObject dao) {
      def template = simpleTemplate
      def binding = [
          name: dao.tablename,
          lowname: dao.tablename.toLowerCase(),
          fields: dao.schema.collect { key, val ->
            "     ${key.padRight(12)} $val" }.join(",\n")
      ]
      def stmt = template.make(binding).toString()
      db.execute stmt
    }
}
```

At first glance, this may look like an oversimplification of SQL table definitions, because we don't have to deal with foreign keys or other constraints, views, joins, and so forth. But it would be easy to expand DbHelper to also cover those scenarios by providing correspondingly amended templates.

Because this class works in collaboration with a DataAccessObject, that's the next class to implement.

IMPLEMENTING DATAACCESSOBJECT

DAOs encapsulate the knowledge of how to do basic CRUD operations with the database, and DataAccessObject is the general superclass that collects common functionality for DAOs. With Groovy SQL, so many operations can be done generally that this superclass grows large in comparison to its subclasses.

In addition to the CRUD operations, DataAccessObject uses the structural information that its subclasses provide through their class names and the getFields method to build the DAOs' meta-information in a general way.

Subclasses are expected to follow the naming convention of MyTableDAO for a table of name MyTable. Their getFields method is expected to return a list of strings, alternating between the fieldnames and their SQL type descriptions.

The following listing shows how DataAccessObject uses this information to expose the table name, fieldnames, schema, and so forth.

Listing 13.22   Athlete example infrastructure: DataAccessObject

```
package layering

abstract class DataAccessObject {
  def db

  abstract List getFields()                                    ❶ Subclass
                                                                 implements this to
                                                                 provide field list

  def dataSet() { db.dataSet(tablename) }                      ❷ Properties for
  def getIdField() { tablename.toLowerCase() + 'Id' }            use in SQL
  private getWhereId() { "WHERE $idField = ?" }                  statements

  String getTablename() {
    def name = this.getClass().name
    return name[name.lastIndexOf('.') + 1..-4]
  }
```

```
    def create(List args) {                                    ◄─┐    Creates
      Map argMap = [:]                                        ③─┘    operation
      args.eachWithIndex { arg, i -> argMap[fieldNames[i]] = arg }
      dataSet().add argMap
    }

  Map getSchema() {
    Map result = [:]
    fieldNames.each {
      result[it] = fields[fields.indexOf(it) + 1]
    }
    return result
  }

  List getFieldNames() {
    List result = []
    0.step(fields.size(), 2) { result << fields[it] }
    return result
  }

  def update(field, newValue, id) {
    def stmt = "UPDATE $tablename SET $field = ? $whereId"
    db.executeUpdate stmt, [newValue, id]
  }

  def delete(id) {
    def stmt = "DELETE FROM $tablename $whereId"
    db.executeUpdate stmt, [id]
  }

  def all(sortField) {                           ◄─┐    Sample read
    def selects = fieldNames + idField          ④─┘    operation
    def result = []
    def stmt = "SELECT " + selects.join(',') +
        " FROM $tablename ORDER BY $sortField"
    db.eachRow(stmt.toString()) { rs ->
      Map businessObject = [:]
      selects.each { businessObject[it] = rs[it] }
      result << businessObject
    }
    return result
  }
}
```

Note that the CRUD operations work with prepared statements. The `update` and `delete` statements both use the `id` column to identify a row, obtaining the appropriate where clause using properties ❷. The creation operation ❸ takes a list of values, which it converts into a map by assuming they're in the same order as the field list provided by the subclass via the `getFields` method ❶. A single read operation ❹ is provided, but because `db` is available as a property, callers can provide their own queries easily enough. For this particular application, we don't need any other read operations anyway.

The `all` method returns business objects transparently as maps.

IMPLEMENTING ATHLETEDAO

With all the hard work already done in `DataAccessObject`, implementing the `Athlete-DAO` is a breeze. It's hardly worth an object.

The following listing shows how `AthleteDAO` needs to do nothing else but subclass `DataAccessObject` and provide the field information.

Listing 13.23   Athlete example infrastructure: `AthleteDAO`

```
package layering

class AthleteDAO extends DataAccessObject {
  List getFields() {
    return [
        'firstname',   'VARCHAR(64)',
        'lastname',    'VARCHAR(64)',
        'dateOfBirth', 'DATE'
    ]
  }
}
```

If you ever need specialized versions of CRUD operations or elaborate finder methods, such a DAO provides the place to put it in. For simple applications, a DAO is overkill and you can get by without one, as you'll see in the next section.

13.4.4 *Using a transparent domain model*

Our application uses transparent business objects, implemented as maps. There is no `Athlete` class as you might expect.

Of course, if we ever needed one, we could easily create it like this:

```
class Athlete {
    def firstname
    def lastname
    def dateOfBirth
}
```

Inside the application, we could create these objects, for example, from an `Athlete-DAO` call like

```
athletes = athleteDAO.all('firstname').collect{ new Athlete(it) }
```

The reason for not introducing such business objects is that they currently add no value. All their information (the fieldnames) is already available in the DAO.

The point at which to start using such business objects is when they begin to depend on other objects in the domain layer or when they provide additional behavior, such as specialized methods.

In the next section, you'll see that simple applications are even easier when using transparent business objects.

13.4.5 *Implementing the application layer*

The application layer is implemented in the `AthleteApplication` class. Listing 13.24 reveals that it does little more than call the infrastructure and display the transparent business objects.

The `mainLoop` method reads the user input from the console, interpreting the first word as the operation and any additional input as parameters. It passes this information to `invokeMethod`, which automatically dispatches to the according method call. Each keyword is implemented by a method of the same name.

Listing 13.24 Athlete example application layer: `AthleteApplication`

```
package layering

class AthleteApplication {
  def helper = new DbHelper()
  def athleteDAO = new AthleteDAO(db: helper.db)       ❶ Initialization.
  def sortBy = 'athleteId'
  def done = false

  def init() { helper.executeDdl(athleteDAO) }

  def exit() { done = true }

  def sort(field) {
    sortBy = field
    list()
  }

  def create(first, last = null, dob = null) {
    athleteDAO.create([first, last, dob])
    list()
  }

  def list() {
    def athletes = athleteDAO.all(sortBy)
    println athletes.size() + ' Athlete(s) in DB: '
    println 'id firstname  lastname     dateOfBirth'
    athletes.each { athlete ->
      println athlete.athleteId + ': ' +
        athlete.firstname.padRight(10) + ' ' +
        athlete.lastname.padRight(12) + ' ' +
        athlete.dateOfBirth
    }
  }

  def update(id, field, newValue) {
    def count = athleteDAO.update(field, newValue, id)
    println count + ' row(s) updated'
    list()
  }

  def delete(id) {
    def count = athleteDAO.delete(id)
    println count + ' row(s) deleted'
    list()
  }
```

```
def mainLoop() {
  def reader = System.in.newReader()
  while (!done) {
    println '\ncommands: create list update delete sort exit'
    def input = reader.readLine().tokenize()
    def method = input.remove(0)
    this."$method"(*input)
  }
}
}
```

Entry point after ❷ **initialization.**

Commands are provided as methods, then arguments.

To use the application, you first need to initialize the database ❶ before calling the main loop of the class ❷. Because the commands are provided as the method name followed by the arguments, you can tokenize each line and treat it as a method call. Of course, you'd have lots of validation in a real system, but it's amazing how a *functional* console interface can be implemented with so little code.

You can see this in action in the following listing, which shows a script that fires up the application, ready for input from the user at the console prompt.

Listing 13.25   Running the `Athlete` example application

```
import layering.*

def app = new AthleteApplication()
app.init()
app.mainLoop()
```

It wasn't intended originally, but this little application effectively implements a *domain-specific language*: a simple line-oriented command language for manipulating the `Athlete` table. This example provides a good way to learn Groovy SQL. It's worth playing with the given code and expanding it in multiple dimensions: more DAOs, relationships between DAOs (one-to-one, one-to-many), views, more operations, and a more sophisticated UI.

You might wonder how to test our `AthleteApplication` class. Because it takes input from the console, you can certainly perform manual testing and we'd encourage you to do so. It always pays to do some exploratory testing[19] in addition to running your test suites. But we can create a test for our regression suites too by intercepting the standard input and output streams as shown in the following listing.

Listing 13.26   Testing the `Athlete` example application

```
import layering.*

def app = new AthleteApplication()
app.init()
ByteArrayOutputStream baos = captureSystemOut()
overrideSystemIn()
```

---

[19] See www.kaner.com/pdfs/QAIExploring.pdf and James Bach, "What is Exploratory Testing? And How it Differs from Scripted Testing," Satisfice Inc., http://www.satisfice.com/articles/what_is_et.shtml.

```
app.mainLoop()
verifyOutput(baos)                          ┌─ Captures standard
                                            │  output stream for
def captureSystemOut() {          ◄─────────┘  testing
    def baos = new ByteArrayOutputStream()
    System.out = new PrintStream(baos)
    baos
}

def overrideSystemIn() {              ◄──┐  Replaces standard
    System.in = new ByteArrayInputStream('''\    │  input stream with
create Paul Tergat 1969-06-17         │  canned input
create Khalid Khannouchi               ┘
update 1 dateOfBirth 1971-12-22
sort firstname
delete 1
exit
'''.bytes)
}

def verifyOutput(output) {
    assert output.toString().readLines()*.trim().join('\n') == '''
commands: create list update delete sort exit
1 Athlete(s) in DB:
id firstname  lastname    dateOfBirth
0: Paul       Tergat      1969-06-17

commands: create list update delete sort exit
2 Athlete(s) in DB:
id firstname  lastname    dateOfBirth
0: Paul       Tergat      1969-06-17
1: Khalid     Khannouchi  null

commands: create list update delete sort exit
1 row(s) updated
2 Athlete(s) in DB:
id firstname  lastname    dateOfBirth
0: Paul       Tergat      1969-06-17
1: Khalid     Khannouchi  1971-12-22

commands: create list update delete sort exit
2 Athlete(s) in DB:
id firstname  lastname    dateOfBirth
1: Khalid     Khannouchi  1971-12-22
0: Paul       Tergat      1969-06-17

commands: create list update delete sort exit
1 row(s) deleted
1 Athlete(s) in DB:
id firstname  lastname    dateOfBirth
0: Paul       Tergat      1969-06-17

commands: create list update delete sort exit'''
}
```

By now, you should have a good idea of how to possibly organize your code around Groovy SQL to work with relational databases. It has become increasingly popular, however, to also consider nonrelational data stores. Groovy shines here as well.

13.5   Groovy and NoSQL

We don't have sufficient space to cover the topic of NoSQL databases at an in-depth level. Such information is covered elsewhere.[20] Instead we plan to whet your appetite by diving straight into showing you how easy it is to use a couple of the popular NoSQL databases: MongoDB, a document database, and Neo4j, a graph database. We'll start with MongoDB.

13.5.1   MongoDB: A document-style database

Relational database systems like you saw earlier in this chapter store data in (typically) highly normalized two-dimensional tables with rows and columns. Data values are (typically) strictly typed and tables can be joined into more complex ones. If you can predict your data use ahead of time, it's relatively straightforward to design appropriate database schemas to allow efficient queries to be carried out.

Document databases take a different tack. Instead of aiming for high levels of normalization, document databases aim to keep related material together in a document or nested map of information. This allows more ad hoc data structures to be used and lends itself to being able to scale in large distributed environments. We'll examine MongoDB[21] (www.mongodb.org) as our exemplar document database.

INSTALLING MONGODB

So let's get started. MongoDB runs as a separate server process. You'll need to download and install it by following the instructions on the MongoDB website. Once it's installed, run the `mongod` executable from the command line. You now have a database server you can talk to. You might want to optionally play with the MongoDB shell to familiarize yourself with some of the database's features but we'll move straight on to accessing it from Groovy via its API.

USING MONGODB

MongoDB has a Java API. Thanks to Groovy's great Java integration, to interact with your MongoDB server from Groovy, you could use that API directly but there's also a special-purpose Groovy API called GMongo (https://github.com/poiati/gmongo). That's what we'll use.

Suppose now we wanted to store our original athlete information in MongoDB. We certainly could mirror our `Athlete` and `Record` tables that we used with our relational database but a more document-style approach would be to keep an athlete and his or her runs as a single document. So we'll choose to store an athlete as a map of properties. One of those properties is the runs, which is a list of maps, each map in the list representing one run. Let's work on a script for entering the athlete information.

---

[20] See *Seven Databases in Seven Weeks*, by E. Redmond and J. R. Wilson (Pragmatic Programmers, 2012) or "NoSQL," https://en.wikipedia.org/wiki/NoSQL.

[21] Another good source is Kyle Banker, *MongoDB in Action*, 2nd edition, (Manning Publications, 2011), www.manning.com/banker/. A second edition is to be published this year.

ENTERING INFORMATION

First, we'll need to access the GMongo library. We'll do that using @Grab. We'll use a field in our script (hence the @Field annotation) to store our reference to the database. For good measure we'll clean out any earlier versions of an athlete collection before adding Paul Tergat and his Berlin run into an athlete collection.

```
@Grab('com.gmongo:gmongo:1.3')
import com.gmongo.GMongo
import groovy.transform.Field

@Field db = new GMongo.getDB('athletes')
db.athletes.drop()
db.athletes << [first: 'Paul', last: 'Tergat', dob: '1969-06-17', runs: [
    [distance: 42195, time: 2*60*60 + 4*60 + 55,
        venue: 'Berlin', when: '2003-09-28']
]]
```

If we want to add lots of athletes and runs (perhaps at different times) it might be useful to define a couple of helper methods:

```
def insertAthlete(first, last, dob) {
  db.athletes << [first: first, last: last, dob: dob]
}

def insertRun(h, m, s, venue, date, lastname) {
  db.athletes.update(
      [last: lastname],
      [$addToSet: [runs: [distance: 42195,
          time: h * 60 * 60 + m * 60 + s,
          venue: venue, when: date]]]
  )
}
```

Note that because we're storing an athlete's runs with the athlete (all one document, remember) we use an update method and a special $addToSet operator, which together will accumulate any runs we add into the runs property. Here's how we might use those methods:

```
insertAthlete('Khalid', 'Khannouchi', '1971-12-22')
insertAthlete('Ronaldo', 'da Costa', '1970-06-07')

insertRun(2,5,38, 'London',  '2002-04-14', 'Khannouchi')
insertRun(2,5,42, 'Chicago', '1999-10-24', 'Khannouchi')
insertRun(2,6,05, 'Berlin',  '1998-09-20', 'da Costa')
```

This should look very familiar to you. The fact that we split out the two helper methods means that we normalized to some extent data entry.

Given that we might want to add any arbitrary document, it should come as no surprise that GMongo supports mechanisms to enter whole documents not just rows. We'll look at entering Paula Radcliffe's information as a JSON document:

```
import com.mongodb.util.JSON

def radcliffe = """{
  first: 'Paula',
```

```
        last: 'Radcliffe',
        dob: '1973-12-17',
        runs: [
            {distance: 42195, time: ${2*60*60+15*60+25},
                venue: 'London', when: '2003-04-13'}
        ]
}"""
```

```
db.athletes << JSON.parse(radcliffe)
```

Now let's look at forms for querying our athlete information.

QUERYING OUR DATABASE

First, we'll check how many athletes we have and then list each athlete we find in the collection:

```
assert db.athletes.count == 4
db.athletes.find().each {
  println "$it._id $it.last ${it.runs.size()}"
}
```

For our system this prints out

```
516b15fc2b10a15fa09331f2 Tergat 1
516b15fc2b10a15fa09331f3 Khannouchi 2
516b15fc2b10a15fa09331f4 da Costa 1
516b15fc2b10a15fa09331f5 Radcliffe 1
```

If you run this yourself, you'll no doubt see something similar but with your own unique IDs. Next, let's confirm the athletes who have run in London:

```
def londonAthletes = db.athletes.find('runs.venue': 'London')*.first
assert londonAthletes == ['Khalid', 'Paula']
```

Now we'll retrieve the first names of the athletes born after 1970 (sorted from youngest to oldest):

```
def youngAthletes = db.athletes.aggregate(
    [$project: [first: 1, dob: 1]],
    [$match: [dob: [$gte: '1970-01-01']]],
    [$sort: [dob: -1]]
)
assert youngAthletes.results()*.first == ['Paula', 'Khalid', 'Ronaldo']
```

Let's look at those steps as a single listing.

Listing 13.27   Athletes stored in MongoDB

```
@Grab('com.gmongo:gmongo:1.3')
import com.gmongo.GMongo
import com.mongodb.util.JSON
import groovy.transform.Field

@Field db = new GMongo().getDB('athletes')
db.athletes.drop()
```

```
db.athletes << [first: 'Paul', last: 'Tergat', dob: '1969-06-17', records: [
    [time: 2 * 60 * 60 + 4 * 60 + 55,
        venue: 'Berlin', when: '2003-09-28']
]]

def insertAthlete(first, last, dob) {
    db.athletes << [first: first, last: last, dob: dob]
}

def insertRecord(h, m, s, venue, date, lastname) {
    db.athletes.update(
            [last: lastname],
            [$addToSet: [records: [time: h * 60 * 60 + m * 60 + s,
                                   venue: venue, when: date]]]
    )
}

insertAthlete('Khalid', 'Khannouchi', '1971-12-22')
insertAthlete('Ronaldo', 'da Costa', '1970-06-07')

insertRecord(2, 5, 38, 'London', '2002-04-14', 'Khannouchi')
insertRecord(2, 5, 42, 'Chicago', '1999-10-24', 'Khannouchi')
insertRecord(2, 6, 05, 'Berlin', '1998-09-20', 'da Costa')

def radcliffe = """{
    first: 'Paula',
    last: 'Radcliffe',
    dob: '1973-12-17',
    records: [
        {time: ${2 * 60 * 60 + 15 * 60 + 25},
            venue: 'London', when: '2003-04-13'}
    ]
}"""

db.athletes << JSON.parse(radcliffe)

assert db.athletes.count == 4
db.athletes.find().each {
    println "$it._id $it.last ${it.records.size()}"
}

def londonAthletes = db.athletes.find('records.venue': 'London')*.first
assert londonAthletes == ['Khalid', 'Paula']

def youngAthletes = db.athletes.aggregate(
        [$project: [first: 1, dob: 1]],
        [$match: [dob: [$gte: '1970-01-01']]],
        [$sort: [dob: -1]]
)

assert youngAthletes.results()*.first == ['Paula', 'Khalid', 'Ronaldo']
```

That sure was a whirlwind tour of MongoDB, but we hope we've given you a flavor for the document style of NoSQL database. Next, we'll look at a graph database.

13.5.2 Neo4J: A graph database

Graph databases store structured data in terms of nodes, edges, and properties. They're ideally suited to data that's highly interrelated. Individual nodes use edges to point to data they're related to. When deep interconnections exist within the data, the extra overheads of storing this additional edge information yield extremely fast query and traversal times compared to more traditional approaches.

We'll use the popular Neo4j (www.neo4j.org/) database to illustrate a graph database.[22] Let's start by defining our athlete information. To make it more interesting from a graph point of view we'll add information about the relationship between marathon records, such as when one record broke an earlier record. Let's have a look at how we might code this in a script. We'll cover adding each piece of information before showing you a complete listing.

ENTERING INFORMATION

First we define the necessary @Grab to make the Neo4j library available. We define a variable in our script to point to the database. We're using Neo4j in its embedded mode so there's no need for any other kind of installation:

```
@Grab('org.neo4j:neo4j-kernel:2.1.6')
import org.neo4j.graphdb.*
import org.neo4j.graphdb.factory.GraphDatabaseFactory

def factory = new GraphDatabaseFactory()
def db = factory.newEmbeddedDatabase("marathon")
```

We also declare an enum to capture the relationships that we'll be representing within our data:

```
enum MyRelationshipTypes implements RelationshipType { set, broke }
```

We've chosen to use a bit of metaprogramming magic here to make our remaining code be more succinct:

```
Node.metaClass {
  propertyMissing { String name, val -> delegate.setProperty(name, val) }
  propertyMissing { String name -> delegate.getProperty(name) }
  methodMissing { String name, args ->
    delegate.createRelationshipTo(args[0], MyRelationshipTypes."$name")
  }
}
```

With these definitions in place, here's how we define Paul Tergat and his Berlin record:

```
def tx = db.beginTx()
def athlete1, record1
try {
  athlete1 = db.createNode()
  athlete1.first = 'Paul'
  athlete1.last = 'Tergat'
  athlete1.dob = '1969-06-17'
  record1 = db.createNode()
  record1.distance = 42195
```

---

[22] Another good source is Aleksa Vukotic et al., *Neo4j in Action* (Manning Publications, 2014), www.manning.com/partner/.

```
record1.time = 2*60*60+4*60+55
record1.venue = 'Berlin'
record1.when = '2003-09-28'
athlete1.set(record1)

def venue = record1.venue
def when = record1.when
println "$athlete1.first $athlete1.last won the $venue marathon on $when"

tx.success()
} finally {
tx.close()
db.shutdown()
}
```

As in previous examples, we might wish to define helper methods to make additional athlete and run definitions easier. First a little bit more metaprogramming will be useful:

```
GraphDatabaseService.metaClass {
  createNode { Map properties ->
    def n = delegate.createNode()
    properties.each{ k, v -> n[k] = v }
    n
  }
}
Relationship.metaClass {
  propertyMissing { String name, val -> delegate.setProperty(name, val) }
  propertyMissing { String name -> delegate.getProperty(name) }
}
```

These will let us use a Map-flavored variant for createNode. Now our helper methods are:

```
def athlete(db, first, last, dob) {
  db.createNode(first: first, last: last, dob: dob)
}

def record(db, h, m, s, venue, when, athlete) {
  def secs = h * 60 * 60 + m * 60 + s
  def record = db.createNode(time: secs, venue: venue, when: when)
  athlete.set(record)
  run
}
```

With these definitions in place, we can add the additional athletes:

```
athlete2 = athlete(db, 'Khalid', 'Khannouchi', '1971-12-22')
record2a = record(db, 2, 5, 38, 'London', '2002-04-14', athlete2)
record2b = record(db, 2, 5, 42, 'Chicago', '1999-10-24', athlete2)

athlete3 = athlete(db, 'Ronaldo', 'da Costa', '1970-06-07')
record3 = record(db, 2, 6, 5, 'Berlin', '1998-09-20', athlete3)

athlete4 = athlete(db, 'Paula', 'Radcliffe', '1973-12-17')
record4a = record(db, 2, 17, 18, 'Chicago', '2002-10-13', athlete4)
record4b = record(db, 2, 15, 25, 'London', '2003-04-13', athlete4)
```

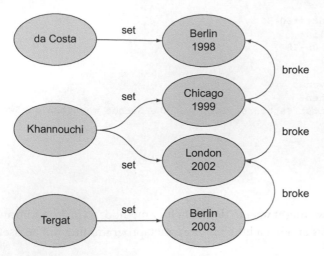

Figure 13.6   Marathon world records showing edge relationships

QUERYING OUR DATABASE

We can perform queries on the athletes and their relationships as follows:

```
def allAthletes = [athlete1, athlete2, athlete3, athlete4]
def londonRecords = allAthletes.findAll { athlete ->
  athlete.getRelationships(MarathonRelationships.set).any {
    record -> record.getOtherNode(athlete).venue == 'London'
  }
}
assert londonRecords*.last == ['Khannouchi', 'Radcliffe']
```

The real power of graph databases comes into play when we have more interesting relationships. Let's add a `broke` relationship to indicate that one marathon world record broke an earlier one:

```
record2b.broke(record3)
record2a.broke(record2b)
record1.broke(record2a)
record4b.broke(record4a)
```

Figure 13.6 illustrates these relationships graphically.

With these relationships in place we can now perform more interesting queries that rely on the graph structure of the data. We can use the API from earlier when we determined which athletes have won a race in London. This API can become a little bit cumbersome with complex graph algorithms. Fortunately, Neo4j comes with special traversal methods especially for when working with graph algorithms. Let's use the traversal facilities to find all records that superseded Ronaldo da Costa's Berlin world record:

```
import org.neo4j.graphdb.traversal.*

println "World records following $record3.venue $record3.when:"
def result = []
  for (Path p in db.traversalDescription().breadthFirst().
      relationships(MarathonRelationships.broke).
      evaluator(Evaluators.fromDepth(1)).
```

```
        uniqueness(Uniqueness.NONE).
        traverse(record3)) {
      def newRecord = p.endNode()
      println "$newRecord.venue $newRecord.when"
  }
```

Running this yields the following output:

```
World records following Berlin 1998-09-20:
Chicago 1999-10-24
London 2002-04-14
Berlin 2003-09-28
```

That took quite a few steps. Let's see it all together in a single listing.

Listing 13.28   Neo4J marathon database

```
@Grab('org.neo4j:neo4j-kernel:2.1.6')
@Grab('org.neo4j:neo4j-lucene-index:2.1.6;transitive=false')
@Grab('org.apache.lucene:lucene-core:3.6.2')
import org.neo4j.graphdb.*
import org.neo4j.graphdb.traversal.*
import static util.Neo4jUtil.*

def db = create()
def tx = null
def athlete1, athlete2, athlete3, athlete4
def record1, record2a, record2b, record3, record4a, record4b
try {
  tx = db.beginTx()

  athlete1 = db.createNode()              Creates
  athlete1.first = 'Paul'                 athlete1
  athlete1.last = 'Tergat'                by hand
  athlete1.dob = '1969-06-17'

  record1 = db.createNode()               Creates
  record1.time = 2 * 60 * 60 + 4 * 60 + 55   record1
  record1.venue = 'Berlin'                by hand
  record1.when = '2003-09-28'

  athlete1.set(record1)

  assert 'Paul Tergat won the Berlin marathon on 2003-09-28' ==
      "$athlete1.first $athlete1.last won the " +
      "$record1.venue marathon on $record1.when"

  athlete2 = insertAthlete(
      db, 'Khalid', 'Khannouchi', '1971-12-22')   Creates nodes
  record2a = insertRecord(                         using utility
      db, 2, 5, 38, 'London', '2002-04-14', athlete2)   methods
  record2b = insertRecord(
      db, 2, 5, 42, 'Chicago', '1999-10-24', athlete2)

  athlete3 = insertAthlete(db, 'Ronaldo', 'da Costa', '1970-06-07')
  record3 = insertRecord(db, 2, 6, 5, 'Berlin', '1998-09-20', athlete3)
```

```
athlete4 = insertAthlete(db, 'Paula', 'Radcliffe', '1973-12-17')
record4a = insertRecord(
    db, 2, 17, 18, 'Chicago', '2002-10-13', athlete4)
record4b = insertRecord(
    db, 2, 15, 25, 'London', '2003-04-13', athlete4)

def allAthletes = [athlete1, athlete2, athlete3, athlete4]
def londonRecords = allAthletes.findAll { athlete ->
  athlete.getRelationships(MarathonRelationships.set).any {
    record -> record.getOtherNode(athlete).venue == 'London'
  }
}
assert londonRecords*.last == ['Khannouchi', 'Radcliffe']
```

Finds athletes holding a record set in London

```
record2b.broke(record3)
record2a.broke(record2b)
record1.broke(record2a)
record4b.broke(record4a)
```

Specifies additional graph edges of interest

```
def result = []
for (Path p in db.traversalDescription().breadthFirst().
    relationships(MarathonRelationships.broke).
    evaluator(Evaluators.fromDepth(1)).
    uniqueness(Uniqueness.NONE).
    traverse(record3)) {
  def newRecord = p.endNode()
  result << "$newRecord.venue $newRecord.when"
}
def expected = ['Chicago 1999-10-24',
                'London 2002-04-14',
                'Berlin 2003-09-28']
assert expected == result

tx.success()
} finally {
  tx?.close()
}
```

Finds world records superseding record3

Such graph-based queries are so common for graph databases that a special Groovy-based DSL called Gremlin[23] has been devised to make writing such queries a bit easier.

USING GREMLIN

Let's use Gremlin and perform some similar queries again. First, we add the necessary @Grab commands to load the Gremlin library and the needed import statements:

```
@Grab('com.tinkerpop.gremlin:gremlin-groovy:2.6.0')
@Grab('com.tinkerpop.blueprints:blueprints-neo4j-graph:2.6.0')
@Grab('com.tinkerpop.blueprints:blueprints-core:2.6.0')
import com.tinkerpop.blueprints.Graph
import com.tinkerpop.blueprints.impls.neo4j.Neo4jGraph
import com.tinkerpop.gremlin.groovy.Gremlin
```

---

[23] Gremlin is a DSL for traversing property graphs. See https://github.com/tinkerpop/gremlin.

Next we need to initialize Gremlin (it enables similar metaprogramming to what we've done manually earlier in this section) and then create a Gremlin `Graph` object, which will let us do our queries:

```
Gremlin.load()

Graph g = new Neo4jGraph(graphDb)
```

The expression `g.V('venue', 'London')` finds all vertices in our graph that have their venue property set to `London`. We can use that expression to find all the records set in London:

```
def pretty = { it.collect{ "$it.venue $it.when" }.join(', ') }
def results = []
g.V('venue', 'London').fill(results)
println 'London world records: ' + pretty(results)
```

For our data this will produce

```
London world records: London 2002-04-14, London 2003-04-13
```

We can also find all world records set immediately after (that is, breaking) a world record set in London:

```
results = []
g.V('venue', 'London').in('broke').fill(results)
println 'World records after London: ' + pretty(results)
```

For our data, this produces

```
World records after London: Berlin 2003-09-28
```

And to see traversal in action, we can find all world records after Ronaldo da Costa's Berlin world record:

```
results = []
def berlin98 = { it.venue == 'Berlin' && it.when.startsWith('1998') }
def emitAll = { true }
def forever = { true }
g.V.filter(berlin98).in('broke').
  loop(1, forever, emitAll).fill(results)
println 'World records after Berlin 1998: ' + pretty(results)
```

For our data, this produces

```
World records after London: Berlin 2003-09-28
World records after Berlin 1998: Chicago 1999-10-24, London 2002-04-14,
    Berlin 2003-09-28
```

Let's see that one more time as a complete listing.

Listing 13.29 Neo4J with Gremlin

```
@Grab('org.neo4j:neo4j-kernel:2.1.6')
@Grab('org.neo4j:neo4j-management:2.1.6')
@Grab('org.neo4j:neo4j-cypher:2.1.6;transitive=false')
@Grab('org.neo4j:neo4j-cypher-commons:2.1.6;transitive=false')
```

```
@Grab('org.neo4j:neo4j-cypher-compiler-1.9:2.0.4;transitive=false')
@Grab('org.neo4j:neo4j-cypher-compiler-2.0:2.0.4;transitive=false')
@Grab('org.neo4j:neo4j-cypher-compiler-2.1:2.1.6;transitive=false')
@Grab('org.neo4j:neo4j-lucene-index:2.1.6;transitive=false')
@Grab('org.apache.lucene:lucene-core:3.6.2')
@Grab('com.tinkerpop.gremlin:gremlin-groovy:2.6.0;transitive=false')
@Grab('com.tinkerpop.gremlin:gremlin-java:2.6.0;transitive=false')
@Grab('com.tinkerpop.blueprints:\
blueprints-neo4j2-graph:2.6.0;transitive=false')
@Grab('commons-configuration:commons-configuration:1.6')
@Grab('com.tinkerpop.blueprints:blueprints-core:2.6.0;transitive=false')
@Grab('com.tinkerpop:pipes:2.6.0;transitive=false')
@Grab('org.parboiled:parboiled-scala_2.10:1.1.6;transitive=false')
@Grab('org.parboiled:parboiled-core:1.1.6')
@Grab('org.scala-lang:scala-library:2.10.4')
@Grab('com.googlecode.concurrentlinkedhashmap:\
concurrentlinkedhashmap-lru:1.4.1')
@GrabExclude('junit:junit')
@GrabExclude('org.hamcrest:hamcrest-all')
@GrabExclude('org.mockito:mockito-core')

import com.tinkerpop.blueprints.Graph
import com.tinkerpop.blueprints.impls.neo4j2.Neo4j2Graph
import com.tinkerpop.gremlin.groovy.Gremlin
import static util.Neo4jUtil.*

def db = create()
def tx = null
def athlete1, athlete2, athlete3, athlete4
def record1, record2a, record2b, record3, record4a, record4b

Gremlin.load()

try {
    tx = db.beginTx()

    // create athlete1 .. athlete4
    athlete1 = insertAthlete(db, 'Paul', 'Tergat', '1969-06-17')
    record1 = insertRecord(
        db, 2, 4, 55, 'Berlin', '2003-09-28', athlete1)

    athlete2 = insertAthlete(db, 'Khalid', 'Khannouchi', '1971-12-22')
    record2a = insertRecord(
        db, 2, 5, 38, 'London', '2002-04-14', athlete2)
    record2b = insertRecord(
        db, 2, 5, 42, 'Chicago', '1999-10-24', athlete2)

    athlete3 = insertAthlete(db, 'Ronaldo', 'da Costa', '1970-06-07')
    record3 = insertRecord(
        db, 2, 6, 5, 'Berlin', '1998-09-20', athlete3)

    athlete4 = insertAthlete(db, 'Paula', 'Radcliffe', '1973-12-17')
    record4a = insertRecord(
        db, 2, 17, 18, 'Chicago', '2002-10-13', athlete4)
    record4b = insertRecord(
        db, 2, 15, 25, 'London', '2003-04-13', athlete4)

    record2b.broke(record3)
    record2a.broke(record2b)
```

```
        record1.broke(record2a)
        record4b.broke(record4a)

        Graph g = new Neo4j2Graph(db)

        def pretty = { it.collect { "$it.venue $it.when" }.join(', ') }
        def results = []
        g.V('venue', 'London').fill(results)
        println 'London world records: ' + pretty(results)

        results = []
        g.V('venue', 'London').in('broke').fill(results)
        println 'World records after London: ' + pretty(results)

        results = []
        def emitAll = { true }
        def forever = { true }
        def berlin98 = { it.venue == 'Berlin' &&
                it.when.startsWith('1998') }
        g.V.filter(berlin98).in('broke').
                loop(1, forever, emitAll).fill(results)
        println 'World records after Berlin 1998: ' + pretty(results)
        tx.success()
} finally {
    tx?.close()
}
```

That wraps up our brief tour of graph databases and Neo4j. We're almost done. On the final pages in this chapter, we want to cover other approaches you might find when persisting data.

13.6 *Other approaches*

For some time now, language and library providers have been trying to make databases easier to use. There have been many approaches, including several along the lines of *object-relational mapping* (ORM). In the most general terms, ORM frameworks allow developers to describe their data models, including the relationships, for use in an object-oriented language. The idea is to retrieve data from the database as objects using an object-oriented search facility, manipulate the objects, and then persist any changes back to the database. The ORM system takes care of adding and deleting records in the right order to satisfy constraints, datatype conversions, and similar concerns.

This sounds wonderful, but reality is more complicated than theory, as always. In particular, new databases can often be designed to be "ORM-friendly," but existing databases are sometimes significantly harder to work with. The situation can become sufficiently complex that the author Ted Neward has referred to ORM as "the Vietnam of computer science."[24]

---

[24] "The Vietnam of Computer Science," June 26, 2006, http://blogs.tedneward.com/2006/06/26/The+Vietnam+Of+Computer+Science.aspx.

There are many different approaches and libraries, both free and commercial, for many different platforms. In the Java world, two of the best-known players in the field are the *Java Data Objects* (JDO) specification and *Hibernate.* The latest *Enterprise Java-Beans* (EJB) (also known as the Java Persistence Architecture (JPA) specification) includes ORM to allow implementation-independent expression of relationships. It has yet to be seen how well this independence will work in practice.

As you've seen, Groovy provides more object-oriented database access than good-old JDBC, but it doesn't implement a full-blown ORM solution. Of course, because it integrates seamlessly with Java, any of the solutions available in Java can be used in Groovy too.

Even within the Groovy library, more can be done without crossing the line into full ORM. We expect future versions of Groovy to ship with `DataSets` that support all CRUD operations, a general DAO implementation, and possibly ready-made Active-Record support.

Beyond the Groovy library are activities to come up with a special *Groovy* ORM (GORM). This is an approach that builds on Hibernate but relieves the programmer of all the configuration work by relying on code and naming conventions. GORM is developed as a part of the *Grails* project.

Finally, we'd like to emphasize that it would be a misconception to see ORM as *the* final solution to database programming and to dismiss all other approaches. ORM is targeted at providing object persistence and transaction support. It tries to shield you from the relational model (to some extent). When selecting an ORM solution, make sure it allows you to exploit the relational model. Otherwise, you're losing most of the power that you paid your database vendor for.

We find the Groovy SQL approach appealing: it provides good means for working with the relational model with an almost ORM-like feeling for the simple cases while keeping all statements under programmatic control.

Before leaving this section we would be remiss if we didn't mention the Spring Data project (www.springsource.org/spring-data). This project aims to provide an overarching framework to make it easier for Spring-based applications to use relational and nonrelational databases, MapReduce frameworks, and cloud-based data services. Groovy integrates well with Spring so you may wish to consider using Spring Data from your Groovy or Grails applications to remove some of the differences between the different persistence options.

13.7 Summary

In this chapter, we've shown you that Groovy has considerable support for database programming within its standard library. Groovy SQL is available wherever Groovy is. You don't need to install any additional modules. It's also easy to integrate with the many available NoSQL databases either via their Java support or in some cases with special Groovy functionality.

Groovy SQL is made from a small set of classes that build on JDBC and make it Groovy-friendly. Important features are as follows:

- Minimal setup for database access
- Simple execution of SQL statements
- Improved reliability through automatic, transparent resource handling (`Data-Source`, `Connection`, `Statement`, `ResultSet`)
- Easy transparent use of prepared statements with GStrings
- Convenience with `DataSets` (adding, nested filtering with expressions)
- Transparent DTOs
- Optionally transparent DAOs and business objects

The filtering available in the `DataSet` class is particularly important in terms of closures being understood not only as a block of code but also as an abstract syntax tree. This can allow logic to be expressed in a manner familiar to the developer without the potentially huge inefficiency of retrieving all the data from the database and filtering it within the application.

You've seen how an example application can be written with the help of Groovy SQL so that the code organization fits into architectural layers and database programming patterns with little work.

Although Groovy doesn't provide any true ORM facilities, it integrates well with existing solutions; and where the full complexities of ORM aren't required, the facilities provided above and beyond straight JDBC can help tremendously.

Groovy doesn't come with NoSQL drivers out of the box but it's easy to find appropriate drivers and often special Groovy support for many of the available NoSQL databases.

Working with XML and JSON

14

This chapter covers

This chapter covers
- Reading and writing XML and JSON
- Transforming treelike structures in-place and as streams
- Navigating inside structured data

Perfection is achieved not when you have nothing more to add, but when you have nothing left to take away.

—Antoine de Saint-Exupéry

Computing means applying logic to data. We retrieve data, process it, and store it again. Processing is the essential activity while retrieving and storing are just necessities. All the aspects of various data formats, encodings, and access protocols can get complex, though, and the required work is likely to distract us. Groovy helps us to stay focused by making the data handling part almost transparent.

We're going to explore two data serialization formats that have special built-in support in the Groovy standard library: XML and JSON. Most of the chapter is devoted to XML, which is the more mature approach and has more options available for its production and consumption. JSON is another popular serialization format for semistructured data. We'll briefly cover the details of processing JSON very efficiently at the end of the chapter.

XML, the eXtensible Markup Language, is so commonly used these days that it's hard to believe there were times without it. The World Wide Web Consortium (W3C) standardized the first version of XML in 1996.

The widespread use of XML and worldwide adoption of Java took place at about the same time. This may be one of the reasons why the Java platform developed such excellent support for working with XML. Not only are there the built-in SAX and DOM APIs, but many other libraries have appeared over time for parsing and creating XML and for working with it using standards such as XPath.

The topic of XML has the unusual property of being simple and complex at the same time. XML is straightforward until you bring in namespaces, entities and the like.

Similarly, although it's feasible to demonstrate *one* way of working with XML fairly simply, giving a good overview of *all* (or even most) of the ways of working with XML would require more space than we have in this book. We'll concentrate on the new capabilities that Groovy brings, as well as mention the enhanced support for the DOM API. Even limiting ourselves to these topics doesn't let us explore every nook and cranny.

This chapter is broadly divided into three parts:

- Techniques for parsing XML in Groovy.
- Tricks for processing and transforming XML.
- Groovy support for parsing JSON, which is probably the most widespread alternative to XML.

We assume you already have a reasonable understanding of XML. If you find yourself struggling with any of the XML concepts we use in this chapter, please refer to one of the many available XML books.[1]

XML processing typically starts with reading an XML document, which is our first topic.

14.1 Reading XML documents

When working with XML, we have to somehow *read* it to begin with. This section will lead you through the many options available in Groovy for parsing XML: the normal DOM route, enhanced by Groovy; Groovy's own `XmlParser` and `XmlSlurper` classes; SAX event-based parsing; and StAX pull-parsers.

Let's suppose we have a little data store in XML format for planning our Groovy self-education activities. In this data store, we capture how many hours per week we can invest in this training, what tasks need to be done, and how many hours each task will eat up in total. To keep track of our progress, we'll also store how many hours are "done" for each task and optionally a little summary of how the task went.

---

[1] We recommend *XML Made Simple* by S. Deane and R. Henderson (Made Simple, 2003) as an introductory text, and *XML 1.1 Bible* by E. R. Harold (Wiley, 2004) for more comprehensive coverage.

The following listing shows our XML data store that resides in a file named data/plan.xml.

Listing 14.1   Example data store data/plan.xml

```
<plan>
  <week capacity="8">
    <task done="2" total="2" title="read XML chapter">easy</task>
    <task done="3" total="3" title="try some reporting">fun</task>
    <task done="1" total="2" title="use in current project"/>
  </week>
  <week capacity="8">
    <task done="0" total="1" title="re-read DB chapter"/>
    <task done="0" total="3" title="use DB/XML combination"/>
  </week>
</plan>
```

We plan for two weeks, with eight hours for education each week. Three tasks are scheduled for the current week: reading this chapter (two hours for a quick reader), playing with the newly acquired knowledge (three hours of real fun), and using it in the real world (one hour done and one still left).

This will be our running example for most of the chapter.

For reading such a data store, we'll present two different approaches: using technologies built into the JRE, and then using the Groovy parsers. We'll start with the more familiar DOM parser.

14.1.1   *Working with a DOM parser*

Why do we bother with Java's classic DOM parsers? Shouldn't we restrict ourselves to show only Groovy specifics here?

First, even in Groovy code, we sometimes need DOM objects for further processing; for example, when applying XPath expressions to an object as we'll explain in section 14.2.4. For that reason, we show the Groovy way of retrieving the DOM representation of our data store with the help of Java's DOM parsers. Second, there's basic Groovy support for dealing with DOM NodeLists, and Groovy also provides extra helper classes to simplify common tasks within the DOM. Third, it's much easier to appreciate how slick the Groovy parsers are after having seen the "old" way of reading XML.

We start by loading a DOM tree into memory.

GETTING THE DOCUMENT

Not surprisingly, the DOM is based around the central abstraction of a *document*, realized as the Java interface org.w3c.dom.Document. An object of this type will hold our data store.

The Java way of retrieving a document is through the parse method of a Document-Builder (that is, a parser). This method takes an InputStream to read the XML from. So a first attempt at reading would look like this:

```
def doc = builder.parse(new FileInputStream('data/plan.xml'))
```

Where does `builder` come from? We're working slowly backward to find a solution. The builder must be of type `DocumentBuilder`. Instances of this type are delivered from a `DocumentBuilderFactory`, which has a factory method called `newDocumentBuilder`:

```
def builder = fac.newDocumentBuilder()
def doc     = builder.parse(new FileInputStream('data/plan.xml'))
```

Where does this factory come from? There's a static method to create one of those. Here it's all together:

```
import javax.xml.parsers.DocumentBuilderFactory

def fac     = DocumentBuilderFactory.newInstance()
def builder = fac.newDocumentBuilder()
def doc     = builder.parse(new FileInputStream('data/plan.xml'))
```

Java's XML handling API is designed with flexibility in mind.[2] A downside of this flexibility is that for our simple example, we have a few hoops to jump through to retrieve our file. It's not too bad, though, and now that we have it we can dive into the document.

WALKING THE DOM
The document object isn't yet the root of our data store. To get the top-level element, which is `plan` in our case, we have to ask the document for its `document-Element` property:

```
def plan = doc.documentElement
```

We can now work with the `plan` variable. It's of type `org.w3c.dom.Node` and so it can be asked for its `nodeType` and `nodeName`. The `nodeType` is `Node.ELEMENT_NODE`, and the `nodeName` is `plan`.

The design of such DOM nodes is a bit unusual (to put it mildly). Every node has the same properties, such as `nodeType`, `nodeName`, `nodeValue`, `childNodes`, and `attributes` (to name only a few; see the API documentation for the full list). But what's stored in these properties and how they behave depends on the value of the `nodeType` property.

We'll deal with types `ELEMENT_NODE`, `ATTRIBUTE_NODE`, and `TEXT_NODE` (see the API documentation for the exhaustive list).

It's not surprising that XML elements are stored in nodes of type `ELEMENT_NODE`, but it's surprising that attributes are also stored in node objects (of `nodeType` `ATTRIBUTE_NODE`). To make things even more complex, each value of an attribute is stored in an extra node object (with `nodeType` `TEXT_NODE`). This complexity is a large part of the reason why simpler APIs such as JDOM, dom4j, and XOM have become popular.

---

[2] The `DocumentBuilderFactory` can be augmented in several ways to deliver `DocumentBuilder` implementations. See its API documentation for details.

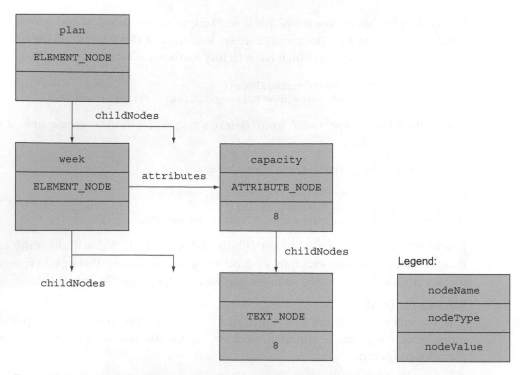

Figure 14.1   Example of a DOM object model (excerpt) for element, attribute, and text nodes

As an example, the nodes and their names, types, and values are depicted in figure 14.1 for the first week element in the data store.

The fact that node objects behave differently with respect to their nodeType leads to code that needs to work with this distinction. For example, when reading information from a node, you need a method such as this:

```
import org.w3c.dom.Node
String info(node) {
    switch (node.nodeType) {
        case Node.ELEMENT_NODE:
            return 'element: '+ node.nodeName
        case Node.ATTRIBUTE_NODE:
            return "attribute: ${node.nodeName}=${node.nodeValue}"
        case Node.TEXT_NODE:
            return 'text: '+ node.nodeValue
    }
    return 'some other type: '+ node.nodeType
}
```

With this helper method, you have almost everything you need to read information from the data store. Two pieces of information aren't yet explained: the types of the childNodes and attributes properties.

The `childNodes` property is of type `org.w3c.dom.NodeList`. Unfortunately, it doesn't extend the `java.util.List` interface but provides its own methods, `get-Length` and `item(index)`. This makes it inconvenient to work with (think error-prone for loops). Fortunately the `groovy-xml` module provides an `iterator` method for `NodeList` that's all that Groovy requires to make its object iteration methods (`each`, `find`, `findAll`, and so on) available on that type (as you already saw in section 12.1.3).

The `attributes` property is of type `org.w3c.dom.NamedNodeMap`, which doesn't extend `java.util.Map` either. We'll use its `getNamedItem(name)` method.

The following listing puts all this together and reads our plan from the XML data store, walking into the first task of the first week.

Listing 14.2 Reading plan.xml with the classic DOM parser

```
import javax.xml.parsers.DocumentBuilderFactory
import static org.w3c.dom.Node.*

def factory = DocumentBuilderFactory.newInstance()
def builder = factory.newDocumentBuilder()
def doc     = builder.parse(new FileInputStream('data/plan.xml'))
def plan    = doc.documentElement

String info(node) {
  switch (node.nodeType) {
    case ELEMENT_NODE:
      return "element: $node.nodeName"
    case ATTRIBUTE_NODE:
      return "attribute: $node.nodeName=$node.nodeValue"
    case TEXT_NODE:
      return "text: $node.nodeValue"
  }
  return "some other type: $node.nodeType"
}

assert info(plan) == 'element: plan'
assert plan.childNodes.length == 5

def firstWeek = plan.childNodes.find { it.nodeName == 'week' }
assert info(firstWeek) == 'element: week'

def firstTask = firstWeek.childNodes.item(1)
assert info(firstTask) == 'element: task'

def firstTaskText = firstTask.childNodes.item(0)
assert info(firstTaskText) == 'text: easy'

def firstTaskTitle = firstTask.attributes.getNamedItem('title')
assert info(firstTaskTitle) == 'attribute: title=read XML chapter'

def firstTaskTitleText = firstTaskTitle.childNodes.item(0)
assert info(firstTaskTitleText) == 'text: read XML chapter'
```

❶ Element and whitespace children visible

❷ Object iteration method

❸ Indexed access

Note how we use the object iteration method `find` ❷ to access the first week element under `plan`. We use indexed access to the first `task` child node ❸. But why is the index 1 and not 0? Because in our XML document, there's a line break between week and `task`. The DOM parser generates a text node containing this line break (and surrounding whitespace) and adds it as the first child node of `week` (at index 0). The `task` node floats to the second position with index 1. These text nodes (three in all) also explain why we have five child nodes at ❶.

> **NOTE** Groovy 2 introduced Modularization (see section B.3 in appendix B) and groovy-xml is one of the available modules. If you're using the groovy-all JAR file or using one of the Groovy distributions, you'll automatically have the groovy-xml module available to you. If, however, you're integrating directly with the core groovy JAR file, then you might need to `@Grab` the groovy-xml module (contained in groovy-xml.jar) or place the JAR file on your classpath.

MAKING DOM GROOVIER

Groovy wouldn't be "groovy" without a convenience method for the lengthy parsing prework:

```
def doc  = DOMBuilder.parse(new FileReader('data/plan.xml'))
def plan = doc.documentElement
```

> **NOTE** The `DOMBuilder` isn't only for convenient parsing. As the name suggests, it's a builder and can be used like any other builder (see chapter 11). It returns a tree of `org.w3c.dom.Node` objects just as if they'd been parsed from an XML document. You can add it to another tree, write it to XML, or query it using XPath (see section 14.2.4).

Dealing with child nodes and attributes as in listing 14.2 doesn't feel "groovy" either. Therefore, Groovy provides a `DOMCategory` that you can use for simplified access. With it, you can index child nodes via the subscript operator or via their node name. You can refer to attributes by getting the `@attributeName` property. A complete listing is shown next.

Listing 14.3   Reading plan.xml with Groovy's `DOMCategory`

```
import groovy.xml.DOMBuilder
import groovy.xml.dom.DOMCategory

def doc  = DOMBuilder.parse(new FileReader('data/plan.xml'))
def plan = doc.documentElement
use(DOMCategory) {
  assert plan.name() == 'plan'                        ❶ Accessing
  assert plan.week[0].name() == 'week'                   node name
  assert plan.week[0].'@capacity' == '8'              ❷ Accessing node
  assert plan.week.task[0].name() == 'task'              attribute
  assert plan.week.task[0].text() == 'easy'           ❸ Accessing
}                                                        node text
```

The example shows some of the additional syntax shortcuts that `DOMCategory` provides, specifically the `name()` method ❶, attribute access ❷, and node text access ❸. Other shortcuts such as `children`, `iterator`, and `parent` will be explained later in this chapter, because they originated in Groovy's purpose-built XML parsing classes. Consult the online Groovy documentation for more details.

This was a lot of work to get the DOM parser to read our data, and we had to face surprises along the way. We'll now do the same task using the Groovy parser with less effort and fewer surprises.

14.1.2 *Reading with a Groovy parser*

The Groovy way of reading the `plan` data store is so simple, we'll dive headfirst into the solution as presented in the following listing.

Listing 14.4 Reading plan.xml with Groovy's `XmlParser`

```
def plan = new XmlParser().parse(new File('data/plan.xml'))      ❶ Parsing in
                                                                     one line
assert plan.name() == 'plan'
assert plan.week[0].name() == 'week'
def firstTask = plan.week[0].task[0]                             ❷ Referring
assert firstTask.name() == 'task'                                   to a node
assert firstTask.text() == 'easy'
assert firstTask.@title == 'read XML chapter'
```

No fluff, just stuff. The parsing is only a one-liner ❶. Because Groovy's `XmlParser` resides in package `groovy.util`, we don't even need an `import` statement for that class. The parser can work directly on `File` objects and other input sources, as you'll see in table 14.2. The parser returns a `groovy.util.Node`. You saw this type in section 11.2. That means we can easily use GPath expressions to walk through the tree, as shown when we reference the first task ❷ and in the various `assert` statements.

Up to this point, you've seen that Groovy's `XmlParser` provides all the functionality you first saw with the DOM parser. But there's more to come. In addition to the `Xml-Parser`, Groovy comes with the `XmlSlurper`. Let's explore the commonalities and differences between those two before considering more advanced uses of each.

COMMONALITIES BETWEEN XMLPARSER AND XMLSLURPER

Let's start with the commonalities of `XmlParser` and `XmlSlurper`: they both reside in package `groovy.util` and provide the constructors listed in table 14.1.

Table 14.1 Common constructors of `XmlParser` and `XmlSlurper`

Parameter list	Note
`()`	Parameterless constructor
`(boolean validating, boolean namespaceAware)`	After parsing, the document can be validated against a declared DTD, and namespace declarations shall be taken into account
`(XMLReader reader)`	If you have an `org.xml.sax.XMLReader` available, it can be reused
`(SAXParser parser)`	If you have a `javax.xml.parsers.SAXParser` available, it can be reused

Besides sharing constructors with the same parameter lists, the types share parsing methods with the same signatures. The only difference is that the parsing methods of XmlParser return objects of type groovy.util.Node; XmlSlurper returns GPathResult objects. Table 14.2 lists the uniform parse methods.

Table 14.2   Parse methods common to XmlParser and XmlSlurper

Signature	Note
parse(InputSource input)	Reads from an org.xml.sax.InputSource
parse(File file)	Reads from a java.io.File
parse(InputStream input)	Reads from a java.io.InputStream
parse(Reader in)	Reads from a java.io.Reader
parse(String uri)	Reads the resource that the uri points to after connecting to it
parseText(String text)	Uses the text as input

These are the most commonly used methods on XmlParser and XmlSlurper. The description of additional methods (such as for using specialized DTD handlers and entity resolvers) is in the API documentation.

The result of the parse method is either a Node (for XmlParser) or a GPathResult (for XmlSlurper). Table 14.3 lists the common available methods for both result types. Note that because both types understand the iterator method, all object iteration methods are also instantly available.

GPathResult and groovy.util.Node provide additional shortcuts for method calls to the parent object and all descendant objects. Such shortcuts make reading a GPath expression more like other declarative path expressions such as XPath or Ant paths.

Table 14.3   Common methods of groovy.util.Node and GPathResult

Node method		GPathResult method		Shortcut
Object	name()	String	name()	
String	text()	String	text()	
String	toString()	String	toString()	
Node	parent()	GPathResult	parent()	'..'
List	children()	GPathResult	children()	'*'
Map	attributes()*	Map	attributes()	

Table 14.3 Common methods of `groovy.util.Node` and `GPathResult`

Node method	GPathResult method	Shortcut
Iterator iterator()	Iterator iterator()	
List depthFirst()	Iterator depthFirst()	'**'
List breadthFirst()	Iterator breadthFirst()	

* Strictly speaking, `attributes()` is a method of `NodeChild`, not `GPathResult`, but this is transparent in most uses.

Objects of type `Node` and `GPathResult` can access both child elements and attributes as if they were properties of the current object. Table 14.4 shows the syntax and how the leading @ sign distinguishes attribute names from nested element names.

Table 14.4 Element and attribute access in `groovy.util.Node` and `GPathResult`

Node (XmlParser)	GPathResult (XmlSlurper)	Meaning
['elementName']	['elementName']	All child elements of that name
.elementName	.elementName	
[index]	[index]	Child element by index
['@attributeName']	['@attributeName']	The attribute value stored under that name
.'@attributeName'	.'@attributeName'	
.@attributeName	.@attributeName	

Note the close similarities between the two APIs (we discuss other differences later). Even though there are a few places where the return types are different, the code using the two APIs will typically be identical. If you wrote the `XmlSlurper` version of listing 14.4 it would only differ where the `XmlSlurper` was created instead of the `Xml-Parser`. The other lines would remain the same. So let's look at some slightly more advanced features using `XmlSlurper` (and even with advanced features it turns out that the `XmlParser` code would also remain identical). The following listing plays with method calls and uses GPath expressions to further process our plan data.

Listing 14.5 Using common methods of `groovy.util.Node` and `GPathResult`

```
def plan = new XmlSlurper().parse(new File('data/plan.xml'))
assert plan.week.task.size() == 5
assert plan.week.task.@done*.toInteger().sum() == 6
assert plan.week[1].task.every{ it.@done == '0' }
```

❶ Five tasks in total
❷ Six hours done so far
❸ No hours done for second week

```
assert plan.breadthFirst()*.name().join('->') ==
    'plan->week->week->task->task->task->task->task'
assert plan.depthFirst()*.name().join('->') ==
    'plan->week->task->task->task->week->task->task'
assert plan.depthFirst()*.name() == plan.'**'*.name()
```

④ **Breadth- and depth-first traversal**

In ❶ `plan.week.task` is a `GPathResult`, which represents all the tasks. Conceptually you treat the result in the same way as if you had used `XmlParser` but there are key differences that we elaborate on later. For now, all you need to know is that `XmlParser` would eagerly create intermediate results (such as `week` and `task` nodes) in a temporary data structure (a node list). But `XmlSlurper` stores whatever *iteration logic* is needed to determine the result and then lazily executes that logic and returns the result (the `size` in this example) only when needed.

At ❷, you see that in GPath, attribute access has the same effect as access to child elements; `node.week.task.@done` results in a list of all values of the `done` attribute of all `tasks` of all `weeks`. We use the spread-dot operator (see section 7.5.2) to apply the `toInteger` method to all strings in that list, returning a list of integers. We finally use the GDK method `sum` on that list.

The line at ❸ can be read as: "Assert that the `done` attribute in *every* task of `week[1]` is `'0'`." What's new here is using indexed access and the object iteration method `every`. Because indexing starts at zero, `week[1]` means the second week.

This example should serve as an appetizer for your own experiments with applying GPath expressions to XML documents.

In addition to the convenient GPath notation, you might wish to make use of traversal methods as shown in ❹.

So far, you've seen that `XmlParser` and `XmlSlurper` can be used in a similar fashion to produce similar results. But there would be no need for two separate classes if there weren't a difference. That's what we cover next.

DIFFERENCES BETWEEN XMLPARSER AND XMLSLURPER

Despite the similarities between `XmlParser` and `XmlSlurper` when used for simple reading purposes, there are differences when it comes to more advanced reading tasks and when processing XML documents into other formats.

`XmlParser` uses the `groovy.util.Node` type and its GPath expressions result in lists of nodes. That makes working with `XmlParser` feel like there always is a *tangible* object representation of elements—something that we can inspect via `toString`, print, or change in place. Because GPath expressions return lists of such elements, we can apply all our knowledge of the `list` datatype (see section 4.2).

This convenience comes at the expense of additional upfront processing and extra memory consumption. The GPath expression `node.week.task.'@done'` generates three lists: a temporary list of weeks[3] (two entries), a temporary list of tasks (five entries), and a list of `done` attribute values (five strings) that's finally returned.

---

[3] This is short for a list of references to objects of type `groovy.util.Node` with `name()=='week'`.

This is reasonable for our small example but hampers processing large or deeply nested XML documents.

XmlSlurper in contrast doesn't store intermediate results when processing information after a document has been parsed. It avoids the extra memory hit when processing. Internally, XmlSlurper uses iterators instead of extra collections to reflect every step in the GPath. With this construction, it's possible to defer processing until the last possible moment.

> **NOTE** This doesn't mean that XmlSlurper would work without storing the parsed information in memory. It still does, and the memory consumption rises with the size of the XML document. But for *processing* that stored information via GPath, XmlSlurper doesn't need *extra* memory.

Table 14.5 lists the methods unique to Node. When using XmlParser, you can use these methods in your processing.

Table 14.5 XmlParser: **Methods of** groovy.util.Node **not available in** GPathResult

Method	Note
Object value()	Retrieves the payload of the node, either the children() or the text()
void setValue(Object value)	Changes the payload
Object attribute(Object key)	Shortcut to attributes().get(key)
NodeList getAt(QName name)	Provides namespace support for selecting child elements by their groovy.xml.QName
void print(PrintWriter out)	Pretty-printing with NodePrinter

Table 14.6 lists the methods that are unique to or are optimized in GPathResult. We could add the following line to listing 14.5 to use the optimized findAll in GPathResult:

```
assert 2 == path.week.task.findAll{ it.'@title' =~ 'XML' }.size()
```

Additionally, some classes may only work on one type or the other; for example, there's groovy.util.XmlNodePrinter with method print(Node) but no support for GPathResult. Like the name suggests, XmlNodePrinter pretty-prints a Node tree to a PrintStream in XML format.

Table 14.6 XmlSlurper: **Methods of** GPathResult **not available in** groovy.util.Node

Method	Note
GPathResult parents()	Represents all parent elements on the path from the current element up to the root
GPathResult declareNamespace (Map newNamespaceMapping)	Registers namespace prefixes and their URIs

Table 14.6 `XmlSlurper:` **Methods of** `GPathResult` **not available in** `groovy.util.Nod` *(continued)*

Method	Note
`List      list()`	Converts a `GPathResult` into a list of `groovy.util.slurpersupport.Node` objects for list-friendly processing
`int       size()`	The number of result elements (memory-optimized implementation)
`GPathResult find(Closure closure)`	Overrides the object iteration method `find`
`GPathResult findAll(Closure closure)`	Overrides the object iteration method `findAll`

You've seen that there are a lot of similarities and some slight differences when reading XML via `XmlParser` or `XmlSlurper`. The real, fundamental differences become apparent when processing the parsed information. In section 14.2 we'll look at these differences in more detail by exploring two examples: processing with direct in-place data manipulation and processing in a streaming scenario. But first we're going to look at event-style parsing and how it can be used with Groovy. This will help better position some of Groovy's powerful XML features in our forthcoming more-detailed examples.

14.1.3 *Reading with a SAX parser*

In addition to the original Java DOM parsing you saw earlier, Java supports what's known as *event-based parsing*. The original and most common form of event-based parsing is Simple API for XML, or SAX. SAX is a push-style, event-based parser because the parser pushes events to your code.

When using this style of processing, no memory structure is constructed to store the parsed information; instead, the parser notifies a *handler* about parsing events. You implement such a handler interface in your program to perform processing relevant to your application's needs whenever the parser notifies you.

Let's explore this for your simple plan example. Suppose you wish to display a quick summary of the tasks that are under way and those that are upcoming; you aren't interested in completed activities for the moment. The following listing shows how to *receive* start element events using SAX and perform your business logic of printing the tasks of interest.

Listing 14.6 Using a SAX parser with Groovy

```
import javax.xml.parsers.SAXParserFactory
import org.xml.sax.*
import org.xml.sax.helpers.DefaultHandler

class PlanHandler extends DefaultHandler {
    def underway = []
    def upcoming = []
    void startElement(String namespace, String localName,
        String qName, Attributes atts) {
```

Declares our handler

Interested in element start events

```
            if (qName != 'task') return
            def title = atts.getValue('title')
            def total = atts.getValue('total')
            switch (atts.getValue('done')) {
                case '0'              : upcoming << title ; break
                case { it != total } : underway << title ; break
            }
        }
    }
}
```

> ⟵ **Interested only in task elements**

```
def handler = new PlanHandler()
def factory = SAXParserFactory.newInstance()
def reader = factory.newSAXParser().XMLReader
reader.contentHandler = handler
new File('data/plan.xml').withInputStream { is ->
    reader.parse(new InputSource(is))
}
```

> ⟵ **Declares our SAX reader**

```
assert handler.underway == [
    'use in current project'
]
assert handler.upcoming == [
    're-read DB chapter',
    'use DB/XML combination'
]
```

Note that with this style of processing, we have more work to do. When our start-Element method is called, we're provided with SAX event information including the name of the element (along with a namespace, if provided) and all the attributes. It's up to us to work out whether we need this information and process or store it as required during this method call. The parser won't do any further storage for us. This minimizes memory overhead of the parser, but the implication is that we won't be able to do GPath-style processing and we aren't in a position to manipulate a treelike data structure. We'll have more to say about SAX event information when we explore XmlSlurper in more detail in section 14.2.

14.1.4 *Reading with a StAX parser*

In addition to the push-style SAX parsers supported by Java, a recent trend in processing XML with Java is to use pull-style event-based parsers. The most common of these are called *StAX-based parsers*[4] (Streaming API for XML). With such a parser, you're still interested in events, but you ask the parser for events (you pull events as needed) during processing,[5] instead of waiting to be informed by methods being called.

The following listing shows how you can use StAX with Groovy. If you're using an old version of Java, you'll need to add a StAX parser to your classpath to run this example.

---

[4] Elliotte Rusty Harold, "An Introduction to StAX," O'Reilly XML.com, 2003, www.xml.com/pub/a/2003/09/17/stax.html.

[5] This is the main event-based style supported by .NET and included with Java 6.

Listing 14.7   Using a StAX parser with Groovy

```
import javax.xml.stream.*

def input = 'file:data/plan.xml'.toURL()
def underway = []
def upcoming = []

def eachStartElement(inputStream, Closure yield) {
    def token = XMLInputFactory.newInstance()            Declares
        .createXMLStreamReader(inputStream)              parser
    try {
        while (token.hasNext()) {                         Loops through
            if (token.startElement) yield token           events of
            token.next()                                  interest
        }
    } finally {
        token?.close()
        inputStream?.close()
    }
}

class XMLStreamCategory {                                 Defines
    static Object get(XMLStreamReader self, String key) { category
        return self.getAttributeValue(null, key)         for simple
    }                                                     attribute
}                                                         access

use (XMLStreamCategory) {
    eachStartElement(input.openStream()) { element ->
        if (element.name.toString() != 'task') return
        switch (element.done) {
            case '0' :
                upcoming << element.title                 Uses
                break                                     category
            case { it != element.total } :
                underway << element.title
        }
    }
}

assert underway == [
    'use in current project'
]
assert upcoming == [
    're-read DB chapter',
    'use DB/XML combination'
]
```

Note that this style of parsing is similar to SAX-style parsing except that we're running the main control loop ourselves rather than having the parser do it. This style has advantages for certain kinds of processing where the code becomes simpler to write and understand.

Suppose you have to respond to many parts of the document differently. With push models, your code has to maintain extra state to know where you are and how to react. With a pull model, you can decide what parts of the document to process at any point within your business logic. The flow through the document is easier to follow, and the code feels more natural.

We've now explored the breadth of parsing options available in Groovy. Next we explore the advantages of the Groovy-specific parsing options in more detail.

14.2 *Processing XML*

Many situations involving XML call for more than just reading the data and then navigating to a specific element or node. XML documents often require transformation, modification, or complex querying. When we look at the characteristics of XmlParser and XmlSlurper when *processing* XML data in these ways, we see the biggest differences between the two. Let's start with a simple but perhaps surprising analogy: heating water.

There are essentially two ways of boiling water, as illustrated in figure 14.2. You can pour water into a tank (called a *boiler*), heat it, and get the hot water from the outlet. Or you can use a continuous-flow heater, which heats the water while it streams from the cold-water inlet through the heating coil until it reaches the outlet. The heating happens only when requested, as indicated by opening the outlet tap.

How does XML processing relate to boiling water? Processing XML means you're not just using bits of the stored information, but retrieving it, adding some new quality to it (making it *hot* in our analogy), and outputting the whole thing. Just like boiling water, this can be done in two ways: by storing the information in memory and processing it in-place, or by retrieving information from an input stream, processing it on-the-fly, and streaming it to an output device.

In general, processing XML with XmlParser (and groovy.util.Node) is more like using a boiler; XmlSlurper can serve as a source in a streaming scenario analogous to continuous-flow heating.

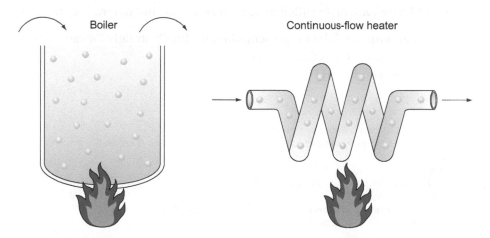

Figure 14.2   Comparing the strategies of boiling versus continuous-flow heating

We're going to start by looking at the "boiling" strategy of in-place modification and processing and then proceed to explore streamed processing and combinations with XPath.

14.2.1 *In-place processing*

In-place processing is the conventional means of XML processing. It uses the `XmlParser` to retrieve a tree of nodes. These nodes reside in memory and can be rearranged, copied, or deleted, and their attributes can be changed. We'll use this approach to generate an HTML report for keeping track of our Groovy learning activities.

Suppose the report should look like figure 14.3. You can see that new information is derived from existing data: tasks and weeks have a new property that we'll call status with the possible values of scheduled, in progress, and finished.

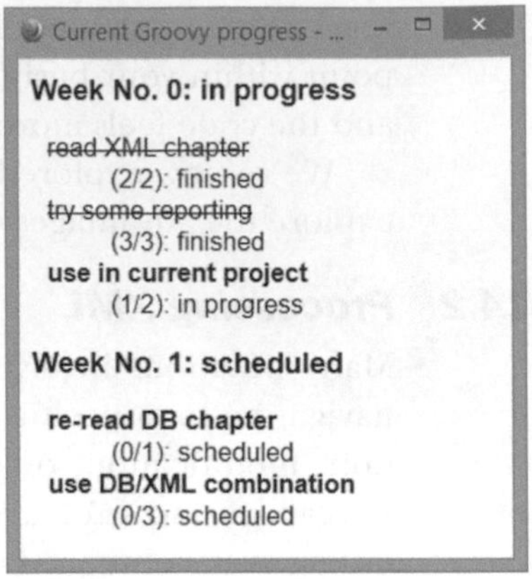

Figure 14.3   An HTML progress report of Groovy learning activities

For tasks, the value of the status property is determined by looking at the done and total attributes. If done is zero, the status is considered scheduled; if done is equal to or exceeds total, the status is finished; otherwise, the status is in progress.

Weeks are finished when all contained tasks are finished. They're in progress when at least one contained task is in progress.

This sounds like we're going to do lots of number comparisons with the done and total attributes. Unfortunately, these attributes are stored as strings, not numbers. These considerations lead to a three-step "heating" process:

1 Convert all string attribute values to numbers where suitable.
2 Add a new attribute called status to all tasks, and determine the value.
3 Add a new attribute called status to all weeks, and determine the value.

With such an improved data representation, it's finally straightforward to use `Markup-Builder` to produce the HTML report.

We have to produce HTML source like

```
<html>
  <head>
    <title>Current Groovy progress</title>
    <link href='style.css' type='text/css' rel='stylesheet' />
  </head>
  <body>
    <h1>Week No. 0: in progress</h1>
    <dl>
      <dt class='finished'>read XML chapter</dt>
      <dd>(2/2): finished</dd>
...
```

```
    </dl>
  </body>
</html>
```

where the stylesheet style.css contains the decision of how a task is finally displayed according to its status. It can, for example, use the following lines for that purpose:

```
dt              { font-weight:bold }
dt.finished { font-weight:normal; text-decoration:line-through }
```

Listing 14.8 contains the full solution. The numberfy method implements the string-to-number conversion for those attributes that we expect to be of integer content. It also shows how to work recursively through the node tree.

The methods weekStatus and taskStatus make the new status attribute available on the corresponding node, where weekStatus calls taskStatus for all its contained tasks to make sure it can work on their status inside GPath expressions.

The final htmlReport method is the conventional way of building HTML. Thanks to the "heating" prework, there's no logic needed in the report. The report uses the status attribute to assign a stylesheet *class* of the same value.

Listing 14.8 Generating an HTML report with in-memory data preparation

```
import groovy.xml.MarkupBuilder
                                              Converts strings
void numberfy(Node node) {                    to numbers
  def atts = node.attributes()
  atts.keySet().grep(['capacity', 'total', 'done']).each {
    atts[it] = atts[it].toInteger()
  }
  node.each { if (it instanceof Node) numberfy(it) }
}

void taskStatus(task) {                       Calculates and
  def atts = task.attributes()                assigns task status
  switch (atts.done) {
    case 0: atts.status = 'scheduled'; break
    case 1..<atts.total: atts.status = 'in progress'; break
    default: atts.status = 'finished';
  }
}
                                              Calculates and
                                              assigns week
void weekStatus(week) {                       status
  week.task.each { taskStatus(it) }
  def atts = week.attributes()
  atts.status = 'scheduled'
  if (week.task.every { it.@status == 'finished'})
    atts.status = 'finished'
  if (week.task.any { it.@status == 'in progress'})
    atts.status = 'in progress'
}
```

```
void htmlReport(builder, plan) {          ←┐  Reports
  builder.html {                            │  building logic
    head {
      title('Current Groovy progress')
      link(rel: 'stylesheet',
           type: 'text/css',
           href: 'style.css')
    }
    body {
      plan.week.eachWithIndex { week, i ->
        h1("Week No. $i: ${week.@status}")
        dl {
          week.task.each { task ->
            dt(class: task.@status, task.@title)
            dd("(${task.@done}/${task.@total}): ${task.@status}")
} } } } } }
def node = new XmlParser().parse(new File('data/plan.xml'))
numberfy(node)                                    │  Prepares data
node.week.each { weekStatus(it) }                 │  for reporting

new File('data/GroovyPlans.html').withWriter { writer ->
  def builder = new MarkupBuilder(writer)
  htmlReport(builder, node)
}
```

After the careful prework, the code isn't surprising. What's a bit unconventional is having a lot of closing braces on one line at the end of `htmlReport`. This isn't only for compact typesetting in the book. We also sometimes use this style in our everyday code. We find it nicely reveals what levels of indentation are to be closed and still allows us to check brace-matching by column. It would be great to have IDE support for toggling between this and conventional code layout.

Now that you've seen how to use the in-memory "boiler," let's investigate the streaming scenario.

14.2.2 *Streaming processing*

To demonstrate the use of streaming, let's start with the simplest kind of processing that we can think of: pumping out what comes in without any modification. Even this simple example can be hard to understand as long as the approach is unfamiliar. We recommend that if you find it confusing, keep reading, but don't worry too much about the details. It's definitely worth coming back later for a second try, though, in many situations, the benefits of stream-based processing are well worth the harder conceptual model.

UNMODIFIED PIPING

You use XmlSlurper to parse the original XML. Because the final output format is XML again, you need some device that can generate XML in a streaming fashion. The groovy.xml.StreamingMarkupBuilder class is specialized for outputting markup on demand—in other words, when an *information sink* requests it. Such a sink is an operation that requests a Writable (for example, the left-shift operator call on streams or the evaluation of GStrings). The trick that StreamingMarkupBuilder uses to achieve this effect is similar to the approach of template engines. StreamingMarkupBuilder provides a bind method that returns a WritableClosure. This object is a Writable and a closure at the same time. Because it's a Writable, you can use it wherever the final markup is requested. Because it's a closure, the generation of this markup can be done lazily on the fly, without storing intermediate results.

Listing 14.9 shows this in action. The bind method also needs the information about what logic is to be applied to produce the final markup. Wherever logic is needed, closures are the first candidate, and so it's with bind. We pass a closure to the bind method that describes the markup logic.

For our initial example of pumping the path through, we use a special feature of StreamingMarkupBuilder that allows us to yield the markup generation logic to a Buildable, an object that knows how to build itself. It happens that a GPathResult (and thus path) is buildable. To yield the building logic to it, we use the yield method. But we cannot use it unqualified because we'd produce a <yield/> markup if we did. The special symbol mkp marks our method call as belonging to the namespace of markup keywords.

Listing 14.9 Pumping an XML stream without modification

```
import groovy.xml.StreamingMarkupBuilder

def path = new XmlSlurper().parse(new File('data/plan.xml'))

def builder = new StreamingMarkupBuilder()
def copier = builder.bind{ mkp.yield(path) }
def result = "$copier"

assert result.startsWith('<plan><week ')
assert result.endsWith('</week></plan>')
```

There's a lot going on here in only a few lines of code. The result variable, for example, refers to a GString with one value: a reference to copier. Note that we didn't call it "copy" because it's not a thing but an actor.

When we call the startsWith method on result, the string representation of the GString is requested, and because the one GString value copier is a Writable, its writeTo method is called. The copier was constructed by the builder so that writeTo relays to path.build().

Figure 14.4 summarizes this streaming behavior.

Note how in figure 14.4, the processing doesn't start before the values are requested. Only after the GString's `toString` method is called does the copier start running and is the `path` iterated upon. Until then, the `path` isn't touched! No memory representation has been created for the purpose of markup or iteration. This is a simplification of what's going on. `XmlSlurper` does have memory requirements. It stores the SAX event information you saw in section 14.1.3 but doesn't process or store it in the processing-friendly `Node` objects.

Calling `startsWith` is like opening the outlet tap to draw the markup from the copier, which in turn draws its source information from the `path` inlet. Any code before that point is only the plumbing.

As a variant of listing 14.9 you can also directly write the markup onto the console. Use the following:

```
System.out << copier
```

Remember that `System.out` is an `OutputStream` that understands the left-shift operator with a `Writable` argument.

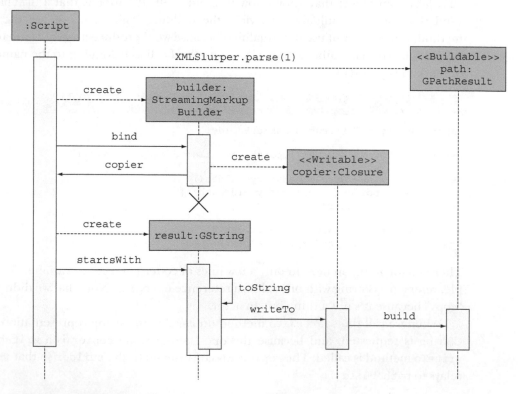

Figure 14.4   UML sequence diagram for streamed building

For this simple example, we could have used the SAX or StAX approaches you saw earlier. They would be even more streamlined solutions. Not only would they not need to process and store the treelike data structures that `XmlParser` creates for you, but they also wouldn't need to store the SAX event information. The same isn't true for the more complicated scenarios that follow. As is common in many XML processing scenarios, the remaining examples have processing requirements that span multiple elements. Such scenarios benefit greatly from the ability to use GPath-style expressions.

HEATING UP TO HTML

Until now, we copied only the "cold" input. It's time to light our heater. The goal is to produce the same GUI as in figure 14.3.

We start with the basics of listing 14.9 but enhance the markup closure that gets bound to the builder. In listing 14.10, the building looks almost the same as in the "boiling" example of listing 14.7; only the evaluation of the week and task status needs to be adapted. We don't calculate the status in advance and store it for later reference, but instead do the classification on the fly when the builder lazily requests it.

Listing 14.10   Streamed heating from XML to HTML

```
import groovy.xml.StreamingMarkupBuilder

def taskStatus(task) {                                    ◁─┤ Calculates
  switch (task.@done.toInteger()) {                            task status
    case 0: return 'scheduled'
    case 1..<task.@total.toInteger(): return 'in progress'
    default: return 'finished'
  }
}
                                                              Calculates
def weekStatus(week) {                                    ◁─┘ week status
  if (week.task.every { taskStatus(it) == 'finished' })
    return 'finished'
  if (week.task.any { taskStatus(it) == 'in progress' })
    return 'in progress'
  return 'scheduled'
}                                                             "Slurps" in
                                                              the XML
def plan = new XmlSlurper().parse(new File('data/plan.xml'))  ◁─┘

Closure markup = {                                        ◁─┐ Expresses the
  html {                                                      processing as
    head {                                                    a closure
      title('Current Groovy progress')
      link(rel: 'stylesheet',
          type: 'text/css',
          href: 'style.css')
    }
    body {
      plan.week.eachWithIndex { week, i ->
        h1("Week No. $i: ${owner.weekStatus(week)}")
```

```
        dl {
          week.task.each { task ->
            def status = owner.taskStatus(task)
            dt(class: status, task.@title)                    Binds parsed
            dd("(${task.@done}/${task.@total}): $status")     XML to
} } } } }                                                     processing logic
def heater = new StreamingMarkupBuilder().bind(markup)  ←┐
def outfile = new File('data/StreamedGroovyPlans.html')   Writes out
outfile.withWriter{ it << heater }                      ←┘ result to a file
```

The cool thing here is that at first glance it looks similar to listing 14.8, but it works very differently:

- All evaluation is done lazily.
- Memory consumption for GPath operations is minimized.
- No in-memory assembly of HTML representation is built before outputting.

This allows you to produce lots of output, because it's not assembled in memory but directly streamed to the output as the building logic demands. But because of the storage of SAX event information on the input, this approach won't allow input documents as large as would be possible with SAX or StAX.

Figure 14.5 sketches the differences between both processing approaches with respect to processing requirements and memory use. The process goes from left to right either in the top row (for "boiling") or in the bottom row (for streaming). Either process encompasses *parsing, evaluating, building,* and *serializing* to HTML, where *evaluating* and *building* aren't necessarily in strict sequence. This is also where the differences are: working on intermediate data structures (trees of lists and nodes) or on lightweight objects that encapsulate logic (iterators and closures).

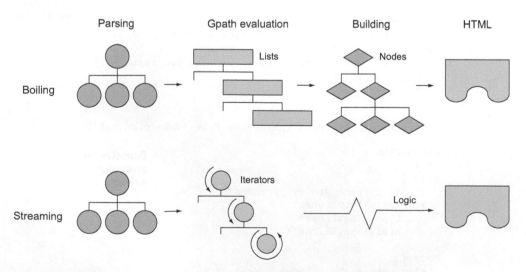

Figure 14.5 Memory use characteristics for the "boiling" versus streaming strategies

That's it for the basics of reading XML and transforming XML into completely new data structures. But sometimes you want to update just a part of an XML document. Groovy has support for that kind of operation too.

14.2.3 *Updating XML*

Suppose you now wanted to update your XML data store programmatically. You've reached the end of the first week in your planned activities. You want to update the first week to record your total progress on the third task and provide a small comment. For the second week you've revised your priorities. You no longer wish to perform the current second task and instead wish to perform two alternative ones.

Let's treat this as an opportunity to exercise test-first development and write a test helper first to reflect how you expect the XML to look like upon completion of the update.

For the first week (remember that's index 0) you expect the hours done to equal the hours in total (that is, seven hours) and you expect that the comment 'time saver' will appear for one of the tasks (the last one but we won't overprescribe the ordering among tasks).

For the second week (index 1) you expect the week to have three tasks. You expect the old task to have gone (no @title will match the old value) and two new tasks should be found—we'll check the @title of one and the @total of the other. Our test code could look something like this:

```
class UpdateChecker {
  static check(text) {
    def updated = new XmlParser().parseText(text)
    updated.week[0].with { w0 ->
      assert w0.task.@done*.toInteger().sum() == 7
      assert w0.find{ it.text() == 'time saver' }
    }
    updated.week[1].with { w1 ->
      assert w1.children().size() == 3
      assert w1.find{ it.@total == "4" }
      assert w1.find{ it.@title == "build web service client" }
      assert !w1.find{ it.@title == "use DB/XML combination" }
    }
  }
}
```

You're using XmlParser in your check, but as you've seen earlier, you could have chosen XmlSlurper or used DOMCategory if you preferred. Something else worth noting here is that your check is assuming that your updated XML is written back out as text ready to be parsed by your test code. For XmlParser and DOMCategory, you could have just as easily done some asserts on the in-memory tree of nodes, but stick with your earlier approach as it works also for XmlSlurper (it does lazy updates) and also shows the end-to-end process for writing XML after an update.

Now consider the following listing, which shows the DOMCategory code needed to update the XML.

Listing 14.11   Updating XML with `DOMCategory`

```
import groovy.xml.DOMBuilder
import groovy.xml.XmlUtil
import groovy.xml.dom.DOMCategory

def doc = DOMBuilder.parse(new FileReader('data/plan.xml'))
def plan = doc.documentElement

use(DOMCategory) {
  plan.week[0].task[2]['@done'] = '2'
  plan.week[0].task[2].value = 'time saver'
  plan.week[1].task[1].replaceNode {
    task(done:'0', total:'4', title:'build web service')
  }
  plan.week[1].task[1] + {
    task(done:'0', total:'1', title:'build web service client')
  }
}

UpdateChecker.check(XmlUtil.serialize(plan))
```

❶ Updates done attribute with new value

❷ Sets the task's text value

We set the new attribute value using Groovy's `putAt` GPath syntax shortcut ❶. The node's text value is set using the `value` property ❷. Then we use `replaceNode` and plus (using the + shorthand) to alter the task nodes.

There are several other ways you could have updated the XML. We chose an approach that illustrated two of the most common operations that are typically used (`replaceNode` and plus) but, if we had wanted to, we could have:

- Used `replaceNode` once but with two task node entries inside it
- Used `appendNode` instead of plus, supplying it the new node name and attributes as a map
- Deleted the original node using the `removeChild` method and then had a plus closure with two nodes or two `appendNode` method calls

Now do the same again with the `XmlParser` as shown in the following listing.

Listing 14.12   Updating XML with `XmlParser`

```
import groovy.xml.XmlUtil

def plan = new XmlParser().parse(new File('data/plan.xml'))

plan.week[0].task[2].@done = '2'
plan.week[0].task[2].value = 'time saver'

plan.week[1].task[1].replaceNode {
  task(done:'0', total:'4', title:'build web service')
}
plan.week[1].task[1] + {
  task(done:'0', total:'1', title:'build web service client')
}
UpdateChecker.check(XmlUtil.serialize(plan))
```

Identical GPath operations are required to perform the update. And similar options also exist as you saw for `DOMCategory`. For example, you could have used `appendNode` or various other options. Now we'll do it one more time with `XmlSlurper` as shown in the following listing.

Listing 14.13 Streamed updating of XML with `XmlSlurper`

```
import groovy.xml.XmlUtil

def plan = new XmlSlurper().parse(new File('data/plan.xml'))

plan.week[0].task[2].@done = '2'
plan.week[0].task[2] = 'time saver'

plan.week[1].task[1].replaceNode {
  task(done:'0', total:'4', title:'build web service')
}
plan.week[1].task[1] + {
  task(done:'0', total:'1', title:'build web service client')
}

UpdateChecker.check(XmlUtil.serialize(plan))
```

The first thing to note is that identical GPath expressions are required again for the update operations. You could have also used `appendNode` (though `XmlSlurper`'s syntax for `appendNode` varies slightly, taking a `Closure` parameter like `plus` does). You could have also used the `leftShift` (syntax shortcut `<<`) to append nodes to the parent node, saving just a little bit of typing.

One other thing to note is that with the `XmlSlurper`, additional streaming behavior is in play. When you call the `replaceNode` and `plus` methods, `XmlSlurper` doesn't actually alter the underlying data structures representing the original tree; instead, it saves away the desired changes that will be applied when you output the XML document to some stream. In this case, this is when you serialize the plan for subsequent checking with your checker.

In section 14.1.1, you saw that classic Java DOM parsers return objects of type `org.w3c.dom.Node`, which differs from what the Groovy parsers return. When using Java to process such nodes, the low-level APIs that you've seen up until now can be a little cumbersome. While Java has nothing akin to the GPath expressions you've seen for Groovy, it does allow a slightly higher-level approach to be used with the help of XPath. The next section shows how Java XPath and Groovy XML processing can be used in combination.

14.2.4 Combining with XPath

XPath is for XML what SQL `select` statements are for relational databases or what regular expressions are for plain text. It's a means to select parts of the whole document and to do so in a descriptive manner.

UNDERSTANDING XPATH

An XPath is an expression that appears in Java or Groovy as a string (exactly like regex patterns or SQL statements do). A full introduction to XPath is beyond the scope of this book, but here's a short introduction from a Groovy programmer's point of view.[6]

Just like a GPath, an XPath selects nodes. Where GPath uses dots, XPath uses slashes. For example,

```
/plan/week/task
```

selects all `task` nodes of all `weeks` below `plan`. The leading slash indicates that the selection starts at the root element. In this expression, `plan`, `week`, and `task` are each called a *node test*. Each node test may be preceded with an *axis specifier* from table 14.7 and a double colon.

Table 14.7   XPath axis specifiers

Axis	Selects nodes	Shortcut
child	Directly below	nothing or *
parent	Directly above	..
self	The node itself (use for further references)	.
ancestor	All above	
ancestor-or-self	All above including self	
descendant	All below	
descendant-or-self	All below including self	//
following	All on the same level trailing in the XML document	
following-sibling	All with the same parent trailing in the XML document	
preceding	All on the same level preceding in the XML document	
preceding-sibling	All with the same parent preceding in the XML document	
attribute	The attribute node	@
namespace	The namespace node	

With these specifiers, you can select all `task` elements via

```
/descendant-or-self::task
```

With the shortcut syntax, you can select all `total` attribute nodes of all `tasks` via

```
//task/@total
```

---

[6]   For a full description of the standard, see www.w3.org/TR/xpath; and for a tutorial, see www.w3schools.com/xpath/. For a good book, see *XSLT 2.0 and XPath 2.0*, 4th edition, by Michael Kay (Wiley, 2008).

A node test can have a trailing *predicate* in square brackets to constrain the result. A predicate is an expression made up from path expressions, functions, and operators for the datatypes `node-set`, `string`, `number`, and `boolean`. Table 14.8 lists what's possible.[7] Table 14.9 shows examples.

Table 14.8 XPath predicate expression cheat sheet

Category	Appearance	Note
Path operators	`/`, `//`, `@`, `[]`, `*`, `..`, `.`	See table 14.7
Union operator	`|`	Union of two node sets
Boolean operators	`and`, `or`, `not()`	`not()` is a function
Arithmetic operators	`+`, `-`, `*`, `div`, `mod`, `idiv` (XPath 2.0)	
Comparison operators	`=`, `!=`, `<`, `>`, `<=`, `>=`	
String functions	`concat()`, `substring()`, `contains()`, `substring-before()`, `substring-after()`, `translate()`, `normalize-space()`, `string-length()`	See the docs for exact meanings and parameters; for example, www.w3schools.com/xpath/ xpath_functions.asp#string
Number functions	`sum()`, `round()`, `floor()`, `ceiling()`	
Node functions	`name()`, `local-name()`, `namespace-uri()`	
Context functions	`position()`, `last()`	`[n]` is short for `[position()=n]`
Conversion functions	`string()`, `number()`, `boolean()`	
Value comparisons (XPath 2.0)	`eq`, `ne`, `lt`, `le`, `gt`, `ge`	

Table 14.9 XPath examples

XPath	Meaning and notes	Note
`/plan/week[1]`	First* week node	Indexing starts at one
`//task[@done<@total]`	All unfinished tasks	Auto-conversion to a number
`//task[@done<@total][@done>0]`	All tasks in progress	Implicit and between brackets
`sum(//week[1]/task/@total)`	Total hours in the first week	Returns a number

* More specifically, the `week` node at position 1 below `plan`.

---

[7] These operators are available in XPath 1.0 and XPath 2.0 unless otherwise indicated.

The next obvious question is how to use such XPath expressions in Groovy code.

USING THE XPATH API

Groovy comes with all the support you need for using XPath expressions in your code, building on Java's `factory` method for accessing the XPath library in a platform-independent way. Use the `javax.xml.xpath.XPathFactory` class to create an instance of an `xpath` object. This object then has methods available for evaluating XPath expressions on your parsed XML (or when efficiency is a major concern we can compile XPath expressions for later evaluation).

In practice, you may want to do something with all weeks. You'll select the appropriate list of nodes via `xpath.evaluate('//week', plan, NODESET)`. The last parameter indicates the expected return type. In your case you want an aggregate of nodes. Because this returns a `NodeList`, you can use the object iteration methods on it to get hold of each week:

```
xpath.evaluate('//week', plan, NODESET).eachWithIndex{ week, i ->
    // do something with week
}
```

For each week, print the sum of the `total` and `done` attributes with the help of XPath. Each week node becomes the new context node for the XPath evaluation and the expected return type is `NUMBER`:

```
xpath.evaluate('//week', plan, NODESET).eachWithIndex{ week, i ->
    out << "\nWeek No. $i\n"
    int total = xpath.evaluate('sum(task/@total)', week, NUMBER)
    int done = xpath.evaluate('sum(task/@done)', week, NUMBER)
    out << " planned $total of ${week.'@capacity'}\n"
    out << " done    $done of $total"
}
```

The following listing puts all this together with a little reporting functionality that produces a text report for each week, stating the capacity, the total hours planned, and the progress in hours done.

Listing 14.14 XPath to text reporting

```
import groovy.xml.DOMBuilder
import groovy.xml.dom.DOMCategory

import javax.xml.xpath.XPathFactory

import static javax.xml.xpath.XPathConstants.NODESET
import static javax.xml.xpath.XPathConstants.NUMBER

def doc = DOMBuilder.parse(new FileReader('data/plan.xml'))
def plan = doc.documentElement
def xpath = XPathFactory.newInstance().newXPath()

def out = new StringBuilder()
use(DOMCategory) {
```

❶ Use DOMCategory for simple attribute access

```
    xpath.evaluate('//week', plan, NODESET).eachWithIndex {
        wk, i ->
        out << "\nWeek No. $i\n"
        int total = xpath.evaluate('sum(task/@total)', wk, NUMBER)
        int done = xpath.evaluate('sum(task/@done)', wk, NUMBER)
        out << " planned $total of ${wk.'@capacity'}\n"
        out << " done     $done of $total"
    }
}
assert out.toString() == '''
Week No. 0
 planned 7 of 8
 done      6 of 7
Week No. 1
 planned 4 of 8
 done      0 of 4'''
```

Selection via XPath, retrieving index and value ❷

❸ **Evaluation using XPath**

Evaluation using DOM attributes directly

XPath is used in two ways here—the querying capability is used to select all the week elements ❶, and then attributes `total` and `done` are extracted with the `evaluate` method ❷. You'll mix and match ways of accessing attributes, using `DOMCategory` to access the `capacity` attribute with the `node.@attributeName` syntax ❸.

Such a text report is fine to start with, but it would certainly be nicer to show the progress in a chart. Figure 14.6 suggests an HTML solution. In a normal situation, we'd use colors in such a report, but they wouldn't be visible in the print of this book. Therefore, we use only a simple box representation of the numbers.

Each box is made from the border of a styled `div` element. The style also determines the width of each box.

This kind of HTML production task calls for a templating approach, because there are multiple recurring patterns for HTML fragments: for the boxes, for each attribute row, and for each week. We'll use template engines, GPath, and XPath in combination to make this happen.

Listing 14.15 presents the template that we're going to use. It's a simple template as introduced in section 12.4.2. It assumes the presence of two variables in the binding: a `scale`, which is needed to make visible box sizes from the attribute values, and `weeks`, which is a list of week maps. Each week map contains the keys 'capacity', 'total', and 'done' with integer values.

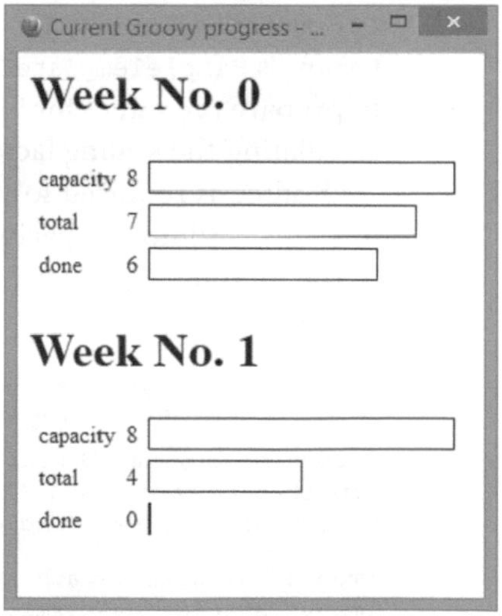

The template resides in a separate file. We like to name such files with the word *template* in the name and ending in the usual file extension for the format they produce. For example,

Figure 14.6 Screenshot of an HTML-based reporting

the name GroovyPlans.template.html reveals the nature of the file, and we can still use it with an HTML editor.

Listing 14.15   HTML reporting layout in data/GroovyPlans.template.html

```
<html>
  <head>
    <title>Current Groovy progress</title>
  </head>
  <body>
    <% weeks.eachWithIndex{ week, i -> %>
    <h1>Week No. $i</h1>
    <table cellspacing="5" >
        <tbody>
            <% ['capacity','total','done'].each{ attr -> %>
            <tr>
              <td>$attr</td>
              <td>${week[attr]}</td>
                <td>
                    <div style=
"border: thin solid #000000; width: ${week[attr]*scale}px">
                         </div>
                </td>
            </tr>
            <% } // end of attribute %>
        </tbody>
    </table>
    <% } // end of week %>
  </body>
</html>
```

This template looks like a JSP file, but it isn't. The contained logic is expressed in Groovy, not plain Java. Instead of being processed by a JSP engine, it'll be evaluated by Groovy's `SimpleTemplateEngine` as shown in listing 14.16. We use XPath expressions to prepare the values for binding. A special application of GPath comes into play when calculating the scaling factor.

Scaling is required so that the longest capacity bar is of length 200, so we have to find the maximum capacity for the calculation. Because we've already put these values in the binding, we can use a GPath to get a list of those and play our GDK tricks with it (calling `max`).

Listing 14.16   Using XPath, GPath, and templating in combination for HTML reporting

```
import groovy.xml.DOMBuilder
import groovy.xml.dom.DOMCategory
import groovy.text.SimpleTemplateEngine as STE

import javax.xml.xpath.XPathFactory
import static javax.xml.xpath.XPathConstants.NODESET
import static javax.xml.xpath.XPathConstants.NUMBER
```

```
def doc   = DOMBuilder.parse(new FileReader('data/plan.xml'))
def plan = doc.documentElement
def xpath = XPathFactory.newInstance().newXPath()

def binding = [ scale:1, weeks:[] ]
use(DOMCategory) {                                                   XPath on
  xpath.evaluate('//week', plan, NODESET).each{ week ->        ◄──┘ DOM nodes
    binding.weeks << [
      total: (int) xpath.evaluate('sum(task/@total)', week, NUMBER),
      done:  (int) xpath.evaluate('sum(task/@done)', week, NUMBER),
      capacity: week.'@capacity'.toInteger()
    ]
  }
}                                                                   GPath on
def max = binding.weeks.capacity.max()                         ◄──┘ binding
if (max > 0) binding.scale = 200.intdiv(max)

def templateFile = new File('data/GroovyPlans.template.html')
def template     = new STE().createTemplate(templateFile)      ◄──── Templating

new File('data/XPathGroovyPlans.html').withWriter {
  it << template.make(binding)
}
```

The code didn't change dramatically between the text reporting in listing 14.14 and the HTML reporting in listing 14.16. But listing 14.16 provides a more general solution, because we can also get a text report from it solely by changing the template.

The kind of transformation from XML to HTML that we achieve with listing 14.16 is classically addressed with XML *Stylesheet Transformation* (XSLT), which is a powerful technology. It uses stylesheets in XML format to describe a transformation mapping, also using XPath and templates. Its logical means are equivalent to those of a functional programming language.

Although XSLT is suitable for mapping tree structures, we often find it easier to use the Groovy approach when the logic is the least bit complex. XPath, templates, builders, and the Groovy language make a unique combination that allows for elegant and concise solutions. There may be people who are able to look at significant amounts of XSLT for more than a few minutes at a time without risking their mental stability, but they're few and far between. Using the technologies you've encountered, you can play to your strengths of understanding Groovy instead of using a different language with a fundamentally different paradigm.

LEVERAGING ADDITIONAL JAVA XML PROCESSING TECHNOLOGIES

Before wrapping up our introduction of processing XML with Groovy, we should mention that although we think that you'll find Groovy's built-in XML features are suitable for many of your processing needs, you're not locked into using just those APIs. Because of Groovy's Java heritage, many libraries and technologies are available for you to consider. We've already mentioned StAX and Jaxen. Here are a few more of our favorites:[8]

- Although `XmlParser`, `XmlSlurper`, and of course the Java DOM and SAX should meet most of your needs, you can always consider JDOM, dom4j, or XOM.
- If you need to compare two XML fragments for differences, consider XMLUnit.
- If you wish to process XML using XQuery, consider Saxon.
- If you need to persist your XML, consider JAXB or Stream.
- If you need to do high-performance streaming, consider Nux.

Our introduction to Groovy XML could finish at this point, because you've seen all the basics of XML manipulation. You should now be able to write Groovy programs that read, process, and write XML in a basic way. You'll need more detailed documentation when the need arises to deal with more advanced issues such as namespaces, resolving entities, and handling DTDs in a customized way.

The final section of this chapter deals with one of the most widespread alternatives to XML—that being JSON.

14.3   Parsing and building JSON

JSON, the JavaScript Object Notation, was originally derived from a subset of the JavaScript language, but the data format itself is language-independent and it's in widespread use with many programming languages. JSON was designed for representing simple data structures. Let's have a look at what's involved with parsing and then building JSON content.

14.3.1   Parsing JSON

Let's revisit our plan example from earlier in the chapter. Suppose we had stored our little database of information in a JSON file instead of the previously discussed XML file. The JSON file would look like this:

```
{ "weeks": [
  {
    "capacity": 8,
    "tasks": [
      { "done": 2, "total": 2,
        "title": "read XML chapter",    "status": "easy" },
      { "done": 3, "total": 3,
        "title": "try some reporting", "status": "fun" },
      { "done": 1, "total": 2,
        "title": "use in current project" }
    ]
  },
```

---

[8] More information is available at http://xmlbeans.apache.org, http://saxon.sourceforge.net, http://dsd.lbl.gov, http://xmlunit.sourceforge.net, http://xstream.codehaus.org, and https://jaxb.java.net.

```
  {
    "capacity": 8,
    "tasks": [
      { "done": 0, "total": 1, "title": "re-read DB chapter" },
      { "done": 0, "total": 3, "title": "use DB/XML combination" }
    ]
  }
]}
```

For this example, we'll assume our file is called plan.json in a data folder. Now let's look at the following listing to see how we can parse it.

```
import groovy.json.JsonSlurper

def plan = new JsonSlurper().parse(new File('data/plan.json'))
assert plan.weeks[0].tasks[0].status == 'easy'
assert plan.weeks[1].capacity == 8
assert plan.weeks[1].tasks[0].title == 're-read DB chapter'
```

That's about as easy as we could expect and follows closely (but not exactly) what we saw for XML. You'll note that the concept of attributes is missing for JSON. We store such information as a list of properties.

The good news is that while easy examples like we just saw are indeed easy, tricky cases are handled too, primarily by switching between parsing implementations with slightly different characteristics. Table 14.10 shows the provided parser implementations.

Table 14.10 `JsonSlurper` parser implementations

Implementation	Description
JsonParserCharArray (default)	Copies character subarrays ("chopping") during parsing
JsonFastParser	An index-overlay parser that avoids or defers creating new char arrays or String instances and keeps pointers to the underlying original character array
JsonParserLax	Supports comments, no-quote strings, and other constructs not officially supported in the ECMA-404 JSON grammar
JsonParserUsingCharacterSource	A special parser for very large files

You can switch to one of the other parsers when calling the constructor like this:

```
new JsonSlurper(type: JsonParserType.LAX)
```

See the online Groovy documentation for more details.[9] That's it for parsing. What if you want to go the other way and actually create some JSON content? Let's look at that next.

---

[9] "Parsing and producing JSON," http://groovy-lang.org/json.html.

14.3.2 *Building JSON*

Let's look at building some JSON. The produced JSON is similar to what we produced when updating our plan with XML, but for simplicity we'll just show directly creating the JSON content rather than updating the original file. The following listing illustrates what's required: simply create a `JsonBuilder` and use it in the same way you've seen for other builders.

Listing 14.18   Building JSON

```
import groovy.json.JsonBuilder

def builder = new JsonBuilder()
builder.weeks {
  capacity '8'
  tasks(
    [{
      done '0'
      total '4'
      title 'build web service'
    }, {
      done '0'
      total '1'
      title 'build web service client'
    }]
  )
}
assert builder.toString() == '{"weeks":{"capacity":"8","tasks":[' +
  '{"done":"0","total":"4","title":"build web service"},' +
  '{"done":"0","total":"1","title":"build web service client"}' +
  ']}}'
```

As you've seen before with other builders, we can also use coding logic intermixed with our synthetic methods when using `JsonBuilder`. Let's again look at our invoice example from earlier chapters.[10] You can generate JSON corresponding to our nested invoice information as shown in the following listing.

Listing 14.19   Invoice example with `JSONBuilder`

```
import groovy.json.JsonBuilder

def builder = new JsonBuilder()
builder {
  invoices(1..3) { day ->          ❶ Pretended method can take collection and closure
    invoice(date: "2015-01-0$day") {
      item(count: day) {           ❷ Closure defines JSON for each item in collection
        product(name: 'ULC', dollar: 1499)
      }
    }
  }
}
```

[10] See section 7.5.1 for GPath examples and section 11.4 for builder examples.

```
assert builder.toPrettyString().startsWith(          ←┐   Check the start
'''{                                                   ❸   of pretty output
    "invoices": [
        {
            "invoice": [
                {
                    "date": "2015-01-01"
''')
```

There's special support for handling lists of maplike structures. For example, our `invoices` will contain a list of three `invoice` maps, so we pass a collection (in this case the range `1..3`) to `invoices` ❶ and also provide a closure to process each item in the collection ❷. Rather than using the normal `toString()` method like we used in listing 14.18, we'll use a `toPrettyString()` variant ❸ that performs appropriate indenting and line-breaking to make the nesting relationships in the result clear.

There's also a streaming JSON builder called (as you might guess) `StreamingJSON-Builder`. Consult the GroovyDoc API documentation for further details.

The final useful JSON class we'll look at is `JsonOutput`. It's used to serialize Groovy objects into JSON. It handles most common datatypes and, importantly, also nested structures of objects and your own domain classes. It's a helper class with static utility methods. It contains numerous `toJson` methods corresponding to the various datatypes it converts and a `prettyPrint` method. Using them is pretty straightforward as shown for a simple athlete data structure in the following listing.

Listing 14.20 Athlete example with `JsonOutput`

```
import static groovy.json.JsonOutput.*

def json = toJson([date: '2015-01-01', time: '6 am'])
assert json == '{"date":"2015-01-01","time":"6 am"}'

class Athlete { String first, last }

def mj = new Athlete(first: 'Michael', last: 'Jordan')
assert toJson(mj) == '{"first":"Michael","last":"Jordan"}'

def pt = new Athlete(first: 'Paul', last: 'Tergat')
def athletes = [basketball: mj, marathon: pt]

json = toJson(athletes)
assert prettyPrint(json) == '''
{
    "basketball": {
        "first": "Michael",
        "last": "Jordan"
    },
    "marathon": {
        "first": "Paul",
        "last": "Tergat"
    }
}
'''.trim()
```

The good news is that most of the time, you don't need to use `JsonOutput` directly. The final example in listing 14.19 could have used `JsonBuilder` as

```
new JsonBuilder(athletes).toPrettyString()
```

and `JsonBuilder` would call `JsonOutput` under the covers. Nevertheless, you might find using `JsonOutput` directly comes in handy for tricky cases like trying to serialize recursive data structures—just don't expect either class to automatically handle such a case.

That wraps up our tour of JSON. Let's have a look at what we covered in this chapter.

14.4   *Summary*

XML and JSON are such big topics that we cannot possibly touch all bases in a book on Groovy. We've covered the most important aspects in enough detail to provide a good basis for experimentation and further reading. When pushing the limits with Groovy XML and JSON, you'll probably encounter topics that aren't covered in this chapter. Don't hesitate to consult the online resources.

At this point, you have a solid basis for understanding the different ways of working with XML and JSON in Groovy.

Using the familiar Java DOM parsers in Groovy enables you to work on the standard `org.w3c.com.Node` objects whenever the situation calls for it. Such nodes can be retrieved from the `DOMBuilder`, conveniently accessed with the help of `DOMCategory`, and investigated with XPath expressions. Groovy makes life with the DOM easier, but it can't rectify some of the design decisions that give surprises or involve extra work for no benefit.

Groovy's internal `XmlParser` and `XmlSlurper` provide access to XML documents in a Groovy-friendly way that supports GPath expressions for working on the document. `XmlParser` provides an in-memory representation for in-place manipulation of nodes, whereas `XmlSlurper` is able to work in a more streamlike fashion. For even further memory reductions, you can also use SAX and StAX.

Finally, it's easy to parse and build JSON for situations where XML isn't required. XML parsers in Java have been optimized over many years and Groovy stands on the shoulder of giants when making XML more accessible. For JSON, the situation is quite different. Here Groovy is currently at the head of the pack in terms of parsing speed.

Whatever your XML- or JSON-based activity, Groovy is likely to have *something* that will ease your work. By now, that shouldn't come as a surprise.

Interacting with Web Services

15

This chapter covers

- Consuming RSS and ATOM feeds
- Using REST and JAX-RS
- Remote operations with XML-RPC
- SOAP Web Services

Service to others is the rent you pay for your room here on earth.

—Muhammad Ali

From the early days of computer networking, we've used a wealth of protocols and data formats to allow computers to interact and exchange information. With the popularity and ubiquity of the World Wide Web, the range of protocols and data formats has consolidated to primarily focus on HTTP, which implements the request–response model you know from your everyday browsing activities, and a small number of markup notations (mainly HTML, XML, and JSON) as the data-exchange format. These are the commonly called *web service* technologies and are the subject of this chapter.

At a simple level, sharing data happens every time you surf the web. With the help of your browser, you *request* a URL. The server *responds* with an HTML document that your browser knows how to display. The server and the browser are interconnected through the HTTP that implements the request–response model, and they use HTML as the data-exchange format.

Now imagine a program that surfs the web on your behalf. Such a program could visit a list of URLs to check for updates, browse a list of news providers for new information about your favorite topics (we suggest "Groovy"), access a stock ticker to see whether your shares have exceeded some target price, and check the local weather service to see if it issued a thunderstorm warning.

Such a program would have significant difficulties to overcome if it had to find the requested information in the HTML of each website. The HTML describes not only what the data is, but also how it should be broadly presented. A change to the presentation aspect of the HTML could easily break the program that was trying to understand the data.

What if instead of using a format intended to present content to human readers, we chose a notation friendlier to computers. Perhaps we could use a binary notation directly matching how our computer represents the data? Unfortunately, interconnected systems can be heterogeneous. They may be written in different languages, run on different platforms (think .NET versus Java), use different OSs, and run on different hardware architectures.

Instead of dealing with the two aspects of content and presentation together, it would be more reliable if there were an XML or JSON description of the pure content. This is what Web Services are about.

XML and JSON describe data in a system-independent way. This makes them obvious candidates for exchanging data across a network. No matter how different these systems are, they can exchange data through XML or JSON, so long as both sides have some idea of how to interpret or serialize the data they're given.

A full description of all web service formats and protocols is beyond the scope of this book, but we'll show how you can use some of them with Groovy. Our focus will be on writing web service clients in Groovy but we'll glimpse a few bits of server technology and techniques along the way. We cover reading XML resources via RSS and ATOM, followed by a more detailed look at using the REST style. Then we cover Groovy's special XML-RPC support on the client and, albeit briefly, the server side. Finally, we'll look at all the ways to use Groovy for writing requests to SOAP services.

In case REST and SOAP make it sound like we're talking about having a bath instead of accessing Web Services, you'll be pleased to hear we're starting with a brief description of some of these protocols and conventions.

15.1   *An overview of Web Services*

Web Services solutions cover a spectrum of approaches from the simple to what some regard as extremely complex. Perhaps the simplest approach is to use the stateless HTTP protocol to request a resource via a URL. This is the basis of the *REpresentational State Transfer* (REST) architecture. The terms REST and RESTful are sometimes used in a very strict sense for Web Services that follow all of the principles espoused in the original Ph.D. thesis[1] by Roy Fielding on the topic, but the terms have also been used more widely to refer to any mechanism for exposing content on the web via simple XML or JSON.

One of the first popular uses of the REST architecture in its most basic form was for making content of web blogs available. Two of the most commonly used formats in this area are *Really Simple Syndication*[2] (RSS) and ATOM (RFC-4287). We'll start our exploration of web services by looking at these formats.

The next logical extension from using a URL to request a resource is to use simple XML embodied within a normal HTTP POST request. This also can be regarded as a REST solution. We'll examine several XML and JSON APIs of this nature as part of our REST tour.

When the focus isn't on the remote resource but on triggering an operation on the remote system, the *XML Remote Procedure Call* (XML-RPC) can be used. XML-RPC uses HTTP but adds context, which makes it a stateful protocol (as opposed to REST).

The SOAP[3] protocol extends the concept of XML-RPC to support not only remote operations but even remote *objects*. Web service enterprise features that build upon SOAP provide other functionality such as security, transactions, and reliable messaging, to name a few of the many advanced features available.

Now that you have your bearings, let's look at how Groovy can access two of the most popular web service formats in use today.

15.2 *Reading RSS and ATOM*

Let's start our day by reading the news. The BBC broadcasts its latest news on an RSS channel. Because we're busy programmers, we're interested only in the top three headlines. A little Groovy program fetches them and prints them to the console. What we'd like to see is the headline, a short description, and a URL pointing to the full article in case a headline catches our interest.

Here is some sample output (edited slightly for brevity):

```
The top three news today:
Cameron challenged on pupil funding ...
http://www.bbc.co.uk/...
David Cameron promises not to cut school budgets ...
----
Litvinenko 'worked as MI6 consultant'
http://www.bbc.co.uk/...
Former Russian spy Alexander Litvinenko  ...
----
```

---

[1] "Architectural Styles and the Design of Network-based Software Architectures," available at www.ics.uci.edu/~fielding/pubs/dissertation/top.htm.

[2] Also called *Rich Site Summary* (RSS 0.9x) or *Resource Description Framework* (RDF) *Site Summary* (RSS 1.0).

[3] SOAP used to stand for *Simple Object Access Protocol*, but this meaning has been dropped since version 1.2, because SOAP does more than access objects, and the word *simple* was questionable from the start.

```
Greste 'angst' for jailed colleagues
http://www.bbc.co.uk/...
Australian Al-Jazeera journalist Peter Greste ...
----
```

The next listing implements this newsreader. It requests the web resource that contains the news as XML. It finds the resource by its URL. Passing the URL to the parse method implicitly fetches it from the web. The remainder of the code can directly work on the node tree using GPath expressions.

Listing 15.1   A simple RSS newsreader

```
def base = 'http://news.bbc.co.uk/rss/newsonline_uk_edition/'
def url  = base +'front_page/rss091.xml'

println 'The top three news items today:'
def items = new XmlParser().parse(url).channel[0].item
for (item in items[0..2]) {
    println item.title.text()
    println item.link.text()
    println item.description.text()
    println '----'
}
```

Of course, for writing such code, we need to know what elements and attributes are available in the RSS format. In listing 15.1, we assumed that at least the following structure is available:

```
<rss ...>
  <channel>
    ...
    <item>
      <title>…</title>
      <description>...</description>
      <link>...</link>
      ...
```

This is only a small subset of the full information. You can find a full description of the RSS and ATOM formats and their various versions in *RSS and ATOM in Action* by Dave Johnson (Manning, 2006).

Reading an ATOM feed is equally easy, as shown in listing 15.2. It reads the ATOM feed from IBM's developerWorks Java Technology topic feed. At the time of writing this chapter, it prints

```
22 Jan 2015  Integrating FindBugs, CheckStyle and Cobertura with Rational
Team Concert build system
21 Jan 2015  Embed rich reports in your applications
17 Dec 2014  Create a coupon-finding app by combining Yelp, Google Maps,
Twitter, and Klout services
   ...
```

One thing that's new in listing 15.2 is the use of XML namespaces. The ATOM format makes use of namespaces like so:

```
<feed xmlns="http://www.w3.org/2005/Atom">
    ...
    <entry>
        <title>Java.next: The Java.next languages</title>
        ...
```

To traverse nodes that are bound to namespaces with GPath expressions, qualified names (QName objects) are used.[4] A QName object can be retrieved from a Namespace object by requesting the property of the corresponding element name. To collect the entries we're interested in we use atom.entry. For each entry we subsequently look up its atom.published date (truncating off time information), its atom.summary (printing out a star for any that mention Groovy), and its atom.title.

Listing 15.2   Reading an ATOM feed

```
import groovy.xml.Namespace

def url = 'http://www.ibm.com/developerworks/views/java/rss/' +       Shows
    'libraryview.jsp?feed_by=atom'                                    latest
def atom = new Namespace('http://www.w3.org/2005/Atom')               three
def numEntries = 3                                                    entries
def entries = new XmlParser().parse(url)[atom.entry][0..<numEntries]
def len = "dd mmm yyyy ".size()                                       Chops
def summaries = entries.collect {                                     published
  it[atom.published].text()[0..<len] +                                date after
      (it[atom.summary].text().contains('Groovy') ? '*' : ' ') +     this many
      it[atom.title].text()                                          chars
}
println summaries.join("\n")
```

That was all fairly easy, right? The next topic, REST, will be more elaborate but covers a wider area of applicability, because it's a more general approach.

15.3   *Using a REST-based API*

Although many Web Services are bound to a standard, REST is an open concept rather than a standard. The common denominators of REST services are the following:[5]

- Formatted data is exchanged between client and server (typically using XML or JSON).
- Communication is done on a stateless request–response model over HTTP(S) using verbs such as GET, POST, and so forth.
- Resources or services are addressed by a URL.

---

[4] XmlParser and XmlSlurper are namespace-aware by default but can be configured to not handle namespaces if you prefer, though you'd typically have more work to do yourself manually in that case.

[5] We could get in-depth here and talk about additional constraints but we'll keep it simple for now.

No binding standard describes the structure of the XML or JSON that's sent around. You need to look into the documentation of each REST service to find out what information is requested and provided. The documentation will describe the available resources, the verbs supported, the XML or JSON structure they expect to receive (for operations that consume a payload), and the result they return.

As a first example, we'll look into the REST services for interacting with The Apache Software Foundation's[6] JIRA[7] used by Groovy for issue tracking. The documentation for these services can be found on the Atlassian website at http://docs.atlassian.com/jira/REST/latest/. It has around 40 different resources listed in the API (some with subresources). For each resource, the supported methods are given. For our purposes, we're interested in the following resource (which will allow us to query the details about a particular JIRA issue of interest[8]):

```
/rest/api/latest/issue/{issueIdOrKey}
```

It supports GET, PUT, and DELETE methods but we're only interested in GET. Looking at the documentation for GET, it has a few options to customize our query (for example, to select which fields are returned). These would be passed in as URL parameters (in general, REST APIs might use JSON- or XML-formatted messages in, for example, a POST method instead of URL parameters). For our purposes, we won't customize our query, so no additional parameters are required.

Invoking the query is simply a matter of performing a GET request at the above URL but substituting in the key for the issue of interest. Since a GET request is the default type of request, we open an HTTP connection to the URL and it will return JSON containing the details we're after. We can use Groovy's JsonSlurper to consume the returned JSON and confirm details about the issue of interest. We might also like to check that we get back a valid response code:

```
def httpConnection = new URL(base + key).openConnection()
assert httpConnection.responseCode == httpConnection.HTTP_OK
def result = slurper.parse(httpConnection.inputStream.newReader())
// do something with result …
```

We'll provide a Groovy-friendly wrapper class (class Jira in listing 15.3) around these calls. That way if we need to swap the JSON parser for an XML one, or the details change about which methods and resources we should be calling, it won't affect the code using our wrapper class. Putting this together can be seen in the following listing.

6 The Groovy project is currently hosted within the Apache incubator as part of moving to the Apache Software Foundation. See www.apache.org for details.
7 The project tracking system from Atlassian. See www.atlassian.com/software/jira/overview for details.
8 One nice aspect of this particular resource is that for simple querying, no authentication is required.

Listing 15.3   Querying JIRA via its REST API

```
import groovy.json.JsonSlurper

class Jira {
  def base = 'https://issues.apache.org/jira/rest/api/latest/issue/'
  def slurper = new JsonSlurper()

  def query(key) {
    def httpConnection = new URL(base + key).openConnection()
    assert httpConnection.responseCode == httpConnection.HTTP_OK
    slurper.parse(httpConnection.inputStream.newReader())
  }
}

def jira = new Jira()
def response = jira.query("GROOVY-5999")
response.fields.with {
  assert summary == "Make @Delegate work with @DelegatesTo"
  assert fixVersions.name == ['2.1.1']
  assert resolutiondate.startsWith('2013-02-14')
}
```

For this simple example, using the JDK URL class was relatively simple and painless, but as the complexity grows, this approach tends to involve a fair bit of boilerplate logic in the solution. We can keep things simple by using a dedicated REST client API. We'll use HTTPBuilder,[9] which provides a RESTClient class. This class makes the GET, POST, and other HTTP methods easily available to us and hides away the underlying details of connection handling. It automatically can determine if a JSON or XML response is returned using MIME-TYPE information in the response and provides us with the necessary slurper without us needing to worry about the details. The end result is cleaner-looking code as shown in the following listing.

Listing 15.4   Querying JIRA using HTTPBuilder

```
@Grab('org.codehaus.groovy.modules.http-builder:http-builder:0.7.2')
import groovyx.net.http.RESTClient

def base = 'https://issues.apache.org/jira/rest/api/latest/'
def jira = new RESTClient(base)
jira.get(path: 'issue/GROOVY-5999') { resp, json ->
  assert resp.status == 200
  json.fields.with {
    assert summary == "Make @Delegate work with @DelegatesTo"
    assert fixVersions.name == ['2.1.1']
    assert resolutiondate.startsWith('2013-02-14')
  }
}
```

---

[9] See https://github.com/jgritman/httpbuilder/wiki.

Let's look at another web service used for finding the conversion rate between two monetary currencies. It's hosted at the popular Web Services portal at www.webservicex.net/. It's very similar to our earlier example but requires query parameters and returns XML instead of JSON. The base URL for this service is:

```
http://www.webservicex.net/CurrencyConvertor.asmx
```

The path and query parameters for conversion from U.S. dollars to Euros are:

```
<baseUrl>/ConversionRate?FromCurrency=USD&ToCurrency=EUR
```

When invoked, XML content containing an appropriate exchange rate will be produced:

```
<double xmlns="http://www.webserviceX.NET/">0.882</double>
```

The HTTPBuilder code to access this web service is shown in the following listing.

Listing 15.5   Using HTTPBuilder with query parameters

```
@Grab('org.codehaus.groovy.modules.http-builder:http-builder:0.7.2')
import groovyx.net.http.RESTClient

def url = 'http://www.webservicex.net/CurrencyConvertor.asmx/'
def converter = new RESTClient(url)
def params = [FromCurrency: 'USD', ToCurrency: 'EUR']
converter.get(path: 'ConversionRate', query: params) { resp, data ->
  assert resp.status == 200
  assert data.name() == 'double'
  println data.text()
}
```

When run, the following output was produced at the time of writing:

```
0.882
```

The example illustrates a nice feature of the HTTPBuilder library. The library examines the MIME type of the web service response and correctly chooses an appropriate slurper to handle the incoming content. Whereas it chose a JSON slurper for our JIRA example in listing 15.4, it has now chosen an XML slurper. When we combine that feature with Groovy's duck-typing we end up with code that's more resilient should the format of the response change in the future. In common with our JIRA example in listing 15.4, this example also used an HTTP GET method but the webservicex currency web service also supports POST method requests as shown in the following listing.

Listing 15.6   Using HTTPBuilder with a POST method

```
@Grab('org.codehaus.groovy.modules.http-builder:http-builder:0.7.2')
import groovyx.net.http.RESTClient
import static groovyx.net.http.ContentType.URLENC

def url = 'http://www.webservicex.net/CurrencyConvertor.asmx/'
def converter = new RESTClient(url)
```

```
def postBody = [FromCurrency: 'USD', ToCurrency: 'EUR']
converter.post(path: 'ConversionRate', body: postBody,
    requestContentType: URLENC) { resp, data ->
  assert resp.status == 200
  assert data.name() == 'double'
  println data.text()
}
```

The examples so far are very simple, but a more typical example might differ in one of two ways:

1 It might involve greater complexity. It may have many more URL parameters, involve authentication, involve JSON or XML POST payloads, etc. The HTTP-Builder library provides markup builders to support these more complex scenarios. See the API documentation for more details.[10]

2 It may be a mashup combining many other services together to provide a more compelling service.

Having said that, you should now have the knowledge to tackle such complex REST applications even with only the few small tools we've shown you in this section.

Before leaving this section, we should briefly look at the latest JAX-RS 2.0 standard (also known as JSR-339).[11] Earlier versions of this standard have been part of the Java EE world for some time. JAX-RS annotations such as @GET, @PUT, @Path, and @QueryParam are added to server-side implementation code. The JAX-RS library takes care of the mapping between the HTTP protocol endpoint and the implementation code. Part of the mapping may involve serialization between domain objects used in the implementation code and their representation as parameters or as a JSON or XML payload.

Obviously this API frees the developer from much low-level detail so it's definitely of interest for endpoint service writers, but this is a chapter focusing on writing web service client code. Why should JAX-RS be of interest? The good news is that as of version 2.0 of this standard, there's now a *unified client API*. In addition, some of the implementations don't require a Java EE container and can be used standalone with Java SE. That makes it ideal for our needs. We'll use the RESTEasy (www.jboss.org/resteasy) client from JBoss.

When using JAX-RS as a client, you use a fluent API provided by a ClientBuilder class to define the details necessary for the builder to make the appropriate HTTP request to your endpoint of interest and understand the returning response. The API has numerous extension points to allow you to cater for custom MIME types or special serialization needs. We'll avoid using those parts of the API. For our example, it's sufficient to specify the target URL and our query parameters and then declare that we

---

[10] See https://github.com/jgritman/httpbuilder/wiki.
[11] See www.jcp.org/en/jsr/detail?id=339 for the final specification.

want a raw string back as the response type. We'll process the response ourselves with Groovy's `XmlSlurper`. The resulting code can be seen in the following listing.

Listing 15.7   Using JAX-RS

```
@Grab('org.jboss.resteasy:resteasy-client:3.0.10.Final')
import javax.ws.rs.client.ClientBuilder

def client = ClientBuilder.newClient()
def base = "http://www.webservicex.net/CurrencyConvertor.asmx"
def response = client.target(base + '/ConversionRate')
    .queryParam("FromCurrency", "USD")
    .queryParam("ToCurrency", "EUR")
    .request().get(String)
def rate = new XmlSlurper().parseText(response)
assert rate.name() == 'double'
println rate.text()
```

❶ Specifies a String response

Specifying we wanted a raw string back was as easy as supplying the `String` class to the get method ❶. Alternatively, we could get the HTTP response object back or a domain object we've previously defined using JAX-RS annotations. Such a class would be available if we had used JAX-RS to define our service.

We should also point out a nice feature of RESTEasy that isn't currently part of the JSR-339 standard. It provides a proxy method that takes an interface class. The interface class is annotated in much the same way as a service endpoint would be with normal JAX-RS conventions, but only the client side mapping is catered for with this technique. This is exactly what we want and the resulting code is shown in the following listing.

Listing 15.8   Using a RESTEasy client proxy

```
@Grab('org.jboss.resteasy:resteasy-client:3.0.10.Final')
import javax.ws.rs.GET
import javax.ws.rs.Path
import javax.ws.rs.Produces
import javax.ws.rs.QueryParam
import javax.ws.rs.client.ClientBuilder

interface CurrencyConvertor {
  @GET
  @Path("ConversionRate")
  @Produces("application/xml")
  String convert(@QueryParam("FromCurrency") String from,
                 @QueryParam("ToCurrency") String to)
}

def client = ClientBuilder.newClient()
def base = "http://www.webservicex.net/CurrencyConvertor.asmx"
def proxy = client.target(base).proxy(CurrencyConvertor)
def response = proxy.convert("USD", "EUR")
def root = new XmlSlurper().parseText(response)
assert root.name() == 'double'
println root.text()
```

Here the `CurrencyConvertor` interface is our declarative description of the details for the web service. Annotations on the `convert` method and its parameters give enough information for the `proxy` method to provide us with an object that satisfies the `CurrencyConvertor` interface but makes the correct HTTP call to the web service when called.

We don't have space within this chapter to deep dive into other details of JAX-RS. For a few more details with a Groovy flavor, we suggest reading *Make Java Groovy* by Kenneth Kousen (Manning, 2013) or visiting the JAX-RS website (https://jax-rs-spec .java.net/) for all the official details.

REST APIs provide a very simple but powerful mechanism for client–server interaction. The downside is that each API is different; you need to understand the details of each one before you use it. You'll see one approach to overcoming this lack of standardization when we look into XML-RPC in the next section.

15.4 Using XML-RPC

The XML-RPC specification is almost as old as XML. It's extremely simple and concise. See www.xmlrpc.com for all details.

Thanks to this specification, Groovy can provide a general implementation for many of the infrastructure details that you have to write for REST. A separate module (groovy-xmlrpc) contains the general implementation and can be easily obtained with a `@Grab` annotation in your class or script or by simply downloading the .jar file.

Perhaps the best way to convince you of its merits is by example. Suppose you have a simple XML-RPC server running on your local machine on port 8080 that exposes an `echo` operation that returns whatever it receives. Using this service from a Groovy client is as simple as

```
import groovy.net.xmlrpc.XMLRPCServerProxy as Proxy
def remote = new Proxy('http://localhost:8080/')
assert 'Hello world!' == remote.echo('Hello world!')
```

Installing a server that implements the `echo` operation is equally easy. Create a server instance, and assign a closure to its `echo` property:

```
import groovy.net.xmlrpc.XMLRPCServer as Server

def server = new Server()

server.echo = { return it }
```

The server must be started on a `ServerSocket` before the client can call it, and it must be stopped afterward. The following listing installs the `echo` server, starts it, requests the `echo` operation, and stops it at the end.

Listing 15.9 Self-contained XML-RPC server and client for the `echo` operation

```
@Grab('org.codehaus.groovy:groovy-xmlrpc:0.8')
import groovy.net.xmlrpc.XMLRPCServerProxy as Proxy
import groovy.net.xmlrpc.XMLRPCServer as Server
```

```
def server = new Server()
server.echo = { return it }

def socket = new ServerSocket(8080)
server.startServer(socket)

remote = new Proxy("http://localhost:8080/")
assert 'Hello world!' == remote.echo('Hello world!')

server.stopServer()
```

Client code

Having the client and server together is useful for testing purposes, but in production these two parts usually run on different systems.

XML-RPC also defines error handling, which in Groovy XML-RPC is available through the XMLRPCCallFailureException with the properties faultString and faultCode.

The areas of applicability for XML-RPC are so wide that any list we could come up with would be necessarily incomplete. It's used for reading and posting to blogs, connecting to instant messaging systems (over the Jabber protocol for systems such as GoogleTalk[12]), newsfeeds, search engines, continuous integration servers, bug-tracking systems, and so on.

It's appealing because it's powerful and simple at the same time. Let's, for example, find out information about the projects managed at the Apache Software Foundatioin (ASF).[13] The ASF provides the JIRA[14] bug-tracking system for its hosted projects.

Printing all project names can be done easily with the following code:

```
import groovy.net.xmlrpc.XMLRPCServerProxy as Proxy

def remote = new Proxy('http://jira.codehaus.org/rpc/xmlrpc')

def loginToken = remote.jira1.login('user','***')
def projects   = remote.jira1.getProjects(loginToken)
projects.each { println it.name }
```

It's conventional for operations exposed via XML-RPC to have a dot-notation like jira1.login. Groovy's XML-RPC support can deal with that.

But if you call a lot of methods, using the remote.jira1. prefix gets in the way of readability. It would be nicer to avoid that. Listing 15.10 has a solution. Calls to proxy methods can always optionally take a closure. Inside that closure, method names are resolved against the proxy. We extend this behavior with a specialized JiraProxy that prefixes method calls with jira1.

---

[12] See Guillaume's excellent article on how to use GoogleTalk through Groovy at http://glaforge.free.fr/weblog/index.php?itemid=142.
[13] The Groovy project is currently hosted within the Apache incubator as part of moving to the Apache Software Foundation.
[14] Find information about the JIRA XML-RPC methods at http://confluence.atlassian.com/display/JIRA/JIRA+XML-RPC+Overview.

To make things a bit more interesting this time, we print information about the Groovy project in the ASF's JIRA.

Listing 15.10 Using the JIRA XML-RPC API on the Groovy project

```
@Grab('org.codehaus.groovy:groovy-xmlrpc:0.8')
import groovy.net.xmlrpc.XMLRPCServerProxy as Proxy

class JiraProxy extends Proxy {
  JiraProxy(url) { super(url) }

  Object invokeMethod(String methodname, args) {
    super.invokeMethod('jira1.' + methodname, args)
  }
}

def jira = new JiraProxy('https://issues.apache.org/jira/rpc/xmlrpc')

// insert your codehaus username and password below
jira.login('username', '****') { loginToken ->
  def projects = getProjectsNoSchemes(loginToken)
  println "${projects.size()} projects found in the Apache jira"
  def groovy = projects.find { it.name == 'Groovy' }
  if (groovy) {
    println "Found the $groovy.name project with key $groovy.key"
    println "Description: $groovy.description"
    println "Led by $groovy.lead and hosted at $groovy.projectUrl"
  }
}
```

This prints

```
519 projects found in the Apache jira
Found the groovy project with key GROOVY
Description: Groovy programming language: a modern dynamic language for the JVM
Led by guillaume and hosted at https://groovy.incubator.apache.org
```

Note the simplicity of the code. Unlike with REST, you don't need to work on XML or JSON nodes, either in the request or in the response. You can just use Groovy data-types such as strings (*user*), lists (*projects*), and maps (*groovy*). Who can ask for more?

There would be a book's worth more to say about XML-RPC and its Groovy module, especially about implementing the server side. But this book has only so many pages, and you need to refer to the online documentation for more details and use scenarios.

You now have the basic information to start your work with XML-RPC. Why not try it right now! Or alternatively, continue on our tour through all the options for distributed processing with an all-embracing solution: SOAP.

15.5 *Applying SOAP*

SOAP is the successor of XML-RPC and follows the approach of providing a binding standard. This standard is maintained by the W3C; see www.w3.org/TR/soap/.

The SOAP standard extends the XML-RPC standard in multiple dimensions. One extension is datatypes. Where XML-RPC allows only a small fixed set of datatypes, SOAP provides means to define new service-specific datatypes. Other frameworks, including CORBA, DCOM, and Java RMI, provide functionality similar to that of SOAP, but SOAP messages are written entirely in XML and are therefore platform- and language-independent. The general approach of SOAP is to allow a web service to describe its public API: where it's located, what operations are available, and the request and response formats (called messages). A SOAP service makes this information available via the Web Services Definition Language (WSDL).

SOAP has been widely adopted by the industry, and numerous free services are available, ranging from online shops through financial data, maps, music, payment systems, online auctions, order tracking, blogs, news, picture galleries, weather services, credit card validation—the list is endless.

Numerous programming languages and platforms provide excellent support for SOAP. Popular SOAP stack implementations on the Java platform include Metro (http://metro.java.net) and Apache CXF (http://cxf.apache.org/). Built-in SOAP support for Groovy is rather basic, but it's used successfully for production projects. First, we'll explore how you can use SOAP with pure Groovy in an effective yet concise manner.

15.5.1 *Doing SOAP with plain Groovy*

Our example uses the currency conversion web service we looked at earlier located at www.webservicex.net, which provides a lot of interesting public Web Services. First, we fetch the service description for its currency converter as shown in the following listing.

Listing 15.11   Listing the operations of a SOAP service

```
import groovy.xml.Namespace

def url  = 'http://www.webservicex.net/CurrencyConvertor.asmx?WSDL'
def wsdl = new Namespace('http://schemas.xmlsoap.org/wsdl/','wsdl')
def doc  = new XmlParser().parse(url)

println doc[wsdl.portType][wsdl.operation].'@name'
```

This prints the available operations:

```
["ConversionRate", "ConversionRate", "ConversionRate"]
```

The service exposes three operations named `ConversionRate` with different characteristics.[15] We're interested in one that takes `FromCurrency` and `ToCurrency` as input parameters and returns the current conversion rate. Currencies can be expressed using a format like `USD` or `EUR`.

---

[15] For advice on how to read a WSDL service description, refer to www.w3.org/TR/wsdl.

SOAP uses something called an envelope format for the request. The details are beyond the scope of this chapter. See the specifications for details. Our envelope looks like this:

```
<?xml version="1.0" encoding="utf-8"?>
<soap:Envelope
  xmlns:xsi="http://www.w3.org/2001/XMLSchema-instance"
  xmlns:xsd="http://www.w3.org/2001/XMLSchema"
  xmlns:soap="http://schemas.xmlsoap.org/soap/envelope/">
  <soap:Body>
    <ConversionRate xmlns="http://www.webserviceX.NET/">
      <FromCurrency>${from}</FromCurrency>
      <ToCurrency>${to}</ToCurrency>
    </ConversionRate>
  </soap:Body>
</soap:Envelope>
```

As you see from the ${} notation, this envelope is a template that we can use with a Groovy template engine.

The code in listing 15.12 reads this template, fills it with parameters for U.S.-dollar-to-Euro conversion, and adds it to a POST request to the service URL. The request needs additional request headers such as the SOAPAction to make the server understand it. We explicitly use UTF-8 character encoding to avoid any cross-platform encoding problems.

The service responds with a SOAP result envelope. We know it contains a node named ConversionRateResult belonging to the service's namespace. We locate the first such node in the response and get the conversion rate as its text value.

Listing 15.12 Using the ConversionRate SOAP service

```
import groovy.text.SimpleTemplateEngine as STE
import groovy.xml.Namespace                             Templated envelope
                                                         of SOAP request
def file     = new File('data/conv.templ.xml')   ◁─┘
def template = new STE().createTemplate(file)
def params   = [from:'USD', to:'EUR']
def request  = template.make(params).toString().getBytes('UTF-8')

def url  = 'http://www.webservicex.net/CurrencyConvertor.asmx'
def conn = new URL(url).openConnection()
def reqProps = [
  'Content-Type': 'text/xml; charset=UTF-8',           Requests
  'SOAPAction'  : 'http://www.webserviceX.NET/ConversionRate',   headers to use
  'Accept'      : 'application/soap+xml, text/*'         every time
]
reqProps.each { key,value -> conn.addRequestProperty(key,value) }

conn.requestMethod = 'POST'
conn.doOutput      = true
conn.outputStream << new ByteArrayInputStream(request)   ◁─┐  Sends the
if (conn.responseCode != conn.HTTP_OK) {                     request
  println "Error - HTTP:${conn.responseCode}"
  return
}
```

```
def resp   = new XmlParser().parse(conn.inputStream)        ⟵┐  Parses the
def serv   = new Namespace('http://www.webserviceX.NET/')      │  response
def result = serv.ConversionRateResult                      ⟵

print   "Current USD to EUR conversion rate: "                 Extracts
println resp.depthFirst().find{result == it.name()}.text()     the result
```

At the time of writing, it prints

```
Current USD to EUR conversion rate: 0.882
```

This is straightforward in terms of each individual step, but taken as a whole, the code is fairly cumbersome. One point to note about the implementation is hidden in locating the result in the response envelope. We use the serv namespace and ask it for its ConversionRateResult property, which returns a QName. We assign it to the result variable and make use of the fact that QName implements the equals method with strings so that we find the proper node.

SOAP is verbose compared to other approaches. It's verbose in the code it demands for execution and—more important—it's verbose in its message format. It's not unusual for SOAP messages to have 10 times more XML markup than the payload size.

But the SOAP standard makes it possible to provide general tools for dealing with its complexity.

15.5.2 *Simplifying SOAP access using HTTPBuilder*

The HTTPBuilder library used earlier for accessing REST Web Services is also capable of accessing SOAP services. HTTPBuilder supports a builder-style notation to build up your SOAP request envelope. This saves you from having those details in a separate template file. The resulting code can be seen in the following listing.

Listing 15.13   Accessing a SOAP service using HTTPBuilder

```
@Grab('org.codehaus.groovy.modules.http-builder:http-builder:0.7.2')
import groovyx.net.http.RESTClient
import static groovyx.net.http.ContentType.XML

def base = 'http://www.webserviceX.NET/CurrencyConvertor.asmx'
def soapEnv = 'http://www.w3.org/2003/05/soap-envelope'
def contentType = 'application/soap+xml; charset=UTF-8'        ❶ Registers a
new RESTClient(base).with {                                       SOAP response
  parser.'application/soap+xml' = parser.'application/xml'   ⟵   parser
  headers = ['Content-Type': contentType]                    ⟵
  post(requestContentType: XML, body: {                          Content-Type
    'soap:Envelope'('xmlns:soap': soapEnv) {                     expected by
      'soap:Body' {                                         ❷ SOAP server
        ConversionRate(xmlns: 'http://www.webserviceX.NET/') {
          FromCurrency('USD')
          ToCurrency('EUR')
        }
      }
    }
  }) { resp, data ->
```

```
      assert resp.status == 200
      println data.text()
    }
}
```

Most of this should look familiar to earlier parsing and builder examples. HTTP-Builder knows how to create XML requests and parse XML responses. You'll use those capabilities and provide the correct elements, attributes, and namespaces expected for a SOAP interaction.

Perhaps the first tricky part is that you need to register an appropriate parser ❶ (using the 'application/soap+xml' MIME type) for the returned response. Given that the SOAP response can be treated as plain-old XML, you can piggyback onto that parser. Also, even though the SOAP request is just plain-old XML, the SOAP server will be expecting a SOAP content type, so you need to set a header to the value the SOAP server is expecting ❷.

Our HTTPBuilder implementation is a big step forward over listing 15.12 but it still contains a fair bit of boilerplate code. Just as one example, the SOAP envelope and body elements would exist for every SOAP service. Our next step to consider is a dedicated SOAP-aware library. That's the subject of the next section.

15.5.3 Simplifying SOAP access using groovy-wslite

The groovy-wslite library knows about SOAP (and REST too if you want to consider an alternative to HTTPBuilder for REST). It uses a builder-style approach to allow us to specify our SOAP body payload but hides away many of the details associated with creating the actual SOAP requests or parsing the SOAP responses. The following listing shows the resulting code.

Listing 15.14 Conversion rates using groovy-wslite

```
@Grab('com.github.groovy-wslite:groovy-wslite:1.1.0')
import wslite.soap.SOAPClient

def url = 'http://www.webservicex.net/CurrencyConvertor.asmx?WSDL'
def client = new SOAPClient(url)
def action = "http://www.webserviceX.NET/ConversionRate"
def response = client.send(SOAPAction: action) {
  body {
    ConversionRate(xmlns: 'http://www.webserviceX.NET/') {
      FromCurrency('USD')
      ToCurrency('EUR')
    }
  }
}
assert response.httpResponse.statusCode == 200
println response.ConversionRateResponse.ConversionRateResult
```

Now, that's a lot groovier! This particular SOAP request will use the default version of SOAP 1.1, but we can swap to SOAP 1.2 just as easily as can be seen in the next listing.

Listing 15.15 Conversion rates using groovy-wslite and SOAP 1.2

```
@Grab('com.github.groovy-wslite:groovy-wslite:1.1.0')
import wslite.soap.*

def url = 'http://www.webserviceX.NET/CurrencyConvertor.asmx?WSDL'
def client = new SOAPClient(url)
def response = client.send {
  version SOAPVersion.V1_2
  body {
    ConversionRate(xmlns: 'http://www.webserviceX.NET/') {
      FromCurrency('USD')
      ToCurrency('EUR')
    }
  }
}
assert response.httpResponse.statusCode == 200
println response.ConversionRateResponse.ConversionRateResult
```

Here we need to explicitly set the version we require but we can drop the SOAPAction information as that isn't required for SOAP 1.2.

We hope you've enjoyed our journey through the variety of web service client technologies. You should have enough information to build a wide variety of web service clients.

15.6 *Summary*

Web Services is such a big topic that we cannot possibly touch all bases in an introductory book on Groovy, but you've seen the most important aspects in enough detail to have a good basis for experimentation and further reading.

It has become increasingly popular to build whole application architectures around small, dedicated, loosely coupled services that cooperate by using the mechanics that we've touched upon in this chapter. They're called microservices.

They can live in their own little container that may even contain their private operating system. Each can have its own way of exposing its service as long as it complies with the web standards. They may run on full-blown Java Enterprise servers, Spring Boot, Grails, Groovy + Jetty as in section 12.5, or something as small and lightweight as Ratpack (www.ratpack.io).

It's not clear whether this trend will continue, but either way, your knowledge of Groovy's web service support enables you to implement conventional architectures just as well as the latest *hip* architectures.

As you've seen, it's easy to send XML and JSON around the world to make networked computers work together, sharing information and computing power. XML-RPC and SOAP have support in the Groovy libraries, although that support is likely to change significantly over time. REST can't benefit from such support as easily (not even in the dynamic world of Groovy) due to a lack of standardization, but you've seen how the use of builders can make the development of an API for a specific REST service straightforward.

Integrating Groovy

In the programming-language world, one rule of survival is simple: dance or die. It is not enough to make a beautiful language. You must also make it easy for programs written in your beautiful language to interact with programs written in other languages.

—Simon Peyton Jones

One of the biggest advantages of Groovy (even one of the reasons for its inception) is that it integrates natively with Java because both languages run on the same platform and for the most part share the same commonly used data structures like lists and maps. It's important to understand what makes Groovy such an attractive option when you need to embed a scripting language in your application.

From a corporate perspective, it makes sense to build on the same platform that most of your projects are already running on. This protects the investment in skills, experience, and technology, mitigating risk and thus costs.

Where Java isn't a perfect fit as a language, Groovy's expressiveness, brevity, and power features may be more appropriate. Conversely, when Groovy falls short because of the inevitable trade-off between agility and speed, performance-critical code can be replaced with raw Java.[1] These balancing decisions can be made early or late with few repercussions due to the close links between the two languages. Groovy provides a transparent integration mechanism that permits a one-to-one mix-and-match of Java and Groovy classes. This isn't always the case with other scripting solutions, some of which just provide wrappers or proxies that break the object hierarchy contract.

16.1   *Prelude to integration*

If Groovy and Java integrate so seamlessly, why is a whole chapter devoted to describing the integration possibilities? To answer, we need to take a step back.

If you already have a Java project that builds using Gradle, then "incorporating" Groovy into your project might be as simple as adding a line at the top of your Gradle build file to enable the Groovy plugin and adding a dependency to the Groovy JAR file. Or, if you're compiling and packaging your Groovy artifacts into class files, then you might be able to add those to your Java classpath. Similarly, if you're mostly using Groovy and want to "incorporate" a bit of Java, it might mean adding a JAR file to your classpath or using the joint compilation flag when calling the Groovy compiler.

But these simple scenarios don't allow for any just-in-time provision of code, whether that's through users entering expressions as they might into a graphing calculator or developers providing replacement scripts for just the bits of code that require frequent changes within a live system. As an idea of how widely used this kind of facility can be, consider Visual Basic (VB). We're not in the business of judging its pros and cons, but it would be hard to deny that VB is popular and has been for a long time. Although many developers write whole applications in VB from scratch, far more use the capability of various products to *embed* pieces of VB code to customize behavior in ways the original developers may never have even considered.

Now consider allowing that kind of flexibility in your application. Instead of hearing people talking about writing VB in Microsoft Office, imagine those same people talking about writing Groovy in *your* application. Imagine them using your product in ways you never contemplated—making it more and more valuable for them.

So, there's a tremendous upside to integration, but it can potentially also add significant complexity depending on which path you take. So let's look at some of the points you should consider when evaluating an integration opportunity, and then what you'd need to do to get started.

---

[1] But make sure you read about `@CompileStatic` in chapter 10, which gives much of your Groovy code Java-like speed.

16.1.1 Integrating appropriately

No one can tell you what your application's needs are or what's going to be suitable for your particular situation. You must look carefully at your requirements and consider whether you'll benefit at all from integrating Groovy. We can't make that decision for you—but we hope we can give a few ideas to guide you.

It's worth explicitly acknowledging that not all applications benefit from integrating a scripting language such as Groovy. We can go as far as saying that many don't require it. If you're writing an e-commerce website, a multimedia player, or an FTP client, chances are that you won't need a scripting language. But don't let us stop you from using Groovy as (one of) your implementation languages for your application. We expect, though, that you'd compile it all in one go in a traditional build process with a single lifecycle.

On the other hand, suppose you were building an advanced word processor, a spreadsheet application, or a complex risk-calculation module for an even more complicated bank software suite that had to evolve quickly to follow the rapid changes of the market, legislation, or new business rules. These applications might need an extension point where end users can customize them to suit their needs. Figure 16.1 shows one example of where you could integrate Groovy.

For instance, the banking application might require the definition of business rules in a script that could be defined at runtime without requiring a new and tedious development/test/qualification phase, reducing the time to market and increasing the responsiveness to changes in financial practices. Another example could be an office suite of applications offering a macro system to create reusable functions that could be invoked with a keystroke. It becomes obvious that a dichotomy of the software world differentiates monolithic applications, which don't need to evolve over time and have a fixed functional scope, from more fluid applications, whose logic can be extended or modified during their lifespan to accommodate context changes.

Before considering using Groovy in your application, analyze whether you need to customize it, and see whether you want to customize, extend, or amend the logic, and not just simple parameters. If parameterization will fulfill your needs, you may be better off with classic configuration mechanisms such as an administration web interface through a set of web services; or, for more advanced monitoring and action

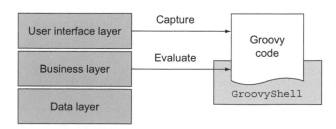

Figure 16.1 One example of an integration solution. Groovy code is entered by the user in the UI layer and then executed in the business layer.

management, you may also consider exposing JMX[2] MBeans. Sometimes, even if the logic has to change, if the choice is between a small and well-defined set of business rules that are known from the beginning, you can also embed all those rules within the application and decide through parameterization which one is to be used.

Once you've examined your needs and come to the conclusion that a scripting environment is what your application requires, this chapter should provide all the information you need to make your application extendable at runtime with logic written in Groovy.[3]

In the following sections, you'll learn how to use the `GroovyShell` class to evaluate simple expressions and scripts, as well as the `GroovyScriptEngine` and the `Groovy-ClassLoader` for further loading of Groovy classes. In addition to the techniques provided by Groovy for integrating your scripts in Java, you'll discover alternatives for leveraging the Spring framework and the scripting API available since Java 6, also known as JSR-223.

16.1.2 *Setting up dependencies*

To use Groovy within your project, you'll need to set it up to use the Groovy libraries. This section covers the dependencies required for Groovy integration. The fact that it's so short should be a source of comfort—there's little work to do to get up and running.

The Groovy distribution comes with a directory containing all the core libraries that form the Groovy runtime. The minimum for embedding Groovy is the groovy-2.4.0.jar file.[4] This contains all of Groovy's core classes plus embedded versions of Antlr, ASM, and Commons-CLI. If you use a feature in one of Groovy's modules such as XML, SQL, or JSON, then you'll also want to incorporate that module's JAR file as well, named groovy-xml.jar, for instance, for the groovy-xml module. See appendix B for a complete list of modules. Alternatively, if you want all of the modules you can use the *embeddable* .jar file, called groovy-all-2.4.0.jar, which resides in the embeddable directory of your distribution. Or you can grab these dependencies from your favored online repository.

> **NOTE** Versions of Groovy prior to 2.3.0 didn't incorporate the Antlr, ASM, and Commons-CLI JAR files except in the embeddable groovy-all JAR file. This meant that you could sometimes get away with a smaller footprint because those third-party JAR files may have been an existing dependency for some other part of your project and therefore already on the classpath. But if you had a noncompatible version of those JAR files on your classpath, there was a risk that Groovy wouldn't work. They're now embedded to avoid such conflicts and you may freely use a different version of those libraries within your application if it makes sense to do so.

---

[2] Java Management Extensions; see www.oracle.com/technetwork/java/javase/tech/javamanagement-140525 .html.

[3] Of course, we don't wish to discourage you from reading the chapter even if you don't have any integration needs right now. Gaining knowledge is a worthy pursuit in and of itself.

[4] The number might be different if you're using a different version.

It's not just Java applications that can benefit from the availability of a scripting engine: you can even integrate custom Groovy scripts and expressions from an application written in Groovy! While explaining the various embedding mechanisms, we'll show you how the Groovy interpreters and classloaders can be exploited from both sides of the language fence. Now that we've set up our environment, we can look at the first of our three ways of directly integrating with Groovy: GroovyShell.

16.2 Evaluating expressions and scripts with GroovyShell

The first Groovy API we'll examine is GroovyShell. This is in many ways the simplest of the integration techniques, and if it covers your situation, it may well be all you need. With all the libraries in place, we'll start dynamically evaluating expressions in a few simple lines of code. We'll then move gradually into more complex scenarios, passing data between the calling code and the dynamically executing script, and then creating classes in the script for use outside. We examine different ways of executing scripts—precompiling them or executing them just once—and the different types of scripts that can be run. Finally, we look at ways you can tweak GroovyShell for more advanced uses. Don't worry if it seems there's a lot to learn—in simple situations, simple solutions often suffice. Also, much of the information presented here is relevant when looking at the other APIs Groovy provides.

16.2.1 Starting simply

The simplest imaginable integration requirement evaluates an expression. For example, some math applications may require users to input arbitrary expressions in a form input field that can't be hardwired at development time in a function or a closure (for instance, a spreadsheet application where formulas are Groovy expressions). Those applications then ask the runtime to calculate the entered formula. In such situations, the tool of choice for evaluating expressions and scripts is the GroovyShell class. The use of this class is straightforward and is similar if you're using it from Java or from Groovy. A simple expression evaluator can be implemented using GroovyShell as shown in the following listing.[5]

> **Listing 16.1   A trivial example of expression evaluation in Groovy**

```
def shell = new GroovyShell()
def result = shell.evaluate("12 + 23")
assert result == 35
```

---

[5] You might wonder why we choose to integrate from Groovy to Groovy. Well, we'd be more likely to do it from Java, but using Groovy simplifies our examples. Doing so can be handy even from Groovy, so that you can organize utility code in external scripts, run scripts with certain security policies in place, or execute user-provided input at runtime.

The equivalent full Java program is naturally somewhat longer due to the scaffolding code and imports required, but the core logic is exactly the same. The following listing gives the complete Java code required to perform the evaluation, albeit it with no error handling. Java examples later in the chapter have been cut down to only the code involved in integration. Imports are usually shown only when they aren't clear from the context.

> **Listing 16.2   Trivial example from listing 16.1, in Java this time**

```java
// Java
import groovy.lang.GroovyShell;

public class HelloIntegrationWorld {
    public static void main(String[] args) {
        GroovyShell shell = new GroovyShell();
        Object result = shell.evaluate("12+23");
        assert result.equals(35);
    }
}
```

In both cases, we first create an instance of groovy.lang.GroovyShell and we call the evaluate method on it, which takes a string as a parameter containing the expression to evaluate. The evaluate method returns an object holding the value of the expression. We won't show the Java equivalent for all the examples in this chapter, but we sometimes provide one, as much as anything to remind you of how easy it is.[6]

Among the evaluate overloaded methods present in GroovyShell, here are the most commonly used ones:

```java
Object evaluate(File file)
Object evaluate(Reader in)
Object evaluate(String scriptText)
Object evaluate(URI uri)
```

You can evaluate expressions coming from a file, a reader, a string, or a URI. There are also some variants we didn't show that take an additional filename parameter that's used to specify the name of the class to be created upon evaluation of the script, because Groovy always generates classes for scripts, too.

---

[6] It's rarely *quite* as easy as the Groovy equivalent, but by now you should realize that this has nothing to do with the features being shown and everything to do with Groovy making life easier in general.

From Groovy scripts, a shortcut can be used: scripts are classes extending the `Script` class, which already has an `evaluate` method. In the context of a script, our previous example can be shortened to the following:

```
assert evaluate("12 + 23") == 35
```

The string parameter passed to `evaluate` can be a full script with several lines of code, not just a simple expression, as you see in the following listing.

Listing 16.3   Evaluating a multiline script with `GroovyShell`

```
def shell = new GroovyShell()
def kineticEnergy = shell.evaluate('''
    def mass = 22.3
    def velocity = 10.6
    mass * velocity**2 / 2
''')
assert kineticEnergy == 1252.814
```

Building on `GroovyShell`, the `groovy.util.Eval` class can save you the boilerplate code of instantiating `GroovyShell` to evaluate simple expressions with zero to three parameters. The following listing shows how to use `Eval` for each case from Groovy (the same applies for Java, of course).

Listing 16.4   `Eval` saves explicitly creating a `GroovyShell` for simple cases

```
assert "Hello" == Eval.me("'Hello'")
assert 1 == Eval.x  (1, "x")
assert 3 == Eval.xy (1, 2, "x+y")
assert 6 == Eval.xyz(1, 2, 3, "x+y+z")
```

The `me` method is used when no parameters are required. The other methods are used for one, two, and three parameters, where the first, second, and third parameters are made available as `x`, `y`, and `z`, respectively. This is handy when your sole need is to evaluate simple expressions or even mathematical functions. Next, you'll see how you can go further with parameterization of script evaluation with `GroovyShell`.

16.2.2   *Passing parameters within a binding*

In listing 16.3, we used a multiline script defining two variables of mass and velocity to compute the kinetic energy of an object of mass 22.3 kilograms with a speed of 10.6 km/h. But notice that this is of limited interest if we can't reuse the expression evaluator. Fortunately, it's possible to pass variables to the evaluator with a `groovy.lang.Binding` object, as shown in the following listing.

Listing 16.5   Making data available to a `GroovyShell` using a `Binding`

```
def binding = new Binding()                          ❶ Creates and
binding.mass = 22.3                                     populates binding
binding.velocity = 10.6

def shell = new GroovyShell(binding)
def expression = "mass * velocity ** 2 / 2"          ❷ Evaluates expression
assert shell.evaluate(expression) == 1252.814          using binding

binding.setVariable("mass", 25.4)                    ❸ Changes binding
assert shell.evaluate(expression) == 1426.972          data and reevaluates
```

To begin with, a `Binding` object is instantiated. Because `Binding` extends `Groovy-ObjectSupport`, we can directly set variables on it as if we were manipulating properties: the `mass` and `velocity` variables have been defined in the binding ❶. The `GroovyShell` constructor takes the binding as a parameter, and further on, all evaluations use variables from that binding as if they were global variables of the script ❷. When we change the value of the `mass` variable, we see that the result of the equation is different ❸. This line is particularly interesting because we've redefined the `mass` variable thanks to the `setVariable` method on `Binding`. That's how we could set or modify variables from Java; Java wouldn't recognize `binding.mass`, because this is a shortcut introduced in Groovy by `Binding` extending `GroovyObjectSupport`.

You may have already guessed that if there is a `setVariable` method available, then `getVariable` also exists. Where the former allows you to create or redefine variables from the binding, the latter is used to retrieve the value of a variable from the binding. The `evaluate` method can return only one value: the value of the last expression of the evaluated script. When multiple values are needed in the result, the script can use the binding to make them available to the calling context. The following listing shows how a script can modify values of existing variables, or how it can create new variables in the binding that can be retrieved later.

Listing 16.6   Data can flow out of the binding as well as into it

```
def binding = new Binding(x: 6, y: 4)          ⟵           Prepopulating
def shell = new GroovyShell(binding)                 ❶     binding data
shell.evaluate('''
    xSquare = x * x                                  ❷     Setting binding data
    yCube   = y * y * y                                    within evaluated script
''')
assert binding.getVariable("xSquare") == 36          ❹     Groovy property
assert binding.yCube == 64              ⟵                  access to binding data
```

Method
access to   ❸
binding
data

In this example, we create a binding instance to which we add two parameters, `x` and `y`, by passing a map to the `Binding` constructor ❶. Our evaluated script creates two new variables in the binding by assigning a value to nondefined variables: `xSquare` and `yCube` ❷. We can retrieve the values of these variables with `getVariable` from both Java and Groovy ❸, or we can use the property-like access from Groovy ❹.

Not all variables can be accessed with `getVariable` because Groovy makes a distinction in scripts between defined variables and undefined variables: if a variable is defined with the `def` keyword or with a type, it will be a local variable, but if you're not defining it and are assigning it a value without prior definition, a variable will be created or assigned in the binding. Here, `localVariable` isn't in the binding, and the call to `getVariable` would throw a `MissingPropertyException`:

```
def binding = new Binding()
def shell = new GroovyShell(binding)
shell.evaluate('''
    def localVariable = "local variable"
    bindingVariable   = "binding variable"
''')

assert binding.getVariable("bindingVariable") == "binding variable"
```

Anything can be put into or retrieved from the binding, and only one return value can be returned as the evaluation of the last statement of the script. The binding is the best way to pass your domain objects or instances of predefined or prepopulated sessions or transactions to your scripts. Let's examine a more creative way of returning a value from your script evaluation.

16.2.3 Generating dynamic classes at runtime

Using `evaluate` can also be handy for generating new dynamic classes on-the-fly. For instance, you may need to generate classes for a web service at runtime, based on XML elements from the WSDL for the service. A contrived example for evaluating and returning a dummy class is shown in the following listing.

Listing 16.7 Defining a class in an evaluated script

```
def shell = new GroovyShell()
def clazz = shell.evaluate('''
    class MyClass {                      Defines a
        def method() { "value" }         new class
    }
    return MyClass                                Creates an
''')                                              instance of
assert clazz.name == "MyClass"                    the class
def instance = clazz.newInstance()
assert instance.method() == "value"           Uses the object
                                              as normal
```

In all the examples you've seen so far, we've used the `evaluate` method, which compiles and runs a script in one go. That's fine for one-shot evaluations, but other situations benefit from separating the compilation (parsing) from the execution, as you'll see next.

16.2.4 Parsing scripts

The `parse` methods of `GroovyShell` return instances of `Script` so that you can reuse scripts at will without reevaluating them each time, without compiling them all over again. (Remember our SwingBuilder plotter from chapter 11.) This method is similar to evaluate, taking the same set of arguments; but rather than executing the code, it generates an instance of the Script class. All scripts you can write are always instances of Script.

Let's take a concrete example. Suppose we're running a bank, and we have customers asking for a loan to buy a house. We need to compute the monthly amount they'll have to pay back, knowing the total amount of the loan, the interest rate, and the number of months to repay the loan. But, of course, we want to reuse this formula, and we're storing it in a database or elsewhere on the filesystem in case the formula evolves in the future.

Let's assume the variables of the algorithm are as follows:

- amount—The total amount of the loan (the principle)
- rate—The annual interest rate
- numberOfMonths—The number of months to reimburse the loan

With these variables, we want to compute the monthly payment. The script in the following listing shows how we can reuse the formula to calculate this important figure.

Listing 16.8 Multiple uses of a monthly payment calculator

```
def monthly = "amount*(rate/12) / (1-(1+rate/12)**-numberOfMonths)"

def shell = new GroovyShell()                    Parses formula into
def script = shell.parse(monthly)                reusable script      Accesses
                                                                       binding
                                                                       variable
script.binding.amount = 154000
script.rate = 3.75/100                           Accesses binding
script.numberOfMonths = 240                      variable using
                                                 shorthand
assert script.run() == 913.0480050387338

script.binding = new Binding(amount: 185000,     Creates new
                             rate: 3.50/100,     binding
                             numberOfMonths: 300)

assert script.run() == 926.1536089487843
```

After defining our formula, we parse it with GroovyShell.parse to retrieve an instance of Script. We then set the variables of the script binding for our three variables. Note how we can shorten script.binding.someVariable to script.someVariable because Script implements GroovyObject and overrides its setProperty method. Once the variables are set, we call the run method, which executes the script and returns the value of the last statement: the monthly payment we wanted to calculate in the first place.

To reuse this formula without having to recompile it, we can reuse the script instance and call it with another set of values by defining a new binding, rather than by modifying the original binding as in the first run.

16.2.5 *Running scripts or classes*

The `run` methods of `GroovyShell` can execute both scripts and classes. When a class is parsed and recognized as extending `GroovyTestCase`, a text test runner will run the test case.

Three of the commonly used variants of the `run` method signatures can take a `String`, a `File`, or a `Reader` to read and execute the script or class, a name for the script, and an array of `String`s for the arguments:

```
run(String scriptText, String scriptName, String[] args)
run(File scriptFile, String[] args)
run(Reader in, String scriptName, String[] args)
```

But there are other variants that read the script from a URI or take the parameters as a list instead of an array. Consult the GroovyDoc for `GroovyShell` for more details.

The execution of `run` is a bit different than that of `evaluate`. `evaluate` evaluates only scripts, but `run` can also execute classes with a `main` method as well as unit tests. The following rules are applied:

- If the class to be run has a `main(Object[] args)` or `main(String[] args)` method, it will be run. Note that a script is a normal Java class that implements `Runnable` and its `run` method is called by an implicit `main` method.
- If the class extends `GroovyTestCase` or is otherwise a JUnit test, then a JUnit test runner executes it.
- If the class implements `Runnable`, it's instantiated with a constructor taking a `String` array, or a default constructor, and the class is run with its `run` method.

The runner mechanism is also extensible, so modules like the groovy-testng module define their own runner.

16.2.6 *Further parameterization of GroovyShell*

We used the `Binding` class to pass variables to scripts and to retrieve modified or new variables defined during the evaluation of the script. We can further configure our `GroovyShell` instance by passing two other objects in the constructor: a parent `Class-Loader` and/or a `CompilerConfiguration`.

For reference, here are the constructor signatures available in `GroovyShell`:

```
GroovyShell()
GroovyShell(Binding binding)
GroovyShell(CompilerConfiguration config)
GroovyShell(Binding binding, CompilerConfiguration config)
GroovyShell(ClassLoader parent)
GroovyShell(ClassLoader parent, Binding binding)
GroovyShell(ClassLoader parent, CompilerConfiguration config)
GroovyShell(ClassLoader parent,
            Binding binding,
            CompilerConfiguration config)
```

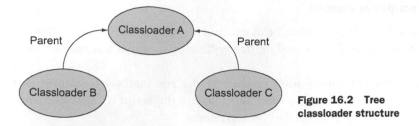

Figure 16.2   Tree classloader structure

While using the `Binding` is easy and self-descriptive, understanding how Groovy handles classloaders, in particular when you instantiate a `GroovyShell` like here, is very important. You could end up creating a memory leak without a proper understanding of the mechanics.

CHOOSING A PARENT CLASSLOADER

Groovy uses classloaders to load Groovy classes. The consequence is that you must have a minimal understanding of how classloaders work when integrating Groovy. Alas, mastering classloaders isn't the most trivial task on a Java developer's journey. When you're working with libraries generating classes or dynamic proxies at runtime with bytecode instrumentation, or with a complex hierarchy of classloaders to make critical code run in isolation in a secured sandbox, the task becomes even trickier. It's important to understand how the hierarchy of classloaders is structured.

A common use case is represented in figure 16.2.

A class loaded by classloader B can't be seen by classloader C. The standard way classloaders load classes is by first asking the parent classloader if it knows the class, before trying to load the class. Classes are looked up by navigating up the classloader hierarchy, but a class loaded by C won't be able to see a class loaded by B, because B isn't a parent of C. Fortunately, by cleverly setting the parent classloader of C to be B, the problem is solved, as shown in figure 16.3. This can be done by using `Groovy-Shell`'s constructors, which permit you to define a parent classloader for the scripts being evaluated.

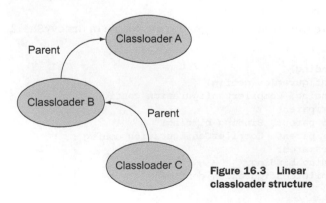

Figure 16.3   Linear classloader structure

To specify `GroovyShell`'s classloader, specify the parent classloader to flatten your hierarchy as follows:

```
def parentClassLoader = objectFromB.classloader
def shellForC = new GroovyShell(parentClassLoader)
```

If you have classloader issues, you'll get a `ClassNotFoundException` or, worse still, a `NoClassDefFoundError`. To debug these issues, the best thing to do is to print the classloader for all affected classes and print each classloader's parent classloader, and so on up to the root of all classloaders. You'll then have a good picture of the whole classloader hierarchy in your application, and the final step will be to set parent classloaders accordingly to flatten the hierarchy. Even better, try to make classes be loaded by the same classloaders if possible.

CONFIGURING THE COMPILATION

In the list of constructors of the `GroovyShell` class, you'll have noticed the `CompilerConfiguration` parameter. An instance of this class can be passed to `GroovyShell` to customize options of the compilation process.

Without studying all the options available, let's review some of the most useful ones, as shown in table 16.1. Some more functionality is covered in section 16.7.

Table 16.1 Some useful methods in `CompilerConfiguration`

Method signature	Description
`setClasspath` `(String path)`	Define your own classpath used to look for classes, allowing you to restrict the application classpath and/or enhance it with other libraries
`setDebug` `(boolean debug)`	Set to `true` to get full, unfiltered stack traces when exceptions are written on the error stream
`setOutput` `(PrintWriter writer)`	Set the writer that compilation errors will be printed to
`setScriptBaseClass` `(String clazz)`	Define a subclass of `Script` as the base class for script instances
`setSourceEncoding` `(String enc)`	Set the encoding of the scripts to evaluate, which is important when parsing scripts from files or input streams that use a different encoding than the platform default
`setRecompileGroovySource` `(boolean b)`	Set to `true` to reload Groovy sources that have changed after they have been compiled—by default, this flag is set to `false`
`setMinimumRecompilationInterval` `(int millis)`	Set the minimum amount of time to wait before checking if the sources are more recent than the compiled classes

Of these methods, `setScriptBaseClass` is particularly worthy of note. If you want all of your scripts to share a common set of methods, you can specify a base class extending `groovy.lang.Script` that will host these methods and then be available inside the scripts. Sharing methods among scripts is a good technique to inject hooks to your own framework services. Let's consider a base script class that extends `Script` and its role will be to inject a global multiplication function[7] into all scripts evaluated by `GroovyShell`:

```
abstract class BaseScript extends Script {
    def multiply(a, b) { a * b }
}
```

`BaseScript` extends `Script`, which is an abstract class, so the class must be declared abstract, because the `run` method is abstract. When compiling or interpreting scripts, Groovy will extend this base script and will inject the script's statements in the `run` method.

To make this class the base class of your scripts, you now need to pass an `org.codehaus.groovy.control.CompilerConfiguration` instance to `GroovyShell`'s constructor, as explained by the following Groovy example:

```
def conf = new CompilerConfiguration()
conf.setScriptBaseClass("BaseScript")
def shell = new GroovyShell(conf)
def value = shell.evaluate('''
    multiply(5, 6)
''')
assert value == 30
```

This isn't the only way to inject functions in all your scripts. Another trick to share functions between scripts is to store closures in the binding of `GroovyShell` without needing to use `CompilerConfiguration`. This can be seen in the following listing.

Listing 16.9 Using the `Binding` to share functions between scripts

```
def binding = new Binding(multiply: { a, b -> a * b })    ◁——— Creates closure
def shell = new GroovyShell(binding)                             within binding
def value = shell.evaluate('''
    multiply(5, 6)              ◁——— Calls closure like a
''')                                 normal method
assert value == 30
```

You also need to be able to write the same code in Java, so we must be able to create closures and put them in the binding. From Java, creating a closure isn't as neat as in Groovy. You must create a class that derives from `groovy.lang.Closure` and implement an `Object doCall(Object arguments)` method. An alternative technique is to

---

[7] Multiplication is easy to demonstrate in a book, but real-world examples might include handling transactional resources, configuration, and logging.

create an instance of org.codehaus.groovy.runtime.MethodClosure, which delegates the call to a multiplication method on a custom multiplicator class instance:

```
// Java
MethodClosure mclos = new MethodClosure(multiplicator, "multiply");
Binding binding = new Binding();
binding.setVariable("multiply", mclos);
GroovyShell shell = new GroovyShell(binding);
shell.evaluate("multiply(5, 6)");
```

We've now fully covered how GroovyShell can be operated both from Java and from
Groovy to extend your application. GroovyShell is a nice utility class to create extension points in your own code and to execute logic that can be externalized in scripts
stored as strings, on the filesystem, or in a database. This class is great for evaluating,
parsing, or running scripts that represent a single and self-contained unit of work, but
it's less easy to use when your logic is spread across dependent scripts. This is where
the GroovyScriptEngine and GroovyClassLoader can help. These are the topics of
the next two sections.

16.3　Using the Groovy script engine

The GroovyShell class is ideal for standalone and isolated scripts, but it can be less
easy to use when your scripts are dependent on each other. The simplest solution at
that point is to use GroovyScriptEngine. This class also provides the capability to
reload scripts as they change, which enables your application to support live modifications of your business logic. We'll cover the basic uses of the script engine and show
you how to tell the engine where to find scripts.

16.3.1　Setting up the engine

The scripting engine has several constructors to choose from when you instantiate it.
You can pass different arguments to these constructors, such as an array of paths or
URLs where the engine will try to find the Groovy scripts, a classloader to be used as the
parent classloader, or a special ResourceConnector that provides URLConnections. In
our examples, we'll assume that we're loading and running scripts from the filesystem:

```
def engine = new GroovyScriptEngine(".")
```

or with an array of URLs or of strings representing URLs:

```
def engine = new GroovyScriptEngine([".", "../folder "])
```

The engine assumes that strings represent filesystem locations. If your scripts are to be
loaded from somewhere other than the filesystem, you should use URLs instead:

```
def engine = new GroovyScriptEngine(
    ["file://.", "http://someUrl"]*.toURL() as URL[])
```

The engine will search the resource following each URL sequentially until it finds the script.

The constructors can also take a classloader, which will then be used by the engine for the parent classloader of the compiled classes:

```
def engine = new GroovyScriptEngine(".", parentCL)
```

The parent classloader can also be defined with the setParentClassLoader method.

Once you've instantiated the engine, you can eventually run your scripts.

16.3.2 *Running scripts*

To run a script, the primary mechanism is the run method of GroovyScriptEngine. This method takes two arguments: the name of the script to run as the relative path of the file and the binding to store the variables that the script will need to operate. The method also returns the value of the last expression evaluated by the script, as GroovyShell does.

If you intend to run a file named MyScript.groovy situated in the test folder relative to the current directory, you might run it as shown here:

```
def engine = new GroovyScriptEngine(".")
def value  = engine.run("test/MyScript.groovy", new Binding())
```

Loaded scripts are automatically cached by the engine and they're updated whenever the resource is updated. The engine can also load script classes directly with the load-ScriptByName method; it returns a Class object representing the class of the script, which is a derived class of groovy.lang.Script. There's a pitfall to watch out for with this method, however. It takes a script with a fully qualified class name notation rather than the relative path of the file:

```
def engine = new GroovyScriptEngine(".")
def clazz  = engine.loadScriptByName("test.MyScript")
```

This example returns the class of the myScript.groovy script situated in the test folder. If you're not using the filesystem, you'll be using URLs instead of files, and in that case it's mandatory to use a special resource connector that's responsible for loading the resources.

16.3.3 *Defining a different resource connector*

If you wish to load scripts from a particular location, you may want to provide your own resource connector. This is done by passing it as an argument to the constructor of GroovyScriptEngine, either with or without the specification of a parent class-loader. The following example shows both overloaded methods:

```
def myResourceConnector = getResourceConnector()
def engine  = new GroovyScriptEngine(myResourceConnector)
def engine2 = new GroovyScriptEngine(myResourceConnector, parent)
```

To implement your own connector, you have to create a class implementing the `groovy.util.ResourceConnector` interface, which contains only one method:

```
public URLConnection getResourceConnection(String name)
    throws ResourceException;
```

The `getResourceConnection` method takes a string parameter representing the name of the resource to load, and it returns an instance of `URLConnection`. If you're also creating your own `URLConnection`, at least three methods need to be implemented properly (you could potentially leave the others aside and throw an `Unsupported-OperationException` or `UnknownServiceException`, like some JDK classes from the `java.net` package do):

```
public long        getLastModified()
public URL         getURL()
public InputStream getInputStream() throws IOException
```

Although usually you'll store your script on the filesystem or inside a database, implementing your own `ResourceConnector` and `URLConnection` allows you to provide a handle on scripts coming from any location: from a database, a remote filesystem, an XML document, or an object data store.

    `GroovyScriptEngine` is perfect for dealing with scripts, but it falls short for more complex manipulation of classes. In fact, both `GroovyShell` and `GroovyScriptEngine` rely on a single mechanism for loading scripts or classes: the `GroovyClassLoader`. This special classloader is what we'll discuss next.

16.4 Working with the GroovyClassLoader

The `GroovyClassLoader` is the Swiss Army knife with all possible tools for integrating Groovy into an application, whether explicitly or via classes such as `GroovyShell`. This class is a custom classloader, which is able to define and parse Groovy classes and scripts as normal classes that can be used either from Groovy or from Java. It's also able to compile all the required and dependent classes.

    This section will take you through how to use the `GroovyClassLoader`, from the simplest uses to more involved situations. We examine how to get around circular dependency issues, how to load scripts that are stored outside the local filesystem, and how to make your integration environment safe and sandboxed, permitting the scripts to perform only the operations you wish to allow.

16.4.1 Parsing and loading Groovy classes

Say you have a simple Groovy class `Hello` like the following:

```
class Hello {
    def greeting() { "Hello!" }
}
```

You want to parse and load this class with the `GroovyClassLoader`. In Groovy, you can do it like so:

```
def    gcl = new GroovyClassLoader()
Class greetingClass = gcl.parseClass(new File("Hello.groovy"))
assert "Hello!" == greetingClass.newInstance().greeting()
```

> ### Instantiating GroovyClassLoader
> In the example, we use the default constructor. But this class offers more construc-tors. `GroovyClassLoader (ClassLoader loader)` lets you define a parent class-loader to avoid problems with a complex hierarchy, as explained in the section about `GroovyShell`. The constructor `GroovyClassLoader(ClassLoader loader, CompilerConfiguration config)` gives you more control over the behavior of the classloader, as explained in the section about `GroovyShell`, thanks to the param-eterization of `CompilerConfiguration`.

An instance of `GroovyClassLoader` is created, and its `parseClass` method is called and passed the Hello.groovy file. The method returns a `Class` object that can then be instantiated by using `Class`'s `newInstance` method, which invokes the default constructor of `Hello`. Once `Hello` is instantiated, because Groovy supports duck typ-ing (section 3.2.4), you can directly call the `greeting` method defined in `Hello`. But in a strongly typed language, you couldn't directly call the method. So, from Java, to invoke a method, you have to either use reflection explicitly—which is usually pretty ugly—or rely on the fact that all Groovy classes automatically implement the `groovy.lang.GroovyObject` interface, exposing the `invokeMethod`, `getProperty`, and `set-Property` methods.

Where `getProperty` and `setProperty` are responsible for accessing properties of your Groovy class from Java, `invokeMethod` allows you to call any method on Groovy classes easily from Java:

```
// Java
GroovyClassLoader gcl = new GroovyClassLoader();
Class greetingClass = gcl.parseClass(new File("Hello.groovy"));
GroovyObject hello  = (GroovyObject) greetingClass.newInstance();
Object[] args    = {};
assert "Hello!".equals(hello.invokeMethod("greeting", args));
```

The `invokeMethod` method takes two parameters: the name of the method to call and one that corresponds to the parameters to pass to the method you're trying to call. If the method takes only one parameter, pass it directly as an argument; if several param-eters are expected, they have to be wrapped inside an array of `Objects`, which becomes the argument. If you wish to call a method that adds two objects together with a signature like `add(a,b)`, you call it like this:

```
a.invokeMethod("add", new Object[] {obj1, obj2}); // Java
```

But if a method you want to call requires an array as its single parameter, you also have to wrap it inside an array:

```
a.invokeMethod("takesAnArray", new Object[] {anArray}); // Java
```

Despite the fact that it's possible to call any method in a Groovy class from Java with invokeMethod, doing so isn't Java friendly because the Java compiler will not know these classes exist and will not let you use the greeting method directly—unless you precompiled your Groovy classes and packed them up inside a JAR file. Fortunately, there's a workaround to circumvent this shortcoming of javac. To make Java understand your Groovy classes, both Groovy and Java have to find a common ground of agreement. This is what we call the chicken and egg problem.

16.4.2 *The chicken and egg dependency problem*

Previous versions of Groovy made it quite difficult to solve the chicken and egg problem. If you had a Java class that was using a Groovy class, itself using a Java class defined in the same project, you had a problem. Fixing this involved code refactoring, such as introducing interfaces to remove cyclic dependencies. The good news is that this is no longer an issue, thanks to *joint compilation*. Joint compilation is the process of compiling Java and Groovy classes in an apparent single pass, only using the groovyc command.

To illustrate, let's consider the Java application in the following listing.

Listing 16.10   A Java/Groovy mixed application

```java
// Java
public class ShapeInfoMain {
    public static void main(String[] args) {
        Square s = new Square(7);
        Circle c = new Circle(4);
        new MaxAreaInfo().displayInfo(s, c);
        new MaxPerimeterInfo().displayInfo(s, c);
    }
}
```

Suppose that the Square and MaxPerimeterInfo classes are written in Java and the Circle and MaxAreaInfo classes are written in Groovy. We might be tempted to try using javac on all the *.java source files followed by groovyc on all the *.groovy files. But this won't work because the displayInfo method in MaxPerimeterInfo requires Circle to be compiled first. We can't swap the order around, either, because we'll have the reverse problem with MaxAreaInfo if Square isn't compiled first.

The solution is quite simple. Instead of calling javac by yourself, let Groovy do it for you, using the -j option:

```
groovyc -j *.java *.groovy
```

Internally, the Groovy compiler will:

- Generate Java stubs for the Groovy files
- Compile the Java sources and the stubs using `javac`
- Compile the Groovy classes

The generation of stubs, which are Java source files corresponding to the "public API" of the Groovy sources, allows the `javac` compiler to compile properly the classes, and the Groovy compiler will replace those stubs with the real Groovy files in the second pass. Note that using the `-j` option is very important: should you forget it, the Java source files would be compiled as if they were written in Groovy!

16.4.3 *Providing a custom resource loader*

The `GroovyClassLoader` has various methods to let you parse and load Groovy classes from different origins: from a file, from an input stream, or from a string. Here are a few of the methods to use when explicitly asking the classloader to load a given class:

```
public Class parseClass(File file)
    throws CompilationFailedException
public Class parseClass(String text, String fileName)
    throws CompilationFailedException
public Class parseClass(InputStream in, String fileName)
    throws CompilationFailedException
```

If you're storing your sources in a database, a possible solution is to retrieve them as a `String` or as an `InputStream`. Then, you can use the classloader's `parseClass` methods to parse and load your classes. But rather than explicitly implementing the plumbing and the lookup and parsing yourself, Groovy provides a better solution, in the form of a `groovy.lang.GroovyResourceLoader`. The resource loader is an interface that you must implement to specify where your sources are to be found: give it a name of a resource, and a URL is returned that points at the location of the resource. This is done by a single method from that interface:

```
URL loadGroovySource(String filename) throws MalformedURLException
```

An implementation of the resource loader in Java will look something like the following class:

```
public class MyResourceLoader extends GroovyResourceLoader {
    public URL loadGroovySource(final String filename)
        throws MalformedURLException {
        URL url = ... // create the URL pointing at the resource
        return url;
    }
}
```

> **TIP** As was the case with `GroovyScriptEngine`, if you're creating your own `URL` and `URLConnection` derived classes, make sure your `URL` overrides its `openConnection` method, which returns an instance of `URLConnection`; and make sure you also override the `getLastModified`, `getURL`, and `getInputStream` methods of the returned `URLConnection`.

Once you've defined this class, you have to register it in your classloader before use like this:

```
GroovyClassLoader gcl = new GroovyClassLoader();
gcl.setResourceLoader(new MyResourceLoader());
```

Your classloader will now use your resource loader to find the resources it needs from wherever you want! At this point, you may find that you have less control than you like over what code is executed. You may need to lock down how much access the code has to the rest of the system, depending on how much you know about the code's origins. This is where the Java and Groovy security model comes into play, as you'll see in the next section.

16.4.4 *Playing it safe in a secured sandbox*

When packaging an application, you know all your source code is trusted. When you open the doors for dynamic code that might evolve over time, such as changing business rules due to a legislation change, you have to be sure that this code can be trusted too. Only trusted users should be able to change the dynamic code by logging in and providing the relevant credentials. But even with authentication and authorization in place, you're never sheltered against human mistakes. That's why Groovy provides a second level of confidence in dynamic code in the form of a secured sandbox that you can set up to load this foreign code.

Modifying, loading, and executing dynamic code at runtime is a nice way to extend your application in an agile way, lessening the time required to adapt it as necessary. Long and tedious repackaging, requalifying, and redeployment scenarios can vanish in no time. This isn't a subject to take lightly, and of course, you'll always have to hand over your application to the acceptance team and pass the relevant integration tests; but embedding code from a scripting language in your application can help you to be more versatile when the requirements are changing.

THE JAVA SECURITY MODEL

However cool embedding a scripting or dynamic language can be, and however well designed your system is in terms of security, you can potentially add another layer of trust by letting this code run in a secured sandbox. Java provides the infrastructure for securing source code through its security model with the help of a *security manager* and the associated *policy* that dictates what permissions are granted to the code. For a simple example of what harm can happen to your application, imagine a user uploads a script containing System.exit(1): your whole system could go down in a second if it's not secured correctly! Fortunately, with some setup, it's possible to protect yourself from such malicious code.

> **NOTE** Covering the whole Java security model with its security managers, permissions, and policy files is beyond the scope of this chapter. We assume that you're familiar with these concepts. If not, we recommend the online resources provided on Oracle's website to get an in-depth view of how security works on the Java platform.

In the Java security model, code sources are granted permissions according to their *code source*. A code source is composed of a codebase in the form of a URL from which the source code was loaded by the classloader, and potentially a certificate used to verify the code when it's obtained from a signed JAR file.

There are two cases you have to consider. If all your Groovy sources are compiled first into .class files and eventually bundled in a JAR file, the standard security mechanisms apply. Those classes are like normal Java-compiled sources, so you can always use the same security managers as normal. But when you're compiling Groovy sources on the fly, through the integration means you've studied so far, extra steps need to be followed.

GROOVYCODESOURCE AND THE SECURITY MANAGER

When scripts and classes are loaded from the filesystem, they're loaded by a Groovy-ClassLoader, which searches the classpath for Groovy files and gives them a code source constructed from a codebase built from the URL of the source file. When Groovy sources are loaded from an input stream or from a string, no particular URL is associated with them. It's possible to associate a codebase with Groovy sources to be compiled by specifying a GroovyCodeSource—as long as the caller loading sources has the permission to specify the codebase. The codebase you associate with the sources need not refer to a real physical location. Its importance is to the security manager and policy, which allocate permissions based on URLs.

A concrete example is always better than long explanations. Say we're running an application on a server, and this application loads Groovy scripts that need to be sandboxed and should only be allowed to access the file.encoding system property. The server application should have all possible permissions, but we have to restrict the loaded Groovy script reading the property. We write a policy file explicitly indicating those rules:

```
grant codeBase "file:${server.home}/classes/-" {
    permission java.security.AllPermission;
};
grant codeBase "file:/restricted" {
    permission java.util.PropertyPermission "file.encoding", "read";
};
```

The first part grants all permissions to our server application, the second part only allows the scripts from the file:/restricted codebase to access the file.encoding property in read-only mode. This policy file should be available in the classpath of the application, and the system property java.security.policy defining the policy file to use should be specified either on the command line that launches the JVM or in code.

A script requesting to read the system property would include code such as:

```
def encoding = System.getProperty("file.encoding")
```

Your server application will load and evaluate the script using `GroovyShell`, using the methods that take a `GroovyCodeSource` to wrap the script and define its code source:

```
def script = '''
    System.getProperty("file.encoding")
'''
def gcs = new GroovyCodeSource(script, "ScriptName", "/restricted")
def shell = new GroovyShell()
    println shell.evaluate(gcs)
```

A `GroovyCodeSource` can be built in various ways depending on how you retrieve the source code: from a string, a file, a reader, or a URI. Here are the four constructors that allow you to build a `GroovyCodeSource`:

```
public GroovyCodeSource(String script, String name, String codeBase)
public GroovyCodeSource(Reader in, String name, String codeBase)
public GroovyCodeSource(File file) throws FileNotFoundException
public GroovyCodeSource(URI uri) throws IOException
```

For the calling application to be able to create a `GroovyCodeSource` with a specific codebase, it must be granted permission by the policy. The specific permission required is a `groovy.security.GroovyCodeSourcePermission`, which the calling application implicitly has because the policy file granted it the `java.security.AllPermission`, which grants all possible rights.

GROOVYSHELL AND GROOVYCLASSLOADER WITH GROOVYCODESOURCE

Both `GroovyShell` and `GroovyClassLoader` allow you to specify `GroovyCodeSources` to wrap scripts or classes that must be secured, but `GroovyScriptEngine` doesn't at the time of writing. If the Groovy source code isn't wrapped inside a `GroovyCodeSource`, the policy will not be enforced, thus letting untrusted code run within the application.

In the sections related to `GroovyShell` and `GroovyClassLoader`, we enumerated several methods that allow you to evaluate, parse, or run Groovy scripts and classes. Let's mention now the methods that take a `GroovyCodeSource`, which you can use to make integrating dynamic code safer.

`GroovyShell` has two methods that take a `GroovyCodeSource`, one for evaluating scripts, and the other for parsing scripts:

```
public Object evaluate(GroovyCodeSource codeSource)
    throws CompilationFailedException
public Script parse(GroovyCodeSource codeSource)
    throws CompilationFailedException
```

`GroovyClassLoader` also has two methods; both parse classes, but the latter also provides an option to control whether the parsed class should be put in the classloader cache:

```
public Class parseClass(GroovyCodeSource codeSource)
    throws CompilationFailedException
public Class parseClass(GroovyCodeSource codeSource,
    boolean shouldCache) throws CompilationFailedException
```

Armed with different means of integrating Groovy securely in your application, you can build extremely flexible applications. Of course, those mechanisms are specific to Groovy. These aren't the only means available, however. If you're using the Spring framework as a common base for your application, or if you're using the scripting support added in Java 6 (JSR-223), you can use the mechanisms provided in these platforms to load your dynamic code in a way that would make it easy to move away from Groovy, should you ever wish to.[8]

16.5   *Spring integration*

As it says on the tin, Spring is an innovative layered Java Enterprise application framework and lightweight container invented by Rod Johnson, which matured while Rod was writing the book *Expert One-on-One J2EE Design and Development* (Wiley, 2004). Spring generalized the concepts and patterns of *Inversion of Control* (IoC) and *Dependency Injection* (DI) and is built from two main building blocks: its IoC container and its AOP system. The framework brings an additional abstraction layer that wraps common APIs such as transactions, JDBC, or Hibernate to help the developer focus on the core business tasks; gives access to AOP; and even provides its own *Model-View-Controller* (MVC) technology. The Spring framework can be used as a whole or piece by piece as needs arise.

Spring lets you wire your application components through DI by instantiating, configuring, and defining the relationships between your objects in a central XML (and since recently Groovy) configuration file, via annotations, or via API calls. Your objects are usually plain-old Java objects (POJOs), but they can also be plain-old Groovy objects (POGOs) because Groovy objects are also standard JavaBeans! This section explores how you can inject Groovy dependencies into your application object model, with options for letting beans refresh themselves automatically and specifying the bodies of scripts directly in the configuration file.

Since version 2.0, the Spring Framework has supported integrating beans written in various scripting languages. Spring supports Groovy and other proven scripting languages for the JVM. With this support, any number of classes written in these languages can be wired and injected into your application as transparently as if they were normal Java objects.

> **NOTE**   It's beyond the scope of this section to explain how Spring can be installed, used, or configured. We're assuming that the interested reader is already familiar with the framework. If this isn't the case, the creators of Spring have comprehensive and detailed online documentation at http://spring.io/docs that should be ideal for discovering what it's all about.

We'll explain how you can wire up POGOs in Spring, discuss reloading Groovy source code on the fly, and cover how Groovy source code can be specified directly in the

---

[8]   Not that we can think of any reason why you'd want to, but we like the principle of avoiding vendor lock-in where possible.

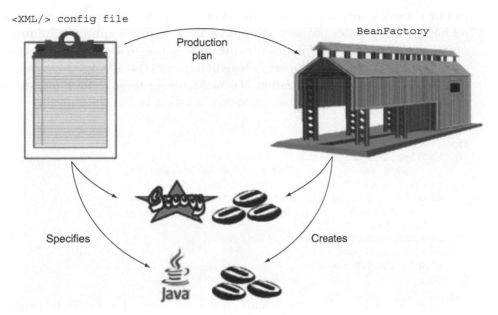

<XML/> config file

Production plan

BeanFactory

Specifies

Creates

Java

Figure 16.4 Spring's `BeanFactory` reads an XML configuration file and creates instances of the JavaBeans and GroovyBeans specified within it.

configuration file, where appropriate. Let's start with the simplest situation before working our way toward more complicated scenarios.

16.5.1 *Wiring GroovyBeans*

Let's take the shape information classes from section 16.4 as an example.

We're going to use Spring's bean factory to create the Groovy objects that our main program needs. All the definitions for our class are captured declaratively in a Spring configuration file, sometimes referred to as a *wiring XML file*. This is illustrated in figure 16.4.

We'd normally wire both Java and Groovy classes in the wiring file and indicate the dependencies between the different parts of our system in this file. In this case, though, we're going to keep it simple. We're going to specify simple definitions in the file to illustrate integration between Spring and Groovy. For now, we assume that all of our Groovy files are precompiled.

Here's what the Spring definition file, called beans.xml in our case, looks like:

```
<?xml version="1.0" encoding="UTF-8"?>
<beans>
  <bean id="circle" class="spring.groovy.Circle">
    <constructor-arg value="4"/>
    <property name="color" value="Black"/>
  </bean>
  <bean id="maxareainfo" class="spring.groovy.MaxAreaInfo"/>
</beans>
```

In our Groovy source file, we have the same constructor that we had previously, and we have added a `color` property to our `Circle` class. In the Spring definition file, the nested `constructor` element indicates the value to pass to the constructor during creation of our `Circle`. The `property` element indicates that the `color` property should also be set as part of initialization. To make use of these definitions, we need to change our `main` method in `ShapeInfoMain` in listing 16.10 to become

```java
// Java
try {
    ApplicationContext ctx =
        new ClassPathXmlApplicationContext("beans.xml");
    Shape s = new Square(7);
    Shape c = (Shape) ctx.getBean("circle");
    ShapeInfo info = (ShapeInfo) ctx.getBean("maxareainfo");
    info.displayInfo(s, c);
    new MaxPerimeterInfo().displayInfo(s, c);
} catch (Exception e) {
    e.printStackTrace();
}
```

Spring provides a number of mechanisms to create beans for you. In this instance, we use what's called the *application context*. It has a `getBean` method that allows us to ask for a bean by name.

As we mentioned earlier, we're assuming here that all of our Groovy classes are precompiled. So, what have we gained? We've begun the process of removing explicit dependencies from our codebase. Over time, we could start moving more dependency information into the wiring file and allow our system to be configured more readily. As a consequence, our design also becomes more flexible, because we can swap our concrete implementations readily. This is particularly important for unit testing, where we might replace concrete implementations with mock implementations.

There's more we can do, though: Spring supports dynamic compilation of our Groovy scripts through a special Groovy factory class. Here's how we'd use it. We'd extend our bean configuration file as follows:

```
...
<lang:groovy id="maxareainfo2"
        script-source="classpath:MaxAreaInfo.groovy">
    <lang:property name="prefix" value="Live Groovy says" />
</lang:groovy>
...
```

Spring 2.0 and above support a number of dynamic scripting languages through special language-specific factories. The namespace `lang:groovy` accesses the special Groovy factory automatically. Now we can use `maxareainfo2` as the name we pass to the bean factory when creating our bean, and Spring will automatically compile the necessary Groovy source files.

16.5.2 Refreshable beans

Another feature that Spring provides is the ability to dynamically detect when Groovy source files change and automatically compile and load the latest version of any Groovy file during runtime. The concept is known as *refreshable beans* and is enabled in our definition file using the `refresh-check-delay` attribute as follows (in this case, setting the delay to five seconds):

```
...
<lang:groovy id="maxareainfo2"
        refresh-check-delay="5000"
        script-source="classpath:MaxAreaInfo.groovy">
    <lang:property name="prefix" value="Live Groovy says" />
</lang:groovy>
...
```

Refreshing beans on-the-fly can make development faster, but you should consider disabling it again for production systems—restarting the system after a change has been made tends to avoid confusing situations where for some period of time (however brief) only *part* of the system has seen the refresh.

16.5.3 Inline scripts

Although it's arguably a bad idea to put code inside Spring's configuration file, Spring offers another way to define scripted beans by *inlining* them—including the source directly in the configuration file. The Spring documentation mentions scenarios for such a case, such as sketching and defining validators for Spring MVC controllers or scripting controllers for quick prototyping or defining logic flow.

In the following listing, we inline a variation of MaxAreaInfo (we need to change our factory getBean call to use maxareainfo3).

Listing 16.11 Spring configuration with inline Groovy class

```
<lang:groovy id="maxareainfo3">                          ⟵  Tells Spring we're
    <lang:inline-script>                                ⟵      using Groovy
    import spring.common.Shape
    import spring.common.ShapeInfo                       Defines the
                                                         class we want
    class SuffixMaxAreaInfo implements ShapeInfo {       an instance of
        String suffix
        void displayInfo(Shape s1, Shape s2) {
            print "The shape with the biggest area is: "
            if (s1.area() > s2.area()) println s1 + ":" + suffix
            else println s2 + ":" + suffix
        }
    }
    </lang:inline-script>
    <lang:property name="suffix"                         Specifies a
                value="Did you guess correctly?"/>       bean property
</lang:groovy>
```

In this case, because the content is hard-coded, setting the refreshable attribute of the script factory doesn't apply for those inline scripted beans. One last remark: if your script contains a less-than sign (<), the XML Spring configuration will be invalid, because the XML parser will think it's the start of a new tag. To circumvent this problem, you should wrap the whole scripted bean in a CDATA section.

This has been a brief introduction to the scripting bean capabilities of the Spring framework. For further details and more in-depth explanations, refer to the project documentation at http://spring.io/docs.

Spring isn't the only recent technology to embrace scripting. The following section looks forward to the next release of the Java platform and explores what support will be provided for Groovy integration.

16.6   *Riding Mustang and JSR-223*

Scripting and dynamic languages are in fashion again thanks to Groovy and the ubiquitous JavaScript in all its flavors. This frenzy originally led Sun and later Oracle to recognize that for certain tasks, scripting languages can help to simplify the development of applications. New JSRs have been accepted by the Java Community Process to standardize languages such as Groovy, JavaScript, and others to create a common API allowing access to various scripting engines from your Java applications.

This section guides you through running Groovy scripts in the new "Java standard" way, highlighting the features of the new API as well as some ways in which it's unavoidably clunky.

16.6.1 *Introducing JSR-223*

JSR-223, titled "Scripting for the Java Platform," provides a set of classes and interfaces used to hold and register scripting engines and to represent scripts, namespaces of key–value pairs available to scripts, or execution contexts. It offers an elegant and simple API that supports a few scripting languages—Groovy being one of them. Since Mustang (Java SE 6), the core JSR-223 (`javax.script.*`) classes and an execution engine for JavaScript have been bundled with the JDK. This makes scripting a first-class citizen on the JVM. The Groovy JSR-223 execution engine is one of Groovy's modules and will already be in your Groovy installation, so you should be ready to get started with using JSR-223.

In addition to incorporating the `javax.script.*` interfaces and classes, the JDK distributes a new command-line tool called `jrunscript` to run scripts, which is a bit like Groovy's own `groovy` and `groovysh` commands. Here's how this new tool is used:

```
Usage: jrunscript [options] [arguments...]
where [options] include:
-classpath, -cp <path>   Specify where to find user class files
-D<name>=<value>         Set a system property
-J<flag>                 Pass <flag> directly to the runtime system
-l <language>            Use specified scripting language
-e <script>              Evaluate given script
```

```
-encoding <encoding>      Specify character encoding used by script files
-f <script file>          Evaluate given script file
-f -                      Interactive mode, read script from
                          standard input
-help, -?                 Print this usage message and exit
-q                        List all scripting engines available and exit
```

Although the command line enables you to execute Groovy through the new API without writing any code to do so, if your application is going to embed Groovy, you'll be using the API directly rather than relying on the tool. Let's meet the core classes involved in running scripts through JSR-223.

16.6.2 *The script engine manager and its script engines*

The main entry point of the JSR-223 API is `javax.script.ScriptEngineManager`. To get started, create an instance of this class from your Java application:

```
ScriptEngineManager manager = new ScriptEngineManager();
```

The manager is able to retrieve script engines through different lookup mechanisms: by file extension, by mime type, or by name, with three dedicated methods:

```
ScriptEngine getEngineByExtension(String extension)
ScriptEngine getEngineByMimeType (String mimeType)
ScriptEngine getEngineByName    (String shortName)
```

So, if you want to retrieve the Groovy script engine supplied with the reference implementation, you can look it up by name:

```
ScriptEngine gEngine = manager.getEngineByName("groovy");
```

With a `ScriptEngine`, you can evaluate Groovy expressions and scripts provided through an instance of `Reader` or of a `String` with the set of `eval` methods, which return an `Object` as the result of the evaluation. You can evaluate a simple expression as follows:

```
ScriptEngineManager manager = new ScriptEngineManager();
ScriptEngine gEngine = manager.getEngineByName("groovy");
String result = (String)gEngine.eval("'+-----' * 3 + '+'");
```

Here are the other eval methods available:

```
Object eval(Reader reader)
Object eval(Reader reader, Bindings b)
Object eval(Reader reader, ScriptContext context)
Object eval(String script)
Object eval(String script, Bindings b)
Object eval(String script, ScriptContext context)
```

They can throw a `ScriptException`, which can contain a root exception cause, a message, a filename, and even a line number and column number where an error occurred, particularly when the error is a compilation error. The optional `ScriptContext` parameter corresponds to the environment within which a script is evaluated, and a `Bindings` is a special map containing an association between a key and an object you want to pass to your scripts. These affect what information is available to your scripts and how different scripts can pass each other data. See the detailed JSR-223 documentation for more information on this topic.

16.6.3 *Compilable and invocable script engines*

Beyond the basic script-evaluation capabilities, the Groovy engine implements two other interfaces: `javax.script.Compilable` and `javax.script.Invocable`. The first lets you precompile and reuse scripts, and the latter lets you execute a method, a unit of execution, rather than executing a whole script as you do with the `eval` method. Implementing these interfaces isn't mandatory, but the Groovy engine provides this feature:

```java
// Java
ScriptEngineManager manager = new ScriptEngineManager();
ScriptEngine gEngine   = manager.getEngineByName("groovy");
Compilable compilable = (Compilable)gEngine;
compilable.put("name", "Dierk");
CompiledScript script = compilable.compile("return name");
String dierksName      = script.eval();
compilable.put("name", "Guillaume");
String guillaumesName = script.eval();
```

Once you've got a handle on the `Compilable` engine (by casting the engine to the `Compilable` interface), you can call two `compile` methods that either take a reader or a string containing the script to precompile. These methods return an instance of `CompiledScript`, which holds a precompiled script that you can execute several times at will without the need to reparse or recompile it. Then, the `CompiledScript` can be evaluated with three `eval` methods: one without any parameters, one taking a `Namespace`, and the last taking a `ScriptContext`.

Even after precompiling a script, you still can't directly call methods declared in that script. The `javax.script.Invocable` interface makes this possible in a manner reminiscent of calling normal Java methods with reflection.

Imagine we have a script the role of which is to change a string parameter into its uppercase representation:

```java
// Java
ScriptEngineManager manager = new ScriptEngineManager();
ScriptEngine gEngine = manager.getEngineByName("groovy");

Invocable invocable  = (Invocable)gEngine;
invocable.eval("def upper(s) { s.toUpperCase() }");
Object s = invocable.invokeFunction("upper", "Groovy");

invocable.eval("def add(a, b) { a + b }");
invocable.invokeFunction("add", new Integer(1), new Integer(2));

assertTrue(invocable.invokeMethod(s, "endsWith", "Y"));
```

The script is evaluated and retained in the script-execution context; then, the defined function can be called with the `invokeFunction` method, which takes the name of the function to call and a `vararg` list of objects to pass to the underlying scripted function as parameters. Be careful, though, because you can only invoke functions defined in the last evaluated script. An `invokeMethod` method goes further and lets you call arbitrary methods on objects resulting from the execution of scripts. This is how we call the `endsWith` method on the string returned by the first function invoked and pass it the letter `Y` as an argument.

Of course, in the last case, we could have cast the return value of `upper` to `String` directly. Although this may seem obvious, it's possible because Groovy plays nicely with Java, returning real and normal classes. Other scripting languages would return some kind of proxy or wrapper, making the integration with Java trickier.

Despite the convenience of being able to call any function defined in a script, it's not yet as Java friendly as we might hope. Nevertheless, the `Invocable` interface gives you another handy method for your toolbox: the `getInterface` method. With this method, you can create a proxy of a given interface that will delegate all method invocations to methods defined in the script.

Say we have a Java interface representing a business service like the following one:

```
// Java
interface BusinessService {
    void   init();
    Object execute(Object[] parameters);
    void   release();
}
```

We create a script that contains functions mapping the same signatures as the ones provided in the `BusinessService` interface:

```
// Groovy
void init() { println "init" }
Object execute(Object[] objs) { println "execute" }
void release() { println "release" }
```

We can make such a script appear to implement the `BusinessService` interface by calling the `getInterface` method of the invocable script engine:

```
// Java
ScriptEngineManager manager = new ScriptEngineManager();
ScriptEngine gEngine = manager.getEngineByName("groovy");
Invocable invocable = (Invocable)gEngine;
invocable.eval(scriptAsAString);
BusinessService service =
        invocable.getInterface(BusinessService.class);

service.init();
Object result = service.execute(new Object[] {});
    service.release();
```

First, we evaluate the script shown earlier, then we call the `getInterface` method with the class of the implementation we want our script to implement, and then we retrieve an instance implementing that interface. Our script doesn't even have to explicitly implement the `BusinessService` interface, but through the proxy mechanism, it appears as if it were the case. With such a mechanism, you can manipulate scripts as if they were normal Java beans, without having to call some kind of `invoke` method.

16.6.4 *Polyglot programming*

So far we've been focused on calling into Groovy from Java, but you can use JSR-223 within your Groovy to call out to other languages. The following code will call into JavaScript from Groovy:

```
def mgr = new ScriptEngineManager()
assert mgr.getEngineByName("javascript").eval('''
function factorial(n) {
    if (n == 0) { return 1; }
    return n * factorial(n - 1);
}
factorial(4)
''') == 24.0
```

The JavaScript engine is bundled with Oracle's JDKs. For other languages you might need to also grab a language's respective JSR-223 execution engine.

That wraps up our discussion of language-neutral integration options using Spring and JSR-223. Shortly we'll discuss all of the pros and cons of language-neutral versus native Groovy integration options and one of the discussion points will be how deeply you need access into the Groovy internals. Before we do that, let's expand on one of the key classes for deep native integration with Groovy, the `CompilerConfiguration` class. We mentioned the class earlier in this chapter but it has advanced abilities that we'll cover next.

16.7 *Mastering CompilerConfiguration*

In the previous sections, we've shown how you could leverage the `GroovyShell`, the `GroovyScriptEngine`, or the `GroovyClassLoader` to integrate Groovy code with different flavors. All those classes have in common the ability to create classes at runtime. Even scripts, as we've shown, are compiled into classes that are loaded, eventually, by the specialized Groovy classloader.

Creating classes at runtime, in this case, doesn't differ much from calling the `groovyc` command-line tool. The compilation process is the same if you call `groovyc` from the command line or use a `GroovyShell`. The difference lies in the way source code is provided (files, strings, or URIs) and the way they're loaded (the classloader).

What makes the `GroovyShell` so powerful is that you implicitly create a `Script` class that can be used, for example, as the core implementation of a DSL:

```
def conf = new CompilerConfiguration()
conf.setScriptBaseClass("BaseScript")
def shell = new GroovyShell(conf)
```

```
def value = shell.evaluate('''
    multiply(5, 6)
''')
assert value == 30
```

In this example, we're explicitly changing the base script class from `Script` to `Base-Script`. This makes all the methods from the `BaseScript` class directly callable from the script text when we call `evaluate`. `setScriptBaseClass` is just one example of what the `CompilerConfiguration` class has to offer in terms of customization of the compilation process.

Wouldn't it be nice, for example, if you could add default imports to your scripts? That is to say, make some classes available to your script without the user needing to add an explicit `import` statement? Groovy, for example, imports by default classes from `groovy.lang` or `java.util`. Maybe you'd want classes of yours to be imported by default too. This is in particular important if you think of DSLs: having to add `import` statements in a DSL doesn't make it look so nice.

In chapter 9, we've shown how you can leverage compile-time metaprogramming to add behavior to your classes at compile time. Using AST transformations like `@ToString`, which generates a `toString()` method for you, it's easy to dramatically reduce the boilerplate code. AST transformations come at a price, which is the use of an annotation, which isn't necessarily user-friendly. What if you could transparently apply AST transformations to the scripts that are evaluated by the `GroovyShell`?

Those two examples—adding imports by default and transparently applying AST transformations—are what we call compilation customizers. Groovy comes with a set of predefined compilation customizers that allow you to hook into the compilation process itself in an elegant way. Of course, compilation customizers aren't limited to what the Groovy distribution offers, so you can write your own.

Applying a compilation customizer is easy. Let's see how you can add an `Import-Customizer`, the class that allows you to add imports by default:

```
def conf = new CompilerConfiguration()
def customizer = new ImportCustomizer()
customizer.addImports('java.util.concurrent.atomic.AtomicInteger',
    'java.util.concurrent.atomic.AtomicLong')
conf.addCompilationCustomizers(customizer)
def shell = new GroovyShell(conf)
def value = shell.evaluate('''
    def myInt = new AtomicInteger(1)
    def myLong = new AtomicLong(2)
''')
```

This example consists of two distinct parts: setting up a `CompilerConfiguration`, which includes the compilation customizer, and evaluating a script. Because the compilation customizer tells the compiler to transparently add imports, when the script is executed it's no longer necessary to add them for the script to compile.

Let's take a short tour of the compilation customizers that Groovy provides.

16.7.1 *The import customizer*

Groovy is great for building DSLs, but there are a few points to consider. Any *internal* Groovy-based DSL is actually Groovy code. The objective of a DSL, however, is to be usable by experts from the domain. There's no reason why the users of your DSL would be programmers. Having that in mind, it would be very unfortunate if users had to add imports to their scripts for them to work.

Let's imagine a DSL that allows the evaluation of mathematical expressions. The natural idea would be to leverage the functions and constants available in the java.lang.Math class. Of course, a user would be able to write this:

```
import static java.lang.Math.*
cos(PI/2)
```

But obviously, the only important part of the script is the mathematical expression itself. The import statement is here for it to be nicer to write or read. The problem is that we ask the user to add the import statement, although because we know that our DSL is meant to evaluate mathematical expressions, it would be normal to make the imports by default and let the user call the cos function as well as the PI constant without hassle. The first obvious solution to the problem is to append imports to the user script:

```
def shell = new GroovyShell()
shell.evaluate('import static java.lang.Math.*\n'+expression)
```

While this works, the solution isn't very elegant and comes with a major problem: scripts, even if they are "evaluated" by a Groovy shell, are in the end compiled and executed by a JVM. This means that if the script contains an error (and it will happen at some time), then an exception will be thrown. In that case, the stack trace will not match the source code: with the preceding example, we're introducing an additional line of code, meaning that when the exception will show an error at line 145, the error will, for the user, really be at line 144 (because of the additional import). Of course, you could filter out the stack trace and fix the line/column numbers yourself, but it wouldn't solve the debugging problem: if the script is compiled, there are some ways of debugging it (for example, setting breakpoints in the IDE), and once again, the line numbers in the bytecode wouldn't match those of the source code. This is definitely a stopper for debugging.

To solve this problem, the import customizer will allow you to plug into the compilation process and make the imports known to the compiler without the need to have them in the form of source code:

```
def conf = new CompilerConfiguration()
def customizer = new ImportCustomizer()
customizer.addStarImports 'java.lang.Math'
conf.addCompilationCustomizers(customizer)
def shell = new GroovyShell(conf)
def value = shell.evaluate('cos(PI/2)')
```

The import customizer allows you to add various types of imports, from "regular" to static star imports, including the ability to use aliases:

```
customizer.addStaticImport 'π','java.lang.Math','PI'
customizer.addStaticImport 'cosine','java.lang.Math','cos'
conf.addCompilationCustomizers(customizer)
def shell = new GroovyShell(conf)
def value = shell.evaluate('cosine(π/2)')
```

Table 16.2 summarizes the methods available through the import customizer.

Table 16.2 Methods offered by the import customizer

Method	Description
`addImport(String className)`	Adds a regular import
`addImport(String alias, String className)`	Adds an import with an explicit alias
`addImports(String... imports)`	Adds multiple regular imports at once
`addStarImport(String packageName)`	Adds a star import for a specific package
`addStarImports(String... packageNames)`	Adds star imports of multiple packages at once
`addStaticImport(String className, String member)`	Adds a static import of a member
`addStaticImport(String alias, String className, String member)`	Adds a static import of a member using an alias
`addStaticStar(String clasName)`	Adds a static star import of all members of a class
`addStaticStars(String... classNames)`	Adds static star imports of multiple classes at once

Using the import customizer is really easy and should help you reduce the amount of setup code users should write to get a DSL up and running. Because it's often the case that users of DSLs aren't programmers, putting them in front of such unfriendly code isn't necessary anymore and you can concentrate on the DSL itself. This is, in general, the goal of compilation customizers, and the next one we're going to analyze is once again aimed toward user-friendliness.

16.7.2 *The source-aware customizer*

A typical Groovy application consists of source files that are compiled by the Groovy compiler, be it using the command-line tool, Gradle, Ant, or Maven. But what if your source files are in fact user scripts? What if those scripts are supposed to be compiled using a specific compiler configuration because, for example, they correspond to a

DSL? In that case, one option you have is to skip those files from compilation and have a wrapper (typically a `GroovyShell`) that will compile the files at runtime using a specific compiler configuration. One problem with this is that scripts are compiled at runtime, meaning you pay the cost of compilation at the application startup or during its lifecycle. In some circumstances this isn't acceptable.

Another typical user requirement is to have different compilation options depending on the file extension. By default, Groovy uses the .groovy file extension, but some users want to be able to use different extensions with different meanings. For example, a .spec file could correspond to an executable specification file that involves AST transformations that aren't necessary for regular .groovy files.

For those use cases, the source-aware customizer provides a powerful configuration mechanism that basically applies different compilation options based on the actual source. In practice, this customizer acts as a guard for another customizer, based on the source file. The following listing creates a source customizer that applies the `ToString` AST transformation to classes whose names end with `Bean`.

Listing 16.12 Apply @ToString to classes whose names end with Bean

```
import groovy.transform.ToString
import org.codehaus.groovy.control.CompilerConfiguration
import org.codehaus.groovy.control.customizers.*                    ①  Creates
                                                                         ToString AST
def conf = new CompilerConfiguration()                                   customizer
def astCustomizer = new ASTTransformationCustomizer(ToString)  ←──────┘
def sourceAwareCustomizer =
    new SourceAwareCustomizer(astCustomizer)
sourceAwareCustomizer.baseNameValidator = {                    ←──────┐
  name -> name.endsWith 'Bean'
}                                                              ③  Creates a base-
conf.addCompilationCustomizers(sourceAwareCustomizer)            name filter

def gcl = new GroovyClassLoader(getClass().classLoader, conf)  ←──────┐
def clazz = gcl.parseClass '''                                          Uses
class MrBean { String first, last }                                     configuration
''', 'MrBean.groovy'                                                    with Groovy-
def result = clazz.newInstance()                               ④  ClassLoader
result.first = 'Rowan'
result.last = 'Atkinson'
assert result.toString() == 'MrBean(Rowan, Atkinson)'
```

Wraps into a source-aware customizer ②

We create the AST transformation customizer ①, which would have been applied to all classes being compiled if we added it directly to the compiler configuration. Instead, we create a source-aware customizer ② that wraps the AST transformation customizer, then we set a predicate on the base name ③ that determines in which condition the AST transformation customizer will be applied. As a last step, we make use of the configuration in conjunction with a `GroovyClassLoader` to compile a class ④.

As is, the source-aware customizers offer three ways to guard another customizer.

- *The base-name validator*—Works on the filename without the extension.
- *The extension validator (extensionValidator)*—Allows you to work specifically on the file extension.
- *The `sourceUnitValidator`*—Works directly on an internal compilation structure called `SourceUnit`. Unlike the previous ones, it's capable of handling more than just the filename, which implies it can work on sources that aren't files. `SourceUnit` gives you access to the concrete syntax tree (CST) or the AST, meaning you can work on the actual classes found in source code.

Using the source-aware customizer is very interesting, but we must warn you that it's a very powerful tool that can lead to results which are difficult to analyze (because the source code doesn't match expectations depending on the file extension, for one).

Groovy comes with many customization options that we present here from an *integration* perspective. In chapter 19, we'll partly revisit them for the purpose of how to create a DSL. There, we'll also discuss the *AST transformation customizer* and the *secure AST customizer,* which would also be relevant in the context of integration.

But you don't have to live by a fixed set of customizers that Groovy gives you. You can just as easily write your own.

16.7.3 *Writing your own customizer*

The last option that Groovy offers to you with regards to compilation customization is writing your own. In terms of complexity, it's somehow easier than AST transformations but almost as powerful. All the customizers we've described so far are extending a base class called `CompilationCustomizer` found in the `org.codehaus.groovy.control` `.customizers` package. This gives you a hint of the incredible possibilities that are now open to you.

As an example, we'll create a compilation customizer that will fail compilation if a class doesn't contain a field of type `String` that's named `name`. The first thing to do is to create the customizer class:

```
class HasNameFieldCustomizer extends CompilationCustomizer {
    HasNameFieldCustomizer() {
        super(CompilePhase.CANONICALIZATION)          Sets the
    }                                              ❶ phase
}
```

This is the minimal code you'll have to write. At ❶, we're setting the compilation phase where the compilation customizer works. As with AST transformations, a compilation customizer has to choose the proper compilation phase and it's often the sooner the better. Now we have to write the code, which will actually check if the field exists:

```
void call(SourceUnit source, GeneratorContext context, ClassNode classNode) {
  def field = classNode.getDeclaredField('name')
```

```
    if (field) {
      if (!field.type.equals(ClassHelper.STRING_TYPE)) {
        source.addError(new SyntaxException("Class ${classNode.name} " +
          "defines field 'name' but using the wrong type"),
          field.lineNumber, field.columnNumber)
      }
    } else {
      source.addError(new SyntaxException("Class ${classNode.name} " +
        "doesn't define a field named 'name' of type 'String'",
        classNode.lineNumber, classNode.columnNumber))
    }
}
```

Calling `source.addError` with a `SyntaxException` will cause the compiler to stop compilation, showing a located error message. In this case, if a field exists but uses the wrong type, then it would show the error on the field, but if the class doesn't define a field named `name`, then the error would be located at the class.

This is a very simple example that shows that a compilation customizer is allowed to do basically what an AST transformation can do, but you have more control on how it's executed. The only restriction behind a compilation customizer is that it exclusively works on class nodes, but it doesn't prevent you from visiting methods inside the compilation customizer itself.

So far, we've shown you how you could use the existing customizers, create your own, and bind them to a `CompilerConfiguration`; now let's see how you can use the same tools with the `groovyc` tool itself.

16.7.4 *The configscript compilation option*

Compilation customizers are very powerful for embedded scripts, such as user DSLs executed through a sandboxed `GroovyShell`. There are some situations where you'd want the same level of customization from the command line itself; that is, using `groovyc` too. This is possible using the `--configscript` compilation option:

```
groovyc --configscript config.groovy MyClass.groovy
```

As you can see, this option requires a configuration file that's itself a Groovy script. This configuration file will give you access to the `CompilerConfiguration` instance that the `groovyc` command creates internally, giving you a chance to plug in your compilation customizers. This compiler configuration instance is exposed in the configuration script using the `config` variable. This means that you can write this in the configuration file:

```
import groovy.transform.Log
import org.codehaus.groovy.control.customizers.ASTTransformationCustomizer

config.addCompilationCustomizers(new ASTTransformationCustomizer(Log))
```

This configuration option is also available on the `groovy` command, as well as in the Ant task. All files compiled will therefore use the configuration as modified by the script.

But what's really nice is that this configuration script also exposes a nice DSL to customize the configuration, dramatically reducing the amount of code that's required to tweak the `CompilerConfiguration`. This DSL is a builder for compilation customizers, which is automatically bound to the `withConfig` method:

```
withConfig(config) {
    ast(Log)
}
```

This code is semantically equivalent to the previous one, despite being much more concise (no more need for imports), but uses the builder syntax instead, meaning that `ast(Log)` creates an AST transformation customizer for the `Log` AST transformation.

Table 16.3 summarizes the mapping between the builder syntax and the traditional syntax.

Table 16.3   Mapping between builder-style and normal customizers creation

Builder	Traditional	Example
ast	ASTTransformation ⤵ Customizer	`ast(Log)` `ast(name:'logger', Log)`

imports	ImportCustomizer	`imports {`
		`    normal 'com.example.Foo'`
		`    star 'com.example.Foo'`
		`    staticStar 'java.lang.Math'`
		`    alias 'Bar', 'com.example.Foo'`
		`    staticMember 'com.Foo.bar'`
		`}`

secure	SecureASTCustomizer	`secure {`
		`    importsWhiteList=[]`
		`}`

source	SourceAwareCustomizer	`source(extension:'sgroovy') {`
		`    ast(CompileStatic)`
		`}`

inline	Custom compilation customizer	`inline(phase:'CONVERSION') {`
		`    source, context, classNode ->`
		`        println "Class $classNode.name"`
		`}`

Tweaking the compiler configuration using the `configscript` command-line option is very powerful, but you should always be careful not to put too much magic in there. Programmers often expect identical-looking code to produce identical-looking classes, but using a tool such as the source-aware customizer, you'll be able to produce very different outputs—such as only depending on the package name. If you ever want to do this, you should always take time to document the configuration, explain why it's done the way it's done, and make sure your build file uses the compiler configuration. In the end, never use a local configuration file and consider compiler configuration scripts as part of the source code. If you don't do so, it's too easy to create unreproducible builds!

You now know about the native Groovy techniques to integrate Groovy in your Java application and the more language-neutral solutions using Spring or JSR-223. The great thing about this is that it presents you with a choice. The downside is that you need to make a decision, so we provide guidance in the last section of this chapter.

16.8 *Choosing an integration mechanism*

This section is similar to the first one in the chapter, in that we can't make any decisions for you. Good guidance *tends* to be right more than it's wrong, but there will always be cases that appear to fit one pattern but that benefit more from another after close examination. We don't know what your needs are, so we can't make that close examination. All we can do is give suggestions and reasons for them.

To give a good rule of thumb, if your application is built on Spring, you should prefer using the Spring integration. If you want to be able to change or mix scripting languages at the same time, or you have the freedom to change at will, using the scripting integration of JSR-223 makes perfect sense. But if you want to do more advanced things or if you're concerned about the potential security hole opened by dynamic code, you should probably choose some of the standard Groovy mechanisms for embedding and executing Groovy code with `GroovyShell`, `GroovyScriptEngine`, or the almighty `GroovyClassLoader`. Table 16.4 shows a summary of the pros and cons of each integration mechanism.

Table 16.4 Sweet spots and limitations of the different integration mechanisms

Mechanism	Sweet spot	Limitations
`Eval.me`	For very simple expressions	Not suited for frequent eval
`GroovyShell`	Perfect for single-line user input, small expressions and DLSs	Will not scale to dependent scripts
`GroovyScriptEngine`	Supports reloading Robust security available Nice for dependent scripts Supports reloading	Doesn't support classes Doesn't support security
`GroovyClassLoader`	Most powerful integration mechanism Supports reloading Robust security available	Trickier to handle in the case of a complex classloader hierarchy
Spring scripting support	Integrates well with Spring Can switch languages easily Supports reloading	Requires Spring

Table 16.4   Sweet spots and limitations of the different integration mechanisms

Mechanism	Sweet spot	Limitations
JSR-223	Can switch languages easily	Requires Java 6 Doesn't support security Doesn't support reloading Doesn't support Groovy-specific configuration
Bean Scripting Framework	Can switch languages easily Doesn't require Java 6	Doesn't support security Doesn't support reloading Doesn't support Groovy-specific configuration More limited capabilities than JSR-223

The basis of Groovy's integration is its excellent compatibility with Java. We've listed the most common ways of integrating Groovy with Java, but anywhere that Java can be integrated, Groovy can work too. Some databases allow stored procedures to be written in Java, for instance, so Groovy can be used in the same way. Additional integration mechanisms may well appear over time in various guises. (See Grengine, http://grengine.ch/.) Don't assume that the options given here are exhaustive!

16.9   *Summary*

This chapter has given you glimpses into how you might allow your applications to become more flexible, giving appropriate users the ability to customize behavior in a way that may enable them to solve the *exact* problem they're facing, rather than the one that was as close as you could imagine when designing the application.

The means of integrating Groovy into your application broadly fall into two camps: those provided directly by the Groovy libraries and those provided in a language-neutral fashion by Spring and, since Java 6, through JSR-223. As is often the case, the more specific solutions prove to be the most powerful ones, but at the cost of language neutrality.

As bookends to the chapter, we discussed the kinds of applications that benefit from this sort of integration and offer guidance as to which integration mechanism might be best for your situation.

There's a good reason why the Spring team made Groovy a first-class citizen and their scripting language of choice in version 4.0: the integration of Groovy with its underlying platform is so deep that it's the natural choice for any dynamic activities on the JVM.

You can benefit from the advantages of both worlds: you can build big and scalable enterprise applications while still using Groovy for smart configuration, adaptable business rules, user-defined logic, and spontaneous runtime inspections.

Part 3

Applied Groovy

We build too many walls and not enough bridges

—Isaac Newton

In the course of this book, you've seen a large portion of Groovyland. Part 1 introduced you to the Groovy language, datatypes, operators, control structures, and even the Meta Object Protocol. Part 2 led you through the Groovy library, showing builders, templates, numerous JDK enhancements, working with databases, and XML support. Your backpack is filled with valuable knowledge that waits to be brought to new horizons.

Part 3 gives you guidance on how to best apply your knowledge with other tools, frameworks, and libraries that embrace Groovy.

It starts with unit testing in chapter 17, an activity that no self-respecting professional developer can work without. With a clever mix of the Groovy wisdom you've already acquired and a bit of guidance through Groovy's excellent testing support, you'll appreciate unit testing as another strength of Groovy.

Chapter 18 prepares you for the to-be-expected multicore era and enables you to take full advantage of all the many processing cores that your machine is likely to have.

Chapter 19 gives you the power of designing your own language so that business aspects can be expressed in the jargon of their domain. You will become the master of domain-specific languages (DSLs).

Chapter 20 comes as a bonus for all the diligent readers who held out until the very end. You will be reimbursed with a sneak peek into a series of tools, libraries, and frameworks that help you with tasks that are as diverse as writing web application, desktop applications, automating Windows, using quality analysis tools, designing by contract, and much more. It's a quick but broad overview to spark your interest in learning more about these projects. We hope you take it as your springboard to dive into the Groovy ocean.

Unit testing with Groovy

17

This chapter covers

- Unit testing Groovy and Java code
- Incorporating code coverage tools
- Integrating IDEs
- Testing with Spock
- Automating the build process

The major difference between a thing that might go wrong and a thing that cannot possibly go wrong is that when a thing that cannot possibly go wrong goes wrong, it usually turns out to be impossible to get at or repair.

—Douglas Adams

Developer unit testing has become a de facto standard in the Java community.[1] The confidence and structure that JUnit[2] and other testing frameworks bring to the development process are almost revolutionary. To those of us who were actively

---

[1] See Kevin Tate, *Sustainable Software Development: An Agile Perspective* (Addison Wesley Professional, 2005) and Greg Smith and Ahmed Sidky, *Becoming Agile* (Manning, 2009).

[2] See Petar Tahchiev, et al., *JUnit in Action, 2nd Ed.* (Manning, 2010); J. B. Rainsberger, *JUnit Recipes* (Manning, 2004), and www.junit.org for more information.

developing Java applications in the latter years of the 20th century, automated unit testing was almost unheard of. Yes, we wrote tests, but they were hardly automated or even a part of a standard build!

Fast-forward to the present, and many people wouldn't think of writing, let alone *releasing*, code without corresponding unit tests. We write tests all the time, and we expect everyone else on our teams to do the same. Moreover, momentum is growing behind the idea of writing code by always writing tests first. Although this isn't universal, it's another indicator that the recent growth in the importance of tests will continue.

We test at all levels, from unit testing to integration testing to system testing. It's sometimes more fun to write the tests than the subject under test, because doing so improves not only the code itself, but also the design of the code. When tests are written often and continually, code has the benefit of being highly extensible, in addition to being obviously freer of defects and easier to repair when needed.

Combine this increased awareness of developer testing with Groovy, and you have a match made in heaven. With Groovy, tests can be written more quickly and easily. It gets even better when you combine the simplicity of unit testing in Groovy with normal Java. You can write Groovy tests for your Groovy-based systems and leverage the many Java libraries and test-extension packages. You can write Groovy tests for your Java-based systems and leverage Groovy's enhanced syntax benefits and extended test functionality.

Groovy makes unit testing a breeze, whichever way you use it, mainly due to four key aspects:

- Groovy embeds JUnit, so you don't have to set up a new dependency.
- Groovy has an enhanced test-case class, which adds a plethora of new assertion methods.
- Groovy has built-in mock, stub, and other dynamic class-creation facilities that simplify isolating a test class from its collaborators.
- Tests written in Groovy can be easily run from Gradle, Maven, or your favorite IDE.

Our focus in this chapter is unit testing; however, many of the ideas can be extended to other kinds of testing as well. We'll mention specific examples throughout the chapter.

17.1 Getting started

The section header implies that you have preparation to do before you can start your testing activities. But you don't. There's no external support to download or install. Groovy treats unit testing as a first-class developer duty and ships with everything you need for that purpose.

Even more important, it simplifies testing by making assertions part of the language,[3] automatically executing test cases by transparently invoking its TestRunner

---

[3] Java also supports assertions at the language level but disables them by default.

when needed, and providing the means to run suites of test cases easily, both from the command line and through integration with your IDE or build environment. This section shows you how simple it can be and introduces you to `GroovyTestCase`, the base class used for most unit testing in Groovy.

17.1.1 *Writing tests is easy*

Assume you have Groovy code that converts temperatures measured in Fahrenheit (F) to Celsius (C). To that end, you define a `celsius` method in a `Converter` class like so:

```
class Converter {
    static celsius (fahrenheit) { (fahrenheit - 32) * 5 / 9 }
}
```

Is this implementation correct? Probably, but you can't be sure. You need to gain additional confidence in this method before the next non-U.S. traveler uses your method to understand the U.S. weather forecast.

A common approach with unit testing is to call the subject under test with static sample data that produces well-known results. That way, you can compare the calculated results against your expectations.

Choosing a good set of samples is key. As a rule of thumb, having a few typical cases and all the corner cases you can think of is a good choice.[4] Typical cases would be 68° F = 20° C for having a garden party or 95° F = 35° C for going to the beach. Corner cases would be 0° F, which is between -17° C and -18° C, the coldest temperature that Gabriel Daniel Fahrenheit could create with a mixture of ice and ordinary salt in 1714. Another corner case is when water freezes at 32° F = 0° C.

Sound complicated? It isn't. The following listing statically imports the method and then adds scripted unit tests using simple assertions that are built into the language itself.

Listing 17.1 Scripted unit tests for the Fahrenheit to Celsius conversion method

```
import static Converter.celsius

assert  20 == celsius(68)
assert  35 == celsius(95)
assert -17 == celsius(0).toInteger()      Rounds down to
assert   0 == celsius(32)                 whole number
```

Scripted tests of this kind are useful. As an example, look at this book: most listings contain such self-checking asserts to ensure the code works and to help reveal your expectations from the code at the same time. Most even work as *inline tests* where assertions live inside the code under test.

---

[4] Finding good test data is a science of its own and involves activities such as structural analysis of the parameter domain. For our purposes, we keep it simple. Refer to the background literature for more information.

But what if a test would fail due to an implementation error? Groovy will report this back in a visual way. Say that instead of converting 95° F to 35° C, we incorrectly assume that the result should be 34° C. If we execute the following:

```
assert 34  == celsius(95)
```

Groovy will report us back the following assertion error:

```
assert 34  == celsius(95)
           |  |
           |  35
           false
```

Here you can see Groovy's Power Assert at work. Power Assert, originally introduced in the Spock Testing Framework, provides a very concise and clear way of reporting errors by outputting the result of each invocation to the console. This makes it easier to understand which parts went right, and which parts wrong.

Whenever the environment of self-testing code changes, the inline tests assert that it is still working. Environmental changes can happen for a number of reasons: evaluating the script on a different machine, using an updated JDK or Groovy version, or running with different versions of packages that the script depends upon.

There are circumstances when tests cannot be *inlined*, such as due to performance requirements. Sometimes *scripted* tests aren't convenient enough because they do not self-organize into trees of test suites. In such cases, it's conventional to pack all the tests of a given script or class into a separate class residing in a separate file. This is where GroovyTestCase appears on stage.

17.1.2 *GroovyTestCase: an introduction*

Groovy bundles an extended JUnit class dubbed GroovyTestCase, which facilitates unit testing in a number of ways. It includes a host of new assert methods, and it also facilitates running Groovy scripts masquerading as test cases.

The added assertions are listed in table 17.1. We won't go into the details of each method, mostly because they're descriptively named. Where it's not absolutely obvious what the meaning is, the description provided in the table should be sufficient. Even though we won't discuss them explicitly, we'll use them in the assertions elsewhere in this chapter, so you'll see how useful they are.

Table 17.1   Enhanced assertions available in GroovyTestCase

Method	Description
void assertArrayEquals(Object[] expected, Object[] value)	Compares the contents and length of each array
void assertContains(char expected, char[] array)	Verifies that a given array of chars contains an expected value

Table 17.1 Enhanced assertions available in GroovyTestCase

Method	Description
void assertContains(int expected, int[] array)	Verifies that a given array of ints contains an expected value
void assertInspect(Object value, String expected)	Similar to the assertToString method, except that it calls the inspect method
void assertLength(int length, char[] array)	Convenience method for asserting the length of an array
void assertLength(int length, int[] array)	Convenience method for asserting the length of an array
void assertLength(int length, Object[] array)	Convenience method for asserting the length of an array
void assertScript(final String script)	Attempts to run the provided script
void assertToString(Object value, String expected)	Invokes the toString method on the provided object and compares the result with the expected string
void shouldFail(Closure code)	Verifies that the closure provided fails
void shouldFail(Class clazz, Closure code)	Verifies that the closure provided throws an exception of type clazz
void shouldFail(String scriptText)	Verifies that the provided script fails when executed
void shouldFail(Class clazz, String scriptText)	Verifies the provided script throws an exception of type clazz when executed
void shouldFailWithCause(Class clazz, Closure code)	Verifies that the closure provided fails and that a particular exception is the cause of the failure

In addition to the methods listed in the previous table, consider the convenient notYet-Implemented method, which you can use to mark a test method as not implemented yet. Here is an example:

```
public void testNotImplementedYet() {
    if (GroovyTestCase.notYetImplemented(this)) return
    fail("will be implemented tomorrow")
}
```

In the previous example, the test case is marked as not yet implemented. If the test somehow passes, which was not yet expected, the test will fail with a descriptive error message.

Groovy doesn't force you to extend GroovyTestCase, and you're free to continue to extend the traditional TestCase class provided by JUnit.[5] Having said that, unless

[5] These methods extend the 4.12 version of JUnit, which is bundled with Groovy.

you need the functionality of a different subclass of `TestCase`, you have plenty of reasons to use `GroovyTestCase` and no reasons to specifically avoid it. Along with the assertions listed in table 17.1, it's easier to work with `GroovyTestCase` than `TestCase`, as you'll see in the next section.

17.1.3 *Working with GroovyTestCase*

To use Groovy's enhanced `TestCase` class, extend it as follows:[6]

```
class SimpleUnitTest extends GroovyTestCase {
    void testSimple() {
      assertEquals("Groovy should add correctly", 2, 1 + 1)
    }
}
```

You can also use the JUnit 4 `@Test` annotation or TestNG's equivalent to mark your test. In that case, you don't have to extend from `GroovyTestCase` unless you want to use `GroovyTestCase`'s convenience methods, nor do you have to start your test method with the "test" prefix:

```
import org.junit.Test
import static org.junit.Assert.assertEquals
class SimpleUnitTest {
    @Test
    void shouldAdd() {
      assertEquals("Groovy should add correctly", 2, 1 + 1)
    }
}
```

Remember, you're free to extend any `TestCase` class you choose, so long as it's in your classpath. You can easily extend JUnit's `TestCase` as follows:

```
import junit.framework.TestCase

class AnotherSimpleUnitTest extends TestCase {
    void testSimpleAgain() {
      assertEquals("Should subtract correctly too", 2, 3 - 1)
    }
}
```

Test cases can be run via the `groovy` command you've used previously for scripts and applications. For example, you can run the `SimpleUnitTest` script seen earlier, by typing the command groovy SimpleUnitTest:

```
> groovy SimpleUnitTest
.
Time: 0

OK (1 test)
```

---

[6] You don't have to import it—it resides in one of the packages imported by default.

If the output looks familiar, that's probably because it is the standard JUnit output you'd expect to see if you ran a normal Java JUnit test using JUnit's text-based test runner.

Now that you've got your feet wet, let's go back and start again from scratch, this time testing a little more methodically.

17.2 *Unit testing Groovy code*

We've introduced Groovy's testing capabilities, but we skipped over some of the details. We'll now explore more of those details by going through a slightly larger Groovy application in need of testing. We'll start with a new example and build up our test class, refactoring tests as we go, validating boundary data, testing that inputs aren't inadvertently changed, even checking that the tests themselves haven't been adversely changed.

Let's imagine we've built a small counter class that determines how many numbers in a list are larger than a target threshold number. The Groovy code is fairly trivial but useful as our example class under test:

```
class Counter {
    int biggerThan(items, threshold) {
        items.grep{ it > threshold }.size()
    }
}
```

Testing this class is easy. First, we define our test case class, `CounterTest`, which extends `GroovyTestCase`:

```
class CounterTest extends GroovyTestCase {
    ...
}
```

Next, we follow the common unit-testing practice of writing a method to set up the variables we'll need in the tests that follow:

```
class CounterTest extends GroovyTestCase {
    private counter
    void setUp() {
        counter = new Counter()
    }
    ...
}
```

We're now in a position to write a test:

```
    void testCounterWorks() {
        assertEquals(2, counter.biggerThan([5, 10, 15], 7))
    }
```

We could continue adding tests in this way, but first let's introduce constants that capture useful boundary case data and refactor out a helper method:

```
static final Integer[ ] NEG_NUMBERS   = [-2, -3, -4]
static final Integer[ ] POS_NUMBERS   = [ 4,  5,  6]
static final Integer[ ] MIXED_NUMBERS = [ 4, -6,  0]
```

```
private check(expectedCount, items, threshold) {
    assertEquals(expectedCount,
                counter.biggerThan(items, threshold))
}
```

This lets us specify more tests in a compact form:

```
void testCountHowManyFromSampleNumbers () {
    check(2, NEG_NUMBERS, -4)
    check(2, POS_NUMBERS, 4)
    check(1, MIXED_NUMBERS, 0)
    …
}
```

Once you've written sufficient tests to cover all the boundary cases you think are important (or to meet your project's coverage requirements, discussed in section 17.7.1), you may think you're finished, but you can do more. First, you can ensure that your method doesn't change the input items. You can provide the correct answer but accidentally modify the input data and cause errors to occur elsewhere. Here's one example of such a test:

```
void testInputDataUnchanged() {
    def numbers = NEG_NUMBERS.clone()
    def origLength = numbers.size()
    counter.biggerThan(numbers, 0 /* don't care */)
    assertLength origLength, numbers
    assertArrayEquals NEG_NUMBERS, numbers
}
```

Tests to assure the input list remains unchanged as a result of biggerThan operations.

You can add items[0] = 0 as the first line of the biggerThan method to show how this test would pick up an accidental bug in the code.

We now have sound tests in place, but we can be more paranoid about our test data and introduce a final test. Over time, we expect further developers to work on the code, and they'll likely change the test constants. To ensure that our key cases remain covered, we can create a test that validates our assumptions about the data:

```
void testInputDataAssumptions() {
    assertTrue NEG_NUMBERS.every { it < 0 }
    assertTrue POS_NUMBERS.every { it > 0 }
    assertContains 0, MIXED_NUMBERS
    int negCount = 0
    int posCount = 0
    MIXED_NUMBERS.each {
        if (it < 0) negCount++ else if (it > 0) posCount++
    }
    assert negCount && posCount
}
```

Test to validate input data

This ensures that our positive, negative, and mixed numbers retain the properties we intend.[7]

---

[7] You could argue that we are being too paranoid here. Maybe, but it gives us a chance to show off a few more example test assertions.

Now for a neat bit of Groovy magic. It turns out that even though we set out to create a calculator for numbers, nothing in our original method was specific to numbers. We'll add another test to illustrate this, using strings with their natural order:

```
void testCountHowManyFromSampleStrings() {
  check(2, ['Dog', 'Cat', 'Antelope'], 'Bird')
}
```

Putting this together results in the code in the following listing.

Listing 17.2 A complete test example, including implementation at the end

```
class Listing_17_02_CounterTest extends GroovyTestCase {
  static final Integer[] NEG_NUMBERS   = [-2, -3, -4]        Constants
  static final Integer[] POS_NUMBERS   = [4,   5,  6]         repeated in
  static final Integer[] MIXED_NUMBERS = [4,  -6,  0]         the test
  private Counter counter

  void setUp() {
    counter = new Counter()
  }

  void testCounterWorks() {
    assertEquals(2, counter.biggerThan([5, 10, 15], 7))
  }

  void testCountHowManyFromSampleNumbers() {
    check(0, NEG_NUMBERS, -1)
    check(0, NEG_NUMBERS, -2)
    check(2, NEG_NUMBERS, -4)
    check(3, NEG_NUMBERS, -5)
    check(0, POS_NUMBERS,  7)
    check(0, POS_NUMBERS,  6)                    Uses a helper
    check(2, POS_NUMBERS,  4)                    method to make
    check(3, POS_NUMBERS,  3)                    code simpler
    check(0, MIXED_NUMBERS,  5)
    check(1, MIXED_NUMBERS,  2)
    check(1, MIXED_NUMBERS,  1)
    check(1, MIXED_NUMBERS,  0)
    check(2, MIXED_NUMBERS, -1)
    check(3, MIXED_NUMBERS, -7)
  }

  void testInputDataUnchanged() {                        Tests proving we don't
    def numbers = NEG_NUMBERS.clone()                    change the array
    def origLength = numbers.size()
    counter.biggerThan(numbers, 0 /* don't care */)
    assertLength origLength, numbers
    assertArrayEquals NEG_NUMBERS, numbers
  }
                                                         Calculator doesn't only
  void testCountHowManyFromSampleStrings() {             work with numbers
    check(2, ['Dog', 'Cat', 'Antelope'], 'Bird')
  }
                                                         Test constants
  void testInputDataAssumptions() {                      sanity check
    assertTrue NEG_NUMBERS.every { it < 0 }
```

```
    assertTrue POS_NUMBERS.every { it > 0 }
    assertContains 0, MIXED_NUMBERS
    int negCount = 0
    int posCount = 0
    MIXED_NUMBERS.each {
      if (it < 0) negCount++ else if (it > 0) posCount++
    }
    assert negCount && posCount
  }

  private check(expectedCount, items, threshold) {
    assertEquals(expectedCount,
        counter.biggerThan(items, threshold)
    )
  }
}
}
```

Looks familiar, doesn't it? It's darn close to normal JUnit test code, but with slight improvements thanks to Groovy's extra assert methods, proper closure support, and more compact syntax. Groovy hasn't made the code much shorter here, only a bit more convenient. As is often true, there's more test code than production code (although in this case, the difference is more pronounced than usual).

It's immediately obvious that Groovy code can test Groovy code, but it may not be as clear that you can test your existing Java using the benefits of GroovyTestCase, too. You'll see this in action in the next section.

17.3   *Unit testing Java code*

At this point in your career, you've probably coded more Java applications than Groovy ones. It stands to reason that one of the quickest ways to experience the pleasures of Groovy is to use this nifty language to test normal Java applications. As it turns out, this process is amazingly simple.

Using Groovy to test normal Java code involves three steps:

1   Write your tests in Groovy.
2   Ensure that the Java .class files you wish to test are on the classpath.
3   Run your Groovy tests in the normal way (on the command line or via your IDE or favorite build environment).

That's it most of the time. Of course, there are more complicated scenarios. If you're running a complicated integration test and want to run your Groovy test code on a server, you can always run groovyc on your test code and then follow the same steps that you'd go through for a Java application.

Let's explore this further by looking at an example. Rather than spend time describing a Java application that you may not have seen before, we'll consider how to write tests for one of the Java collection classes: HashMap.

One of the first things you'd do if you wrote Java tests for HashMap is set up test fixtures. You do the same thing in Groovy, but you have Groovy's convenient syntax to make your tests shorter and easier to understand. This is how we set up our test fixtures for an arbitrary key object and a sample map:

```
static final KEY = new Object()
static final MAP = [key1: new Object(), key2: new Object()]
```

One of the complicated things to test with Java-based tests is proper exception handling. Groovy's built-in `shouldFail` assert method can be of great assistance for such tests. It's part of HashMap's expected behavior to disallow a null value when constructing the HashMap. Creating a HashMap by passing in a null value as in `new HashMap(null)` should lead to a `NullPointerException`. The `shouldFail` method asserts that this exception is thrown from within its closure:

```
void testHashMapRejectsNull() {
    shouldFail(NullPointerException) {
        new HashMap(null)
    }
}
```

If the attached closure fails to throw any exception (say you accidentally left out `null` as the parameter), the test would fail with a message like:

```
junit.framework.AssertionFailedError: testHashMapRejectsNull() should
have failed with an exception of type java.lang.NullPointerException
```

If the closure fails but with an incorrect exception, say you accidentally had -1 instead of `null` as the parameter, the test would fail with a message like:

```
testHashMapRejectsNull() should have failed with an exception of type
java.lang.NullPointerException, instead you got exception
java.lang.IllegalArgumentException: Illegal initial capacity: -1
```

The `shouldFail` method (inherited from `GroovyTestCase`) additionally returns the exception message so you can test that the correct message is generated by the exception, as in the following example:

```
void testBadInitialSize() {
    def msg = shouldFail(IllegalArgumentException) {
        new HashMap(-1)
    }
    assertEquals "Illegal initial capacity: -1", msg
}
```

If the incorrect exception message was returned (say you accidentally had -2 in the constructor call instead of -1), your test fails with a message similar to the following:

```
junit.framework.ComparisonFailure:
expected:<... initial capacity: -[1]>
but was:<... initial capacity: -[2]>
```

Groovy's object-inspection methods (see section 9.1.1 for further details) also prove useful for writing our Groovy tests. Here is how you might use dump:

```
assert MAP.dump().contains('java.lang.Object')
```

We can put all this together into a complete test class as shown in the following listing.

Listing 17.3 Testing HashMap from Groovy

```
class Listing_17_03_HashMapTest extends GroovyTestCase {
  static final KEY = new Object()
  static final MAP = [key1: new Object(), key2: new Object()]

  void testHashtableRejectsNull() {
    shouldFail(NullPointerException) {
      new Hashtable()[KEY] = null
    }
  }

  void testBadInitialSize() {
    def msg = shouldFail(IllegalArgumentException) {      ◁─┐ Checks that
      new HashMap(-1)                                          the right kind
    }                                                          of exception is
    assertEquals "Illegal initial capacity: -1", msg    ◁─┐ thrown
  }                                                          Checks the
                                                             message
  void testHashMapAcceptsNull() {
    def myMap = new HashMap()
    myMap[KEY] = null
    assert myMap.keySet().contains(KEY)
  }

  void testHashMapReturnsOriginalObjects() {
    def myMap = new HashMap()
    MAP.entrySet().each {
      myMap[it] = MAP[it]
      assertSame MAP[it], myMap[it]                      ◁─┐ Uses Groovy
    }                                                          inspection to
    assert MAP.dump().contains('java.lang.Object')    ◁─┘ examine the map
    assert myMap.size() == MAP.size()
  }
}
```

None of the behavior here is unexpected—after all, the classes we're testing are familiar ones. Using shouldFail is more compact and readable than the equivalent in Java with a try/catch, which fails if it reaches the end of the try block. It's also safer than the JUnit4 annotation for exception testing, which only checks whether *anything* in the method throws the desired exception, rather than the line of code we want to check.

The use of dump in this test isn't as elegant as it tends to be in real testing. When you know the internal structure of the class, you can perform more useful tests against the introspected representation.

The final point we'll mention about using Groovy to test your Java code is related to the agile software development practice of *test-driven development* (TDD).[8] Using this practice, code is developed by first writing a failing test and then writing production code to make that test pass, followed by refactoring and then repeating the process. Modern IDEs provide strong support for this practice, by offering to automatically create a nonexistent class mentioned in a test.

You can still adopt TDD using a hybrid Groovy/Java environment. Current IDEs provide decent support to assist making this as streamlined as for pure Java environments.

Having considered individual test classes, you'll now see how to run sets of tests together.

17.4 Organizing your tests

Until now, we've run our Groovy tests individually. For large systems, tests typically aren't run individually but are grouped into test suites that are run together. Or sometimes you want to run the same test but with multiple (perhaps large) sets of data. We'll look at ways to create suites, write parameterized or data-driven tests, and use property-based testing. These techniques let you scale up your testing ambitions. We'll start with test suites.

17.4.1 Test suites

JUnit has built-in facilities for working with suites. These facilities allow you to add individual test cases (and other nested suites) to test suites. JUnit's test runners know about suites and run all the tests they contain. Unfortunately, these facilities require you to manually add all of your tests to a suite and assume you're using Java classes for your tests. We'll look at ways of making life easier with Groovy.

Because grouping tests into suites is so important, numerous solutions have popped up in the Java world for automatically creating suites, but these too typically assume you're using Java classes. The good news is that because Groovy classes compile to Java classes, you don't have to abandon any of your current practices for grouping tests—as long as you're willing to compile your Groovy files using groovyc first. The even better news is that solutions exist that allow you to work more naturally directly with your Groovy files.

First, we should mention GroovyTestSuite, which is a Java class. It allows you to invoke Groovy test scripts from the command line as follows:

```
> java groovy.util.GroovyTestSuite src/test/Foo.groovy
```

GroovyTestSuite, because it is a Java class, can be used with any conventional Java IDE or Java build environment for running JUnit tests. It allows you to add Groovy files

---

into your test suites, as shown in the following listing. This creates a suite containing the two previous tests. You could also add Java tests to the same suite.

Listing 17.4   Adding Groovy scripts to a JUnit suite with `GroovyTestSuite`

```
import junit.framework.*
import junit.textui.TestRunner

static Test suite() {
  def suite = new TestSuite()
  def gts = new GroovyTestSuite()
  suite.addTestSuite(gts.compile("Listing_17_02_CounterTest.groovy"))
  suite.addTestSuite(gts.compile("Listing_17_03_HashMapTest.groovy"))
  return suite
}

TestRunner.run(suite())
```

We create a normal JUnit `TestSuite` and call `GroovyTestSuite`'s compile method to compile the Groovy source code so that `TestSuite` knows how to run it. We then use the normal JUnit console UI to run the tests. It isn't aware that it's running anything other than normal Java.

Next, we look at `AllTestSuite`, which can be thought of as an improved version of `GroovyTestSuite`. It allows you to specify a base directory and a filename pattern, and then it adds all the matching Groovy files to a suite. The following listing shows how you'd use it to run the same tests as we did in listing 17.4.

Listing 17.5   Adding Groovy scripts to a JUnit suite with `AllTestSuite`

```
def suite = AllTestSuite.suite(".", "Listing_17_*Counter*Test.groovy")
junit.textui.TestRunner.run(suite)
```

This time, we use the return value of the `suite` method directly, but if we want to add multiple directories or patterns, we can call `suite` multiple times, adding the tests to a suite before running them all together.

We'll have more to say about grouping tests into suites and running test suites when we look at IDE, Gradle, and Maven integration later in this chapter, but first let's look at scaling up your test input data.

17.4.2 *Parameterized or data-driven testing*

JUnit 4, TestNG, and Spock (which we'll cover shortly) all provide facilities for data-driven tests. The following listing shows how to write such a test for JUnit 4.

Listing 17.6   Using `Parameterized` data with JUnit 4

```
import org.junit.Test
import org.junit.Test
import org.junit.runner.RunWith
```

```
import org.junit.runners.Parameterized
import org.junit.runners.Parameterized.Parameters
import static Converter.celsius

@RunWith(Parameterized)
class Listing_17_06_DataDrivenJUnitTest {
  private c, f, scenario

  @Parameters static scenarios() {[
      [0,   32,  'Freezing'],
      [20,  68,  'Garden party conditions'],
      [35,  95,  'Beach conditions'],
      [100, 212, 'Boiling']
  ]*.toArray() }

  Listing_17_06_DataDrivenJUnitTest(c, f, scenario) {
    this.c = c
    this.f = f
    this.scenario = scenario
  }

  @Test void convert() {
    def actual = celsius(f)
    def msg = "$scenario: ${f}°F should convert into ${c}°C"
    assert c == actual, msg
  }
}
```

1 Special test runner

2 Array of test data

3 Constructor parameters consume a row of test data

JUnit uses the `Parameterized` test runner **1** to invoke data-driven tests. The `@Parameter` annotation **2** earmarks an array of test data. The test class constructor **3** is parameterized so that its parameters match one row of test data.

Our example used a hard-coded array of test values, but there's no reason this couldn't have come from a file, Excel spreadsheet, or database. TestNG and Spock also have similar capabilities. Before leaving this topic, we want to look at a technique you can use to write many fewer tests with potentially large sets of auto-generated test data.

17.4.3 Property-based testing

When applying agile developer practices, such as TDD, and working with imperative code, we often end up playing a little game. We try to work out the minimum tests we can write to steer the design of the production code being produced to have the desired "business" functionality but also to achieve 100% code coverage.[9] It makes perfect sense. Because we know a little bit about our implementation's internal workings, we craft our tests to cover every branch—effectively validating the assumptions we make in each and every part of our implementation. An effective pair programmer will try to bring any hidden assumptions about the implementation to the surface. Best to deal with such assumptions up front and not when they become an issue in production.

---

[9] For the impatient, you don't have long to wait to learn more; we'll cover that topic in the next section.

When working with functional languages this practice is rarely used, at least not in the same way. A slightly different slant is often taken on the testing process. Instead of trying to test assumptions about inner workings, the focus is about validating the external behavior of the code. Are there any hidden assumptions about its behavior that might cause unexpected results in the future? In this context, *property-based testing* as a concept has arisen and flourished.

With property-based testing, we try to establish expected properties of part of our system. We then hit it with a large amount of input data and see if those properties hold. As an example consider this code:

```
@Grab('net.java.quickcheck:quickcheck:0.6')
import static net.java.quickcheck.generator.PrimitiveGenerators.*
import static net.java.quickcheck.generator.CombinedGeneratorsIterables.*

for (words in someNonEmptyLists(strings())) {
    assert words*.size().sum() == words.sum().size()
}
```

Here, we use two inbuilt generators from the QuickCheck for Java library: one that produces arbitrary strings and another one that produces non-empty lists of items from another generator. Putting them together, we get lists of non-empty strings.

The *property* or *invariant* that we want to hold is that if we take any such list and concatenate all the strings and find the length of the concatenated string, then we should get the same value that we would obtain by finding the length of each individual string and summing the lengths together. This makes sure nothing is lost (or incorrectly added) when we concatenate strings together.

We can use the same library and apply that same concept to our temperature converter as shown in the following listing.

Listing 17.7   Property-based testing using QuickCheck for Java with Groovy

```
@Grab('net.java.quickcheck:quickcheck:0.6')
import static net.java.quickcheck.generator.PrimitiveGenerators.*
import static java.lang.Math.round
import static Converter.celsius

def gen = integers(-40, 240)          ❶  Selects integers
def liquidC =  0..100                      from this range
def liquidF = 32..212
100.times {                           ❷  Gets the next
    int f = gen.next()                     integer        ❸  Celsius less
    int c = round(celsius(f))                                 than Fahrenheit
    assert c <= f                                             (above -40 degrees)
    assert c in liquidC == f in liquidF   ❹
}                                          Water should be
                                     ❹  liquid in this range
```

We use a generator, in this case for integers ❶, to provide a random set of test values for the temperature in Fahrenheit. Then looping 100 times, we obtain the next temperature from the generator ❷ and pass it through the converter.

In general at this point, we need a way to determine if the result we got was correct. We manually created the expected value when doing TDD, but here we won't have that option. We could have an oracle of some kind, perhaps another algorithm we know produces the correct result but may be too slow to use in production, or perhaps a database of correct answers is available. But in general with property-based testing, we give up on the goal of trying to validate fixed *values*. Instead we'll check that certain *properties* hold.

For our converter we'll check two properties:

- That the Celsius value is smaller than or equal to the Fahrenheit value ❸ which holds true for temperatures above -40 degrees. That conveniently matches what our generator is producing.
- That any Fahrenheit temperature and its converted Celsius value pass a little sanity check. We know the range of temperatures in which water is a liquid for both Fahrenheit and Celsius scales.[10] A Fahrenheit temperature corresponding to the liquid phase, once converted, should be in the liquid range we know for Celsius and vice versa ❹.

Each time we run the test, it uses 100 different random test values, so over time we'll get increasingly good data coverage of our system.[11] While our water liquidity test might seem a little strange, it reveals the nature of property-based testing. It's up to you to determine what properties are important in your system.

We used simple inbuilt generators in our examples. In general, if you dive into property-based testing, you'll likely create your own generators and combine your own generators with the provided ones to build composite generators. The end result of using property-based testing is that you'll end up having much fewer data values encoded in your tests, which eases refactoring and maintenance.

This approach to testing can feel "harder" as long as its underlying functional thinking is unfamiliar. The benefit is that you're led to detect behavioral characteristics of your system by making them explicit in your tests. Writing such tests is often an enlightening experience.

As you can see, property-based testing is a powerful technique available in our testing toolbox. Speaking of useful techniques, let's examine a few more advanced techniques, which you'll also want to stash away in a corner of your Groovy testing toolbox.

17.5 *Advanced testing techniques*

Let's switch into "Groovy expert mode" and look at advanced testing techniques. Several of the techniques will help you test hard-to-test systems by leveraging Groovy's dynamic nature. You'll also learn how to gain knowledge about your test coverage and

---

[10] We're keeping the underlying science nice and simple for this example.
[11] And if needed, many property-based libraries have ways to seed the randomness for repeatable tests.

about the performance of small parts of your system in isolation. Let's start with exploring why systems can be hard to test.

Automated testing is easy if you develop your automated tests in close interplay with your production code, because you immediately design your system for testability. Unfortunately, this level of test awareness isn't universal, and you'll sometimes find yourself in the position where you have to write tests for code that already exists. This is when you need advanced testing techniques, the same way you'd need a more specialized tool than a dinner fork to efficiently extract a single strand of spaghetti from a bowl of pasta.

A number of bad programming habits can make testing difficult. One is writing incoherent classes and methods that do more than they should, resulting in overly long classes and methods. Even worse is code with many dependencies to other classes that we'll call *collaborators*. Unit testing your *subject under test* (SUT) in its purist form means that you test it in isolation without the collaborators so you're focused on finding errors in your code.[12]

The first set of advanced testing techniques we're about to explore is mainly concerned with replacing such collaborators for the purpose of unit testing the SUT in isolation. To that end, we first show how you can employ Groovy's core language features to provide "fake" collaborators. We then explore Groovy's special support for so-called stubs and mocks, which allow flexible simulation of collaborator behavior, as well as let you specify exactly *how* the collaborators must be used. We finish our first wave of techniques by considering an approach that can be used when all else fails: using logs to test that your classes are behaving as you expect them to.

17.5.1 *Testing made groovy*

Once, I (Dierk) gave a lecture on unit testing where I asked the audience to challenge me with the most difficult testing problem they could think of, something they believed would be impossible to unit test. Their proposal was to test the load-balancer of a server farm. How could we test this in Groovy?

The core logic of a load balancer is to relay a received request to the machine in the server farm that currently has the lowest load. Suppose we already have collaborator classes that describe *requests*, *machines*, and the *farm*; a Groovy load balancer could have the following method:

```
def relay(request, farm) {
    farm.machines.sort { it.load }[0].send(request)
}
```

The method finds the machine with the lowest load by sorting all machines in the farm by the load property, taking the first one, and calling the send method on that machine object.

---

[12] Other kinds of integration tests should pick up errors that come from integrating your code with the collaborators.

To unit test this logic, we need to somehow call the `relay` method to verify its behavior. We can do this only if we have `request` and `farm` objects, but we don't want our test to depend on any of the production collaborator classes. Luckily, our Groovy solution doesn't demand any specific types, and we can use any type we fancy.

What would be a good object to use for the `farm` parameter? Thanks to Groovy's duck typing of the relay parameters, any object that we can ask for a `machines` property will do—a map for example. The `machines` property, in turn, needs to be something that can be *sorted* by a `load` property and understands the `send(request)` method. Listing 17.8 follows this route by testing the load balancer logic with a map-based farm of fake machines made using a `FakeMachine` class. Fake machines return a self-reference from their send method to allow subsequent asserts to verify that the send method was called on the expected machine.

Listing 17.8 Unit-testing a load balancer with Groovy collaborator replacements

```
import static org.junit.Assert.assertSame

def relay(request, farm) {                              Subject
    farm.machines.sort { it.load }[0].send(request)     under test
}

class FakeMachine {                          Replacement
    def load                                 class
    def send(request) { return this }
}

final LOW_LOAD = 5, HIGH_LOAD = 10
def farm = [machines: [                      Map
    new FakeMachine(load:HIGH_LOAD),         replaces
    new FakeMachine(load:LOW_LOAD)]]         farm

assertSame(LOW_LOAD, relay(null, farm).load)
```

Note that we don't need to create a special stub for the `request` parameter. Because it's relayed and no methods are ever called on it, `null` is fine.

The important point about the previous listing is that the load-balancing logic is tested in full isolation. No accidental change to any of the collaborator classes can possibly affect this test. When this test fails, we can be sure that the load-balancing logic and nothing else is in trouble.

17.5.2 Stubbing and mocking

Until now, our load balancer was fairly easy to test in isolation because we could feed all collaborator objects into the `relay` method. That wasn't a real challenge. Things get more interesting when we need to replace objects that cannot be set from the outside.[13]

---

[13] In UML terms: when the collaborator is *composed*, not *aggregated*.

EXAMPLE PROBLEM: COLLABORATOR CONSTRUCTION

Suppose our load balancer directly creates its collaborator `farm` object:

```
def relay(request) {
    new Farm().getMachines().sort { it.load }[0].send(request)
}
```

The Farm class looks like this:

```
class Farm {
    def getMachines() {
        /* some expensive code here */
    }
}
```

From an implementer's perspective, such a solution could be justifiable for a number of reasons. Perhaps the `Farm`'s `getMachines` method provides support for finding all machines via a network scan and then caches that information. Anyway, we wouldn't want to perform an expensive operation if we didn't need it, so placing the `new Farm().getMachines()` statement within `relay` seems like the way to go. From a tester's perspective, however, even allowing for potential caching, calling the real code is going to be too expensive an operation for a unit-test environment, where tests should execute in the blink of an eye if developers are expected to run them often. Also, we need to run our tests even when no real machines are available.

The implementation isn't easily testable. We can't use the fake implementation techniques in the way you saw earlier, because we have no way to sneak such a subclass into our subject under test. One common trick when testing would be to subclass `Farm`. That won't help us here either, for the same reasons. Should we give up? No!

STUBBING OUT THE COLLABORATOR

Groovy's Meta-Object capabilities come to the rescue in the form of Groovy stubs. The trick provided by Groovy stubs is to intercept all method calls to instances of a given class (`Farm` in this case) and return a predefined result. Here's how it works.

We first construct a *stub* object for calls to the `Farm` class:

```
import groovy.mock.interceptor.StubFor

def farmStub = new StubFor(Farm)
```

Next, we create two fake machines to help define our expectations from the stub:

```
def fakeOne = new Expando(load:10, send: { false } )
def fakeTwo = new Expando(load:5,  send: { true } )
```

Then, we demand that when the `getMachines` method is called on our stub, our fake machines are returned. Registering this behavior is done by calling the respective method on the stub's `demand` property and passing a closure argument to define the behavior:

```
farmStub.demand.getMachines { [fakeOne, fakeTwo] }
```

Finally, we pass our test code as a closure to the stub's use method. This ensures that the stub is in charge when the test is executed: any call to any `Farm` object will be intercepted and handled by our stub. The full test scenario is given in the following listing.

Listing 17.9 Using Groovy stubs to test an otherwise untestable load balancer

```
import groovy.mock.interceptor.StubFor

def relay(request) {
    new Farm().getMachines().sort { it.load }[0].send(request)
}

def fakeOne = new Expando(load:10, send: { false } )          Creates
def fakeTwo = new Expando(load:5,  send: { true } )           stub

def farmStub = new StubFor(Farm)
farmStub.demand.getMachines { [fakeOne, fakeTwo ] }           Specifies
                                                              demanded
farmStub.use {                                                behavior
    assert relay(null)        Calls the class under
}                             test using stub
```

Note that for the use of Groovy stubs, it makes no difference whether the collaborator class is written in Java or Groovy. The class under test, however, must be a Groovy class.

STUB EXPECTATIONS

Groovy stubs support a flexible specification of the demanded behavior. To demand calls to different methods, do so in sequence:

```
someStub.demand.methodOne { 1 }
someStub.demand.methodTwo { 2 }
```

When calls to the stubbed method should yield different results per call, add the respective demands in sequence:

```
someStub.demand.methodOne { 1 }
someStub.demand.methodOne { 2 }
```

You can provide a range to specify how often the demanded closure should apply; the default is (1..1):

```
someStub.demand.methodOne(0..35) { 1 }
```

Finally, it's also possible to react to the method argument that the SUT passes to the collaborator's method. Each argument of the method call is passed into the demand closure and can thus be evaluated inside it. Suppose you expect that the stubbed method is called only with even numbers, and you'd like to assert that *invariant* while testing. You can achieve this with

```
someStub.demand.methodOne {
    number -> assert 0 == number % 2
    return 1
}
```

Of course, you can also combine all these kinds of demand declarations, producing an elaborate specification of call sequences on the collaborator and returned values. The more elaborate that specification is, the more likely it is that you'll want to also assert that all demanded method calls happened. For stubs, this isn't asserted by default, but you can enforce this check by calling

```
someStub.expect.verify()
```

after the use closure.

Stubs use a `LooseExpectation` for verifying the demanded method calls. It's called *loose* because it only verifies that all demanded methods were called, not whether they were called in the sequence of the specification.

COMPARING STUBS AND MOCKS

Strict expectations are used with *mocks*. A mock object has all the behavior of a stub and more. The strict expectation of a mock verifies that all the demanded method calls happen in exactly the sequence of the specification. The first method call that breaks this sequence causes the test to fail immediately. Also, with mocks you have no need to explicitly call the `verify` method, because that happens by default when the use closure ends.

At first glance, it appears that mocks and stubs are almost the same thing, with mocks being a bit more rigorous. But a deep fundamental difference exists in the purpose behind their use:[14] Stubs enable your SUT to run in isolation and allow you to make assertions about state changes of the SUT. With mocks, the test focus moves to the interplay of the SUT and its collaborators. What gets asserted is whether the SUT follows a specified *protocol* when talking with the outside world. A protocol defines the rules that the SUT has to obey when calling the collaborator. Typical rules would be: the first method call must be `init`, the last method call must be `close`, and so on.

Consider a new variant of our load balancer that uses a `SortableFarm` class, which provides a `sort` method to change its internal representation of machines such that any subsequent call to `getMachines` returns them sorted by load:

```
class SortableFarm extends Farm {
    def sort() {
        /* here the Farm would sort its machines by load */
    }
}
```

Our SUT now has to follow a certain protocol when using `SortableFarm`: first sort must be called, and then `getMachines`:

```
def relay(request) {
    def farm = new SortableFarm()
    farm.sort()
    farm.getMachines()[0].send(request)
}
```

---

[14] See www.martinfowler.com/articles/mocksArentStubs.html for more details.

Listing 17.10 uses a mock as constructed with the `MockFor` class to verify that our SUT exactly follows this protocol. Only the compliance to the protocol is tested and nothing else; for this special test, we don't even verify that the call is relayed to the machine with the lowest load.

Listing 17.10   Using Groovy mock support to verify protocol compliance

```
import groovy.mock.interceptor.MockFor

class SortableFarm extends Farm {
    void sort() {
        /* here the Farm would sort its machines by load */
    }
}

def relay(request) {
    def farm = new SortableFarm()
    farm.sort()
    farm.getMachines()[0].send(request)
}

def farmMock = new MockFor(SortableFarm)          ← Creates mock

farmMock.demand.sort(){}                           Specifies demanded
farmMock.demand.getMachines { [new Expando(send: {} )] }   behavior

farmMock.use {
    relay(null)
}
```

If you're unfamiliar with mock objects, protocol-based testing (also called interaction-based testing) will probably appear strange to you. In traditional testing, we tend to focus on state changes and return values rather than on the effects caused to collaborating objects. In particular cases, interactions with collaborators are implementation details and shouldn't be tested. If they are part of the object's guaranteed behavior, mock testing is appropriate.

Groovy's clever way of providing stubs and mocks even for objects that cannot be passed to the SUT is a double-edged sword. Testing should lead you into a design of high coherence and low coupling. Without resorting to clever Java tricks, Java mocks work only if you can pass them to the SUT, forcing you to expose the collaborator, which usually leads to a more flexible design. Groovy has no such restriction, because you can more easily test even a rotten design. The implication is that Groovy won't stop you from building a less-flexible design even when using the latest development practices.

Conversely, Java projects often suffer from the deadlock that appears when developers find large sections of untestable code. They cannot easily refactor such a section of code because it has no tests. They cannot easily write tests without refactoring the code to make it more testable. With Groovy's built-in mocking facilities, you have a better chance of escaping this deadlock.

17.5.3 *Using GroovyLogTestCase*

Sometimes, even with stubs and mocks, testing a particular object can be difficult. The amount of work involved in setting up all the mocked interactions in a tricky scenario may outweigh the benefits of your testing efforts. To be realistic, if your system (and resulting tests) is that complex, perhaps you have a bug in your tests. In such cases, another useful feature provided by Groovy is GroovyLogTestCase. You saw in listing 17.2 that it was relatively easy to test the fictitious countHowManyBiggerThan calculator. Suppose, though, that it was much harder to test. We could resort to writing information to a log file, and then we could manually check the log file to see if it appears to contain the correct information. In these scenarios, GroovyLogTestCase can be extremely useful. Consider the following modified LoggingCounter:

```
import java.util.logging.*

class LoggingCounter {
    static final LOG = Logger.getLogger('LoggingCounter')
    def biggerThan(items, target) {
        def count = 0
        items.each{
            if (it > target) {
                count++
                LOG.finer "item was bigger - count this one"
            } else if (it == target) {
                LOG.finer "item was equal - don't count this one"
            } else {
                LOG.finer "item was smaller - don't count this one"
            }
        }
        return count
    }
}
```

Note that the calculator outputs log messages for each of three scenarios: the item being tested was smaller than, equal to, or bigger than the target value. We can now test this class with the assistance of GroovyLogTestCase, as shown in the following listing.

> **Listing 17.11 Using GroovyLogTestCase for tricky cases**

```
import java.util.logging.Level

class Listing_17_11_LoggingCounterTest extends GroovyLogTestCase {
    static final MIXED_NUMBERS = [99, 2, 1, 0, -1, -2, -99]          ◁─┘ Test data
    private count

    void setUp() {                                                    Sets up
        count = new LoggingCounter()                                  stringLog
    }

    void testCounterAndLog() {                                        Invokes SUT
        def log = stringLog(Level.FINER, 'LoggingCounter') {    ◁──┘
            def bigger = count.biggerThan(MIXED_NUMBERS, -1)    ◁──         Traditional
            assertEquals(4, bigger)                             ◁─┘        JUnit style
        }                                                                  assert
```

```
        checkLogCount(1, "was equal", log)
        checkLogCount(4, "was bigger", log)
        checkLogCount(2, "was smaller", log)
        checkLogCount(4, /[^d][^o][^n][^'][^t] count this one/, log)
        checkLogCount(3, "don't count this one", log)
    }

    private checkLogCount(expectedCount, regex, log) {        ◁─┐  Helper method
        def matcher = (log =~ regex)                             │  asserting patterns
        assertTrue log, expectedCount == matcher.count           │  within the log
    }
}
```

If you look at the test data in the MIXED_NUMBERS list, you expect four entries to be bigger than -1, two to be smaller, and one to be the same. Log messages corresponding to these cases will be stored in the log variable thanks to the stringLog statement. Our test then uses regular expressions to ensure that the log contains the correct number of each kind of log message.

GroovyLogTestCase makes use of the *Log String* testing pattern[15] in a test scenario that would otherwise be cumbersome and error-prone to implement. It relieves you of the work of setting the appropriate log levels and registering string appenders for the SUT logger. After the test, it cleans up properly and restores the old logging configuration.

That finishes our wave of techniques for tackling hard-to-test systems. Up next we look at performance testing.

17.5.4 *Unit testing performance*

There may be many performance characteristics of your system that are important and worthy of being tested. But in the context of this chapter, we'll limit ourselves to looking at one library that lets you perform simple load and performance tests at the unit test level. JUnitPerf is an extension framework for JUnit that offers the ability to ascertain fine-grained performance and scalability of your objects and its methods. For instance, JUnitPerf enables scenarios such as "the findTrades method must return a list of Trade objects within one second and the test fails if it performs too slowly (even if the test did return a valid list of Trade objects)." The framework also adds scalability via threading. Using this scenario, you can add the requirement that under a load of 100 invocations, the findTrades method must return a collection of Trade objects within one second.

Understandably, there are scenarios within Groovy where this type of framework could come in handy:

- Testing the performance and scalability of Groovy applications
- Testing the performance and scalability of normal Java code in tests *written in Groovy*

---

[15] Described in chapter 27 of *Test-Driven Development: By Example.*

Using JUnitPerf with Groovy can be a little tricky. JUnitPerf is a decorator-based framework. It decorates test cases by individually wrapping them with a decorator. This is typically done within a `suite` method. Groovy's `GroovyTestSuite` and `AllTestSuite` test runners, however, ignore `suite` definitions and provide alternative mechanisms for determining which tests to run.

To allow JUnitPerf to work with Groovy involves following a few simple steps. First, you need a way to select a single JUnit test that you want to decorate. If you look at JUnit's `TestCase` class, you'll notice that it provides a constructor that takes the name of a test method and allows a single test case to be selected. We can make use of this for JUnitPerf by declaring a constructor that takes a method name and have it call `super(testName)`:

```
Listing_17_12_JUnitPerf(String testName) {
  super(testName)
}
```

Then we create a `suite` method that defines a test case using this constructor:

```
static Test suite() {
  def testCase = new Listing_17_12_JUnitPerf("testConverter")
  // decorate testCase and return decorated version
}
```

Now we can apply the appropriate decorators on the test case according to JUnitPerf's documentation for load and stress testing scenarios:

```
def loadTest = new LoadTest(testCase, numUsers, stagger)
```

It sounds complicated, but really it's the same steps you'd follow to use JUnitPerf in Java. As an example, the next listing utilizes JUnitPerf to test our temperature converter. It verifies that invoking `testConverter` 20 times in concurrent threads (with each thread staggered by 100 milliseconds) returns within 2100 milliseconds.

Listing 17.12   Using JUnitPerf decorators to perform load and time tests

```
@Grab('junitperf:junitperf:1.9.1')
@GrabResolver('https://repository.jboss.org/')
import com.clarkware.junitperf.*
import junit.framework.*
import junit.textui.TestRunner
import static Converter.celsius

class Listing_17_12_JUnitPerf extends TestCase {
  Listing_17_12_JUnitPerf(String testName) {
    super(testName)                            ← Calls super
  }

  void testConverter() {            ← Traditional nontimed JUnit test
    assert 0 == celsius(32)       Class under test
    assert 100 == celsius(212)
  }
```

```
                static main(args) {
                  TestRunner.run(suite())
                }

                static Test suite() {                              ┐  Defines
                  def testCase = new Listing_17_12_JUnitPerf("testConverter")  ◄─┘  test case

  Decorates
test case to      def numUsers = 20                                ┐  20 users for load
 simulate         def stagger = new ConstantTimer(100)             │  staggered at 100 ms
    load  └─▷     def loadTest = new LoadTest(testCase, numUsers, stagger)

                  def timeLimit = 2100                          ◄─┐  Must return
                  return new TimedTest(loadTest, timeLimit)  ◄─┐     within 2100 ms
                }                                              │
              }                                   Returns decorated
                                                  time-constrained test
```

When you run this program, you should see output indicating that the program is running your tests, followed by the time it took to complete the tests. Because there are 20 users starting 100 ms apart, we expect the test to run for at least 2 seconds. If the time is less than 2.1 seconds, then the test will be successful:

```
...................TimedTest (WAITING): LoadTest (NON-ATOMIC):
ThreadedTest: testConverter(Listing_17_12_JUnitPerf): 2014 ms
Time: 2.014
OK (20 tests)
```

If the test takes too long to run (suppose we expect it to complete in 2.01 seconds), it will fail:

```
There was 1 failure:
1) LoadTest (NON-ATOMIC): ThreadedTest:
testConverter(Listing_17_12_JUnitPerf)junit.framework.AssertionFailedError:
Maximum elapsed time exceeded! Expected 2010
ms, but was 2020ms.
```

The next time you need to figure out the performance of Groovy code or you want to test the performance and scalability of your Java application with Groovy, give JUnitPerf a try!

17.5.5 *Code coverage with Groovy*

Code-coverage tools are now a mainstream part of any serious Java engineer's toolkit. They provide useful feedback on how well your testing efforts are going. To leverage any existing Java code coverage tool for Groovy, you need to compile your Groovy into bytecode and then run the tool as before.

If you're interested in the coverage of your Groovy code and you try this technique with an older coverage tool, you'll probably not have the ability to see reports indicating which lines of code were executed, because the tool or its reporting infrastructure doesn't know about Groovy source files.

The good news is that efforts are being made to provide native Groovy support in code-coverage tools. One open source tool that has gained Groovy support is Cobertura (http://cobertura.sourceforge.net).

Cobertura works in a similar way to many other coverage tools for the JDK.[16] During the build process, it modifies our bytecode so that later when our code executes, it will write out information about which code paths have been executed. This information will be stored away in a form suitable for later processing by the coverage tool reporting.

Consider the following Groovy class:[17]

```
class BiggestPairCalc {
  int sumBiggestPair(a, b, c) {
    def op1 = a
    def op2 = b
    if (c > a) {
      op1 = c
    } else if (c > b) {
      op2 = c
    }
    return op1 + op2
  }
}
```

Here's a test for this code:

```
class BiggestPairCalcTest extends GroovyTestCase {
    void testSumBiggestPair() {
        def calc = new BiggestPairCalc()
        assertEquals(9, calc.sumBiggestPair(5, 4, 1))
    }
}
```

At this stage, we could run our test and make sure it passes. To get coverage, however, requires a few extra steps. We used a Gradle build file to capture these steps. The entire build file, build.gradle,[18] is fairly simple and looks like the following:

```
plugins {
  id 'net.saliman.cobertura' version '2.2.6'
}

apply plugin: 'groovy'

repositories {
  mavenCentral()
}

dependencies {
  compile 'org.codehaus.groovy:groovy-all:2.4.0'
  testCompile 'junit:junit:4.12'
}
```

---

[16] But tools such as Clover actually hook into Groovy's compiler phases.

[17] If we were trying to be really Groovy, we could write [a,b,c].sort()[-2..-1].sum(), but that would have made it harder to show some lines covered and some not!

[18] Within the cobertura directory of the book's sample code.

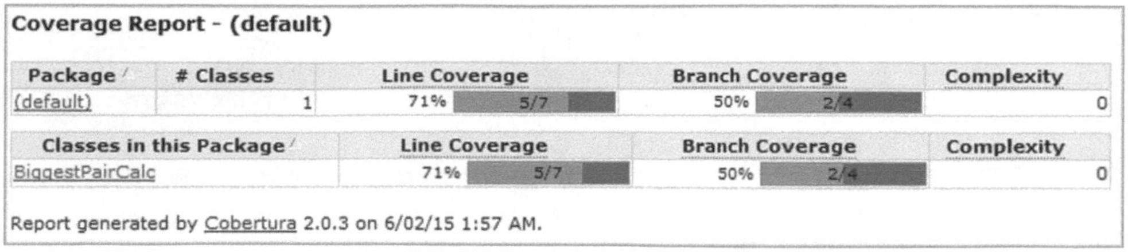

Coverage Report - (default)

Package	# Classes	Line Coverage	Branch Coverage	Complexity
(default)	1	71% 5/7	50% 2/4	0

Classes in this Package	Line Coverage	Branch Coverage	Complexity
BiggestPairCalc	71% 5/7	50% 2/4	0

Report generated by Cobertura 2.0.3 on 6/02/15 1:57 AM.

Figure 17.1 Cobertura code-coverage summary report

The Cobertura plugin makes numerous tasks available to Gradle. The one we want is `gradle cobertura`. This will compile our code, execute our tests, and generate a Cobertura report as shown in figure 17.1. Note that nothing special was required to get the Groovy coverage. All Java classes (if any) and Groovy classes in our project will be part of the coverage analysis.

If we go deeper into the report by clicking an appropriate link for one of our source files, we can see which lines are covered by tests. Figure 17.2 shows that lines 6 and 8 are not covered yet by tests and 5 and 7 are only partially covered.

Now that we can see where we're missing coverage, we can add more tests to our test method:

```
assertEquals(15, calc.sumBiggestPair( 5, 9, 6))
assertEquals(16, calc.sumBiggestPair(10, 2, 6))
```

We can run the tests to make sure they all still work and then check the coverage again to see how our coverage is going. The result is shown in figure 17.3.

Is the code correct? The tests all pass, and we have 100% coverage—that means we don't have any bugs, right? For fun, let's add one more test:

```
assertEquals(11, calc.sumBiggestPair(5, 2, 6))
```

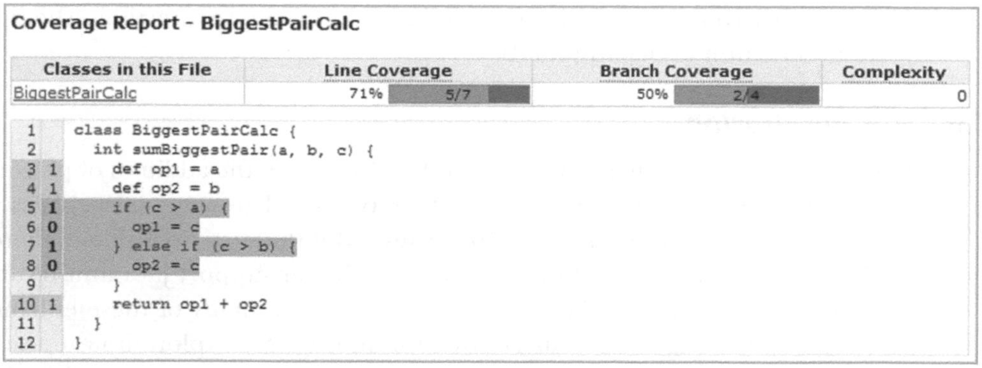

Coverage Report - BiggestPairCalc

Classes in this File	Line Coverage	Branch Coverage	Complexity
BiggestPairCalc	71% 5/7	50% 2/4	0

```
1     class BiggestPairCalc {
2       int sumBiggestPair(a, b, c) {
3  1      def op1 = a
4  1      def op2 = b
5  1      if (c > a) {
6  0        op1 = c
7  1      } else if (c > b) {
8  0        op2 = c
9         }
10 1      return op1 + op2
11      }
12    }
```

Figure 17.2 Cobertura code-coverage file report showing partial coverage

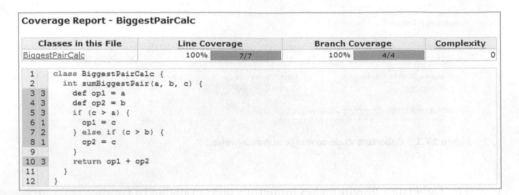

Figure 17.3 Cobertura code-coverage file report showing full coverage

If we run our tests again, they now fail! There was an error in our original algorithm. That was nothing to do with Groovy, but is a reminder that coverage is a necessary but not sufficient condition to show that you have all the tests that you need. We can fix the calculator as shown in figure 17.3.

```
int sumBiggestPair(int a, int b, int c) {
    int op1 = a
    int op2 = b
    if (c > [a,b].min()) {
        op1 = c
        op2 = [a,b].max()
    }
    return op1 + op2
}
```

Now we can run all our tests. They should all pass, and Cobertura should report 100% coverage.

You have seen that Groovy makes even advanced testing techniques easily available through core language features. The running theme of improving developer convenience with Groovy finds its logical continuation in the next section, where we integrate Groovy unit testing in Java IDEs.

17.6 *IDE integration*

In section 1.6, you saw that several major Java IDEs (with the addition of plug-ins) have useful support for editing and running Groovy code. The same mechanisms are suitable for editing and running your Groovy tests. But the story doesn't end there.

Java IDEs often have additional features to better support Java unit testing, such as enhanced test runners. Fortunately, you'll see that many of these enhanced features can be leveraged for your Groovy unit testing. We explore how to use the two test suite classes you saw earlier within an IDE, before taking a brief look at how

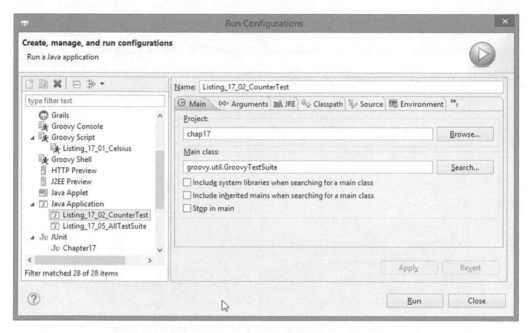

Figure 17.4   Eclipse run configuration for `Main` tab using `GroovyTestSuite`

Groovy's close relationship with Java allows it to be used with cutting-edge IDE testing features.

17.6.1 *Using GroovyTestSuite*

While editing a Groovy test file within your IDE, you can run it like any other Groovy file. Eclipse users with the Groovy plug-in installed might right-click, select Run As, and then select Groovy. IntelliJ IDEA users with the Groovy plug-in installed might press Ctrl-Shift-F10. In both cases, the corresponding tests within the current file would run. If your Groovy file was several `assert` statements in a script file, as in listing 17.1, then you wouldn't see any output—this is expected because `assert` statements make noise only when something goes wrong. If you don't want to run your tests individually or want additional feedback when running your tests, `GroovyTest-Suite` may be what you're after.

In section 17.4, you saw that `GroovyTestSuite` could be used to invoke a Groovy test from the command line. You also saw how it could be used to add Groovy files into a standard JUnit suite.[19] We now look at another way to use `GroovyTestSuite`: as part of an IDE run configuration. Figure 17.4 shows how to configure Eclipse to use

---

[19] Test suites remain an important concept you typically use in conjunction with other IDE integration.

Name: Listing_17_02_CounterTest

ⓖ Main (x)= Arguments ▣ JRE ⚙ Classpath ⬚ Source ▦ Environment ⬚ Common

Program arguments:

```
Listing_17_02_CounterTest.groovy
```

Variables...

VM arguments:

Variables...

Working directory:
- ○ Default: ${workspace_loc:chap17}
- ● Other: ${workspace_loc:chap17}

Workspace...   File System...   Variables...

Figure 17.5 Eclipse run configuration for the Arguments tab using GroovyTestSuite

GroovyTestSuite as part of a run configuration. Select Run -> Run, and create a new Java Application configuration. Set the Project to be your current project, and select groovy.util.GroovyTestSuite as the Main class.

Next, click the Arguments tab; in the Program Arguments box, include the path to your Groovy script, as shown in figure 17.5.

When you run this configuration, you should see output similar to that shown in figure 17.6.

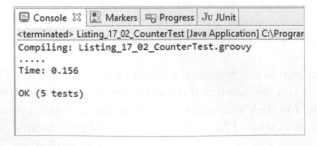

```
🖵 Console ✕  Markers  Progress  Ju JUnit
<terminated> Listing_17_02_CounterTest [Java Application] C:\Progran
Compiling: Listing_17_02_CounterTest.groovy
.....
Time: 0.156

OK (5 tests)
```

Figure 17.6 Eclipse GroovyTestSuite example run output

Users of JUnit's text-based runner should now feel at home and will see a bit more feedback than the previously empty output.

17.6.2 *Using AllTestSuite*

JUnit's green/red bar reporting mechanism found in graphical test runners can be addictive when you are "in the groove." The default behavior of Groovy's `GroovyTestSuite`, however, doesn't easily fit into the graphical runner model, because those runners usually prefer to run normal Java classes, rather than Groovy files.

One strategy is to rely on `groovyc` to compile all test cases and then run them via a Java-aware GUI runner; however, that takes an extra step. It's more fun to see the green bar *immediately* after coding! This is where `AllTestSuite`, which we discussed in section 17.7, really shines. In addition to its uses for organizing your tests into suites, `AllTestSuite` can also be used as part of configuring your test runs.

To configure Eclipse to use `AllTestSuite`, create a new JUnit run configuration, select your project, and set the Test class to `groovy.util.AllTestSuite`, as shown in figure 17.7.

Then, in the Arguments tab, define two properties that tell `AllTestSuite` which Groovy tests to run. These properties need to be supplied as two `VM` Arguments. The properties need to be adjusted for your system but will look something like `-Dgroovy`

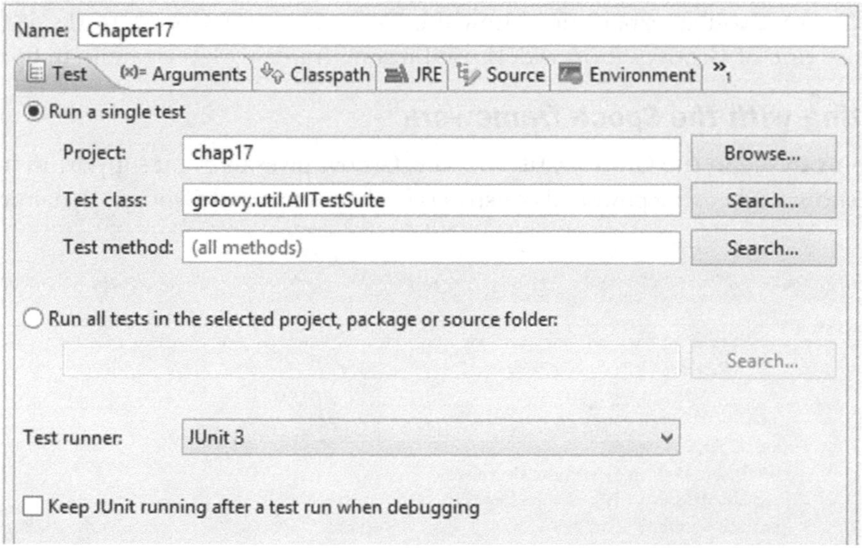

Figure 17.7   Eclipse `AllTestSuite` run configuration Test tab

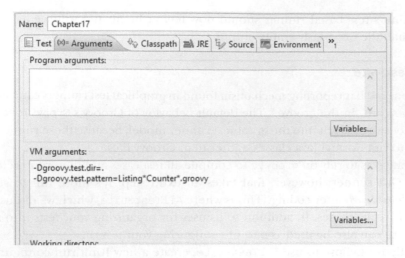

Figure 17.8   Eclipse `AllTestSuite` run configuration Arguments tab

`.test.dir=.` for the directory and `-Dgroovy.test.pattern=Listing*Counter*.groovy` for the filename pattern. Your configuration will be similar to that shown in figure 17.8.

When you run this configuration, you should see the familiar green and red bars, as shown in figure 17.9. We don't have time to illustrate how to set up other IDEs, but you'll see IntelliJ IDEA screenshots when we cover Spock.

Now that you've experienced how the IDE support for Groovy works, it's time to explore one of Groovy's most widely used testing framework—say hello to Spock.

17.7   Testing with the Spock framework

As you can see in the Groovy GDK chapter, Groovy gives us great support to more easily test our code using powerful constructs such as maps and Groovy's dynamic nature.

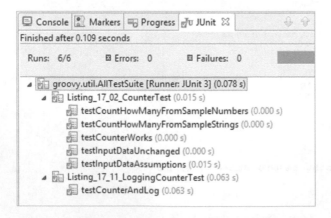

Figure 17.9   Eclipse `AllTestSuite` example test run output

The flexibility of the Groovy language made things possible that are often hard to do in the Java programming language.

We can go further in this and create an even more readable and compact test. Meet Spock (www.spockframework.org), a testing and specification framework for Java and Groovy applications. Spock supports a diversity of testing styles and one of the most well-known approaches is a Behavior-Driven Development (BDD)[20] style approach, characterized by its Given-When-Then format. The following listing introduces the Spock Given-When-Then style.

Listing 17.13   A simple Spock specification

```
@Grab('org.spockframework:spock-core:1.0-groovy-2.4')
import spock.lang.Specification

class GivenWhenThenSpec extends Specification {

  def "test adding a new item to a set"() {
    given:
    def items = [4, 6, 3, 2] as Set

    when:
    items << 1

    then:
    items.size() == 5
  }
}
```

What's most interesting to know is that the code in the previous listing is completely valid Groovy code and makes great use of the flexibility Groovy provides when writing software. Groovy labels are used to separate the Given-When-Then blocks. Also note that you can use spaces in the method name, a feature provided by Spock, which is implemented using an AST transformation.

In the setup part of the test, marked with the `given` label, we create a set of numbers. In the `when` part of the test we execute an action on our test subject. In our case, we add a number. Then, in the last part of the test, we check if the item has been added. Note that no assert statement is needed here to verify the result; all expressions in the `then` block are checked automatically for being true.

17.7.1   Testing with mocks

The test described in the previous section is a simple one. In the real world, the class you're testing usually has dependencies on other classes that can make testing often a bit trickier. Luckily, Spock provides excellent mocking[21] support.

---

[20] For more information, see http://en.wikipedia.org/wiki/Behavior-driven_development.

[21] For more information, see "Mocks Aren't Stubs," http://martinfowler.com/articles/mocksArentStubs.html.

Consider a more complex example. Instead of testing `java.util.Set`'s, we'll test the purchasing of movie tickets. It's a fairly simple domain model with a `MovieTheater` and a `Purchase` class. In this example, we'll mock out the `MovieTheater` and focus on the `Purchase` class.

Given those assumptions, let's use an interface as follows for the `MovieTheater`:

```
interface MovieTheater {
  void purchaseTicket(name, number)
  boolean hasSeatsAvailable(name, number)
}
```

In a separate test, when testing the `MovieTheater`, we wouldn't mock it out, but focus on the `MovieTheater` instead. In this case, the `MovieTheater` is a mock, and we'll validate that the `Purchase` will call the right methods when buying a movie ticket.

What should happen when the fill method is called on an instance of the `Purchase` class is that we should check if the theater has availability and, if so, buy a ticket. A skeleton for such a class is as follows:

```
@TupleConstructor
class Purchase {
  def name, number, completed = false

  def fill(theater) {
    if (theater.hasSeatsAvailable(name, number)) {
      theater.purchaseTicket(name, number)
      completed = true
    }
  }
}
```

With these definitions in place, we can now write our test, as shown in the following listing.

Listing 17.14 Testing with mocks

```
@Grab('org.spockframework:spock-core:1.0-groovy-2.4')
import spock.lang.Specification

class MovieSpec extends Specification {                    Creation of
  def "buy ticket for a movie theater"() {                 mock theater
    given:
    def purchase = new Purchase("Lord of the Rings", 2)
    MovieTheater theater = Mock()                          Mock hasSeats-
    theater.hasSeatsAvailable("Lord of the Rings", 2) >> true   Available call
                                                           returning true
    when:
    purchase.fill(theater)

    then:                                                  Assert
    purchase.completed                                     purchaseTicket has
    1 * theater.purchaseTicket("Lord of the Rings", 2)     been called one time
  }
}
```

In listing 17.14, you can see that the then block contains one assertion and one inter-action. An interaction consists of four distinct parts: a cardinality, a target constraint, a method constraint, and an argument constraint:

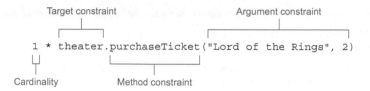

Diving into all options here goes a bit beyond the scope of this chapter, but if you want to learn more about Spock interactions, you can do so in the excellent documentation online.[22]

The next listing has a similar approach, but describes the case when all of the movies are sold out. There are no tickets for any movie. In the test, you see the usage of the Spock wildcard operator (_), which can be read as "any". In our test we don't care which movie is purchased; none are available, and because of this, no purchase can be completed.

Listing 17.15 Using wildcards to ignore arguments

```
@Grab('org.spockframework:spock-core:1.0-groovy-2.4')
import spock.lang.Specification

class Listing_17_15_SpockMockWildcards extends Specification {
  def "cannot buy a ticket when the movie is sold out"() {
    given:
    def purchase = new Purchase("Lord of the rings", 2)
    MovieTheater theater = Mock()

    when:
    theater.hasSeatsAvailable(_, _) >> false          ← Mock hasSeatsAvailable
    purchase.fill(theater)                              call, any args, returns
                                                        false

    then:                                             ← The purchaseTicket
    !purchase.completed                                 method has not
    0 * theater.purchaseTicket(_, _)                    been called
  }
}
```

To create a bit more flexibility, we can also use wildcard matchers in combination with Groovy closures. The closure can be used to check the argument passed to the method, failing the test if the argument doesn't match. In listing 17.16, one such approach is demonstrated. Here we basically have the same scenario as listing 17.14 but this one runs as part of a special "couples night" scenario we're trying to test. As part of this scenario, we might not care what movies are watched, only that the tickets are sold in

---

[22] For more information, see http://docs.spockframework.org/.

pairs. We'll ignore the first argument with a wildcard and check the second argument by injecting a closure ❶ that will validate the argument passed to the purchaseTicket method, as seen in the following listing.

Listing 17.16   Argument checking with injected closures

```
@Grab('org.spockframework:spock-core:1.0-groovy-2.4')
import spock.lang.Specification

class Listing_17_16_SpockMockClosureChecks extends Specification {
  def "on couples night tickets are sold in pairs"() {
    given:
    def purchase = new Purchase("Lord of the Rings", 2)
    MovieTheater theater = Mock()
    theater.hasSeatsAvailable("Lord of the Rings", 2) >> true

    when:
    purchase.fill(theater)

    then:
    1 * theater.purchaseTicket(_, { it % 2 == 0 })      ❶ Closure argument
  }                                                          checking
}
```

17.7.2 Data-driven Spock tests

In section 17.4 we looked briefly at data-driven tests. Spock also supports that approach and in fact has a special notation for capturing such test case data elegantly, as can be seen in the following listing.

Listing 17.17   Data-driven testing

```
@Grab('org.spockframework:spock-core:1.0-groovy-2.4')
import spock.lang.*

import static Converter.celsius

class Listing_17_17_SpockDataDriven extends Specification {
  def "test temperature scenarios"() {
    expect:
    celsius(tempF) == tempC

    where:
    scenario                   | tempF || tempC
    'Freezing'                 |    32 ||     0
    'Garden party conditions'  |    68 ||    20
    'Beach conditions'         |    95 ||    35
    'Boiling'                  |   212 ||   100
  }
}
```

A little syntactic sugar is going on here. Note that the variables defined in the where clause are automatically available in the expect block. Also, there's the use of the || symbol, which is used as a separator between input and output separators. Note that the || could have been replaced by the | symbol, but the || are used here to visually set them apart.

REPORTING FAILURES

But what if our implementation contains an error (we'll momentarily alter one figure), and we want to get feedback about it? In that case, the following output is:

```
Condition not satisfied:

celsius(tempF) == tempC
|       |       |  |
35      95      |  34
             false
```

It's a pretty clear explanation, but is it clear which iteration caused this error? Because we only have four iterations, it's not that hard to find out that iteration three caused the error, and we can easily fix that. In other cases, for example when dealing with external data, or when we have lots of data, the solution might be less obvious. To handle this, we can use the `@Unroll` annotation.

@UNROLL ANNOTATION

A method annotated with `@Unroll` will have its iterations reported independently. The test execution isn't changed; the only thing that has changed is how Spock reports each test iteration. We can annotate the method in the following way:

```
@Unroll
def "test temperature scenarios"() { … }
```

Executing the same test now using IntelliJ will produce the output shown in Figure 17.10.

As you can see in the figure, each test is now reported separately. With a small change, we can do even better though:

```
@Unroll
def "Scenario #scenario: #tempF°F should convert to #tempC°C"() { … }
```

When running the test now (again in IntelliJ), the report produced now looks as shown in Figure 17.11.

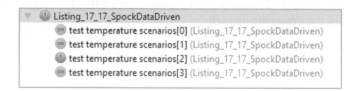

Figure 17.10   **IntelliJ IDEA** `Listing_17_17_SpockDataDriven` **test unrolled.**

> Listing_17_17_SpockDataDriven
>   Scenario Freezing: 32°F should convert to 0°C (Listing_17_17_SpockDataDriven)
>   Scenario Garden party conditions: 68°F should convert to 20°C (Listing_17_17_SpockDataDriven)
>   Scenario Beach conditions: 95°F should convert to 34°C (Listing_17_17_SpockDataDriven)
>   Scenario Boiling: 212°F should convert to 100°C (Listing_17_17_SpockDataDriven)

Figure 17.11   **IntelliJ IDEA** `Listing_17_17_SpockDataDriven` **test unrolled with parameter values.**

Now, the @Unroll annotation uses the method variables from the test. Using the placeholders, we can tell at a glance which iteration is causing the problem and what our actual expectation would be.

As demonstrated in this section, Spock provides a flexible way of writing tests and should be considered when writing code on a software project, be it in Java or in Groovy. Making sure your software works correctly is crucial and writing tests for it is one of the best ways to assert that your software behaves the way you want it to, and that it keeps doing that. To do so, we can make use of build automation, which is described in the next section.

17.8   Build automation

We looked at how to run tests individually or in suites from the command line and using IDEs. For a team environment, however, the automated build environment should also run all the tests.[23] Two of the more popular build automation technologies in the Java world are Gradle and Maven. We'll look briefly at how to integrate Groovy with each of these technologies.

17.8.1   Build integration with Gradle

Gradle is a new and flexible build automation tool, capable of building, testing, publishing, and deploying software, much like Maven. Gradle accomplishes this by providing a declarative Groovy DSL and sensible defaults, making a build file not bigger than is needed, thus improving readability.

We'll talk about Gradle again in chapter 20 to cover its general use for build automation. Here, we'll focus on its use for integrating unit tests in the build.

Before we start, we need to install Gradle. This can be done in multiple ways, one of which is downloading Gradle from the Gradle website (www.gradle.org). An easier way is to use the GVM tool to manage the set of software installations, such as Groovy, Grails, Gradle, and more. The GVM can be downloaded from the GVM tool website (www.gvmtool.net) using a simple command:[24]

```
curl -s get.gvmtool.net | bash
```

Once GVM is installed, installing Gradle is as easy as typing:

```
gvm install gradle
```

This will download and install the newest version of Gradle, which at the moment of writing is version 2.2.1. Gradle uses a build file named build.gradle that contains all the instructions to create a correct build.

---

[23] See *Pragmatic Project Automation: How to Build, Deploy, and Monitor Java Apps* by Mike Clark (The Pragmatic Programmers, 2004) for more details on why this is important.

[24] Windows users might want to use Cygwin or posh-gvm or download Gradle manually.

The basic `build.gradle` we'll use is the following:

```
apply plugin: 'groovy'
repositories {
    mavenCentral()
}
dependencies {
    compile 'org.codehaus.groovy:groovy-all:2.4.0'
    testCompile group: 'junit', name: 'junit', version: '4.12'
}
```

This is the basic set of information needed to build our Groovy project. This build file adds the Groovy plugin, which makes is possible to mix Groovy and Java code by enabling joint compilation; adds the Groovy dependency to compile the Groovy files; and adds the latest version of the JUnit 4 dependency.

To create the project structure, we need to add a Gradle task, which will create the complete project structure for us. Add the following lines of code to the `build.gradle` file as shown in the following listing.

Listing 17.18 Adding a Gradle task

```
task initProject () << {
    if (hasProperty(initPlugins)) {
        initPlugins.split(',').each { plug ->
            project.apply {
                plugin(plug.trim())
            }
        }
    }
    project.sourceSets*.allSource.srcDirTrees.flatten().dir.each { dir ->
        dir.mkdirs()
    }
}
```

Now we can easily create a complete project structure without having to create it by hand. Executing the Gradle `initProject` task will create everything we need. We can execute the task by typing:

```
gradle initProject -PinitPlugins=groovy
```

The result is the following project structure:

```
.
├── build.gradle
└── src
    ├── main
    │   ├── groovy
    │   ├── java
    │   └── resources
    └── test
        ├── groovy
        ├── java
        └── resources
```

As you can see, Gradle created a directory structure well known by Maven users that contains source and test folders for Groovy as well as for Java. If you're not going to use any Java source files in your project, you can of course remove those directories, but for now, we'll leave them in.

The next task is creating the test and the SUT. For this, we'll use a simple calculator. Place the `Calculator.groovy` with the following contents in the `src/main/groovy` directory, as shown in the next listing.

Listing 17.19   Using Calculator.groovy

```groovy
class Calculator {
    def add(number1, number2) {
        return number1 + number2
    }
}
```

And its test class, `CalculatorTest.groovy`, in the `src/test/groovy` directory:

```groovy
import org.junit.Test

class CalculatorTest {
    @Test
    void testAdd() {
        def calculator = new Calculator()
        assert 10 == calculator.add(3, 7)
    }
}
```

We've now created a simple test for our Calculator. By running the Gradle test task, Gradle will compile our source code and run the tests to validate whether the outcome is what we expect. Running the Gradle test task is done with the following command.

```
gradle test
```

This creates the following output:

```
:compileJava UP-TO-DATE
:compileGroovy
:processResources UP-TO-DATE
:classes
:instrument SKIPPED
:compileTestJava UP-TO-DATE
:compileTestGroovy
:processTestResources UP-TO-DATE
:testClasses
:test

BUILD SUCCESSFUL
```

As you can see here, everything built correctly, and we now have a successful build. To accomplish this, all we had to do was enable the Groovy plugin and provide the right dependencies, and we're ready to integrate in our build. Can't be much easier than that, can it?

Next up, we'll integrate the build with Maven, another Open Source build tool.

17.8.2 Build integration with Maven

Apache Maven is a software project-management framework that can help you manage the many activities associated with producing a project's deliverable artifacts. This may include acquiring your project's dependent software, compiling your software, testing it, packaging it, and generating test and metrics reports. Two main versions of Maven are in use today: Maven 2 (versions 2.0 and above) and Maven 3 (versions 3.0 and above).

Maven supports the concept of plug-ins to perform many of the project lifecycle activities that it manages for you. For example, there are plug-ins to compile Java files, test them, package them up as jar files, and so forth. Because Groovy tests are easily compiled to normal Java bytecode, it should come as no surprise that you can leverage many of the existing Maven Java tasks to assist you. Plus, there are purpose-built Maven tasks for Groovy that you can utilize.

If you're already a Maven user you can use the Groovy-Eclipse compiler.[25] Using the plugin you can compile your Java and Groovy projects. In the approach we're going to use to ensure that our Groovy tests automatically run as part of our Maven build, we first need to compile the Groovy files down to bytecode. First we need to enable the Groovy compiler. We can do this by adding the following to the pom.xml, so that our Groovy sources are compiled, and can then be used in the test phase, as shown in the following listing.

Listing 17.20 Enabling the Groovy compiler

```
<build>
    <plugins>
        <plugin>
            <artifactId>maven-compiler-plugin</artifactId>
            <version>3.2</version>
            <configuration>
                <compilerId>groovy-eclipse-compiler</compilerId>
            </configuration>
            <dependencies>
                <dependency>
                    <groupId>org.codehaus.groovy</groupId>
                    <artifactId>groovy-eclipse-compiler</artifactId>
                    <version>2.9.1-01</version>
                </dependency>
            </dependencies>
        </plugin>
        <plugin>
            <groupId>org.codehaus.groovy</groupId>
            <artifactId>groovy-eclipse-compiler</artifactId>
            <version>2.9.1-01</version>
            <extensions>true</extensions>
        </plugin>
    </plugins>
</build>
```

---

[25] See http://docs.groovy-lang.org/latest/html/documentation/tools-groovyeclipse.html for more details.

For the Maven groovy compiler to work, we need Groovy to be in our Java classpath. In Maven terms, we've introduced Groovy as a dependency, so we'll also have to update Maven's pom.xml file and add the Groovy (as well as the JUnit framework) dependency as shown in the following listing.

Listing 17.21   Updating Maven's pom.xml file and adding a Groovy dependency
---

```
<dependencies>
    <dependency>
        <groupId>org.codehaus.groovy</groupId>
        <artifactId>groovy-all</artifactId>
        <version>2.4.0</version>
    </dependency>
    <dependency>
        <groupId>junit</groupId>
        <artifactId>junit</artifactId>
        <version>4.12</version>
        <scope>test</scope>
    </dependency>
</dependencies>
```

We are now ready to run our tests. This can be done from a DOS or UNIX command shell:

```
$> mvn test
```

The output should look something like this:

```
-------------------------------------------------------
 T E S T S
-------------------------------------------------------
Concurrency config is parallel='none', perCoreThreadCount=true,
    threadCount=2, useUnlimitedThreads=false
Running CalculatorTest
Tests run: 1, Failures: 0, Errors: 0, Skipped: 0, Time elapsed: 0.351 sec

Results :

Tests run: 1, Failures: 0, Errors: 0, Skipped: 0

[INFO] ------------------------------------------------------
[INFO] BUILD SUCCESS
[INFO] ------------------------------------------------------
[INFO] Total time: 2.794 s
[INFO] Finished at: 2015-02-06T05:16:34+10:00
[INFO] Final Memory: 10M/219M
[INFO] ------------------------------------------------------
```

Configuring Maven to run test cases in Groovy is fairly straightforward, and as you can see, plugging Groovy into your normal Java build processes is a cinch, whether they're Gradle or Maven based.

17.9 *Summary*

That wraps up our exploration of how Groovy adds immense value to your unit-testing activities.

In any serious project it's recommended you use a build tool. Whether you want to use Gradle or Maven is up to you, but build tools provide great functionality for creating build artifacts, managing dependencies or deploying software to servers. Having a standard way of building software in a team is often crucial and should be done in a central and standard way.

We believe that unit testing is not only a worthwhile activity but also sometimes even more demanding and full of variations and engineering challenges than writing production code. Our experiences with Groovy are that it assists with meeting those demands and challenges. We hope you felt this too when we examined the benefits that Groovy brings to unit testing: the automatic availability of JUnit, the enhanced test case class with its additional assert methods, and the in-built support for mocks, stubs, and other dynamic classes.

Groovy's integrated unit-test support lets you test Groovy and Java code alike. Our more detailed examination of how to unit test Groovy code with Groovy tests, how to test Java code with Groovy tests, and how to organize your tests into meaningful suites gave you the grounding to begin testing your own systems using Groovy.

Our investigation of advanced testing techniques led us to explore how to use stubs, mocks, and other dynamic classes such as maps and `GroovyLogTestCase`. With the help of these advanced features, it's possible to test complex scenarios with minimal to moderate effort. Previously tricky scenarios can sometimes be tackled with much less work. This can often be the difference between justifying unit testing and it being too expensive. By augmenting these techniques with data-driven and property-based testing you have enormous flexibility and no reason not to have an appropriate testing regime and quality production code.

For sustainable software development with a high level of test coverage, unit testing must be both pleasant and efficient. What makes it pleasant is seamless integration into the developer's IDE of choice to provide immediate feedback in develop/test/refactor cycles. What makes it efficient is the frequent unsupervised self-running execution of the test suite in an automated build process. In the Groovy world, both of these have excellent support.

Groovy gains much from its Java heritage. This was shown clearly when we looked at additional Java-level tool integration: in particular, one technology that enabled us to do code coverage and another that enabled us to do stress and performance testing. We examined only two tools, but hundreds are available for Java, and there are many yet-unexplored possibilities for leveraging them in Groovy.

To advocates of unit testing, Groovy can only be seen as a powerful and positive addition to the Java and Groovy developer's toolkit. With Groovy, you can write your tests more quickly and easily. Just think, with all the time you'll save by writing tests in Groovy, you can now go back to your customer and ask for more feature requests!

Concurrent Groovy with GPars

This chapter covers

- Making concurrency more approachable with Groovy
- Using different types of task coordination
- Putting these concepts to work with the GPars library

> *The tools we use have a profound (and devious!) influence on our thinking habits, and, therefore, on our thinking abilities.*

Edsger Dijkstra
How do we tell truths that might hurt? Published as part of *Selected Writings on Computing: A Personal Perspective*, Springer-Verlag, 1982.

We'll start our exploration with general considerations about concurrency followed by moving from the simple to the more advanced usages of concurrency. We'll visit waypoints that show various means of coordinating concurrent tasks, from predefined coordination to implicit and explicit control. We'll move on to investigate how to safeguard objects in a concurrent environment and wrap up the topic with a final showcase. But let's start by considering why we might want to enter this challenging landscape in the first place.

Public wisdom has it that we'll no longer see the major speed-ups in processor cycle times that we are so used to. In the past, the safest way to improve software performance was to wait 18 months, get a new computer, and enjoy the doubled speed.

These days, it's more likely that you'll see a slight decrease in processor speed but with the benefit of having twice as many processing units (cores). Our programs must now be prepared to take advantage of the new direction of hardware evolution.

This *could* mean putting the burden of managing concurrency on the application programmer. But considering the huge number of difficulties that come with classical approaches to concurrency, this doesn't seem like a wise choice.

An alternative approach is to put the burden on framework designers so that we can run our code in a managed environment that handles concurrency for us. The Java Servlet framework may serve as an example: the Servlet programmer—and this includes Servlet-based technologies such as JSP, GSP, JSF, and Wicket—doesn't care much about concurrency, but the web server executes the application for many requests in parallel. The programmer only has to obey restrictions such as not spawning threads on his own and only sharing mutable state in dedicated scopes. Admittedly, projects can break these restrictions because they're not technically enforced, but by and large this has been a successful model.

The concurrency concepts we'll look at in this chapter follow the successful Servlet approach in that they introduce an elevated level of abstraction. This allows the application programmer to focus on the task at hand and leave the low-level concurrency details to the framework.

18.1 Concurrency for the rest of us

Your job as an application programmer is to get the sequential parts of your code right, including their test cases. When concurrency is required, you can choose one of the tools explained in this chapter, passing it your sequential code for execution. Understanding the concepts is a prerequisite for choosing the most appropriate one for the situation. You don't have to understand the inner workings of each implementation, but you need to understand its approach and constraints.

18.1.1 Concurrent != parallel

A full exposition of concurrency is beyond the scope of this chapter, given that there are whole books devoted to the topic. Also, it's not our job to explain the concurrency support provided by the Java language and the `java.util.concurrent` package in the Java standard library. We'll approach the topic from a Groovy point of view and assume that you are at least somewhat familiar with the Java basics. The Groovy view starts with the observation that concurrency is more than parallelism.

> **NOTE** Concurrency allows better utilization of resources, higher throughput, and faster response times, but the real value is in the coherence of the programming model. Each concurrent task fulfills one single coherent purpose; multiple tasks may run sequentially, in intermixed time slices, or in parallel.

Let's start with resource utilization. The obvious resource that you want to use efficiently is your processing capacity: spreading calculations over many processing cores to get the results faster. Note that this only makes sense if those cores would be otherwise idle! With a dual-core machine you're often better off leaving the second core to the OS to run its other processes. Prominent examples of "other processes" are your database and web server.

Spreading computation over many cores, processors, or even remote machines is what we call *parallelism*. Concurrency goes beyond parallelism. It allows asynchronous access to the database, filesystem, external devices, the network, and foreign processes in general, whether they're managed by the OS or other applications. If you're into service-oriented architectures (SOA), you can think of all of these resources as services that are typically slow. If we worked in a synchronous fashion—waiting for each service to complete before progressing to the next step—we wouldn't exploit other resources to their maximum, especially not our processing capacity.

One special service that's particularly slow but has a low tolerance for latency is the user. The user's input may be notoriously slow but as soon as they submit it, they expect a response immediately. A responsive UI may be the best example of concurrency. Even on a single-core machine, the user legitimately expects that they can move the mouse, enter text, click a button, and so on while the application fetches web pages or sends them to a printer. This may well make the overall task marginally *slower* as the processor spends time switching context between background threads and the UI, but the experience is a much more pleasant one for the user.

All this may sound as if asynchronous resource consumption is the only goal of concurrency. It's the most obvious one but certainly not the only one, and possibly not even the most important one. At its heart, concurrency is a great enabler for a coherent programming model.

Imagine writing a graphical application from scratch. You wouldn't want to intermix your application code with checking every tenth of a second whether the mouse has moved and the cursor on the UI needs repainting. Nor would you want to repeatedly check for garbage collection from within your application. Luckily, Java comes with a concurrent solution that takes care of updating the UI and running the garbage collector. The main point here is that this allows each piece of the system—your application code, the UI painter, and the garbage collector—to focus on its own responsibility while remaining blissfully unaware of the others.

CONCURRENCY FOR SIMPLER CODE   Concurrency enables you to write simple, small, coherent actions that implement exactly one task. Simple actions such as these are easier to test, easier to maintain, and easier to implement in the first place.

These benefits don't come free. There is controlling effort for starting and stopping each task, mutually exclusive assignment of resources (scheduling), safeguarding shared resources, and coordination of control when, for example, one task consumes what a second task has produced.

Far too many developers are obsessed with performance improvements, overlooking the other benefits that a well-designed concurrent programming model yields.

JAVA'S BUILT-IN CAPABILITIES

Java has supported concurrency at the language and library level right from the first version. Starting a new `Thread` and waiting for its completion is simple. Groovy sprinkles a little sugar on top with the GDK so that you can start a new `Thread` more easily using the `start` method with a closure argument.

```
def thread = Thread.start { println "I'm in a new thread" }
thread.join()
```

The introduction of the `java.util.concurrent` package brought many improvements, including thread pools, the executor framework, and many datatypes with support for concurrent access. If you haven't yet looked at this package, now is the time to do so. You'll find excellent tutorials on the web as well as good books such as *Java Concurrency in Practice* by Brian Goetz et al., (Addison-Wesley Professional, 2006) and *Concurrent Programming in Java* by Doug Lea (Addison-Wesley Professional, 1999).

Reading these books can also be a scary experience, though. The authors walk through examples of seemingly simple code and explain how it fails when called concurrently. I guess this is the reason why many developers shy away from concurrency. They don't want to appear incompetent and leave those fields to the experts who can manage this black art. Well, we have to overcome this fear somehow, and the concepts introduced in this chapter are targeted at giving you an enjoyable pathway into concurrency.

The first notable difference is that we're rarely going to use the concept of a thread. Instead, we'll think in terms of *tasks*. A task is a piece of sequential code that may run concurrently with other tasks. This may involve thread management and pooling under the covers but you don't have to care.

We'll free you from dealing with Java language features such as `volatile` and `synchronized`. They require advanced knowledge of the Java memory and threading model and are all too easy to get wrong. Likewise, this eliminates the need for wait/notify constructions for thread coordination, which are an infamous source of errors. Because we don't expose threads, we can offer less error-prone task coordination mechanics.

18.1.2 *Introducing new concepts*

To make concurrent programming easier, we'll introduce concepts that are new in the sense that they're not yet widely known, even though most of them were developed a long time ago and have implementations in other languages as well. They cover three main areas:

- Starting and stopping concurrent tasks
- Coordinating concurrent tasks
- Controlling access to shared mutable state

Parallel collections with *fork/join* and *map/filter/reduce* operations are concepts that hide the work of starting and stopping concurrent tasks from the programmer and coordinate these tasks in a *predefined* manner.

Actors create a frame in that tasks can run without interference but they start, stop, and coordinate *explicitly*.

Dataflow variables, operators, and streams coordinate concurrent tasks *implicitly* such that downstream data consumers automatically wait for data providers.

If your tasks need to access shared mutable state, you can *delegate* the coordination of concurrent state changes to an *agent*.

We'll use Groovy features to make the above possible, particularly closures, metaprogramming, and AST transformations. The real heavy lifting is done by the implementation in the GPars library.

USING GPARS

GPars is an external library that comes bundled with the Groovy installation and is thus readily available in most cases. If you happen to run an embedded Groovy without the standard installation then you can still refer to GPars as

```
@Grab('org.codehaus.gpars:gpars:1.2.1')
<some import statement here>
```

This statement will transparently download and cache the specified version of the library (1.2.1 as of now) and its dependencies. If you'd like to add GPars as a dependency to your Gradle or Maven build or download its jars manually, please refer to http://gpars.org, which is also the place to find additional information, including many demos and the comprehensive documentation.

Now we've set the stage, let's visit a common application of concurrency: processing all the items in a collection concurrently.

18.2   *Concurrent collection processing*

Processing collections is particularly auspicious when each item in the collection can be processed independently. This situation also lends itself naturally into processing the items concurrently.

Groovy's object iteration methods (each, collect, find, and else) all take a closure argument that's responsible for processing a single item. Let's call such closures *tasks*. Naturally, GPars builds on this concept with the capability to process these tasks concurrently in a fork/join manner.

> **FOR CLARIFICATION**   In this chapter, the term fork/join always indicates that several items are each processed in their own "forked" task and all tasks are immediately "joined" after execution. The same term may have different meanings in other contexts.

The following listing uses the fork/join approach to concurrently calculate the squares of a given list of numbers by using the collectParallel method that the withPool method adds through metaprogramming to a list of numbers. This method works exactly the same as Groovy's `collect` besides that, we collect concurrently now, as shown in the following listing.

Listing 18.1 Calculating a list of squares concurrently

```
import static groovyx.gpars.GParsPool.withPool

def numbers = [1, 2, 3,  4,  5,  6]
def squares = [1, 4, 9, 16, 25, 36]

withPool {
   assert squares == numbers.collectParallel { it * it }
}
```

The concurrency is almost invisible: no thread creation, no thread control, and no synchronization on the resulting list are visible in the code. This is all safely handled under the covers.

> **DISCLAIMER** Calculating squares concurrently is only an introductory example for educational purposes. In practice, the overhead of concurrency only makes sense if the tasks can be split up into reasonably sized, time-consuming chunks.

You may wonder how many threads listing 18.1 uses for calculating the squares. You shouldn't care, but GPars uses a default that's calculated from the number of available cores plus one. That makes three for a dual-core machine, for example. Alternatively, you can explicitly supply the number of threads to use as the first argument to the with-Pool method:

```
withPool(10) {
   // do something with a thread pool of size 10
}
```

GParsPool doesn't create threads. Instead, it takes them from a fork/join thread pool of the Java standard library (formerly jsr166y). GPars uses this Java library feature extensively, especially its support for parallel arrays that are the basis for all parallel collection processing in GPars.

18.2.1 Transparently concurrent collections

Having the `*Parallel` counterparts of the Groovy object iteration methods is nice and convenient. However, the method names are a bit lengthy and don't feel groovy. Couldn't we use the standard method names and give them a concurrent meaning?

The following listing makes the list of numbers transparently subject to concurrent treatment with a method name that `withPool` adds to collections and that's aptly named `makeConcurrent`.

Listing 18.2 Calculating a list of squares with transparent concurrency

```
import static groovyx.gpars.GParsPool.withPool

def numbers = [1, 2, 3,  4,  5,  6]
def squares = [1, 4, 9, 16, 25, 36]
```

```
withPool {
    assertSquares(numbers.makeConcurrent(), squares)
}
def assertSquares(numbers, squares) {
    assert squares == numbers.collect { it * it }
}
```

Groovy metaprogramming is again in action here. When called from within the with-
Pool closure, the standard `collect` method is modified to delegate to the `collect-
Parallel` method for collections that have been made transparent.

Note that the `assertSquares` method knows nothing about concurrency! In fact,
when this method is called from outside the `withPool` closure, it will calculate the
squares sequentially. When called from inside the `withPool` closure, the calculation
runs concurrently.

> **IN OTHER WORDS** Transparently concurrent collections enable you to pass
> collections into methods written for sequential execution and make them
> work concurrently for a specific caller. The caller can even decide about the
> "amount" of concurrency by passing the pool size argument to the `withPool`
> method.

Think how much easier this makes unit testing of methods such as `assertSquares`. Of
course, this approach has its limits. If we do something really silly, let's say side-effecting
from inside our task, then our code may run fine sequentially but not when passed a
transparently concurrent collection.

The following code *does not* construct an ordered String of squares:

```
def assertSquares(numbers, squares) {
    String result = ''
    numbers.each { result += it * it }  // This is wrong, don't do it!!!
    assert squares.join('') == result
}
```

When called with `numbers.makeConcurrent()` the previous code may work accidentally, but at times a higher number will be processed before a smaller number and the
assertion will fail. Even worse, modifying a variable in this way isn't a thread-safe operation! Three separate operations are involved: reading the current value from the
variable, computing the new value, and writing the new value to the variable. If these
operations are interrupted by another task, the results may be inconsistent, with one
task overwriting the result of another. This is a special case of a race condition: a missing update.

Therefore, when you run the above code multiple times, you'll see that the result
string is often missing squares.

For the record, the correct and concurrency-friendly solution would be

```
def assertSquares(numbers, squares) {
    assert squares.join('') == numbers.collect{ it * it }.join('')
}
```

The good news is that you can easily avoid errors such as the one above by simply sticking to the rule of avoiding state changes from inside the iteration methods.

Transparent concurrency has interesting characteristics. First, it's *idempotent.* Calling makeConcurrent on a collection that's already transparently concurrent returns the collection unmodified. Second, it's *transitive.* When you call a method such as collect on a transparently concurrent collection, the returned list is again transparently concurrent so that you can chain calls. The following listing chains calls to collect and grep with the effect that grep is also called concurrently. The code first collects all squares and then filters the small ones.

Listing 18.3   Using transitive transparent concurrency to find squares < 10

```
import static groovyx.gpars.GParsPool.withPool

withPool {
    def numbers = [1, 2, 3,  4,  5,  6].makeConcurrent()
    def squares = [1, 4, 9]
    assert squares == numbers.collect{ it * it }.grep{ it < 10 }
}
```

The collect and grep methods use the same fork/join thread pool. In fact, every concurrent collection method called from the same withPool closure will do so, regardless of whether they appear as transparent or *Parallel invocations.

The fork/join approach is probably the simplest step into concurrent programming, but for the small squares problem, we could do better. Listing 18.3 first collects all squares, stores them in a list, and then processes the temporary list to filter the small squares. It's more efficient to spare the temporary list and do the squaring and filtering in one task. We'll revisit this approach in section 18.3.

18.2.2 Available fork/join methods

The full list of available concurrent methods is in class groovyx.gpars.GParsPool-Util. The transparent methods are in groovyx.gpars.TransparentParallel. Table 18.1 puts the two versions next to each other.

Table 18.1   Concurrency-aware methods in "withPool"

Transparent	Transitive?	Parallel
any { ... }		anyParallel { ... }
collect { ... }	yes	collectParallel { ... }
collectMany { ... }	yes	collectManyParallel { ... }
count(filter)		countParallel(filter)
each { ... }		eachParallel { ... }
eachWithIndex{ ... }		eachWithIndexParallel { ... }
every { ... }		everyParallel { ... }

Table 18.1   Concurrency-aware methods in "withPool" *(continued)*

Transparent	Transitive?	Parallel
find { ... }		findParallel { ... }
findAll { ... }	yes	findAllParallel { ... }
findAny { ... }		findAnyParallel { ... }
fold { ... }		foldParallel { ... }
fold(seed) { ... }		foldParallel(seed){ ... }
grep(filter)	yes	grepParallel(filter)
groupBy { ... }		groupByParallel { ... }
max { ... }		maxParallel { ... }
max()		maxParallel()
min { ... }		minParallel { ... }
min()		minParallel()
split { ... }	yes	splitParallel { ... }
sum()		sumParallel()

Contrasting table 18.1 with the Groovy object iteration methods shows a few notable differences that are due to the concurrent processing.

- In addition to find, there's also findAny. While find always returns the first matching item in the order of its collection, findAny may return whatever matching item it finds first.
- The GDK inject method is replaced by fold. While inject runs through the collection in strict order, no such order exists in concurrent processing and thus the contract differs. The fold method acts like inject but you have to be aware that its task closure may be invoked with any combination of items and/ or temporary results.
- Transparent concurrent methods are only transitive when they return a collection as their return type. Note that using the transparent find method on a list of lists also returns a collection but this won't be transparent automatically.
- Not all Groovy object iteration methods have a concurrent counterpart. Several iteration methods are simply missing at the time of writing, while others don't make sense in a concurrent context.

Finally, it's worth noting that this approach to concurrent processing isn't restricted to collections but can be used with any Java or Groovy object—the Groovy object iteration logic applies.

We'll now elaborate on this approach further by investigating the map/filter/ reduce concept.

18.3 Becoming more efficient with map/filter/reduce

We've seen concurrent tasks of calculating squares and filtering in listing 18.2 with the fork/join approach. First, we had to collect all the squares; only then could we proceed with the filtering part. This isn't ideal: we don't really need the intermediate results as a collection.

Fortunately, there's an alternative. The *map/filter/reduce* approach allows us to chain tasks in a way that doesn't restrict us to finish all the squaring before filtering. To make the difference even more obvious, listing 18.4 shows a map/filter/reduce performing a variant of the squaring problem. We've made two changes: incrementing the value before squaring it and adding the squares instead of filtering. What was `collect` and `fold` in fork/join, becomes `map` and `reduce` for map/filter/reduce. The methods are used in a similar fashion, but as we'll see they work quite differently.

> **Listing 18.4 Using map/filter/reduce to increment each number in a list, square it, and add up the squares—all concurrently**

```
import static groovyx.gpars.GParsPool.withPool

withPool {
    assert 55 == [0, 1, 2, 3, 4].parallel
        .map    { it + 1  }
        .map    { it ** 2 }
        .reduce { a, b -> a + b }
}
```

The `map` and `reduce` methods are available on parallel collections. We get such an instance by holding onto the `parallel` property of our list. This property is available inside the `withPool` closure.

Figure 18.1 depicts the difference in the workflow. Assume that time flows from left to right, bubbles denote states of execution, and arrows show scheduled tasks. If you imagine a sweeping vertical line, you can see which tasks can be executing at any

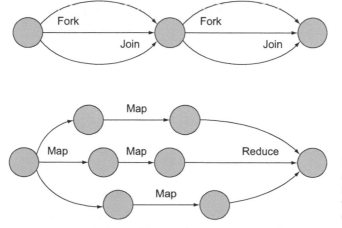

Figure 18.1 Contrasting task concurrency for fork/join vs. map/filter/reduce where map/filter/reduce can achieve a higher degree of concurrency

point. While fork/join always has the same order, the map/filter/reduce example is only one of many possible execution orders. Its inner bubbles can freely flow horizontally like pearls on a string.

In the map/filter/reduce example there are many valid execution orders. On one run all the increments may be calculated before all squares, effectively giving you fork/join workflow, but this is an unlikely coincidence.

On another run we could end up with one increment and its square being calculated, then a second one, and then both being passed into the reduce task even before the third increment starts!

Either way, GPars makes sure that all the increments, squares, and their sum are calculated correctly in the end. But the many different possible workflows open more possibilities for different tasks running concurrently. The task coordination is still predefined even though the coordination scheme spans over more tasks and allows for more variability in scheduling.

With fork/join, a collect task could only run concurrently with other invocations of that collect task. With map/filter/reduce, any task can run concurrently with any other one, thus providing a higher degree of concurrency.

> **FOR THE GEEKS: THE MERITS OF MORE CONCURRENCY**   If the scheduler has more options for assigning a task to a thread, there's a lower probability that a few slow task invocations thwart the overall execution. With more options in the workflow, map/filter/reduce offers more concurrency over fork/join.

We've seen that map/filter/reduce works on a parallel abstraction that comes with the concurrency-aware methods listed in table 18.2. Note that only map and filter return a parallel datatype that allows further map/filter/reduce processing.

Table 18.2   Concurrency-aware methods for map/filter/reduce

Method	Chainable	Analogous to
`combine(initialValue) { ... }`		
`filter { ... }`	True	`findAll`
`getCollection()`		
`groupBy { ... }`		
`map { ... }`	True	`collect`
`max { ... }`		
`max()`		
`min { ... }`		
`min()`		
`reduce { ... }`		`inject, fold`
`reduce(seed) { ... }`		`inject, fold`

Table 18.2   Concurrency-aware methods for map/filter/reduce

Method	Chainable	Analogous to
size() sort { ... } sum()	True	

This gives us enough knowledge to finally present the small squares problem with map/filter/reduce in listing 18.5.

We use the `filter` method that only passes temporary results down the execution stream if they satisfy the given closure. This is analogous to the `findAll` method for sequential code. The `filter` method is such an important part of the concept that we've included it in the name. This also distinguishes it from the more commonly known "map/reduce" label that's also used in different contexts. (For comparison see http://en.wikipedia.org/wiki/MapReduce.)

For the assertion in the next listing we need to refer to the `collection` property to unwrap our parallel datatype and make it comparable to the list of expected numbers.

Listing 18.5   Collecting the small squares with map/filter/reduce

```
import static groovyx.gpars.GParsPool.withPool

withPool {
    def numbers = [1, 2, 3,  4,  5,  6]
    assert [1, 4, 9] == numbers.parallel
        .map    { it * it }
        .filter { it < 10 }
        .collection
}
```

Up to this point, fork/join and map/filter/reduce have proved to be concurrency concepts that are fairly easy to use. This is mostly due to their baked-in, predefined task coordination that implements a well-known flow of data. When one task needs to wait for data from a preceding one, this is all known in advance and handled transparently. This leaves no room for errors to creep in.

The map/filter/reduce approach is also available in Java because Java 8 parallel streams were introduced. You can harness their power from Groovy as well—passing Groovy closures where Java expects lambda expressions. It looks amazingly similar:

```
// Groovy with Java 8
def numbers = [1, 2, 3,  4,  5,  6]
assert [1, 4, 9] == numbers.parallelStream()
    .map    { it * it }
    .filter { it < 10 }
    .collect()
```

In the next section, we'll investigate how to coordinate tasks when we need more flexibility in the flow of data.

18.4 *Dataflow for implicit task coordination*

Both fork/join and map/filter/reduce work on collection of items that are transformed and processed. That makes their data flow predictable and allows for an efficient implementation.

In the more general case, we may need to derive a value from data delivered by concurrent tasks. For this to work, we need to ensure that all the affected tasks are scheduled in a sequence that allows data to flow from assignment to usage. This may sound difficult, but with the Dataflow concept it's a snap.

The following listing demonstrates a simple sum where the input data isn't known at the time when we declare the logic of the task. Therefore, each reference is wrapped within a dataflow. Assignments to dataflow references happen in concurrent tasks.

Listing 18.6   A basic Dataflow adds numbers that are assigned in concurrent tasks

```
import groovyx.gpars.dataflow.Dataflows
import static groovyx.gpars.dataflow.Dataflow.task

final flow = new Dataflows()
task { flow.result = flow.x + flow.y }         ❶ Assigns
task { flow.x = 10 }                              derived value
task { flow.y = 5 }                            ❷ Assigns    ❸ Reads
assert 15 == flow.result                          value         value
```

We start with the calculation in ❶ where a dataflow variable `result` is derived from dataflow variables x and y, even though x and y are not yet assigned. This calculation happens in a new task that is started by the `task` factory method. It has to wait until x and y are assigned values.

Assignments to x and y in two other concurrent tasks ❷ make these values available so that ❶ can execute.

The main thread waits at ❸ until `result` can be read. This means that ❶ has to finish, which can only happen after both the tasks in ❷ have finished. The dataflow from ❷ to ❶ to ❸ happens regardless of which task is started first. This is implicit thread coordination in action.

18.4.1 *Testing for deadlocks*

Predefined coordination schemes like fork/join and map/filter/reduce are deadlock-free. It's guaranteed that the task coordination itself never produces a *deadlock*—the situation when concurrent tasks block each other in a way that prohibits any further progress.

It's still possible to write code that uses fork/join mechanics and runs into a deadlock anyway, but this wouldn't be the result of the coordination scheme. Instead it would be an error elsewhere in the code. If the forked code blocks on shared resources, you can still end up with a deadlock in the normal way.

With dataflow concurrency, we cannot guarantee the absence of deadlocks in the coordination itself. The following example demonstrates a dataflow deadlock due to circular assignments:

```
def flow = new Dataflows()
task { flow.x = flow.y }
task { flow.y = flow.x }        ◁─┘  Deadlock!
```

For all practical cases, dataflow-based deadlocks are reproducible. The previous example will *always* deadlock.

This has a huge benefit: it makes the coordination scheme unit-testing friendly! Aside from pathological cases, you can be sure that your code does not deadlock if your test cases do not deadlock.

> **FOR THE GEEKS: A PATHOLOGICAL CASE** Testability fails as soon as assignments to dataflow variables happen at random, like this: `flow.x = Math.random() > 0.5 ? 1 : flow.y`

Beside testability, dataflow variables have another nice feature that makes them convenient to use in the concurrent context: their references are immutable. They never change the instance they refer to after the initial assignment. This makes them not only safe to use but also efficient because no protection is needed for reading (nonblocking read). The benefit is greatest when the dataflow variable refers to an object that is also immutable, such as a number or a string.

Because dataflow variables can refer to any kind of object, which may happen to have mutable state, we may run into problems such as the following example where a (mutable) list is assigned to a dataflow variable but possibly changes its state after assignment:

```
def flow = new Dataflows()          ❶  Bad idea!
task { flow.list    = [0] }
task { flow.list[0] = 1    }   ◁─    ❷  Prints [0] or [1]
println flow.list              ◁─┘       without guarantee
```

> **NOTE** Dataflow variables work best when used with immutable datatypes. Consider using the `asImmutable()` methods, use types that are handled by the `@Immutable` AST transformation, or safeguard your objects with agents (see section 18.6).

Deterministic deadlocks and variable immutability add to the safety and robustness of the Dataflow Concurrency model.

18.4.2 *Dataflow on sequential datatypes*

Until now, we've only seen the merits of implicit task coordination with the dataflow concept for simple datatypes. This naturally leads to the question of whether we can use this concept for processing more than simple data—and yes, we can.

Think about it like this: implicit task coordination means that we automatically calculate a `result` *as soon as* dataflow variables x and y have assigned values. We can easily expand this concept to calculating a result *whenever* x and y are available!

In other words, we have an input channel that we can ask for x and a second one that gives us the next y to process. Whenever we have a pair of x and y, we calculate the result.

Listing 18.7 leads us into this concept by calculating statistical payout values that derive from the amount of a possible payout and the chance that this payout might happen. Think of this as a gambling situation where you weigh the possible payout against your ante. Insurance companies follow a comparable approach when calculating risks.

The `operator()` method creates a `DataflowOperator` and starts it immediately. The `chances` and `amounts` variables represent the input channels, and `payouts` represents the output channel. All the channels are of type `DataflowQueue` for implicitly coordinated reading and writing of input and output data. The closure that's passed to the `operator()` method defines the action to be taken on the input data. The next available unprocessed item of each input channel is passed into it (`chance`, `amount`), as shown in the following listing.

Listing 18.7   Dataflow streams and operators for implicit task coordination over sequential input data

```
import static groovyx.gpars.dataflow.Dataflow.*
import groovyx.gpars.dataflow.DataflowQueue

def chances = new DataflowQueue()
def amounts = new DataflowQueue()
def payouts = new DataflowQueue()

operator( inputs: [chances, amounts],
         outputs: [payouts],
         { chance, amount -> payouts << chance * amount }
)

task { [0.1, 0.2, 0.3].each { chances << it } }
task { [300, 200, 100].each { amounts << it } }

[30, 40, 30].each { assert it == payouts.val }
```

Note that the operator and the value assignments for the input channels all work concurrently, but thanks to the implicit task coordination, we still have a predictable outcome.

The `DataflowOperator` and `DataflowQueue` APIs are rather wide-ranging and full coverage is beyond the scope of this chapter. Refer to the API documentation, the reference guide, and the GPars demos for more details. One feature that shouldn't go unnoticed, though, is that dataflow operators are *composable*.

It's no coincidence that input and output channels are both of the same type. The output channel of one operator can be wired as the input channel of a second operator. One can make a whole network of concurrent, implicitly coordinated operators.

18.4.3 Final thoughts on dataflow

Dataflow variables are lightweight. You can easily have millions of them in a standard JVM.

They're also efficient. A scheduler for dataflow tasks has additional information that allows picking tasks "sensibly" for execution.

Dataflow abstractions can help when writing unit tests for concurrent code. They can easily replace Atomic* variables, latches, and futures in many testing scenarios.

Most of all, dataflow is an abstraction that lends itself naturally for all those concurrent scenarios where the primary concern is the flow of data. Take the classical producer-consumer problem where a consumer processes data that a producer delivers concurrently. It is all about the flow of data. Listing 18.7 is a specialized form of the same pattern, combining two producers, synchronizing on them effortlessly: we've solved the "consumption" part of the problem without even thinking about it! The consumer always patiently waits until he gets something to do.

This is only one half of the story. Imagine the producers are much faster than the consumer. This leads to a waste of memory and badly distributed consumption of CPU time. The full solution also needs a throttling mechanism for the producers. Luckily, we can easily build such a mechanism on top of dataflow operators by applying the efficient KanbanFlow pattern (http://people.canoo.com/mittie/kanbanflow.html).

Concurrent programming is all about modeling. We either model the flow of data indirectly through the concurrent operations that we perform on it or directly through dataflow abstractions.

Several experts go so far as to claim that without the need for data handling, concurrency is trivial; otherwise, dataflow should be the first solution approach to consider. This claim may be a little bit too bold, however. We need more control over task coordination at times than dataflow can provide. This is where actors enter the stage.

18.5 Actors for explicit task coordination

We've seen *predefined* task coordination with fork/join and map/filter/reduce and *implicit* task coordination with dataflow. The actor abstraction fills the hole of how to coordinate concurrent tasks *explicitly*.

Actors were introduced many decades ago and have undergone a rollercoaster ride of academic popularity, great hopes, challenges, disillusions, sleeping beauty, rediscovery, and recently resurgence in popularity. They've been at the heart of the Erlang concurrency and distribution model for a long time, proving the concept's value for parallel execution, remoting, and fault-tolerance.

Actors provide a controlled execution environment. Each actor is like a frame that holds a piece of code and calls that code under the following conditions:

- A message is waiting in the actor's inbox.
- The actor isn't concurrently processing any other message.

This description is the lowest common denominator between the available actor concepts and implementations. Beyond it, you'll find all kinds of variations about whether or not an actor is allowed to have mutable state, whether messages have to be immutable, whether the actor and/or the messages have to be serializable, how their lifecycle is controlled, and so on. For the remainder of this chapter, we'll avoid such controversy. When we use the word actor, we mean the GPars definition.

Listing 18.8 gets us started by creating three actors: `decrypt`, `audit`, and `main`. The `main` actor sends an encrypted message to the `decrypt` actor, which replies with the decoded message. When the `main` actor receives that reply, it reacts to it by sending it to the `audit` actor, which in turn prints

```
top secret
```

Listing 18.8   Three actors for explicit coordination of decrypting and printing tasks

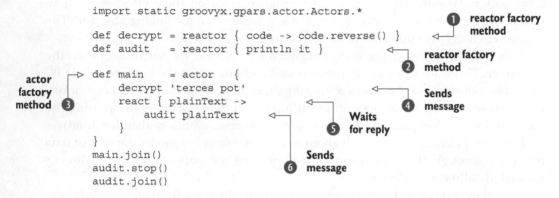

```
import static groovyx.gpars.actor.Actors.*

def decrypt = reactor { code -> code.reverse() }         ❶ reactor factory method
def audit   = reactor { println it }                     ❷ reactor factory method

def main    = actor {                                    ❸ actor factory method
    decrypt 'terces pot'                                 ❹ Sends message
    react { plainText ->                                 ❺ Waits for reply
        audit plainText                                  ❻ Sends message
    }
}
main.join()
audit.stop()
audit.join()
```

Hopefully by now you're comfortable with the static factory methods that GPars has consistently provided. The `actor` ❶ and the `reactor` ❷ methods are two more examples of the same, living in the `Actors` class. They each return an `Actor` instance, which is started right away.

They both have a closure argument, telling them what the generated actor should do when its `act()` method is called, which happens as part of starting the actor. This is straightforward for the `actor{}` ❸ factory method but a bit more involved in the case of `reactor{}`. Here, the given closure is wrapped so that it's executed concurrently whenever a message is waiting in the inbox and the actor is not already busy. The message is passed to the closure and the closure result is replied to the sender. You can think of a reactor as having an `act()` method of

```
loop { react { message -> reply reactorClosure(message) } }
```

This construction is needed so often that the GPars team has put it into the `reactor` factory method for your convenience.

NOTE   You never call the `act()` method directly! This would undermine the actor's concurrency guarantees. Instead, you call the actor's `send(msg)` facility that puts the given message in its inbox for further processing. Sending is available in various shortcuts: the send(msg) method, leftShift(msg) to implement the << operator, and call(msg), which enables the transparent method call[1] (see section 5.4.1) that we use in listing 18.8 for sending messages ❹ and ❻.

Sending a message to an actor takes the form of an asynchronous request. The actor is free to process our message at any time. We do not wait for its response, unless we use the sendAndWait() method. When an actor replies to a message, it sends the reply to the originating actor. In listing 18.8, you see the main actor sending a message to the decrypt actor ❹ and going into react mode ❺, waiting for the reply message to arrive. The decrypt actor replies to the main actor, effectively sending the decrypted plain text as a message.

REACT MODE IS A STATE Using an actor facility that makes the actor wait for a reply is an example of state. GPars supports such actor states but this isn't common between various actor implementations. It's up to you to decide whether or not to use this kind of state.

Actors can be seen as asynchronous services. They wait idly until they have a message to process, do their job, and either stop or wait again. Running actors don't prevent the JVM from exiting; they're backed by a pool of daemon threads. This is why we need the last three lines in listing 18.8.

The main.join() waits until the main actor is finished. We can be sure that it has received the plain text and has sent it to the audit actor. But because the audit actor handles the request asynchronously, we cannot be sure that the printing has been done. We have to wait for the audit actor to finish as well by audit.join(). The audit actor is a reactor, though. It never finishes until we send it the stop() message as shown in the following code.

```
main.join()
audit.stop()
audit.join()
```

These commands are the necessary coordination control that makes sure that the decrypted message appears on the console before our program exits. Try the program without these lines. If you run it several times you'll see the output appearing at random.

There are so many conceivable applications of actors that we cannot possibly do them justice in this chapter. Table 18.3 lists actor capabilities by method name.

---

[1] When it's possible to execute x.call() then Groovy syntax allows us to write this as x(). Such a transparent call may have any number of arguments that the call method understands.

Table 18.3   Actor capabilities (excerpt)

Method	Capability
start()	Starts the actor. Automatically called by the factory methods.
stop()	Accepts no more messages, stops when finished.
act()	Contains the code to execute safely per message.
send(msg)	Passes a message to the actor for asynchronous sequential processing. Aliases for actor x: `x.leftShift(msg)`, `x << msg`, `x.call(msg)`, `x(msg)`.
sendAndWait(msg)	Passes a message to the actor for synchronous sequential processing. Waits for the reply. Comes with timeout variants.
loop{}	Does work until stopped.
react{msg->}	This is only available on subtypes of `SequentialProcessingActor`. It waits for a message to be available in the inbox, pops one message out of the inbox, and passes it into the given closure for execution. Comes with timeout variants.
msg.reply(replyMsg)	Sends the `replyMsg` back to the sender of the msg. Most useful inside a react closure where it is delegated to the processed msg so that it can be called without knowing the receiver.
receive()	Like `react` but without a closure parameter to process. Returns the message. Comes with timeout variants.
join()	Waits for the actor to be finished before proceeding with current task.

Although this should give you an initial feeling for the Actor API, using it wisely isn't quite as easy as it might seem. Of all the concepts in this chapter, this is possibly the one at the lowest level of abstraction and with the highest potential for errors.

First, it's often suggested that actors should be free of side-effects, which is restrictive because this doesn't allow printing to a console, storing a file, modifying a database, updating a UI, writing to the network, and so on. A more practical requirement is that only one actor should access one such device to avoid concurrent access. This is exactly what the audit actor in listing 18.8 does. The next time you see an actor presentation without such a safeguard, shout out loud!

Second, keep it simple. With many actors sending and replying to messages it's all too easy to run into deadlocks from circular references and other concurrency traps that we're here to avoid. They can also be difficult to debug and unit test. If you cannot sketch your actor dependencies as easily as in figure 18.2, consider whether any of the other concurrency concepts may yield a simpler solution. They often do.

Third, sendAndWait() is a troublesome feature. You may wait forever. Give it a timeout at least. But if it times out, what do we do? Try again? The rule of thumb is that if you're using actors together with sendAndWait(), you've probably chosen the wrong concept.

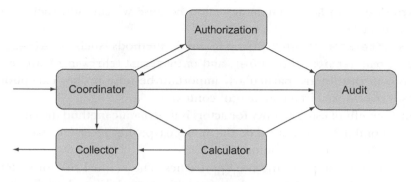

Figure 18.2 A simple example network of actors for processing a request. A coordination actor waits for the authorization reply and triggers a calculation. Many actors inform the audit actor. A collector returns the result.

When creating a network of actors you may get some inspiration for tailoring responsibilities along the lines of enterprise integration patterns as implemented in the Apache Camel project (see http://camel.apache.org/enterprise-integration-patterns.html and *Camel in Action* by Claus Ibsen and Jonathan Anstey (Manning, 2010), http://manning.com/ibsen/). If you think in terms of Enricher, Router, Translator, Endpoint, Splitter, Aggregator, Filter, Resequencer, and Checker, you're on the right track.

18.5.1 *Using the strengths of Groovy*

We've seen that Groovy provides a clean and concise API for creating and using actors. Listing 18.8 is pretty much the most compact piece of actor code that one can think of without sacrificing readability.

But two more Groovy features make our language particularly interesting in this context: assigning event hooks through metaprogramming and using dynamic dispatch for reacting appropriately based on the message type.

Let's start with metaprogramming. Listing 18.9 uses a standard reactor that calls its own stop() method as soon as it receives a message. We'd like to be notified when the actor stops and look into its inbox. What we'll see is the remaining stop message:

```
[Message from null: stopMessage]
```

Listing 18.9 Hooking into the actor lifecycle through metaprogramming

```
import static groovyx.gpars.actor.Actors.*

def stopper = reactor { stop() }
stopper.metaClass.afterStop = { inbox -> println inbox }
stopper.send()
```

Actors can implement the optional afterStop() message for that purpose but the standard reactor that we used in the previous listing has no such method. We don't need to write our own `Actor` implementation because we can add such a method through the metaclass.

Besides `afterStop()` other lifecycle hook methods such as `afterStop()`: `onTimeout()`, `onException(throwable)`, and `onInterrupt(throwable)` are available. The final two in this list are particularly important because proper exception handling is easily overlooked in a concurrent context.

The third benefit of using Groovy for actors is its dynamic method dispatch. Whenever actors respond differently based on the message type they receive, dispatch remains to be done—either manually or automatically.

The next listing compares the two approaches. The manual reactor switches on the message type, effectively taking a do-it-yourself approach to method dispatch. The auto message handler in the second part of the example defines when clauses for each message type and leaves the dispatch to Groovy.

Listing 18.10   Comparing manual and automatic methods for dispatching

```
import static groovyx.gpars.actor.Actors.*

def manual = reactor { message ->           ❶  Self-made
    switch (message) {                          dispatch
        case Number: reply 'number'; break
        case String: reply 'string'; break
    }
}

def auto = messageHandler {                 ❷  Groovy method
    when { String message -> reply 'string' }   dispatch
    when { Number message -> reply 'number' }
}
```

The difference may not look significant in this small example, but it makes a considerable difference when managing any reasonably sized actor of that kind. The `message-Handler` is again a factory method that returns an `Actor`, which happens to be a `DynamicDispatchActor`. You can use it in a number of different ways: through the factory method, by calling various constructors that allow registering of `when` closures, or by subclassing and implementing `onMethod(messageType)` hooks.

> **BY THE WAY** Static languages—the ones that have no dynamic method dispatch—have a hard time supporting actors with dispatch on the message type in a way that doesn't compromise their static language characteristics.

Actors can be difficult to handle but compared to other low-level constructs for explicit task coordination they have a pleasant structure and the send-reply-react scheme is easier to understand and handle than most of Java's built-in facilities.

Now that we've seen predefined, implicit, and explicit task coordination, we have the difficulty of choosing between them. Luckily, we have yet another candidate that we can delegate to.

18.6 Agents for delegated task coordination

Delegation is my favorite strategy. Whenever I don't know what to do, don't want to do it, or simply don't want to decide, I happily hand the work to a delegate. Delegates are abundant. They often appear as agents (think "real-estate") that are happy to work on your behalf. GPars can also create such helpful fellows and we use them for working on shared mutable state.

When it comes to shared mutable state, many concurrency experts shiver with disgust. But it's totally unavoidable as long as we integrate with Java, use its common datatypes, and call its methods—not only in the JDK but also in the vast space of open source, commercial, and home-grown APIs that we rely upon.

Rather than deny reality, it's more pragmatic to look for ways to safeguard our valuable assets. Listing 18.11 uses an agent to safeguard access to a string that we change in a concurrency-safe manner. We'll update the value by sending update instructions to our agent that does all the tiring work for his client.

> **IMMUTABILILITY IS NOT ENOUGH** Note that we don't need to safeguard the string as such because strings are immutable. Anyway, we have to safeguard the reference that holds the string to make sure that the concatenation has been done on our original string, and not a concurrently changed one.

Listing 18.11 Safeguarding a string for concurrent modifications

```
import groovyx.gpars.agent.Agent

def guard = new Agent<String>()

guard { updateValue('GPars') }
guard { updateValue(it + ' is groovy!') }

assert "GPars is groovy!" == guard.val
```

Agents protect a secure place where the safeguarded object cannot be changed by anyone but the agent. Instructions on how to change the object are sent to the agent. Again, the usual methods are available; listing 18.11 demonstrates `send`, `leftShift`, `<<`, `call`, and a transparent method. The `updateValue()` message is used when the safeguarded object itself is replaced by a new one.

Agents can easily be used in combination with all the other concurrency concepts we've seen in this chapter. They are a simple yet ubiquitously useful tool for the concurrent programmer.

18.7 Concurrency in action

Let's round up our tour through Groovy concurrency with an example that fetches stock prices from the web in order to find the most valuable one. This task has recently gained some popularity for a number of reasons:

- Fetching web pages is slow compared to local calculations; therefore, using concurrency is promising no matter how many processing cores we have.

- The effect can be achieved with many different approaches, which gives us freedom of choice.
- Many solutions have been published for different languages that we can compare our solution against.

We start with the easy part: fetching the year-end closing price of a given stock ticker. Listing 18.12 connects to a Yahoo! service that provides this information in CSV format. The result of fetching its URL looks like this:[2]

```
Date,      Open,  High,   Low,   Close, Volume,  Adj Close
2009-12-01,202.24,213.95,188.68,210.73,19068700,210.73
```

From that data, we need the fifth entry in the second line (the closing price), which is what the getYearEndClosingUnsafe method returns. This method doesn't handle any problems with connecting to the service, so we've created an exception-safe variant getYearEndClosing for convenience.

Listing 18.12   Fetching the year-end closing price for a given stock ticker symbol

```
class YahooService {
  static getYearEndClosingUnsafe(String ticker, int year) {
    def url = "http://real-chart.finance.yahoo.com/table.csv?" +
        "s=$ticker&a=11&b=1&c=$year&d=11&e=31&f=$year&g=d&ignore=.csv"
    def data = url.toURL().text
    return data.split("\n")[1].split(",")[4].toFloat()
  }

  static getYearEndClosing(String ticker, int year) {
    try {
      getYearEndClosingUnsafe(ticker, year)
    } catch (all) {
      println "Could not get $ticker, returning -1. $all"
      return -1
    }
  }
}
```

Providing an exception-safe variant in addition to an unsafe method allows both convenience and caller-specific exception handling where each is required.

The API design of YahooService goes for static methods with immutable parameter types, which makes it concurrency-friendly even though the code shows no trait of being concurrency-aware. It almost entirely avoids access to foreign objects with the exception of println. Printing this way is considered a concurrency design flaw and only acceptable when printing a single line, knowing that the PrintStream synchronizes internally.

Stateless methods are often frowned upon as being against traditional object-oriented style, but for concurrency-friendly services, they make sense.

---

[2] Slightly reformatted for better readability.

Now, let's assume we wish to check the prices for Apple, Google, IBM, Oracle, and Microsoft using the following stock ticker symbols:

```
def tickers = ['AAPL', 'GOOG', 'IBM', 'ORCL', 'MSFT']
```

Then we could sequentially find the most valuable one by collecting all prices together with their ticker symbols and selecting the one with the maximum price:

```
def top = tickers
    .collect { [ticker: it, price: getYearEndClosing(it, 2014)] }
    .max { it.price }
```

Nothing fancy here. This is all plain non-concurrent code that connects to the Yahoo-Service for one stock ticker after the other.

Listing 18.13 makes one small addition to turn this into a concurrent solution: by calling makeConcurrent() on the tickers, which results in calling the collect logic concurrently. This fork/join approach requires us to put the code inside a withPool scope.

Listing 18.13 Fetching prices concurrently with fork/join

```
import static groovyx.gpars.GParsPool.withPool
import static YahooService.getYearEndClosing

def tickers = ['AAPL', 'GOOG', 'IBM', 'ORCL', 'MSFT']

withPool(tickers.size()) {
  def top = tickers.makeConcurrent()
      .collect { [ticker: it, price: getYearEndClosing(it, 2014)] }
      .max { it.price }
  assert top == [ticker: 'GOOG', price: 526.4f]
}
```

Note that we use the withPool method with an argument to define the pool size. We want to have a concurrent task for processing each ticker so that we don't limit our network usage by our processing capacity. We go for highest concurrency even on a machine with a single core.

The solution in listing 18.13 is arguably the simplest one that we can get, and it's so close to optimal that if you're a practitioner, you may want to skip the rest of this section and go right to the summary. The concurrency-addicted developer may want to read on. We have interesting variants coming!

Calculating the maximum once we have all prices available is a quick operation and usually not worth optimizing, but for the sake of exploring the concepts, we do it anyway. Listing 18.13 first collects all prices and starts calculating the maximum only after all the prices have been fetched. We could do a little bit better.

Suppose that AAPL and GOOG have been fetched but the remaining ones are still loading. We could use that network delay to eagerly calculate the maximum of the prices we already know. The following listing introduces what looks like a minimal change in the code to make this happen, but which is a rather fundamental change in scheduling.

Listing 18.14   Fetching prices concurrently with map/filter/reduce

```
import static groovyx.gpars.GParsPool.withPool
import static YahooService.getYearEndClosing

def ticker = ['AAPL', 'GOOG', 'IBM', 'ORCL', 'MSFT']

withPool(ticker.size()) {
  def top = ticker.parallel
      .map { [ticker: it, price: getYearEndClosing(it, 2014)] }
      .max { it.price }
  assert top == [ticker: 'GOOG', price: 526.4f]
}
```

We have gone from fork/join to a map/filter/reduce approach because finding a price is conceptually a mapping from a ticker symbol to its price, and finding the maximum is a special logic of reducing the result set.

Note that neither max nor any other reduction method guarantees that we process prices as soon as two of them are available. In the worst case, we wait for the two candidates that finally turn out to be the slowest ones. But on average, we win.

Now, is listing 18.14 the best we can get? Well, so many options exist and we're entering the space of personal taste. Interesting variants come with dataflow. Let's explore at least one in the next listing that spawns a task for each ticker symbol, which is used as the dataflow index. When calculating the maximum, we refer to the price dataflow entry, thus implicitly waiting if the price hasn't yet been fetched.

Listing 18.15   Fetching prices concurrently with Dataflows

```
import groovyx.gpars.dataflow.Dataflows
import static YahooService.getYearEndClosing
import static groovyx.gpars.dataflow.Dataflow.task

def tickers = ['AAPL', 'GOOG', 'IBM', 'ORCL', 'MSFT']

def price = new Dataflows()                                      Sets when
tickers.each { ticker ->                                         available
  task { price[ticker] = getYearEndClosing(ticker, 2014) }   ◁──┘
}                                                                Reads
def top = tickers.max { price[it] }                          ◁── sequentially
assert top == 'GOOG' && price[top] == 526.4f
```

We get the same concurrency characteristics as with map/filter/reduce in listing 18.14 but without the need for the extra ticker/price mapping.

This example is well suited to investigate further concepts and you'll find more demos in the GPars codebase. Look for the `DemoStockPrices*` scripts. Actor-based solutions exist but I personally find them less attractive because the problem doesn't really call for explicit coordination. They also tend to be lengthier in terms of the code required.

Another interesting approach would be to use the dataflow `whenBound` feature, where one can deposit a closure that's executed asynchronously after a value is bound to a dataflow variable. This comes with considerable effort in terms of coordinating the tasks to assert that all prices have been processed and also shielding the temporary maximum against concurrent access. This approach has the appeal of always calculating the currently best-known maximum as early as possible, but it's anything but simple.

Weighing algorithmic appeal against simplicity is a design choice that we often encounter in concurrent scenarios. Don't think twice. Go for simplicity!

18.8 *Summary*

As a Groovy or Java programmer, you don't have to be afraid of the multicore era. Java has provided us with a solid, battle-tested foundation for concurrent programming that Groovy uses to build more high-level abstractions upon.

Now is the time to make yourself comfortable with the approaches to coordinate concurrent tasks. The predefined control flow on collections through fork/join and map/filter/reduce is possibly the easiest one to understand and start with. Implicit coordination with dataflow should be your choice whenever your focus is on the flow of data rather than the manipulation steps. Explicit control with actors should be your last consideration when no other concept applies. And regardless of how you coordinate your concurrent tasks, always consider using agents to protect shared mutable state.

It goes without saying that a mere chapter that tries to cover so many concepts cannot do justice to the full API of such a rich project as GPars and necessarily fails to present such a wide topic as concurrency in all its beauty.

Even more concepts are expected in the near future and may be available by the time you read this. Keep an eye on http://gpars.org to get the latest updates.

Please allow me to point your attention to the grace and elegance that Groovy has shown once again in this chapter. The functional nature of closures blends naturally with the need to demarcate pieces of code for concurrent execution. Object iteration methods provide a perfect base for fork/join. Last but not least, actors profit from dynamic method dispatch and metaprogramming. I'm so glad we have this language!

Domain-specific languages

19

This chapter covers

- Understanding domain-specific languages (DSLs)
- Writing DSLs in Groovy
- Creating readable and expressive languages
- Testing, securing, and providing good error reporting when creating DSLs

> *The limits of my language are the limits of my world.*
>
> —Ludwig Wittgenstein

Domain-specific languages are languages tailored toward representing a particular domain of knowledge. Proponents of development methodologies suggest that what leads to success or failure of a project is the quality of communication and a common goal of producing software that delivers on promises of solving a particular domain problem.

Languages are at the root of any kind of communication and involve two interlocutors. A *subject matter expert* (SME) can write specifications in their mother tongue, say, English, with tons of domain-specific words and concept names that will be read by software developers. A developer can also speak to a computer using different languages to tell it about the business rules of the application the SME is longing to play with. The former will use a natural language while the latter will use one or several general-purpose programming languages.

A translation process is obviously involved to codify requirements into executable code. And this process isn't usually that straightforward because there may be ambiguities in the natural language used and different approaches exist for implementing the same behavior—using different patterns, algorithms, or idioms. More so than typing issues or lacking `null` pointer checks, what introduces bugs in our machinery is the imperfection of our understanding of each other's words and their meaning.

Let's step back and reflect on these considerations. In this Babel of languages, what if we had one language that everybody could unambiguously understand? What if this language contained words that all stakeholders could put the same meaning on, that is both readable and expressive? And imagine if Esperanto could even be understood by computers themselves? But does such a dreamed-up ubiquitous language exist? We wouldn't write that prose if we didn't think Groovy could play a central role here, and this chapter wouldn't be named "domain-specific languages" if one couldn't create a special language in Groovy that would help reduce the gaps in understanding each other and help us make our project succeed.

19.1 Groovy's flexible nature

The grammar of the Groovy language directly derives from Java 5; you can often copy and paste Java code into your Groovy programs and run it without any modification. However, as a Java developer, as you learn Groovy, you'll progressively write more idiomatic Groovy code. Over the course of the past chapters, you've discovered many language features and APIs that will make your code groovier and more concise! For instance, you'll get rid of and even forget about those boring semicolons—isn't the compiler supposed to be clever enough to figure out when a statement ends? You'll also quickly omit parentheses in your `println` statements, among other places. You're rapidly benefiting from Groovy's flexible nature at the syntax level as well as the API level—after all, `println` is already a shortcut notation for `System.out.println`! Let's review what Groovy offers out of the box for making your code look nicer to the eye.

19.1.1 Back to omitting parentheses

In Groovy, the parentheses can be omitted under certain circumstances. All top-level statements or expressions, called *command expressions*, can benefit from that rule.

Imagine you're a NASA engineer, and you've sent a rover on the ground of planet Mars. In the comfy seat of Mission Control, from miles and miles away—certainly with a delay due to the speed of light at which information travels—you're planning the journey of your little robot on the rocky soil. You'll tell your robot to move left and right. In Java, you'd need to create a class (lots of surrounding boilerplate code) and describe the orders in a method; in Groovy, you could put all the orders in a simple script. Let's put all the accompanying code aside. What could the orders look like?

In Java, you'd need parentheses and a final semicolon:

```
move(left);
```

In Groovy, the code looks look like an imperative sentence:

```
move left
```

We don't gain that much, but the Groovy variant is free of punctuation noise.

In either case, you need to have a method named `move()` defined in your script or class taking one parameter of type `Direction`, perhaps even an Enum value.

But here we're only showing the command the operator sends to the remote robot. If we have the `move left` order in our Groovy script and execute it, we get an exception telling us the `left` variable isn't found, and if it's found, we get another exception afterward indicating the `move()` method couldn't be found. The following listing contains the full script.

Listing 19.1 Our naïve approach with a self-contained script

```
package v01

import static Direction.*          ❷ Makes constants
                                       available in script

enum Direction {                    ❶ The enum
   left, right, forward, backward       definition
}
class Robot {                       ❸ Defines class
   void move(Direction dir) {       ❹ Method
     println "robot moved $dir"         definition
   }
}
def robot = new Robot()             ❺ Creates instance

robot.move left                     ❻ Instructs robot
                                       to move
```

We define an enum for the directions ❶, so our robot can understand the left, right, forward, and backward movements. We use a static `import` to import all the enum constants ❷, so they're available in the body of our script. Who receives the commands? Ah yes, the robot! We obviously need a robot! We create a `Robot` class ❸ and out robot has a `move()` method ❹, taking a `Direction` value. We instantiate our `Robot` class ❺ to create a robot. And at last ❻, we can tell our robot to move left.

That's quite a bit of code for telling our robot to move left, isn't it? Wasn't a key goal of a DSL to be concise and readable? For a single move, we need an enum definition, a static import, an instantiation, and the final command. Twelve lines of code for a mere command which doesn't look like the one we mentioned earlier: there's a robot prefix! Have we lied to you? Can't we do better? Of course, we can!

We can start by speaking of integration. We should differentiate the infrastructural code from the business code: the code of the robot, the directions, the instantiation of the robot are all about infrastructure, and the order we send to the robot is the business code, our DSL code.

Cleanly separating the kinds of code is good practice, plus it allows us to streamline the DSL bits, so they remain short, concise, and readable. All the cleverness of the DSL will come from the infrastructural code and how we integrate everything. This dichotomy is also a separation of concerns: the infrastructure stays the same, or evolves at its own pace. The same is true for the business code: the orders sent to the rover vary depending on where the robot is and where we want it to go.

Let's start work on version 2 of our robot example. `GroovyShell` will be our weapon of choice for evaluating our business rules. This will be the class that will be integrated in our back end (it could be a pure Java or Groovy back end or a mix of the two). The `Direction` enum and the `Robot` class will be part of our infrastructural code, already precompiled on our classpath as part of the build process of our overall application. Compared with our full script from earlier, they'll be removed from their specific files (see the following two listings), and will be part of our domain model package (`v02.model`).

Listing 19.2 Our enum for directions: `projectmars.model.Direction`

```
package v02.model

enum Direction {
  left, right, forward, backward
}
```

Listing 19.3 Our core robot class: `projectmars.model.Robot`

```
package v02.model

class Robot {
  void move(Direction dir) {
    println "robot moved $dir"
  }
}
```

Given those domain model classes, our business rules, in the form of a Groovy script, are already shorter, as shown in the following listing.

Listing 19.4 Our updated business rules

```
package v02

import v02.model.Robot          ⟵ Imports Robot class from model package
import static v02.model.Direction.*   ⟵ Uses static import for directions

def robot = new Robot()

robot.move left
```

What's still missing in our big picture is the code using the `GroovyShell` class we mentioned earlier. For simplicity's sake, we keep business rules in a simple multiline Groovy string, but they can come from a configuration file, from a database, or entered interactively in a kind of console application. The following listing shows our concrete integration. As our overall application is pretty simple so far, we keep our application main entry point inside a Groovy script, but this could also be a more involved, full-blown class with additional responsibilities.

Listing 19.5   The integration and main entry point of our application

```
package v02

def shell = new GroovyShell(this.class.classLoader)    ①  Instantiates
shell.evaluate '''                                         the shell
import v02.model.Robot
import static v02.model.Direction.*                    ②  Shell
                                                          evaluates
def robot = new Robot()                                   inline script

robot.move left
'''
```

Our main script instantiates the `GroovyShell` class ① ensuring that it has the same classloader as our script. Setting up the classloader in this way isn't necessary for this simple example but it's a good practice to get into for many integration scenarios. Any classes we define in our main script will be visible within the shell and any classes that our shell creates could be passed back to our main script. We then call our shell's `evaluate()` method, which takes a string—here a multiline string—as parameter ②.

External DSL file

In our example from listing 19.5, we evaluated a DSL that was in the form of a string. But the idea here is that your DSL might come from an external file. You could also store this DSL in a database or elsewhere. Instead of the verbatim string, you can call other variants of the evaluate method that take a `Reader`, `URI`, or `File`. Here's an example pulling the file from a folder relative to where the script runs:

```
def shell = new GroovyShell()
shell.evaluate 'v02/CommandScript.groovy' as File
```

Here's another loading the file from the classpath:

```
def shell = new GroovyShell()
def script = Robot.getResource("/v02/CommandScript.groovy")
shell.evaluate new File(script.toURI())
```

And of course you can use the Reader or URI variants to retrieve a remote script.

Given that we're done with our infrastructural code (our domain model classes and our application main entry point integrating the business rules), let's have another look back at our business logic from listing 19.4. We have an import and a static import, a robot instantiation, and eventually the command we send to our robot. Is it perfect? Well, we could consider the two imports as undesirable boilerplate code (at least from the perspective of the person writing the business rules). The same goes for the instantiation of the robot: it's probably boilerplate as well. On the one hand, we'd like references to the robot to disappear, but we don't want our reference to the robot to completely disappear. It could definitely help us test our business code if we inject a mock robot, and if one day our robot is upgraded to a newer version, we could later inject a different instance of the robot. Finally, the style used for sending our commands to the robot isn't looking like what we promised in the introduction of our chapter, because we've got this robot prefix.

To summarize, we want to:

- Get rid of the imports
- Inject the robot more transparently
- Improve the way we send orders to the robot

We'll take care of those three points in the next sections.

19.2 *Variables, constants, and method injection*

Tackling the injection first permits us to remove the instantiation of the class and the related import. How can we achieve this? By using the script's binding: every script has a special kind of map in which dynamic variables can be saved and looked up.

Before applying this idea to our robot example, let's look at a simple example, evaluating math expressions. Listing 19.6 shows how the binding can be created ❶ and passed to the `GroovyShell` in its constructor ❷. We create distance and time variables in the binding, and those two variables are available when we evaluate our math formula. No `MissingPropertyException` is thrown; the variables are present globally in the body of that script, without any prior definition or particular explicit lookup. Notice we assign the quotient of distance over time into a speed variable ❸. We have neither "def-ed" that variable nor used a different approach than a plain assignment to pass the result of the calculation to the binding. In ❹, the variables we put into the binding are still there—and we haven't updated their values, but we could have done that. And in ❺, we discover that the binding now contains an additional variable: our speed variable is here, containing the result of the computation.

Leveraging the script's binding is a great technique to exchange variables and values during the execution of a script.

Listing 19.6   Exchanging variables and values through a script's binding

```
def binding = new Binding([distance: 11400, time: 5 * 60])     ◁──┐  Creates and
                                                                  ❶  populates binding
   ┌─▷ def shell = new GroovyShell(binding)
Passes │  shell.evaluate '''                        ❸  Calculation only
binding to │      speed = distance / time        ◁──┘   involves binding
GroovyShell ❷                                          variables
```

```
'''
assert binding.distance == 11400
assert binding.time == 5 * 60
assert binding.speed == 38
'''
```

④ **Inputs variables unchanged**

⑤ **Results also in binding**

With that knowledge in mind, you've guessed—correctly—that the binding is going to be the approach we'll use for injecting the robot instance into our command script. Thanks to duck-typing, we can use that robot instance without specifying that it is of type Robot, without having to import the Robot class! As the following listing demonstrates, we can remove one import and inject the robot into our DSL script through a binding object.

Listing 19.7 Injecting a robot variable into the script's binding

```
package v02

import v02.model.Robot

def binding = new Binding(robot: new Robot())

def shell = new GroovyShell(this.class.classLoader, binding)
shell.evaluate '''
    import static v02.model.Direction.*

    robot.move left
'''
```

Creates binding using named params or map

Passes binding to GroovyShell constructor

We've injected a robot into our DSL script. We don't need to instantiate a Robot object, and we managed to get rid of one import. But we're left with the static import for the directions and the prefixed move method.

We managed to inject the robot variable; we can apply the same technique to inject the direction constants. This is a first approach that we'll take, but we'll also have a look at a couple of additional options.

19.2.1 *Injecting constants through the binding*

In the following listing, we enumerate the directions manually, adding them in the binding to pass to the shell.

Listing 19.8 Injecting constants through the binding

```
package v02

import v02.model.*

def binding = new Binding(
    robot:      new Robot(),
    left:       Direction.left,
    right:      Direction.right,
    forward:    Direction.forward,
```

① **Inject directions**

```
    backward:  Direction.backward
)
def shell = new GroovyShell(this.class.classLoader, binding)
shell.evaluate '''
    robot.move left
'''
```
◁─┐ **Import free**
❷   **script**

This approach is certainly the simplest one: we add each and every direction manually into the binding ❶, and we notice that the static import for the constants has disappeared from the script DSL ❷. It's a bit fragile. What happens if we add a new direction value? We'd have to update the enum definition as well as the integration where we inject the enum values into the binding. Fortunately, Groovy's magic empowers us to make things less brittle by using the collectEntries() method and spread map operator.

The following listing shows how we can inject all the Direction enum constants into the binding automatically, rather than manually. The collectEntries() method creates a map that is the association of the name of the enum values and the respective values. The spread map operator will merge those entries into the binding map.

Listing 19.9 Injecting enum values

```
package v02

import v02.model.*

def binding = new Binding(
    robot: new Robot(),
    *: Direction.values().collectEntries { [(it.name()): it] }   ◁─┐
)

def shell = new GroovyShell(this.class.classLoader, binding)
shell.evaluate '''
    robot.move left
'''
```
Injects directions using spread map operator

This new binding definition still injects the robot and spreads the content of a map into the binding map to form one consistent map. The obvious benefit is that if ever you need more directions, maintenance will be easier because you need to update the Direction enum and not need to touch your integration code. No duplication!

With enums, we managed to solve the problem of maintenance and duplication elegantly, but sometimes, you don't have enums at your disposal—perhaps legacy classes and interfaces you have no control over, or you don't want to import all of the enum values. You can go with manually adding each constant as we did in listing 19.8, injecting constants through the binding. You have other ways to add variables and constants into your DSL scripts. We'll look at those shortly, but first let's look at simple techniques for injecting methods into a script.

19.2.2   *Injecting methods into a script*

Let's come back to our original goals with our Mars rover. From our original script, we managed to get rid of the imports, and to inject the robot instance. However, the movement of the robot is still "prefixed", and isn't as concise as it could be:

```
robot.move left
```

We want the movements to be sent to the robot, but we'd like the code to look as if we were speaking directly to the robot, telling it explicitly "move left", because it knows we are talking to it—a pretty clever robot understanding human speech! But a move method would be a method on the current script that's running, not on the robot. Can we redirect the methods to the robot?

A naïve approach would be to append methods at the end of our script code, before it gets evaluated, as illustrated by the approach in the next listing. You'd create your own evaluation method that would call `GroovyShell#evaluate`, but which would in turn do string concatenation to append each method definition you'd need to be carried over to our robot instance.

Listing 19.10   Appending method definitions to script code

```
shell.evaluate '''
    move left
''' + '''
    def move(dir) {
        robot.move dir
    }
'''
```

This naïve approach isn't ideal for a number of reasons. The implementation is fragile because you put code in a String that isn't easy to refactor. For maintenance, this is problematic because you have to update those appended method definitions when the `Robot` class is evolving. If the scripts that end users are sending you are bogus and don't compile properly, you may get weird compilation error messages, as the parser would see the `def` token afterward. Although this approach is easy, it should be avoided.

A proper way to add methods to the script class is to use a custom base script class. Scripts extend the `groovy.lang.Script` base abstract class, and the Groovy compiler allows us to define a different base class for our scripts (as long as it's extending `groovy.lang.Script`).

First we need to create our own script base class, as shown in listing 19.11. Our class is declared `abstract` like its parent ❶, and extends `groovy.lang.Script`. We then add a `move()` method with the same signature as the one of the robot ❷ that will be accessible from the DSL script as a script method not requiring any prefix for being called. We retrieve the robot ❸ from the script's `Binding`—the same binding that we pass to `GroovyShell`.

Listing 19.11 Defining a custom base script class

```
package v02.integration

import v02.model.Direction

abstract class RobotBaseScript extends Script {          Defines base
  void move(Direction dir) {                          ① script class
    this.binding.robot.move dir                          Defines move()
  }                                          Retrieves  ② method
}                                            robot from the
                                          ③ script's binding
```

Now that our base script class is ready, let's put it to good use. We have a number of options to apply this base class. Let's first look at using the @BaseScript AST transformation, as shown in the following listing.

Listing 19.12 Using a custom base script class

```
package v02

import v02.model.*

def binding = new Binding(
    robot: new Robot(),
    *: Direction.values().collectEntries { [(it.name()): it] }
)

def shell = new GroovyShell(this.class.classLoader, binding)
shell.evaluate '''
@BaseScript(v02.integration.RobotBaseScript)
import groovy.transform.BaseScript

move left
'''
```

It's nice that we can use an annotation to tweak the base class but, at least for our example, we've introduced as many lines as we've saved. Instead, let's look at additional ways to customize the compilation process. It'll be handy for automatically adding imports to our script, and as we'll see later, also provides us with a better approach for specifying a base script class.

19.2.3 Adding imports and static imports automatically

Until now our examples used GroovyShell for evaluating our robot moves, and we see that we can pass parameters, such as a Binding to pass variables and constants, that will be available during the execution of the script. But GroovyShell's constructor also takes a CompilerConfiguration as a parameter. Through the latter, we can define *compiler customizers* (three kinds exist, and you can create your own), as well as a *custom base script class*.

Let's start by looking at one special customizer: the import customizer from chapter 16, where we looked at it from an integration perspective. The name is explicit: an import customizer helps you customize the imports of your scripts and classes. With it,

you can add imports and static imports, as well as star imports and star static imports.
You can also do type aliasing for your imports and static imports.

Listing 19.13 shows how we continue improving our integration script by injecting
the robot variable ❶, by creating an import customizer ❷, then adding a static star
import for the direction enum values ❸, specifying the customizer to be used by the
compiler configuration ❹, and eventually passing the configuration to the Groovy-
Shell constructor ❺.

Listing 19.13   Using import customizers to add imports transparently

```
package v02

import org.codehaus.groovy.control.CompilerConfiguration
import org.codehaus.groovy.control.customizers.*
import v02.model.Robot

def binding = new Binding(robot: new Robot())

def importCustomizer = new ImportCustomizer()
importCustomizer.addStaticStars 'v02.model.Direction'

def config = new CompilerConfiguration()
config.addCompilationCustomizers importCustomizer

def shell = new GroovyShell(this.class.classLoader, binding, config)
shell.evaluate '''
    robot.move left
'''
```

❶ Injects only variables into binding

❷ Creates import customizer

❸ Direction.* enum values statically imported with star import

❹ Imports customizer added to compiler configuration

❺ Passes compiler configuration to GroovyShell

Once you've instantiated an ImportCustomizer, you can add:

- *Normal imports*—addImports(String… fqnClassNames)
- *An aliased import*—addImport(String alias, String fqnClassName)
- *A static import*—addStaticImport(String fqnClassName, String fieldName)
- *An aliased static import*—addStaticImport(String alias, String fqnClassName, String fieldname)
- *Star imports*—addStarImports(String… packageNames)
- *Static star imports*—addStaticStars(String… fqnClassNames)

In our case, we needed only the latter variant that allowed us to add a static star import
for all the enum constant values.

Compiler configuration customizers are useful for DSL purposes. Later in the chapter we'll discover more customizers for securing your scripts and applying transformations, and even how to create your own customizers.

What we want is a way to inject methods. We've got several interesting approaches
for doing that.

19.2.4 *Injecting methods (revisited)*

Let's look at another option of `CompilerConfiguration`, which allows us to specify a base class. It's an alternative way to use the base class that we defined in listing 19.11. The compiler configuration has a `scriptBaseClass` property that we can use to point to our robot base script as shown in the following listing.

Listing 19.14   Configuring and using a custom base script class

```
package v02

import org.codehaus.groovy.control.CompilerConfiguration
import org.codehaus.groovy.control.customizers.*
import v02.integration.RobotBaseScript
import v02.model.*

def binding = new Binding(robot: new Robot())

def importCustomizer = new ImportCustomizer()
importCustomizer.addStaticStars Direction.name

def config = new CompilerConfiguration()
config.addCompilationCustomizers importCustomizer          Specifies script
config.scriptBaseClass = RobotBaseScript.name      ◁──┘    base class

def shell = new GroovyShell(this.class.classLoader, binding, config)
shell.evaluate '''
    move left
'''
```

NOTE When you add a getter in your base script class, such as `getMyConstant()`, you can then access it with `myConstant` in your script, as if it were passed through the binding. That's another way of injecting a constant in the binding. However, if you defined a `setMyConstant()` setter method, this method would not be called upon assignment of `myConstant`, as the variable would go into the binding. If you wanted to call that setter, you'd have to call it explicitly in the form of its method call.

Coming back to our abstract base script class, you certainly noticed that we replicated the `move()` method from the `Robot` class. The script base class serves as a façade. The decoupling is valuable in itself even though we currently only have one method; otherwise, you'd have to put a delegate method in place for each method of the `Robot` class.

  If you remember AST transformations from previous chapters, you might find that using the `@Delegate` transformation is a good fit for delegating methods. The following listing shows how to implement this idea. The transformation automatically adds all methods from `Robot` at compile-time in your script base class. You'll also notice that we employed the `@Lazy` transformation, because the binding is populated after the class initialization and instance construction.

Listing 19.15   Using @Delegate for method injection and delegation

```
package v02.integration

import v02.model.Direction

abstract class RobotBaseScript extends Script {
    @Delegate @Lazy Robot robot = this.binding.robot
}
```

The delegation approach is good if you want to delegate all method calls, but if you're interested in a specific set of methods, our previous solution worked well (by copying the signatures of our robot and delegating to the robot's methods). You can also use the same approach that we used earlier for injecting variables, through the binding, by adding method closures into the binding. You'll see this in more detail when you want to manually pick methods or add dynamic routines and don't want to have to use a custom base script class.

19.2.5   *Adding closures to the binding*

The script binding is a mere wrapper around a map. In that map of variables, we have the keys that represent the variable names, and the values that are the variable values. A value can be anything, including closures! And calling closure variables looks like an ordinary method call.[1]

You can quickly wrap method calls to a certain object instance as method closures (sometimes called *method pointers*), using the .& notation. If we revisit our previous examples, we can get a reference to the move() method of Robot ❶ and add it to the binding of our script, as the following listing shows.

Listing 19.16   Using a method closure to inject a method

```
package v02

import v02.model.*

def robot = new Robot()
def binding = new Binding(                                   ❶ Method closure
    robot: robot,                                               reference to robot's
    move: robot.&move,                                          move() method
    *: Direction.values().collectEntries { [(it.name()): it] }
)

def shell = new GroovyShell(this.class.classLoader, binding)
shell.evaluate '''
    move left
'''
```

In this case, we inject only one method. If we had to add all of them (Robot's methods), we'd have to manually add every one, or resort to using a reflection to find out all the available methods. But for one-off utility methods that need to be available to the script, using the binding in that way is easy without necessitating the need for a

---

[1] We've seen that before. Closures have a call() method (they even implement Callable) and thus references to closures are subject to the *transparent method call*.

custom base script class. Furthermore, when the functions that we need are totally dynamic, depending on the context, the ability to add any closure, referenced under any name, can be useful.

Taking this idea further, what if our DSL were case-insensitive? Users of that DSL could make mistakes in their entered case and still have the robot obey their orders. In that situation, we wouldn't want to add all possible methods and constants in all the possible combinations of uppercase and lowercase letters in the script base class or in the binding. How can we proceed? We have two solutions. For entering an arbitrary case for method calls, we leverage our custom base script class, and for constants or variables, we use a custom binding class.

For entering an arbitrary case for our methods, listing 19.17 shows how we added an invokeMethod() implementation ❶ to our base script class to intercept method calls. The calls are then delegated to the robot variable stored in the binding ❷. We use the GString method calls, putting the name into lowercase, and we *spread* the argument of the calls (using the spread operator *) back in the call of the method of our rover.

Listing 19.17 Implementing `invokeMethod()` in the script base class

```
package v02.integration

abstract class CaseRobotBaseScript extends RobotBaseScript {
  def invokeMethod(String name, args) {
    getBinding().robot."${name.toLowerCase()}"(*args)
  }
}
```

❶ Intercepts method invocation

❷ Mixed-case script calls become lowercase robot calls

For our direction constants, we use a custom binding class, overriding the getVariable(String name) method so that we handle our own logic for retrieving variables from the binding, as displayed in the following listing.

Listing 19.18 A custom binding overriding `getVariable(String)`

```
package v02.integration

import v02.model.Direction

class CustomBinding extends Binding {
  private Map variables

  CustomBinding(Map vars) {
    this.variables = [
        *: vars,
        *: Direction.values().collectEntries { [(it.name()): it] }
    ]
  }

  def getVariable(String name) {
    variables[name.toLowerCase()]
  }
}
```

Merges constructor variables and Direction constants

Variable lookup via lowercase key

Putting these classes to use is shown in the following listing.

Listing 19.19   Using custom binding with lowercased variable names

```
package v02

import org.codehaus.groovy.control.*
import v02.integration.*
import v02.model.*

def binding = new CustomBinding(robot: new Robot())

def config = new CompilerConfiguration()
config.scriptBaseClass = CaseRobotBaseScript.name      ◁── Specifies script
                                                            base class
def shell = new GroovyShell(this.class.classLoader, binding, config)
shell.evaluate '''
    mOVe lEfT
'''
```

The techniques we've used so far were centered more around integration aspects. They allowed us to properly integrate our business rules using our DSL, and cleanly separate them from our domain model and from the infrastructural code, for a better design, easier maintenance, and better overall readability, without the usual boilerplates of imports and too much punctuation.

But we'll discover many more techniques in the next sections to add more flesh to our examples.

19.3   *Adding properties to numbers*

Assume you want to be more precise in your robot movements and specify distance. We'll create a third version of our robot system with a revamped and more powerful domain model.

How would you tell your rover to move right by two meters? We need to update our move() method to support a direction and a distance, and we need to implement the concept of distance in our domain model. For the latter, we can represent it as a combination of an amount (a number such as 2) and a unit (meters). Let's start with the unit that we can represent in the form of an enum, as shown in the following listing.

Listing 19.20   Unit enum

```
package v03.model

enum DistanceUnit {

    centimeter('cm', 0.01),
    meter     ( 'm',    1),
    kilometer ('km', 1000)

    String abbreviation
    double multiplier
```

```
  DistanceUnit(String abbr, double mult) {
    this.abbreviation = abbr
    this.multiplier = mult
  }

  String toString() { abbreviation }
}
```

For the `Distance` class, we'll use our `Unit` enum and also have an amount, as shown in this listing.

```
package v03.model

import groovy.transform.TupleConstructor

@TupleConstructor
class Distance {
  Number amount
  DistanceUnit unit

  String toString() { "$amount$unit" }
}
```

We update our `Robot` class to support a movement with a direction and a distance by adding an overloaded `move()` method like this:

```
void move(Direction dir, Distance d) {
    println "robot moved $dir by $d"
}
```

In our DSL script, we can now call the new method with:

```
move right, new Distance(3, DistanceUnit.meters)
```

Is it satisfying? We're back with a feeling of "programming" rather than giving plain English commands to our robot. What can we do to make things better? We can inject the `Unit` constants with another start static import injection, to have something like the following:

```
move right, new Distance(3, meters)
```

We still have the `new` keyword, and the class name `Distance`, which are perhaps slightly redundant: when a robot operator sees 3 and meters, it knows it's a distance. An increasing trend in the Java ecosystem is toward "fluent APIs," that is, APIs that "read" well, closer to what a spoken language is building. With a factory method on `Distance`, we could turn our order into:

```
move right, Distance.of(3, meters)
```

This is already more pleasing to the eye, even if the overall command doesn't yet sound like an English sentence. But what we suggest now is that we support the following syntax in our DSL:

```
move right, 3.meters
```

This notation is much more concise, reads well, and is closer to plain English. Later, we'll also provide the shortcut notation of 3.m in the international measures format. But how can we add properties to numbers in Groovy? We have a couple of approaches, actually. As we've discovered in chapter 8 on the Groovy MOP, we can modify the meta class or use a Groovy Category to add new methods and properties to any type, including number types.

We can add the meters property to the meta class of Number with a statement like:

```
Number.metaClass.getMeters = { new Distance(delegate, Unit.meters) }
```

But modifying the meta class has a drawback: its reach is pretty much global to our JVM, and we'd pollute the namespace of numbers even outside the reach of our DSL. We'd also need a place to register that method: we can obviously do that in our integration script as usual. As an alternative, we'd like to explore with you the idea of using a Category. Categories have the nice quality of providing more fine-grained control over the scope of the "monkey patching" we're doing on numbers: changes to the affected classes are only available under the runtime scope of the use() method, and in the current thread exclusively. As soon as you leave the block, the changes disappear.

The following listing shows the implementation of our Category.

Listing 19.22   Implementing a distance category

```
package v03.integration

import v03.model.*

class DistanceCategory {
    static Distance getCentimeters(Number num) {
        new Distance(num, Unit.centimeter)
    }

    static Distance getMeters(Number num) {
        new Distance(num, Unit.meter)
    }

    static Distance getKilometers(Number num) {
        new Distance(num, Unit.kilometer)
    }
}
```

Given our DistanceCategory implementation, we need to apply that Category to the execution of our DSL script. To do that, we wrap the evaluation of the script with a use() block as follows:

```
use(DistanceCategory) {
    shell.evaluate '''
        move left
        move right, 3.meters
    '''
}
```

Now we're talking! Or that's our DSL speaking for itself. Perhaps the DSL could also let us express the logic with more formalism by allowing the following form:

```
move right, by: 3.meters
```

Notice that our method now takes a normal argument as well as a named argument. Mixing named and non-named arguments is also a nice technique for making our DSLs more fluent. In the next section, we'll look at leveraging this approach.

19.4 *Leveraging named arguments*

Groovy's support for named arguments in method calls helps clarify the meaning of the parameters that are given to a method, instead of relying purely on the position of those parameters.

When a method call is made using a mix of named and non-named arguments, Groovy follows a convention[2] for the signature of the method to call. All named arguments are put in a map, which is passed as the first argument of the call, and all the other non-named arguments are passed afterward in the order they appear in the call. More concretely, given a hypothetical call like:

```
method argOne, keyOne: valueOne, argTwo, keyTwo: valueTwo, argThree
```

Groovy's runtime will interpret the call as:

```
method([keyOne: valueOne, keyTwo: valueTwo], argOne, argTwo, argThree)
```

and will in the end call the method with the signature:

```
def method(Map m, argOne, argTwo, argThree)
```

With that new knowledge in our bag of tricks, let's see how we can apply that to our Robot class by adding a new move() method variant with that approach:

```
void move(Map m, Direction dir) {
    println "robot moved $dir by $m.by"
}
```

That's straightforward. All named arguments (here, only the by argument) are passed in the first Map parameter of the method, and all the non-named arguments (here, only the direction argument) are passed in the order they appear in the call, after the Map.

To go further with named arguments, we could imagine defining a speed of movement, to support a usage such as:

```
move right, by: 3.meters, at: 5.km/h
```

---

[2] As explained in chapter 7.

Our `move()` method can cope with an additional named argument, which will go into the `Map` parameter. We need to adapt our dummy `println` statement for now:

```
void move(Map m, Direction dir) {
    println "robot moved $dir by $m.by at ${m.at ?: '1 km/h'}"
}
```

If no particular speed is provided, we assume the default speed is one kilometer per hour by using the Elvis operator.

Two things are not yet going to work: first, we haven't defined abbreviations in our distance category to support m, km, and so forth. The following listing shows an updated distance category. Second, we have a notion of speed here, which is a distance divided by a duration. But we have neither the notion of speed nor of duration.

Listing 19.23   New unit shortcuts for distances

```
package v03.integration

import v03.model.*

class DistanceCategory {
  // getCentrimeters, getMeters, getKilometers as before

  static Distance getCm(Number num) { getCentimeters(num) }

  static Distance getM(Number num) { getMeters(num) }

  static Distance getKm(Number num) { getKilometers(num) }
}
```

Let's start with the notion of speed with the `Speed` class in the following listing, where we assume that speed is always measured per hour.

Listing 19.24   `Speed` class

```
package v03.model

import groovy.transform.TupleConstructor

@TupleConstructor
class Speed {
  Number amount
  Unit unit

  String toString() { "$amount $unit/h" }
}
```

Now we need to figure out how to construct our speed objects from our DSL. You noticed that we used the division operator /, and an h constant. We'll need two things: operator overloading (seen in chapter 3) to call the `div()` method on distances and a new constant in the binding of the script to provide the h hour unit.

This time, we'll start with the second point: we'll introduce a duration concept and inject the hour constant in the binding. For that we need a `Duration` enum as displayed in the following listing.

Listing 19.25 Duration enum

```
enum Duration {
    hour
}
```

And we can inject the hour constant manually into the binding, since we really only care for that specific constant of time, with:

```
def binding = new Binding([
    robot: new Robot(),
    h: Duration.hour
])
```

When writing `5.km/h`, we have the shortcut equivalent of `5.getKm().div(h)`. The `getKm()` method comes from the `DistanceCategory`. And we need to amend the `Distance` class to support the division as shown in the following listing.

Listing 19.26 Updated distance with an overloaded division operator

```
package v03.model

import groovy.transform.TupleConstructor

@TupleConstructor
class Distance {
    double amount
    DistanceUnit unit

    Speed div(Duration dur) {
        new Speed(amount, unit)
    }

    String toString() { "$amount$unit" }
}
```

Supporting the familiar notation of speed as `5.km/h` involved three techniques at the same time: adding properties to number, operator overloading, and binding constant injection. Sometimes, for more concise elements in your DSLs, you'll need to combine several techniques simultaneously to achieve your goals of readability and expressivity.

Our more complex command now looks like this:

```
move right, by: 3.m, at: 5.km/h
```

It's readable, like plain English, when we read that sentence aloud, but visually, something could be annoying: the quantity of punctuation needed to separate the elements of that sentence. What if we could get rid of commas and colons? Thanks to Groovy's *command chains*, we can go as far as writing this kind of statement:

```
move right by 3.m at 5.km/h
```

We got rid of the commas and colons, leaving the dots between the numbers and units as the only punctuation. In the following section, we'll look at these command chains, so we can learn how to construct them for the benefit of our DSLs.

19.5 *Command chains*

We started our journey about DSLs by talking about Groovy's flexible nature, and particularly the fact we can drop parentheses (and semicolons) for top-level method calls. A standalone call to a method that takes arguments can be written that way, making our println's a bit nicer on the eye. These language elements are called *command expressions* or *top-level statements,* because they look more like commands or orders than like usual Java programming. Method calls in a command chain can also take named arguments, or a mix of named and non-named arguments, as we saw in our examples.

When the Groovy developers designed that specific aspect of the syntax, they always felt that we could probably go beyond top-level statements and find a way to expand those simple command expressions into more complex constructs, where we'd chain or nest method calls with that parentheses-free syntax. It took several years before a proposal emerged providing an approach that sounded good enough, with a good dose of groove, and that would help developers write even more beautiful DSLs.

Let's step back and analyze a simple command. It's a method name (the method to call), whitespace, and a comma-separated list of named and non-named arguments:

```
methodName argOne
methodName argOne, argTwo
methodName argOne, keyOne: valueOne, argTwo, keyTwo: valueTwo
```

We always have those two parts: method name and arguments.

Now, what if we expanded that concept to chained method calls. What could the syntax look like?

```
methodOne argOne methodTwo argTwo
methodOne argOne methodTwo argTwo methodThree argThree
methodOne argOne, keyOne: valueOne methodTwo argTwo, keyTwo: valueTwo
```

and how would they be interpreted? As chained method calls with the usual syntax:

```
methodOne(argOne).methodTwo(argTwo)
methodOne(argOne).methodTwo(argTwo).methodThree(argThree)
methodOne(argOne, keyOne: valueOne).methodTwo(argTwo, keyTwo: valueTwo)
```

Notice the alternation and repetition of a method name and arguments (named and non-named). This is the essence of command chains as introduced in Groovy 1.8.

For example, a syntax such as the one we want to achieve:

```
move right by 3.meters at 5.km/h
```

is equivalent to:

```
move(right).by(3.meters).at(5.km/h)
```

Once we've mentally managed to parse that new syntax with the correct added parentheses and dots, the implementation becomes trivial. We change the implementation of the Robot class to have a move() method that takes a Direction, which returns an object (instead of void currently) on which we can call a method named by() that takes a `Distance` and returns yet another object (or the same!) that then has a method called `at()` that takes a `Speed` as argument.

This pattern is often used in Java fluent APIs, where we can chain method calls on the same object, as all the methods in the chain return `this`, the current object on which we operate. We could follow this approach of returning `this`, but instead, we'll show you a nice trick with nested maps and closures. The following listing shows what our new `move()` method can look like.

Listing 19.27 Chained method calls with nested maps and closures

```
def move(Direction dir) {
    [by: { Distance dist ->
        [at: { Speed speed ->
            println "robot moved $dir by $dist at $speed"
        }]
    }]
}
```

Let's decompose that implementation in simple steps. First, our method is called `move(right)`. This call returns a map whose sole key is `by`. From that map, you get the value associated with the `by` key; that's a closure you call with the `3.meters` distance as a parameter, which in turn returns a new map with the `at` key, which then corresponds to a last closure that we call, passing it the `5.km/h` speed argument. This sequence of calls is decomposed as shown in the following listing.

Listing 19.28 Decomposition of an extended command expression call sequence

```
def map1 = move(right)
def byClosure = map1['by']
def map2 = byClosure(3.meters)
def atClosure = map2['at']
atClosure(5.km/h)
```

Knowing the Groovy syntax rules, we can equally write this as

```
move right by 3.meters at 5.km/h
```

Obviously, you'll prefer the abbreviated version to the expanded one! At least I hope so. Command chains allow you to write more English-friendly sentences with a minimum amount of clutter.

We discovered the pattern of the sequence of method name and arguments, with an even number of elements (always a method and arguments), but it's also possible to have an odd number, with a series of method names and arguments, and a *final* property access. Let's look at that with a concrete example: our robot moves, but it also has arms to examine the rocky soil, so we can tell it to deploy its left or right arm:

```
deploy left arm
```

Now we have a "sentence" with three words. It no longer fits our pattern of method name/arguments. But when faced with an odd number of "elements," command chains have their own tricks! The last element is a property access. The previous command is equivalent to:

```
deploy(left).arm
```

If you want to implement that chain of calls, you can apply our technique with nested maps and closures, but with a little twist, as the last element isn't a method call:

```
def deploy(Direction dir) {
    [arm: {-> println "deploy $dir arm" }()]
}
```

Notice here how the `arm` property from the map is associated with a closure call—see the parentheses after the closure definition. Otherwise, the `.arm` part of the expression would return the closure without executing it.

Similarly with the odd number of words, we can use silent words as parameters of chained method calls, and use maps with default values in the place of method names as shown in the following listing with a trading DSL.

Listing 19.29   An order DSL

```
def of = "silent word"              ←─┐  Defines
                                      ❶  silent word
def buy(n) {
  [shares: { of ->
    [:].withDefault { ticker ->       ←─   Map with Closure
      println "buy $n shares of $ticker"   defining behavior for
    }                                  ❸  unknown keys
  }]
}

buy 200 shares of GOOG
```

Unused parameter ❷

We define a dummy variable called `of` ❶, to which we assign a random value (it could as well be `null`). This variable is passed as a parameter of the closure value of the `shares` key of the map ❷, but we don't use that parameter through the rest of the implementation. Because we may have an infinite set of stock tickers (unlike in the case of the Mars rover with only a finite set of instruments like its arm), we use a map with default values, thanks to the GDK method `withDefault()` ❸. Each time we try to access a key that wasn't in the original empty map on which that method is called, we execute the closure (which simply prints a message here).

With this style of implementing command chains, we can tackle DSL sentences that are more varied in style, and can correspond to proper English. But DSLs aren't only about the ability to write English phrases, and we can go beyond imperative commands and add various forms of control flow to our minilanguages. It's possible to use all the control flow logic from Groovy in your DSLs (`if/else`, `for` loops, `while` loops, etc.), but in the next section, we'll also discover how to create your own control structures.

19.6 *Defining your own control structures*

The ubiquitous `if` branching instruction is available in virtually all programming languages. It takes a `boolean` expression as parameter, and a block of code that is executed when the `boolean` expression is evaluated to true. For some reason, perhaps your business users are more comfortable with *when* than *if?* Could we have a control structure like `if`, but with a `when` as keyword? What would we need to achieve that goal? A method taking a `boolean` expression and a closure to represent our code block to execute, as this listing shows.

> **Listing 19.30 An alternative to `if`**

```
def when(boolean condition, Closure block) {
  if (condition) block()
}
def a = 1
def b = 2

when(a < b, { println "a < b" })
```

❶ **Closure is the last parameter.**

Our `when()` method does take a `boolean` expression as first parameter and a closure as second parameter ❶, but this doesn't look the same as our `if` statement yet. What's missing? You guessed it, we remember about the syntactical rule that allows us to put the last closure argument outside the parentheses, such as `inject(seed){}`, and so forth. By following this rule, we can rewrite our control structure as:

```
when (a < b) { println "a < b" }
```

This is exactly what we wanted to achieve; we now have created a synonym for `if`. You can also imagine implementing an `unless` method that would be like `if`, but when negating the Boolean expression: `unless (condition) {}`.

The astute reader might, however, notice one thing: because that's a closure we pass as last argument, the curly braces are always needed even when the closure only contains one instruction. Some will say it's a nice way of enforcing the good practice of always requiring curly braces, but others could think it's a lack of flexibility.

Cases like this, where mere method calls with nice Groovy syntax tweaks exist, still differ in one way or another, but we can find workarounds; for example, by using AST transformations to alter the structure of our programs to reach our syntactical goals. As a developer, you should also remember that it can come at a certain price. If you want to have your `when` statement support single block statements without curly braces, you have to implement an AST transformation. You'd have more code to develop, test, and maintain, and it'll take more time.

As a developer, and as the guiding hand of the syntax of the DSL, you might have to make compromises. Do your users want as much flexibility of syntax as possible but at the expense of more time spent implementing the feature and more code to develop and maintain? Are your users happy with a little sacrifice (such as requiring curly

braces) but want their DSL implemented more rapidly and have it be easier to develop
and maintain for the developers?

You have to keep those considerations in mind when crafting your DSL. Sometimes,
as developers, we tend to overengineer code because we think it'll please the end users,
but we forget the agile mantra of "YAGNI" (You Ain't Gonna Need It), as those end users
don't necessarily need that added flexibility of the language you're creating for them.

After this little warning stance, you may still want to know the solution on how to
get rid of curly braces? We'll get to that shortly! First let's look at another example
where curly braces might be good to remove, because the behavior of the code might
be surprising otherwise and where mandating the curly braces makes the statement
look weirder than it should.

Let's introduce the until construct. Like while, until is a looping construct. The
sole difference is that instead of looping while a condition is true, we'll loop until the
condition's evaluation *becomes* true. The problem here is that the condition should be
evaluated each time we iterate and call the block of code to see if we must still continue to iterate or stop. If we tried the naïve approach of the following listing, we'd get
an infinite loop, because the condition is evaluated once as false, and the condition
isn't re-evaluated later on.

Listing 19.31   Erroneous implementation of the until construct

```
def until(boolean condition, Closure closure) {
  while (!condition) closure()
}

def counter = 0                               ❶ Eagerly
                                                 calculated
until(counter == 10) {                           expression
  counter++
}
```

When the call to the until() method is made ❶, the Boolean expression is evaluated
only once, at that specific moment. It's not re-evaluated each time. The consequence
is that our while loop in the implementation will loop forever, which is definitely not
the outcome we wished for. How can we have an expression that is re-evaluated each
time? By using a closure, as the following listing illustrates.

Listing 19.32   Implementation of until() using a closure condition

```
def until(Closure condition, Closure closure) {
  while (!condition()) closure()      ❶ Evaluating closure
}                                        for each iteration
def counter = 0

until({ counter == 10 }) {            ❷ Passing a closure
  counter++                              as first parameter
}

assert counter == 10
```

In this implementation, we pass a closure as the first parameter in the `until()` method call ❷ and we negate the result of evaluating this closure condition during each loop iteration ❶. But we also notice that the `until()` usage has become somewhat less appealing because we require curly braces for the condition ❷, making the look different from our goal of creating a construct like `while()`. Obviously, as in our when case, we wouldn't mind also getting rid of the curly braces for the block of code as well (the one increasing the counter).

We've already come up with three cases where it could be handy if we could treat a simple statement or expression as if it were a closure, by managing to find a solution where we could abandon the surrounding curly braces.

In the case of the when statement, we'd have to transform:

```
when (condition);
statement;
```

into:

```
when (condition) {
    statement
}
```

Whereas in the case of `until`, we'd like to transform:

```
until ({ condition }) {
    statement
}
```

into the following:

```
until (condition) {
    statement
}
```

Or if we wanted to get rid the curly braces of the single statement case that means transforming:

```
until (condition);
statement;
```

into this form:

```
until ({ condition }) {
    statement
}
```

Have you fastened your seat belt? Okay, let's have fun transforming nodes of the AST that the Groovy parser creates!

In the following paragraphs, we'll focus on one particular transformation: allowing curly-braces-free when calls. We'll let you have fun with implementing all the cases—otherwise we'd have to kill a couple more trees for producing the book with the increased number of pages.

In chapter 9, you learned about the two kinds of transformations Groovy supports: local and global transformations. Global transformations, in our case, are interesting because they're applied everywhere without the need of decorating elements of our business code with annotations, but that's also the drawback of the global application of the transformation, so everywhere we might have a until or when, the transformation kicks in. Conversely, although local transformations exhibit annotations that may be foreign to business users' eyes, they have the advantage that the transformations are local.

For the purpose of this example, we'll use local transformations, but as we don't want to impose on our business users to have to use an explicit annotation, you'll also learn how to *hide* the annotation, by injecting the local transformation transparently, thanks to *compilation customizers*. We'll get the benefits of both kinds of transformations without their drawbacks: locality and transparency of application.

We'll start by defining an annotation for our local transformation. The following listing shows our annotation definition.

Listing 19.33 CustomControlStructure annotation

```
package xform

import java.lang.annotation.*
import org.codehaus.groovy.transform.*

@Retention(RetentionPolicy.SOURCE)
@Target(ElementType.TYPE)
@GroovyASTTransformationClass(classes = [WhenUntilTransform])
@interface CustomControlStructure {}
```

1 Annotation thrown away before runtime

2 Class annotation

3 Reference to transform implementation class

Our annotation doesn't have to be available at runtime through reflection, so the source retention policy **1** will be sufficient for our needs. The annotation will be put on types (that is, classes) **2** and we'll see how to inject that annotation on the base script of our business rules. We instruct the compiler **3** that the transformation is implemented by the class called WhenUntilTransform.

Let's build an empty skeleton for our transformation, as shown in the following listing, that we'll flesh out as we progress on our journey.

Listing 19.34 The WhenUntilTransform class

```
import org.codehaus.groovy.ast.*
import org.codehaus.groovy.control.*
import org.codehaus.groovy.transform.*

@GroovyASTTransformation(phase = CompilePhase.SEMANTIC_ANALYSIS)
class WhenUntilTransform implements ASTTransformation {
    void visit(ASTNode[] nodes, SourceUnit unit) {
        // we'll fill in the gaps!
    }
}
```

To take care of our new control structure, we use a technique we've already used, with a base script class implementing our special when() method, taking a Boolean and a closure as parameters, as shown in the following listing.

Listing 19.35 A base script class for our business logic's control structure

```
package xform

abstract class BusinessLogicScript extends Script {
    def when(boolean condition, Closure closure) {
        if (condition) closure()
    }
}
```

As we flesh out our overall solution, we need a little infrastructure to test our transformation as shown in the following listing.

Listing 19.36 Testing our transformation

```
package xform

import org.codehaus.groovy.control.CompilerConfiguration
import org.codehaus.groovy.control.customizers.ASTTransformationCustomizer

def binding = new Binding([customer: [name: 'John Doe', age: 32]])

def config = new CompilerConfiguration()
config.scriptBaseClass = BusinessLogicScript.class.name
config.addCompilationCustomizers(
    new ASTTransformationCustomizer(CustomControlStructure))

def shell = new GroovyShell(this.class.classLoader, binding, config)
def result = shell.evaluate '''
    when (customer.age >= 21) {
        "Alcohol allowed for ${customer.name}"
    }
'''
assert result == "Alcohol allowed for John Doe"
```

- ① Populates binding with customer
- ② Config instance
- ③ Defines base script
- ④ Injects transform annotation
- ⑤ Creates configured shell
- ⑥ Evaluates script
- ⑦ Confirms result

We'll define a binding containing the data on which our business rule will work ①. We inject a variable called customer corresponding to a simple map (but you can use plain classes, numbers, or whatever you want). We instantiate a CompilerConfiguration object that we'll use to define a base script class ②, for our business logic (that we defined) ③ and a compiler customizer that will inject our local AST transformation ④. GroovyShell will be our weapon of choice again for evaluating our business rules using our new control structure. When instantiating the shell, we pass the current classloader of the script as a parameter ⑤. As we scaffold this example in the Groovy console, and I put everything (annotation and transformation) in the same compilation unit (that is, in the same script), the shell needs to know all the classes that we're working on. We pass the binding for sharing the information that our business rules need and for the compiler configuration object. The business rule using our custom control structure ❻ is executed with the evaluate() method of the shell. We can then check the result returned by the evaluation of the business rule ❼.

So far so good, but what happens if we remove the curly braces to implement our *no-curlies* requirement? We get the following exception:

```
groovy.lang.MissingMethodException: No signature of method:
BusinessLogic.when() is applicable for argument types: (java.lang.Boolean)
values: [false]
Possible solutions: when(boolean, groovy.lang.Closure), wait(), …
at BusinessLogic.run(Script1.groovy:9)
```

What's happening here? As we hinted before, Groovy thinks the when method call takes only a Boolean argument and treats the supposed body of the when as another statement, not part of the when call. It treats that code as if it were written as follows (semicolons helps better visualize what Groovy understands here):

```
when (customer.age >= 21);
"Alcohol allowed for ${customer.name}";
```

The goal of our transformation is to analyze this AST to recognize the when calls, to wrap the following standalone statement within a closure expression, and to pass that expression as a second parameter of the when calls, while removing that free-standing statement from the code block it belongs to.

Let's put that plan into action by filling the gaps of our transformation's visit() method, by creating our own implementation of ClassCodeVisitorSupport, as shown in the following listing.

Listing 19.37   Implementing ClassCodeVisitorSupport

```
@GroovyASTTransformation(phase = CompilePhase.CONVERSION)
class WhenUntilTransform implements ASTTransformation {
    void visit(ASTNode[] nodes, SourceUnit unit) {
        ClassNode annotatedClass = nodes[1]
        new ClassCodeVisitorSupport() {
            def currentMethod
            def currentBlock
            def currentStatement
            void visitMethod(MethodNode method) {
                currentMethod = method
                super.visitMethod(method)
            }
            void visitBlockStatement(BlockStatement block) {
                currentBlock = block
                super.visitBlockStatement(block)
            }
```

```
        void visitExpressionStatement(ExpressionStatement statement) {
            currentStatement = statement
            super.visitExpressionStatement(statement)
        }
        void visitMethodCallExpression(MethodCallExpression mCall) {
            super.visitMethodCallExpression(mCall)
        }
        protected SourceUnit getSourceUnit() { unit }
    }.visitClass(annotatedClass)
    }
}
```

ClassCodeVisitorSupport will be handy for us, for visiting the data structure that is the AST. It implements the famous Visitor pattern, calling many visit* methods, as it encounters a particular node in the AST.

In our situation, we're interested in four methods: visitMethod(), visitBlock-Statement(), visitExpressionStatement(), and visitMethodCallExpression().

To illustrate why those four methods are the ones we'll pay attention to, let's look at the structure of the AST for the following when instruction:

```
when (a > b) {
    println "a > b"
}
```

When parsed into its AST, this code will be represented as shown in Figure 19.1.

The when MethodCallExpression is wrapped in an ExpressionStatement, which is an element of the list of statements of the BlockStatement, that is in turn child of a MethodNode. We'll track this structure by implementing the four adequate visitor methods.

Note that we're always calling the super methods of the same name, as the parent class of our anonymous inner class knows all the traversing logic, and you don't have to take care of that logic yourself.

Let's focus on the visitMethodCall() implementation now, as the other methods are here only to track where we are in the AST, and have the right pointers for the

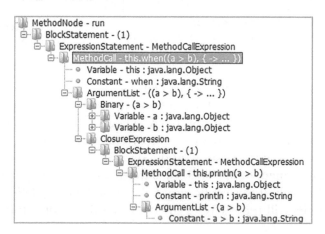

Figure 19.1 Structure of a when() call

places where the modifications of the AST will happen. Here's how we can find the relevant when() calls we want to look at.

```
void visitMethodCallExpression(MethodCallExpression mCall) {
    if (
        mCall.objectExpression instanceof VariableExpression &&
        mCall.objectExpression.variable == 'this' &&
        mCall.method instanceof ConstantExpression &&
        mCall.method.value == 'when' &&
        mCall.arguments.expressions.size() == 1
    ) {}
        super.visitMethodCallExpression(mCall)
}
```

❶ Matches "this" part of this.when(args)

❷ Matches constant name "when" of this.when(args)

Matches one arg form of when(args)

Such when() calls are actually method calls on the this variable expression ❶, and the name of the method being called is a constant expression with value "when" ❷. We also differentiate calls when the normal Boolean/closure pair is used as arguments, or when we trick the compiler into believing a when(boolean) call followed by a plain statement is another form of our control structure. Here we don't want to modify the Boolean/closure call at all, only the latter one.

We found the calls we want to act upon, now what? First, we should check that there's another statement after the when call that will be our single-statement when body. Otherwise, if there were no following statement, the when instruction wouldn't be complete, and that would be flagged as a compilation error. But how do we know there's no following statement?

We'll look at the list of statements contained in the block statement and find the index of the expression statement wrapping the method call ❶ to check if its index is the last one of the block ❷. If the index is the last one, the associated when statement is missing, and we're instructing the compiler that a compilation error should occur.

```
def idx = currentBlock.statements.findIndexOf {
    it == currentStatement
}
if (idx + 1 >= currentBlock.statements.size()) {
    addError("The when instruction has no body.", mCall)
} else { /* ... */ }
```

❶ Finds statement's position in current block

Flags ❸ error

❷ Checks if statement is last in block

As usual, the GDK offers useful methods that we can take advantage of. For example, the findIndexOf() method allows us to find the index of the statement wrapping the when call, in the list of statements of the current block of code ❶. As you realize, the other visitor methods helped us track where we were (current code block and current statement). With the knowledge of the position of the statement in the block, we verify that the call isn't the last element of the block ❷, otherwise no following statement can be attached to our when call. If this verification fails, we add a compilation error message ❸ that the compiler will report! You can check that the error is thrown by temporarily commenting out the last statement of the business rule. In the `else` part, we'll continue our implementation with the transformation per se.

What's left to do? We want to find the statement associated with our when call, wrap it in a closure, and modify the when call to take that closure a second parameter.

We know the index of the when call, so the statement to be attached is the one following when:

```
def whenCode = currentBlock.statements[idx + 1]
```

We wrap that code within a `ClosureExpression`, whose constructor takes two arguments: an array of parameters that the closure can receive, and the statements forming the body of the closure:

```
def closureExp = new ClosureExpression(Parameter.EMPTY_ARRAY, whenCode)
```

With that closure expression we created, we can push it as a second parameter of our when call with:

```
mCall.arguments.addExpression(closureExp)
```

The statement that we wrapped in a closure is still present in the list of statements of the block of code containing our when call, so we need, as a last step, to remove it from the list of statements with:

```
currentBlock.statements.remove(idx + 1)
```

Now, if you run the business rule again, you'll notice that the new syntax is allowed: a when call and a curly-braces-free single statement. Our final transformation class is shown in the following listing.

Listing 19.38   The complete AST transformation to allow brace-free when statements

```
import org.codehaus.groovy.ast.*
import org.codehaus.groovy.ast.expr.*
import org.codehaus.groovy.ast.stmt.*
import org.codehaus.groovy.control.*
import org.codehaus.groovy.transform.*

@GroovyASTTransformation(phase = CompilePhase.SEMANTIC_ANALYSIS)
class WhenUntilTransform implements ASTTransformation {
    void visit(ASTNode[] nodes, SourceUnit unit) {
        ClassNode annotatedClass = nodes[1]
        new ClassCodeVisitorSupport() {
            def currentMethod
            def currentBlock
            def currentStatement
            void visitMethod(MethodNode method) {
                currentMethod = method
                super.visitMethod(method)
            }
```

```
    void visitBlockStatement(BlockStatement block) {
        currentBlock = block
        super.visitBlockStatement(block)
    }
    void visitExpressionStatement(ExpressionStatement statement) {
        currentStatement = statement
        super.visitExpressionStatement(statement)
    }
    void visitMethodCallExpression(MethodCallExpression mCall) {
        if (
            mCall.objectExpression instanceof VariableExpression &&
            mCall.objectExpression.variable == 'this' &&
            mCall.method instanceof ConstantExpression &&
            mCall.method.value == 'when' &&
            mCall.arguments.expressions.size() == 1
        ) {
            def idx = currentBlock.statements.findIndexOf {
                it == currentStatement
            }
            if (idx + 1 >= currentBlock.statements.size()) {
                addError(
                    "The when instruction has no body.", mCall)
            } else {
                def whenCode = currentBlock.statements[idx + 1]
                def closureExp = new ClosureExpression(
                    Parameter.EMPTY_ARRAY, whenCode)
                closureExp.variableScope = new VariableScope()
                closureExp.variableScope.parent =
                    currentBlock.variableScope
                mCall.arguments.addExpression(closureExp)
                currentBlock.statements.remove(idx + 1)
            }
        }
        super.visitMethodCallExpression(mCall)
    }
    protected SourceUnit getSourceUnit() { unit }
  }.visitClass(annotatedClass)
  }
}
```

Such a transformation isn't necessarily a big amount of code, but the explanations usually take longer than what it takes in lines of code. The hardest part we would say is to get to know better the internals of the Groovy compiler and its machinery, and how the AST is structured.

We solved one of the cases we listed, and we'll leave, as an exercise to the reader, fleshing out this transformation to cover the other cases. This would also be a good time to go back to listing 19.36, delete the braces after the when condition, and see John Doe still getting his drink.

Before closing this section on custom control structures, let's look at one more, where we can take advantage of command chains. Many testing frameworks follow the

BDD approach, adopting the vocabulary of user stories: given/when/then. Let's consider the scenario:

- *Given* two numbers, a and b, whose values are 1 and 2
- *When* you add a and b together
- *Then* the result of the addition is 3

We can interpret that scenario with the custom control structure shown next. It's a similar construct as if / else:

```
given {
    a = 1
    b = 2
} when {
    result = a + b
} then {
    result == 3
}
```

Such a structure is a chained method call structure equivalent to:

```
given({ … }}.when({ … }).then({ … })
```

We'll apply the technique that we've learned with nested maps and closures:

```
def given(Closure g) {
    g()
    [when: { Closure w ->
        w()
        [then: { Closure t ->
            t()
        }]
    }]
}
```

The three closures are called and executed serially.

In the context of a script, when you assign values to variables that haven't been defined, then the script binding is used to store those values. Our example works fine inside a script. But if you'd run this inside a class, you'd get the following error message:

```
groovy.lang.MissingPropertyException: No such property: a for class: Test
```

To make it work for classes as well, you should use a value holder object, for example a map, as delegate of all the closures. And to have the assignments be done on that value holder object, you should also set the resolve strategy of closures to use the delegate first. Otherwise, the containing class would be used, as shown in the following listing:

Listing 19.39   given/when/then with closure delegation

```
def given(Closure g) {
    def valueHolder = [:]
    g.delegate = valueHolder
    g.resolveStrategy = Closure.DELEGATE_FIRST
    g()
    [when: { Closure w ->
        w.delegate = valueHolder
        w.resolveStrategy = Closure.DELEGATE_FIRST
        w()
        [then: { Closure t ->
            t.delegate = valueHolder
            t.resolveStrategy = Closure.DELEGATE_FIRST
            t()
        }]
    }]
}
```

Taking advantage of the way properties are resolved in the context of a closure is often used in DSLs, for builders for example, for switching the context of execution. In the next section, it's worth investigating what you can do with this technique, and particularly, how you can use Groovy's with{} method.

19.7   *Context switching with closures*

When you use POJOs (Plain Old Java Objects) or POGOs (Plain Old Groovy Objects) with many properties or when you assign values to many of those properties, your code can become quite verbose.

Consider an address bean like this:

```
class Address {
    String line1
    String line2
    String city
    String zipCode
    String country
}
```

If you instantiate such a class the "Java-way," you'd get the following code:

```
def addr      = new Address()
addr.line1    = '1st, Main Street'
addr.line2    = 'Suite 345'
addr.city     = 'Metropolis'
addr.zipCode  = '12345'
```

The verbosity shows itself with the repetition of the addr. prefix. Constructors with named arguments improve the situation:

```
addr = new Address(
    line1:    '1st, Main Street',
    line2:    'Suite 345',
```

```
city:    'Metropolis',
zipCode: '12345'
)
```

Groovy also adopts the context switching technique with closure delegation in the form of the with{} method:

```
addr = new Address()
addr.with {
    line1   = '1st, Main Street'
    line2   = 'Suite 345'
    city    = 'Metropolis'
    zipCode = '12345'
}
```

All the assignments are done on the properties of the object. They aren't done on certain fields or local variables.

Coming back to our examples with our Mars rover, a simple context switching might have been good enough for our users, as demonstrated by the following listing. This example also proves this context switching works as well with method calls.

Listing 19.40   Robot and context switching with closures

```
package v03

import v03.model.Robot
import static v03.model.Direction.*        ❶ Demarcates block
                                              where robot will
def robot = new Robot()                       be delegate

robot.with {                               ❷ Streamlined syntax
  move left                                  available within block
  move forward
}
```

We again use the with{} method with our robot instance ❶, and we can give it its orders with the streamlined syntax ❷.

One little downside, though, is that perhaps the usage of with as a method name doesn't look ideal within the context of the rover, but we can alias this method by adding (or injecting by metaprogramming) a method on Robot that would delegate to Groovy's with{} method:

```
void execute(Closure actions) {
    this.with actions
}
```

Then you'd be able to send your commands that way:

```
robot.execute {
    move left
    move forward
}
```

Let's finish this section with a concrete example of how we can improve the usage of a library, using command chains, and using with{} again. In recent years, we've seen many projects using the fluent API approach that we mentioned when we spoke about command chains. To illustrate, we'll take inspiration from a class called FetchOptions from the Google App Engine SDK that's used to parameterize how data is fetched from the datastore used for storing nonrelational information. This class can be easily replicated by the class presented in the following listing.

Listing 19.41 A fluent API example

```
final class FetchOptions {                                      ❷ Non-extensible
  private int limit, offset, chunkSize, prefetchSize               class

  private FetchOptions() {}                                    ❸ Private
                                                                  constructor
  FetchOptions limit(int lim) {
    this.limit = lim
    return this                                            ❶ Enables
  }                                                           chaining

  FetchOptions offset(int offs) {
    this.offset = offs
    return this
  }

  FetchOptions chunkSize(int cs) {
    this.chunkSize = cs
    return this
  }

  FetchOptions prefetchSize(int ps) {         ❺ Non-extensible
    this.prefetchSize = ps                       class
    return this
  }                                                     ❻ Private
                                                         constructor
  static final class Builder {
    private Builder() {}
    static FetchOptions withDefaults() {              ❹ Default factory
      new FetchOptions()                                 method
    }

    static FetchOptions withLimit(int lim) {       A specialized
      new FetchOptions().limit(lim)             ❼ factory method
    }

    static FetchOptions withOffset(int offs) {
      new FetchOptions().offset(offs)
    }

    static FetchOptions withChunkSize(int cs) {
      new FetchOptions().chunkSize(cs)
    }

    static FetchOptions withPrefetchSize(int ps) {
      new FetchOptions().prefetchSize(ps)
    }
  }
}
```

The FetchOptions class is an implementation of the classic Gang of Four Builder pattern. You can find variants with slightly different approaches, but the key aspect and common gene between implementations is the fact that you have several methods always returning this, the current instance ❶. That way, you can chain calls to methods of that instance that you're building and create sentences that read well, although with a bit too much punctuation that hinders the reading of those sentences.

Looking at ❷, you quickly realize that you cannot extend the class at will because the class is final, and you cannot easily instantiate it as the constructor is private ❸. The sole class allowed to instantiate FetchOptions is the internal Builder class, which does so in various places, such as within the default factory method ❹, but unfortunately, this class is once again final ❺ and has got a private constructor ❻. It's not friendly for hacking!

The Builder class then gives you specialized static factory methods (such as ❼) so you can create FetchOptions instances, and then chain calls easily on FetchOptions once your first instance is created.

Let's use this FetchOptions class and its Builder:

```
def options = FetchOptions.Builder.withLimit(10).offset(60).chunkSize(1000)
```

Having to prefix all options creations with FetchOptions.Builder isn't necessarily beautiful. But if you use a static import on the methods of the Builder, then the situation improves nicely with:

```
import static FetchOptions.Builder.*

def options = withLimit(10).offset(60).chunkSize(1000)
```

Combine that with command chains, and you can remove much of the punctuation noise:

```
def options = withLimit 10 offset 60 chunkSize 1000
```

What happens if you have such fluent APIs with a long list of methods we need to call in a chain? You'll have to split the statement across several lines. Without command chain expressions, you can get away[3] with:

```
def options = withLimit(10)
              .offset(60)
              .chunkSize(1000)
```

With command chains, you'd have to use a backslash to split over several lines; otherwise the Groovy compiler might think these are individual method calls (that is, not chained):

```
def options = withLimit 10      \
              offset 60         \
              chunkSize 1000
```

---

[3] Beware of automatic code formatters that often get this so wrong that you need to fall back to tricks such as trailing every line with a // comment so that they leave your carefully crafted code alone.

Using backslashes is probably not intuitive for business users. Furthermore with a static import, we don't necessarily remember that we're creating fetch options, because all we see is a long list of options.

What are we trying to achieve here? We want to have a concise and readable way of expressing the creation of fetch options. We'd like to define the options on one line or many, transparently, but not at the expense of odd characters or abandoning command chain expressions, and still be able to recognize them at a glace as fetch options. Fortunately, there's a solution for that: by combining static imports, command chains, and context switching with `with{}`.

Let's create our own fetch options builder utility class that will wrap the use of `FetchOptions.Builder`, as shown in the following listing.

Listing 19.42   The `FetchOptionsBuilder` class

```
class FetchOptionsBuilder {
    static FetchOptions fetchOptions(Closure c) {
        def opts = FetchOptions.Builder.withDefaults()
        opts.with c
        return opts
    }
}
```

Our `FetchOptionsBuilder` class contains a single static method called `fetchOptions`. We can static import it too. What's more interesting are the three lines of code from this single method. The first one hides the slightly noisy code for creating the first fetch options instance. The second one then uses `with` to delegate all method calls and property accesses from within the body of the closure passed as a parameter, so that the calls and access are routed to the `FetchOptions`. The last one returns that `FetchOptions` instance.

Let's see this in action in the following listing.

Listing 19.43   The `FetchOptionsBuilder` in action

```
import static FetchOptionsBuilder.fetchOptions

fetchOptions {
    limit 10 offset 60
    chunkSize 1000
}
```

You can create a `FetchOptions` instance by importing and calling our newly created utility class and its static method, passing a closure to that method call, in which you can then define all the options you need, and chaining calls on a single line with command chains, or by stacking them up spanning several lines, or even a combination of both. Furthermore, you can assign the result of that call to variables, or use such calls verbatim as parameters of the datastore commands.

All of that without the standard method call syntax of Java or too much punctuation or weird line continuation characters. We managed to enhance our library with a more Groovy-friendly builder class to instantiate a complex object.

Speaking of builders, we've talked about closure delegation and resolve strategy, a technique used by Groovy's with{} method and by many builders in the wild (like Grails's), and you also learned about them in the chapter about Groovy builders, on how to use existing ones provided by Groovy or how to create your own. Groovy builders are great for creating hierarchical data structures. In the next section, I'll show you another handy trick to creating such trees of data.

19.8   *Another technique for builders*

Hierarchical data is everywhere. Groovy builders can come to the rescue for implementing a DSL for hierarchical representations (extending BuilderSupport, FactoryBuilderSupport, or using ObjectGraphBuilder), but you can also take advantage of the @Newify transformation. But first, a few words about this transformation.

The standard way of instantiating a class is to use the new keyword that calls one of the constructors of the class. Several languages beyond Groovy use this notation, but others adopt different syntaxes. Ruby prefers a factory-like approach where new is a class method, so you can call MyObject.new(). Python appends parentheses and arguments to the name of the class with MyObject(). The @Newify transformation is designed to add those syntaxes to Groovy, as shown in the following listing.

Listing 19.44   Ruby-style instantiation

```
import groovy.transform.ToString

@ToString
class Car {
    String make
    String model
}

@Newify
def car = Car.new(make: 'Porsche', model: '911')

assert car.toString() == 'Car(Porsche, 911)'
```

To use the Ruby-style approach, you annotate a class, a method, a field, or a local variable with @Newify, as shown in listing 19.44. Then in the scope of application of that annotation, a new static method new() appears on all types so that you can instantiate objects by calling that factory method.

For Python-style notation, you need to use the @Newify annotation[4] with a class or array of classes as a parameter, as demonstrated in the following listing.

---

[4] Contrast what @Newify achieves in these examples with the addition of the make() method we achieved through metaprogramming in section 8.5.2.

Listing 19.45 Python-style instantiation

```
import groovy.transform.Canonical

@Canonical
class Country {
    String name
}

@Canonical
class City {
    String name
    String zipCode
    Country country
}

@Newify([City, Country])
def paris = City('Paris', '75000', Country('France'))

assert paris.toString() == 'City(Paris, 75000, Country(France))'
```

Given the `Country` and `City` classes, and using the `@Canonical` transformation to have a nice `toString()` output and a Java-like tuple constructor, we can then apply the `@Newify` transformation to the classes for which we want to abandon the usage of the new keyword altogether.

You see in that example how we can build something from its parts with a more concise instantiation notation. Let's push that further with another example where we can have an arbitrarily nested structure. As we're in the chapter about DSLs, and the L stands for *language*, we're going to build a term expression language to represent a formula.

We need a base interface for representing terms, as well as several implementations of that term: one for a value, one for representing an addition, and another one for a multiplication (and you can add others if you so desire). The following listing gives you those interfaces and classes to get started building your term structures.

Listing 19.46 `Term`, `Value`, `Add`, and `Mult` types

```
import groovy.transform.*

interface Term {}

@Canonical
class Value implements Term {
    def content
}

@Canonical
class Add implements Term {
    def left, right
}

@Canonical
class Mult implements Term {
    def left, right
}
```

With a Java-like instantiation, to represent the expression *a * (b + c)*, you'd need to write it as follows:

```
def term =
    new Mult(new Value('a'), new Add(new Value('b'), new Value('c')))
```

That's a lot of new keywords! But if you apply the @Newify transformation, the expression becomes easier to read:

```
@Newify([Value, Mult, Add])
def term2 = Mult(Value('a'), Add(Value('b'), Value('c')))
```

Well, the expression itself is nice, but you pay the price of the annotation for the local transformation. You're familiar with CompilerConfiguration and its compilation customizer to transparently inject local transformations to make their use invisible from the user's perspective. We won't let you do this one as an exercise, because it's important to look at how we can inject a local transformation that takes parameters—so far, the ones we injected didn't need any. The following listing shows you how do that.

Listing 19.47   Injecting a local transformation that takes parameters

```
import org.codehaus.groovy.control.CompilerConfiguration
import org.codehaus.groovy.control.customizers.ASTTransformationCustomizer

def config = new CompilerConfiguration()
config.addCompilationCustomizers(
    new ASTTransformationCustomizer(                   ❶ Passes annotation and
        value: [Value, Mult, Add], Newify)                parameters to customizer
)
def shell = new GroovyShell(                           ❷ Passes config
    this.class.classLoader, new Binding(), config)        to GroovyShell
def term3 = shell.evaluate '''
    Mult(
        Value('a'),
        Add(
            Value('b'),                                ❸ Implicit
            Value('c')                                    Newify
        )
    )
'''
assert term3.toString() == 'Mult(Value(a), Add(Value(b), Value(c)))'
```

We define an ASTTransformationCustomizer for the @Newify local transformation ❶, and pass the parameters needed by the transformation in the form of a map or named parameters. @Newify has a value parameter, which needs a list of classes for values. When instantiating the GroovyShell, we need to pass the compiler configuration ❷, and the class loader of the script. (We ran these examples in one compilation unit inside the Groovy console.) Then we can evaluate our term expression without needing to use the @Newify annotation explicitly ❸.

All the techniques that we learned up to now are more about empowering developers to create nicely crafted DSLs, and end users to code their business rules with a more concise and readable language, than with a plain programming language. But as the saying goes, with power comes great responsibilities! As a developer of the DSL, you could trust your users to do no harm, but you could protect yourself from mistakes or intentional misbehavior by securing your DSLs. That's the purpose of the next section.

19.9   Securing your DSLs

The nice aspect of an embedded or internal DSL is that you have all the underlying language at your disposal for coding your business rules: using branching constructs, loop constructs, the wealth of the JDK APIs and third-party libraries, and so on. But sometimes, certain DSLs are reduced in scope and shouldn't use anything beyond the area this DSL is supposed to cover. Furthermore, situations exist where malicious use of the DSL, the underlying language or the APIs, could wreak havoc in your running application, or the overall system, and open up breaches of security.

Because we're on the Java platform, an obvious solution is to use a Java security manager. You can grant permissions or prevent access to certain methods (System .exit(0) anyone?), to system properties, to the filesystem, and many more things. Ample documentation on this topic exists elsewhere, and it's not the goal of this chapter to cover aspects of Java itself. But be sure to remember this facility when you try to secure your DSL. Also think of the cost of a security manager. As the security checks are happening at runtime, this may lead to longer execution times for your business rules. This might not be acceptable if your code needs to execute as fast as possible.

19.9.1   Introducing SecureASTCustomizer

In the previous sections, we had the opportunity to use compiler customizers for injecting imports or AST transformations. But there's more! You can even create your own customizer by extending the CompilationCustomizer class, but here we'll investigate another existing customizer: SecureASTCustomizer.

As with the other customizers, this one should be set on the CompilerConfiguration object. It sports several setters to tell if the scripts and classes are allowed to:

- Define a package name
- Define a method
- Define a closure

And it has a white list/black list mechanism to say if the scripts and classes can use:

- Simple imports, static imports, star imports, static star imports
- Statements, expressions, tokens, constant types, and receivers

To get our feet wet, let's dive in with a concrete use case. When you offer an extension point in your application, you expose an API (better yet, a DSL) that you can use to interact with your software. If users should only use those classes from that API, you can forbid them to access any other class, thanks to our secure customizer. In that case, the whitelist approach is interesting, because you can specify you only want to allow the use of classes coming from a certain package. Progressively, you can open other utility classes users may need. With the blacklist approach, you allow everything, except certain classes. Your end users shouldn't have access to the filesystem (this is a case that's covered by security managers as well). The following listing shows how you can prevent access to classes from the `java.io` package.

Listing 19.48   Prevent access to `java.io` classes

```
import org.codehaus.groovy.control.*
import org.codehaus.groovy.control.customizers.*

def secure = new SecureASTCustomizer()                    ❶ Disallow
secure.starImportsBlacklist = ['java.io.*']                  java.io imports
secure.indirectImportCheckEnabled = true                  ❷ Disallow explicit
                                                             java.io class
def config = new CompilerConfiguration()                     references
config.addCompilationCustomizers(secure)

def shell = new GroovyShell(config)

groovy.test.GroovyAssert.shouldFail {
  shell.evaluate '''
    new File('.')                                         ❸ Evaluate
  '''                                                        violating script
}
```

We specify the list of star imports that are forbidden ❶. We also enable the indirect import check ❷ because someone may use fully qualified class names instead of an import. We add the customizer to the compiler configuration object, and then we evaluate the script ❸. Because we use `File`, which is in the blacklist, we expect an error. Because we don't want to break the self-testing nature of our listings, we wrap our evaluate call within a `shouldFail` block.

The error message tells us the import of the file class isn't allowed. We didn't import it, but Groovy has an implicit import for `java.io` classes, and the indirect import checks helped us catch this case. It's a good practice to use the indirect check flag, especially in the cases where people use fully qualified names.

This first example was a bit trivial, but the samples offered within the Groovy project's source repository provide a more elaborate case study: the arithmetic shell.

19.9.2 *The ArithmeticShell*

You can use Groovy as an arithmetic expression evaluator. But if you do, what would prevent users from doing things such as `System.exit(0)` in your formulas? The secure customizer comes to the rescue here. It allows you to limit a particular invocation of the shell to allow only arithmetic expressions, effectively forbidding anything else, be it using closures, creating classes, importing classes other than `java.lang.Math`, and so forth. The following listing illustrates what's involved in creating a shell with a locked-down version of the Groovy language using the secure customizer.[5]

Listing 19.49   Configuration of the `ArithmeticShell` secure customizer

```
import org.codehaus.groovy.ast.expr.*
import org.codehaus.groovy.ast.stmt.*
import org.codehaus.groovy.control.CompilerConfiguration
import org.codehaus.groovy.control.customizers.ImportCustomizer
import org.codehaus.groovy.control.customizers.SecureASTCustomizer

import static org.codehaus.groovy.syntax.Types.*

def imports = new ImportCustomizer().addStaticStars('java.lang.Math')
def secure = new SecureASTCustomizer()

secure.with {                                            ❶ Disables closures
  closuresAllowed = false          ❷ Disables methods
  methodDefinitionAllowed = false

  importsWhitelist = []                                  ❸ Disables imports and
  staticImportsWhitelist = []                              static imports except
  staticStarImportsWhitelist = ['java.lang.Math']          java.lang.Math

  tokensWhitelist = [                                    ❹ Allows mathematical tokens
    PLUS, MINUS, MULTIPLY, DIVIDE, MOD, POWER, PLUS_PLUS,
    MINUS_MINUS, COMPARE_EQUAL, COMPARE_NOT_EQUAL,
    COMPARE_LESS_THAN, COMPARE_LESS_THAN_EQUAL,
    COMPARE_GREATER_THAN, COMPARE_GREATER_THAN_EQUAL,
  ]

  constantTypesClassesWhiteList = [                      ❺ Allows number types
    Integer, Float, Long, Double, BigDecimal,
    Integer.TYPE, Long.TYPE, Float.TYPE, Double.TYPE
  ]

  receiversClassesWhiteList = [                          ❻ Allows number receivers
    Math, Integer, Float, Double, Long, BigDecimal
  ]

  statementsWhitelist = [                                ❼ Allows only blocks and statements
    BlockStatement, ExpressionStatement
  ]

  expressionsWhitelist = [                               ❽ Allows only math-related expressions
    BinaryExpression,          ConstantExpression,
    MethodCallExpression,      StaticMethodCallExpression,
    ArgumentListExpression,    PropertyExpression,
    UnaryMinusExpression,      UnaryPlusExpression,
    PrefixExpression,          PostfixExpression,
    TernaryExpression,         ElvisOperatorExpression,
    BooleanExpression,         ClassExpression
  ]
}
```

---

[5] Listing 19.49 is based on the Groovy project's `ArithmeticShell` example class.

```
def config = new CompilerConfiguration()
config.addCompilationCustomizers(imports, secure)
def shell = new GroovyShell(config)                    9  Runs the
def result = shell.evaluate('1+cos(PI/2)')          ⟵⎤    shell
assert result == 1
```

Allowing arithmetic expressions only isn't such an easy task when you have to somehow dumb down a full-blown programming language to allow such expressions. To commence, using or defining closures ❶ and defining methods ❷ has nothing to do with arithmetic expressions, so they're disabled. The whitelist mechanism ❸ is used to disable imports except for the static star import of the java.lang.Math static methods, which provides methods such as sine, cosine, and friends. The tokens recognized by the Groovy lexer ❹ are filtered to only allow the ones that could make up math expressions, such as all the arithmetic operators, increment/decrement operators, and comparison operators. Numbers literals (*.TYPE elements) and the use of the Number classes are allowed ❺. The receiver classes ❻ are classes that can be used and that can *receive* method calls. Block statements and expression statements ❼ are allowed because an expression is wrapped in an expression statement, part of a block statement, which is the body of your script (your formula is the body of the run() method of Script). And to finish, a list of expressions that are whitelisted ❽.

Once all the customizer information is in place, we create a shell and use it ❾.

That was quite a ride! When you want to restrict precisely what users can do with the language, crafting the right rules of exclusions and inclusions can be a long task.

As an exercise in hacking, you could have a go at trying to find a workaround to do things that shouldn't be allowed by this secured arithmetic shell. Remember that hackers are more malicious than you can be, and they can find back doors easily. They could put your system down by doing something as simple as running an infinite loop doing nothing but consuming precious CPU cycles. How can you stop this?

19.9.3 *Stopping the execution of your programs*

Your application provides an extension point with a nice DSL that your users can use. For example, imagine a wiki engine that would allow authors to make their pages dynamic with Groovy scripting inside the wiki markup of the pages. What if a malicious or not careful user creates an infinite loop? What can you do to prevent this? Neither security managers nor a secure customizer can help there much. But Groovy provides three interesting AST transformations that you can apply to the sources of your scripts so that you can stop their execution when a thread is called to be interrupted, after an elapsed period of time, or after a custom condition is met (for instance, when too much of a resource is used, etc.).

Chapter 9 on AST transformations covers the @ThreadInterrupt, @TimedInterrupt, and @ConditionalInterrupt local transformations in section 9.2.6, so we won't go into much detail about their use. We'll remind you how to make local transforms transparent to the users. Because those transformations are local, users need to put the annotations into their scripts.

> **NOTE** Before going further, remember that such transformations can only be applicable on scripts and classes that are going to be compiled. You cannot apply them after the compilation has already happened—if you wanted to post-process classes from a JAR file, for example.

We learned this technique in previous sections, but we can apply it again here, by looking at how we inject the `@TimedInterrupt` in the script of the following listing.

Listing 19.50　Stopping script execution with a reliable timeout

```
import groovy.transform.*
import org.codehaus.groovy.control.*
import org.codehaus.groovy.control.customizers.*
import java.util.concurrent.TimeoutException
import static groovy.test.GroovyAssert.shouldFail

def config = new CompilerConfiguration()         ❷ Adds 2 second
config.addCompilationCustomizers(                   timeout to
    new ASTTransformationCustomizer(value: 2, TimedInterrupt)  our script
)
def shell = new GroovyShell(config)
def te = shouldFail(TimeoutException) {
    shell.evaluate '''
        for (i in 1..1000) {          ❶ Creates
          sleep 1000                    lengthy loop
        }
    '''
}
println te.message
```

A script such as ❶ would loop a thousand times, sleeping one second at each iteration, totaling more than 16 minutes of execution time. That can be a bit long for code that's not doing anything useful! Thus, we define and configure an `ASTTransformation-Customizer` for the `@TimedInterrupt` transformation, which will wait for 2 seconds before the script is interrupted ❷. As usual, this customizer is specified on the `CompilerConfiguration` that we pass in the constructor of the `GroovyShell`.

　Now what happens when you execute that program? You get a `TimeoutException` after 2 seconds:

```
Execution timed out after 2 units. Start time: Wed Feb 04 00:42:19 CET 2015
```

Please note that this interruption does *not* rely on a supervisor thread with a higher priority because that wouldn't lead to a reliable solution.

　We saw how to filter the AST with the secure customizers or how to stop the execution of long-running or resource-consuming business rules, but malicious code could try to cheat by using metaprogramming tricks. Let's see what you can do to prevent this from happening.

19.9.4 *Preventing cheating with metaprogramming*

A customer we worked with didn't want to use security managers to forbid calls to `System.exit(0)` in their business rules, as security managers would almost double the runtime execution speed of those rules. They ended up hooking into the Groovy compiler to filter the AST to check for method call expressions that would happen on the `java.lang.System` class, with a method name of `exit`. They did that before the compilation customizers even existed. We'll replicate with customizers what they did. Interestingly, we'll also learn how to create our own customizer beyond the three we've already learned about.

The following listing creates a custom customizer for `System.exit()`.

Listing 19.51 Failing compilation on `System.exit()`

```
import org.codehaus.groovy.ast.*
import org.codehaus.groovy.ast.expr.*
import org.codehaus.groovy.control.*
import org.codehaus.groovy.control.customizers.*          ❶ Extends
import org.codehaus.groovy.classgen.*                        Compilation-
import org.codehaus.groovy.syntax.*                          Customizer
import static groovy.test.GroovyAssert.shouldFail
import static org.codehaus.groovy.control.CompilePhase.*

def config = new CompilerConfiguration()                  ❷ Overrides
def filter = new CompilationCustomizer(CANONICALIZATION) {    call
  void call(SourceUnit src, GeneratorContext ctxt, ClassNode cn) {  method
    new ClassCodeVisitorSupport() {
      void visitMethodCallExpression(MethodCallExpression call) {
        if (call.objectExpression.text == 'java.lang.System' &&   ❺ Detects
        call.method.text == 'exit') {                               System.exit
          src.addError(new SyntaxException(
              'System.exit() forbidden',              ❻ Flags error
              call.lineNumber, call.columnNumber))
        }
        super.visitMethodCallExpression(call)
      }
      SourceUnit getSourceUnit() { src }
    }.visitClass(cn)
  }
}
config.addCompilationCustomizers(filter)

def shell = new GroovyShell(config)
def ce = shouldFail(CompilationFailedException) {
  shell.parse '''
    System.exit(0)
  '''
}
println ce.message
```

❸ Defines visitor

❹ Overrides method call visits

To create your own customizer, you need to extend `CompilationCustomizer` ❶ by creating an anonymous inner class. You must then implement the `call()` abstract method ❷. This method has the `ClassNode` of the script or class to be introspected as an argument for finding the offending method call. To do that, we're creating a `ClassCodeVisitorSupport` object ❸ that will visit all the method call expressions in ❹. For each such call, we'll check if the receiver type is `java.lang.System` and if the method name is `exit` ❺. If this is the case, ❻, we add a compilation error that will fail the compilation of the script or class. We'll come back in the next section on error reporting.

When compilation fails, you get a message similar to the following:

```
System.exit() forbidden at line: 2, column: 5
```

It's more verbose than using a security manager, but it has no performance cost, which is good. You might think, "Job done!" But are we done with it here? We indeed fail the compilation when someone explicitly and literally writes `System.exit()` in the source code. Fine, and that's something along those lines that my customer did. But when we did the code review, we noticed this wouldn't cover all the cases—a case that the security manager would have caught though. As you start to know Groovy pretty well, you might find out how to call `System.exit(0)` and bypass our new customizer.

If you try our customizer on the following code (without `shouldFail` assertion), the compilation will work, and running the code your program will exit:

```
shell.parse '''
    def clazz = 'java.lang.System' as Class
    def method = 'e' + 'x' + 'i' + 't'
    def params = [0]
    clazz."${method}"(*params)
'''
```

The last line is an offending call to `System.exit()` that our customizer couldn't spot, since the values of the class, method name, and parameters could not really be figured out until runtime, until the execution of the code itself.

Apart from using a security manager, what could we do? In this case, you could add checks in your code, checking the method call expressions to disallow those whose method expression is a `GStringExpression`:

```
if (call.method instanceof GStringExpression) {
    source.addError(new SyntaxException('GString method names forbidden',
        call.lineNumber, call.columnNumber))
}
```

Then the compilation will fail as expected even in that odd forged case. But it comes at the price of disallowing GString method calls, which may have been useful in your DSL in certain contexts. As usual, there's no free lunch. Also, clever Groovy users can forge innovative method calls by abusing other Groovy constructs. Securing your scripts and classes isn't that trivial, but it also depends on how secure it needs to be in the first place.

With a similar approach, you'd want to prevent DSL users from doing any meta-programming in the business rules they author. For example, to filter access to the metaclass to alter the behavior of certain classes, you might add the following checks in your customizer to prevent metaClass property access as well as GString property access (that could forge a metaClass property name):

```
void visitPropertyExpression(PropertyExpression expr) {
    if (expr.property.text == 'metaClass') {
        src.addError(new SyntaxException('Accessing metaClass forbidden',
            expr.lineNumber, expr.columnNumber))
    }
    if (expr.property instanceof GStringExpression) {
        src.addError(new SyntaxException('GString access forbidden',
            expr.lineNumber, expr.columnNumber))
    }
    super.visitPropertyExpression(expr)
}
```

For metaprogramming alterations that would use categories, you could add checks in the method `call` expression as shown in the following:

```
if (call.objectExpression.text == 'this' && call.method.text == 'use') {
    src.addError(new SyntaxException('use(category){} forbidden',
        call.lineNumber, call.columnNumber))
}
```

Securing DSLs is an important aspect of their design, but another often overlooked aspect is the testing and error reporting phases, which are key to the quality and success of your endeavor. The next section looks into this topic a bit more.

19.10 *Testing and error reporting*

As software developers, we often test the nominal cases first to check that we properly implemented a feature. Oftentimes the logic to handle edge cases is shoehorned into our solution as an afterthought. It's particularly important in the context of DSLs not to do this but to put sufficient emphasis on testing various cases, including error cases such as typos a user could make throughout your design and development. As developers, we're used to reading stack traces, even large ugly nested ones, but we shouldn't push that burden onto our DSL users.

Let's focus on making our DSLs more robust. We aren't going to use any DSL-specific techniques per se, but by applying general robustness principles, we expect to make the life of our users better. We'll start by exploring ways to better handle those edge cases and give better and more meaningful error messages.

For our journey, we'll work on an SQL-like query language, with verbs and words such as select, from, and where. We want to issue queries like this:

```
query {
    select all from users
    where lastname == 'Guillaume'
}
```

In the following listing we scaffold our DSL.

Listing 19.52   Query language

```
class Query {
  static query(Closure c) {              ❶ DSL entry
    def q = c.clone()                        point
    q.resolveStrategy = Closure.DELEGATE_FIRST   ❷ Defines delegate
    q.delegate = new Query()                        and resolution
    q()                                             strategy
  }

  def getProperty(String name) { name }    ←┐ Trivial
                                              implementation of
  Query select(column)    { this }   ❹ Enables  ❸ property resolution
  Query from(table)       { this }     method
  Query where(condition)  { this }     chaining
}
```

Our `Query` class features a query method that takes a closure as argument ❶. We'll use a static import of that method later on (that we can inject with the approaches seen earlier in this chapter). We specify the closure resolve strategy to have the `Query` instance to receive all the method calls and property lookups first ❷. The parameters to our verbs are looked up through the `getProperty()` method, which returns strings for now ❸—we're not building the full-blown DSL! Finally, all our verbs are methods returning `this` ❹ to chain method calls as commands.

Now what happens when you execute a query where you make a typo in the verbs? For example:

```
query { selct all }
```

In the Groovy Swing console, you'd see an error like the following:

```
groovy.lang.MissingMethodException: No signature of method: Query.selct() is
applicable for argument types: (java.lang.String) values: [all]
    Possible solutions: select(java.lang.Object), split(groovy.lang.Closure),
getAt(java.lang.String), sleep(long), each(groovy.lang.Closure), wait()
    at errorreporting$_run_closure2.doCall(errorreporting.groovy:23)
    at errorreporting$_run_closure2.doCall(errorreporting.groovy)
    at Query.query(errorreporting.groovy:6)
    at Query$query.callStatic(Unknown Source)
    at errorreporting.run(errorreporting.groovy:23)
```

Highlighted in bold, you see that a `MissingMethodException` is thrown. The `select()` method doesn't exist, and Groovy even suggests possible alternatives, such as the right `select()` method. You also notice the line information where the problem occurred, although the class/method parts of the stack trace are perhaps a bit obscure.

Should you want to provide your own exception and message, you could add a `methodMissing()` method to your `Query` class, so that query methods that are mistyped would go through that trap:

```
def methodMissing(String name, args) {
    throw new SyntaxException(
        "No query verb '$name', only select/from/where allowed"
    )
}
```

This method uses your own custom syntax exception:

```
import groovy.transform.*

@InheritConstructors
class SyntaxException extends Exception {}
```

When you run your query, you'll get the following trace:

```
SyntaxException: No query verb 'select', only select/from/where allowed
    at Query.methodMissing(errorreporting2.groovy:18)
    at Query.invokeMethod(errorreporting2.groovy)
    at errorreporting2$_run_closure2.doCall(errorreporting2.groovy:35)
    at errorreporting2$_run_closure2.doCall(errorreporting2.groovy)
    at Query.query(errorreporting2.groovy:12)
    at Query$query.callStatic(Unknown Source)
    at errorreporting2.run(errorreporting2.groovy:35)
```

With this approach, you get your own custom exception with an even more explicit message, rather than the ones provided by Groovy itself. You'll notice, however, that the exception is coming directly from the `methodMissing()` method, and not from the place that issued the call, which happens only a couple of stack trace elements later.

The stack traces shown in this section are already filtered in the Groovy Swing console to only show relevant elements of your own programs, and the full stack trace outputted in your shell is much longer. You could still filter out more by removing the stack trace elements that hide the right method call site by changing the `methodMissing()` implementation like this:

```
def methodMissing(String name, args) {
    def se = new SyntaxException(
        "No query verb '$name', only select/from/where allowed"
    )
    se.stackTrace = se.stackTrace.findAll { StackTraceElement ste ->
        ste.className != 'Query' &&
        !(ste.methodName in ['invokeMethod', 'methodMissing'])
    }
    throw se
}
```

We rewrite the stack trace elements array of the exception by removing the offending elements we don't want the user to see, so as to only see where the problematic

DSL usage is situated. Then the filtered trace is more obvious and shows the relevant line first:

```
SyntaxException: No query verb 'selct', only select/from/where allowed
    at errorreporting3$_run_closure2.doCall(errorreporting3.groovy:41)
    at errorreporting3$_run_closure2.doCall(errorreporting3.groovy)
    at Query$query.callStatic(Unknown Source)
    at errorreporting3.run(errorreporting3.groovy:40)
```

Whether you let Groovy throw its method missing error and suggestion fixes, or you choose to use your own explicit custom exception possibly with a filtered stack trace, there's one common downside: the exception happens at runtime and not at compile time!

Usually, developers coming from a statically typed language prefer catching errors as early as possible, and compilation would be the perfect moment. Similarly, business users using your DSL would appreciate that you offer them a tool (through mere compilation) letting them know they made a mistake such as a typo, early on, rather than when the business rules are deployed in the production environment. For generating compile-time errors, nothing's better than an AST transformation or a compilation customizer. Using a customizer, you could get out with the following listing.

Listing 19.53   Checking query method names usage

```
// imports not shown
new CompilationCustomizer(SEMANTIC_ANALYSIS) {
  void call(SourceUnit src, GeneratorContext ctxt, ClassNode cn) {
    new ClassCodeVisitorSupport() {
      boolean inQueryClosure = false

      void visitStaticMethodCallExpression(                        ❶ Tracks
          StaticMethodCallExpression call) {                          when inside
        if (call.method == 'query' && call.ownerType.name == 'Query')  Query.query
          inQueryClosure = true
        super.visitStaticMethodCallExpression(call)
        if (inQueryClosure)
          inQueryClosure = false
      }

      void visitMethodCallExpression(MethodCallExpression call) {
        def methName = call.method.text
        if (                                                        ❷ Checks method
          inQueryClosure &&                                            calls are to known
          call.objectExpression.text == 'this' &&                     methods
          !(methName in ['select', 'from', 'where'])) {
            src.addError(new SyntaxException(                       ❸ Adds error
                                                                       if unknown
              "No query verb ${methName}, only select/from/where",     methods
              call.lineNumber, call.columnNumber))                     found
        }
        super.visitMethodCallExpression(call)
      }
```

```
      SourceUnit getSourceUnit() { src }
    }.visitClass(cn)
  }
}
```

With the static import of the `Query.query{}` method, we check that we're in the context of such a call by implementing the `visitStaticMethodCallExpression()` method ❶, keeping a Boolean flag up to date. We check that all method calls within that context have the correct spelling ❷.

What's more important here is we'll have a closer look at where we add the error message ❸. We're calling the `addError()` method on the `SourceUnit`. When you use a customizer or an AST transformation, that's the method to use if you want to create a compilation error. This method takes a `SyntaxException` as an argument to the constructor, to which you can pass not only the error message, but also the position of where the error is supposed to happen. There you can reuse the current AST node's line and column information, so the compiler delivers a nice error message with proper location.

The `SourceUnit` class also provides an `addException()` method which lets you pass an exception as an argument, but we would argue this method is less interesting because it's not generating the usual syntax errors IDEs would expect, nor does it give a change to properly specify position information. We'd avoid using this version.

For more control over the error reporting from the `SourceUnit` when you're using a customizer or transformation, you can retrieve its error collector with the `getError-Collector()` method, and then call more fine-grained methods than the two provided directly, as a shortcut, on `SourceUnit`. You can, for example, say if the error you're creating should fail the compilation right away or continue to find other potential errors.

> **When to use a transform vs. a customizer**
>
> For compilation errors, you might wonder whether to use an AST transformation or a compilation customizer, as transforms and customizers offer pretty much the same approach—introspecting the AST. The usual consultant's answer is...it depends! It depends on the techniques you used to implement your DSL, as well as on the integration strategy you've chosen to compile and execute your business rules. If you're already using a transform for implementing your DSL or parts of it, you should seize your chance to also add proper compilation errors there. If you're integrating your business rules using Groovy's shell, classloader, scripting engine, and so forth, then you can define a compiler configuration object to configure the compilation, and thus add your customizers at that point. If you're using global or local transformations without a particular integration mechanism (that is, your code is precompiled, not compiled on the fly), your sole option is to use an AST transformation.

We saw the case where a DSL user makes a typo in a method name, but we can also take a quick look at what happens if they use the wrong arguments for the methods forming the verbs of the DSL. More concretely, what happens if a user passes a string instead of a date argument?

To try that, let's go back to our initial `Query` class. We'll need a new verb for our experiment: an `after()` action to check that some database result is after a certain date. We need to add that method to our class:

```
Query after(Date d) { this }
```

This time, this method takes a `Date` instance. What happens if we pass a string instead of a date? A string representing a date such as `'2014/02/04'`? With neither a method missing trap nor an AST transformation checking for mistyped verbs, you'd get an exception like the following one:

```
groovy.lang.MissingMethodException: No signature of method: Query.after() is
applicable for argument types: (java.lang.String) values: [2014/02/04]
Possible solutions: after(java.util.Date), ...
```

The message is as informative as before, so you could get away with it, even if it's not your custom exception showing up here.

If you put in place a missing method trap, the error you'd get would be more misleading:

```
SyntaxException: No query verb 'after', only select/from/where/after allowed
```

Because the method with the proper signature wasn't found, it goes through our trap, and our error message is indeed misleading as the user typed `after` in their query, but the message seems to indicate `after` doesn't exist. You could improve the error message to make it clearer that a verb is not only the name of that verb, but also the type of arguments that it takes. You could also investigate using our earlier customizer to add proper checks for types, but sometimes the Groovy AST doesn't always have enough type information at compile time to figure out if there's an error. For now, we'll consider an alternative way of taking advantage of multimethods.

If you have overloaded methods taking different arguments, Groovy will always try to call at runtime the most appropriate method according to the runtime types of the arguments. In a nutshell, that's what we call multimethods. The idea is to play on that specific aspect of the multiple dispatch logic to lead your DSL to give better error messages.

In our case, we have an `after(Date)` method, but we can add an `after(Object)` method:

```
Query after(Object d)  {
    throw new SyntaxException(
        "The after method takes a Date as argument, " +
        "not ${d} of type ${d.class.name}")
}
```

Which yields a nicer error message:

```
SyntaxException: The after method takes a Date as argument, not 2015/02/04 of
type java.lang.String
    at Query.after(errorreporting5.groovy:25)
```

By overloading your DSL methods with ones taking a mere object type, if the user makes a mistake in terms of type, they'll get a more precise and meaningful error message, as the multiple dispatch will route the call to that trap method, rather than letting the Groovy runtime not find a matching method to call.

19.11 Summary

The main purpose of DSLs is to bridge the communication gap that leads to misunderstanding end users, software bugs, delays in delivery, and inadequacy with the real requirements. To bridge this gap, we've learned in this chapter how to combine many features and techniques to build your own DSLs.

We covered a lot of ground: Groovy's flexible syntax and command chains, static imports, constant and method injection, custom control structures, closure delegation strategy, AST transformations, compilation customizers, integration approaches, security concerns, and error reporting. Often, building a DSL in Groovy is a clever way of complying with the various call conventions to pimp an existing library to turn it into an easy to use DSL from Groovy.

By cleverly mixing these techniques, our business rules achieve a high-level readability, and more conciseness without necessarily verging into ASCII art. The form of the DSL matters, and we need to keep in mind that one form or another might be more approachable for our end users. That's why we need to work as a team, involving users early in the process, and work iteratively toward crafting the right language that everybody will understand.

As a parting thought, remember that as a knowledgeable Groovy developer and responsible barman shaking ingredients for a nice DSL cocktail, you must care for your customer. Mixing too many flavors only leads to headaches. We recommend a solid body of fruitful API design with a lacing of metaprogramming and a pinch of syntax sugar on top.

The Groovy ecosystem

20

This chapter covers

- Incorporating tools for automation
- Improving startup time
- Analyzing code
- Developing code on the web, on the desktop, or in the cloud

> *"I can't imagine why anyone would need X" is a statement about your imagination, not X.*
>
> —Dan Piponi, via Twitter

Groovy is a rich and flexible language and every day Groovy programmers are finding new, novel, and exciting ways to bend Groovy to their needs. The Groovy Ecosystem refers to all of the projects built around Groovy, projects that solve a particular problem for a particular group of people, and projects that are essential to being a productive Groovy programmer.

This chapter starts by examining projects that make using Groovy as a scripting language and automation tool easier: Grapes for managing dependencies within scripts, Scriptom for working with Windows components, GroovyServ for making scripts run faster, and Gradle for project and task automation.

Groovy is a good choice to use as a system scripting language. Groovy scripts are easily executed from the command line and can automate repetitive tasks. Groovy is far less verbose than Java, can easily spawn new threads and processes, and has many convenience methods for interacting with the filesystem. But the biggest advantage of scripting with Groovy is that you have access to every library you use in development. Need a script to access a SOAP-based web service? You can use the same library from your development project within your script. Need to download and manipulate web pages? You can use XmlParser and the TagSoup Java library. Any Java library is available to Groovy and it's available within a script.

After scripting, we'll look at two interesting projects meant to bring a higher level of quality for larger Groovy projects: CodeNarc for static analysis of Groovy code and GContracts for design-by-contract within Groovy. For full-blown application development we'll look at three popular application development platforms tailor-made around Groovy: Grails for web application development, Griffon for desktop development, and Gaelyk for Google App Engine cloud applications.

Buckle up and hold on—the whirlwind tour is about to start.

20.1 Groovy Grapes for self-contained scripts

A common use of scripts is working with other teams, such as the quality assurance or operations team. Assume you have a hard to reproduce defect and you need someone to execute a script on a remote machine. It's easy to email them a script, but if the script has a dependency on several jar files, then how do you easily package all into something executable? How do you get libraries onto the classpath correctly? This is the problem Grapes was invented to solve.

Grapes lets you add Maven dependencies to your classpath from within a .groovy file. The script can then be executed without downloading the dependencies and constructing a lengthy command line. Consider a script that uses the TagSoup library to read data out of poorly formatted HTML files. The following listing gives an example of this, reading the twitter coordinates of your book authors from the publisher's book page.

Listing 20.1   Using Grapes in the parse Twitter.groovy script

```
@Grab(group='org.ccil.cowan.tagsoup', module='tagsoup', version='1.2')
import org.ccil.cowan.tagsoup.Parser

def parser = new XmlParser(new Parser())
def html = parser.parse("http://manning.com/koenig2")

def twitterUrls = html.body.'**'.a.@href.grep(~/.*twitter.*/)
println twitterUrls.join("\n")

assert 'http://www.twitter.com/mittie' in twitterUrls
```

This script declares a dependency on TagSoup version 1.2 using the `@Grab` annotation. To execute this script, simply invoke it with the command `groovy parseTwitter.groovy` and you'll see a set of URLs printed to the console.

Clearly the script is importing and invoking objects from the TagSoup library, but where did this dependency come from and how was it resolved? The answer is that the Grapes module system is aware of the `@Grab` annotation. Before a script is executed, Groovy reads the `@Grab` annotations and resolves the parameters as Maven dependencies. Those dependencies are downloaded, resolved, and added to the classpath of the script. Only once all of the dependencies are resolved and in-scope does the script execution begin. There's no need to ever email another JAR file to someone or construct a long classpath statement from the command line so they can run your script. Grapes has you covered.

> **NOTE** Groovy uses Ivy to download the declared dependencies into your Grape cache, which is located in the `.groovy/grape` directory of your User Home directory. You can change this directory by passing a JVM parameter to groovy named `grape.root`. For example, passing `-Dgrape.root=/home/.m2/repository` configures Grapes to use your local Maven repository for the cache.

Many companies maintain their own internal Maven repository for their own proprietary software or because they don't want developers downloading files from the internet. You can tell Grapes about your own repositories using the `@GrabResolver` annotation. If TagSoup were located in your own repository hosted at http://myrepo.my-company.com, then you would add the `@GrabResolver` annotation to your script, like so:

```
@GrabResolver(name='myrepo', root='http://myrepo.my-company.com/')
@Grab('org.ccil.cowan.tagsoup:tagsoup:1.2')
import org.ccil.cowan.tagsoup.Parser
```

These two annotations give you pretty much everything you need for working with Grapes. Also, notice how we specified the Maven dependency using the short form that separates the common parameters using a colon. More customization is available. Grapes is controlled by the .groovy/grapeConfig.xml file in your User Home directory. You can edit this file to permanently add Grape resolvers, change the local repository directory, and configure network proxies. Dependencies can also be manually installed, removed, and listed using the Grapes command line interface.

Grapes is becoming more popular, and it provides a simple way to manage dependencies. It puts the abundance of Java libraries directly in the hands of the Groovy programmer. Tooling is becoming more frequent as well. IntelliJ IDEA has explicit support for Grapes and can automatically configure your project structure. The website MvnRepository (http://mvnrepository.com) allows you to search for dependencies and displays the correct `@Grab` use for any library you find through their site.

That's all you need to know about Grapes to get started, and it makes life easier when working with the libraries in the rest of this chapter. Next up we'll see how Scriptom makes COM and ActiveX scripting easier.

20.2 *Scriptom for Windows automation*

Scriptom's name stems from a mix of the word scripting and the acronym COM, Microsoft's component object model. Scriptom allows you to manipulate COM and ActiveX objects as simply as if you're using Visual Basic or JavaScript. Combining Scriptom and Groovy means that you can take advantage of the Java world and its libraries and at the same time control applications such as Microsoft Word or Excel from Groovy.

Scriptom is an add-on that you can install if you're running Windows. It ships with Groovy's Windows installer, or you can download and install it manually. Scriptom is composed of standard Java classes and native DLLs for both 32-bit and 64-bit architectures. The native code does the heavy lifting needed for COM integration and the Groovy and Java classes provide a dynamic DSL for the components. To test the installation, let's write our first ActiveX Groovy script:

```
import org.codehaus.groovy.scriptom.*
def wshell = new ActiveXObject('WScript.Shell')
wshell.popup('Scriptom is Groovy!')
```

If everything is installed correctly then running the code displays a short message in a native dialog box, as seen in figure 20.1. You run this code like any other Groovy script; you don't need classpath changes or anything else.

The Scriptom module uses Jacob (Java COM Bridge), an open source Java/COM bridge that allows you to call COM automation components from Java. Jacob offers a generic API that can be used to access any native object. Scriptom builds on top of the Jacob API to provide a more intuitive syn-

Figure 20.1 A native message

tax, similar to the kind that VB programmers are used to. You can set and read properties and invoke methods using the standard Groovy syntax. The following listing shows how to instantiate an instance of Internet Explorer, set properties, and then invoke the `Navigate` method to display a page.

Listing 20.2 Working with ActiveX objects

```
import org.codehaus.groovy.scriptom.ActiveXObject

def explorer = new ActiveXObject('InternetExplorer.Application')
explorer.Visible    = true
explorer.AddressBar = true
explorer.Navigate('http://www.groovy-lang.org/')
```

Most Microsoft applications can be automated with Scriptom using a COM interface. Access, Excel, FrontPage, Notepad, and all the other members of the Microsoft Office suite can be manipulated with Scriptom. In addition to applications, several utilities available on the Windows platform let you interact with the OS in a simple fashion. This is handy when your automation tasks include activities such as reading and writing keys in the registry, sending keystrokes to running applications, or popping up file dialogs, which is shown in the following listing.

Listing 20.3   Working with ActiveX objects

```
import org.codehaus.groovy.scriptom.ActiveXObject

def PARENT = 0
def OPTS   = 0
def sh     = new ActiveXObject('Shell.Application')
def folder = sh.BrowseForFolder(PARENT, 'Choose a folder', OPTS)
println "Chosen folder: ${folder.Items().Item().Path.value}"
```

With the `Shell.Application`, you can call the `BrowseForFolder` method, which shows a file-chooser widget to allow you to select a directory. The `PARENT` and `OPTS` values are the parent window (where 0 means no parent) and the option flags to use, respectively. On the last line, you can see that the method returns an object representing a file selection. On this object, you can call the `Items` method to retrieve the selected files and `Item` to select the chosen one. This item has a property called `Path` to retrieve the path of the chosen file. Finally, `value` is a Groovy property that lets you unmarshal the value of the `Path`.

You may wonder how to know which methods and properties are available on a given native object or application. Unfortunately, you have to dive into the documentation of the application you're driving and see what's available through its exposed APIs. For instance, for Microsoft applications, the best source of information is the Microsoft Developer Network (MSDN) website at http://msdn.microsoft.com/library/.

The ability to script running applications is one side of the story; the other side is that Scriptom can receive events when the person in front of the computer clicks buttons, types in text, or executes shortcuts. Also, Scriptom can receive and react to application events, such as reaching the end of a media stream in Windows Media Player. Registering for events isn't straightforward, and the Scriptom website lists the full instructions on how to do so.

Groovy and Scriptom are a powerful combination to bridge two worlds: the Java world with its many free libraries and server-side applications, and Microsoft's platform and its end-user-rich native applications. Scriptom allows you to interact almost intuitively with the host environment to create complex automation tasks and control multiple applications and external Java libraries at the same time.

20.3 GroovyServ for quick startup

We've seen how Grapes and Scriptom make Groovy an excellent choice for a scripting language. However, one challenge of the JVM we haven't yet addressed is the relatively long startup time. You can use the time command along with Groovy from the command line to write a small one-liner to display the current time, along with how long the command took to execute, shown next.[1]

Listing 20.4   Timing plain old Groovy

```
$ time groovy -e "println new Date()"
Thu Jun 02 13:37:15 CEST 2011

real 0m0.631s
user 0m0.700s
sys  0m0.130s
```

Notice two things about the output: the one-liner prints the current date and time, and the elapsed user-space time to execute this was 0.7 seconds. Compare this with how quickly the same Python script executes on the same machine, shown here.

Listing 20.5   Timing Python

```
$ time python -c 'import datetime;print str(datetime.datetime.now()) '
2011-06-02 13:36:46.542847

real 0m0.024s
user 0m0.030s
sys  0m0.000s
```

The Python version takes 0.3 seconds, which is considerably faster. Critics of the JVM point to these startup times and claim that JVM languages are not fit for scripting because of these excesses. Luckily, a Groovy project called GrooyServ fixes this situation. GroovyServ replaces the groovy client application with its own client called groovyclient. It has the same API and command line parameters, and you can see from the output that its speed is comparable to Python's, shown next.

Listing 20.6   Timing GroovyServ

```
time groovyclient -e "println new Date()"
Thu Jun 02 13:46:58 CEST 2011

real 0m0.036s
user 0m0.020s
sys  0m0.000s
```

Why so much faster? groovyclient is only half of the GroovyServ project, the other half is groovyserver. The groovyserver application starts up a JVM as a TCP/IP server and waits for groovyclient applications to connect. When a client connects, the existing JVM is reused to execute the script, which is much faster than starting up a new

---

[1]   Windows users can use Cygwin or Measure-Command from within PowerShell.

JVM process. In practice, you only need to know about `groovyclient` because it automatically starts the server the first time it's needed. The first time you use `groovyclient` the request takes longer, but all subsequent uses are fast.

GroovyServ is partially a native application, not a pure Java application, and it's available for Windows, Mac, and Ubuntu Linux. GroovyServ properly tracks the current working directory, executing your scripts out of the directory from which they were called, which is why a native application is required. GroovyServ should function like the `groovy` command even though it's a TCP/IP server. The `System.in`, `out`, and `err` are all properly streamed to the client, and calls to `System.exit()` are sent to the client as well. Environment and classpath variables are also properly propagated from script instance to script instance.

Because GroovyServ behaves the same way as normal `groovy`, people can create an alias to GroovyServ that replaces their normal `groovy` command. For Mac and Linux users, add the following line to your profile:

```
alias groovy=groovyclient
```

Windows users can use the `doskey` command to create aliases:

```
doskey groovy=groovyclient $*
```

You should understand the limitations before replacing the `groovy` command. Every script does execute in its own GroovyClassLoader, but the JVM and ContextClassLoader are shared. Commands such as `System.getProperties()` are shared between scripts, and metaprogramming changes to classes in one script may affect another. For example, adding a new method to `java.lang.String` makes that new method visible to all future scripts. You can only clear the classloader memory by restarting or killing `groovyserver`. To do this call `groovyserver -r` to restart or `groovyserver -k` to kill it. GroovyServ is under active development and the limitations described here may have been addressed by the time you read this.

Despite these limitations, GroovyServ goes a long way toward overcoming the startup time problems of the JVM. Future versions of Java might one day reduce startup times to a tolerable level, but until then GroovyServ is good enough and usable enough to be a simple solution to the problem. The next technology we'll look at is Gradle, which can help you with all sorts of automation and deployment concerns.

20.4 *Gradle for project automation*

We've seen several approaches for making Groovy a more effective scripting and task automation language. But clearly, Gradle is the *must-have* application for project automation on the Groovy platform. Gradle is a project build system designed to allow simple projects to have simple, convention-based builds, while still supporting the most complex builds for those that need it. Gradle's motto is, "Make the simple things easy and the complex things possible."

The build script for Gradle builds is a Groovy-based DSL, which allows you to write builds in either a declarative or imperative manner, as well as write plain old Groovy code whenever you need it. Gradle integrates easily with Maven repositories for dependency management, supports multiproject and multiartifact builds, has a rich plugin system, and is based around a real object-oriented domain model for projects. The easiest way to see the power of Gradle is with examples. The following listing builds a full Groovy project, integrating with Maven repositories for finding dependencies.

Listing 20.7   Groovy build script (build.gradle)

```
apply plugin: 'groovy'

repositories {
    mavenCentral()
}

dependencies {
    compile      'org.codehaus.groovy:groovy-all:2.4.0'
    testCompile 'junit:junit:4.12'
}
```

This is the entire content of a typical build.gradle file. You can run it from the command line by typing `gradle build`. This script applies the Groovy plugin, declares Maven Central as a dependency repository, and then configures the versions for Groovy and JUnit. With this build you get all the standard build targets such as `clean`, `build`, `check` (run the unit tests), and `assemble` (build the JAR files), along with several more. The build conventions are the same as in Maven: put the production source code in the /src/main/groovy directory, test source in the src/test/groovy directory, and any resources in the /src/main/resources directory.

If you're going to build a JAR file, then it's sensible to set a version number and include a manifest in the JAR file. Gradle allows you to specify this declaratively within your build file by adding the content of the following listing.

Listing 20.8   Building a JAR file

```
version = '1.0'
jar {
    baseName="mySample"
    manifest {
        attributes  'Implementation-Title': 'My Sample',
                    'Implementation-Version': version
    }
}
```

You can build the JAR file from the command line by typing `gradle assemble`, and the build will produce a file named mySample-1.0.jar. Inside the JAR is the correct MANIFEST.MF file. If you need to build a .war file, then use the war plugin and the .war file will be generated for you.

Typical modern builds, especially in the enterprise, don't only test and assemble JAR files, they also upload them to a repository so that others can use the new code. Gradle includes a standard `uploadArchives` task for this, and you should configure the task to know where to copy the new files. In the following listing, we publish to a local directory, but it's easy to publish to a remote location or several locations at once.

Listing 20.9   Publishing a JAR file

```
uploadArchives {
    repositories {
        flatDir(dirs: file('my_repository'))
    }
}
```

After running `gradle uploadArchives` you'll see that mySample-1.0.jar was copied to the `my_repository` directory.

No whirlwind tour of Gradle is complete without mentioning the Gradle Wrapper. Gradle knows how to download and install itself on client machines, eliminating the need for users to ever install Gradle once you've written your build file. This is perfect for Continuous Integration servers because you have nothing to install or configure on the remote machines. It's also convenient for open source projects where many users build the software infrequently and don't want long setup times. Perhaps more importantly than the convenience factor, using the Gradle wrapper ensures a consistent environment for everyone on your team and reproducible builds should you ever need to go back to an old version and rebuild it. To enable the Gradle Wrapper for your build, you need to add the wrapper task to your script, run the task once, and then check the results into version control. The task is fairly short and only changes when you want to upgrade Gradle:

```
task wrapper(type: Wrapper) {
    gradleVersion = '2.4'
}
```

Run the wrapper once using the `gradle wrapper` command. This creates several files on disk that need to be checked in: gradle-wrapper.jar, gradle-wrapper.properties, and the gradlew.bat and gradle shell scripts. Now any user can run the wrapper for any build task by typing `gradlew` instead of `gradle`. The wrapper will download and install Gradle, and then run any targets the user has invoked.

Many Gradle features exist, so many that they can't be covered in this short space. For a more thorough coverage we happily point you to *Gradle in Action* by Benjamin Muschko (Manning, 2014) (www.manning.com/muschko/). The online documentation is also excellent and includes a lengthy user guide, several cookbooks and tutorial-style documents, and more. There are many features to explore, such as multiproject and multiartifact builds, the Gradle Daemon (to increase performance), parallel unit test execution, multiple language integration, and dozens of plugins. If you need an automated Groovy build, then Gradle is one of the best products to consider. In the process of building the code for this book, we've used it as well. You can see that when looking at the sources of chapter 9, for example.

That's the end of the scripting and automation technologies. In the next section, we change gears and take a look at a static analysis tool that can help your Groovy code stay maintainable and of high quality.

20.5　*CodeNarc for static code analysis*

The CodeNarc project analyzes Groovy code and warns you of possible defects, bad practices, dead code, or poor Groovy style. It's a flexible system based around rules that find violations in your code, and it generates reports so you can fix problems either before checking code into version control or before the release. Consider the following innocent looking Groovy script, and then we'll see what CodeNarc thinks of it:

```
Map map = [a: 1, b: 2, "$c": 3, 'b': 4 ];
```

CodeNarc finds four violations in this one small example. Try to find them yourself before reading on. Ready for the answers?

- *Duplicate map key*—The map literal includes the key "b" twice. The value set in a Map must be unique, so the resulting Map instance only contains three elements instead of the four specified.
- *GString as map key*—The element "$c" is a GString, which should never be used as a Map key. The hashcode of a GString is unstable, so you may not find this element again!
- *Unnecessary semicolon*—The line ends in a semicolon, which is unnecessary in Groovy.
- *Unused variable*—The variable map is never used after being created.

This small example shows a good range of the issue types CodeNarc can catch. A duplicate map entry and an unused variable are examples of dead, or meaningless, pieces of code. They're probably not bugs, but they could be masking a subtle problem where the code isn't exactly doing what you think it should. The GString as map key is almost always a bug and should never be used in code.

The unnecessary semicolon is a style issue. Semicolons appear frequently with new developers used to working with Java code. The rules about style issues, such as this one, are used to help you convert to writing more Groovy code and relying less on Java idioms and practices.

Let's see a more advanced example that highlights the power and intelligence of CodeNarc. The following listing shows a closure that squares all the values of a map.

Listing 20.10　Squaring map values

```
def squareMapValues = { map ->
    if (map == null) { return null }
    if (!map) { return [] }
```

```
    return map.values().collect { it * it }
}
assert [1, 4, 9] == squareMapValues([a: 1, b: 2, c: 3])
```

CodeNarc produces two violations for the `squareMapValues` closure. One is a simple style issue and the other is more subtle.

- *Unnecessary return keyword*—The last line of the method includes the return keyword, which is unnecessary in Groovy.
- *Return `null` instead of empty collection*—If passed `null` the closure returns `null`. This means the user of the API has to perform `null` checks on the method result. It's a better practice to return an empty list when there's no result rather than a `null`.

What makes this an interesting example is that the `doubleMapValues` closure doesn't specify a return type, yet CodeNarc was smart enough to infer that the closure does return a collection and the closure could also return `null`. CodeNarc analyzes the return paths of dynamically typed methods and closures and attempts to infer their type.

CodeNarc has nearly 350 rules, and the list is constantly growing. The rules are grouped into different rulesets, or categories, such as basic, design, concurrency, security, exceptions, and others. Framework-specific rules exist, such as rules targeted at Grails or the Spock Framework. One of the most interesting categories is the concurrency ruleset. Concurrency is easy to get wrong, and many bad practices can be found automatically. The Groovy language provides nice shortcuts, but it's always good to understand the fundamentals. Consider the concurrency-related example in the following listing.

Listing 20.11 Using `@Synchronized`

```
class Person {
    List addresses

    @groovy.transform.Synchronized
    void setAddresses(List addresses) {
        this.addresses.clear()
        this.addresses.addAll(addresses)
    }
}
```

The violation generated for this code is "Inconsistent Property Synchronization." The method `setAddresses` is synchronized, but the method `getAddresses` isn't. Remember, Groovy generates a getter and a setter for each property, and this code has a synchronized setter but the hidden getter isn't synchronized. The problem is subtle and clearly needs correcting. And while you're creating the getter, remember to return a copy of the internal `List` so the code remains thread-safe.

CodeNarc can be run in numerous ways. You can use the command line runner that's simple to get working for small projects, or use the Maven, Gradle, and Ant plugins so you can run CodeNarc as part of your regular build process. Also, Grails and

Griffon users have a CodeNarc plugin that automatically runs against the codebase. But the simplest way is to run it as a unit test from a GroovyTestCase. All of these methods are fully documented on the CodeNarc website at http://codenarc.sourceforge.net/. CodeNarc's output is text, XML, or HTML. You can use the default HTML reports or define your own style sheets. Configuring CodeNarc, choosing which rules to run, and changing rule properties can all be done via Groovy markup, XML, or a plain text properties file, and again the CodeNarc website contains complete documentation. If you receive false positives or want to ignore violations, you're always free to apply the standard java.lang.SuppressWarnings annotation on classes or methods.

CodeNarc is a mature and positive addition to the Groovy ecosystem. It can be used by teams to ensure high code quality and consistency, and used by single developers to help migrate to the Groovy way of coding. CodeNarc is like a good pair programming partner, making recommendations when needed and being quiet when not. Because it's so easy to add to Groovy projects, why not give it a try?

The next project we'll review is also focused on code quality. The GContracts project allows you to follow an interesting design approach that encourages you to think about object interactions and contracts.

20.6 GContracts for improved design

The GContracts project brings the concepts of design-by-contract to the Groovy language. Design-by-contract (DbC) is a software design approach that specifies how components interact with each other. The unique part of DbC is that the specifications, or contracts, are defined as source code within the program, rather than simply in documentation. Creating classes, fields, and a public API is one way to specify a contract within Groovy. DbC extends your design capabilities by allowing you to specify class invariants, method preconditions, and method postconditions. The following listing shows these contracts applied to a kettle object. For those unfamiliar, a kettle heats water, and you can either add water to a kettle or pour water out of a kettle.

> **Listing 20.12 Using GContracts's @Invariant**

```
@Grab('org.gcontracts:gcontracts-core:1.2.12')
import org.gcontracts.annotations.*

@Invariant({ waterVolume >= 0; waterVolume <= maxVolume })
class Kettle {
    int waterVolume = 0
    int maxVolume = 1000

    // ...
}
```

The example starts by grabbing the latest version of GContracts from Maven Central using the @Grab annotation, and declaring the Kettle class with two properties: waterVolume (the current amount of water in the kettle) and maxVolume (how much the kettle can hold). The interesting part of `Kettle` is the `@Invariant` annotation. This specifies logic that must always hold true for the object. It must be true after the constructor is called or after any method is invoked. Here the invariant states the water volume cannot be negative and the water volume cannot be more than the maximum volume of the kettle. `@Invariant` is an extension of the type system, and you can define how your type behaves using whatever Groovy code you like. If the invariant is ever violated, an exception is thrown from the object. There should be no way for a programmer to end up with an object whose invariant is violated. Beyond `@Invariant`, GContracts also provides `@Requires` and `@Ensures` annotations, which can be applied to methods, as shown in the following listing.

Listing 20.13 Using GContracts's `@Requires` and `@Ensures` annotations

```
// inside listing 20.12
@Requires({ amount > 0 })
@Ensures({ waterVolume == maxVolume || waterVolume > old.waterVolume })
void addWater(int amount) {
    waterVolume = Math.min(maxVolume, amount + waterVolume)
}
```

The `addWater` method from the listing adds water to the kettle, making sure not to overflow the container. The `@Requires` code is a statement about what must be true *before* this method is called: the method parameter (`amount`) must be greater than zero. Violating the `@Requires` precondition produces an exception. The `@Ensures` code is a statement about what must be true *after* this method has been called: the water volume must be at the maximum level (`waterVolume == maxVolume`) or the volume must be greater than whatever the volume was at the beginning of the method call (`waterVolume > old.waterVolume`).

   You may wonder where `old` comes from in the expression `old.waterVolume`. The `old` variable is a snapshot, or copy, of the object's state before the method call. You also have access to the return value of the method using the `result` variable, as seen in the following listing.

Listing 20.14 Using GContracts's `result` value

```
// inside listing 20.12
@Requires({ desiredAmount > 0 })
@Ensures({
  result >= 0;
    result == 0 ? waterVolume==old.waterVolume : waterVolume<old.waterVolume
})
int pour(int desiredAmount) {
    int amountPoured = (desiredAmount <= waterVolume
            ? desiredAmount
            : waterVolume)
    waterVolume = waterVolume - amountPoured
    amountPoured
}
```

The `pour` method attempts to pour water from the kettle, returning the amount poured (`amountPoured`) to the user as an `int`. You can see in the `@Ensures` code that the result will always by zero or greater (`result >= 0`) and the final `waterVolume` of the kettle will be less than or equal to the original `waterVolume`. This `@Ensures` code is a combination of two Groovy statements separated by a semicolon. You can put as much code as you'd like within the annotation parameters, either chaining all the expressions together with `&&`, `||`, and parentheses, or by separating them with semicolons. Any valid Groovy code is a valid contract expression.

Contracts can be inherited from parent types. If you specify a contract on an interface or parent class, then all implementations and subclasses inherit that contract. You can also finely control when to apply the contracts. The JVM has several assertion enabling and disabling mechanisms built in, and GContracts honors them. Passing `-da` to the JVM disables all assertions and `-ea` enables all assertions. Also, you can enable and disable assertions based on package name. Any contracts you write for objects appear in the generated Groovydoc for that object.

DbC is a well-respected design approach that is often envied by the Java community. At one point, adding DbC was the highest voted issue in Sun's Java issue tracker. GContracts brings the core DbC features to Groovy, and Groovy's flexibility allows you to write contracts in a clean and code-centric way. GContracts is definitely a project to check out.

Next up is the jewel in the crown of Groovy: Grails. If you write web applications then you owe it to yourself to discover Grails.

20.7   *Grails for web development*

We've looked at a few libraries and applications that make working in Groovy a more productive experience. Now we'll look at a few application development platforms, starting with Grails, that make writing and deploying full applications a breeze.

Grails is a platform for writing Groovy web applications, and at its core is a Model-View-Controller (MVC) design based on Spring, database persistence on top of Hibernate, view templating with SiteMesh, project and deployment automation, and a heavy dose of metaprogramming. The underlying technology is mature and stable enough for the needs of any enterprise environment, and the use of Groovy as a language within all tiers of the MVC make it a pleasure to work with. Seeing Grails in action is the best way to appreciate it.[2]

Getting a web application up and running requires running a few command line statements and editing one or two files. Grails handles almost all the hard work for you. After installing Grails, you create an application using the `create-app` command,

---

[2] *Grails in Action, 2nd Edition,* by Glen Smith et al. (Manning Publications, 2014) at www.manning.com/gsmith2/.

as shown in the following listing. For a quick prototype, we'll create a simple contacts manager application that lets you add, edit, and delete contacts from a list.

Listing 20.15   Creating a Grails application

```
$ grails create-app contacts
Welcome to Grails 1.3.7 - http://grails.org/
Licensed under Apache Standard License 2.0
...
Created Grails Application at /home/hdarcy/contacts
cd contacts
contacts $
```

This script creates a new application template for you and configures your environment with reasonable defaults, such as an in-memory database for development and an acceptable-looking set of CSS style sheets. At this point, you could run the application successfully, but there wouldn't be much to see without defining any models, views, or controllers. Creating these is a simple step and again done from the command line, as shown in the following listing.

Listing 20.16   Creating a domain object and a controller

```
contacts $ grails create-domain-class contacts.Person
...
Created DomainClass for Person
Created Tests for Person
contacts $ grails create-controller contacts.Person
...
Created Controller for Person
Created Tests for Person
contacts $
```

As you can see from the output, not only were classes created, but also unit tests. All these files are on disk, and to see a meaningful contacts application we need to give the Person domain class a few properties and constraints and also tell the controller to provide the standard create, read, update, and delete (CRUD) actions for the Person object. The following listing shows the updated Person class.

Listing 20.17   The /grails-app/domain/contacts.Person.groovy domain object

```
package contacts

class Person {
    String name
    String email

    static constraints = {
        name  blank: false
        email email: true
    }
}
```

The application, when run, reads the properties from the object and displays a default user interface based on the class. The constraints DSL is a way to specify validations for your properties. In this case, a name is required, and the email field must be in a format for an email address. There are many more options for constraints and you can customize them yourself. The last step before running the app is to tell the controller to provide the default scaffolding, as shown in the following listing.

Listing 20.18   The /grails-app/controller/PersonController.groovy scaffolding

```
package contacts

class PersonController {
    def scaffold = Person
}
```

With this in place, we can run the app (using the `grails run-app` command) and get a reasonable UI for a `Person`. You can view all the people, add new people, edit an existing person, and delete a person. The web page displays an error if any of the domain constraints are violated, making sure your data is always consistent. Figure 20.2 shows the Person list and the detail view for a single person, all of which Grails generated for us.

There is much more you can do with Grails, such as define custom view pages, override the default controller behavior, or declare complex relationships between domain classes. But one of the most powerful features of Grails is its database interface. To interact with the database you use the Groovy Object Relational Mapping

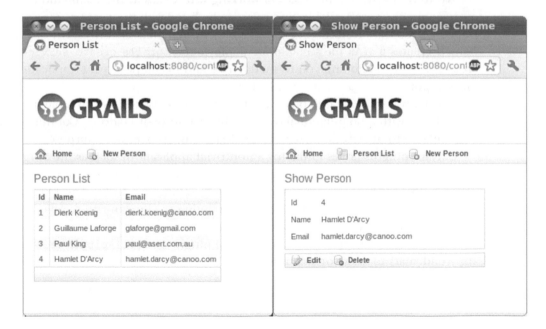

Figure 20.2   Generated list and detail view

(GORM) interface. In short, Grails automatically provides methods on your domain objects for working with the database. For instance, each domain object has a save() method that persists the object to the database, and the domain classes have a dynamic query API built into them. You can use the Grails console (run with grails console) to try queries interactively. The following listing shows GORM in action.

Listing 20.19 Accessing a database with GORM

```
import contacts
new Person(name: 'Dierk',  email: 'dierk@canoo.com').save()      ❶ Creates
new Person(name: 'Hamlet', email: 'hamlet@canoo.com').save()        persons

def people = Person.findAllByEmailLike('%canoo%')
assert people.size() == 2
def person = Person.findByEmailLikeAndNameLike('%canoo%', 'Ham%')   Finds one
assert person instanceof Person                                    ❸ person
```

Finds multiple persons ❷

The listing starts ❶ by creating two Person objects and persisting to the database (or at least the Hibernate cache) using the save() method provided by Grails. But the real magic is in the dynamic finders on the Person class. The findAllByEmailLike ❷ and findByEmailLikeAndNameLike method ❸ are dynamically created at runtime. You can use any of the properties from your domain class to invoke such a dynamic finder method, and many other comparators are supported, such as between, lessThan, and notEqual. The full DSL is one of the most powerful features of Grails.

We've only covered the basics of working with Grails at the command line. Many more commands are available, and they can be listed with the grails help command. Important commands are grails test-app (which runs all the tests), grails war[3] (which creates a WAR file suitable for deployment), grails create-service (which creates a service, allowing you to modularize and decompose your application), and most importantly, grails install-plugin.

Internally, Grails is based on a plugin architecture. GORM itself is a plugin and can be replaced with a nonrelational database like Gemfire or Hadoop. Countless plugins are available to be downloaded and installed for any conceivable purpose.

Certain plugins are essential for a nontrivial application, such as the Spring Security Core plugin (install-plugin spring-security-core), which provides your application with role based security for controller actions and URLs. The Quartz plugin (install-plugin quartz) provides job scheduling so you can run regular tasks. The Searchable plugin (install-plugin searchable) adds easy search integration from the UI for your domain classes, and the Mail plugin (install-plugin mail) lets your app send mail to users or administrators. You can choose, as we said earlier, from many, many more.

---

[3] Since Grails 3 named grails package.

Grails is the premier web application platform within the Groovy community, and is growing in use as more developers see the productivity gains and make the switch. If you're writing web applications then Grails is a must-know platform. This section is only the smallest taste of the power of Grails, and many topics were skipped entirely. If you're interested to know more, then we strongly suggest you pick up one of the many books devoted solely to Grails, such as *Grails in Action* from Manning Publications.

Grails is a great framework, but not everybody develops web applications. If you like Grails but write desktop applications, then Griffon is the framework for you. We'll look at that next.

20.8 Griffon for desktop applications

Griffon is an application development platform for desktop applications, and its goal is to bring all the benefits of Grails to desktop developers. Griffon started life as a fork of the Grails codebase, so many of the conventions and features are exactly the same between the two platforms. Today Griffon is definitely its own beast and is evolving in parallel with Grails, with its own distinct and active community. To learn all about it, we recommend—not surprisingly—*Griffon in Action* by Andres Almiray et al., (Manning Publications, 2012) (www.manning.com/almiray/).

The core concepts behind Griffon are MVC groups, services, events, and plugins. Applications are divided into several MVC groups, and the groups can themselves be composed of other MVC groups. We'll make an MVC group ourselves to see how it works. Services are a way to move shared functionality into a component, similar to how they are used in Grails. The Griffon events system allows you to send and receive events between components, both synchronously and asynchronously. Events can be application lifecycle events, like starting up and shutting down, or you can define your own in-application events. Finally, plugins are a way to bundle and deploy reusable functionality.

To demonstrate the power of Griffon, we'll create an email client that allows you to send emails through a Gmail account. The main window lets you type in typical email fields, and pressing Send sends the email through a Gmail account. Figure 20.3 shows the finished application.

To get started, create a Griffon app in the same way as a Grails app, using the `create-app` command. You'll also install two plugins: MigLayout for easier form layout and Mail for SMTP mail integration. The following listing shows these commands.

Figure 20.3 A simple Griffon application

Listing 20.20   Creating a Griffon app and installing plugins

```
$ griffon create-app mailer
...
$ cd mailer
...
mailer $ griffon install-plugin mail
...
mailer $ griffon install-plugin miglayout
...
mailer $
```

At this point we have a basic "Hello World"-style desktop application with a single model, view, and controller. We'll write the controller code first that sends emails. Controllers have public closures that are invoked from the UI. The controller has an automatic reference to both the view and the model in the following listing, which shows the code that sends an email using the Mail plugin.

Listing 20.21   Sending email in /griffon-app/controllers/mailer/MailerController.groovy

```
package mailer

class MailerController {

    def model

    def action = {
        sendMail(transport: 'smtps', auth: true,
            mailhost: 'smtp.gmail.com',
            user:     model.yourEmail,
            from:     model.yourEmail,
            password: model.yourPassword,
            to:       model.to,
            subject:  model.subject,
            text:     model.text)
    }
}
```

The `sendMail` method is provided automatically by the plugin, and the rest of the parameters are mostly moving data from our data model to the service call. The model does not yet have all of these properties, and we need to add them next. A Griffon model isn't a domain model, but is an application model. An application model allows the view and controller to exchange data, and a domain model is a way to describe the concepts and entities in your system. For example, an application model might have a field called enabled or busy, while a domain model is more concerned with being a higher level description of the system. The following listing shows our application model.

Listing 20.22   The application model in /griffon-app/model/mailer/MailerModel.groovy

```groovy
package mailer

import groovy.beans.Bindable

class MailerModel {
    @Bindable String yourEmail
    @Bindable String yourPassword
    @Bindable String to
    @Bindable String subject
    @Bindable String text
}
```

The `@Bindable` annotation exists so that properties can be automatically bound to widgets. When a widget value (like a text box) changes, the bound domain object is automatically updated. You have no need to manually write any `PropertyChange-Listener` code; Griffon handles it all for you.

The last piece of the puzzle is the view, as shown in the following listing. The view layer is a DSL for Swing components. You can declaratively specify the layout of the form and supply constraints. In this case we're using MigLayout to achieve proper alignment of components.

Listing 20.23   The view in /griffon-app/views/mailer/MailerView.groovy

```groovy
package mailer

import net.miginfocom.swing.*

application(title: 'mailer', pack: true) {

    migLayout(layoutConstraints:'wrap 2', columnConstraints:'[left][fill]')

    label('Your Email:')
    textField(text:bind(target:model, 'yourEmail'))
    label('Your Password:')
    passwordField(text:bind(target:model, 'yourPassword'))
    label('To:')
    textField(text:bind(target:model, 'to'))
    label('Subject:')
    textField(text:bind(target:model, 'subject'))
    textArea(text:bind(target:model, 'text'), rows: 6, columns: 30,
            constraints: 'span, grow, wrap')
    button(text: 'Send', actionPerformed: controller.action,
            constraints: 'span, right')
}
```

❶ Property binding

❷ Button to controller wiring

The property binding for the widgets is within the `bind` method calls at the ❶ annotations, and wiring a button to a controller action is as simple as adding the `action-Performed: controller.action` parameter to the button ❷. The UI for our mailer is displayed when you launch it with the `griffon run-app` command.

Griffon automates much of the application lifecycle, especially around deployments and packaging. Griffon has built-in support for generating Java Web Start applications, applets, and standalone apps. Additionally, the Installer plugin can be used to create native installers for a variety of platforms, such as Windows, Mac, and Linux. Griffon also handles the dirty work of signing JAR files; your application can be securely signed after placing your credentials in the correct configuration files. You can still use Griffon even if you want to commit to writing Java code. Many of the artifacts, such as the controllers and services, can still be written in plain old Java.

Desktop developers should take a long look at using Griffon for their next project. Griffon provides a strong design by basing applications on MVC groups, and plugins and services allow applications to naturally decompose into small, reusable pieces. The short-term benefits of using the numerous plugins and project automation scripts are obvious, but Griffon apps have a long-term advantage as well. The Griffon way is a blueprint for well-factored and maintainable long-term desktop apps.

The next project we'll look at is Gaelyk, a framework for building lightweight web applications on top of Google App Engine. Gaelyk is a good choice for simpler web applications that benefit from a cloud data store and free, easy deployments.

20.9   *Gaelyk for Groovy in the cloud*

Gaelyk is a lightweight yet powerful framework designed for running Groovlets and Groovy Templates Pages in the cloud using Google App Engine (GAE). With Gaelyk you have access to all the GAE services like the data store, task queue, and Jabber API, and you also benefit from the power of using Groovy as a templating engine to generate your website. Whether you need to generate HTML for a UI or JSON for an Ajax server, Gaelyk has you covered.

To demonstrate Gaelyk and GAE, we'll build a simple hello-world style HTML site that integrates with Google authentication, as shown in figure 20.4. Once you have the basics of security, routing, and Gaelyk's take on MVC, then you should have an easy time moving on to harder tasks such as working with the data store.

The first step is to download and install the Google App Engine for Java SDK; you should check the Gaelyk website to see which version is supported by Gaelyk. After

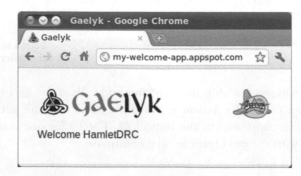

Figure 20.4   A simple
Gaelyk application

that you need to register with GAE and create an application. You register at and select an app name at http://appengine.google.com/. Our sample app is named "my-welcome-app." The last part of the setup is to download and unzip the Gaelyk template project from the Gaelyk website (gaelyk.appspot.com) .

Now that everything is installed, we can run the application locally to make sure that everything is working correctly. Gaelyk and GAE come with many helpful scripts that automate running and deploying apps. The following code snippet shows how to build and run the app locally:

```
$ groovy build.groovy
$ dev_appserver.sh
...
INFO: The server is running at http://localhost:8080/
```

At this point you can open your browser and see the standard welcome page of a Gaelyk app. With the installation verified, it's time to configure the application to use our ID and enable security. The app ID is defined in the file appengine-web.xml. Open this file with a text editor and write your app ID into the `<application>` tag, like so:

```
<application>my-welcome-app</application>
<version>1</version>
```

Also notice the version number. Over time, you'll want to increase this number each time you make a deployment or release. GAE lets you run several versions of your app at once, so managing the version number lets you test new versions in the cloud while your users continue to use the stable release.

Now let's update the web.xml to enable security. GAE uses a web.xml file, which is the standard way to define servlets, filters, and security constraints within a Java application server. By default, a Gaelyk site is public and open to anyone. We'll want to enable security so that users are required to be logged in through Google. Open the web.xml file and copy in the security description from the following listing.

Listing 20.24   Enabling security in war/WEB-INF/web.xml

```
<security-constraint>
    <web-resource-collection>
        <url-pattern>/*</url-pattern>
    </web-resource-collection>
    <auth-constraint>
        <role-name>*</role-name>
    </auth-constraint>
</security-constraint>
```

The GAE website has more information about the security constraints, but for now this is all we need. Anyone visiting our web page will need to be signed into Google first, and GAE handles the redirects and authentication for us.

At last we're ready to code application logic. Gaelyk is based on a MVC pattern that separates the UI logic into .gtpl template files and business logic into Groovy-based controllers. The key is in URL routing. As a URL is accessed, Gaelyk internally redirects that request to your controller, which performs logic and then renders a template view. In our simple app we're going to route all traffic to the "/" URL to the "welcome.groovy" controller. That controller will access the currently logged-in user information and then forward the information to the view template. The view template needs to print out a welcome message.

The first step is to edit the routes.groovy table to forward requests to our controller by adding the following line:

```
get "/", forward: "/welcome.groovy"
```

This configures the container so that any HTTP GET request is forwarded to welcome.groovy. The next step is to define the welcome controller. The controller is where you would normally access the data store, start tasks, or perform other complex logic. Our controller is simple; it exposes the current user in the request and renders the default view, which is done with two lines of code:

```
request.currentUser = user
forward 'index.gtpl'
```

The last piece of the puzzle is editing the index.gtpl view. This is a Groovy Template page, and by default the text is markup. Your tag syntax is similar to JSP syntax, and you can include scripts using the <% %> or the ${} notation:

```
<% include '/WEB-INF/includes/header.gtpl' %>
<p>Welcome ${request.currentUser.nickname}</p>
<% include '/WEB-INF/includes/footer.gtpl' %>
```

Those are the basics of Gaelyk. We can build and test locally using the groovy build.groovy and dev_appserver.sh .war commands. Google even provides mock account authentication for testing. When you're satisfied that everything is working locally then it's time to deploy to the cloud. Run the command appcfg.sh update .war to push the deployment to GAE. You'll be prompted for your Google credentials, and after a short wait you can access your application using the public App Engine URL.

This tutorial presents the bare minimum functionality of Gaelyk, but more exists. Anything you can do with GAE is accessible with Gaelyk: the data store, task queue, Jabber, image and file services, and more. GAE is a great way to get apps up and running in the cloud, and Gaelyk is the best way to use Groovy to do so. The community is active and more Gaelyk apps are being deployed all the time. Now is a great time to give it a spin.

20.10 *Summary*

This concludes our whirlwind tour of the Groovy ecosystem: those projects that aren't exactly part of Groovy itself but are essential for being a productive Groovy programmer.

If you use Groovy as a scripting and automation language, then consider mastering Grapes, Scriptom, GroovyServ, and Gradle. Grapes is a great way to easily manage script dependencies and makes sharing easy. Scriptom provides a good way to automate Windows-specific work. For frequent scripters, GroovyServ can speed up the startup time a noticeable amount. Gradle is an import technology for not only building your Groovy and Java projects, but also for project automation in general.

On the surface, CodeNarc and GContracts are different technologies. CodeNarc is focused on finding and preventing bugs in your code and helping with the enforcement of coding standards. GContracts brings DbC to Groovy, allowing you to design objects and interactions based on the expected contract of those objects. But the two technologies are similar in that both are focused on improving the overall quality of a system written in Groovy.

For web application developers, Grails is an important technology to master because it uses Groovy in several unique ways in order to make web apps fast to write, easy to maintain, and a joy to work on. Griffon does the same for desktop applications. For cloud developers, Gaelyk is a good platform for running Groovy on the Google App Engine. You can get up, running, and deployed quickly with minimum investment.

The tools presented in this chapter are useful, but you have plenty of room for innovation in the Groovy ecosystem. Two recent innovations have gone as far as compiling Groovy to different target platforms: GrooScript (http://grooscript.org) compiles Groovy code to JavaScript and the *gooid* version of the Groovy compiler produces the Android flavor of Java. This way, Groovy becomes a "native" web and mobile language. Some even call it the Swift for Android.

We pointed you to different places where Groovy applies so that you can select the one where you'll find your groove.

Let the sparks of inspiration ignite your fire, try something new, and regardless of whether it's one of these technologies or one of your own inventions: keep groovin'!

appendix A
Installation and documentation

This appendix covers

- Installing Groovy
- Finding more information

A.1 Installing Groovy

The only prerequisite for running Groovy 2.4 is that you must first have a Java Runtime Environment (JRE) for Java versions 6, 7, or 8 installed, available free from https://www.java.com/en/download and the `JAVA_HOME` environment variable set to the location of your Java installation. For any serious development work with Groovy, we recommend to not only use the JRE, but the full JDK.

To install Groovy check out http://groovy-lang.org/install.html. This will give you the latest installation instructions. We'd also like to share our experiences with you.

We like to use the Groovy enVironment Manager (GVM, http://gvmtool.net). It makes it simple keeping up to date with new versions of not only Groovy but also Grails, Griffon, Gradle, Groovyserv, and more.[1] Installing, using, and switching between versions is as easy as

```
> gvm use groovy 2.4.0
```

---

[1] Windows users might try running GVM on Cygwin or consider Posh-GVM.

using Groovy version 2.4.0 in this shell.

Each terminal window can use a different version of Groovy. To see whether your installation works correctly try

```
> groovysh
Groovy Shell (2.4.0, JVM: 1.7.0_51)
Type ':help' or ':h' for help.
----------------------------------------
groovy:000>
```

and—whoosh!—you can try Groovy code in a nice, interactive shell. GVM conveniently cares for all the grunt work of setting environment variables such as PATH, GROOVY_HOME, and so on.

GVM downloads and caches the Groovy version of your choice under your user home folder as

```
.gvm/groovy/2.4.0
```

with subfolders for .jar files to embed all of Groovy in one JAR or pick any of the Groovy modules (see appendix B) from the lib folder. This is sometimes helpful for setting up your IDE, classpath, or manual bundles. We recommend using declarative dependency management for that purpose, though.

A.2 Obtaining up-to-date documentation

This book aims to provide the necessary documentation for Groovy; however, other sources can provide more detailed, up-to-date, and responsive information. We only list a few starting points here—the community has expanded so much that the online output is difficult to put under one umbrella.

A.2.1 Using online resources

Groovy's home page is http://groovy-lang.org. This is where you can find links to all the latest information, including:

- The awesome new documentation: http://groovy-lang.org/documentation.html.
- The famous and invaluable Groovy Quick-Reference, also available under http://refcardz.dzone.com/refcardz/groovy.
- A short language description and the official Groovy Language Specification (GLS), along with the official Groovy grammar in a browser-friendly format.
- Links to the source code repository, together with live-update feeds of latest changes for those who prefer to live on the edge.
- Many articles, blogs, and tutorials about Groovy on the web where the know-it-all Groovy blog aggregator is www.groovyblogs.org, also comprising the "Groovy Weekly."
- YouTube, SlideShare, Parleys, and their equivalents are full of presentations and videos of Groovy being used for all kinds of purposes. Search for "Groovy" or the name of your favorite *Groovy in Action* author.
- http://groovyconsole.appspot.com/, where you can do live-coding in the browser.

For any questions concerning the normal use of Groovy, post questions at Stack-Overflow.com with the "groovy" tag or subscribe to user@groovy.codehaus.org. Other mailing lists (replace *user* with *dev, announce, eclipse-plugin-user,* or *scm*) deal with these respective topics.

We're constantly surprised by the responsiveness of these lists and the quality of answers that everybody receives. All mailing list participants and especially project manager Guillaume Laforge make this community a fun place to be.

A.2.2 *Connecting to the book's forum*

For questions about this book, Manning has a forum at http://www.manning.com/koenig2 where you can meet the authors. We'd love to hear from you!

appendix B
Groovy language
information

This appendix covers

- Understanding operator precedence
- Using Groovy keywords
- Using Groovy modules

B.1 Operator precedence

Table B.1 lists all the Groovy operators in order of their precedence. Most of these operators can be overridden. See table 3.4.

Table B.1 Groovy operators in order of precedence

Level	Operator	Note
1	new () () {} [] . .& .@ ?. * *. *: ~ ! (type) [] ++ --	Object creation, explicit parentheses Method call, closure, literal list/map Member access, method closure, field/attribute access Safe dereference, spread, spread-dot, spread-map Negate, not, typecast List/Map/Array index, Post inc/decrement
2	**	Power

Table B.1 Groovy operators in order of precedence *(continued)*

Level	Operator	Note
3	`++ -- + -`	Preincrement/decrement, unary sign
4	`* / %`	Multiply, div, modulo
5	`+ -`	Addition, subtraction
6	`<< >> >>> .. ..<`	Shift, range
7	`< <= > >= in instanceof as`	Relational, in instanceof, type coercion
8	`== != <=>`	Equals, not equals, compare to
	`=~ ==~`	Regex find, regex match
9	`&`	Binary and
10	`^`	Binary xor
11	`|`	Binary or
12	`&&`	Logical and
13	`||`	Logical or
14	`? :, ?:`	Ternary conditional, Elvis operator
15	`= **= *= /= %= += -=` `<<= >>= >>>= &= ^= |=`	Assignments

B.2 *Keyword list*

The list of Groovy language keywords is shown in table B.2. Not all of these keywords are used. Some keywords are reserved for future use; however, no keyword may be used as an identifier, with the exception of in.

`System.in`

Table B.2 Groovy keywords

Keywords
`abstract, any, as, assert`
`boolean, break, byte`
`case, catch, char, class, const, continue`
`def, default, do, double`
`else, enum, extends`
`false, final, finally, float, for,goto`
`if, implements, import, in, instanceof, int, interface, it, long`

Table B.2 Groovy keywords

Keywords
native, new, null
package, private, protected, public, return
short, static, strictfp, super, switch, synchronized
this, threadsafe, throw, throws, traits, transient, true, try
void, volatile, while

B.3 Modules

As part of modularization in Groovy 2.0, Groovy was split into a core module and the following (sub)modules:

```
groovy-ant
groovy-bsf
groovy-console
groovy-docgenerator
groovy-groovydoc
groovy-groovysh
groovy-jmx
groovy-json
groovy-jsr223
groovy-nio
groovy-servlet
groovy-sql
groovy-swing
groovy-templates
groovy-test
groovy-testng
groovy-xml
```

Each module is packaged into a separate JAR file. Most people use the *groovy-all* JAR, which combines the classes from all these modules plus embedded versions of ANTLR, ASM, and Commons CLI. The normal (non-all) groovy JAR doesn't have these modules but does have the embedded ANTLR, ASM, and Commons CLI classes. In earlier versions of Groovy, the non-all JAR didn't have embedded versions of ANTLR, ASM, and Commons CLI and required you to have compatible versions of at least the first two of these in your classpath. If you use Groovy in an embedded context, you can either use the *groovy-all* JAR or you can mix and match the non-all JAR files with whichever of these modules are appropriate for your circumstances.

For all JAR files mentioned, additional versions make use of the *invoke dynamic* feature of Java 7 and above. They're marked with an *–indy* suffix. Those versions can run considerably faster, but you should measure the effect for your environment. They only work when your code is executed with Java versions 7 or 8.

appendix C
GDK API quick reference

This appendix covers

■ Understanding Groovy primitives

■ Listing Groovy packages

See http://docs.groovy-lang.org/2.4.0/html/groovy-jdk/ and http://docs.groovy-lang.org/2.4.0/html/gapi/ for further information, including parameter details and API documentation.

Array of primitives

Table C.1 Groovy primitives

Primitive type	Method name	Parameter types	Return type
byte[]			
	asBoolean	–	Boolean
	contains	Object	Boolean
	count	Object	Number
	eachByte	Closure	void
	encodeBase64	–	Writable

Table C.1 Groovy primitives

Primitive type	Method name	Parameter types	Return type
	encodeBase64	Boolean	Writable
	encodeHex	_--	Writable
	flatten	_	Collection
	getAt	Collection	List
	getAt	IntRange	List
	getAt	ObjectRange	List
	getAt	Range	List
	size	_	int
	swap	int, int	byte[]
	toList	_	List
	toSet	_	Set
	toString	_	String
char[]			
	asBoolean	_	Boolean
	contains	Object	Boolean
	count	Object	Number
	flatten	_	Collection
	getAt	Collection	List
	getAt	IntRange	List
	getAt	ObjectRange	List
	getAt	Range	List
	size	_	int
	swap	int, int	char[]
	toList	_	List
	toSet	_	Set
	toString	_	String
double[]			
	asBoolean	_	Boolean
	contains	Object	Boolean

Table C.1   Groovy primitives *(continued)*

Primitive type	Method name	Parameter types	Return type
	count	Object	Number
	flatten	—	Collection
	getAt	Collection	List
	getAt	IntRange	List
	getAt	ObjectRange	List
	getAt	Range	List
	size	—	int
	swap	int, int	double[]
	toList	—	List
	toSet	—	Set
	toString	—	String
float[]			
	asBoolean	—	Boolean
	contains	Object	Boolean
	count	Object	Number
	flatten	—	Collection
	getAt	Collection	List
	getAt	IntRange	List
	getAt	ObjectRange	List
	getAt	Range	List
	size	—	int
	swap	int, int	float[]
	toList	—	List
	toSet	—	Set
	toString	—	String
int[]			
	asBoolean	—	Boolean
	contains	Object	Boolean
	count	Object	Number

Table C.1 Groovy primitives

Primitive type	Method name	Parameter types	Return type
	equals	int[]	Boolean
	flatten	—	Collection
	getAt	Collection	List
	getAt	IntRange	List
	getAt	ObjectRange	List
	getAt	Range	List
	size	—	int
	swap	int, int	int[]
	toList	—	List
	toSet	—	Set
	toString	—	String
long[]			
	asBoolean	—	Boolean
	contains	Object	Boolean
	count	Object	Number
	flatten	—	Collection
	getAt	Collection	List
	getAt	IntRange	List
	getAt	ObjectRange	List
	getAt	Range	List
	size	—	int
	swap	int, int	long[]
	toList	—	List
	toSet	—	Set
	toString	—	String
short[]			
	asBoolean	—	Boolean
	contains	Object	Boolean
	count	Object	Number

Table C.1   Groovy primitives *(continued)*

Primitive type	Method name	Parameter types	Return type
	flatten	—	Collection
	getAt	Collection	List
	getAt	IntRange	List
	getAt	ObjectRange	List
	getAt	Range	List
	size	—	int
	swap	int, int	short[]
	toList	—	List
	toSet	—	Set
	toString	—	String
boolean[]			
	asBoolean	—	Boolean
	contains	Object	Boolean
	count	Object	Number
	flatten	—	Collection
	getAt	Collection	List
	getAt	IntRange	List
	getAt	ObjectRange	List
	getAt	Range	List
	size	—	int
	swap	int, int	Boolean[]
	toList	—	List
	toSet	—	Set
	toString	—	String
	double		
	downto	Number, Closure	void
	upto	Number, Closure	void
	float		
	downto	Number, Closure	void

Table C.1 Groovy primitives

Primitive type	Method name	Parameter types	Return type
	upto	Number, Closure	void
long			
	downto	Number, Closure	void
	upto	Number, Closure	void

The groovy.lang package

Table C.2 groovy.lang package

Type	Method name	Parameter types	Return type
Closure			
	asType	Class	Object
	print	Object	void
	println	—	void
	println	Object	void
GString			
	asType	Class	Object
	drop	int	String
	dropWhile	Closure	String
	getAt	IntRange	String
	getAt	Range	String
	getAt	int	String
	take	int	String
	takeWhile	Closure	String
GroovyObject			
	getMetaClass	—	MetaClass
	setMetaClass	MetaClass	void
ListWithDefault			
	getAt	Collection	List
	getAt	EmptyRange	List
	getAt	Range	List

Table C.2 groovy.lang package *(continued)*

Type	Method name	Parameter types	Return type
MetaClass			
	mixin	Class	void
	mixin	Class[]	void
	mixin	List	void

The groovy.sql package

Table C.3 groovy.sql package

Type	Method name	Parameter types	Return type
GroovyResultSet			
	asBoolean	—	Boolean

The java.awt package

Table C.4 java.awt package

Type	Method name	Parameter types	Return type
Container			
	clear	—	void
	getAt	int	java.awt.Component
	iterator	—	Iterator
	leftShift	java.awt.Component	java.awt.Container
	size	—	int

The java.io package

Table C.5 java.io package

Type	Method name	Parameter types	Return type
Buffered-Reader			
	getText	—	String

Table C.5   java.io package

Type	Method name	Parameter types	Return type
Buffered- Writer			
	writeLine	String	void
Closeable			
	closeQuietly	—	void
	closeWithWarning	—	void
	withCloseable	Closure	Object
DataInput- Stream			
	iterator	—	Iterator
File			
	append	InputStream	void
	append	Object	void
	append	Object, String	void
	append	Reader	void
	append	Reader, String	void
	append	Writer	void
	append	Writer, String	void
	append	byte[]	void
	asType	Class	Object
	asWritable	—	File
	asWritable	String	File
	static createTempDir	—	File
	static createTempDir	String, String	File
	deleteDir	—	Boolean
	directorySize	—	long
	eachByte	Closure	void
	eachByte	int, Closure	void
	eachDir	Closure	void
	eachDirMatch	Object, Closure	void

Table C.5   java.io package *(continued)*

Type	Method name	Parameter types	Return type
	eachDirRecurse	Closure	void
	eachFile	Closure	void
	eachFile	groovy.io.File-Type, Closure	void
	eachFileMatch	Object, Closure	void
	eachFileMatch	groovy.io.File-Type, Object, Closure	void
	eachFileRecurse	Closure	void
	eachFileRecurse	groovy.io.File-Type, Closure	void
	eachLine	Closure	Object
	eachLine	String, Closure	Object
	eachLine	String, int, Closure	Object
	eachLine	int, Closure	Object
	eachObject	Closure	void
	filterLine	Closure	Writable
	filterLine	String, Closure	Writable
	filterLine	Writer, Closure	void
	filterLine	Writer, String, Closure	void
	getBytes	–	byte[]
	getText	–	String
	getText	String	String
	leftShift	InputStream	File
	leftShift	Object	File
	leftShift	byte[]	File
	newDataInputStream	–	DataInputStream
	newDataOutputStream	–	DataOutputStream
	newInputStream	–	BufferedInput-Stream

Table C.5   java.io package

Type	Method name	Parameter types	Return type
	newObjectInputStream	_	ObjectInputStream
	newObjectInputStream	ClassLoader	ObjectInput-Stream
	newObjectOutput-Stream	_	ObjectOutput-Stream
	newOutputStream	_	BufferedOutput-Stream
	newPrintWriter	_	PrintWriter
	newPrintWriter	String	PrintWriter
	newReader	_	BufferedReader
	newReader	String	BufferedReader
	newWriter	_	BufferedWriter
	newWriter	String	BufferedWriter
	newWriter	String, Boolean	BufferedWriter
	newWriter	Boolean	BufferedWriter
	readBytes	_	byte[]
	readLines	_	List
	readLines	String	List
	renameTo	String	Boolean
	setBytes	byte[]	void
	setText	String	void
	setText	String, String	void
	size	_	long
	splitEachLine	String, Closure	Object
	splitEachLine	String, String, Closure	Object
	splitEachLine	java.util.regex.Pattern, Closure	Object
	splitEachLine	java.util.regex.Pattern, String, Closure	Object
	traverse	Closure	void

Table C.5   java.io package (continued)

Type	Method name	Parameter types	Return type
	traverse	Map	void
	traverse	Map, Closure	void
	withDataInputStream	Closure	Object
	withDataOutputStream	Closure	Object
	withInputStream	Closure	Object
	withObjectInput-Stream	ClassLoader, Closure	Object
	withObjectInput-Stream	Closure	Object
	withObjectOutput-Stream	Closure	Object
	withOutputStream	Closure	Object
	withPrintWriter	Closure	Object
	withPrintWriter	String, Closure	Object
	withReader	Closure	Object
	withReader	String, Closure	Object
	withWriter	Closure	Object
	withWriter	String, Closure	Object
	withWriterAppend	Closure	Object
	withWriterAppend	String, Closure	Object
	write	String	void
	write	String, String	void
Input-Stream			
	eachByte	Closure	void
	eachByte	int, Closure	void
	eachLine	Closure	Object
	eachLine	String, Closure	Object
	eachLine	String, int, Closure	Object
	eachLine	int, Closure	Object

Table C.5   java.io package

Type	Method name	Parameter types	Return type
	filterLine	Closure	Writable
	filterLine	String, Closure	Writable
	filterLine	Writer, Closure	void
	filterLine	Writer, String, Closure	void
	getBytes	—	byte[]
	getText	—	String
	getText	String	String
	iterator	—	Iterator
	newObjectInputStream	—	ObjectInput-Stream
	newObjectInputStream	ClassLoader	ObjectInput-Stream
	newReader	—	BufferedReader
	newReader	String	BufferedReader
	readLines	—	List
	readLines	String	List
	splitEachLine	String, Closure	Object
	splitEachLine	String, String, Closure	Object
	splitEachLine	java.util.regex.Pattern, Closure	Object
	splitEachLine	java.util.regex.Pattern, String, Closure	Object
	withObjectInput-Stream	ClassLoader, Closure	Object
	withObjectInput-Stream	Closure	Object
	withReader	Closure	Object
	withReader	String, Closure	Object
	withStream	Closure	Object

Table C.5 java.io package *(continued)*

Type	Method name	Parameter types	Return type
Object-Input-Stream			
	eachObject	Closure	void
Object-Output-Stream			
	leftShift	Object	void
Output-Stream			
	leftShift	InputStream	OutputStream
	leftShift	Object	Writer
	leftShift	byte[]	OutputStream
	newObjectOutput-Stream	—	ObjectOutput-Stream
	newPrintWriter	—	PrintWriter
	newWriter	—	Writer
	newWriter	String	Writer
	setBytes	byte[]	void
	withObjectOutput-Stream	Closure	Object
	withPrintWriter	Closure	Object
	withStream	Closure	Object
	withWriter	Closure	Object
	withWriter	String, Closure	Object
Print-Stream			
	print	Object	void
	println	Object	void
Print-Writer			
	print	Object	void
	println	Object	void

Table C.5   java.io package

Type	Method name	Parameter types	Return type
Reader			
	eachLine	Closure	Object
	eachLine	int, Closure	Object
	filterLine	Closure	Writable
	filterLine	Writer, Closure	void
	getText	—	String
	iterator	—	Iterator
	readLine	—	String
	readLines	—	List
	splitEachLine	String, Closure	Object
	splitEachLine	java.util.regex .Pattern, Closure	Object
	transformChar	Writer, Closure	void
	transformLine	Writer, Closure	void
	withReader	Closure	Object
Writer			
	leftShift	Object	Writer
	newPrintWriter	—	PrintWriter
	withPrintWriter	Closure	Object
	withWriter	Closure	Object
	write	Writable	void

The java.lang package

Table C.6   java.lang package

Type	Method name	Parameter types	Return type
Byte[]			
	eachByte	Closure	void
	encodeBase64	—	Writable
	encodeBase64	Boolean	Writable

Table C.6   java.lang package *(continued)*

Type	Method name	Parameter types	Return type
	encodeHex	—	Writable
Object[]			
	asBoolean	—	Boolean
	asType	Class	Object
	collectEntries	—	Map
	collectEntries	Closure	Map
	collectEntries	Map	Map
	collectEntries	Map, Closure	Map
	collectMany	Closure	List
	contains	Object	Boolean
	count	Closure	Number
	count	Object	Number
	countBy	Closure	Map
	drop	int	Object[]
	dropRight	int	Object[]
	dropWhile	Closure	Object[]
	equals	List	Boolean
	find	Closure	Object
	findAll	—	Collection
	findAll	Closure	Collection
	first	—	Object
	flatten	—	Collection
	getAt	Collection	List
	getAt	EmptyRange	List
	getAt	IntRange	List
	getAt	ObjectRange	List
	getAt	Range	List
	getIndices	—	IntRange
	grep	—	Collection

Table C.6   java.lang package

Type	Method name	Parameter types	Return type
	grep	Object	Collection
	groupBy	Closure	Map
	groupBy	List	Map
	groupBy	Object[]	Map
	head	—	Object
	init	—	Object[]
	inject	Closure	Object
	inject	Object, Closure	Object
	iterator	—	Iterator
	join	String	String
	last	—	Object
	max	—	Object
	max	Closure	Object
	max	Comparator	Object
	min	—	Object
	min	Closure	Object
	min	Comparator	Object
	minus	Iterable	Object[]
	minus	Object	Object[]
	minus	Object[]	Object[]
	plus	Collection	Object[]
	plus	Iterable	Object[]
	plus	Object	Object[]
	plus	Object[]	Object[]
	reverse	—	Object[]
	reverse	Boolean	Object[]
	reverseEach	Closure	Object[]
	size	—	int
	sort	—	Object[]

Table C.6   java.lang package *(continued)*

Type	Method name	Parameter types	Return type
	sort	Closure	Object[]
	sort	Comparator	Object[]
	sort	Boolean	Object[]
	sort	Boolean, Closure	Object[]
	sort	Boolean, Comparator	Object[]
	sum	—	Object
	sum	Closure	Object
	sum	Object	Object
	sum	Object, Closure	Object
	swap	int, int	Object[]
	tail	—	Object[]
	take	int	Object[]
	takeRight	int	Object[]
	takeWhile	Closure	Object[]
	toArrayString	—	String
	toList	—	List
	toSorted	—	Object[]
	toSorted	Closure	Object[]
	toSorted	Comparator	Object[]
	toSpreadMap	—	SpreadMap
	toString	—	String
	toUnique	—	Object[]
	toUnique	Closure	Object[]
	toUnique	Comparator	Object[]
String[]			
	execute	—	Process
	execute	List, File	Process
	execute	String[], File	Process

Table C.6   java.lang package

Type	Method name	Parameter types	Return type
Appendable			
	leftShift	Object	Appendable
	withFormatter	Closure	Appendable
	withFormatter	Locale, Closure	Appendable
Boolean			
	and	Boolean	Boolean
	asBoolean	—	Boolean
	implies	Boolean	Boolean
	or	Boolean	Boolean
	toBoolean	—	Boolean
	xor	Boolean	Boolean
CharSequence			
	asBoolean	—	Boolean
	asType	Class	Object
	bitwiseNegate	—	java.util.regex.Pattern
	capitalize	—	String
	center	Number	String
	center	Number, CharSequence	String
	contains	CharSequence	Boolean
	count	CharSequence	int
	denormalize	—	String
	drop	int	CharSequence
	dropWhile	Closure	CharSequence
	eachLine	Closure	Object
	eachLine	int, Closure	Object
	eachMatch	CharSequence, Closure	CharSequence
	eachMatch	java.util.regex.Pattern, Closure	CharSequence

Table C.6 java.lang package *(continued)*

Type	Method name	Parameter types	Return type
	expand	_	String
	expand	int	String
	expandLine	int	String
	find	CharSequence	String
	find	CharSequence, Closure	String
	find	java.util.regex.Pattern	String
	find	java.util.regex.Pattern, Closure	String
	findAll	CharSequence	List
	findAll	CharSequence, Closure	List
	findAll	java.util.regex.Pattern	List
	findAll	java.util.regex.Pattern, Closure	List
	getAt	Collection	String
	getAt	EmptyRange	String
	getAt	IntRange	CharSequence
	getAt	Range	CharSequence
	getAt	int	CharSequence
	getChars	_	char[]
	isAllWhitespace	_	Boolean
	isBigDecimal	_	Boolean
	isBigInteger	_	Boolean
	isCase	Object	Boolean
	isDouble	_	Boolean
	isFloat	_	Boolean
	isInteger	_	Boolean
	isLong	_	Boolean

Table C.6   java.lang package

Type	Method name	Parameter types	Return type
	isNumber	—	Boolean
	leftShift	Object	StringBuilder
	matches	java.util.regex.Pattern	Boolean
	minus	Object	String
	minus	java.util.regex.Pattern	String
	multiply	Number	String
	next	—	String
	normalize	—	String
	padLeft	Number	String
	padLeft	Number, CharSequence	String
	padRight	Number	String
	padRight	Number, CharSequence	String
	plus	Object	String
	previous	—	String
	readLines	—	List
	replaceAll	CharSequence, CharSequence	String
	replaceAll	CharSequence, Closure	String
	replaceAll	java.util.regex.Pattern, CharSequence	String
	replaceAll	java.util.regex.Pattern, Closure	String
	replaceFirst	CharSequence, CharSequence	String
	replaceFirst	CharSequence, Closure	String

Table C.6   java.lang package *(continued)*

Type	Method name	Parameter types	Return type
	replaceFirst	java.util.regex.Pattern, Char-Sequence	String
	replaceFirst	java.util.regex.Pattern, Closure	String
	reverse	–	String
	size	–	int
	split	–	String[]
	splitEachLine	CharSequence, Closure	Object
	splitEachLine	java.util.regex.Pattern, Closure	Object
	stripIndent	–	String
	stripIndent	int	String
	stripMargin	–	String
	stripMargin	CharSequence	String
	stripMargin	char	String
	take	int	CharSequence
	takeWhile	Closure	CharSequence
	toBigDecimal	–	java.math.BigDecimal
	toBigInteger	–	java.math.BigInteger
	toDouble	–	Double
	toFloat	–	Float
	toInteger	–	Integer
	toList	–	List
	toLong	–	Long
	toSet	–	Set
	toShort	–	Short
	toURI	–	java.net.URI
	toURL	–	java.net.URL

Table C.6   java.lang package

Type	Method name	Parameter types	Return type
	tokenize	—	List
	tokenize	CharSequence	List
	tokenize	Character	List
	tr	CharSequence, CharSequence	String
	unexpand	—	String
	unexpand	int	String
	unexpandLine	int	String
Character			
	asBoolean	—	Boolean
	compareTo	Character	int
	compareTo	Number	int
	div	Character	Number
	div	Number	Number
	intdiv	Character	Number
	intdiv	Number	Number
	isDigit	—	Boolean
	isLetter	—	Boolean
	isLetterOrDigit	—	Boolean
	isLowerCase	—	Boolean
	isUpperCase	—	Boolean
	isWhitespace	—	Boolean
	minus	Character	Number
	minus	Number	Number
	multiply	Character	Number
	multiply	Number	Number
	next	—	Character
	plus	Character	Number
	plus	Number	Number

Table C.6   java.lang package *(continued)*

Type	Method name	Parameter types	Return type
	previous	–	Character
	toLowerCase	–	char
	toUpperCase	–	char
Class			
	getMetaClass	–	MetaClass
	isCase	Object	Boolean
	metaClass	Closure	MetaClass
	mixin	Class	void
	mixin	Class[]	void
	mixin	List	void
	newInstance	–	Object
	newInstance	Object[]	Object
	setMetaClass	MetaClass	void
ClassLoader			
	getRootLoader	–	ClassLoader
Comparable			
	numberAware-CompareTo	Comparable	int
Double			
	abs	–	double
	downto	Number, Closure	void
	round	–	long
	round	int	double
	trunc	–	double
	trunc	int	double
	upto	Number, Closure	void
Float			
	abs	–	float
	downto	Number, Closure	void

Table C.6   java.lang package

Type	Method name	Parameter types	Return type
	round	—	int
	round	int	float
	trunc	—	float
	trunc	int	float
	upto	Number, Closure	void
Integer			
	power	Integer	Number
Iterable			
	any	Closure	Boolean
	asCollection	—	Collection
	asList	—	List
	collate	int	List
	collate	int, Boolean	List
	collate	int, int	List
	collate	int, int, Boolean	List
	collectEntries	—	Map
	collectEntries	Closure	Map
	collectEntries	Map	Map
	collectEntries	Map, Closure	Map
	collectMany	Closure	List
	collectMany	Collection, Closure	Collection
	collectNested	Closure	List
	collectNested	Collection, Closure	Collection
	combinations	—	List
	combinations	Closure	List
	contains	Object	Boolean
	containsAll	Object[]	Boolean

Table C.6   java.lang package *(continued)*

Type	Method name	Parameter types	Return type
	count	Closure	Number
	count	Object	Number
	countBy	Closure	Map
	disjoint	Iterable	Boolean
	drop	int	Collection
	dropRight	int	Collection
	dropWhile	Closure	Collection
	each	Closure	Iterable
	eachCombination	Closure	void
	eachPermutation	Closure	Iterator
	eachWithIndex	Closure	Iterable
	every	Closure	Boolean
	findResults	Closure	Collection
	first	—	Object
	flatten	—	Collection
	flatten	Closure	Collection
	getAt	int	Object
	groupBy	Closure	Map
	groupBy	List	Map
	groupBy	Object[]	Map
	head	—	Object
	indexed	—	Map
	indexed	int	Map
	init	—	Collection
	intersect	Iterable	Collection
	join	String	String
	last	—	Object
	max	—	Object
	max	Closure	Object

Table C.6 java.lang package

Type	Method name	Parameter types	Return type
	max	Comparator	Object
	min	—	Object
	min	Closure	Object
	min	Comparator	Object
	minus	Iterable	Collection
	minus	Object	Collection
	multiply	Number	Collection
	permutations	—	Set
	permutations	Closure	List
	plus	Iterable	Collection
	plus	Object	Collection
	size	—	int
	sort	—	List
	sort	Closure	List
	sort	Boolean	List
	sort	Boolean, Closure	List
	sort	Boolean, Comparator	List
	sum	—	Object
	sum	Closure	Object
	sum	Object	Object
	sum	Object, Closure	Object
	tail	—	Collection
	take	int	Collection
	takeRight	int	Collection
	takeWhile	Closure	Collection
	toList	—	List
	toSet	—	Set
	toSorted	—	List

Table C.6   java.lang package *(continued)*

Type	Method name	Parameter types	Return type
	toSorted	Closure	List
	toSorted	Comparator	List
	toSpreadMap	—	SpreadMap
	toUnique	—	Collection
	toUnique	Closure	Collection
	toUnique	Comparator	Collection
	withIndex	—	List
	withIndex	int	List
Long			
	abs	—	long
	downto	Number, Closure	void
	power	Integer	Number
	upto	Number, Closure	void
Number			
	abs	—	int
	and	Number	Number
	asBoolean	—	Boolean
	asType	Class	Object
	bitwiseNegate	—	Number
	compareTo	Character	int
	compareTo	Number	int
	div	Character	Number
	div	Number	Number
	downto	Number, Closure	void
	intdiv	Character	Number
	intdiv	Number	Number
	isCase	Number	Boolean
	leftShift	Number	Number
	minus	Character	Number

Table C.6 java.lang package

Type	Method name	Parameter types	Return type
	minus	Number	Number
	mod	Number	Number
	multiply	Character	Number
	multiply	Number	Number
	next	—	Number
	or	Number	Number
	plus	Character	Number
	plus	Number	Number
	plus	String	String
	power	Number	Number
	previous	—	Number
	rightShift	Number	Number
	rightShiftUnsigned	Number	Number
	step	Number, Number, Closure	void
	times	Closure	void
	toBigDecimal	—	java.math.BigDecimal
	toBigInteger	—	java.math.BigInteger
	toDouble	—	Double
	toFloat	—	Float
	toInteger	—	Integer
	toLong	—	Long
	unaryMinus	—	Number
	unaryPlus	—	Number
	upto	Number, Closure	void
	xor	Number	Number
Object			
	addShutdownHook	Closure	void

Table C.6   java.lang package *(continued)*

Type	Method name	Parameter types	Return type
	any	—	Boolean
	any	Closure	Boolean
	asBoolean	—	Boolean
	asType	Class	Object
	collect	—	Collection
	collect	Closure	List
	collect	Collection, Closure	Collection
	dump	—	String
	each	Closure	Object
	eachWithIndex	Closure	Object
	every	—	Boolean
	every	Closure	Boolean
	find	—	Object
	find	Closure	Object
	findAll	—	Collection
	findAll	Closure	Collection
	findIndexOf	Closure	int
	findIndexOf	int, Closure	int
	findIndexValues	Closure	List
	findIndexValues	Number, Closure	List
	findLastIndexOf	Closure	int
	findLastIndexOf	int, Closure	int
	findResult	Closure	Object
	findResult	Object, Closure	Object
	getAt	String	Object
	getMetaClass	—	MetaClass
	getMetaProperty-Values	—	List
	getProperties	—	Map

Table C.6   java.lang package

Type	Method name	Parameter types	Return type
	grep	—	Collection
	grep	Object	Collection
	hasProperty	String	MetaProperty
	identity	Closure	Object
	inject	Closure	Object
	inject	Object, Closure	Object
	inspect	—	String
	invokeMethod	String, Object	Object
	is	Object	Boolean
	isCase	Object	Boolean
	iterator	—	Iterator
	metaClass	Closure	MetaClass
	print	Object	void
	print	PrintWriter	void
	printf	String, Object	void
	printf	String, Object[]	void
	println	—	void
	println	Object	void
	println	PrintWriter	void
	putAt	String, Object	void
	respondsTo	String	List
	respondsTo	String, Object[]	List
	setMetaClass	MetaClass	void
	static sleep	long	void
	static sleep	long, Closure	void
	split	Closure	Collection
	sprintf	String, Object	String
	sprintf	String, Object[]	String
	toString	—	String

Table C.6   java.lang package *(continued)*

Type	Method name	Parameter types	Return type
	use	Class, Closure	Object
	use	List, Closure	Object
	use	Object[]	Object
	with	Closure	Object
	withTraits	Class[]	Object
Process			
	closeStreams	_	void
	consumeProcess-ErrorStream	Appendable	Thread
	consumeProcess-ErrorStream	OutputStream	Thread
	consumeProcess-Output	_	void
	consumeProcess-Output	Appendable, Appendable	void
	consumeProcess-Output	OutputStream, OutputStream	void
	consumeProcess-OutputStream	Appendable	Thread
	consumeProcess-OutputStream	OutputStream	Thread
	getErr	_	InputStream
	getIn	_	InputStream
	getOut	_	OutputStream
	getText	_	String
	leftShift	Object	Writer
	leftShift	byte[]	OutputStream
	or	Process	Process
	pipeTo	Process	Process
	waitForOrKill	long	void
	waitForProcess-Output	_	void

Table C.6　java.lang package

Type	Method name	Parameter types	Return type
	waitForProcess-Output	Appendable, Appendable	void
	waitForProcess-Output	OutputStream, OutputStream	void
	withOutputStream	Closure	void
	withWriter	Closure	void
String			
	asType	Class	Object
	collectReplacements	Closure	String
	decodeBase64	—	byte[]
	decodeHex	—	byte[]
	eachMatch	String, Closure	String
	eachMatch	java.util.regex.Pattern, Closure	String
	execute	—	Process
	execute	List, File	Process
	execute	String[], File	Process
	getAt	IntRange	String
	getAt	Range	String
	getAt	int	String
	leftShift	Object	StringBuffer
	plus	CharSequence	String
	size	—	int
	toBoolean	—	Boolean
	toCharacter	—	Character
	toURI	—	java.net.URI
	toURL	—	java.net.URL
StringBuffer			
	leftShift	Object	StringBuffer
	plus	String	String

Table C.6   java.lang package *(continued)*

Type	Method name	Parameter types	Return type
	putAt	EmptyRange, Object	void
	putAt	IntRange, Object	void
	size	—	int
StringBuilder			
	leftShift	Object	StringBuilder
System			
	static current-TimeSeconds	—	long
Thread			
	static start	Closure	Thread
	static start	String, Closure	Thread
	static startDaemon	Closure	Thread
	static startDaemon	String, Closure	Thread

The java.math package

Table C.7   java.math package

Type	Method name	Parameter types	Return type
BigDecimal			
	downto	Number, Closure	void
	multiply	Double	Number
	multiply	java.math.Big-Integer	Number
	power	Integer	Number
	upto	Number, Closure	void
BigInteger			
	downto	Number, Closure	void
	power	Integer	Number
	power	java.math.Big-Integer	java.math.Big-Integer
	upto	Number, Closure	void

The java.net package

Table C.8   java.net package

Type	Method name	Parameter types	Return type
ServerSocket			
	accept	Closure	java.net.Socket
	accept	Boolean, Closure	java.net.Socket
Socket			
	leftShift	Object	Writer
	leftShift	byte[]	OutputStream
	withObject-Streams	Closure	Object
	withStreams	Closure	Object
URL			
	eachByte	Closure	void
	eachByte	int, Closure	void
	eachLine	Closure	Object
	eachLine	String, Closure	Object
	eachLine	String, int, Closure	Object
	eachLine	int, Closure	Object
	filterLine	Closure	Writable
	filterLine	String, Closure	Writable
	filterLine	Writer, Closure	void
	filterLine	Writer, String, Closure	void
	getBytes	—	byte[]
	getText	—	String
	getText	Map	String
	getText	Map, String	String
	getText	String	String
	newInput-Stream	—	BufferedInput-Stream

Table C.8   java.net package (continued)

Type	Method name	Parameter types	Return type
	newInput-Stream	Map	BufferedInput-Stream
	newReader	_	BufferedReader
	newReader	Map	BufferedReader
	newReader	Map, String	BufferedReader
	newReader	String	BufferedReader
	readLines	_	List
	readLines	String	List
	splitEach-Line	String, Closure	Object
	splitEach-Line	String, String, Closure	Object
	splitEach-Line	java.util.regex.Pattern, Closure	Object
	splitEach-Line	java.util.regex.Pattern, String, Closure	Object
	withInput-Stream	Closure	Object
	withReader	Closure	Object
	withReader	String, Closure	Object

The java.nio.file package

Table C.9   java.nio.file package

Type	Method name	Parameter types	Return type
Path			
	append	InputStream	void
	append	Object	void
	append	Object, String	void
	append	Reader	void
	append	Reader, String	void

Table C.9 java.nio.file package

Type	Method name	Parameter types	Return type
	append	Writer	void
	append	Writer, String	void
	append	byte[]	void
	asType	Class	Object
	asWritable	—	java.nio.file.Path
	asWritable	String	java.nio.file.Path
	deleteDir	—	Boolean
	eachByte	Closure	void
	eachByte	int, Closure	void
	eachDir	Closure	void
	eachDirMatch	Object, Closure	void
	eachDirRecurse	Closure	void
	eachFile	Closure	void
	eachFile	groovy.io.FileType, Closure	void
	eachFileMatch	Object, Closure	void
	eachFileMatch	groovy.io.FileType, Object, Closure	void
	eachFileRecurse	Closure	void
	eachFileRecurse	groovy.io.FileType, Closure	void
	eachLine	Closure	Object
	eachLine	String, Closure	Object
	eachLine	String, int, Closure	Object
	eachLine	int, Closure	Object
	eachObject	Closure	void
	filterLine	Closure	Writable
	filterLine	String, Closure	Writable
	filterLine	Writer, Closure	void

Table C.9   java.nio.file package *(continued)*

Type	Method name	Parameter types	Return type
	filterLine	Writer, String, Closure	void
	getBytes	_	byte[]
	getText	_	String
	getText	String	String
	leftShift	InputStream	java.nio.file.Path
	leftShift	Object	java.nio.file.Path
	leftShift	byte[]	java.nio.file.Path
	newDataInput-Stream	_	DataInputStream
	newDataOutput-Stream	_	DataOutput-Stream
	newInputStream	_	BufferedInput-Stream
	newObjectInput-Stream	_	ObjectInput-Stream
	newObjectInput-Stream	ClassLoader	ObjectInput-Stream
	newObjectOutput-Stream	_	ObjectOutput-Stream
	newOutputStream	_	BufferedOutput-Stream
	newPrintWriter	_	PrintWriter
	newPrintWriter	String	PrintWriter
	newReader	_	BufferedReader
	newReader	String	BufferedReader
	newWriter	_	BufferedWriter
	newWriter	String	BufferedWriter
	newWriter	String, Boolean	BufferedWriter
	newWriter	Boolean	BufferedWriter

Table C.9   java.nio.file package

Type	Method name	Parameter types	Return type
	readBytes	—	byte[]
	readLines	—	List
	readLines	String	List
	renameTo	String	Boolean
	renameTo	java.net.URI	Boolean
	setBytes	byte[]	void
	setText	String	void
	setText	String, String	void
	size	—	long
	splitEachLine	String, Closure	Object
	splitEachLine	String, String, Closure	Object
	splitEachLine	java.util.regex.Pattern, Closure	Object
	splitEachLine	java.util.regex.Pattern, String, Closure	Object
	traverse	Closure	void
	traverse	Map	void
	traverse	Map, Closure	void
	withDataInput-Stream	Closure	Object
	withDataOutput-Stream	Closure	Object
	withInputStream	Closure	Object
	withObjectInput-Stream	ClassLoader, Closure	Object
	withObjectInput-Stream	Closure	Object
	withObjectOutput-Stream	Closure	Object
	withOutputStream	Closure	Object

Table C.9   java.nio.file package *(continued)*

Type	Method name	Parameter types	Return type
	withPrintWriter	Closure	Object
	withPrintWriter	String, Closure	Object
	withReader	Closure	Object
	withReader	String, Closure	Object
	withWriter	Closure	Object
	withWriter	String, Closure	Object
	withWriterAppend	Closure	Object
	withWriterAppend	String, Closure	Object
	write	String	void
	write	String, String	void

The java.sql package

Table C.10   java.sql package

Type	Method name	Parameter types	Return type
Date			
	clearTime	—	java.sql.Date
	minus	int	java.sql.Date
	next	—	java.sql.Date
	plus	int	java.sql.Date
	previous	—	java.sql.Date
ResultSet			
	toRowResult	—	groovy.sql.GroovyRowResult
ResultSetMetaData			
	iterator	—	Iterator
Timestamp			
	minus	int	java.sql.Timestamp
	plus	int	java.sql.Timestamp

The java.util package

Table C.11   java.util package

Type	Method name	Parameter types	Return type
Abstract-Collection			
	toString	—	String
AbstractMap			
	toString	—	String
BitSet			
	and	BitSet	BitSet
	bitwiseNegate	—	BitSet
	getAt	IntRange	BitSet
	getAt	int	Boolean
	or	BitSet	BitSet
	putAt	IntRange, Boolean	void
	putAt	int, Boolean	void
	xor	BitSet	BitSet
Calendar			
	clearTime	—	Calendar
	copyWith	Map	Calendar
	downto	Calendar, Closure	void
	format	String	String
	getAt	int	int
	minus	Calendar	int
	next	—	Calendar
	previous	—	Calendar
	putAt	int, int	void
	set	Map	void
	updated	Map	Calendar
	upto	Calendar, Closure	void

Table C.11   java.util package *(continued)*

Type	Method name	Parameter types	Return type
Collection			
	addAll	Iterable	Boolean
	addAll	Iterator	Boolean
	addAll	Object[]	Boolean
	asBoolean	—	Boolean
	asImmutable	—	Collection
	asSynchronized	—	Collection
	asType	Class	Object
	collect	—	List
	collect	Closure	List
	collect	Collection, Closure	Collection
	collectNested	Closure	List
	each	Closure	Collection
	eachWithIndex	Closure	Collection
	find	—	Object
	find	Closure	Object
	findAll	—	Collection
	findAll	Closure	Collection
	findResult	Closure	Object
	findResult	Object, Closure	Object
	flatten	—	Collection
	getAt	String	List
	getIndices	—	IntRange
	grep	—	Collection
	grep	Object	Collection
	inject	Closure	Object
	inject	Object, Closure	Object
	intersect	Collection	Collection

Table C.11   java.util package

Type	Method name	Parameter types	Return type
	isCase	Object	Boolean
	leftShift	Object	Collection
	minus	Collection	Collection
	plus	Collection	Collection
	plus	Iterable	Collection
	plus	Object	Collection
	removeAll	Closure	Boolean
	removeAll	Object[]	Boolean
	removeElement	Object	Boolean
	retainAll	Closure	Boolean
	retainAll	Object[]	Boolean
	split	Closure	Collection
	toListString	—	String
	toListString	int	String
	toSet	—	Set
	unique	—	Collection
	unique	Closure	Collection
	unique	Comparator	Collection
	unique	Boolean	Collection
	unique	Boolean, Closure	Collection
	unique	Boolean, Comparator	Collection
Date	clearTime	—	Date
	copyWith	Map	Date
	downto	Date, Closure	void
	format	String	String
	format	String, TimeZone	String
	getAt	int	int

Table C.11   java.util package *(continued)*

Type	Method name	Parameter types	Return type
	getDateString	_	String
	getDateTimeString	_	String
	getTimeString	_	String
	minus	Date	int
	minus	int	Date
	next	_	Date
	static parse	String, String	Date
	static parseToStringDate	String	Date
	plus	int	Date
	previous	_	Date
	putAt	int, int	void
	set	Map	void
	toCalendar	_	Calendar
	toTimestamp	_	java.sql.Time- stamp
	updated	Map	Date
	upto	Date, Closure	void
Enumeration			
	asBoolean	_	Boolean
	iterator	_	Iterator
	toList	_	List
	toSet	_	Set
Iterator			
	any	Closure	Boolean
	asBoolean	_	Boolean
	collectEntries	_	Map
	collectEntries	Closure	Map
	collectEntries	Map	Map
	collectEntries	Map, Closure	Map

Table C.11 java.util package

Type	Method name	Parameter types	Return type
	collectMany	Closure	List
	count	Closure	Number
	count	Object	Number
	countBy	Closure	Map
	drop	int	Iterator
	dropRight	int	Iterator
	dropWhile	Closure	Iterator
	each	Closure	Iterator
	eachWithIndex	Closure	Iterator
	every	Closure	Boolean
	getAt	int	Object
	indexed	—	Iterator
	indexed	int	Iterator
	init	—	Iterator
	inject	Object, Closure	Object
	iterator	—	Iterator
	join	String	String
	max	—	Object
	max	Closure	Object
	max	Comparator	Object
	min	—	Object
	min	Closure	Object
	min	Comparator	Object
	reverse	—	Iterator
	size	—	int
	sort	—	Iterator
	sort	Closure	Iterator
	sort	Comparator	Iterator
	sum	—	Object

Table C.11   java.util package *(continued)*

Type	Method name	Parameter types	Return type
	sum	Closure	Object
	sum	Object	Object
	sum	Object, Closure	Object
	tail	—	Iterator
	take	int	Iterator
	takeWhile	Closure	Iterator
	toList	—	List
	toSet	—	Set
	toSorted	—	Iterator
	toSorted	Closure	Iterator
	toSorted	Comparator	Iterator
	toUnique	—	Iterator
	toUnique	Closure	Iterator
	toUnique	Comparator	Iterator
	unique	—	Iterator
	unique	Closure	Iterator
	unique	Comparator	Iterator
	withIndex	—	Iterator
	withIndex	int	Iterator
List			
	addAll	int, Object[]	Boolean
	asImmutable	—	List
	asSynchronized	—	List
	drop	int	List
	dropRight	int	List
	dropWhile	Closure	List
	each	Closure	List
	eachWithIndex	Closure	List
	equals	List	Boolean

Table C.11 java.util package

Type	Method name	Parameter types	Return type
	equals	Object[]	Boolean
	execute	—	Process
	execute	List, File	Process
	execute	String[], File	Process
	findAll	—	List
	findAll	Closure	List
	first	—	Object
	flatten	—	List
	getAt	Collection	List
	getAt	EmptyRange	List
	getAt	Range	List
	getAt	int	Object
	grep	—	List
	grep	Object	List
	head	—	Object
	init	—	List
	intersect	Iterable	List
	last	—	Object
	leftShift	Object	List
	minus	Collection	List
	minus	Iterable	List
	minus	Object	List
	multiply	Number	List
	plus	Collection	List
	plus	Iterable	List
	plus	Object	List
	plus	int, Iterable	List
	plus	int, List	List
	plus	int, Object[]	List

Table C.11   java.util package *(continued)*

Type	Method name	Parameter types	Return type
	pop	—	Object
	push	Object	Boolean
	putAt	EmptyRange, Collection	void
	putAt	EmptyRange, Object	void
	putAt	IntRange, Collection	void
	putAt	IntRange, Object	void
	putAt	List, List	void
	putAt	List, Object	void
	putAt	int, Object	void
	removeAt	int	Object
	reverse	—	List
	reverse	Boolean	List
	reverseEach	Closure	List
	split	Closure	List
	subsequences	—	Set
	swap	int, int	List
	tail	—	List
	take	int	List
	takeRight	int	List
	takeWhile	Closure	List
	toSpreadMap	—	SpreadMap
	toUnique	—	List
	toUnique	Closure	List
	toUnique	Comparator	List
	transpose	—	List
	unique	—	List
	unique	Closure	List
	unique	Comparator	List

Table C.11   java.util package

Type	Method name	Parameter types	Return type
	unique	Boolean	List
	unique	Boolean, Closure	List
	unique	Boolean, Comparator	List
	withDefault	Closure	List
	withEagerDefault	Closure	List
	withLazyDefault	Closure	List
Map			
	any	Closure	Boolean
	asBoolean	—	Boolean
	asImmutable	—	Map
	asSynchronized	—	Map
	asType	Class	Object
	collect	Closure	List
	collect	Collection, Closure	Collection
	collectEntries	Closure	Map
	collectEntries	Map, Closure	Map
	collectMany	Closure	Collection
	collectMany	Collection, Closure	Collection
	count	Closure	Number
	countBy	Closure	Map
	drop	int	Map
	dropWhile	Closure	Map
	each	Closure	Map
	eachWithIndex	Closure	Map
	equals	Map	Boolean
	every	Closure	Boolean
	find	Closure	Entry

Table C.11   java.util package *(continued)*

Type	Method name	Parameter types	Return type
	findAll	Closure	Map
	findResult	Closure	Object
	findResult	Object, Closure	Object
	findResults	Closure	Collection
	get	Object, Object	Object
	getAt	Object	Object
	groupBy	Closure	Map
	groupBy	List	Map
	groupBy	Object[]	Map
	groupEntriesBy	Closure	Map
	inject	Object, Closure	Object
	intersect	Map	Map
	isCase	Object	Boolean
	leftShift	Entry	Map
	leftShift	Map	Map
	max	Closure	Entry
	min	Closure	Entry
	minus	Map	Map
	plus	Collection	Map
	plus	Map	Map
	putAll	Collection	Map
	putAt	Object, Object	Object
	reverseEach	Closure	Map
	sort	—	Map
	sort	Closure	Map
	sort	Comparator	Map
	spread	—	SpreadMap
	subMap	Collection	Map
	subMap	Object[]	Map

Table C.11   java.util package

Type	Method name	Parameter types	Return type
	take	int	Map
	takeWhile	Closure	Map
	toMapString	_	String
	toMapString	int	String
	toSorted	_	Map
	toSorted	Closure	Map
	toSorted	Comparator	Map
	toSpreadMap	_	SpreadMap
	withDefault	Closure	Map
ResourceBundle			
	static getBundle	String	ResourceBundle
	static getBundle	String, Locale	ResourceBundle
Set			
	asImmutable	_	Set
	asSynchronized	_	Set
	each	Closure	Set
	eachWithIndex	Closure	Set
	equals	Set	Boolean
	findAll	_	Set
	findAll	Closure	Set
	flatten	_	Set
	grep	_	Set
	grep	Object	Set
	intersect	Iterable	Set
	leftShift	Object	Set
	minus	Collection	Set
	minus	Iterable	Set
	minus	Object	Set
	plus	Collection	Set

Table C.11   java.util package *(continued)*

Type	Method name	Parameter types	Return type
	plus	Iterable	Set
	plus	Object	Set
	split	Closure	List
SortedMap			
	asImmutable	—	SortedMap
	asSynchronized	—	SortedMap
	sort	—	SortedMap
	toSorted	—	Map
SortedSet			
	asImmutable	—	SortedSet
	asSynchronized	—	SortedSet
	drop	int	SortedSet
	dropRight	int	SortedSet
	dropWhile	Closure	SortedSet
	each	Closure	SortedSet
	eachWithIndex	Closure	SortedSet
	flatten	—	SortedSet
	init	—	SortedSet
	intersect	Iterable	SortedSet
	leftShift	Object	SortedSet
	minus	Collection	SortedSet
	minus	Iterable	SortedSet
	minus	Object	SortedSet
	plus	Collection	SortedSet
	plus	Iterable	SortedSet
	plus	Object	SortedSet
	sort	—	SortedSet
	tail	—	SortedSet
	take	int	SortedSet

Table C.11   java.util package

Type	Method name	Parameter types	Return type
	takeRight	int	SortedSet
	takeWhile	Closure	SortedSet
	toSorted	—	Set
Timer			
	runAfter	int, Closure	TimerTask

The java.util.concurrent package

Table C.12   java.util.concurrent package

Type	Method name	Parameter types	Return type
BlockingQueue			
	leftShift	Object	BlockingQueue

The java.util.regex package

Table C.13   java.util.regex package

Type	Method name	Parameter types	Return type
Matcher			
	asBoolean	—	Boolean
	getAt	Collection	List
	getAt	int	Object
	getCount	—	int
	static getLastMatcher	—	java.util.regex.Matcher
	hasGroup	—	Boolean
	iterator	—	Iterator
	matchesPartially	—	Boolean
	setIndex	int	void
	size	—	long

Table C.13   java.util.regex package *(continued)*

	Method name	Parameter types	Return type
Pattern			
	isCase	Object	Boolean

The javax.swing package

Table C.14   javax.swing package

Type	Method name	Parameter types	Return type
AbstractButton			
	setMnemonic	String	void
ButtonGroup			
	getAt	int	AbstractButton
	iterator	_	Iterator
	leftShift	AbstractButton	ButtonGroup
	size	_	int
DefaultComboBox-Model			
	clear	_	void
DefaultListModel			
	clear	_	void
	iterator	_	Iterator
	leftShift	Object	DefaultListModel
	putAt	int, Object	void
JComboBox			
	clear	_	void
	getAt	int	Object
	iterator	_	Iterator
	leftShift	Object	JComboBox
	size	_	int
JMenu			
	getAt	int	java.awt.Component

Table C.14 javax.swing package

Type	Method name	Parameter types	Return type
	iterator	—	Iterator
	leftShift	Action	JMenu
	leftShift	GString	JMenu
	leftShift	JMenuItem	JMenu
	leftShift	String	JMenu
	leftShift	java.awt.Component	JMenu
	size	—	int
JMenuBar			
	getAt	int	JMenu
	iterator	—	Iterator
	leftShift	JMenu	JMenuBar
	size	—	int
JPopupMenu			
	iterator	—	Iterator
	leftShift	Action	JPopupMenu
	leftShift	GString	JPopupMenu
	leftShift	JMenuItem	JPopupMenu
	leftShift	String	JPopupMenu
	leftShift	java.awt.Component	JPopupMenu
JTabbedPane			
	clear	—	void
	getAt	int	java.awt.Component
	iterator	—	Iterator
	size	—	int
	JToolBar		
	getAt	int	java.awt.Component
	leftShift	Action	JToolBar
	ListModel		

Table C.14   javax.swing package *(continued)*

Type	Method name	Parameter types	Return type
	getAt	int	Object
	iterator	_	Iterator
	size	_	int
MutableComboBox- Model			
	iterator	_	Iterator
	leftShift	Object	MutableComboBox- Model
	putAt	int, Object	void

The javax.swing.table package

Table C.15   javax.swing.table package

Type	Method name	Parameter types	Return type
DefaultTableModel			
	iterator	_	Iterator
	leftShift	Object	javax.swing.table .DefaultTableModel
	putAt	int, Object	void
TableColumnModel			
	getAt	int	javax.swing.table .TableColumn
	iterator	_	Iterator
	leftShift	javax.swing.table .TableColumn	javax.swing.table .TableColumnModel
	size	_	int
TableModel			
	getAt	int	Object[]
	iterator	_	Iterator
	size	_	int

The javax.swing.tree package

Table C.16 **javax.swing.tree package**

Type	Method name	Parameter types	Return type
`DefaultMutable-TreeNode`			
	`clear`	—	`void`
	`leftShift`	`javax.swing.tree.DefaultMutable-TreeNode`	`javax.swing.tree.DefaultMutable-TreeNode`
`MutableTreeNode`			
	`leftShift`	`javax.swing.tree.MutableTreeNode`	`javax.swing.tree.MutableTreeNode`
	`putAt`	`int, javax.swing.tree.Mutable-TreeNode`	`void`
`TreeNode`			
	`getAt`	`int`	`javax.swing.tree.TreeNode`
	`iterator`	—	`Iterator`
	`size`	—	`int`
`TreePath`			
	`getAt`	`int`	`Object`
	`iterator`	—	`Iterator`
	`leftShift`	`Object`	`javax.swing.tree.TreePath`
	`size`	—	`int`

The org.w3c.dom package

Table C.17 org.w3c.dom package

Type	Method name	Parameter types	Return type
org.w3c.dom.Element			
	serialize	_	String
org.w3c.dom.NodeList			
	iterator	_	Iterator

appendix D
Cheat sheets

This appendix covers

- Understanding GStrings
- Using lists, closures, and regular expressions
- Notating XML GPath

Cheat sheets provide you with quick information and examples to get you up and running quickly. For more details about any topic, refer to the corresponding section in the book or the Groovy documentation.

D.1   GStrings

For more information, see chapter 3.

```
// normal use
def    g1 =  "1 + 1 equals ${1 + 1}"
assert g1 == '1 + 1 equals 2'
assert g1 instanceof CharSequence
assert g1 instanceof GString

def x = 10

def    g2 =  "$x"   // reference
assert g2 == "10"

def    g3 =  "${x}" // expression
assert g3 == "10"
```

819

```
// lazy evaluation with a writeable closure!
def g4 = "${ -> x}" // closure
x = 20              // value change after definition
assert g4 == "20"   // lazy evaluation!
```

D.2   *Lists*

For more information, see section 4.2.

```
assert [1,2,3,4]        == (1..4)
assert [1,2,3] + [1]    == [1,2,3,1]
assert [1,2,3] << 1     == [1,2,3,1]
assert [1,2,3,1] - [1] == [2,3]
assert [1,2,3] * 2      == [1,2,3,1,2,3]
assert [1,[2,3]].flatten() == [1,2,3]
assert [1,2,3].reverse()    == [3,2,1]
assert [1,2,3].disjoint([4,5,6])
assert [1,2,3].intersect([4,3,1]) == [3,1]
assert [1,2,3].collect{ it+3 }    == [4,5,6]
assert [1,2,3,1].unique().size()  == 3
assert [1,2,3,1].count(1) == 2
assert [1,2,3,4].min()    == 1
assert [1,2,3,4].max()    == 4
assert [1,2,3,4].sum()    == 10
assert [4,2,1,3].sort()   == [1,2,3,4]
assert [4,2,1,3].findAll{ it%2 == 0 } == [4,2]

def animals = ['cat','kangaroo','koala','dog']
assert animals[2] == 'koala'
def kanimals = animals[1..2]
assert animals.findAll{ it =~ /k.*/ } == kanimals
assert animals.find{ it =~ /k.*/ }    == kanimals[0]
assert animals.grep(~/k.*/)           == kanimals

// parallel assignment as swap
def a = 1, b = 2
(a, b)   = [b, a]
assert a == 2
assert b == 1

// lesser known methods

assert animals.sort    { it.size() } == ['cat', 'dog', 'koala', 'kangaroo']
assert animals.max     { it.size() } == 'kangaroo'
assert animals.groupBy { it.size() } == [ 3:['cat','dog'], 5:['koala'],
      8:['kangaroo'] ]

assert [1,2,3].permutations().toList() == [
      [1, 2, 3], [3, 2, 1], [2, 1, 3], [3, 1, 2], [1, 3, 2], [2, 3, 1]
]
assert (1..10).collate(3)   == [[1, 2, 3], [4, 5, 6], [7, 8, 9], [10]]

def matrix = [
    ['a', 'b'],
    [ 1 ,  2 ]
]
assert matrix.transpose()    == [ ['a', 1], ['b', 2] ]
assert matrix.combinations() == [ ['a', 1], ['b', 1], ['a', 2], ['b', 2] ]
```

D.3 *Closures*

For more information, see chapter 5.

```
def add  = { x, y -> x + y }
def mult = { x, y -> x * y }
assert add(1,3)  == 4
assert mult(1,3) == 3
def min = { x, y -> [x,y].min() }
def max = { x, y -> [x,y].max() }
def atLeastTen = max.curry(10)
assert atLeastTen(5)  == 10
assert atLeastTen(15) == 15
def pairWise(list, Closure invoke) {
    if (list.size() < 2) return []
    def next = invoke(list[0],list[1])
    return [next] + pairWise(list[1..-1], invoke)
}
assert pairWise(1..5, add)  == [3, 5, 7, 9]
assert pairWise(1..5, mult) == [2, 6, 12, 20]
assert pairWise(1..5, min)  == [1, 2, 3, 4]
assert pairWise(1..5, max)  == [2, 3, 4, 5]
assert 'cbaxabc' == ['a','b','c'].inject('x'){
        result, item -> item + result + item
}
assert [1,2,3].grep{ it<3 } == [1,2]
assert [1,2,3].any{ it%2 == 0 }
assert [1,2,3].every{ it<4 }
assert (1..9).collect{it}.join()   == '123456789'
assert (1..4).collect{it*2}.join() == '2468'
```

D.4 *Regular expressions*

For more information, see section 3.5.

Table D.1 Regular expressions

Symbol	Meaning
.	Any character
^	Start of line (or start of document, when in single-line mode)
$	End of line (or end of document, when in single-line mode)
\d	Digit character
\D	Any character except digits
\s	Whitespace character
\S	Any character except whitespace
\w	Word character

Table D.1   Regular expressions *(continued)*

Symbol	Meaning
`\W`	Any character except word characters
`\b`	Word boundary
`()`	Grouping
`(x|y)`	x or y as in (Groovy|Java|Ruby)
`\1`	Backmatch to group one; for example, find doubled characters with (.)\1
`x*`	Zero or more occurrences of x
`x+`	One or more occurrences of x
`x?`	Zero or one occurrence of x
`x{m,n}`	At least m and at most n occurrences of x
`x{m}`	Exactly m occurrences of x
`[a-f]`	Character class containing the characters *a*, *b*, *c*, *d*, *e*, *f*
`[^a]`	Character class containing any character except *a*
`[aeiou]`	Character class representing lowercase vowels
`[a-z&&[^aeiou]]`	Lowercase consonants
`[a-zA-Z0-9]`	Uppercase or lowercase letter or digit
`[+|-]?(\d+(\.\d*)?)|(\.\d+)`	Positive or negative floating-point number
`^[\w-\.]+@([\w-]+\.)+[\w-]{2,4}$`	Simple email validation
`(?is:x)`	Switches mode when evaluating x; i turns on ignore-Case, s is single-line mode
`(?=regex)`	Positive lookahead
`(?<=text)`	Positive lookbehind

EXAMPLES

```
def twister = 'she sells sea shells by the sea shore'

// contains word 'shore'
assert twister =~ 'shore'

// contains 'sea' twice (two ways)
assert (twister =~ 'sea').count == 2
assert twister.split(/ /).grep(~/sea/).size() == 2

// words that start with 'sh', \b = word boundary
def shwords = (twister =~ /sh[a-z]*\b/).collect{it}.join(' ')
assert shwords == 'she shells shore'
```

```
// sh-words by parallel assignment
def (a, b, c) = twister =~ /sh[a-z]*\b/
assert a == 'she'
assert b == 'shells'
assert c == 'shore'

// four words have three letter, \S = non-Space letter
assert (twister =~ /\b\S{3}\b/).count == 4

// three words start with 's' and have 4, 5, or 6 letters
assert (twister =~ /\bs\S{4}\S?\b/).count == 3

// replace words with 'X', \w = word character
assert twister.replaceAll(/\w+/,'X') == 'X X X X X X X X'

// starts with 'she' and ends with 'shore'
def pattern = ~/she.*shore/
assert pattern.matcher(twister).matches()

// replace 'sea' with 'ocean' but only if preceded by word 'the'
def ocean = twister.replaceAll('(?<=the )sea','ocean')
assert ocean == 'she sells sea shells by the ocean shore'

// swap 1st and 2nd pairs of words
def pairs = twister =~ /(\S+) (\S+) ?/
assert pairs.hasGroup()
twister = [1, 0, 2, 3].collect{ pairs[it][0] }.join()
assert twister == 'sea shells she sells by the sea shore'
```

D.5   XML GPath notation

For more information, see chapter 14.

Groovy supports special notation for common XML processing activities. Consider the following delicious XML:

```
def recipeXml = '''
<recipe>
    <ingredients>
        <ingredient amount='2 cups'>Self-raising Flour</ingredient>
        <ingredient amount='2 tablespoons'>Icing sugar</ingredient>
        <ingredient amount='2 tablespoons'>Butter</ingredient>
        <ingredient amount='3/4 - 1 cup'>Milk</ingredient>
    </ingredients>
    <steps>
        <step>Preheat oven to 230 degrees celsius</step>
        <step>Sift flour and icing sugar into a bowl</step>
        <step>Melt butter and mix into dry ingredients</step>
        <step>Gradually add milk to the mixture until moist</step>
        <step>Turn onto floured board and cut into portions</step>
        <step>Bake for 15 minutes</step>
        <step>Serve with jam and whipped cream</step>
    </steps>
</recipe>
'''
```

Initialization for XmlSlurper looks like this:

```
def recipe  = new XmlSlurper().parseText(recipeXml)
/* … processing steps … */
```

Initialization for XmlParser looks like this:

```
def recipe  = new XmlParser().parseText(recipeXml)
/* … processing steps … */
```

Initialization for DOMCategory looks like this:

```
def reader  = new StringReader(recipeXml)
def doc     = groovy.xml.DOMBuilder.parse(reader)
def recipe  = doc.documentElement
use (groovy.xml.dom.DOMCategory) {
    /* … processing steps … */
}
```

Using XmlSlurper, XmlParser, or DOMCategory, you can write the following notation to process this XML:

```
assert 4 == recipe.ingredients.ingredient.size()

// should be 14 elements in total
assert 14 == recipe.'**'.findAll{true}.size()

// step 4 (index 3 because we start from 0) involves milk
assert recipe.steps.step[3].text().contains('milk')
assert '2 cups' == recipe.ingredients.ingredient[0].'@amount'.toString()

// two ingredients have '2 tablespoons' amount attribute
def ingredients = recipe.ingredients.ingredient.grep{
    it.'@amount' == '2 tablespoons'
}
assert ingredients.size() == 2

// every step has at least 4 words
assert recipe.steps.step.every{
    step -> step.text().tokenize(' ').size() >= 4
}
```

appendix E
Annotation parameters

This appendix covers the available parameters for the annotations known by the Groovy compiler. This includes Groovy AST transformations and related annotations.

Table E.1 Annotation groupings

AST transform	Parameter details, chapter coverage
Code generation transformations	
`@groovy.transform.builder.Builder`	Table E.6, Section 9.2.1
`@groovy.transform.EqualsAndHashCode`	Table E.16, Section 9.2.1
`@groovy.transform.IndexedProperty`	none, Section 9.2.1
`@groovy.transform.InheritConstructors`	Table E.24, Section 9.2.1
`@groovy.lang.Lazy`	Table E.25, Section 9.2.1
`@groovy.lang.Newify`	Table E.32, Section 19.8
`@groovy.transform.ToString`	Table E.41, Section 9.2.1
`@groovy.transform.TupleConstructor`	Table E.42, Section 9.2.1
Class design and design pattern annotations	
`@groovy.transform.Canonical`	Table E.8, Section 9.2.1
`@groovy.lang.Category`	Table E.9, Section 8.4.7
`@groovy.lang.Delegate`	Table E.14, Section 9.2.2
`@groovy.transform.Immutable`	Table E.23, Section 9.2.2
`@groovy.transform.Memoized`	Table E.30, Section 9.2.2

Table E.1 Annotation groupings (continued)

AST transform	Parameter details, chapter coverage
`@groovy.transform.Mixin`	Deprecated, use traits instead
`@groovy.lang.Singleton`	Table E.34, Section 9.2.2
`@groovy.transform.TailRecursive`	none
Logging improvements	
`@groovy.util.logging.Commons`	Table E.10, Section 9.2.3
`@groovy.util.logging.Log`	Table E.27, Section 9.2.3
`@groovy.util.logging.Log4j`	Table E.28, Section 9.2.3
`@groovy.util.logging.Log4j2`	Table E.29, Section 9.2.3
`@groovy.util.logging.Slf4j`	Table E.36, Section 9.2.3
Declarative concurrency	
`@groovy.transform.Synchronized`	Table E.38, Section 9.2.4
`@groovy.transform.WithReadLock`	Table E.44, Section 9.2.4
`@groovy.transform.WithWriteLock`	Table E.45, Section 9.2.4
Easier cloning and externalizing	
`@groovy.transform.AutoClone`	Table E.4, Section 9.2.5
`@groovy.transform.AutoExternalize`	Table E.5, Section 9.2.5
`@groovy.transform.ExternalizeMethods`	See @AutoExternalize
`@groovy.transform.ExternalizeVerifier`	See @AutoExternalize
Scripting support	
`@groovy.transform.BaseScript`	Table E.6
`@groovy.transform.ConditionalInterrupt`	Table E.13, Section 9.2.6
`@groovy.transform.Field`	none
`@groovy.transform.SourceURI`	Table E.37
`@groovy.transform.ThreadInterrupt`	Table E.39, Section 9.2.6
`@groovy.transform.TimedInterrupt`	Table E.40, Section 9.2.6
Compiler directives	
`@groovy.transform.AnnotationCollector`	Table E.2
`@groovy.transform.ClosureParams`	Table E.10
`@groovy.transform.CompileDynamic`	none

Table E.1 Annotation groupings

AST transform	Parameter details, chapter coverage
`@groovy.transform.CompileStatic`	Table E.12
`@groovy.lang.DelegatesTo`	Table E.15
`@groovy.lang.DelegatesTo.Target`	Table E.16
`@groovy.transform.PackageScope`	Table E.33
`@groovy.transform.SelfType`	Table E.34
`@groovy.transform.TypeChecked`	Table E.43
JavaBean/Swing patterns	
`@groovy.beans.Bindable`	none
`@groovy.beans.ListenerList`	Table E.26
`@groovy.beans.Vetoable`	none
Test assistance	
`@groovy.transform.ASTTest`	Table E.3
`@groovy.lang.NotYetImplemented`	none
Grape handling	
`@groovy.lang.Grab`	Table E.18
`@groovy.lang.GrabConfig`	Table E.19
`@groovy.lang.GrabExclude`	Table E.20
`@groovy.lang.GrabResolver`	Table E.21
`@groovy.lang.Grapes`	Table E.22

Table E.2 Parameters for `@AnnotationCollector`

Parameter name	Purpose
`processor`	This parameter can be used to define a custom processor for determining the replacement annotations for an alias annotation. By default the processor is `org.codehaus.groovy.transform.AnnotationCollector-Transform`. Custom processors need to extend that class.
`value`	A list of replacement annotations. The default processor adds these replacement annotations (if any) to the other annotations (if any) defined on the alias annotation.

Table E.3   Parameters for @ASTTest

Parameter name	Purpose
phase	This parameter specifies the compile phase after which the test code should run. By default, CompilePhase.SEMANTIC_ANALYSIS.
value	A closure which is executed against the annotated node after the specified phase has completed.

Table E.4   Parameters for @AutoClone

Parameter name	Purpose
excludes	This parameter contains a comma-separated list of property names that should be excluded from the cloning process. By default, all properties are included.
includeFields	This parameter indicates that fields, and not only properties, should be included in the cloning process. By default, only properties are included.
style	This parameter sets the style of cloning, which defaults to AutoClone-Style.CLONE. Other valid options are AutoCloneStyle.COPY_CONSTRUCTOR and AutoCloneStyle.SERIALIZATION.

Table E.5   Parameters for @AutoExternalize

Parameter name	Purpose
excludes	This parameter contains a comma-separated list of property names or a literal list of String property names that should be excluded from the read and write process. By default, all properties are included.
includeFields	This parameter indicates the fields, and not only properties, that should be included in the read and write process. By default, only properties are included.
checkPropertyTypes	Turns on strict type checking for property (or field) types. In strict mode, such types must also implement Serializable or Externalizable. If your properties have interface types that don't implement Serializable but all the concrete implementations do, or the type is of a non-Serializable class but the property will be null at runtime, then your instances will still be serializable but you can't turn on strict checking.

Table E.6   Parameter for @BaseScript

Parameter name	Purpose
value	The name of the base script class

Table E.7 Parameters for `@Builder`

Parameter name	Purpose
forClass	A class for which builder methods should be created.
builderStrategy	A class capturing the builder strategy. Default: `DefaultStrategy`.
prefix	The prefix to use when creating the setter methods.
builderClassName	For strategies that create a builder helper class, the class name to use for the helper class.
buildMethodName	For strategies that create a builder helper class that creates the instance, the method name to call to create the instance.
builderMethodName	The method name to use for a builder factory method in the source class for easy access to the builder helper class for strategies that create such a helper class.
excludes	List of field and/or property names to include within the generated builder methods.
includes	List of field and/or property names to include within the generated builder methods.

Table E.8 Parameters for `@Canonical`

Parameter name or overriding annotation	Purpose
excludes	Exclude certain properties or fields by specifying their names as a `String` with comma-separated values or a literal list of `String` values. By default, no properties are excluded. Incompatible with `includes`.
includes	Include only a specified list of properties by specifying the desired property names as a `String` with comma-separated values or a literal list of `String` values. Incompatible with `excludes`.
@ToString	Can be used in conjunction with `@Canonical` to customize behavior. See table E.41 for details. The `includes` and `excludes` parameters for `@Canonical` will be ignored for `toString()` if this annotation is present.
@EqualsAndHashCode	Can be used in conjunction with `@Canonical` to customize behavior. See table E.16 for details. The `includes` and `excludes` parameters for `@Canonical` will be ignored for `equals()` and `hashCode()` if this annotation is present.
@TupleConstructor	Can be used in conjunction with `@Canonical` to customize behavior. See table E.42 for details. The `includes` and `excludes` parameters for `@Canonical` will be ignored for the constructor if this annotation is present.

Table E.9   **Parameter for** `@Category`

Parameter name	Purpose
`value`	This required annotation parameter indicates the type of the `self` parameter of the generated category class.

Table E.10   **Parameters for** `@ClosureParams`

Parameter name	Purpose
`value`	Defines a `ClosureSignatureHint` class that the compiler will use to infer the parameter types.
`options`	A set of options passed to the hint when the type is inferred.

Table E.11   **Parameters for** `@Commons`

Parameter name	Purpose
`value`	Used to set the name of the logging variable. Defaults to `log`.
`category`	Used to set logging category name. Default is to use the class name as logging category.

Table E.12   **Parameters for** `@CompileStatic`

Parameter name	Purpose
`TypeCheckingMode value`	Used to indicate whether type checking should be performed (PASS) or skipped (SKIP).
`String[] extensions`	An optional list of classpath resource paths to type checking extensions.

Table E.13   **Parameters for** `@ConditionalInterrupt`

Parameter name	Purpose
`applyToAllClasses`	When Groovy finds the `@ConditionalInterrupt` annotation it tries to augment every class and every script in the source file. You can change this behavior by setting the `applyToAllClasses` parameter to false. When false, Groovy augments only the specific type that was annotated. For instance, annotating a class with `@Conditional-Interrupt(applyToAllClasses=false, { ... })` augments the annotated class but not any inner classes or public classes from the same source file. Annotating an import statement with `@ConditionalInterrupt(applyToAllClasses=false, { ... })` augments only the `Script` object instance and not any surrounding classes from the script file.

Table E.13 Parameters for @ConditionalInterrupt

Parameter name	Purpose
applyToAllMembers	Set this to false if you have multiple methods/closures within a class or script and only want conditional checks on some of them. Place annotations on the methods/closures that you want enhanced. When false, applyToAllClasses is automatically set to false. Set to true (the default) for blanket coverage of conditional checks on all methods, loops, and closures within the class/script.
checkOnMethodStart	Set this parameter to false to turn off the interrupt check made at the beginning of each method. By default, this check is made.
value	The value of the parameter is a closure. This closure is executed at the start of every method, closure, and loop within the specified scope. The closure return value is interpreted to a boolean using Groovy Truth.
thrown	The type of exception that should be thrown if the timeout is reached. By default an InterruptedException is thrown.

Table E.14 Parameters for @Delegate

Parameter name	Purpose
interfaces	Set this parameter to true to make the owner class implement the same interfaces as the delegate, which is the default behavior. To make the owner *not* implement the delegate interfaces, set this parameter to false.
deprecated	Set this parameter to true to have the owner class delegate methods marked as @Deprecated in the delegate. By default @Deprecated methods are not delegated.
methodAnnotations	Set to true if you want to carry over annotations from the methods of the delegate to your delegating method. By default, annotations are not carried over. Currently Closure annotation members are not supported.
parameterAnnotations	Set to true if you want to carry over annotations from the method parameters of the delegate to your delegating method. By default, annotations are not carried over. Currently Closure annotation members are not supported.
excludes	List of method and/or property names to exclude when delegating. Must not be used if includes is used. For convenience, a String with comma-separated names can be used in addition to an array (using Groovy's literal list notation) of String values. If interfaces is true (the default), you will need to manually supply any methods excluded from delegation that are required for the interface.
excludeTypes	List of interfaces containing method signatures to exclude when delegating. Only includes or includeTypes or excludes or excludeTypes should be used. If interfaces is true (the default), you will need to manually supply any methods excluded from delegation that are required for the interface.

Table E.14 Parameters for @Delegate (continued)

Parameter name	Purpose
includes	List of method and/or property names to include when delegating. Must not be used if excludes is used. For convenience, a String with comma-separated names can be used in addition to an array (using Groovy's literal list notation) of String values. If interfaces is true (the default), you will need to manually supply any methods not included via delegation that are required for the interface.
includeTypes	List of interfaces containing method signatures to exclude when delegating. Only includes or includeTypes or excludes or excludeTypes should be used. If interfaces is true (the default), you will need to manually supply any methods excluded from delegation that are required for the interface.

Table E.15 Parameters for @DelegatesTo

Parameter name	Purpose
value	Used to specify the Class that will be delegated to within the Closure parameter.
strategy	Indicates the delegating strategy with default Closure.OWNER_FIRST.
target	Indicates that we are delegating to another parameter of the method call.
genericTypeIndex	Indicates that we are delegating to a particular generic type of the target.
type	A String representation of the type.

Table E.16 Parameter for @DelegatesTo.Target

Parameter name	Purpose
value	Optional ID

Table E.17 Parameters for @EqualsAndHashCode

Parameter name	Purpose
excludes	Exclude certain properties from the calculation by specifying them as a comma-separated list or literal list of String name values. This is commonly used with an object that has an ID field. By default, no properties are excluded. Incompatible with includes.
includes	Include only a specified list of properties by specifying them as a comma-separated list or literal list of String name values. Incompatible with excludes.

Table E.17   Parameters for `@EqualsAndHashCode`

Parameter name	Purpose
cache	Set to true to cache `hashCode()` calculations. Use only for immutable objects. By default the `hashCode()` is recalculated whenever the `hashCode()` method is called.
callSuper	Include properties from the super class by setting this parameter to true. By default, the super class is not used as part of the calculation.
includeFields	Include the class's fields, not just the properties, in the calculation by setting this parameter to true. By default, fields are not taken into account.
useCanEqual	Set to false to disable generation of a `canEqual()` method to be used by `equals()`. By default the `canEqual()` method is generated. The *canEqual* idiom[a] provides a mechanism for permitting equality in the presence of inheritance hierarchies. For immutable classes with no explicit super class, this idiom is not required.

a. "How to Write an Equality Method in Java," by Martin Odersky et al., 2009, www.artima.com/lejava/articles/equality.html.

Table E.18   Parameters for `@Grab`

Parameter name	Purpose
group	The organization or group (for example, org.apache.ant).
module	The module or artifact (for example, ant-junit).
version	The revision or version (for example, 1.7.1).
classifier	The classifier if in use (for example, jdk14).
transitive	Defaults to `true` but set to `false` if you don't want transitive dependencies also to be downloaded.
force	Defaults to `false` but set to `true` to indicate to the underlying Ivy conflict manager that this dependency should be forced to the given revision.
changing	Defaults to `false` but set to `true` to indicate that an underlying artifact may change without a corresponding revision change. Sometimes useful for snapshot artifacts.
conf	The configuration if in use (normally only used by internal Ivy repositories).
ext	The extension of the artifact (normally safe to leave at default value of .jar but other values like .zip are sometimes useful).
type	The type of the artifact (normally safe to leave at default value of "jar" but other values like "sources" and "javadoc" are sometimes useful).
value	Allows more compact String representations of dependencies in Ivy or Maven formats: `junit:junit:*;transitive=false` or `junit#junit;4.8.2`.
initClass	Set to `false` to disable automatically placing static initialization code in a Grab-annotated class to add any dependencies to the classpath (downloading if needed).

Table E.19   Parameters for @GrabConfig

Parameter name	Purpose
systemClassLoader	Set to true if you want to use the system classloader when loading the grape.
initContextClassLoader	Set to true if you want the context classloader to be initialized to the classloader of the current class or script.
autoDownload	Set to false if you want to disable automatic downloading of locally missing .jars.
disableChecksums	

Table E.20   Parameters for @GrabExclude

Parameter name	Purpose
group	The organization or group (for example, org.apache.ant).
module	The module or artifact (for example, ant-junit).
value	String convenience format (for example, org.apache.ant:ant-junit).

Table E.21   Parameters for @GrabResolver

Parameter name	Purpose
name	A name for the resolver.
root	The URL for the resolver repository root.
value	Shorthand to specify the name and root. The supplied String will be used for both.
m2Compatible	Whether the resolver is Maven compatible. Defaults to true.
initClass	Whether initialization code will be added to a Grab-annotated class to register the resolver with the Ivy runtime.

Table E.22   Parameters for @Grapes

Parameter name	Purpose
value	An array of Grab annotations
initClass	To set the default for all child annotations

Table E.23 Parameters for `@Immutable`

Parameter name or overriding annotation	Purpose
`copyWith`	If true, this adds a method `copyWith` that takes a `Map` of new property values and returns a new instance of the `Immutable` class with these values set.
`knownImmutableClasses`	Allows you to specify a list of `Classes` which are to be considered immutable.
`knownImmutables`	Allows you to specify a list of `Class` names which are to be considered immutable.
`@ToString`	Can be used in conjunction with `@Immutable` to customize behavior. See table E.41 for details.
`@EqualsAndHashCode`	Can be used in conjunction with `@Immutable` to customize behavior. See Parameter in table E.16 for `@DelegatesTo.Target` details.

Table E.24 Parameters for `@InheritConstructors`

Parameter name or overriding annotation	Purpose
`constructorAnnotations`	Set to true if you want to carry over annotations from the parent constructors to your constructors. By default, annotations are not carried over. Currently `Closure` annotation members are not supported.
`parameterAnnotations`	Set to true if you want to carry over annotations from the method parameters of the parent constructors to your constructors. By default, annotations are not carried over. Currently `Closure` annotation members are not supported.

Table E.25 Parameter for `@Lazy`

Parameter or modifier name	Purpose
`soft`	If the field should be a `SoftReference`, and therefore eligible for garbage collection, then set this parameter to true. By default, the field is not a soft reference.

Table E.26 Parameters for `@ListenerList`

Parameter name	Purpose
`name`	A suffix for creating the `add`, `remove`, and `get` methods if the default isn't suitable.
`synchronize`	Whether or not the methods created should be synchronized at the method level. Defaults to `false`.

Table E.27   Parameters for `@Log`

Parameter name	Purpose
value	Used to set the name of the logging variable. Defaults to `log`.
category	Used to set logging category name. Default is to use the class name as logging category.

Table E.28   Parameters for `@Log4j`

Parameter name	Purpose
value	Used to set the name of the logging variable. Defaults to `log`.
category	Used to set logging category name. Default is to use the class name as logging category.

Table E.29   Parameters for `@Log4j2`

Parameter name	Purpose
value	Used to set the name of the logging variable. Defaults to `log`.
category	Used to set logging category name. Default is to use the class name as logging category.

Table E.30   Parameters for `@Memoized`

Parameter name	Purpose
protectedCacheSize	Number of cached return values to protect from garbage collection.
maxCacheSize	The maximum size the cache can grow to.

Table E.31   Parameter for `@Mixin`

Parameter name	Purpose
value	The list of class types to mixin to this class. Static mixins have been deprecated in favor of traits (`trait` keyword).

Table E.32 Parameters for `@Newify`

Parameter name	Purpose
value	A list of classes which, if found in code in Python-style object creation format, will be turned into Groovy (Java compatible) constructor calls. If not present, only Ruby-style new method calls will be converted.
auto	Set to `false` to disable automatic conversion of Ruby-style new method calls.

Table E.33 Parameter for `@PackageScope`

Parameter name	Purpose
value	If present, allows a context to be defined for whether a class, its methods, and/or its fields should be left as package scope.

Table E.34 Parameter for `@SelfType`

Parameter name	Purpose
value	Class array declaring the list of types that a class implementing that trait is supposed to extend.

Table E.35 Parameters for `@Singleton`

Parameter name	Purpose
lazy	Set this parameter to true to lazily instantiate the instance the first time it is accessed. This marks the instance volatile and correctly performs double-checked locking during initialization. The default is no lazy initialization.
strict	By default, no explicit constructors are allowed. To create one or more explicit constructors set `strict=false`.
property	Used to alter the property name of the singleton. Defaults to `instance`.

Table E.36 Parameters for `@Slf4j`

Parameter name	Purpose
value	Used to set the name of the logging variable. Defaults to `log`.
category	Used to set logging category name. Default is to use the class name as logging category.

Table E.37   Parameter for @SourceURI

Parameter name	Purpose
allowRelative	By default the URI will be made absolute (it will have an authority) in the case where a relative path was used for the source of the script. If you want to leave relative URIs as relative, then set `allowRelative=true`. Defaults to `false`.

Table E.38   Parameter for @Synchronized

Parameter name	Purpose
value	If a user-specified lock object with the given name should be used instead of the default privately created lock.

Table E.39   Parameters for @ThreadInterrupt

Parameter name	Purpose
applyToAllClasses	When Groovy finds the `@ThreadInterrupt` annotation it tries to augment every class and every script in the source file. You can change this behavior by setting the `applyToAllClasses` parameter to false. When false, Groovy only augments the specific type that was annotated. For instance, annotating a class with `@ThreadInterrupt(applyToAllClasses=false)` augments the annotated class but not any inner classes or public classes from the same source file. Annotating an import statement with `@ThreadInterrupt(applyToAllClasses=false)` augments only the Script object instance and not any surrounding classes from the script file.
applyToAllMembers	Set this to false if you have multiple methods/closures within a class or script and only want thread interrupt checks on some of them. Place annotations on the methods/closures that you want enhanced. When false, `applyToAllClasses` is automatically set to false. Set to true (the default) for blanket coverage of thread interrupt checks on all methods, loops, and closures within the class/script.
checkOnMethodStart	Set this parameter to false to turn off the thread interrupt check made at the beginning of each method. By default, this check is made.
thrown	The type of exception that should be thrown if the thread interrupt is detected. By default an `InterruptedException` is thrown.

Table E.40   Parameters for @TimedInterrupt

Parameter Name	Purpose
applyToAllClasses	When Groovy finds the @TimedInterrupt annotation it tries to augment every class and every script in the source file. You can change this behavior by setting the applyToAllClasses parameter to false. When false, Groovy only augments the specific type that was annotated. For instance, annotating a class with @TimedInterrupt(value = 1L, applyToAll-Classes=false) augments the annotated class but not any inner classes or public classes from the same source file. Annotating an import statement with @TimedInterrupt (value = 1L, applyToAllClasses=false) augments only the Script object instance and not any surrounding classes from the script file.
applyToAllMembers	Set this to false if you have multiple methods/closures within a class or script and only want timeout checks on some of them. Place annotations on the methods/closures that you want enhanced. When false, applyToAllClasses is automatically set to false. Set to true (the default) for blanket coverage of timeout checks on all methods, loops and closures within the class/script.
checkOnMethodStart	Set this parameter to false to turn off the timeout check made at the beginning of each method. By default, this check is made.
value	This parameter controls how long to wait before timing out. There is no default value and you must specify a value.
unit	This parameter controls the unit of measure for the value parameter. The default unit of measure is TimeUnit.SECONDS.
thrown	The type of exception that should be thrown if the timeout is reached. By default a TimeoutException is thrown.

Table E.41   Parameters for @ToString

Parameter Name	Purpose
excludes	Exclude certain properties from toString() by specifying the property names as a comma-separated list or literal list of String name values. By default, all properties are included. Incompatible with includes.
includes	Include only the specified properties by specifying the property names as a comma-separated list or literal list of String name values. Incompatible with excludes.
includeSuper	Include the toString() for the super class by setting this parameter to true. By default, it is not included.
includeSuperProperties	Include the properties from any super classes by setting this parameter to true. By default, they are not included.

Table E.41   Parameters for `@ToString` **(continued)**

Parameter Name	Purpose
includeNames	Include the names of the properties by setting this parameter to true. By default, the names are not included.
includeFields	Include the class's fields, not just the properties, by setting this parameter to true. By default, fields are not included.
ignoreNulls	Exclude any properties that are null. By default null values will be included.
includePackage	Set to false to print just the simple name of the class without the package. By default the package name is included.
cache	Set to true to cache toString() calculations. Use only for immutable objects. By default the toString() is recalculated whenever the toString() method is called.

Table E.42   Parameters for `@TupleConstructor`

Parameter Name	Purpose
excludes	Exclude certain properties or fields from constructor parameters by specifying their names in a comma-separated list or literal list of String name values. By default, no properties are excluded. Incompatible with includes.
includes	Include only a specified list of properties by specifying the desired property names as a comma-separated list or literal list of String name values. Incompatible with excludes.
includeFields	Include fields, not just properties, in the constructor parameters by setting this parameter to true. By default, fields are not included.
includeProperties	Exclude properties in the constructor parameters by setting this parameter to false. By default, properties are included.
includeSuperFields	Include super class fields in the constructor parameters by setting this parameter to true. When true, the super class fields come first in the constructor parameter list, starting with the most super type. By default, super class fields are not included.
includeSuperProperties	Include super class properties in the constructor parameters by setting this parameter to true. When true, the super class properties come first in the constructor parameter list, starting with the most super type. By default, super class properties are not included.
callSuper	Invoke the super class constructor with parameters by setting this property to true. By default, properties on the super class are set using that property's setter method. When set to true, the super class's constructor is called rather than relying on property manipulation.

Table E.42 Parameters for @TupleConstructor

Parameter Name	Purpose
force	By default, tuple constructors are not created if the class provides its own constructor. Force these tuple constructors to be created even when a custom constructor is present by setting this parameter to true. Be careful: It is your responsibility to avoid constructor overloading conflicts.

Table E.43 Parameters for @TypeChecked

Parameter Name	Purpose
TypeCheckingMode value	Used to indicate whether type checking should be performed (PASS) or skipped (SKIP).
String[] extensions	An optional list of classpath resource paths to type checking extensions.

Table E.44 Parameter for @WithReadLock

Parameter Name	Purpose
value	If a user-specified lock object with the given name should be used instead of the normal default.

Table E.45 Parameter for @WithWriteLock

Parameter Name	Purpose
value	If a user-specified lock object with the given name should be used instead of the normal default.

appendix F
Compiler phases

This appendix describes the phases of the Groovy compiler.

Conway's Law is a well-known maxim from the 1960s that states roughly that the organization of a software system will match the communication structure of the group creating the system. Or, as Eric Raymond's more famous restatement[1] puts it: "If you have four groups working on a compiler, you'll get a 4-pass compiler." Groovy's compiler is a counterpoint to this law: one group maintains it yet it has nine phases. Something unique happens in each phase, and there are good reasons for each one's existence. The nine phases, presented in the order in which they execute, are:

1. *Initialization*—Opens the source files or input stream and configures the compilation environment.
2. *Parsing*—Uses the language grammar to convert the source code into a tree of tokens. Under the covers, Groovy uses ANTLR to help with this task.
3. *Conversion*—Where the token tree is converted into an AST, and is the first place where we can begin to write AST visitors.
4. *Semantic analysis*—Performs consistency and validity checks beyond what the grammar can provide. Also, classes are resolved during this phase.
5. *Canonicalization*—Writes any final changes into the complete AST. This is typically the last point at which you want to run a transformation.
6. *Instruction selection*—Chooses an instruction set for the generated bytecode; for instance, Java 5 versus pre-Java 5 bytecode instructions.
7. *Class generation*—Creates the bytecode-based Class in memory.

---

[1] Eric S. Raymond, *The New Hacker's Dictionary*, 3rd Ed. (MIT Press, 1996).

8 *Output*—Finally, the binary output is written to the filesystem in the form of a .class file.

9 *Finalization*—Used only to clean up any resources no longer needed.

In the early phases of the compiler, the AST is sparse and holds less information, making it an ideal time to write information into the tree. In the later phases the AST is denser and holds type information, making it a good time to read information from the tree. The best way to learn about the different phases is to use the AstBrowser within the Groovy Console. The AstBrowser lets you view the AST at different phases of the compilation.

appendix G
AST visitors

After reading chapter 9, you should have a general idea of what types of tasks compile-time metaprogramming can offer, how Groovy gets compiled into AST and eventually bytecode, and which tools you'll need for further exploration. We're all set to dig in and see some of the details of AST. This appendix focuses on walking and reading an AST. We'll look at the options for code visitors and the implementation of a static analysis tool for Groovy.

The examples in chapter 9 are focused on writing new information into the AST of a class. Transformations give you the class and method nodes you need to work with as parameters. This is enough when you want to write AST. But things aren't always so simple. Often, we need to read the AST to discover more information about it, such as which statements are next to each other, or which variables are in scope. To answer more complex questions about the AST content you will need to walk the tree.

G.1 *Walking and reading a tree*

The standard way to walk and read a tree in Java is with the venerable Visitor pattern from the Gang of Four. The Visitor pattern separates the object being walked (the tree) from the behavior of the walker (the visitor). We'll use the `ASTNode` class hierarchy as a concrete example of how this works. If you want to walk (or visit) every statement and expression in the AST then you need to implement `GroovyCodeVisitor`. Figure G.1 shows some of the classes you'll need to know in order to visit AST.

The `GroovyCodeVisitor` interface has one method for every subclass of `AST-Node`, and each subclass of `ASTNode` has a `visit(GroovyCodeVisitor)` method. When you tell an `ASTNode` to visit your visitor, then it dutifully calls the correct method on your object. Ask to visit a `ConstructorCallExpression` and it calls back your `visitConstructorCallExpression` method. `MethodCallExpressions` calls back your `visitMethodCallExpression` method. With this pattern, the `ASTNode`

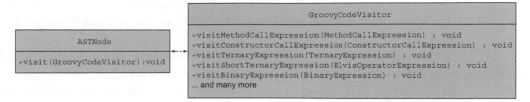

Figure G.1 `GroovyCodeVisitor` **is used to discover information about the source code.**

classes stay general, and only know that they can be visited, while all of the specific behavior resides in the visitor classes. Low coupling and high cohesion: classic traits of good object-oriented design.

One last piece of information: `GroovyCodeVisitor` visits every statement or expression in the tree; `GroovyClassVisitor` visits the structure of a class. Figure G.2 shows the `GroovyClassVisitor` class diagram.

The classes shown in figure G.2 are the general interfaces for the visitors. In practice, you will use the abstract classes defined to help you implement this pattern. That way you won't have to worry about any method dispatch or implementing a whole bunch of uninteresting methods. Normally you want to subclass `CodeVisitorSupport` or `ClassCodeVisitorSupport`, shown in figure G.3.

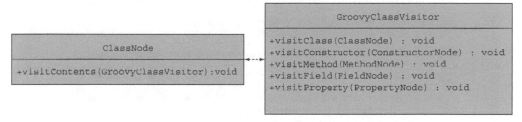

Figure G.2 `GroovyClassVisitor` **is used to discover information about the class structure.**

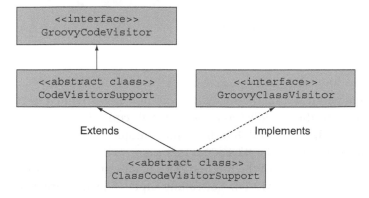

Figure G.3 `GroovyCodeVisitor` **is used for visiting AST.**

To boil it down to one simple rule: extend the class `ClassCodeVisitorSupport` and override whatever method you need. That's the easiest approach and exactly how `CodeNarc` works.

`CodeNarc` is an open source static analysis tool for Groovy. It analyzes the AST of Groovy classes and searches for bugs, inconsistencies, bad practices, or just unclean code. It's meant to be run as part of your automated build and integrates with all the major build systems, and it can both fail the build and create a report of any problems encountered. At its core is a set of configurable rules based on this Visitor pattern that walks the AST of your source code. A useful example is the `SynchronizedOnGetClass` rule. The code in the following listing creates a violation.

Listing G.1   Synchronizing on `getClass()`

```
synchronized(getClass()) {
        println 'doing something...'
}
```

Can you spot the problem? It is a subtle concurrency error. If your class is subclassed then this code might end up synchronizing on the wrong lock (the class of the child class instead of the `this` reference), possibly leading to a live-lock! There are many other rules as well, in categories like concurrency, unit testing, and unused code. Rules are simple visitors, and it should be easy to understand the implementation of the `SynchronizedOnGetClass` rule shown in the following listing.

Listing G.2   Visiting synchronized statements

```
class SynchronizedOnGetClassAstVisitor extends AbstractAstVisitor {

    void visitSynchronizedStatement(SynchronizedStatement statement) {

        if (statement.expression instanceof MethodCallExpression) {
            def method = statement.expression
            def argumentCount = 0
            if (AstUtil.isMethodNamed(method, 'getClass', argumentCount)) {
                addViolation statement
            }
        }
        super.visitSynchronizedStatement(statement);
    }
}
```

This method analyzes any usage of `SynchronizedStatement`. If the expression within the synchronized statement is a method call, that method call is named `getClass()`, and takes zero arguments, then a violation is created. This code cheats a little by defining an `isMethodNamed` helper method, but the implementation is a straightforward `if` statement against the contents of the `MethodCallExpression` instance. Notice that the super method is called at the end of the method. This makes sure than any nested elements later in the source are also visited. Not calling super will short-circuit your visit. In most cases it should be called.

The point of this example is to demonstrate that writing a useful AST visitor can be simple, straightforward, and understandable. Writing `CodeNarc` rules is a good starting point for learning more about AST because the problems are small and contained, and the code and results are easily testable. Plus, it handles the problem of wiring your AST into the compilation process, a necessary step we have not yet covered.

Visitor Gotchas

Writing AST visitors is fun and rewarding; it's one of those rare tasks where you spend most of your time thinking. Thinking deeply about the language, the edge cases, and how it can be used is a superb way to gain a deep understanding of Groovy. Before jumping in and writing visitors, there are a few gotchas to consider.

- *Types*—Groovy is a dynamic language, and a lot can happen at runtime. In most cases, it is not possible to know definitively the type of an object, and it is especially hard to determine what type a method will return. Practically anything can happen at runtime; this is a feature of the language. Be conservative when thinking you know the type of an object: often you cannot.
- *Scope*—The rules for variable and field scope are complex in Java. We have local variables, parameters, fields, constants, and static references. These become more complex when adding closures and delegates to the language. Remember, a closure may be executed far away from the point it was declared, and any variables it references can be overwritten by the closure's delegate. It is very difficult to reason about what is in scope for a closure at compile time. Be careful not to make assumptions.
- *State*—Managing state within a visitor is tricky because of all the scoping and nesting rules. Often you want to keep track of some variable, but the recursive nature of trees means you risk overwriting that state the next time your method is invoked, which can occur before your method is finished running! There are two options. Make your visitor immutable, and when state is needed create a new instance of your visitor to process any further tree nodes. The second option is to hold all state in a `Stack` object. When saving state add an element to the stack, and when reading state read only the topmost element. Examples of both approaches can be found in the source code of the open source projects previously mentioned, particularly in `CodeNarc`.

G.1.1   *Wiring in a Visitor*

There are several ways to wire a `Visitor` into the Groovy compilation process. Local and global transformations handle the wiring for you. As long as you declare your transformation correctly then it gets invoked. But sometimes you need more control and need to wire a transformation into the compile process using a `ClassLoader`. This happens most commonly for DSL writers or users of GroovyShell.

Including a visitor with a `ClassLoader` is a more verbose approach than global and local transformations. It requires more code; however, most of the code involves subclassing a few classes so the compiler checks your work. If your program accepts user input and evaluates it as Groovy, or if it already uses GroovyShell for execution, then this `ClassLoader` approach is the best approach to take. The `ArithmeticShell` previously discussed uses this approach, and a full unit test and build script is available in all Groovy distributions. For our examples we'll use something simpler. We are going to write and execute a transformation that takes a Groovy script as input, and turns any `String` literals into the words "Hello from our Visitor!" Before showing the transformation, let's look at how `ClassLoader` objects can be used to compile scripts, as shown in the following listing.

Listing G.3   Creating a `Script` from a `String` with `GroovyClassLoader`

```
GroovyClassLoader loader = new GroovyClassLoader()
Class clazz = loader.parseClass(' "Hello from Groovy!" ')
Script script = clazz.newInstance()
assert "Hello from Groovy!" == script.run()
```

A `GroovyClassLoader` has several public methods to turn `Strings` and `InputStreams` into instances of `Script`, which are runnable via the `run()` method. In this listing we turn the Groovy code "Hello from Groovy!" into a `Script`, execute it, and assert the correct result. Our `Visitor` class example is going to subclass `GroovyClassLoader` in order to wire in the transformation. The following listing shows how our code will behave when we're finished.

Listing G.4   Simple unit test for a new AST visitor

```
GroovyGlassLoader loader = new MyClassLoader()
Class clazz = loader.parseClass(' "Hello from Groovy!" ')
Script script = clazz.newInstance()
assert "Hello from our Visitor!" == script.run()
```

The only difference is that we defined our own `GroovyClassLoader` subclass called `MyClassLoader`, and when we execute the produced `Script` we get a different result. The `Visitor` for this is small; it simply searches the AST for any `String` constant and replaces it with our Groovy message. Constants could be numeric or `null` as well, so it is safest to only change the value of `Strings`. The entire `Visitor` can be seen in the following listing and is an example of how you can use the abstract `ClassCodeVisitorSupport` class.

Listing G.5   Using a `Visitor` to replace constants' values

```
import org.codehaus.groovy.ast.*
import org.codehaus.groovy.ast.expr.*

class MyAstVisitor extends ClassCodeVisitorSupport {
    def source

    void visitConstantExpression(ConstantExpression exp) {
        if (exp.value instanceof String) {
            exp.value = 'Hello from our Visitor!'
        }
    }
}
```

```
    SourceUnit getSourceUnit() {
        source
    }
}
```

After showing a sample use script and a quick visitor, we're finally able to get to wiring the transformation together with the new `ClassLoader`. A `GroovyClassLoader` has a `CompilationUnit` that stores all of the information about the compile, like the source, AST, and compiled classes. It also stores a list of `PhaseOperations`. A `PhaseOperation` is just a bit of code (for instance, a visitor) that gets executed during one of the compiler phases. So a `GroovyClassLoader` creates a `CompilationUnit`, a `CompilationUnit` has `PhaseOperations`, and your `PhaseOperation` can be an AST visitor, as shown in the following listing.

Listing G.6 Wiring an AST visitor into a GroovyClassLoader

```
import java.security.CodeSource
import org.codehaus.groovy.classgen.*
import org.codehaus.groovy.control.*
import org.codehaus.groovy.control.CompilationUnit.PrimaryClassNodeOperation

class MyClassLoader extends GroovyClassLoader {
    protected CompilationUnit createCompilationUnit(
                            CompilerConfiguration cfg,
                            CodeSource src) {

        CompilationUnit cu = super.createCompilationUnit(cfg, src)
        def operation = new MyClassNodeOperation()
        def phase = Phases.SEMANTIC_ANALYSIS
        cu.addPhaseOperation(operation, phase)
        cu
    }
}

private class MyClassNodeOperation extends PrimaryClassNodeOperation {

    void call(SourceUnit src, GeneratorContext ctx, ClassNode node) {
        node.visitContents(new MyAstVisitor(source: src))
    }
}
```

In this example you can see that we subclass `GroovyClassLoader` in order to get at the `CompilationUnit`, and we subclass `PrimaryClassNodeOperation` in order to add in our visitor. All in all it is a bit of boilerplate code to write, and we have not covered any of the exceptions you'll want to catch (hint: `MultipleCompilationErrorsException`). But this is the best approach if you're already using GroovyShell, need to execute text-based scripts as a DSL, or are directly using `ClassLoaders` to compile user input. If this isn't your scenario, then a local or global transformation is much easier to write.

appendix H
Type checking extensions

In chapter 10, we introduced the optional type checking features that were added in Groovy 2. We showed that even if Groovy remains primarily a dynamic language, it offers a powerful type system, including the ability to hook directly into the compilation process, more precisely during the type checking phase to help the compiler or even add custom static analysis. This feature allows Groovy to become a powerful statically typed language, capable of performing deep static analysis at compile time; but more importantly, type checking extensions allow the programmer to improve it, in particular for DSL analysis.

We've seen that type checking extensions relied on an event-based API. In this appendix, we'll analyze the API and give insight on how you can combine those events to achieve impressive static analysis extensions.

The type checking extension writer should be aware of the fact that this feature is only available since Groovy 2.1.0.

H.1 Type checking extension API

Groovy isn't bound to a specific implementation of type checking APIs. However, it's definitely easier to write extensions using the type checking extension DSL that it provides. Supported out of the box, it also provides shortcuts for common tasks that would be complicated to implement without the DSL. It's possible to write an extension in pure Java, but it would require more code and you couldn't load the extension using the extensions parameter of the @TypeChecked annotations. For those reasons, this appendix focuses on only the type checking extension DSL and won't explain the alternatives.

H.1.1 The GroovyTypeCheckingExtensionSupport class

Internally, all type checking extension scripts inherit the `org.codehaus.groovy` `.transform.stc.GroovyTypeCheckingExtensionSupport` class. This class offers many helper methods that you can use in your extensions, as shown in table H.1.

Table H.1 Helper methods available in the DSL

Method	Description
`isXXXExpression(expr)`	Tests if an expression is an instance of XXX expression. For example: ■ if (expr instanceof `BinaryExpression`) { ... } can be rewritten ■ if (`isBinaryExpression(expr)`){ ... }
`isDynamic(var)`	Tests if a variable is a dynamic variable (unresolved variable) if (`isDynamic(var)`){ ... }
`getTargetMethod(call)`	Given a method call expression, returns the target method (`MethodNode`) selected by the type checker. Note that depending on the event where you use it, it's possible that the method has not yet been selected.
`getType(expr)`	Returns the inferred type of an expression. This method should always be used instead of `expr.getType()` if you want to use the inferred type of an expression instead of the declared type.
`storeType(expr, type)`	Use this method to store the inferred type of an expression. If you want to tell the type checker that the type of an unresolved variable is String, you can use: `storeType(var, STRING_TYPE`[a]`)`
`addStaticTypeError(msg, node)`	This method is very important if you want to throw custom type checking errors. In that case, you must provide: ■ msg: an error message string, which will appear as the compilation error ■ node: the AST node from which the error is issued The AST node is important to provide the code location in compilation error messages (line and column number information).
`classNodeFor(clazz)`	Returns the class node that corresponds to the provided class. It's important to understand that type checking extensions work at the AST level. You shouldn't use class literals directly (for example to compare the inferred types) but instead use a `ClassNode`. This method allows you to return the `ClassNode` corresponding to a `Class`. There are two variants of this method: one takes a `Class` as an argument and the other takes a `String`. It's important to understand that this method should only be used for classes that are compiled before the type checking extension works, that is to say, classes that are on the compile classpath. For classes that are, for example, defined in the script being type checked, use the `lookupClassNodeFor` method instead.

Table H.1   Helper methods available in the DSL *(continued)*

Method	Description
`lookupClassNodeFor(clazz)`	Returns the `ClassNode` corresponding to a class being compiled. This method should be used whenever you need a handle on a class that's defined in the script being type checked itself.
`isAnnotatedBy(node, clazz)`	Tests if an AST node is annotated by the supplied annotation. You can use a `Class` or a `ClassNode` as the annotation parameter.
`isGenerated(MethodNode)`	This method lets the extension writer know if the supplied method node was generated by the type extension itself (see virtual methods in the next section).
`delegatesTo(clazz)`	This method can be used to emulate the behavior of `@DelegatesTo` in the context of the type checking extension; for example, if the original method isn't annotated. See chapter 10 for details.

a. The `STRING_TYPE` constant comes from the `org.codehaus.groovy.ast.ClassHelper` class.

H.1.2   *Virtual methods*

Virtual methods are an important concept in type checking extensions. It's possible in Groovy to write code that calls nonexistent methods. One could implement the `methodMissing` method to implement dynamic method calls. If a DSL uses such a feature, it's normally not compatible with type checking because the method calls cannot be resolved statically. It's possible, however, for the DSL designer, given the name of a method and its inferred argument types, to determine if a call is valid or not, and therefore infer a return type. In that case, a type checking extension needs to define a virtual `MethodNode`. It's called virtual because it isn't attached to a class: it's only used so the type checker knows a method call is valid and that it returns a specific type.

While it's possible (and sometimes required) for an extension to create a method node from scratch, the type checking extension DSL offers helper methods dedicated to this task. Each method created using one of these helper methods is automatically added to the list of generated methods of the extension, so calling `isGenerated(node)` on such a method would return true:

- *newMethod(String name, ClassNode returnType)*—Defines a method whose name is name and whose return type is returnType.
- *newMethod(String name, Class returnType)*—Defines a method whose name is name and whose return type is returnType.
- *newMethod(String name, Closure returnType)*—Defines a method whose name is name, but whose return type computation is deferred.

| Listing H.1   Find by name method returns the enclosing class node |

```
newMethod('findByName') {
    typeCheckingContext.enclosingClassNode
}
```

The last method is interesting if it's not possible to determine the return type immediately. In that case, the closure will be called whenever the type checker needs to find the return type of the method. This is why it's deferred: the computation of the return type is lazy and done on demand. (It's lazy, but it's not cached: the closure is called each time the type checker calls getReturnType on the method node.) In listing H.1, we're supposing that the dynamic method returns the enclosing class node (the class that's currently being type checked).

Note that none of those helper methods care about the argument types because, in general, once a method call has been resolved (thus when you return such a generated method), the argument types are no longer important. Should you need them, you need to create a method node from scratch (using new MethodNode). Note that you don't even need to give a method body because it's virtual. It is used internally by the type checker to perform type safety computations.

Be warned that because those methods are virtual, you cannot rely on the fact that you generate such methods to have extensions that will allow a DSL to be compiled statically! In general, statically compiling a DSL requires an AST transform, which is beyond the scope of type checking extensions.

One more important thing to know before digging into the type checking handlers that you can write is dealing with the type checking context and the scoping of your extension.

H.1.3   *Type-checking extension scope*

It would be rare to write a type checking extension that can run in any context. In general, a type checking extension should be active only once a precondition is met; for example, once you've found an introduction verb followed by a closure:

```
doLater { // doLater is an introduction verb
    … // here goes custom type checking
}
```

More complex examples can involve deep nesting. Imagine that you want to perform type checking of a builder, but inside the body of the builder you use a Markup-Builder. In that case, the extension should be active when you enter the scope of the custom builder, temporarily switched off once you visit MarkupBuilder code, then reactivated once the visit of the MarkupBuilder closure is finished. As you can see, defining the scope of an extension in a declarative manner is barely impossible.[1] As an

---

[1] This is also why type checking extensions in Groovy don't follow the pointcut pattern that is famous to AspectJ users.

alternative, the type checking extension DSL provides an API that allows the use of custom scopes.

Scopes can be used to collect and store temporary data, and they're organized as a stack. Creating a new scope puts it on top of the stack, and you can pop a scope from the stack too. Scopes are also organized in a hierarchy; the scope on the stack inherits data from the scopes beneath it in the stack. You can create a new scope using the `scopeEnter` method and remove a scope from the stack using `scopeExit`, as shown in the following listing.

Listing H.2   Creating a scope to store custom data

```
def scope = scopeEnter()                                        Pushes a new
scope.extraChecks = []          Initializes an empty list for the   scope on stack
...                             extraChecks custom variable
onMethodSelection {
    currentScope.extraChecks << { println 'Extra check' }       Event handler
}                                                               adds a custom
...                            Pops scope                    ❶ check to the list
scopeExit {                    from stack
    extraChecks*.run()
}                              Calls deferred
                               actions
```

Listing H.2 shows that a custom event handler can access the current scope and store additional metadata in it. There's no limit to what data you can store. A scope basically acts like a map, but inherits keys from its parent scope. This scoping mechanism is powerful because it allows you to perform deferred checks, allowing complex type checks such as forward references in a DSL.

Forward references are a typical use case that type checkers cannot resolve normally: declarative languages are fond of declarations and normally order doesn't matter. But imperative languages suppose that statements are executed in order and don't allow the use of a variable before it's declared. Using a list of closures (`extraChecks`) here, we allow several checks to be performed after all the code has been visited. This is done by calling `scopeExit`, which takes an optional closure as argument. This closure lets you perform work before the scope is removed. Here, it's used to call the closures of the `extraChecks` list.

The call to `currentScope` ❶ gives access to the scope that's currently on top of the stack. This is contextual data, but there's much more than the scope offered by the type checker as contextual data. Often, it's interesting to know what method you're in, or if you're in a binary expression, and so forth, so you can react appropriately. For that, the type checker provides a context, available through the `org.codehaus.groovy .transform.stc.TypeCheckingContext` class. This context gives interesting information such as the stack of visited class nodes, the stack of enclosing binary expressions, and others. All methods from this class are immediately available in the DSL. In particular, this class is also the one that stores all error messages before they're transmitted to the compiler. It's possible for you to temporarily change the error collector.

This means that if you want to intercept all errors thrown by the type checker and replace them with custom error messages, the type checking extensions will allow you to do that using the type checking context!

The type checking context is a sensitive model. It's used in many places of the type checker, so be careful if you need to manipulate it.

Now that we've seen the basics of type checking extensions, it's time to dig into the various handlers that you can write and combine to perform DSL type checking. Those handlers correspond to events sent by the type checker.

H.2 Type checking events

This section describes the events that a type checking extension can react to. Several of those events are sent when the type checker would normally throw a type checking error. If your type checking extension is meant to remove this error, then you should know about the handled flag.

The handled flag must be set by your type checking extension to tell it that you care about the error. If the type checker fails to resolve a variable, it will call your extension. If your extension sets the handled flag to true, then the type checker will consider that you have fixed the error, and it won't be shown to the user at compile time. This is exactly what type checking extensions are meant for: handle unexpected errors or, in certain cases, throw errors when the type checker would normally not. The reason why you need to set a flag is that you can have preconditions. Your extension may not resolve all unresolved variables. In the following listing, the handled flag is only set if we find a variable named 'robot'.

Listing H.3 The handled flag

```
unresolvedVariable { var ->
    handled = ('robot'==var.name)
}
```

In general, it isn't required to set this flag, but not doing so may lead to surprising results. For example, you may help the type checker by telling it the type of variable, but if you forget to set the flag, the error is still shown to the user. Because cases exist where this can be useful, the flag isn't automatically set, so you should always take care of it explicitly. The events the type checking extension can handle are explained in the following sections.

H.2.1 setup

Arguments: none

The setup event is always called after the type checker completes its initialization. It gives you the chance to perform custom initialization steps before type checking starts.

H.2.2   *finish*

Arguments: none

The `finish` event is triggered once static type checking is completed. It allows the programmer to perform cleanup tasks.

H.2.3   *unresolvedVariable*

Arguments: `var` (`VariableExpression`), the unresolved variable

This event allows you to react to an unresolved variable. An unresolved variable is a variable that isn't defined in the context of the script. In the following code:

```
def variable1 = 'foo'
varable2 = 'unresolved'
```

variable1 is resolved, because it is declared (using `def`) in the context of the script. The variable2 variable is, on the other hand, undeclared. It's a dynamic variable and typically the type checker doesn't know anything about it. When the type checker encounters such a variable in a method, you're given the chance to tell it what type it is, for example:

```
unresolvedVariable { var ->
  if (var.name == 'variable2'){
    storeType(var, STRING_TYPE)
    handled=true
  }
}
```

H.2.4   *unresolvedProperty*

Arguments: `pexp` (`PropertyExpression`), the unresolved property expression

Groovy allows the programmer to resolve properties at runtime (for example, using `propertyMissing`), meaning that it's possible that a property isn't statically defined. When the type checker encounters such an unresolved property, it throws the `unresolvedProperty` event, giving the extension writer a chance to resolve its type.

H.2.5   *unresolvedAttribute*

Arguments: `aexp` (`AttributeExpression`), the unresolved attribute expression

In a similar manner to unresolved properties, it's possible for the extension writer to react on missing attributes. In that case, an `unresolvedAttribute` message is sent by the type checker.

H.2.6   *beforeMethodCall*

Arguments: `methodCall` (`MethodCallExpression` or `StaticMethodCallExpression`)

This event is systematically sent before the type checker tries to resolve a method call, that is to say, before it tries to determine the types of the arguments, then tries to find an appropriate method. This handler can be used if the user wants to perform custom analysis of a method call, bypassing the type checker. In that case, the extension writer should set the `handled` flag to true.

H.2.7 *afterMethodCall*

Arguments: methodCall (`MethodCallExpression` or `StaticMethodCallExpression`)

This event is systematically sent after the type checker has completed the analysis of a method call. It's particularly interesting to perform additional type checks once the method has been resolved by the type checker. Indeed, before the type checker resolves a method call, there's no guarantee that the call is valid. Once it's resolved, the extension writer can have access to the target method (the real method that will be called) and therefore perform additional analysis.

It's worth noting that the `afterMethodCall` event is also sent if the user set the `handled` flag to true using the `beforeMethodCall` event.

H.2.8 *onMethodSelection*

Arguments:

- *expr (Expression)*—The expression that triggered a method selection event
- *methodNode (MethodNode)*—The selected method node

The `onMethodSelection` event is sent by the type checker each time a method is selected. Various cases exist where a method is selected. The first one is whenever a method call is analyzed and when a method with the appropriate name and arguments is found on the call receiver. The second case is when using symbols such as "+" that can be used as shortcuts for method calls.[2] This explains why the `onMethodSelection` event gives access to the original expression, instead of a method call. The second argument is the method that has been selected.

The `onMethodSelection` event is particularly important for reacting to specific method calls that may be used to define the scope of the type checking extension analysis. Imagine that you're performing type checking of a builder. Then the custom type checking analysis should only be active when the builder body is found; for example, whenever the `builder.build(Closure)` method is selected.

H.2.9 *methodNotFound*

Arguments:

- *receiver (ClassNode)*—The inferred type of the receiver
- *name (String)*—The name of the method being called
- *argList (ArgumentListExpression)*—The arguments of the call
- *argTypes (ClassNode[])*—The inferred types of the arguments
- *methodCall (StaticMethodCallExpression or MethodCallExpression)*—The method call that couldn't be resolved

---

[2] Here, a + b is equivalent to a.plus(b).

This event is thrown by the type checker if it cannot find any appropriate method on the receiver that matches the name of the call and the arguments. In general, it will correspond to two different cases: a user error such as a typo (the method doesn't exist) or dynamic methods (which by definition cannot be resolved statically). Using the `methodNotFound` handler, the extension writer can help the type checker by resolving a dynamic method call. The behavior of the type checker depends on what you will return:

- An empty list means that the type checking extension didn't find a method either, so the type checker will throw a compilation error (no such method).
- A single `MethodNode` or a list of one `MethodNode` means that the type checker did find a corresponding method. It isn't necessary that the `MethodNode` you return is defined on an existing class. It can be totally virtual, because its role is only to remove a type checking error and give the type checker a hint about the return type of the method so that it can perform the rest of the analysis.
- A list of multiple method nodes. In that case, the type checker will throw an ambiguous method selection error.

H.2.10   beforeVisitMethod

Arguments: `methodNode` (`MethodNode`), the visited method

This event is sent before the type checker starts analyzing a method body. It may be interesting to define the scope of the analysis of the extension (for example, if the extension should only apply to a specific method), or it can be used to totally change the behavior of the type checker for this method node by bypassing the normal type checking. In that case, the extension writer should set the `handled` flag to `true` and the type checking extension will take care of visiting the method body itself. Normal type checking of the method body will be totally bypassed in that case.

H.2.11   afterVisitMethod

Arguments: `methodNode` (`MethodNode`), the method visited by the type checker.

This event is sent whenever the type checker has finished the analysis of a method body. It can be used to perform additional checks once a method is visited, for example, if you collect information during the visit, but that information can only be used once the visit is complete (typical use case: a second pass).

H.2.12   beforeVisitClass

Arguments: `classNode` (`ClassNode`), the class visited by the type checker

This event is sent before the type checker starts visiting a class node that's type checked. It can be used to initialize custom type checking scopes, as well as implement a different type checking mechanism for a specific class. If the extension writer wants to perform such a custom visit, he has to set the `handled` flag to `true`. In that case, the type checker won't visit the class and it's the responsibility of the type checking extension to perform the analysis.

H.2.13 afterVisitClass

Arguments: `classNode (ClassNode)`, the class visited by the type checker

In symmetry with `beforeVisitClass`, the `afterVisitClass` event is thrown once the type checker has completed the analysis of a class. It gives the extension writer the ability to perform additional static checks once a class is visited, when performing a second pass analysis.

H.2.14 incompatibleAssignment

Arguments:

- `lhsType (ClassNode)`—The type of the left-hand side of the assignment
- `rhsType (ClassNode)`—The type of the right-hand side of the assignment
- `expr (Expression)`—The expression representing an assignment

The type checker performs type checks with regard to assignments. If it ever determines that the type of the right-hand side isn't compatible with the type of the left-hand side of an assignment, the `incompatibleAssignment` event is thrown. A typical use case for this includes the implementation of the `setProperty` method, which allows the DSL developer to write complex strategies to assign properties. As an example, the Grails `BeanBuilder`[3] allows the following syntax:

```
myProp = { AnotherBean -> … }
```

where `myProp` is the property of a bean, and the right-hand side is an anonymous bean definition. In that case, the type of the left-hand side is `AnotherBean`, but the right-hand side is a `Closure`, which is normally not allowed. Because the builder uses `setProperty` to handle this case, the `incompatibleAssignment` event can be used to tell the type checker that the assignment is in fact valid. For that, the extension writer needs to set the handled flag to true.

H.2.15 ambiguousMethods

Arguments:

- `nodes (List<MethodNode>)`—The list of ambiguities
- `origin (Expression)`—The expression that triggered the ambiguity

This handler has only been available since Groovy 2.2. It allows the extension writer to react on an ambiguous method call, for example, by implementing a custom resolution strategy. The event carries the list of ambiguities, and the extension is supposed

---

[3] For more information, see http://grails.org/doc/latest/api/grails/spring/BeanBuilder.html.

to return a single element. If it doesn't, then the ambiguity remains and the type checker throws the error to the user.

H.2.16 *incompatibleReturnType*

Arguments:

- `returnStmt (ReturnStatement)`—The return statement that is incompatible
- `returnType (ClassNode)`—The inferred return type of this statement

This handler has only been available since Groovy 2.2. It works in a similar fashion as `handleIncompatibleAssignment` but is dedicated to return types. It allows the extension writer to handle the case where the inferred return type isn't compatible with the declared return type of the method. If the assignment is deemed to be valid in the context of the DSL, the extension may set the handled flag to true and the error will go away. Note that the return statement carried in this event doesn't necessarily correspond to an explicit return: implicit returns may also trigger this event.

H.3   *Extensions aren't AST transformations*

The last advice that we can give you with regard to type checking extensions is to remember that they are not meant to replace AST transformations. Because the DSL is rich and provides direct access to the AST, the temptation to modify the AST from the extension is great. You should never do that, as it can lead to unexpected results. Especially remember that type checking is the last phase before bytecode generation, while AST transformations can be run in much earlier phases. Even if you think your code is safe, even if adding a field seems to work, never trust what you see. Type checking extensions are not meant to modify the AST.

appendix I
Android support

This appendix covers
- Getting started with Android
- Getting more information

Getting started

It's possible to write an Android application in Groovy. To target Android bytecode, you must use a special version of the compiler rather than the normal groovyc command line tool. In particular, when targeting the Android platform, you must use specific .jar files that have a classifier of grooid. To make things easier, a Gradle plugin adds support for the Groovy language in the Android Gradle tool chain.

Figure I.1 Android phone running Groovy

861

The plugin is used by adding the following lines to the start of your Gradle build file:

```
buildscript {
    repositories {
        jcenter()
    }
    dependencies {
        // ...
        classpath 'org.codehaus.groovy:gradle-groovy-android-plugin:0.3.5'
    }
}

apply plugin: 'groovyx.grooid.groovy-android'
```

Then you need to add a dependency to the grooid version of the Groovy compiler:

```
dependencies {
    compile 'org.codehaus.groovy:groovy:2.4.0:grooid'
}
```

Note that if a Groovy JAR (such as a submodule JAR) doesn't provide a special grooid classifier alternative, the JAR is directly compatible with Android. In that case, you can add the dependency directly:

```
dependencies {
    compile 'org.codehaus.groovy:groovy:2.4.0:grooid'        // special version
    compile ('org.codehaus.groovy:groovy-json:2.4.0') {      // normal version
        transitive = false
    }
}
```

Note that the transitive=false parameter for groovy-json tells Gradle not to download the normal Groovy JAR as a dependency of the JSON dependency.

   Please go to the plugin homepage in order to find the latest, news, documentation and version information: https://github.com/groovy/groovy-android-gradle-plugin.

index